OUTPUT, INFLATION AND GROWTH

Other books by D. C. Rowan

Australian Monetary Policy 1950–1975
Money and Banking in British Colonial Africa
(with W. T. Newlyn)

OUTPUT, INFLATION AND GROWTH

AN INTRODUCTION TO MACROECONOMICS

Third edition

D. C. ROWAN

M

MACMILLAN PRESS
LONDON

First edition 1968
Second edition 1974
Reprinted 1976, 1978, 1979
Third edition 1983

Published by
THE MACMILLAN PRESS LTD
London and Basingstoke
Companies and representatives throughout the world

ISBN 0 333 35154 1 (paper cover)

Typeset by Photo-Graphics, Honiton, Devon

Printed and bound in Great Britain at
The Camelot Press Ltd, Southampton

To My Wife

Contents

Foreword to the Third Edition

The revisions incorporated in the new edition amount to a fairly substantial rewriting. The basic reasons for this are the collapse of the 'neo-Keynesian' consensus which dominated macroeconomics up to the early 1970s, the increasing importance of 'monetarism' and the emergence of 'stagflation', a phenomenon not easily accommodated by the early analysis. A subsidiary reason is the introduction of 'floating' exchange rates and the major shift in the emphasis of official policy *away* from the objective of maintaining 'full' or 'high' employment and *towards* a reduction in the rate of inflation.

Attempting to deal with these changes raises very considerable problems, particularly because no consensus view of macroeconomics now exists. I have sought to deal with this difficulty by presenting both a 'neo-Keynesian' and a 'monetarist' analysis. Of necessity, in a book aimed at first-year undergraduates, both views are presented in a simplified form. The objectives throughout have been to give a clear and non-polemical account of both theories, and to indicate, as far as possible, what evidence we need to discriminate between them. I can only hope that I have succeeded in doing this in a way those who read and use this book will find helpful.

Over the years I have received many helpful criticisms of the book from students and teachers. Once again I cannot thank them all individually. I must, however, express my thanks to my present and past colleagues at Southampton, and more particularly to David Heathfield, Peter Smith, Alan Hamlin, John Driffill and George McKenzie for their generous advice. Even if the result is not precisely what they would wish, the book is certainly the better for it.

I owe a special debt to my colleague Tim Harrison, who very kindly helped me with the simulations reported in Chapter 27.

The data employed in the book have been brought up to date and both the exercises and references have been substantially revised. Bearing in mind that few departments or schools can now afford to purchase any comprehensive array of statistical material or learned journals, I have endeavoured, wherever possible, to refer to the more readily accessible and inexpensive sources. Among these the *Economic Progress Reports* issued by HM Treasury are particularly helpful, as are the publications of the National Institute and the London Business School and the Reviews put out by the major banks and, of course, by the Bank of England.

To find space for additional material, the chapters on monetary and fiscal policy have had to be deleted and the coverage of both is now more skeletal. With regret I have been unable to discuss the many changes in the UK's monetary and financial system since to do so effectively would lengthen the book beyond any reasonable limit. This may not be the perfect decision; it seemed to me, however, the wisest course and I have tried to make good the resulting omission by very full references to the controversies regarding the money supply and its control.

Finally I would like to thank Mrs J. Hepburn, who has so patiently, skilfully and uncomplainingly typed most of the book, at a time when the financial pressures on the university have entailed correspondingly severe pressures on clerical staff.

February 1983 D. C. Rowan

A Note on Statistics

Many of the figures in this book employ published economic statistics relating to the British economy. In each case I have followed the usual practice and given a reference to the source whether official or unofficial.

Every care has been taken to make the figures and their reproduction as accurate as possible. Readers are, however, warned that because of minor differences in series, the inevitable revisions which are made from time to time in published economic data and the difficulties of reproduction, the figures should be taken as illustrative of economic behaviour rather than precise quantitative descriptions of it.

Preface to the Third Edition

The primary purpose of this book is to provide an introduction to macroeconomics suitable for undergraduates in the first year of a degree course in economics or social science. The book should also be useful to schools and other educational institutions and some professional bodies, for I have tried, as best I can, to keep the language and exposition simple and I have assumed that my readers have no previous acquaintance with the subject.

The approach of the book emphasises that economics is a social science which aims to develop testable predictions in terms of measurable concepts. Although it contains a good deal of theory, I have tried consistently to develop the view that theory is meant to be tested. To this end each chapter is supplemented by questions and exercises, many of which require the reader to select data from published sources and use them to make simple tests of economic predictions or hypotheses. *This means that the student is asked not only to read through the book but also to work through it.* It also gives students the opportunity to learn economics in the best of all possible ways – by working out problems for themselves. By this approach I hope not only to encourage an appropriate methodological outlook but also to discourage students from thinking, as many do, that economic theory is empty and arid and applied economics mainly unstructured description only loosely related to theory.

Many students are drawn to economics initially by an entirely natural and creditable concern with social problems. Unfortunately many introductory courses, in their anxiety to give an adequate grounding in theory, devote little time to the application of theory to policy issues. The result is sometimes disenchantment. I have tried, by devoting the last few chapters of the book largely to short-run policy, to give the reader ample opportunity to apply the theory of the earlier chapters to policy problems. In these chapters I have placed the emphasis on the difficulty of conducting macroeconomic policy rather than the capacity of a relatively simple theory to grind out apparently satisfactory answers to complex questions.

Economics is commonly studied by many students who do not continue the subject after completing their 'A' Level examination or the first year of their university course. With this in mind I have tried to make this book self-contained, in the sense that those who read and use it properly should be able to take an informed and critical interest in such valuable publications as *Economic Trends* and the *NIESR Review*. At the same time, since many students do proceed further in economics, I have sought to provide a suitable foundation for further work in macroeconomics. In particular I have tried to avoid teaching, in the interests of simplicity, things which must subsequently be untaught. At the same time I have tried to avoid concealing difficulties.

Two problems inevitably face the writer of any introductory text: the first and most awkward of these is to decide what use to make of mathematics; the second is how far to describe the institutional framework within which the theory is developed.

As far as the first problem is concerned, the decision taken is to assume no knowledge of mathematics beyond that required for GCE 'O' Level and, in particular, no knowledge of the differential calculus. This point is important, for many people are discouraged from any systematic study of economics by the belief that the subject is now accessible only to well-trained mathematicians. Obviously those who possess a grasp of mathematical methods of analysis, the most powerful tools for thinking yet developed, are in an advantageous position. Nevertheless it remains true that 'O' Level mathematics is enough for the whole of this book.

Not infrequently the fear of mathematics is misplaced. What looks like 'mathematics' is simply the plentiful use of symbols (rather than words) and the frequent employment of the notion of a function. Few students would regard as unintelligible the proposition that 'consumption depends upon income'. Many, however, regard as 'mathematics' and *therefore incomprehensible*, the statement $C = f(Y)$. I have attempted to eliminate this 'pseudo-fear' or 'symbol phobia' by two methods. The first is to devote Chapter 7 to discussing and illustrating the use of symbols, functions and identities. The second is to use symbols and functional notation wherever I can in the hope, which my experience suggests to be not entirely unjustified, that growing familiarity with this means of expression (which is becoming increasingly common in the literature) will breed confidence in its interpretation. To some readers the result may seem excessively formal, pedantic or even forbidding. I believe it represents a sensible way of meeting an awkward and unavoidable problem.

As regards the description of institutions I have, after a good deal of cogitation, decided that this must be kept to a minimum. As a result there is very little institutional material (in the narrow sense) in the text. There is, however, a good deal in the questions and exercises at the end of chapters in that, where appropriate, questions have been devised that require the reader to relate the theory of the text to the behaviour of particular groups of institutions. This may not prove to be the ideal decision, but in view of the high opportunity cost of including purely descriptive matter it is the one I find most strongly supported.

The first edition of this book appeared in 1968. At that time there was, in the economic profession itself as well as among policy-makers, a fairly complete acceptance of what may be called 'neo-Keynesian' macroeconomic analysis. The book reflected this consensus, which was still operative when the second edition came out in 1974. This consensus has now broken down. And no new one has replaced it. This circumstance has considerably increased the difficulty of writing a useful introduction to macroeconomics, since quite apart from the divergence of views between 'neo-Keynesians' as a whole and 'monetarists' as a whole, neither of these major groups is even approximately homogeneous. We can indeed distinguish 'post-Keynesians' and 'new Keynesians' among the former and a number of sub-groups – including the 'new classicals' – among the latter.

Readers of an introductory text are entitled to an account, as far from polemics and special pleading as the author can contrive, of at least the principal approaches. This is what I have tried to provide. Whether I have succeeded or not readers, of course, must judge for themselves.

The attempt to give an account of both neo-Keynesian and 'monetarist' approaches has made it necessary to revise the structure of the book fairly considerably. Chapters 1–7 remain, as in earlier editions, primarily introductory. Chapters 8–15* set out the 'neo-

Keynesian' model in static form and Chapters 16–18 the main elements of the 'monetarist' position. As in earlier editions Chapters 19–21 are explicitly dynamic and deal with economic growth (again emphasising the supply side), the business cycle and the problem of inflation, with, of course, particular emphasis on UK experience.

Chapters 22–25 are concerned with the functions of money and the determination of the nominal money supply. The treatment here is somewhat formal in the sense that there is no discussion of recent UK controversies in this area and no description of the evolution of Bank of England policy. There are, however, ample references to articles on these topics and the exercises include questions on these issues and, in particular, on the role of the public sector borrowing requirement (PSBR).

As in earlier editions, the last three chapters are concerned with policy and the controversy surrounding it. At this point I have sought to give a brief account of the way in which existing macroeconometric models such as those of HM Treasury, the London Business School and the National Institute of Economic and Social Research may be used to generate economic forecasts or to simulate the consequences of particular macroeconomic policies. Again, I have tried to stress the limitations of these models and the extent to which their forecasts rely upon the skilled 'judgements' of their operators rather than suggest that any particular model can grind out simple answers to policy issues.

The book now contains two chapters which are marked with a star. At a first reading, or for a shortened course, these chapters can, if necessary, be omitted. The first of the starred chapters (14*) deals with the introduction to the basic theory of a 'floating' – as opposed to a 'pegged' – exchange rate. Its omission therefore restricts the relevance of the analysis to the period before the breakdown of Bretton Woods. Clearly this reduces its contemporary relevance and, to some extent, reduces the interest of the later (Chapter 27) discussion of the results of certain 'model simulations'. When the length of the course permits it, inclusion is therefore desirable.

The second starred chapter (15*), represents an attempt to relate the behaviour of output, and in particular its response to perceived changes in aggregate demand, to the microeconomic decisions of firms and thus to their expectations. Though brief, it is my hope that this chapter will provide some corrective to the somewhat 'mechanical' view of output responses which are typically found in simple expositions of the multiplier process and which are implicit in static analysis. This seems to me to be a worthwhile objective in that it reminds the reader of the limitations of formal static analysis and suggests that the short-term results of expansionary policies are not as clear cut as some of their advocates appear to assume. By the same token it suggests that recovery from the present recession is likely to be a more difficult business than is frequently assumed. Again, however, in a shortened course, the chapter can be omitted

Analytically the book is planned, as were the earlier editions, to follow what I then called 'the principle of increasing difficulty'. In the early chapters basic ideas are spelled out in considerable detail. There are many illustrations and not a little repetition. As the book proceeds, the reader is assumed to acquire facility with economic analysis. Exposition becomes briefer and the demands made upon the reader correspondingly more severe, though never, I hope, too severe.

The exercises and reading lists are integral parts of the book. The latter have been kept as short as possible and aim to provide references which supplement, criticise and extend the analysis in the text.

The choice of references presents an increasingly difficult problem since university and other libraries are currently experiencing financial strain, while many valuable official publications are now too costly for individuals to purchase or for libraries to duplicate. I have therefore, apart from the Blue Book, referred principally to *Economic Trends* and the *Economic Progress Reports* published by the Treasury. Readers are strongly urged to cultivate the habit of consulting these offical publications, plus the *Bank of England Quarterly Bulletin* (*BEQB*). Other valuable publications are the *Quarterly Review of the National Institute of Economic and Social Research* (*NIESR Review*), the *Economic Outlook* of the London Business School and the Reviews published by the major banks, among which that of the Midland Bank is particularly helpful.

Economics, though a difficult and regrettably imprecise subject, is nevertheless exciting and rewarding to study. Despite the lack of any contemporary professional consensus, this remains true of macroeconomics. I hope that, if they use this book well, readers will find that some of the excitement of studying economics has communicated itself to them. They should also find themselves better able to evaluate contemporary disagreements among economists and contemporary controversies regarding policy.

February 1983 D. C. Rowan

Note: special subscription rates are available to students for the *BEQB* and the *NIESR Review*.

PART I

PROBLEMS AND METHODS

Chapter 1
The Scope of the Book

The social result of economic activity is the satisfaction of human wants. In any period of time, say a year, an immense *variety* of goods (cars, clothes, books and beer) and services (such as those of doctors, dentists, politicians and pop singers) becomes available in varying *quantities*. These goods and services satisfy the wants of those who purchase them. Obviously not all wants are satisfied by this economic activity, for wants are virtually insatiable and resources are scarce. But if we think of the 'economic system' of a country in this way we can, subject to some obvious safeguards, regard it as a 'machine' for organising the production of goods and services which ultimately satisfy human wants.

The machine analogy is useful but has its dangers. It is essential to avoid too mechanistic a view of the economic system. This is best done by reminding ourselves that the annual flow of goods and services depends upon *human action*. Retaining our machine analogy we may think of economics as

> the *scientific* study of the principles determining the operations of the economic 'machine'

which, since the 'machine' is really a complicated set of social and technical relations between human beings, can alternatively be thought of as

> the *scientific* study of *man's behaviour* in the everyday business of earning his living.

This second definition forcibly reminds us that economics is concerned with human behaviour. Economics is therefore a social science – that is, one of the group of disciplines which studies human behaviour. Others are sociology, psychology and anthropology. Each of these selects a particular aspect of human behaviour for study much as, in the natural sciences, physics and chemistry study particular aspects of the physical world.

This division of the social sciences into economics, sociology and psychology is not of course immutable. Its justification is simply convenience. The division has, so far, proved fruitful and helpful. As long as it does it will be retained. As soon as it does not it will be abandoned.

Both our definitions of economics contain the italicised adjective *scientific*. The precise meaning we attach to this term is set out in Chapter 2. For the present, however, it is sufficient to note that, in terms of our machine analogy, the purpose of economics is to explain why the machine (or economic system) operates to produce the results that we observe and not some other set of results.

In short the questions which concern economists, as social scientists, are questions involving 'how' or 'why'. As such they form part of what is called *positive economics*. By contrast, questions involving the word 'ought' form part of what is called *normative economics*. These distinctions are elaborated in Chapter 2. At this stage the student is asked merely to note that there *is* a significant distinction betwen the two types of question and to remind himself that much popular discussion of economic questions belongs to 'normative' rather than 'positive' economics. This, of course, does not mean that normative economics is unimportant or that economists do not discuss normative questions.

When, retaining our machine analogy, we ask the positive question 'why does the machine operate as it does and not in some other way?', we are not being very precise. To make any progress we need to clarify the meaning of the word 'operate'. What is it that the economic system does that we seek to explain?

In the first place, as we have already noted, the economic machine organises, in any period, the production of a flow of goods and services. Suppose that we can measure this flow by a single magnitude called 'output'. Since output satisfies wants and human wants are insatiable we would like to have twice, three times or ten times the annual flow of output we are currently (1983) obtaining. We cannot because 'resources' are scarce. The available resources set an upper limit to output. But, since it is a matter of common knowledge that output fluctuates, it does not seem plausible to think that the flow of output is always at the maximum level obtainable with the existing resources. We can then ask:

1. What, in any given period (say 1983), determines the magnitude or the flow of total output?

In the second place, as a casual reading of the newspapers will remind us, output grows over time. In the last decade it seems that output in the UK has grown rather more slowly and less steadily than it used to do and than it has in many other countries. Our second question is then:

2. What determines the rate at which output grows?

We introduced the concept 'output' as a convenient means of measuring the annual flow of goods and services made available by our economic machine. Since resources are scarce (in relation to wants) somehow or other the commodity composition of this 'output' has to be determined. If we want more missiles we must, in general, agree to have less butter. Our third question is therefore:

3. What determines the commodity and service composition of output in any period?

It is a familiar observation that there is more than one way of doing most things. Cats *can* be choked with cream. They can also be shot, drowned, starved, or poisoned. In the same way most commodities can be produced in ways which, from the economist's point of view, differ significantly. For example, forty men with thirty shovels and ten wheelbarrows can move the same amount of earth in a day as either 400 men working with their bare hands or one man equipped with bulldozer. It would be easy, but tedious, to multiply examples of this kind. Clearly where more than one method of production is possible the question arises:

4. What determines the ways in which resources are combined to produce goods?

Even the least curious observer of developed economic systems cannot fail to notice that some persons (who can often be classified into professional groups) obtain a larger share of the flow of goods and services per period ('output') than others. Dentists, on average, receive more than dustmen. Doctors, on average, receive more than drivers of delivery vans. Why is this? Or, to put the question in the form which we have hitherto used:

5. What determines the way in which output is distributed between persons and groups?

It is these five questions which economists try to answer by discovering the principles upon which the economic system works. The questions, as the reader may readily convince himself, are common to all human societies.

The five questions listed have been set out, as the reader will have noticed, in what are called 'real' terms. That is we have spoken of the flow of goods and services – not its money value. In short, we have said nothing whatever about the absolute level of prices. Nevertheless the behaviour of the price level is a problem of considerable interest. Indeed, since the end of the Second World War, and particularly in recent years, there has probably been as much effort devoted to examining the determination of the price level, and its rate of growth, as to any questions in economics. Accordingly we add to our list of questions:

6. What determines the level of prices?
7. What determines the direction in which and the rate at which prices change?

These two questions, by definition, relate only to societies which use money rather than barter and whose prices are therefore expressed in terms of a monetary unit such as the pound, the dollar, the rouble, the franc, the mark or the rupee. They are therefore not necessarily common to all human societies as the first five are, for it is possible to conceive of a society which makes no use of any monetary unit. This point, however, need not worry us, for in this book we are concerned only with the workings of the 'mixed' capitalist-collectivist economies of Western Europe and the USA. That is, we are assuming, though we shall not attempt to describe it in any detail, a particular type of institutional framework. Economies of this type express all prices in terms of an abstract monetary unit. They thus possess a price level. It follows that questions (6) and (7) are relevant to the frame of reference in which we have chosen to work.

Although we cannot discuss the institutional framework of the mixed economy in any detail it is worth while considering a few of its major features. Overwhelmingly its most important characteristic is the dominance of the market.

A market is an organisation which makes it possible for those who wish to buy to get into touch with those who wish to sell. Modern communities contain an immense array of markets, some of them very highly specialised. There are 'money markets' in which those who have funds available for short periods offer loans to those who have a temporary need for money. The price at which these loans are made is the short-term rate of interest. There are highly organised markets in meat, fruit, vegetables, fish, wheat, tin, rubber, tea and in many other commodities. There are markets for services such as air freight space. In a broad sense there is a market for labour. There is, indeed, a market for virtually every good and service produced and demanded in a modern community.

In such a system of markets everything has a price. The price of labour, for example, is a wage or salary. With the money received from the sale of labour the individual worker demands goods or services and can obtain them, up to the limit imposed by the income he receives and the wealth he possesses, in whatever combination he wishes. The market system thus makes it possible for an individual to specialise completely at his work and get in return whatever combination of goods and services he wants and can pay for. For this reason in modern communities it is rare to find an individual who makes, by himself, a complete commodity.

The prices ruling in the markets reflect the availability of commodities (or services) on the one hand and the community's requirements for them on the other. Suppose, for example, the community wants, and is willing to pay for, more washing-machines than are currently being produced. The price of such machines tends to rise. As a result producing them becomes more profitable. The firms making them expand output, and to do this bid for more labour in the labour market. Wages in the washing-machine-producing industry tend to rise relative to wages elsewhere and labour is attracted into the washing-machine industry. In short the mechanism of the market provides signals in the form of profits (losses) which tell producers what kinds of output are to be expanded (contracted). In responding to these signals producers redeploy the productive resources of the economy by attracting labour (and other resources) into more profitable lines and withdrawing it (and other resources) from less profitable or unprofitable lines. Thus, as a consequence of individual decisions, reconciled by the market system, the pattern of production gets determined. By a similar process operating in the labour market so do wages and salaries, and since each commodity has a price the market system also determines not only what is to be produced but how much of what is produced is to go to each individual.

This, of course, is a highly simplified account of how any market economy actually operates. It is useful only at a very general level of discussion. How any market actually operates requires detailed and systematic study. For our present purpose, however, a simplified sketch is sufficient provided the reader is aware not only how simplified it is but also of the need, when studying any particular market, to confront our generalities with careful observation of what actually occurs.

Our economy, despite the degree of government intervention, government controls and government planning which justifies the adjective 'mixed', still conforms to a very large extent to the simplified picture of the 'market system' sketched above. Indeed what is remarkable is not the extent of government intervention and planning but the very restricted role they play in the modern 'mixed economy'. Overwhelmingly our economic system is still based upon individual enterprise. To confirm this statement the reader has only to walk through the shopping area in any large city, note the immense variety of goods and services available, and ask himself what proportion of these arises out of the planned activities of state enterprise. The answer, obviously enough, is a very small proportion. Overwhelmingly the immense variety of goods and services needed to sustain contemporary urban life are available in appropriate quantities in modern urban communities as the result of many millions of individual decisions made effective by the market process.

Thus although the economic system may be said to determine the rate of output, the composition of output, the methods by which output is produced, the distribution of output and the rate of growth of output over time, it does so not as the result of *conscious direction* by a group of planners but as the result of many millions of individual decisions acting through (and being reconciled by) the market process. Broadly speaking no one concerns himself with our five original questions. Producers pursue profit. Consumers arrange their expenditure, subject to the limits imposed by their income and wealth, to get that collection of goods and services which they prefer. Workers seek the highest price they can get for their labour. The result may not be ideal from some social points of view. But the market system demonstrably does work – as a visit to Marks & Spencer's will confirm – and it is the market system, operating within the framework defined by law and social custom, which provides the answers to our seven questions.

Broadly speaking the seven questions set out above define the subject-matter of positive economics which we examine against the particular background of a *market economy*. But just as it has been found convenient to subdivide the social sciences so economists have found it convenient to subdivide economics. As a result, in the technical language of economics, it is now usual to speak of *macro*economics and *micro*economics.

The former is that part of economics which studies the behaviour of *aggregates*. Examples of these are 'output', 'employment', 'consumption', 'investment', 'the general level of prices', 'exports' and 'imports'. *Macroeconomics* thus seeks to explain the values these aggregates take in any period. Again speaking rather broadly, macroeconomics may be said to embrace the *theory of output and employment*, the *theory of the price level* and the *theory of economic growth*: that is, to be concerned with the questions we have listed as (1), (2), (6) and (7).

The concentration on aggregates entailed in macroeconomics results, again speaking broadly, in the deliberate neglect of those problems we have listed as (3), (4) and (5). We simplify our task of explaining the level of total 'output' by either assuming its commodity composition to be invariant or assuming that changes in its composition do not have a significant effect on its total. The justification for this procedure is that, within limits, it has proved useful.

By contrast *microeconomics* seeks to provide answers to the questions we have numbered (3), (4) and (5). It seeks to explain not the general 'level of prices' but the output of particular commodities. Broadly speaking microeconomics embraces the *theory of demand*, the *theory of supply* and the *theory of distribution*.

We now begin to see how macro- and microeconomics complement each other. The former neglects individual prices and concentrates on the determination of the 'general price level'. The latter takes the general price level as given and seeks to explain the determination of a particular price in relation to all other prices. A precisely similar approach is made to problems of output; here macroeconomics seeks a method of explaining the general level while microeconomics takes the general level of output as given and seeks to explain, on this assumption, what determines the quantity of a particular commodity which is produced.

In this book we shall discuss only macroeconomics. This means that we shall consider only the *theory of employment and output*, the *theory of the price level* and the *theory of economic growth*. This does not mean that microeconomics is of less importance. On the contrary a reference back to our questions (3), (4) and (5) will convince the student of the importance of this branch of economics. This decision to concentrate on one branch of the subject is again one of convenience. It is simply not possible to extract a quart from a pint pot. In the same way, it is not possible to deal usefully with the whole of positive economics within the confines of this book.

Summary

1. Economics is a social science which seeks to explain why the economic system operates as it does and not in some other way.
2. Every society, whatever the stage of its development, must provide answers to five questions. These are

What, in any given period, determines the magnitude or rate of total output?

What determines the rate at which 'output' grows between any two periods?

What determines the commodity and service composition of 'output' in any period?

What determines the ways in which resources are combined to produce goods?

What determines the way in which 'output' is distributed between persons and groups?

3. In the 'mixed capitalist-collectivist' economies found in Western Europe and North America these questions are 'answered' by the economic system as the result of countless millions of individual decisions which are reconciled in the market.
4. Since mixed economies (as here defined) express prices in terms of a monetary unit there emerges the concept of a 'price level' and the derived concept of its rate of change. These lead to our questions (6) and (7).
5. The purpose of positive economics is to explain why the economic system provides the answers which it does to these seven questions and not some other set of answers.

Questions and exercises

1. We are often told that there is a serious national need for engineers, scientists and technologists. In a *market* economy what evidence would you look for to test this statement? Does 'need' mean 'shortage'? If not what does it mean?

2. If there was a 'shortage' of engineers, how do you think the *market* system would tend to eliminate it?

3. The prices people are prepared to pay for goods and the costs of producing them determine what is produced. What is produced determines what enterprises are prepared to pay for different kinds of labour. Extend this argument to explain the relative incomes of (i) the top pop group; (ii) Michael Edwards; (iii) your doctor; (iv) postmen.

4. If it is true that producers are always pursuing profit, how can this help to explain the *methods* by which a good is produced?

5. Discuss the contention that the market system works badly because a successful salesman receives a higher income than a great physicist. What is meant by 'badly'? Is this question one for positive or normative economics?

Suggested reading

J. Robinson, *Economic Philosophy* (Penguin, 1962) ch. 1.

F. Zeuthen, *Economic Theory and Method* (Longman, 1955) ch. 1.

Chapter 2
The Process of Economic Analysis

In Chapter 1 we defined the four main problems with which this book deals as being to explain:

(i) what determines the level of 'output' in any period;
(ii) what determines the rate at which 'output' grows between any two periods;
(iii) what determines the general level of prices in any period;
(iv) what determines its rate and direction of change between any two periods.

We have thus *selected* particular aspects of the economic system for intensive study. How are we to set about analysing these problems?

Since our aim is to develop a theory which explains the determination of output – that is why output is what it is in any period and not some greater (or smaller) magnitude – our first task is that of economic *description*.

Since we hope to develop a theory which will explain the facts we need to know what the facts are. The purpose of *economic description* is to give a systematic account of the facts which is, at one and the same time, sufficiently detailed for our purposes and sufficiently simple for us to comprehend. Two processes are involved here: (i) the definition, in operational terms, of a set of concepts with which a complex economic reality can conveniently be described; and (ii) the use of these concepts to provide a description.

All this no doubt sounds somewhat confusing. We shall now try to clarify it by an example.

What the economic system produces, in any period of time we may use for accounting purposes, is a flow of dissimilar goods and services. In principle it would be possible to make a detailed list of the quantity of each good and service produced in any given period. But such a list would contain several millions of dissimilar items, many of which would need to be measured in different units. The result would be comprehensive but not readily comprehensible. Moreover there is no obvious way in which the quantities of the various heterogeneous goods and services could be added together to produce a single total. What, for example, is the sum of 1.2 million cars, 97 million cabbages, 7 million 'books' (themselves not homogeneous), three new aircraft carriers, a new cathedral and two new atomic warheads?

To deal with this difficulty we make use of an abstract concept of output. This has two characteristics:

1. It possesses the capacity to satisfy human wants.[1]
2. It requires the use of scarce resources to produce it.

This definition, it should be noted, is derived directly from the observation that all scarce goods – that is goods which command a price – share the common property of being able in some degree to satisfy human wants, a point which we established in Chapter 1.

Thus defined, output cannot be observed directly. All that *can* be observed is the flow of heterogeneous goods and services which are scarce (that is, command a price) and which are produced in any period. In addition to our definition we therefore need to write down a set of rules which will enable us to say that a given flow of heterogeneous goods and services is equal to a particular flow of output. Once this has been done, output is, in principle, *measurable*: that is, the abstract notion of 'output' has been made operational. Provided we are prepared to undertake the work of measurement, or find someone to do it for us, we can then give a comprehensive, comprehensible and numerical description of the facts in which we are interested.

In the next two chapters we shall discuss in some detail the concepts (of which 'output' is only one) that we shall need to use to describe those facets of economic behaviour which interest us. We shall also discuss how these concepts can be measured. At this stage, however, we anticipate some of our later results by introducing a graph (Figure 2.1) on which three variables are plotted against time. These three variables are

1. The output of the UK for each quarter from 1955 to 1982.
2. The industrial output of the UK for each quarter from 1955 to 1982.
3. The percentage of the work-force unemployed for each quarter from 1955 to 1982.

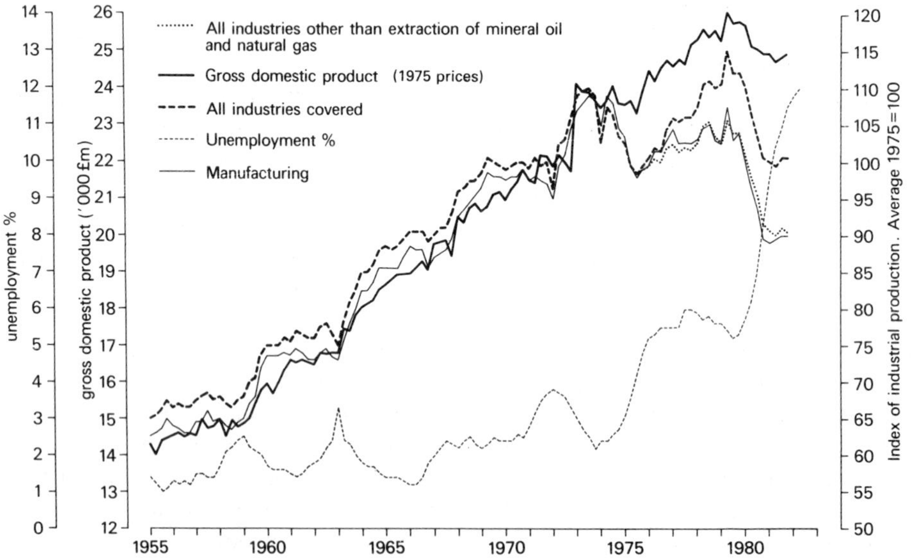

Source: *Economic Trends*, Annual Supplements.

Figure 2.1 Output and employment

[1]Wants may be satisfied directly or indirectly. Hence a shoe-manufacturing machine indirectly, by aiding in the process of shoe production, satisfies wants.

We shall not now comment on this set of observations of recent economic events. The reader, however, is invited to make a list of those problems in positive economics suggested by the diagram.

Economic description provides us with a systematic account of what we believe to be the relevant facts. Without some preliminary theory, that is without some notion of what it is we want to investigate, we have, of course, no idea what facts are relevant. Theory and fact in this sense are complementary, not opposed, concepts as the loose expression of everyday speech might lead us to suppose. Description, however, is not itself theory. For description can do no more than summarise for us, within the framework of a chosen conceptual scheme, what *has* happened. It does nothing directly to explain to us *why* whatever it was that happened actually did happen, though it may suggest possible lines of enquiry to us. To explain events is the task of theory. What then *is* a *theory*?

Since economics is a social science, any economic theory must

> *contain hypotheses concerning the way in which human beings behave. It is these hypotheses, which may obviously be correct or incorrect, which give economic theory its operational significance.*

These hypotheses must be expressed in terms of the conceptual framework in which the economic events are described. From these hypotheses by a process of logical deduction, we derive *predictions*[1] in terms of the conceptual framework which we have used to describe events. These *predictions* can then be tested against actual observations. If our observations conform to our predictions we may say that our theory is *not refuted by events*. We cannot say that it is 'correct', for other observations may, and eventually will, be made which force us to modify or abandon it. On the other hand if our *predictions* are not in conformity with observations, our theory *is refuted* and must be abandoned or modified.

All this sounds very difficult and possibly rather dull. In some cases it *is* difficult though it is *never* dull. A simple example may aid in clarification. Suppose that we are interested in explaining the monthly production of beer. We first define beer in such a way that the monthly production of it can be measured: that is, we provide an operational definition. This is not quite so simple as it sounds, for beer, like goods and services, is not homogeneous. Our definition must be in some degree arbitrary. Armed with our definition we can measure 'beer' production in each month and plot it on a graph.

Let us assume that the resultant curve looks like that in Figure 2.2. How are we to develop a theory to explain the fluctuations in production revealed by this graph?

From our discussion of the workings of a market economy we can argue that beer producers will try and adjust the quantity of beer produced in any month to the quantity consumed. For if they produce more than this, either stocks of unsold beer will accumulate (and deteriorate) or beer prices will fall. Either way producers will make *less* profit than they otherwise would. Equally if they produced less beer than the public wanted to consume the producers would be *forgoing* profits. Since, as we have seen, producers pursue profits and seek to avoid losses we may assume that they aim to produce the quantity the public wants to purchase at the ruling market price. Accordingly we may adopt the hypothesis that beer producers will plan to produce in any month the quantity of beer they *expect* that the public will want to buy. How do they form their expectations?

The main guide we have to the future is what has happened in the past. We can thus think of *brewers in general* as adjusting their production of beer in each month to the

[1] Sometimes called 'theorems'.

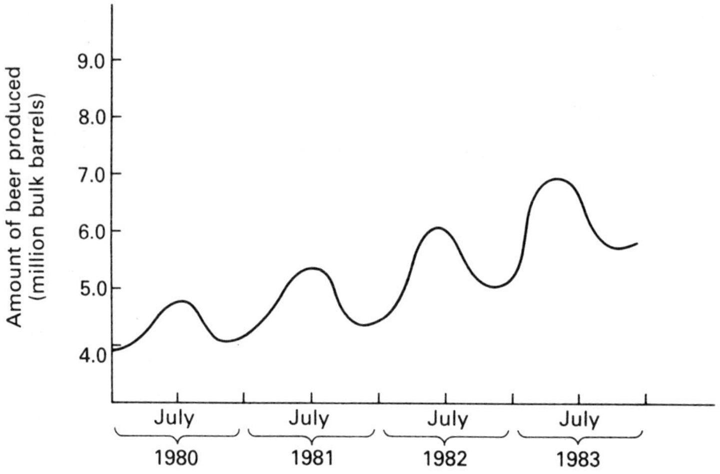

Figure 2.2 The quantity of beer produced over a period of four years (hypothetical data)

consumption of beer in the *previous* month. Hence, we can write our first hypothesis about human behaviour thus:

beer production in January = beer consumption in December

We now need to formulate some hypothesis about the beer-drinking decisions of *people in general* in order to explain consumption.

It is a familiar observation that public houses and bars are more crowded in summer than in winter. We should therefore expect some systematic seasonal variation in monthly beer consumption due ultimately to variations in climatic conditions. It also seems reasonable to argue that, given the 'weather' conditions, people drink more beer when they are more 'prosperous'. But surely, given the 'weather' and the 'degree of prosperity', the more beer people will drink the 'cheaper' it is in relation to other forms of alcohol? If whisky cost, per pint, the same as beer, would not people drink more whisky and less beer?

These considerations lead to a simple hypothesis about human behaviour which states that

The quantity of beer consumed in any month	*depends upon*	(i) The 'weather' in that month (ii) The general degree of 'prosperity' in that month (iii) The 'cheapness' of beer in relation to other forms of alcohol in that month

We now have to give operational meaning to our notions of 'the weather', 'the general degree of prosperity' and the relative 'cheapness' of beer. This is not hard. In any month we can measure the weather by the average hours of sunlight or average daily temperature. Similarly since the 'general level of prosperity' is likely to be inversely related to the percentage of the work-force unemployed we can measure the 'degree of prosperity' by the reciprocal of this percentage. To measure the 'cheapness' of beer let us take the price of whisky as a proxy for the price of other forms of alcohol. Then the 'cheapness' of beer is measured by price of whisky (per bottle)/price of beer (per pint):

$$\frac{\text{price of whisky (per bottle)}}{\text{price of beer (per pint)}}$$

We now have three behaviour hypothesis. These are:

1. Beer producers (brewers) pursue profits and seek to avoid losses; hence they try to adjust production to expected consumption.
2. The rule they follow to do this is to make production in any month equal to consumption of the previous month.
3. Consumption in any month depends upon:
   (i) average temperature
   (ii) the reciprocal of the percentage of the work-force unemployed
   (iii) the ratio of the price of whisky to the price of beer

We can now use our theory – in which every variable is operationally defined – to generate a number of *predictions*. Some typical predictions are as follows:

> if, in any month, with no change in the 'weather' (temperature) and no change in the relative 'cheapness' of beer (price of whisky in relation to price of beer) unemployment rises as a percentage of the work-force, then
> (i) beer consumption in the *same* month will fall; and
> (ii) beer production in the *following* month will fall by an equivalent amount.

Predictions of this kind can be tested against observations of what actually occurs. If the observations conform with our predictions we may continue to hold our theory. If they do not we must abandon our prediction.

The example is, of course, artificially simplified. As a result the process of deducing predictions logically from the behaviour assumption is extremely easy. It consists in saying:

If	**A** increase in the percentage of the work-force unemployed	*occurs in context*	**C** no change in average temperature no change in the ratio $\frac{\text{whisky prices}}{\text{beer prices}}$
then	**B** decrease in beer consumption	*will occur.*	

If **B** *occurs then* { **D** fall in beer production } *occurs one month later.*

An alternative way of putting the same thing is to say:

> If, other things being equal (often written *ceteris paribus*), the percentage of the work-force unemployed in any month *rises*
> *then*, in the same month, beer consumption will fall
> *and*, in the next month, beer production will fall by an equivalent amount.

In many economic theories the chain of reasoning, though ultimately reducible to this form, may be much more complicated. We may, for example, have to argue that, *on our behaviour hypotheses*,

If **A** *occurs in context* **C** *then* **Z** *will occur.*
If **Z** *occurs* **Q***will occur.*
If **Q** *occurs* **R** *will occur.*
If **R** *occurs* **S** *will occur.*
If **S** *occurs* **B** *will occur.*

Here again we can make the same predictions as before – *If* **A** *then* **B** – but only after a good deal more intellectual effort. But the greater complexity of the second example does not alter the fundamental nature of the process. This is the derivation of testable (or meaningful) predictions from hypotheses about human behaviour. It is because positive economics seeks to develop testable predictions of this kind that it can lay claim to the adjective 'scientific' – for the essential nature of scientific enquiry is precisely the development of predictions which can conceivably be tested by observation and experiment.

Two further points of great importance also emerge from this example. *Notice that the basic assumption of our method is that there is regularity in human behaviour – in this case human beer-drinking behaviour and the production planning of brewers.* If there were no regularity, our behaviour hypotheses would be false. Beer consumption would fluctuate capriciously from month to month and no systematic explanation would be possible. The assumption of regularity is, of course, familiar enough in the natural sciences. Is it a reasonable assumption in the social sciences?

To answer this question consider what would happen if there were *no* regularities in economic phenomena. Not only would beer consumption fluctuate capriciously – so would the consumption of all other commodities. Whatever producers tried to do, business planning would be virtually impossible. Now as a matter of common observation business planning, though difficult, is not impossible. Hence we may argue that regularity is present in sufficient degree to make some prediction conceivable.

The second point to notice is that, in expressing our behaviour assumption, we spoke deliberately of *people in general.* We are trying, in other words, to formulate hypotheses about group behaviour – *not individual behaviour.* Predicting individual behaviour is notoriously difficult even if we choose individuals whom we have known intimately for most of our lives. Predicting group or average behaviour is, however, far simpler. Why is this?

To see why consider the case of an insurance company which receives a proposal for life assurance from a man of 30. The proposal is to mature at age 60. Medical examination of the proposer shows no obvious physical defects. The proposer is, let us say, a librarian. Now the insurance company has no means of knowing at what age any particular proposer will die. Our librarian may be run over and killed ten minutes after the policy comes into force. Alternatively he may live to 90. On the other hand, from the statistics of deaths, the insurance company can easily calculate the percentage of 'average healthy' adult male librarians who die at any given age. The percentages can be plotted on a graph like Figure 2.3.

The next step is simply to interpret these percentages as 'probabilities'. The *most* probable age bracket in which death occurs is, on this figure, shown to be 61–70. Equally the probability of the average adult male librarian dying before the age of 31 is 0.03. The insurance company can now readily calculate the number of cases per cent in which

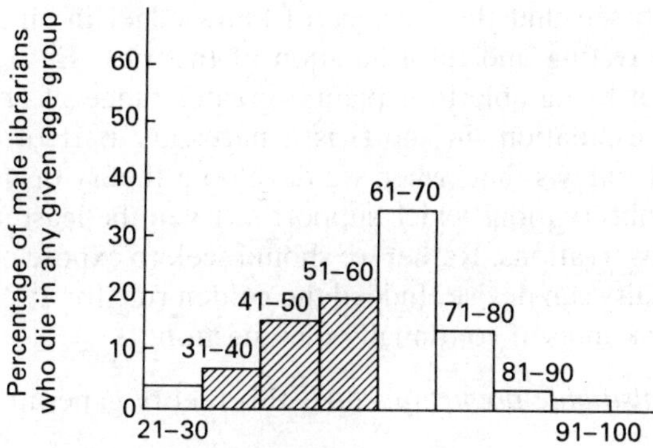

Figure 2.3 The percentage of 'average healthy' adult male librarians who die at any given age (hypothetical data)

30-year-old males will die before the age of 61. This is the sum of the probabilities in the shaded area. All it then has to do is (i) charge a premium sufficient to cover this risk and leave it a margin of profit, and (ii) write life policies for a sufficiently large number of librarians for the average behaviour to be applicable. In short. life insurance, indeed all insurance, can be conducted profitably because though it is impossible to forecast what will happen in individual cases, it *is* possible to predict what will happen, on average, in a large number of cases.

A similar situation exists in physics where the physicist, though he cannot predict the response of an individual electron to a given stimulus, can predict, with a useful degree of accuracy, the average response of a large group of electrons.

We may sum up what we have learned about the process of economic analysis so far as follows:

1. The first stage is to *select* a problem.
2. The second stage is *economic description*, which consists in:
   (a) *defining* operational (or measurable) concepts in terms of which the problem is to be examined
   (b) *measurement*
3. The third stage is to formulate, in terms of these concepts, *hypotheses* (or *assumptions*) about human behaviour.
4. The fourth stage is to derive, by logical processes, *conclusions* or *predictions* in terms of the concepts already defined.

The four stages are sometimes referred to as the development of a 'model' of the economy (or a part of the economy).

5. The fifth stage is to *test* the *predictions* of the theory or model against observations.

If the predictions are shown to be in conformity with the observations the theory is *not* shown to be correct. *It is merely shown not to be incorrect.* We can continue to hold it until its predictions cease to correspond with observation. When this happens we need to develop a new theory or model which generates predictions consistent not only with observations which the old model *could* explain but also with observations which the old model *could not* explain. Our new theory (model) must therefore be more general in its scope than the old.

From this it is easy to see that the advance of knowledge, in all sciences, takes place through the continuous testing and reformulation of theories. Each new theory is more powerful, in the sense of being able to explain a greater range of observations, than the theory it replaces. Reformulation, in short, is a necessary part of the advancement of knowledge. From this it follows that, when we develop a theory or model, we should not simply look around for observations which support it. Even the least useful of theories can be supported by *some* observations. Rather we should seek to expose our model to the most stringent tests our ingenuity can devise. Indeed the golden rule for anyone studying positive economic theory is to ask himself continually the question:

> What *testable or falsifiable predictions* does this theory generate?

This, as we shall see in later chapters, is often a difficult question to answer.

We have now said enough about the process of economic analysis to make it clear that what we have called 'positive economics' deals with issues which can be settled ultimately only by an appeal to the facts. This indeed is the characteristic of what we earlier called 'how' or 'why' questions.

By contrast, 'normative economics' deals with questions which *cannot* be settled by an appeal to the facts. Consider, for example, the statement:

> The government ought to raise taxes on cigarettes by 6p per packet of 20 in order to reduce lung cancer.

This, on analysis, consists of three propositions:

1. *If* a tax of 6p per packet is imposed, *then* cigarette consumption per year will fall by a certain amount;
2. *If* cigarette consumption falls by this amount, *then* the incidence of lung cancer will decline;
3. It is *desirable* that the incidence of lung cancer should decline.

Proposition (1) is easily recognisable as a *prediction* about the way the economic system works. It is a proposition in *positive economics*. Proposition (2) is similarly a *prediction* in human biology. Both these propositions can, in principle, be tested by an appeal to observation.

Proposition (3) is, however, of an altogether different kind. It asserts that a reduction in the incidence of lung cancer is 'good' or 'desirable'. We may agree with this. *But if we do not the disagreement can never be settled by any appeal to the facts.* This is because Proposition (3) is what is called a 'value judgement'. It reflects the 'value judgement' that one state of affairs is 'better' than another. In general, though possibly not in this case, many people will disagree over judgements of this kind. Their disagreements, however, cannot be resolved by observation or research.

It follows that normative propositions in economics involve not only propositions in positive economics, which can be tested by an appeal to the facts, but also value judgements, which cannot. This does not mean that normative propositions are unimportant. They are of very great importance and we shall devote part of this book to the examination of some 'normative' issues. What it does mean is that the student, particularly in his reading of the popular and semi-technical press, should be careful to distinguish positive economic statements from value judgements. For the former he should demand evidence. For the latter he can merely offer agreement or disagreement. In the same way, he should draw the same distinction in his own thinking and writing and, where his value judgements are inevitably involved, seek to make it clear precisely what they are and where they enter the argument.

The terminology employed here seeks to distinguish between positive and normative economics because this distinction, though ultimately invalid, is useful pedagogically. The reader, however, must not fall into the trap of thinking that normative economics, as we have used the term, is in any sense inferior to positive economics. This view can all too easily be arrived at through excessive contemplation of the rather elementary examples used to illustrate what is meant by 'normative'. By definition, normative propositions involve a value judgement and the value judgements involved are frequently unacceptable to the reader. At the same time the examples offered, in the interests of simplicity, often appear to require very little positive economic analysis. It is thus only too easy to assume that disputes over normative economic propositions are largely non-technical disputes over value judgements. Any assumption of this kind is entirely unjustified. Indeed some of the most promising (and most technical) modern developments in economics, including linear and other programming techniques, are concerned precisely with the problem of how best to reach a given objective and are thus, in the general sense, normative.

Properly speaking, therefore, normative economics is concerned with economic problems in which some objective (or target) is either given explicitly or implied. Thus if the objective of a business is to maximise profits then given this target the problem is to discover how to do it. This is frequently a complicated programming problem.

By contrast, positive economics is concerned to describe, explain and ultimately predict what actually occurs in the economic system.

Summary

1. Positive economic analysis of a selected problem consists of
   - (i) economic description, which entails
     - (a) the definition of measurable concepts
     - (b) measurement
   - (ii) formulation of behaviour hypotheses in terms of these definitions
   - (iii) generation of testable or falsifiable predictions (in terms of the definitions) from the behaviour assumptions
   - (iv) testing the predictions against observations
2. Positive economics is thus concerned with issues which can, in principle, be settled by the examination of evidence.
3. The fundamental assumption of positive economics is that, on average, the behaviour of people in the everyday business of earning a living exhibits sufficient regularity to make possible a predictive science of economics.
4. That there are observable regularities in economic behaviour is beyond dispute. What matters, however, is the degree of precision in prediction these regularities permit and whether positive economics can attain a useful degree of precision.
5. Normative economics consist of
   - (i) predictions derived from positive economics which are, in principle, testable, coupled with
   - (ii) value judgements which cannot be tested

Questions and Exercises

1. Using the theory of beer production outlined in the text, generate *ceteris paribus* predictions for the results of (i) a 'heat wave' in July; (ii) an additional 10 per cent tax on whisky in April; (iii) a social survey published in March showing that beer is the most popular drink of the aristocracy. In each case what is the precise meaning in terms of the theory of *ceteris paribus*?

2. What do we mean by saying that our predictions are in conformity with the facts? Plot on a graph the predicted values given by the table below and compare them with the observed values. Plot also the difference between the predicted and observed values. Which is the 'better' theory? Why? Give your reasons. What can you learn from examining the errors?

Year	*Actual value*	*Value predicted by: Theory 1*	*Theory 2*
1	100	100	101
2	51	51	50
3	43	44	42
4	43	44	41
5	47	49	49
6	62	64	61
7	81	83	82
8	111	113	112

3. Develop, on the general principles of our theory of beer production, an operational theory to explain the monthly production of automobiles in the UK. Use your theory to generate *ceteris paribus* predictions for the results of (i) an increase in the minimum deposit on hire-purchase transactions; (ii) a reduction in car tax; (iii) a reduction in UK tariffs on imported cars. Treat each case separately and, for each prediction, give a precise meaning, in terms of your theory, to *ceteris paribus*.

4. Can you develop an operational theory which would make it possible to test the proposition that 'The root cause of juvenile delinquency is simply broken homes'?

5. 'A tax on the television advertising of cigarettes, tobacco and alcohol could not fail to bring immense social benefits.' Analyse the propositions implied in this statement. Has it any meaning?

6. Is there any way of testing the following propositions?
   (i) Honesty is, in the long run, always the best policy.
   (ii) The higher the rate of tax on increments in income, the less the professional classes will be disposed to work.
   (iii) Virtue is always rewarded — in this world or the next.
   (iv) Women are inferior (superior) to men.

7. Suppose you are the son or daughter of a brewer who tells you that he *neither* seeks to maximise his profits *nor* plans his monthly beer production to be equal to the previous month's consumption. Does his statement invalidate the theory put forward in this chapter? If not, why not?

8. According to Figure 2.2, beer production has a general tendency (trend) to rise from 1980 to 1983, for each successive seasonal peak (and trough) is higher than its predecessor. Can this be explained in terms of the model in the text? If so, how? If not, what additions would you make to the theory to explain it? Give your reasons.

9. What are the obvious objections to the beer model in the text? How would you seek to improve it? In what way do your modifications change its predictions?

10. Assume that brewers commonly hold stocks of beer. On the basis of the model in the text – and Figure 2.2 – graph the path of these stocks over time. Does this graph help you to answer question 9?

11. 'No theory predicts with complete accuracy; there is always *some* error.' Do you agree? If so, what is the difference btween a 'prediction' derived from a theory and a 'guess'?

12. If the statement quoted in question 11 is correct, how does science advance?

13. Meteorologists predict the weather. So do witch doctors. In what sense, if any, do they differ? If they do not, is it correct to regard a witch doctor as a scientist? And vice versa?

14. 'That experience of privation in youth gives sound character in middle age is amply attested by research.' Consider this statement. Do you think it reasonable? Can you think of the way in which research might have led to this conclusion?

15. 'Research has shown that those university departments that select their undergraduate entry by interview would have done better if they had picked them out with a pin.' How do you think this result could have been reached? Explain the logical processes involved.

16. 'The essence of science consists in specifying the range of error of a prediction. The advance of science consists in reducing the error.' Consider these statements carefully.

17. To many philosophers the distinction between positive and normative economics made in this chapter is unacceptable. Can you think of reasons why the distinction might break down?

18. 'Spare the rod and spoil the child.' 'Corporal punishment should be retained in schools because, while there is evidence that schoolmasters and senior boys enjoy inflicting it, there is no evidence that it does any harm to those who suffer it.' Are either of these arguments scientific?

Suggested reading

M. Friedman, *Essays in Positive Economics* (Chicago University Press, 1953) ch. 1.
*T. W. Hutchinson, *The Significance and Basic Postulates of Economic Theory* (Macmillan, 1938).
A. R. Louch, *Explanation and Human Action* (Oxford University Press, 1966) chs 4, 5.
J. Robinson, *Economic Philosophy* (Penguin, 1962) ch. 1.
F. Zeuthen, *Economic Theory and Method* (Longman, 1955) chs 1–5.

*More advanced reference.

Chapter 3

Definition of Concepts and Measurement of Output

In this chapter we define some of the concepts which we shall need to employ in describing how the economy operates and developing a theory to explain why the economy operates as it does.

Our picture of the economy, which is very much simplified, is this. Resources, which we shall call *factors of production*, are combined in various ways by *firms* or *enterprises* to produce an annual flow of *goods* and *services*. We define these terms as follows:

1. The *factors of production* are defined to be *land, labour* and *capital*.
2. *Land* consists of natural resources provided free by nature; examples are mineral deposits, forests and, surprisingly enough, water in the form of rivers and natural lakes.
3. *Capital* consists of all those aids to production which have been made by people. Examples are machinery, roads, houses, railways, tools, canals and man-made lakes.
4. *Labour* consists of human resources. These are partly mental and partly physical. They are also partly inherited and partly acquired.
5. *Production* is the process of making goods and services which is organised by *enterprises*.
6. *Enterprises* are organisations (which may take various legal forms such as public companies, private companies, partnerships, nationalised corporations) which take economic decisions.
7. Those enterprises which take decisions relating to production we call *productive enterprises*.

This system of classification is set out schematically in Figure 3.1. Here we see the factors of production, i.e. services of land, labour and capital, being organised as *inputs* by enterprises so as to produce an *output* of goods and services.

This flow of goods and services (or output) is available for the satisfaction of human wants. The process of using these goods and services for the satisfaction of immediate wants is called *consumption*; and goods that are used for this purpose we assume to be used up (or consumed) either at the moment of purchase or a very short while afterwards. Beer, for example, is an obvious type of consumption good and the purchase of beer an obvious form of *consumption expenditure*. In other cases such as expenditure on durable goods the distinction between *consumption* and *investment* is more difficult to draw.

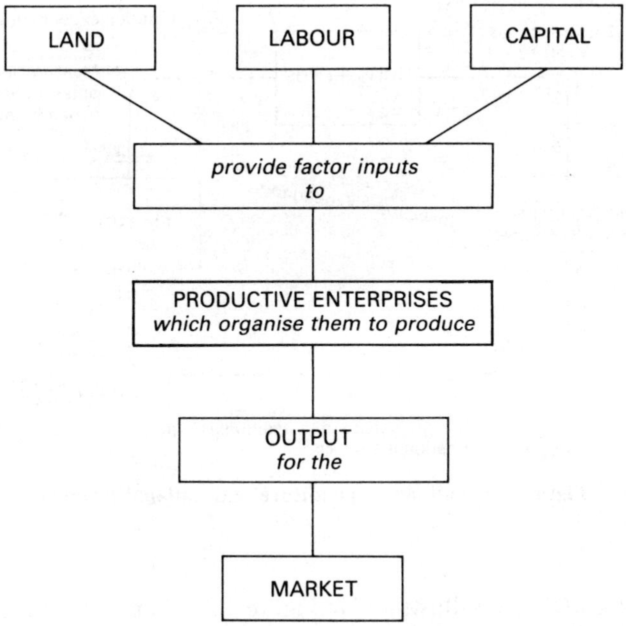

Figure 3.1 The organisation of production

Not all goods produced by the economy in any period are *consumed*. Some are added to the capital stock of the economy existing at the beginning of the period. This process of adding to the capital stock is called *investment*. Notice that this definition differs from popular usage.

Obviously, in any period, that part of output which is not *consumed* must be added to the capital stock existing at the beginning of the period. This increment in capital is, by definition, *investment*. Hence the total flow of output becoming available to the community in any period is, again by definition, equal to the sum of the flows of *expenditure* on *consumption* and *investment*. This equality, which is illustrated in Figure 3.2, can be simply expressed as follows:

$$pO \equiv pC + pI$$

where pO is money value of the flow of goods and services in a given period; pC is money value of the flow of consumption expenditure in that period; pI is money value of the flow of investment expenditure in that period; p is the price level, i.e. the price of a unit of output.

Thus

O is the real flow of goods and services
C is the real flow of consumption expenditure
I is the real flow of investment expenditure

This equality is written with three horizontal lines instead of the usual two to indicate that it is an *identity which is always true*, not an equation which is satisfied only for certain values of O, C and I.

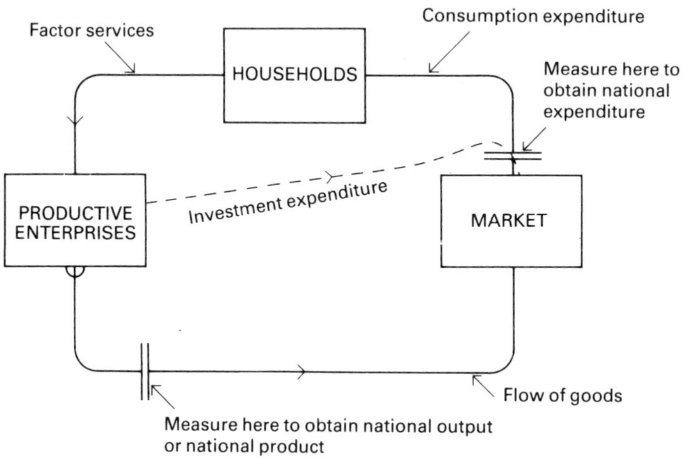

Figure 3.2 National expenditure and national product

The identity $pO \equiv pC + pI$ is illustrated in Figure 3.2, where we have introduced the new concept of *households*. A household is defined as an individual (or group of individuals) that receives income from the sale of factor services and engages in consumption expenditures. Although in practice the household sector of the economy does engage in investment expenditure also, we have assumed here, and in general shall continue to assume that (i) all consumption expenditure is made by *households*; and (ii) all investment expenditure is made by *productive enterprises*.

There is one difficulty here which needs to be faced if it is not to cause confusion. It relates to the meaning of investment expenditures.

As far as consumption expenditures are concerned, there is, in general, little difficulty in relating these expenditures to a money flow. By and large consumption goods are bought (by consumers) and sold (by enterprises) at identifiable market prices. As goods flow from enterprises to households, money flows from households to enterprises.

This analogy holds satisfactorily for investment where the investment of an enterprise consists in expenditure on some good (say a machine-tool) which is produced and sold by some other enterprise. Again there is a money flow and an identifiable price.

Now consider the case (say of a farmer) where the investment by the farmer consists of the accumulation of inventories (stocks). Suppose, for example, the farmer grows a crop of which some part is sold to consumers. Again a money flow exists and there is an identifiable price. The remainder of the crop, that which is *unsold*, the farmer retains. It is thus an addition to the farmer's capital stock and, *by definition*, constitutes investment. But there is no money flow. The farmer does not purchase this part of the crop for his own use. Moreover there is *no* identifiable market price.

To deal with this situation we assume a *notional* expenditure by the farmer on the unsold part of the crop: that is, an *investment* in the form of inventory accumulation. Moreover we value this investment at the price at which the remainder of the crop was sold in the market. On this basis the value of output in any period is, *by definition*, equal to the value of expenditure on output, though not all expenditures now can be identified with *actual* money flows. Some consist in *notional* money flows.

Now $C + I$, if we measure it as a money flow, is simply the sum of the *expenditure*, valued at the prices ruling in the period, on output produced in the period and thus available for the satisfaction of human wants. Hence in any period the value of output, at the prices ruling in the period, is always by definition equal to the value of expenditure on that output. Thus for the economy of any country we may write:

> the value of national output ≡ the value of national expenditure ≡ the value of consumption *plus* the value of investment.

The upshot of these simple considerations is that we have now developed a *set of rules* for measuring output. We add together the heterogeneous collection of goods and services becoming available in any period of the satisfaction of human wants by valuing each at its price. The resultant total is then expressible in terms of monetary units. It is simply the money value of national output or national product. For example, suppose we picture a simple community which produces, in a given period, the following goods which become available for the satisfaction of human wants:

1,000 loaves of bread
10 wheelbarrows
800 suits of clothes

If the price of a loaf of bread is 20p, that of a wheelbarrow £10 and that of a suit £60 then the value of national output, at these prices, is

$$£[1{,}000 \times 1/5] + £[10 \times 10] + £[800 \times 60] = £48{,}300$$

We have thus established a method of adding together a heterogeneous collection of goods so as to produce a single readily comprehensible measure.

At this stage it is convenient to introduce four assumptions which are of considerable importance. In what follows we shall continue to assume (as we have in Figure 3.2) that

1. All *consumption* expenditure is made by *households*.
2. All *investment* expenditure is made by *enterprises*.
3. There is no government sector.
4. The economy does not engage in international trade.

On the basis of these assumptions we can now draw Figure 3.3. This shows a flow of *factor services* from *households* to *enterprises*. *Enterprises* use these services in *production*. The result is a flow of *goods* and *services* on to the *market*. The expenditure on goods and services is shown as a flow from *households* in the form of *consumption* plus a flow from *enterprises* in the form of *investment*.

If we measure the flow of goods and services from enterprises to the market, we obtain the value of *national output*. If we measure the flow of expenditure,[1] we obtain the value of *national expenditure*. These two totals are equal by definition. Or, as this proposition is usually stated and as we have stated it above,

$$\begin{aligned}\text{national output} &\equiv \text{national expenditure}\\ &\equiv \text{consumption} + \text{investment}\end{aligned}$$

Figure 3.3 is considerably more satisfactory than Figure 3.2, for it shows where *households* obtain the incomes they spend on *consumption* and where *enterprises* obtain the resources they devote to *investment*. These two problems can now be explained more fully.

The factors of production used by enterprises are owned by the individuals who constitute households. In return for selling their factor services to enterprises these

[1]Including the notional expenditure on stock accumulation.

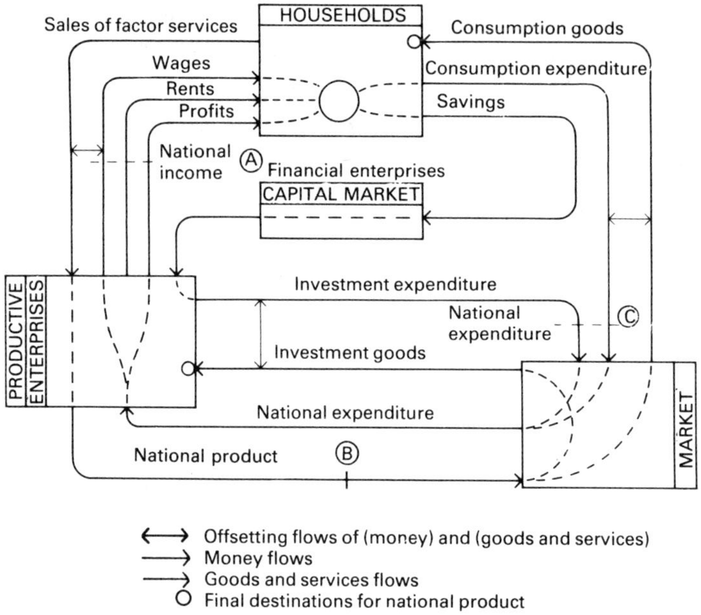

Figure 3.3 The circular flow of income, output and expenditure

individuals receive rewards which constitute their *incomes*. For the sale of labour services, the reward is *wages*; for the sale of the services of land and buildings the reward is *rent*; for the sale of the services of capital (other than buildings) the reward is *profit*. These are definitions of *factor incomes* or, to the enterprise, *factor costs*. What is cost to one is income to another.

Two of these costs, *wages* and *rent*, are contractual. The third, *profit*, is a *residual*. *Profit* is now *defined* as the difference between the value of output and the sum of *wages* plus *rents*, the contractual costs incurred in producing it. That is,

$$\text{the value of output} \equiv \text{the values of wages} + \text{rent} + \text{profits}$$

National income may now be *defined* as the *sum of factor incomes generated by the process of production*. Hence:

$$\begin{matrix}\text{the value of}\\ \text{national output}\end{matrix} \equiv \text{wages} + \text{rent} + \text{profits} \equiv \begin{matrix}\text{national}\\ \text{income}\end{matrix}$$

Combining this *identity* with those on earlier pages we have:

$$\begin{matrix}\text{national}\\ \text{output}\end{matrix} \equiv \begin{matrix}\text{national}\\ \text{income}\end{matrix} \equiv \begin{matrix}\text{wages} + \text{rent}\\ + \text{profits}\end{matrix} \equiv \begin{matrix}\text{consumption}\\ + \text{investment}\end{matrix} \equiv \begin{matrix}\text{national}\\ \text{expenditure}\end{matrix}$$

This is the fundamental identity of what is called national income accounting. It is always true because we have defined our terms so that it must be. In short, the three aggregates national income, national output and national expenditure are simply three ways of looking at the same thing.

The simple extension of our conceptual scheme shows where households obtain the income they spend, in part, upon consumption. How do they dispose of the whole of it?

Households do not invest. Hence their income must either be *consumed* or *not consumed*. The act of abstaining from consumption we define as *saving*. Hence, from the income disposal side,

$$\text{national income} \equiv \text{sum of wages} + \text{rent} + \text{profits} \equiv \text{consumption } \textit{plus} \text{ saving}$$

However, we already know that national income is identically equal to national expenditure, which is identically equal to consumption *plus* investment. Hence:

$$\text{national income} \equiv \text{consumption} + \text{saving} \equiv \text{national expenditure} \equiv \text{consumption} + \text{investment}$$

So it is obvious that

$$\text{saving} \equiv \text{investment}$$

We thus reach the conclusion that, *as far as our national income accounting framework is concerned, saving and investment are always identically equal. That is, they are equal by definition.*

The common sense of this result should be obvious. If in some period a part of the national product is not consumed, then, by definition, it is saved. It must therefore be added to the capital stock existing in the economy at the beginning of the period. But we have already defined the process of adding to the capital stock as investment. Hence saving and investment, *as we have here defined them*, are simply two different ways of looking at the same quantity of output.

Now this *identity* between the accounting concepts of savings and investment has, surprisingly enough, caused a lot of confusion. The student should remember (i) that it is an identity which is true by definition; (ii) that it refers to the *results* of past decisions and does not tell us whether those results were expected or unexpected, wanted or unwanted. These are important points, for in the accounting sense precisely the same identity holds between demand and supply. This can easily be seen as follows. The value of demand in any period can be defined as the value of purchases on the market, for all that is purchased must be demanded. That is:

$$\text{value of demand} \equiv \text{value of purchases}$$

The value of supply, on the other hand, must be equal to the value of sales, for all that is sold must be supplied. Hence:

$$\text{value of supply} \equiv \text{value of sales}$$

Now, since sales ≡ purchases (they are merely two aspects of the same set of transactions), demand must equal supply, *by definition*. This means that, in accounting terms, demand and supply are always identically equal.

Although this last statement is correct, *on these definitions*, it does not prevent our arguing that demand and supply may be unequal, for when we do *we are using the terms in different senses*. Analogously there are, as we shall see, senses in which saving and investment can be unequal. In later chapters we shall refer to saving and investment in the accounting sense as actual saving and actual investment. Hence the identity above merely states that

$$\text{actual } \textit{or} \text{ accounting saving} \equiv \text{actual } \textit{or} \text{ accounting investment}$$

and does not preclude there being other important senses in which saving and investment *need not* be equal except in special circumstances.

We have now answered the question of where the *enterprises* obtain the real resources to devote to *investment*. The answer is, in our conceptual scheme, from the *saving of households*. The financial flows by which the saving of households is made available to enterprises does not at present concern us. We merely note that they usually occur through the medium of *financial enterprises* – such as banks, building societies and finance houses – which we define as constituting the *capital market*.

Thus Figure 3.3 sets out the full conceptual framework which we have elaborated. This diagram depicts what is often called the circular flow of income, expenditure and output. If we enter the diagram at the point *A*, we measure the sum of wages *plus* profits *plus* rents – that is, national income. If we enter at *B* we measure the value of the flow of goods and services produced by enterprises – that is, national output or national product. If we enter at *C* we measure the value of consumption *plus* investment – that is, national expenditure. Whichever point of entry we choose, the total we arrive at will be the same for, as we have seen,

$$\begin{array}{c}\text{the value of}\\ \text{national output}\\ \text{(or national product)}\end{array} \equiv \begin{array}{c}\text{the value of}\\ \text{national income}\end{array} \equiv \begin{array}{c}\text{the value of}\\ \text{national expenditure}\end{array}$$

Questions and exercises

1. 'It is evident that everything produced in an economy during a period such as a year must have been used up by someone during the period or added to what someone possessed at the beginning of the period. Therefore national output must be equal to national expenditure.' Explain.

2. What is the purpose of measuring national product and expenditure? How far do expenditure estimates represent money flows?

3. Can consumption exceed national income? If so what are the implications of such an excess for saving and investment? Illustrate your answer by reference to a situation in which

   national income ≡ £10,000m
   consumption ≡ £11,500m

4. 'Driving tests do not measure driving skill. They measure whatever qualities are necessary to pass driving tests. In the same way national income is whatever it is that the national income estimates measure.' Discuss critically.

5. 'The national income is a measure of the money value of goods and services becoming available to the nation from economic activity. It can be regarded in three ways: as a sum of incomes derived from economic activity...; as a sum of expenditure...; or as a sum of the products of the various industries of the nation' (*National Accounts Statistics: Sources and Methods*). Explain.

6. From *Economic Trends*, prepare a table showing quarterly estimates of gross domestic product at factor cost for 1962–82 (i) at current prices; (ii) at constant prices; (iii) unadjusted; (iv) seasonally adjusted. Why do you think the authorities provide four estimates in this way? What is the point of providing a 'seasonally adjusted' series?

7. Express consumers' expenditure, gross fixed capital formation at home and the value of physical increase in stocks and work in progress as proportions of gross domestic product. What item shows the 'greater fluctuations'?

8. What is the meaning of negative investment in stocks? In what periods do you observe it? Can gross fixed capital formation ever be negative?

9. From *Economic Trends* show that gross domestic expenditure is gross expenditure on the domestic product and not gross expenditure by home nationals. What is the distinction? In what circumstances would the two concepts be identical?

10. Why do we have four estimates of real GDP? Which do you prefer and why?

Suggested reading

Central Statistical Office, *National Accounts Statistics: Sources and Methods* (HMSO, 1968) chs i–iv.

Central Statistical Office, *National Income and Expenditure* (HMSO, annual).

Central Statistical Office, *The National Accounts: A Short Guide*, Studies in Official Statistics no. 36 (HMSO).

E. Devons, *An Introduction to British Economic Statistics* (Cambridge University Press, 1958) chs i, ix.

*H. C. Edey and A. T. Peacock, *National Income and Social Accounting* (Hutchinson, 1969).

*J. R. Hicks, *The Social Framework* (Oxford University Press, 1971)

*Alternative references.

Chapter 4

National Income and National Product

In the last chapter we erected a consistent set of definitions which provided us with a conceptual scheme in terms of which we can (and shall) describe economic behaviour. How do we measure the concepts we have defined? The easiest way of answering this question is to construct, and work through, a simple example.

National output or national product

Suppose we assume an economy with only two firms and that, at the end of the period for which we wish to prepare accounts, the books of these concerns reveal the information shown in Table 4.1.

Table 4.1 Hypothetical data: firms A and B

	FIRM A		
Allocations		*Receipts*	
Purchases from *B*	2,300	*Sales*	
Wages	15,000	to households	20,000
Rent	3,000	to firm *B*	14,000
Profit (residual)	13,700		
	34,000		34,000
	FIRM B		
Purchases from *A*	14,000	*Sales*	
Wages	15,300	to households	24,000
Rent	3,300	to firm *A*	2,300
Profit (residual)	5,700	Addition to stocks*	6,000
		Addition to fixed capital	6,000
	38,300		38,300

*Notional sale.

We now wish to prepare an estimate of national product (or output). If we sum the sales of the two firms we obtain the figure £72,300. Is this a correct estimate of the national product?

Looking back to our conceptual framework we know that

national product ≡ national income ≡ wages + rents + profits

If, however, we add the factor incomes we obtain:

national income ≡ wages + rent + profits
≡ £(15,000 + 15,300) + £(3,000 + 3,300) + £(13,700 + 5,700)
≡ £56,000

This result is, *by definition*, impossible. What has gone wrong? The answer is simply that the total value of sales is *not* the same thing as the value of national product. The latter is correctly interpreted as the sum of the values produced by *each firm alone*. This we have not measured. For, as the table shows, in estimating the value of output of firm *A* we have included the value of output it purchased from firm *B*. And, demonstrating consistency in error, we have repeated this procedure with *B*. We have thus double-counted.

We avoid this difficulty by defining

national output ≡ national product ≡ sum of the value added by firms in the economy

and

value added (of any firm) ≡ sales of the firm – purchases from other firms
≡ addition to the value of the product attributable to the firm in question alone

Applying these definitions to Table 4.1 we obtain:

national product ≡ value added by *A* *plus* value added by *B*
≡ [sales by *A* – purchases from *B*] + [sales by *B* – purchases from *A*]
≡ £[34,000 – 2,300] + £[38,300 – 14,000]
≡ £31,700 + £24,300
≡ £56,000.

The reasoning behind this procedure is readily demonstrated by considering (say) a pint of beer selling at 60p. We trace this back through the productive process in Table 4.2.

Table 4.2

Stages of productive process	*Value of sales*	*Cost of materials*	*Value added*
1. Farmer sells hops to dealer	15p	Nil	15p
2. Dealer sells hops to brewer	24p	15p	9p
3. Brewer sells beer to publican	42p	24p	18p
4. Publican sells beer to consumer	60p	42p	18p

In Table 4.2 the total value of all sales is 141p; the total value of intermediate sales is 81p. Hence the total *value added* by the farmer, dealer, brewer and publican is: the sum of sales minus purchases from other firms = 60p. What this means is that we cannot count in the national product the value of the hops sold by the farmer *and* the whole value of the beer of which they become part. And this, as the reader can see, is precisely the error we made in summing the sales of firms *A* and *B* to obtain national product. It was this error which resulted in arithmetic inequality of national product and national income: an inequality inadmissible by definition.

National expenditure

National expenditure is the total expenditure on the national product. As we know, national expenditure ≡ consumption *plus* investment. Consumption expenditure is recorded as sales to households by both firms. This amounts to £44,000. We know also that firm *B* added to its stocks by £6,000. There is thus a *notional* expenditure of £6,000 on investment since, as we have defined investment, an addition to stocks constitutes investment. There is also a £6,000 addition to the fixed capital of firm *B*. Hence we have:

national expenditure ≡ expenditure on the national product ≡ consumption *plus* investment
≡ £44,000 + £12,000
≡ £56,000

National income and depreciation

In the previous chapter we stated that:

national income ≡ national product ≡ national expenditure
national income ≡ wages + rent + profits

We now need to examine this more closely.

The concept of national income is of interest because it measures the flow of factor incomes generated by the production of output in the current period available to satisfy human wants. What, then, do we mean by 'income'?

What we usually mean by income in any period is the amount which income recipients themselves *could* consume and leave themselves as well off at the end of the period as they were at its beginning. There are, of course, immense difficulties in saying what is meant by 'as well off as'. Nevertheless it is clear that, to obtain a measure of income, allowance must be made for that part of the output of the current period which is due *not* to economic activity in the current period but to economic activity *in past periods*. How does this arise?

In any period some part of the output produced is attributable to the using up of capital equipment existing at the beginning of the period. To arrive at income, therefore, it is necessary to subtract from output of the current period a sum which is sufficient to restore the capital at the end of the period to what it was at the beginning of the period. Failure to make such a subtraction results in an overestimate of income and hence of the flow of goods and services which can be consumed without becoming worse off and, what is the same thing, the flow attributable to the economic activity of the current period.

To make this correction we set aside an annual sum to cover *depreciation*. Our identities now become:

$$\begin{aligned}\text{national income} &\equiv \text{wages} + \text{rents} + [\text{profits} - \text{depreciation}]\\ &\equiv \text{wages} + \text{rents} + \textit{net}\ \text{profits}\end{aligned}$$

where

$$\textit{net}\ \text{profits} \equiv \text{gross profits} - \text{depreciation}$$

On the expenditure side we have:

$$\begin{aligned}\text{gross national expenditure} &\equiv \text{consumption} + \textit{gross}\ \text{investment}\\ \text{net national expenditure} &\equiv \text{consumption} + [\textit{gross}\ \text{investment} - \text{depreciation}]\\ &\equiv \text{consumption} + [\textit{net}\ \text{investment}]\\ &\equiv \text{gross national expenditure} - \text{depreciation}\end{aligned}$$

And on the output side we have:

$$\begin{aligned}\text{gross national product} &\equiv \text{gross values added}\\ \text{net national product} &\equiv \text{gross national product} - \text{depreciation}\end{aligned}$$

So that:

$$\text{national income} \equiv \textit{net}\ \text{national expenditure} \equiv \textit{net}\ \text{national product}$$

Formally speaking these adjustments are simple enough. But this is because we have avoided the problem of saying *how the value of depreciation should be calculated*. This is a difficult question the discussion of which would take us too far afield. It is worth noting, however, that in the UK, because of the difficulty of calculating the proper annual allowance for depreciation, the estimates of national income and expenditure did not contain an estimate of *net investment* until 1956. Since that date the Central Statistical Office has been prepared to publish a figure based upon rather detailed calculations of 'capital consumption'.[1] The caution of the CSO in this matter serves to remind us of the complex problems involved in the calculation of the appropriate adjustment.

The introduction of government

So far we have proceeded on the convenient assumption that our economic system contains no government. This assumption we shall now relax. As a result our conceptual system will become more realistic. The cost of this additional realism is additional complication.

[1] On this point the reader should consult *National Accounts Statistics: Sources and Methods*, and *National Income and Expenditure* – the latter published annually by HMSO and hereafter referred to as the Blue Book.

In a modern 'mixed economy' the government (or, as we shall call it, the *public sector*) undertakes the following activities:

1. Through the nationalised corporations the public sector produces a part of output which is sold on the market like the output of any private enterprise.
2. The public sector undertakes expenditure on the provision of common services such as defence, education, law and justice which are, in general, not sold on any market.
3. In addition the public sector makes payments to individuals in the form of social service benefits. These payments, as we shall presently explain, are called *transfer payments*.
4. Finally, the public sector imposes taxes.

Our problem is how to integrate these activities into the system of national accounts.

Item (1) causes no difficulty. The ownership of an enterprise is clearly irrelevant in determining its contribution to national product. Public enterprises are thus to be dealt with precisely like private enterprises and their values added, calculated in the usual way, form part of national product. Hence the expenditure and the factor incomes generated by their activities form part of national income. This accords with common sense since it would obviously be absurd to include the operations of (say) the coal industry in national product if it were privately owned and exclude them if it were publicly owned.

Item (2) is more troublesome. The first problem is a conceptual one. Should the common services performed by the public sector be regarded as part of national product or not? Alternatively, does it make more sense to regard, let us say, the provision of education as an intermediate rather than a final product – an expense which must be incurred if output is to be produced at all? In practice the statisticians responsible for the UK national income estimates solve this problem by *adopting the convention* of including *all* common services provided by the public sector as part of national product. This convention thus disposes in practice of the question of principle involved. But now a second problem arises. If we are to include these common services in national product, how are we to value them?

This valuation problem arises because these services are not sold upon a market. They therefore have no identifiable price. *The solution adopted is to value such services at the cost of providing them.* This cost is, of course, the value of the factor incomes (wages and rents) paid to the persons who provide them. Hence the value of the common services provided by the public sector appears

(a) in national expenditure as *public sector expenditure on goods and services*
(b) in national output as *the value of the output of common services*
(c) in national income as *the factor incomes generated by their production*.

In short, once we have agreed to the convention that includes these services in output, we have *defined* expenditure on them as part of national expenditure and the factor costs of providing them as part of national income.

If we now incorporate these modifications into our basic identities we have:

gross national product	≡	gross value of output of private sector	+	gross value of output of public sector		
	≡	gross value of output of private sector	+	gross value added by public enterprises	+	value of public sector's common services

On the expenditure side the adjustment is straightforward. We have:

$$\text{gross national expenditure} \equiv \text{consumption} + \text{gross investment} + \begin{array}{c}\text{government}\\ \text{expenditure on}\\ \text{common services}\end{array}$$

In practice, however, some part of gross investment is undertaken by the public sector. Hence the national expenditure identity can be expanded to read:

$$\begin{array}{l}\text{gross}\\ \text{national}\\ \text{expenditure}\end{array} \equiv \text{consumption} + \left\{\begin{array}{c}\text{gross investment by private sector}\\ +\\ \text{gross investment by public sector}\end{array}\right\}$$
$$+ \begin{array}{l}\text{government (public-sector) expenditure}\\ \text{on common services}\end{array}$$

On the income side:

$$\text{national income} \equiv \text{wages} + \text{rents} + (\text{gross profits} - \text{depreciation})$$

$$\equiv \left\{\begin{array}{c}\text{wages bill}\\ \text{of private}\\ \text{sector}\\ +\\ \text{wages bill}\\ \text{of public}\\ \text{sector}\end{array}\right\} + \left\{\begin{array}{c}\text{rents paid by}\\ \text{private sector}\\ +\\ \text{rents paid by}\\ \text{public}\\ \text{sector}\end{array}\right\} + \left\{\begin{array}{c}\textit{net}\text{ profits of}\\ \text{private}\\ \text{enterprises}\\ +\\ \textit{net}\text{ profits of}\\ \text{public-}\\ \text{sector}\\ \text{enterprises}\end{array}\right\}$$

As we have seen, the problems so far raised by government economic activity are twofold. The basic conceptual problem is that of *defining* product. The subsidiary problem is that of *valuing* product. Once conventions are adopted to deal with these, the adjustment of our original identities presents no difficulties. The result is to make our main aggregate slightly more complicated. In return the information they provide is more comprehensive. That is all.

We now turn to consider items (3) and (4) and ask the question: What complications occur as the result of the raising of taxation by the public sector and the payment of transfers by the public sector?

We begin by classifying taxes into two groups: *direct* and *indirect*. *Direct taxes* are those imposed upon persons or enterprises. The most important example of them is *income tax*. *Indirect taxes* are levied not upon persons but on commodities. The most familiar example here is value added tax.

In addition to levying taxes the government also makes what are called *transfer payments*. These are defined as payments made to persons which are not classifiable as payments made for the provision of a productive service. *Old-age pensions*, *unemployment benefits* and *disability pensions* are examples of such payments. So, too, is the *interest on the National Debt*.

Transfer payments of this kind can be regarded as negative direct taxes. Neither type of transaction modifies any of the concepts we have so far defined. Taken together, however, direct taxes and transfer payments cause what are called *personal incomes* and *personal disposable incomes* to differ from the sum of net factor incomes (≡ national income). It is easy to see why this should be. Consider some (hypothetical) individual called Smith who receives the following *factor incomes* in a given year:

	£
Wages	4,800
Profits	240
Rents	100
	£5,140

From this factor income he must pay £1,000 in income tax. Smith also receives a disability pension of £50 per year and interest on his holding of government bonds amounts to £100 per year. We then define Smith's personal income as:

personal income ≡ wages + profits +rent + transfer receipts
≡ £4,800 + £240 + £100 + £100 + £50
≡ 5,290

and his personal disposal income as:

personal disposable income ≡ personal income − direct taxation
≡ wages + rent + profits + transfer receipts−direct taxation
≡ £5,290 − £1,000
≡ £4,290

We must now take account of indirect taxes and subsidies. The effect of an indirect tax is to raise the *market prices* of a commodity above its *factor cost*. A subsidy, which is from this point of view a negative indirect tax, simply does the reverse. For example, suppose the factor cost of a packet of twenty cigarettes is 30p, made up as follows

Wages	20p
Rent	7p
Profits	3p
	30p

If the government now imposes a tax of 50p per packet, the *market price* becomes 30p + 50p ≡ 80p.

The effect of indirect taxes (and subsidies) is therefore to complicate matters slightly by giving us two sets of prices at which output, expenditure and income may be valued: namely, *market prices* and *factor costs*. The two are related by the definition:

market price ≡ factor cost + (indirect taxes − subsidies)
≡ factor cost + net indirect taxes

The adjustment defined by this identity may be applied to a single commodity (as we have applied it) or to any one of our aggregates. Thus:

gross national product (at market prices) *less* net indirect taxes *equals* gross national product (at factor cost) ≡ gross national expenditure (at market prices) *less* net indirect taxes *equals* gross national expenditure (at factor cost)

We have not shown the corresponding adjustment on the income side since, by convention, national income, which is simply the sum of net factor income, is always valued at *factor cost*.

These, in outline, are the principal modifications to our conceptual scheme made necessary by the introduction of public-sector activity. None of the changes is unduly complicated in principle and, as the example at the end of this chapter makes clear, it is a simple matter to handle the modifications in practice.

The introduction of international trade

So far, simply as a matter of convenience, we have proceeded on the assumption that our hypothetical economy does not engage in international trade – that is, it is a 'closed' economy. This assumption is unrealistic. Accordingly we must relax it. This requires that we adjust our system of accounts to allow for the influence of the sale of goods to foreigners, i.e. *visible* exports; the sale of services to foreigners i.e. *invisible* exports; and the corresponding purchases from foreigners, i.e. *visible and invisible imports*.

To see what is necessary here, consider the expenditure side. Without international trade we have:

gross national expenditure
(at market prices)

$$\equiv \text{consumption} + \text{gross investment} + \text{public-sector expenditure on final output (all at market prices)}$$

$$\equiv C + I + G$$

Now the expenditure of foreigners on our goods and services is, by definition, *exports*, which we write as E. Clearly this forms part of the total expenditure on our national product. E must therefore be *added* to $C+I+G$.

Equally some part of $C+I+G$ will be spent on goods and services produced by foreigners. By definition, the sum of these expenditures is equal to the value of *imports*, which we write as M. To arrive at the value of expenditure on our national product we must *subtract* M from $C+I+G+E$. Hence we have:

gross national expenditure $\equiv C+I+G+E-M$.

On the *output* side we now need to calculate *value added* for each firm as:

total sales (including exports) *less* purchases from other firms (including imports)

Obviously the sum of the value added by all firms, since intermediate purchases and sales cancel out, is then:

Sales to	*Less purchases from*
households (consumption) enterprises (investment) government (government expenditure) foreigners (exports)	foreigners (imports)

which is identical with $C + I + G + E - M$, as it must be.

Table 4.3 National income accounting: principal aggregates

	Consumers' expenditure		Income from employment
plus	public authorities' current expenditure	*plus*	income from self-employment
plus	gross fixed capital formation at home	*plus*	gross trading profits of companies
plus	value of physical increase in stocks and work in progress	*plus*	gross trading surplus of public corporations
		plus	gross profits of other public enterprises
plus	exports and income received from abroad	*plus*	rent
minus	imports and income paid abroad	*plus*	residual error
		minus	stock appreciation
equals	gross national expenditure at market prices	*equals*	gross domestic product at factor costs
minus	taxes on expenditure	*plus*	income from abroad (net)
plus	subsidies		
		equals	gross national product at factor cost
equals	gross national expenditure at factor cost	*minus*	capital consumption
minus	capital consumption		
		equals	national income
equals	net national expenditure at factor cost	*plus*	transfers to persons
		minus	undistributed profits
		minus	surpluses of public enterprises and corporations
		equals	personal income
		minus	direct taxes on persons
		equals	personal disposable income

Finally, national income can be obtained from the factor incomes generated in producing gross national product or output. To obtain these we first adjust GNP to a net basis by subtracting depreciation or capital consumption. Next we subtract net indirect taxes to obtain NNP at factor cost. This, as we have already seen, is equal to the sum of factor incomes, which is, by definition, national income.

We can now summarise the relationships between the principal aggregates in tabular form (see Table 4.3). Before we do this, however, we need to make an adjustment due to the fact that in some countries, of which the UK is one, a part of the income received by households is derived from the ownership of property overseas. Analogously some property in the UK is owned by foreigners, and hence the income arising out of its productive services is paid to overseas residents. We thus have an item:

$$\begin{matrix}\text{net income} \\ \text{from abroad}\end{matrix} \equiv \begin{matrix}\text{income receipts} \\ \text{from abroad}\end{matrix} - \begin{matrix}\text{income payments} \\ \text{to abroad}\end{matrix}$$

Clearly this item is part of national income. Equally clearly it does not rise out of production within the domestic economy. To meet this problem we distinguish between gross domestic product (the result of the productive process within the economy) and gross national product. These are related as follows:

GNP	≡ GDP + net income from abroad
national income	≡ net domestic product + net income from abroad
gross national expenditure	≡ $G + I + G + E - M$ + net income from abroad
net domestic product	≡ gross domestic product − depreciation

The reader should now carefully examine Table 4.3 and compare it with the latest Blue Book.

The saving–investment identity

In our simple system of accounting identities we showed that:

S	≡	I
saving		investment

where these two concepts were defined net (of depreciation) or gross. How must this identity be modified to take account of our introduction of government and international trade?

Let us begin by recalling that we now have three sources of *net* saving:

(a) households
(b) enterprises
(c) public sector

and three classifications of *net* investment:

(d) *net* investment of private enterprises } *net* investment at home
(e) *net* investment of public sector }
(f) *net* investment overseas

Our identity therefore expands to:

net household saving	+	*net* saving of enterprises	+	*net* saving of public sector	≡	*net* investment at home	+	*net* investment overseas

To show how this extension occurs, consider first the net saving of households. This is given by:

net personal saving	≡	personal disposable income	−	household consumption						
	≡	national income	−	undis-tributed profits	+	transfer incomes	−	direct taxes on persons	−	household consumption

Now

$$\text{national income } (Y_n) \equiv \begin{array}{c}\text{net national product}\\ \text{at market prices } (Y)\end{array} - \text{net indirect taxes } (T_i)$$

So, writing:

$$\begin{aligned} U &\equiv \text{undistributed profits}\\ R &\equiv \text{transfer incomes}\\ T_h &\equiv \text{direct taxes on households}\end{aligned}$$

we have:

$$\text{net personal saving } (S_h) \equiv$$

$$\begin{array}{c}\text{national}\\ \text{income}\\ (Y - T_i)\end{array} - \begin{array}{c}\text{undis-}\\ \text{tributed}\\ \text{profits } (U)\end{array} + \begin{array}{c}\text{transfer}\\ \text{incomes } (R)\end{array} - \begin{array}{c}\text{direct}\\ \text{taxes on}\\ \text{households } (T_h)\end{array} - \begin{array}{c}\text{consumption}\\ \text{of}\\ \text{households } (C_h)\end{array}$$

The *net* saving of the public sector we define as S_g:

$$S_g \equiv \begin{array}{c}\text{total tax}\\ \text{receipts } (T_i + T_h)\end{array} - \text{transfers } (R) - \begin{array}{c}\text{public-sector current}\\ \text{expenditure on goods}\\ \text{and services } (C_g)\end{array}$$

The *net* saving of enterprises is a new concept to us, for so far we have assumed enterprises not to save. However, where profits are not distributed – and thus do not enter personal disposable income – enterprises, whether public or private, are saving. Hence we define

$$\text{net saving of enterprises } (S_e) \equiv \text{undistributed profits } (U)$$

Adding household, public-sector and enterprises' saving we have:

$$\begin{aligned} S &\equiv S_h + S_g + S_e\\ &\equiv \begin{array}{c}\text{net saving}\\ \text{of households}\\ (Y - T_i - U + R - T_h - C_h)\end{array} + \begin{array}{c}\text{net saving}\\ \text{of public}\\ \text{sector}\\ (T_i + T_h - R - C_g)\end{array} + \begin{array}{c}\text{net}\\ \text{saving of}\\ \text{enterprises } (U)\end{array}\\ &\equiv Y - (C_h + C_g)\end{aligned}$$

which is obviously net national product (Y) minus consumption (C), as before. In short we still have $S \equiv Y - C$ just as we did in our earliest set of accounts.

On the investment side we have:

$$\begin{aligned} I_e &\equiv \textit{net} \text{ investment of enterprises}\\ I_g &\equiv \textit{net} \text{ investment by public sector}\\ I_f &\equiv \textit{net} \text{ investment overseas} \equiv \text{exports } (E) - \text{imports } (M)\end{aligned}$$ [1]

Our saving–investment identity therefore becomes:

$$\begin{aligned} S &\equiv I\\ S_h + S_g + S_e &\equiv I_e + I_g + I_f\\ Y - C &\equiv I_e + I_g + (E - M)\end{aligned}$$

or, rearranging the items slightly,

[1] An excess of exports (receipts) over imports (payments) means that domestic nationals are accumulating assets overseas (usually in the form of foreign currency, bank balances or securities). These claims on foreigners form part of the capital of the country. Hence an increase in them constitutes investment.

$$Y \equiv C + (I_e + I_g) + (E - M)$$
$$\equiv (C_h + C_g) + (I_e + I_g) + (E - M)$$

Now total public-sector expenditure on goods and services (G) is obviously $G \equiv C_g + I_g$. Hence:

$$Y \equiv C_h + I_e + G + (E - M)$$

which is the net national expenditure identity we have already met.

All this may seem a trifle complicated but in practice all we have done is:

1. To expand the basic definition of *net* saving ($S = Y - C$) into three elements:
   (a) S_h $\equiv$ *net* savings of households
   (b) S_e $\equiv$ *net* savings of enterprises
   (c) S_g $\equiv$ *net* savings of public sector
2. To show that *net* investment now consists of three elements:
   (a) I_e $\equiv$ *net* investment by enterprises
   (b) I_g $\equiv$ *net* investment by the public sector
   (c) I_f $\equiv$ *net* investment overseas
3. To demonstrate, what should be obvious, that our fundamental identity of $S \equiv I$ still remains.

Money and 'real' values

We have now set out a conceptual framework in terms of which we can (i) describe how the economic system has behaved; and (ii) seek to develop a theory to explain *why* it behaved as it did. This conceptual system defines for us, and tells us how, in principle, we are to measure the money value of certain flows in any given accounting period. This is helpful. But it does not give us all the information we want. For many purposes, particularly when we seek to compare different years (*or* quarters *or* months) it is not the *money value of output* which primarily interests us but its *real* value – the *quantity* of (different) goods and services to which the measured money value corresponds. For it is *real* output that satisfies human wants, and it is to produce *real* output that enterprises must organise the input of *real* factor services. Accordingly we need a measure of real output or a method of converting our money value of output – and, of course, other associated aggregates – into real terms.

In practice there are four methods of obtaining such estimates.

The first is to revalue the quantities of goods and services *produced* in each year in terms of the prices of some particular base year. This is called the *output* or *production* method.

The second is to conduct a similar exercise from the *expenditure side*. In this case we revalue each item of expenditure in any year at the prices ruling in some base year.

The third, obviously enough, is to perform the same exercise from the *income side*.

Since income, expenditure and output are defined to be equal, whether measured in money or 'real' terms, if we had complete information the results of these methods would be identical. Each would provide an estimated value of output (expenditure) in any year valued at constant (base-year) prices. In practice our information is not complete. The

Table 4.4 Index numbers of gross domestic product: 1975 = 100 (selected years)

	Constant factor costs					
	1959	1964	1969	1974	1979	1980
Expenditure method	64.7	77.6	88.7	100.5	109.0	107.3
Income method	64.2	77.8	90.1	100.9	111.3	109.2
Output method	68.1	81.2	91.9	101.9	110.3	107.2
Average estimate	65.1	78.9	90.3	101.1	110.2	107.9

Source: Blue Book (1981) table 1.11.

methods therefore provide slightly different results, as they do for estimates in money terms. But as Table 4.4 shows, the results are in close conformity.

The fourth method is to estimate the extent to which *prices* have changed, from one period to another, by a *price index number*. This simply expresses the prices of any given year as a ratio of the prices in some chosen *base year* in which the price index is taken to be 100 (or unity).

Armed with this estimate we can then *deflate* the value estimates of any year by dividing them by the *index number* of prices in that year and multiplying by 100.

For example, gross domestic product at *current* factor cost in the United Kingdom was:

	£m
1969	38,557
1970	42,229
1971	47,491

In the same years the index of *retail* prices was:

1969	127.2
1970	135.3
1971	148.1

We can now obtain estimates of *real* gross national product at constant (1963) *factor cost* by *deflating* the values of these years as shown in Table 4.5.

Table 4.5

Year	Value in £m (1)	Index of retail prices (2)	Estimated 'real' value in 1963 prices col. (1) ÷ col. (2) £m.
1969	38,557	127.2/100	30,312
1970	42,229	135.3/100	31,211
1971	47,491	148.1/100	32,067

These estimated 'real' values can now be compared with those given in the Blue Book. They differ – which tells us that the *index of retail prices* has moved differently from the *index of factor costs*. The example, however, is simply offered to illustrate the process of *deflating* – that is, in this case, of *revaluing* gross national product at 1963 (base-year) prices.

In principle all four methods are the same in that they involve revaluation and thus an *explicit*, or *implicit*, price index number. In the fourth case the index number of prices was calculated independently of the estimates of GNP at *current factor prices* and then applied to them to obtain 'real' or constant price GNP. In the first and second cases 'real' or 'constant' GNP was obtained by revaluing quantities of output (production method)[1] or expenditure (expenditure method) directly. The resultant 'real' values define an 'implicit price index' by the following relation:

$$\frac{\text{GNP (current prices)}}{\text{GNP (constant prices)}} \equiv \text{implicit index of final product prices}$$

$$\equiv \text{implicit GNP deflator}$$

Table 4.6, derived from the Blue Book, gives the value of this implicit *price index* as well as the values of other well-known indexes of various types of prices. In general, as one might expect, price indexes tend to move together but the movements are not identical.

Table 4.6 Price index numbers, UK, selected years (1975 = 100)

	Total home costs	Consumers' expenditure	Imports	Retail prices		All manufactured products (wholesale)
				All items	Food	
1959	34.8	36.7	35	36.1	33.8	39.2
1964	39.9	41.9	37	41.4	37.3	43.5
1969	47.3	51.9	44	51.0	45.3	50.5
1974	78.7	80.9	88	80.5	79.6	81.8
1979	161.7	163.4	155	165.8	171.3	172.0
1980	190.9	189.5	169	195.6	191.9	200.0
1981	212.0	n.a.	n.a.	218.9	208.2	221.3

Sources: Blue Book (1981) table 2.6; *Economic Trends Annual Supplement*; *Economic Trends* (July 1982).

The theory of index numbers cannot be discussed here. All we need to remember at this stage is that from our aggregate estimates in terms of current prices (market or factor) we can obtain, by deflating, estimates in terms of constant prices (or relative '*real*' values) and that, for many purposes, it is 'real' values which concern us.

Questions and exercises

1. Suppose you were interested in the change in 'economic welfare' in the UK between 1948 and 1980. How would you seek to define it? Which aggregate or aggregates would you use to estimate it? Why?

[1]In principle this method requires the revaluation, in constant prices, of all 'values added'. This requires the revaluation of all input and output prices.

2. Assume that the authorities replace *all* direct taxation by indirect taxes producing an equivalent yield. What would be the consequences for the estimates of gross domestic product, national income and personal disposable income? Would your estimate of economic welfare be affected? If so, how and why?

3. 'If a householder repairs his own leaking roof national income is unaltered; if he hires a builder to do it, national income is increased.' Is this so? If it is, does it imply any serious criticism of national income estimates? Can we increase economic welfare by doing each other's washing?

4. Suppose that an output of lawlessness makes it necessary to put 250,000 additional men into the police force where they are paid (in total) precisely what they were paid in their previous occupations. What would happen to national income? What would be the effect on economic welfare? In the light of your answers discuss the limitations of the national income concept.

5. Interest on the National Debt is treated as a transfer payment. Why is this? Where the expenditure financed by the government borrowing was used to build factories, is the procedure sensible?

6. Net investment is defined as gross investment *minus* depreciation. Explain the theoretical relationship between net investment and the community's stock of real capital. Can net investment be negative? If so, in what periods of British history would you expect to find negative net investment? Can gross investment ever be negative? Give your reasons.

7. In a particular period an economy consisting of two firms (*A* and *B*) and a public sector records the data shown in Table 4.7:
   (a) Prepare estimates of gross national product and gross national expenditure at both market prices and factor costs.
   (b) From your results in (a), prepare estimates of national income, personal income and personal disposable income.
   (c) Next prepare a capital account showing the saving and investment identity on page 37. What is the saving of households, enterprises and government? Has the government a surplus or deficit? What is the value of *net* investment?
   (d) Finally prepare an account showing transactions with the rest of the world. Is the balance of trade favourable or unfavourable? What is the value of investment overseas?

8. Use the Blue Book to provide data for the national expenditure identity on page 36 for the years 1950–80. What are the *average* ratios over the period of the following sub-aggregates to gross national expenditure:

   (a) consumers' expenditure
   (b) public authority's current expenditure
   (c) investment (gross and net)
   (d) exports
   (e) imports

   Do any of the ratios show fluctuations around their average? Can you suggest and defend a simple way of comparing the extent to which the different ratios fluctuate? Do you get a different picture if you distinguish between fixed capital formation and the increase in stocks? What is the most 'volatile' series?

9. Distinguish carefully between (i) the increase in the value of stocks; (ii) the value of the increase in stocks. Write:

   P_1 for the price of a unit of stocks in year 1
   P_2 for the price of a unit of stocks in year 2
   Q_1 for the quantity of stocks in year 1
   Q_2 for the quantity of stocks in year 2,

Table 4.7

Allocations		*Receipts*	
		FIRM A	
Purchases from		Sales to	
firm *B*	6,000	households	10,000
foreigners	5,000	firm *B*	21,000
Wages	20,000	government	5,000
Rents	1,000	foreigners	8,000
Indirect taxes	1,000		
Taxes on profits	2,000	Additions to	
Depreciation	5,000	fixed capital	6,000
Dividends	7,000	stocks	4,000
Undistributed profits	7,000		
	54,000		54,000
		FIRM B	
Purchases from		Sales to	
firm *A*	21,000	households	45,000
foreigners	19,000	firm *A*	6,000
Wages	22,000	foreigners	21,000
Rents	500		
Indirect taxes	1,500	Additions to	
Taxes on profits	700	stocks	−1,000
Depreciation	3,300		
Dividends	1,000		
Undistributed profits	2,000		
	71,000		71,000
		GOVERNMENT	
Interest on National		Taxes:	
Debt	1,000	direct taxes on	
Wages and salaries	6,000	companies	2,700
Purchases from *A*	5,000	direct taxes on	
Net decrease in		persons	7,000
indebtedness	200	indirect taxes	2,500
	12,200		12,200

and formulate expressions for (i) and (ii). Use your answer to explain the significance of the item 'stock appreciation'. Compare your discussion with that in *National Accounts Statistics: Sources and Methods*, particularly ch. 13.

10. 'The concept of depreciation is difficult enough. Its measurement is more difficult still.' Explain. Compare your explanation with that given in *National Accounts Statistics*.

11. Use the latest Blue Book to extend Table 4.4. Graph the relationship betwen the expenditure and production output indexes. Do the differences between the two indexes show any systematic pattern?

12. Which aggregate would you expect to be most closely related to domestic unemployment? Why? Test your conclusions by plotting GNP, GDP and national income against the percentage of the work-force unemployed for the years 1960–70.

13. 'Quarterly data on gross domestic product will always tell us whether output is expanding or contracting.' Do you agree? Compare your answer with the GDP estimates in *Economic Trends* for all three methods of calculation. Does each tell the same story? Are the discrepancies increasing?

14. Distinguish between 'profits' and the 'rate of profit'. How would you measure both?

15. 'North Sea oil and gas contribute immensely to our national product. And will continue to contribute at a growing rate for many years.' Estimate the North Sea contribution in current years and express it as a proportion of real GDP. Will it continue to grow?

Suggested reading

Bank of England, 'Trends in Company Profitability', *BEQB* (March 1976).

Central Statistical Office, *The National Accounts: A Short Guide,* Studies in Offical 1968).

Central Statistical Office, *The National Accounts: A short Guide*, Studies in Official Statistics no. 36 (HMSO).

*H. C. Edey and A. T. Peacock, *National Income and Social Accounting* (Hutchinson, 1969).

W. A. H. Godley and C. Gillon, 'Measuring National Product', *NIESR Review*, no. 27 (1964).

*J. R. Hicks, *The Social Framework* (Oxford University Press, 1971).

HM Treasury, *Revenue from the North Sea*, Economic Progress Report no. 143 (March 1982).

*Alternative references.

Chapter 5
Output and Capacity

We have now defined a set of accounting concepts in terms of which we can describe, in a systematic and unambiguous way, the behaviour of the UK economy. To do this we had to spend some time and effort in looking at purely accounting problems. There is therefore a risk that in concentrating on the development of a conceptual framework we have lost sight of our main objective. Accordingly this is a good point at which, before looking at the behaviour of the UK economy in Chapter 6, to take stock of what we have learned.

We began, in Chapter 3, by picturing the simplest possible economic system. In this there was no governmental economic activity and no international trade. Our sketch of the economy in operation was correspondingly simple. Households sold factor services to enterprises. Enterprises organised these services to produce a flow of goods and services. These passed, via the market, either to households (as consumption) or to enterprises (as investment). For convenience we produce as Figure 5.1 our earlier figure describing this.

The whole of Chapters 3 and 4 were concerned to develop a consistent and unambiguous set of concepts in terms of which we could give a numerical description of economic activity in a model of this kind. Description, however, presupposes analysis. Our first aim was to measure the flow of goods and services becoming available, in any given period, to satisfy human wants while leaving the community as well off at the end of the period as it was in the beginning. Measurement of this flow – which we called real national income or real net national product – is obviously an important problem. For real national income is a measure of the potential economic welfare of society in any given period.

Our second aim, however, was rather more ambitious. We sought to answer the questions:

(1) What determines the magnitude of real national income in any period?
(2) What determines the rate at which real national income grows from one period to another?

Logically this second aim was prior to our first. It was *because* we wanted to explain the level of potential economic welfare in any period and its rate of growth between periods that we embarked on the tasks of defining national income and its associated aggregates and sub-aggregates and elaborating a set of rules for measuring them. Asking our two questions – that is, posing our two problems for analysis – told us what facts were likely to be relevant to our enquiry. Now we have defined our facts – which we shall shortly need to explain – we can take a more systematic look at the analytical problem from which we started.

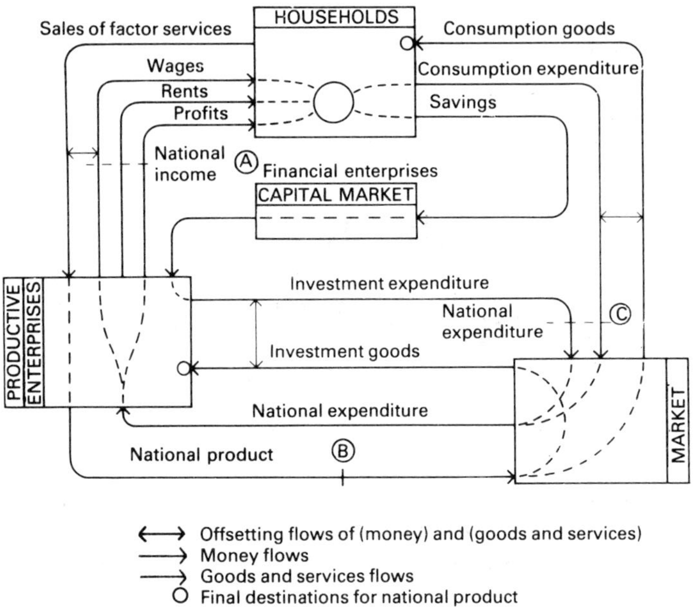

Figure 5.1 The circular flow of income, output and expenditure

Obviously enough the level of real output produced in the economy in any accounting period depends upon:

(a) the *capacity* of the economic system to produce output
(b) the *extent* to which the capacity in existence is utilised

Equally clearly the growth in output between two accounting periods depends upon:

(c) the growth in *capacity* between the two periods
(d) the change between the two periods in the *extent* to which capacity is utilised

It is therefore convenient to begin our enquiry into the determination of the level of output and its rate of growth by making these two notions – capacity and its degree of utilisation – rather more precise.

The determinants of capacity

We have already spoken of the economy as possessing, at any given time, a given endowment of the factors of production, which we shall in future call 'labour' and 'capital'. It is also clear that, at any given time, the community will have a certain degree of technical knowledge about the way in which the services of these factors *may* be combined to produce a flow of output in any period. Accordingly we can think of the productive *capacity* of the system, in any short period such as a year or a quarter, as being determined by (i) the endowments of the two factors; and (ii) the state of technique – and the actual output produced as being determined by the extent to which this capacity is utilised.

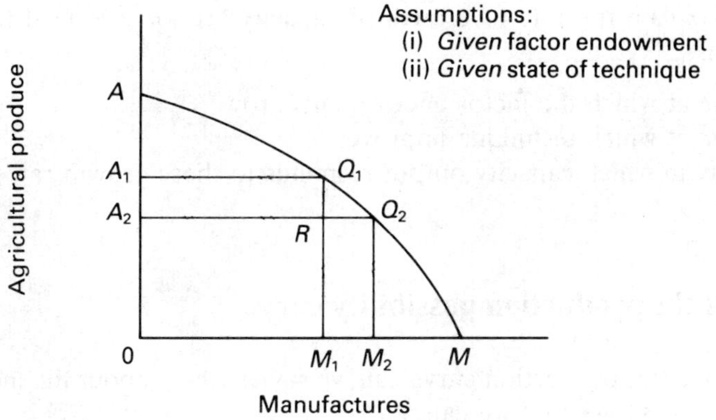

Figure 5.2 Production possibility curve

Output, in terms of commodities and services, is, as we know, multi-dimensional. To fix our ideas, however, we may think of output as consisting of only two commodities. These we can call 'manufactures' and 'agricultural produce'. Approaching matters along these lines we can then construct a simple diagram showing the various combinations of these two outputs which the economy can produce with its 'capacity' fully and optimally utilised. This is done in Figure 5.2.

Interpreting this diagram is relatively straightforward. Suppose only agricultural produce is to be produced. If the whole of capacity is employed, output of agricultural produce is *OA* and output of manufactures is zero. Suppose now that the community's preferences change in favour of manufactures. Through the working of the market, enterprises redeploy factors so as to produce more manufactures and less agricultural produce. If this process continues we shall trace out a curve showing all the combinations of the two commodities which can be produced by the community on the assumptions that (i) both factors are fully employed; (ii) the production of each commodity is optimally organised; (iii) the state of technique is given. Of these three assumptions only (ii) has a meaning which is not self-evident. What does 'optimal' organisation mean? The answer, which at this stage we ask the reader to take on trust, is that at all points on the curve *AM*: (i) enterprises, in the search for profit, are using factors in such a way as to keep costs at a minimum and that, provided they do this, (ii) at no point on *AM* is it possible to have more of either commodity without giving up a *greater* value of the other. The curve *AM* is thus not defined simply by the technical conditions of production and the factor endowment. It also depends on the implicit assumption that the market processes, which underlie the curve, produce an 'optimal' allocation of resources in the sense defined above.

Given this assumption – which in future we shall continue to make – the shape and position of the curve *AM*, which we call *the production possibility curve*, depends upon (i) the state of technique, and (ii) the factor endowment. In formal terms it represents a first attempt at answering the question 'What determines the capacity of the economy to produce output?'

On this approach the *growth* of capacity over time takes the form of an outward shift in the curve. Clearly it can occur because the process of *net investment* increases the endowment of capital, because *technique is improving* or because the work-force is *growing*. To explain the rate of growth of capacity economists need to develop a theory which explains:

(a) the *rate* at which the factor endowments grow
(b) the *rate* at which technique improves
(c) the way in which capacity output responds to these growth rates

The slope of the production possibility curve

Before we leave this production curve can we say anything about the meaning of its slope? A little reflection shows that we can.

Consider the points Q_1 and Q_2 on the curve. If we move from Q_1 to Q_2 we obtain an additional output of manufactures of M_1M_2 at the *cost* of giving up A_1A_2 of 'agricultural produce'. We then say that the *opportunity cost* of M_1M_2 of 'manufactures' is A_1A_2 of 'agricultural produce'. Their ratio, that is the 'opportunity cost' of M_1M_2 in terms of A_1A_2, is given by the *slope* of Q_1Q_2. Clearly if the distance M_1M_2 is made smaller and smaller, then A_1A_2 is also made smaller, and by the same token the line Q_1Q_2 is shortened. As this process is continued, the slope of the line Q_1Q_2 becomes closer and closer to the slope of the production possibility curve. Where the distance Q_1 to Q_2 is indefinitely small, the 'opportunity cost' of manufactures in terms of agricultural produce is simply the slope of the production possibility curve at the point under consideration.

This concept of 'opportunity cost' is of considerable importance in economics. *It is a valid concept if, and only if, choice between alternatives is enforced by some limitation – in this case the capacity output of the system*. A precisely similar situation arises for a man who is acceptable in marriage to Joan and Jean and is strongly attracted to both. If it is not legally possible to marry both girls, Joan is the opportunity cost of Jean and Jean the opportunity cost of Joan. Where society permits polygamy the man can marry both and the concept of opportunity cost does not arise. The polygamous situation is depicted in economic terms by the point R in Figure 5.2. If the economic system is at a point like R *inside the production possibility curve* (as it was throughout the 1930s) capacity is *not* fully utilised. Here 'agricultural produce' can be increased *without* reducing the output of manufactures. There is no opportunity cost of increasing either form of output simply because the whole of productive capacity is not being used.

In terms of Figure 5.2, we can now rephrase our questions, which become:

1. What determines the position of the production possibility curve in any given period?
2. What determines whether the economy operates, in any given period, at a point (such as Q_1) *on* the production possibility curve or at a point (such as R) *inside* it?
3. What determines the rate at which, through time, the production *possibility curve* moves outwards (to the right)?
4. What determines the rate at which, through time, actual output grows?

Finally, there remains one last point about the *production possibility curve* itself. We have seen that at any point on it (say Q_1) the *slope* of the curve is the opportunity cost ratio. As the curve in Figure 5.2 is drawn, the opportunity cost of manufactures in terms of agricultural produce rises as the output of manufactures grows. Conversely, if we move *down* the curve the opportunity cost of agricultural produce in terms of manufactures also grows. Figure 5.2 thus depicts a situation of increasing opportunity cost.

Why should costs be increasing? In general this will follow even if the factors of production are homogeneous[1] and equally well adapted to the production of either agricultural produce or manufactures. A formal proof of this is a little complicated. But the following argument should serve to clarify the issue.

Suppose we are at some point (say Q) on the production possibility curve and we wish to give up a unit of agricultural produce to gain an extra unit of manufactures. Suppose also that, at Q, the factors labour and capital are used in the two forms of production as follows:

	Unit of agricultural produce	*Unit of manufactures*
Units of labour	1	1
Units of capital	4	10

If we give up a unit of agricultural produce we release 1 unit of labour and 4 of capital. But to produce a unit of manufactures we require 1 unit of labour and 10 of capital. Too little capital is therefore released to maintain the same cost of manufactures. In producing manufactures the ratio of labour to capital must rise above the ratio of 1:10. Since this was, *because businesses choose the least-cost combination in order to earn maximum profit*, the cheapest method (optimal factor ratio) for producing manufactures cost *must* rise. Hence there are increasing costs as we move *down* the production possibility curve AM towards M, for what is true of point Q is true of any point on AM.

Now move the other way from Q – that is, give up manufactures to obtain *more* agricultural produce. Now inputs are *required* in the ratio 1 labour/4 capital and *released* in the ratio 1 labour/10 capital. Too little labour is released. The ratio of labour to capital must *fall* in agricultural produce. Hence, by the argument above, the cost of agricultural produce must rise.

It follows that (i) *whichever* direction we move from Q we encounter increasing costs, provided only that (ii) factors are *not* used in the *same* proportion in producing *both* types of output. The second condition will be satisfied if both types of output do not possess the same production function – a reasonable enough assumption.

Since we have not yet met the concept of a *production function* a brief explanation of this statement is necessary.

Consider the output of 'agricultural produce'. This depends upon (i) the inputs of labour and capital, and (ii) the state of technique. Given (i) and (ii) there will be a single value of output of 'agricultural produce'. Thus we may write a *production function*[2] for agricultural produce as:

$$Y_{ag} = f(N_{ag}, K_{ag}). \tag{5.1}$$

where

Y_{ag} ≡ the output of agricultural produce
N_{ag} ≡ the labour input to the industry
K_{ag} ≡ the capital employed in the industry

[1]Homogeneity simply means that one unit of any factor is indistinguishable (economically) from any other unit of the same factor.

[2]The notion of a 'production function' is more fully explained in Chapter 7.

This equation may be read as follows:

output of agricultural produce	*is a function of, i.e. systematically dependent upon*	the inputs of labour and capital

What about 'technique'? We could have included a symbol (say T) in this function to stand for the 'state of technique'. Indeed, in later chapters – as a pedagogic device – we adopt this procedure. In the equation 5.1, however, we simply regard the functional relation – denoted by the letter f in front of the bracket – as reflecting a given state of technique. If technique changes, so does the function. For manufacturing there will be a function of similar type written formally:

$$Y_{\text{man}} = f(N_{\text{man}}, K_{\text{man}}) \tag{5.2}$$

For our earlier argument to hold we simply require these two functions (systematic relationships) to be different in the sense that, given the prices of the factor inputs, the *ratios* in which they are employed in order to minimise costs differ in the two uses. As the reader will see, this is not a strong assumption since agricultural output is likely, in general, to require very different factor inputs, at any given set of factor prices, from manufactured goods.

At this stage some readers may find this argument hard to follow. They should take courage for, in the questions and exercises which follow Chapter 7, they will find themselves proving, with great ease, most of the propositions which we have here asserted.

From this argument in terms of ratios it is easy to see that if, given the price of factor inputs, the ratios in which factors are employed in order to minimise costs *are the same in each use*, then the opportunity cost curve will be a straight line and costs will be constant. This is illustrated in Figure 5.3b.

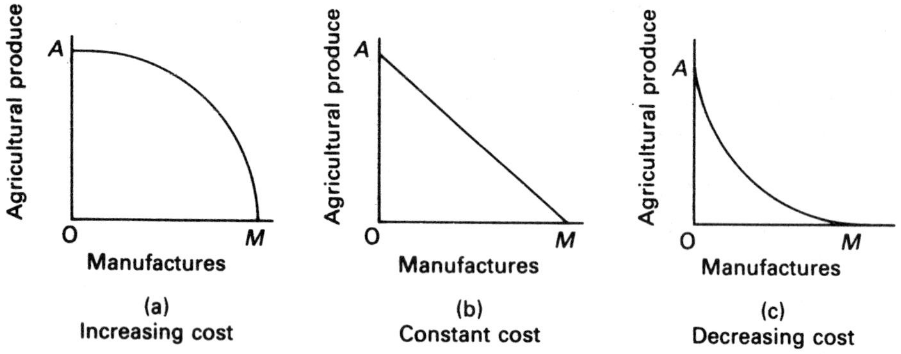

Figure 5.3 Production possibility curves: increasing, constant and decreasing cost

How can we have decreasing costs? At first sight our two ratio arguments seem to exclude this possibility. But suppose the production function for manufacturing is of the particular form:

$$Y_{\text{man}} = AN_{\text{man}}K_{\text{man}}$$

where A is some constant. To fix ideas put $A = 1$, $N = 100$, $K = 1{,}000$. Then:

$$
\begin{aligned}
Y_{\text{man}} &= 1 \times 100 \times 1{,}000 \\
&= 100{,}000
\end{aligned}
$$

Now suppose both N_{man} and K_{man} to double. We have:

$$
\begin{aligned}
Y_{\text{man}} &= 1 \times 200 \times 2{,}000 \\
&= 1 \times 100 \times 1{,}000 \times 2 \times 2 \\
&= 4[1 \times 100 \times 1{,}000] \\
&= 400{,}000
\end{aligned}
$$

Doubling factor inputs has *more than doubled output – it has in fact quadrupled it. When this occurs, or more generally when a doubling of factor inputs leads to more* than doubling output, we say that there are *economies of scale* or *increasing returns to scale*. Conversely when a doubling of inputs leads to *less* than doubling output we say that there are *decreasing returns to scale* or *diseconomies of scale*.

Our earlier arguments assumed, implicitly, that both production functions were of a form which ensured *constant returns to scale*: that is, a doubling of inputs exactly doubled output. They are valid on that assumption. If, however, manufacturing has a production function which exhibits increasing returns to scale, then, even if input ratios differ (the case we assumed to argue increasing costs of one output in terms of another), the effect of these ratios in raising costs as resources are transferred into manufacturing will be offset in whole or in part, *or even more than offset*, by the influence of the *economies of scale*. Increasing returns to scale thus make it *possible* for the production possibility curve to be concave to the origin. They are a necessary but not a sufficient condition for Figure 5.3c to be the appropriate one.

Thus each of the production possibility curves we have drawn is logically permissible. Which is appropriate is a question of fact. In general we shall proceed on the assumption that the production functions in our economy (i) exhibit constant returns to scale, and (ii) differ in the sense explained on pages 49–50.

It thus follows that the reader may picture the production possibility curve – or, as it is sometimes called, 'the transformation curve' – as it is drawn in Figure 5.2.

The three problems

Now that we have restated our three problems concerning the determination of output in terms of the production possibility curve, we can develop a convenient method of approach to them. We shall begin by examining the question – what determines whether the economy operates *on* the production possibility curve (i.e. at full capacity) or at some point R inside it (i.e. at less than full capacity)?

In considering this problem we shall take the position of the production possibility curve as given and invariant. Since the position of this curve depends upon:

(a) the real capital stock – which we know is increasing as the result of net investment
(b) the work-force – which we know is also growing as the result of population growth and the increasing proportion of the population which seeks employment
(c) the state of technique – which is also improving

we are taking as constant and unchanged variables which we know in practice to be changing. To do this is obviously convenient, for it enables us to leave the problem of the growth of capacity for later examination. But is it justified? Provided we restrict the time period involved, it is a reasonable procedure for although capacity does grow over time, in any period of (say) a year it grows relatively little – probably by about 3 per cent or even less. We proceed, in other words, like a man buying a new suit. He knows that, in fact, his measurements are changing. He is getting heavier. His stomach muscles are weakening. Nevertheless he proceeds on the assumption (sometimes shown to be unjustified) that over the expected life of the suit these changes can be ignored. In economic terms the man buying the suit undertakes a *short-run* analysis. That is, he obtains a garment which fits his existing contours on the assumption that in the short run they are constant even though he knows that, in practice, they are changing.

Our analysis of question 2 on page 45 will be a *short-run* analysis in this sense. For we shall take, as given and invariant, the determinants of *the position of the production possibility curve* even though we know that, over time, these are changing: that is, *economic growth* in capacity is proceeding. This device simplifies matters but requires the reader to make the proper intellectual allowances for its limitations and the artificiality it inevitably introduces.

In much of what follows we shall make a further simplification in that we shall not in general explicitly introduce time into our analysis. To see what this means consider Figure 5.4.

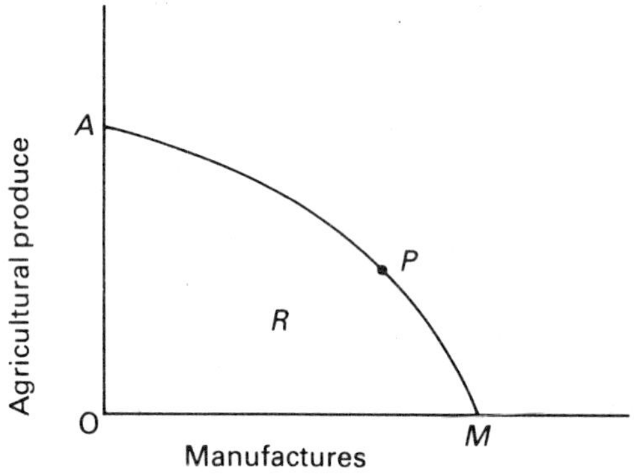

Figure 5.4 Capacity and its utilisation

Suppose we succeed in developing a theory which explains why the economy operates at the point R. Let us suppose that this theory tells us that *if* some variable (let us call it x) takes the value x_1 we shall be at R while *if* it takes the value x_2 we shall be at P. On the basis of this theory we can work out that if x changes from x_1 to x_2 the economy will move from R to P. This information is obviously useful. But it is equally obviously incomplete, for it does *not* tell us (i) *how long* the system takes to get from R to P; (ii) by *what path* it gets from R to P; (iii) whether, once at P, the system will stay there. Economic theories that only compare positions such as R and P we call *static* theories. Theories which also explain the path the system takes from R to P – and how long it takes to get there – we call *dynamic* theories since they involve time in an *explicit* way.

Dynamic theories, since they tell us more, are obviously likely to be (and in practice are) more complicated than static theories. For simplicity therefore we begin by developing a static theory. Once again the reader, who intuitively thinks in dynamic terms, must make the necessary intellectual adjustment. Above all he must avoid mixing statics with dynamics. Since static analysis is artificial this requires a continuous intellectual effort.

These warnings do not imply that this book contains no discussion of dynamic problems. It does. Those chapters, however, which develop a short-run macroeconomic theory of the determination of output are largely *static*, while those which discuss economic growth, economic fluctuations and rising prices respectively are explicitly *dynamic*.

We are now almost ready to embark upon the development of our *short-run* and *static* theory of the determination of output. Before we do so, however, we shall first examine the record of the UK economy (in Chapter 6) and then (in Chapter 7) say something about the analytical and expository techniques employed by economists and, in particular, about the use of mathematics.

Questions and exercises

1. Why do we describe real national income as a measure of 'potential economic welfare' rather than 'economic welfare'? What limitations are there to the validity of either description?

2. From the data shown in Table 5.1 plot the production possibility curves. Do they describe increasing, decreasing or constant costs?

Table 5.1 Three production possibility curves: numerical data

1 Output of		2 Output of		3 Output of	
Agricultural products	Manufactured products	Agricultural products	Manufactured products	Agricultural products	Manufactured products
(i)	(ii)	(iii)	(iv)	(v)	(vi)
1,000	nil	1,000	nil	1,000	nil
950	24.5	950	34	950	15
900	49.0	900	67	900	31
850	73.5	850	99	850	48
800	98.0	800	130	800	66
750	122.5	750	160	750	85
700	147.0	700	189	700	105
650	171.5	650	217	650	126
600	196.0	600	244	600	148
550	220.5	550	270	550	171
500	245.0	500	295	500	195
450	269.5	450	319	450	220
400	294.0	400	342	400	246
350	318.5	350	364	350	273
300	343.0	300	385	300	301
250	367.5	250	405	250	330
200	392.0	200	424	200	360
150	416.5	150	442	150	391
100	441.0	100	459	100	423
50	465.5	50	475	50	456
nil	490.0	nil	490	nil	490

3. Construct a diagram similar to Figure 5.4. Show, geometrically, how you would seek to measure the proportion of capacity employed at the point *R*. With what observable phenomena, for which statistical data are usually available, would you expect your measure to be related? Give your reasons.

4. 'As a nation we spend far too little on education. We should increase our expenditure on it by at least £1bn. a year.' Discuss this statement in the light of the concept of 'opportunity cost'.

5. 'In the short run, by definition, some variable or variables which are known to be changing over time are assumed to be constant. How misleading short-run analysis is, is therefore a question of fact.' Elucidate.

6. A tank is connected to a hose through a valve controlled by a ball cock. Initially the water in the tank is at a level of 3 inches. The hose is turned on at 11.00 a.m. Give (i) a static and (ii) a dynamic analysis of the operation of this system. What is the new equilibrium level?

7. Table 5.2 gives estimates of the rate of growth in real output in eleven countries over the period 1950–9. In terms of a production possibility analysis how would you seek to explain the relative position of the UK?

Table 5.2 Percentage growth in output: selected countries 1950–9

Country	Growth rate	Country	Growth rate
Japan	8.6	Norway	3.4
USA	3.4	Germany	7.4
Canada	4.0	France	4.1
Sweden	3.3	Italy	5.7
Denmark	2.6	UK	2.2
Netherlands	4.6		

Source: *NIESR Review* (July 1961).

8. Construct hypothetical production possibility curves, in terms of agricultural produce and manufactures for (i) the UK; (ii) New Zealand. Would you expect their shapes to differ? If so, in what way? Justify your hypothetical curves.

9. Suppose the community, with a production possibility curve defined by cols (i) and (ii) of the data in question 2 is in equilibrium at the following point:

Output of agricultural products	*Output of manufactured products*
550	*220.5*

What is the price of agricultural output in terms of manufactures? Why? Interpret your answer in the light of the earlier discussion of the working of a market economy.

10. What statistical data would be relevant to any attempt to test your answer to question 8? Why?

Suggested reading

P.A. Samuelson, *Economics*, 11th edn (McGraw-Hill, 1979) chs 1, 2.

Chapter 6
A Sketch of British Economic Experience

In the last chapter we made use of the concept of a 'production possibility curve' to distinguish two macroeconomic problems.

The first of these was the *short-run* problem of explaining the determination of the extent to which *existing* productive capacity is utilised. In other words, *what determines whether the economy operates at some point on or inside the given 'production possibility curve'*.

The second, which we called the *long-run* problem, was to explain the determinants of the rate at which the 'production possibility curve' moves to the right over time: that is, *to explain the rate of growth over time in the economy's capacity to produce output*.

The 'production possibility curve' is a piece of geometry which helps us to distinguish between the two problems. But geometry is all that it is. We now need to enquire whether our two problems are real problems: that is, whether productive capacity *does grow over time at rates which, even on average over longish periods, vary, and whether, over shortish periods of time, the extent to which existing capacity is utilised varies*. For if productive capacity were always fully utilised (i.e. the economy did operate *on* the 'production possibility curve') *and* output (and hence capacity) grew at a rate which never varied, our analysis in Chapter 5, though logically correct, would be of little practical interest.

The primary aim of this chapter is therefore to sketch the economic experience of the UK in terms of macroeconomic concepts we have either met already or shall soon meet in order to see the broad pattern of the facts that our theory needs to explain.

Output, capacity and employment

We begin our examination by setting out the behaviour of annual output. To do this, we make use of series giving index numbers of real gross domestic product and divide experience into:

(a) the interwar years (1921–1938) – set out in Figure 6.1
(b) the postwar years (1955–1981) – set out in Figure 6.2

The years 1939–49 have been exluded simply because, in them, the performance of the economy was dominated by the war and/or its immediate aftermath and was thus atypical.

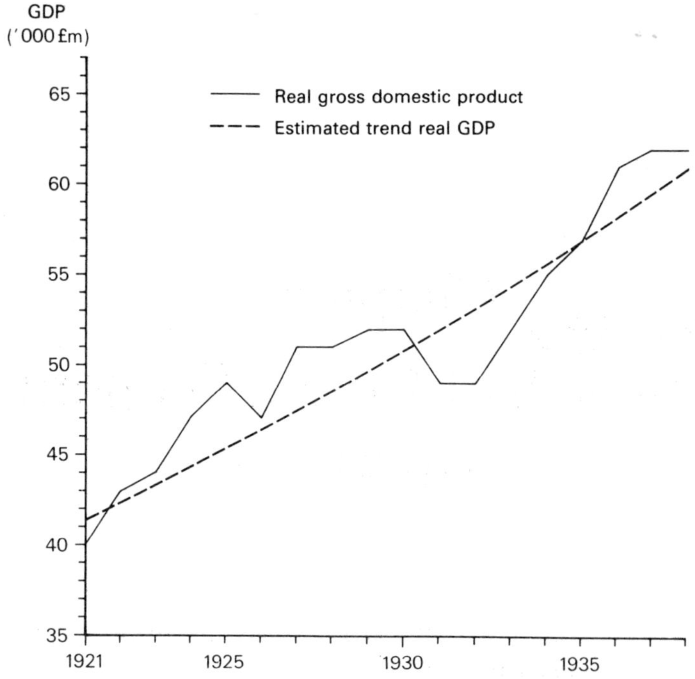

Source: *The British Economy – Key Statistics 1900–1966* (Times Newspaper for London and Cambridge Economic Services).

Figure 6.1 Real GDP and its trend in the interwar period

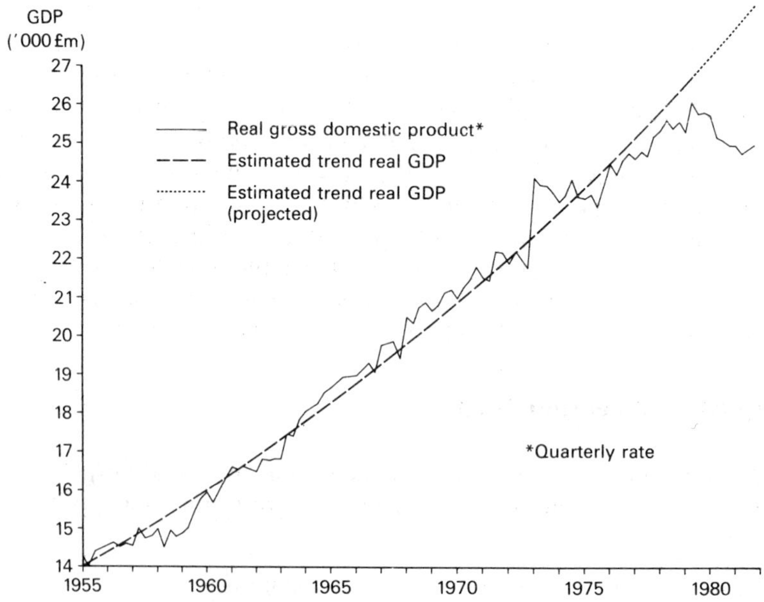

Source: *Economic Trends*, Annual Supplements.

Figure 6.2 Real GDP and its trend since 1955

What do these diagrams tell us?

In the first place, in both periods, output clearly displayed a *long-run* tendency to grow. The 'trend' or average rate of growth in each period is represented by the *dashed* line, the slope which assumes a constant percentage rate of growth. Simply by eye it is easy to see that the 'trend' rate of growth between 1955 and 1980 was appreciably higher than between 1921 and 1938: in fact, around 3.0 per cent per annum as against some 2.3 per cent – an improvement of about 30 per cent. However, since 1973, output has grown much more slowly, and by 1981 was only 2–3 per cent above its 1973 level – thus suggesting a 'trend' rate of growth since 1973[1] of perhaps 1 per cent, or a little more, about one-third of the 'trend' from 1955–1973.

As we know, the observed growth in real output reflects not only the growth in capacity but also the variation in the extent to which capacity was utilised. Can we determine, at least up to an acceptable degree of approximation, the rate at which, on average, productive capacity grew?

Any direct attempt to measure the rate of growth in capacity by, say, measuring the growth in factor availability is fraught with difficulties. We can, however, make some progress by finding an observable variable which can serve as an indicator of the extent to which capacity is utilised. A variable commonly used in this way is the percentage of the work-force unemployed – the assumption being that the *higher* the percentage of recorded unemployment, the *lower* is the ratio of observed output to capacity output. On this argument, any two periods which record the same percentage of unemployment have the same percentage of capacity utilisation. Hence the observed growth in output between them and the growth in capacity are identical so that the former gives an estimate of the latter.

Plainly this procedure is extremely rough and ready and, at best, gives us only a very crude approximation to the rate of growth in capacity. The reader is invited to list all the objections to it which in his or her view are likely to be important and to suggest in which way they are likely to bias the estimates. In the meantime, using this procedure, we obtain the following rather rough estimates for the rate of growth in the UK's productive capacity:

(a) interwar years (1921–38) 2.3 per cent
(b) postwar years (1955–73) 3.1 per cent

For the latest period, our simple method is inapplicable since recorded unemployment has typically risen in each of the ten years up to 1982 for which observations are available. We therefore accept the common view that, for reasons which have not yet been satisfactorily explained, the rate of growth in capacity has fallen dramatically since the early 1970s to a figure which is within the range 1–2 per cent, and probably of the order of 1.75 per cent.

We may thus conclude that:

(a) in the longer run (i.e. ten years or more), the rate of growth in output is *primarily* – but not exclusively – to be explained by the rate of growth in productive capacity
(b) the rate of growth in productive capacity has varied quite considerably and is, contemporaneously, thought to be no more than two-thirds – and perhaps less – of its value between 1955 and 1973.

Our 'long-run' approach thus does appear to be relevant to UK experience. What of our *short-run* argument that variations in output over the short run are to be explained primarily by variation in the extent to which capacity is actually used to produce output?

[1]Output grew by some 7–8 per cent from 1973 to 1979. The growth rates given here are illustrative approximations.

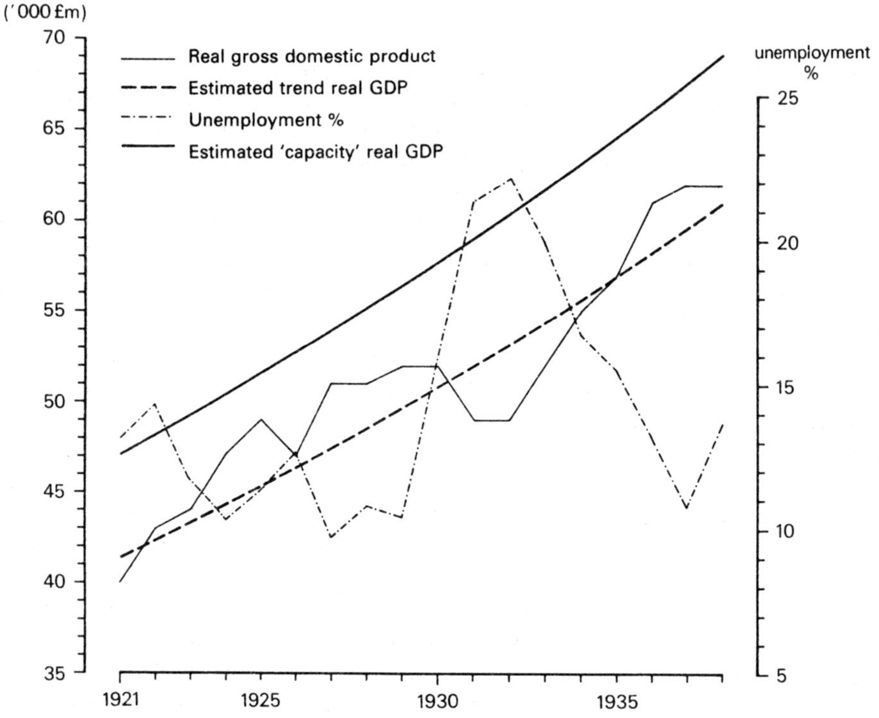

Source: as for Figure 6.1.

Figure 6.3 Real GDP and 'capacity' in the interwar period

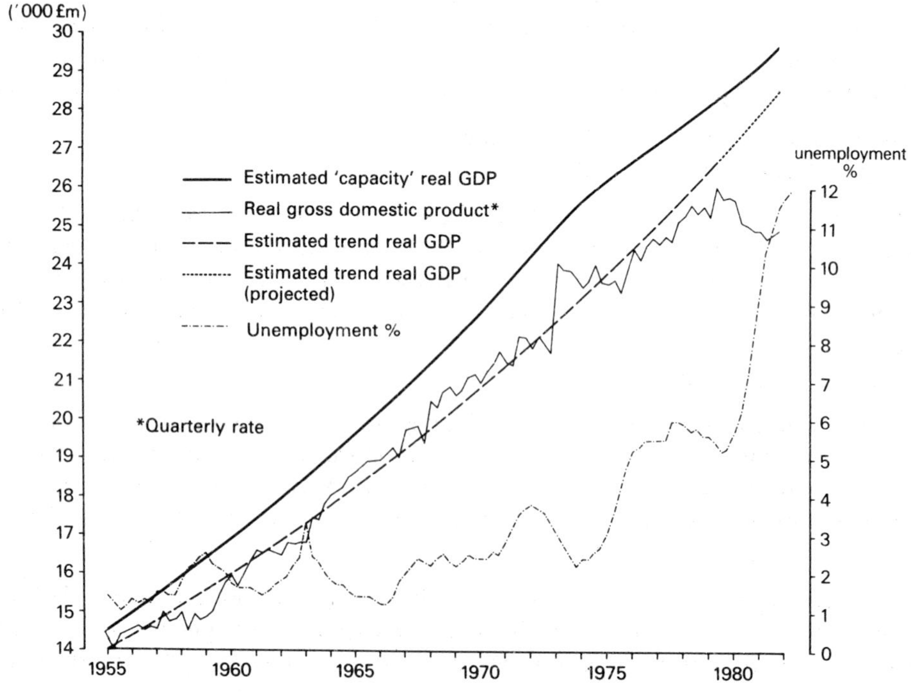

Source: as for Figure 6.1.

Figure 6.4 Real GDP and 'capacity' since 1955

In Figures 6.3 and 6.4 we have repeated the GDP series of our earlier graphs and *added* our series for the percentage of the work-force unemployed – a series we have used as an indicator of the extent of unused (or excess) productive capacity. What do these graphs tell us?

In the first place, output did not grow smoothly. In some short periods it grew faster than either the trend rate or the capacity rate. In others it grew more slowly. Typically, in the former periods, the percentage of employment declined, while in the latter it rose. For examples of the first type we have 1922–5 and 1932–7 in the interwar period, and in the postwar period 1958–61 and 1971–3. In all four, unemployment fell. Conversely in 1929–33 growth was negative, as it has been more recently between 1979 and 1981. In both these periods unemployment rose very sharply. In the short run, what explains output explains employment: a theory of the former is a theory of the latter.

We may therefore conclude that *short-run* changes in output owe a great deal to changes in capacity utilisation. This is obvious when output is falling – as, for example, between 1979 and 1981. But it also holds when output is rising faster than trend: for example, between 1972 and 1973 output rose by some 6.75 per cent – more than twice as fast as capacity on our approximate estimate.

Over all, then, it seems that the approach of Chapter 5, which entails a sharp distinction between short- and long-run aspects of output variation, is a useful way of looking at experience: both the short- and long-run problems it identifies are real problems.

Notice that we have, at no stage, sought to identify 'full-capacity' working. We have not, for example, regarded some particular percentage of unemployment as indicating 'full capacity' – merely arguing that *similar* percentages of unemployment indicate *similar* percentages of capacity employed.

It is, of course, possible to identify some particular percentage of recorded unemployment with 'full-capacity' utilisation. Professor Paish, for example, used to argue that:

(a) 'full-capacity' working was defined by 1 per cent of recorded unemployment
(b) 'unused (or excess) capacity' rose by 5 per cent for every 1 per cent increase in the unemployment percentage (i.e. 3 per cent unemployment indicated 10 per cent 'excess capacity').

The second approximation was, of course, only applicable within a 'small' range of unemployment (say 1–3 per cent). Moreover, neither of these is likely to be relevant to the UK after, say, 1973 since it is widely agreed that, among other things, entry into the EEC and the sharp rise in oil prices have combined to raise the percentage of unemployment and it is reasonable to associate 'full-capacity' working to perhaps as high as 3–4 per cent. In short, the identification of 'full-capacity' output is a complex matter about which economists are likely to disagree – particularly when the period *after* 1973 is in question.

On the other hand, if we are prepared to be rather arbitrary, we can, by adopting this or some similar approach, make calculations of 'full-capacity' output, and these, when plotted against actual output, will give a visual index of the importance of fluctuations in the utilisation of capacity. Some calculations of this type are illustrated in Figures 6.5 and 6.6.

In these graphs 'full capacity' – shown by the dotted line – grows at the rates we have already estimated for 'capacity'.[1] The gap between actual output (the hard line) and 'full-capacity' output (the heavy black line) is thus output, which (by assumption) could have been produced but was not. The reader is reminded here that our 'capacity' estimates are very rough approximations indeed. The figures are thus approximations which are only illustrative and suggestive; they are certainly not definitive.

[1]The estimated rates are 'reasonable' approximations, *not* precise calculations.

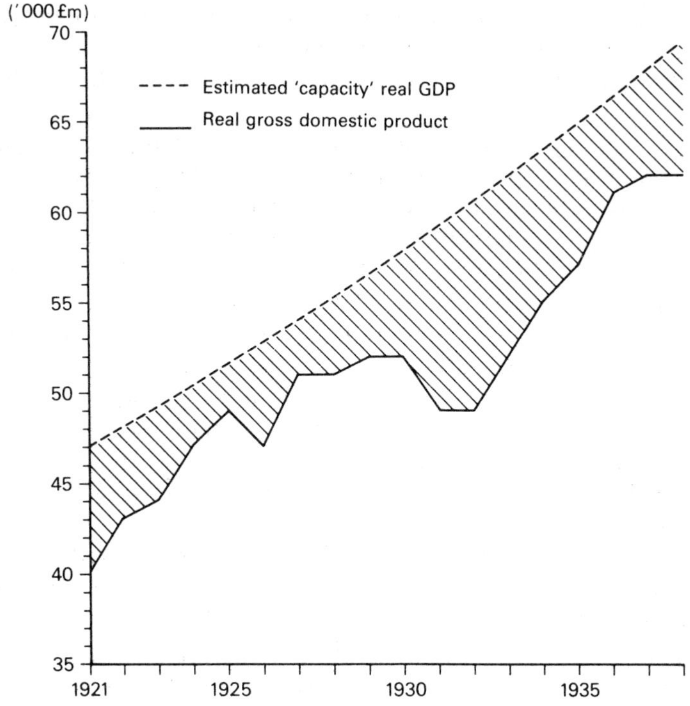

Source: as for Figure 6.1.

Figure 6.5 Real GDP and estimated 'capacity' GDP in the interwar period

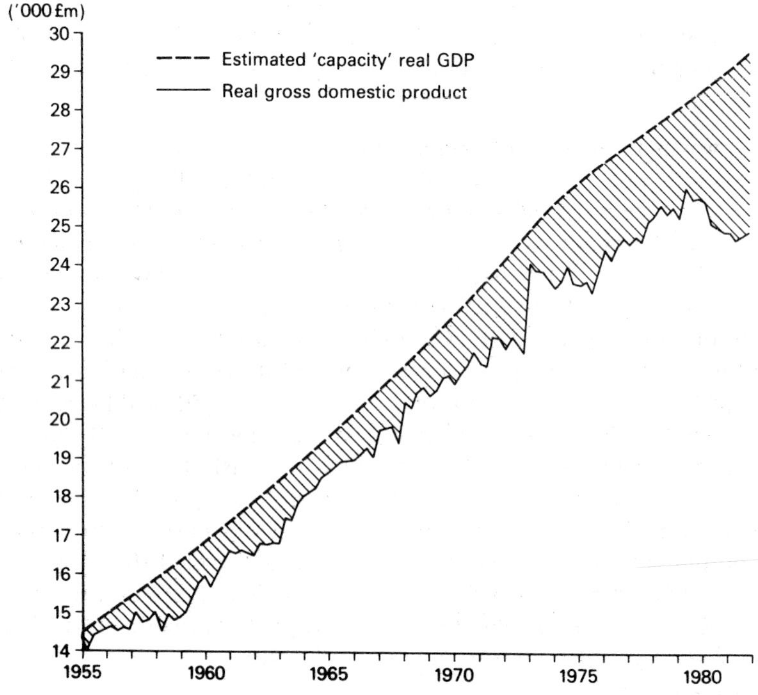

Source: as for Figure 6.1.

Figure 6.6 Real GDP and estimated 'capacity' GDP since 1955

What can we learn from these graphs?

In the interwar years there were severe fluctuations in the extent to which capacity was utilised. Moreover, the *average level* of capacity utilisation was relatively low. For example, one estimate has suggested that 'full-capacity' output in 1938 was some *11 per cent above* recorded output. This suggests, since 1938 was a relatively 'good' year, a high average annual loss of potential output; and this is confirmed by the high average percentage of unemployment.

In the postwar period – at least up to 1973 – output was typically much closer to 'full-capacity' output.[1] There were, of course, fluctuations in the extent to which capacity was utilised; but compared with the interwar years these were minor. The percentage of unemployment, though it fluctuated, did so within a remarkably narrow range and around an average value markedly lower than in the interwar years.

Since 1973 economic performance has deteriorated dramatically. The extent of 'excess capacity' has increased – more particularly since 1979 – and recorded unemployment, which probably *understates* unemployment compared with 1955–73, has risen very sharply indeed. The economy is not yet performing as badly as it did in the interwar years; but it is performing more like it did then and much less like it did between 1955 and 1973.

Although our calculations are, as we have stressed, only very rough approximations, they confirm that:

> fluctuations in the extent of capacity utilisation *are* important in explaining *short-term* changes in output

which was a proposition we derived in Chapter 5.

Moreover, if our calculations are useful approximations, it seems that the losses in output due to failure to utilise the whole of productive capacity can be large. Clearly they were so in the interwar years; and they have been increasingly significant since 1973 and, more particularly, since 1979. And this would remain true even if our approximations were adjusted downwards.

We can now list the questions, suggested by our graphs and our discussion, for which we may reasonably require our theory to suggest explanations. These are:

1. What explains the level of output (and employment) in the *short period*?
2. What explains the rate at which productive capacity grows over *the long run*?
3. What explains the wavelike fluctuations in output and employment?
4. Why did the economy operate (a) with only small fluctuations about (b) a high level of capacity utilisation (low level of unemployment) between 1955 and 1973 when it so conspicuously failed to do so in the interwar years and has begun to repeat this failure since 1974?

Our comparison of the postwar period with the interwar years is brief. It leaves a great deal out of account. Clearly, in the interwar years potential output was lost on a gigantic scale. Mass unemployment was tragically endemic and the talents and lives of many men and women stunted and wasted. No statistical series can adequately tell this story. For a real understanding of the period the reader should consult the works of social historians or, better still, some of the novels and biographies of the time.

[1] It may well have been closer than our very rough 'capacity' estimates suggest.

'Cycles' and the UK economy

As we have seen, both output and unemployment exhibit what we can call 'wavelike' movements over time. For example, for a time output rises faster than capacity and the trend. At some point its growth rate falls to that of the trend and subsequently falls below it. For a time it grows more slowly than the trend. Then growth once again accelerates and the process repeats itself. We define these 'wavelike' movements as 'cycles'. A schematic illustration of a cycle is given in Figure 6.7.

In Figure 6.7 B and B' are the *lower turning-points* (or troughs) in the output series; A and A' are the *upper turning-points* (or peaks). At *all* turning-points in a growth cycle it is mathematically the case that output is growing at the trend rate. Between B and A and B' and A' output is growing faster than the trend and the cycle is in its *upswing*: between A and B', the reverse is true and it is in its *downswing*. In the *downswing* output may – or may not – decline absolutely, but it falls in relation to capacity just as it increases in relation to capacity in *upswings*.

The *length* of a cycle – sometimes called its *periodicity* – is measured from peak to peak (AA') or trough to trough (BB'). By definition, cycles are repetitive. Cycles in economic variables do not, however, repeat themselves precisely. Hence their length varies and so does the deviation between peak and trend (Aa) and trough and trend ($b'B'$), which is a rough indicator of what is usually called *amplitude*.

In Figure 6.8 we have plotted quarterly data for real GDP industrial production, manufacturing production and unemployment. As can be seen, not all the series move precisely together. Unemployment, for example, follows (or 'lags') output, and it would be possible to find some series which typically 'lead' output. Identifying 'the' cycle of the UK

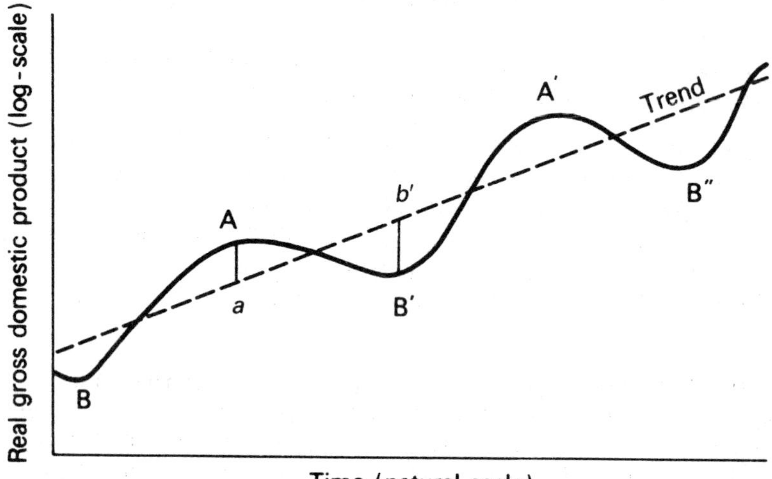

Figure 6.7 The cycle in real GDP

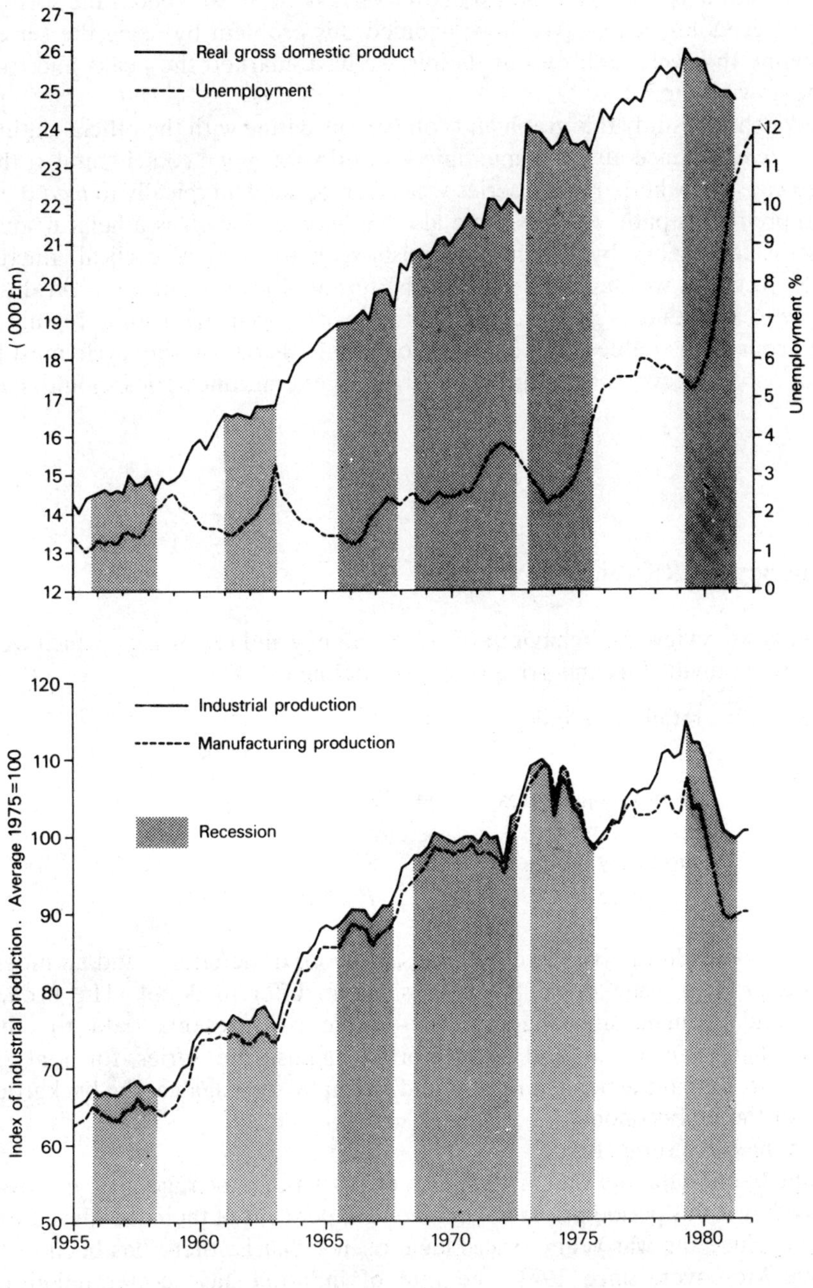

Sources: *Economic Trends*, Annual Supplements; *The British Economy – Key Statistics.*

Figure 6.8 Cycles in the UK economy

economy as a whole is thus an awkward matter since to do so we need some sort of index of a number of economic series. We have avoided this problem by using the series for real GDP to define the cycle and, on our dating, we have marked the peaks and troughs and shaded the *downswings*.

The reader should study this graph and compare its dating with the official dating given in *Economic Trends*.[1] Since all economic time series do not move coincidentally, the student should also consider whether some series which can be shown typically to *lead* the cycle can be used to predict its path. On this issue also, *Economic Trends* is a helpful source.

We discuss the theory by which economists seek to explain 'cyclical' fluctuations in Chapter 20, in which we shall make use of the terminology set out here. At this stage we need simply to note that cyclical fluctuations appear to occur with some regularity among the major economic variables and that any worthwhile theory of 'the' cycle must be able to explain not only why cycles occur but also why, in general, one series should lead (or lag) another.

Prices, money wages and real wages

In this section we review the behaviour of prices, money and real wages, which we define as the money wage divided by the price level. We define:

$$\text{prices} \equiv \text{retail price index} \equiv P$$

$$\text{money wages} \equiv \text{money wage rates} \equiv W$$

$$\text{real wages} \equiv \frac{\text{money wage index}}{\text{price level}} \equiv \frac{W}{P}$$

Had we used some alternative price index – say the GDP deflator – and an index of wage earnings rather than wage rates, the results might differ in detail. The broad outline, however, would remain unchanged. Thus Figure 6.9 presents data for the annual percentage change in W, P and W/P plotted against the series for real GDP and unemployment, so that the behaviour of P and W can be seen against the background of the behaviour of the real economy.

Consider the price series first.

According to our data, the rate of change in prices was, on average, *negative* from 1920 to 1935. Indeed over this period prices *fell* by about 40 per cent of their 1920 level. Since 1935, even if we exclude the war years, prices have risen – that is, there has been *inflation* – in every year. Moreover, since 1971, the rate of inflation has accelerated dramatically, exceeding 20 per cent in both 1974–5 and 1979–80.

We shall naturally require any macroeconomic theory we develop to be able to explain *both*

(a) the determination of the price *level*
(b) its *rate* and (direction) of change

[1]See also *NIESR Review*, no. 98 (November 1981) table 1, p. 7.

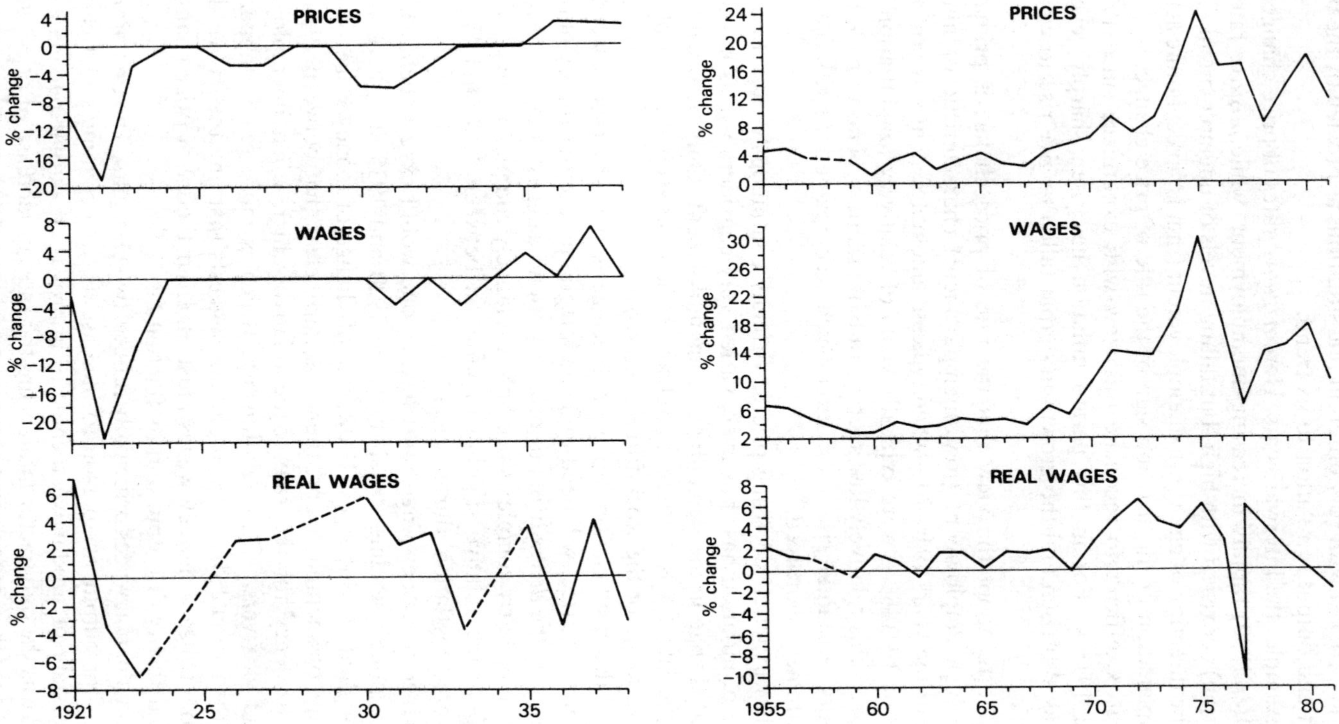

Source: as for Figure 6.8.

Figure 6.9 Rates of change in prices, nominal wages and real wages

What a glance at Figure 6.9 immediately suggests is that developing such a theory – and more particularly a theory of inflation – is not likely to prove at all simple since rising prices clearly can – and do – coexist with very different real situations as proxied by the percentage of unemployment and output in relation to its trend.

Consider, for example, the interwar years. Here *negative* rates of price change coexisted with high and (after 1930) rapidly increasing unemployment, while *positive* rates of price change (i.e. inflation) coexisted with high, but falling, levels of unemployment. This might suggest that it is the direction of change in unemployment (that is, in economic activity) that dominates the explanation of the size and sign of the rate of price change.

Unfortunately it is difficult to reconcile this view with experience since 1971–2, and particularly since 1973–4. For in this period inflation has risen sharply, even though unemployment has also risen and the growth in output fallen to give rise to what is often called 'stagflation'.

Nor is it possible to adopt the view that the rate of price change is primarily to be explained by the high employment (low unemployment) characteristic of much of the postwar period. For the years 1946–70 – when typically unemployment *was* low in relation to *either* 1920–39 *or* 1971–81 – were typically years of relatively *low* inflation by recent standards. Moreover, this relatively low average rate of inflation seems to have been fairly stable since the very substantial rise in inflation which accompanied the Korean war boom of 1950–1 was extremely shortlived.

Thus the UK has experienced rising prices, virtually continuously, for close on half a century. The rate of inflation has, however, varied very considerably, as has its relation to the level of and change in the percentage of unemployment. Only between the Second World War and the late 1960s is there any clear relation between the rate of change of prices and the percentage of the work-force unemployed.

The existence of this last relationship strongly suggests that any theory we develop to explain the behaviour of prices will need to be an integral part of our theory of output and its fluctuations. Equally the *diversity* of our price experience suggests that any theory we put forward will have to be fairly complex since only a relatively complex theory is likely to be able to explain *both* the relative stability of inflation between 1946 and 1970 *and* the emergence of severe 'stagflation' during the 1970s.

The rate of change in money wage rates has, as one would expect, behaved in a way broadly similar to prices: tending to fall between 1920 and 1935 and thereafter to rise continuously, though at varying rates. If the rate of change of money wages is compared with the percentage of unemployment, then it is fairly clear that between 1946 and 1968 there was some tendency for the rate to be relatively high when unemployment was relatively low and vice versa. This relationship, which is more readily apparent when quarterly rather than annual data are employed, suggests that any theory we develop to explain the rate of change of money wages must, like our theory of price changes, be an integral part of our theory of output and its fluctuations.

The rate of change in real wages principally reflects two elements. The first of these is the *long-run* tendency for output per person to increase as the economy's real capital stock increases and the state of productive technique improves. If output per man grew at a constant rate *and* was the only factor influencing the rates of increase of prices and money wages, the rate of growth in money wages would equal the rate of growth in prices plus the rate of growth in output per man. In practice this does not happen. In the short run, therefore, there is no simple and invariant relation between the rates of growth in money wages and prices. Hence real wages grow on average – as *long-run* influences require. But the rate of growth varies in the *short run* and is sometimes negative, while it is not hard to find periods in which an increase in the rate of growth in money wages was associated with a reduction in the rate of growth in real wages.

Interest rates

A macroeconomic variable to which we shall need to devote considerable attention is 'the rate of interest'. A glance at the *Financial Times* makes it clear that there is no single interest rate any more than there is a single price of 'output'. With 'output' we deal with this problem by making use of an index number which tells us the price of a defined 'basket' of goods. We could follow a similar procedure in defining 'the interest rate'. Instead we shall adopt the convention that:

rate of interest ≡ rate of return on irredeemable bonds issued by the UK government.

The most important of these irredeemables is 2½% Consols, so that, by our convention:

rate of interest ≡ rate of return on 2½% Consols

We plot annual values of this rate on Figure 6.10, together with the rate on Treasury bills (a three-month debt issued by the government) and our usual indicators of the behaviour of the real economy.

Both these interest rates are nominal rates. If the Consol rate is, say, 4.79 per cent, then £100 spent on purchasing Consols entitles the purchaser to £4.79 per year gross of income tax. If the price level rises so that the *real* value of his Consol (in terms of goods and services) falls, the *real rate* of *interest* will be *less* than 4.79 per cent. Indeed the real rate of interest – as is explained in Chapter 10 – is usually written:

real rate of interest ≡ nominal rate of interest *minus* rate of change of prices

so that if, in our earlier example, prices rose by 10 per cent, we should have:

$$\begin{aligned}\text{real rate of interest} &\equiv \text{nominal rate} - \text{rate of price change}\\ &\equiv 4.79 - 10.0\\ &\equiv -5.21\end{aligned}$$

This is, we should have a *positive* nominal rate but a *negative* real rate.

In the diagram we plotted *nominal* rates. How did they behave?

In the interwar years rates at both long-term (Consols) and short-term (Treasury bills) fell as unemployment rose to its 1932 peak. The decline continued, however, in the long-term rate as unemployment fell from 1932 to 1936. In the minor boom of 1937 the long rate rose again. This suggests no clear-cut pattern in relation to real activity.

In the postwar period both long- and short-term rates have fluctuated about a rising trend. They have tended to move together, though movements in short rates have been more severe. The common upward trend in both is almost certainly related to the rise in the rate of price increases. This is particularly clear in the period after 1972.

The annual series set out in Figure 6.10 does not make it easy to identify short-term movements about the rising trend. This is particularly the case with the Consol rate. If,

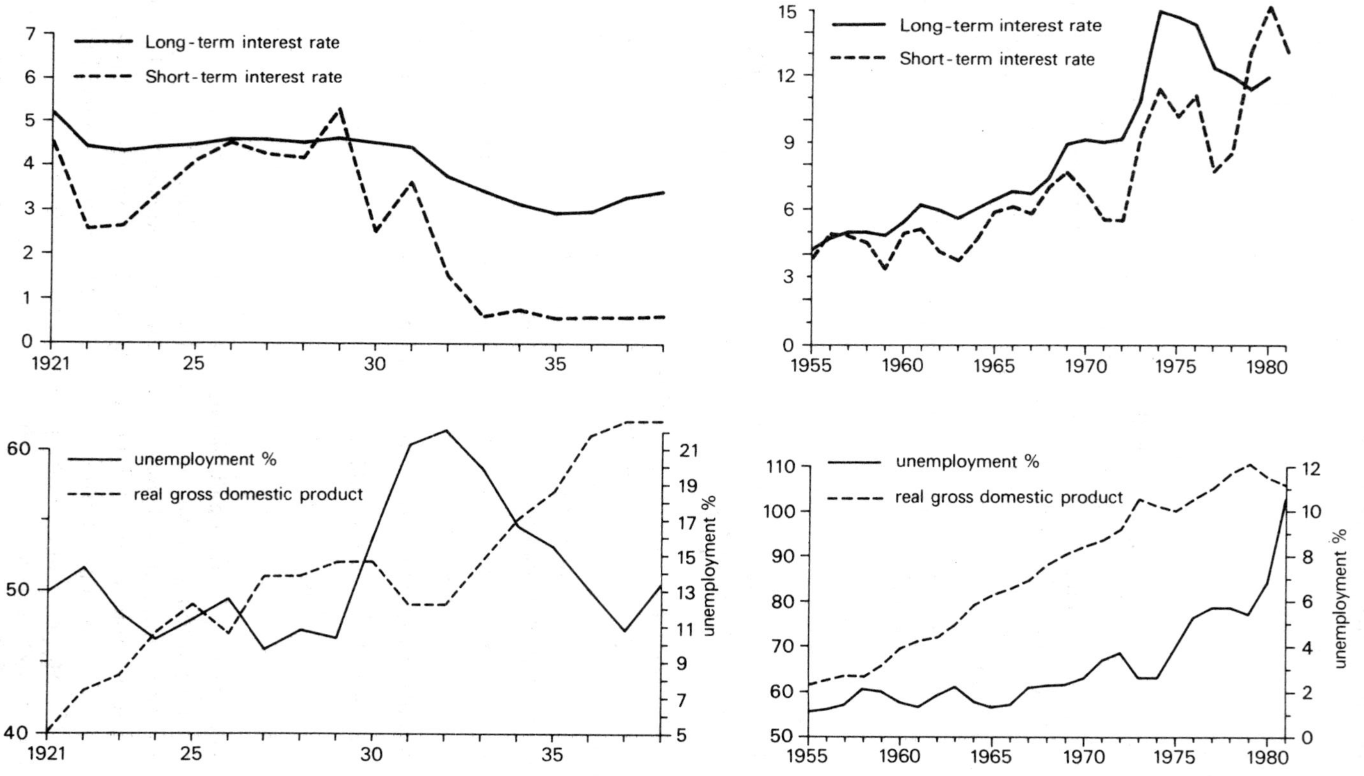

Figure 6.10 Output, unemployment and nominal interest rates

however, we make use of short-term rates and consider only their deviations from trend, high levels of the short-term rate seem to coincide with or follow shortly upon cyclical peaks in the output series, and low rates behave similarly with troughs. This correspondence, or slightly delayed correspondence, is only approximate and short rates exhibit fluctuations not related to the cycle in this sense. The relationship is, nevertheless, sufficiently close to suggest that any theory we develop to explain output and its fluctuations must also explain the behaviour of nominal interest rates.

Since nominal rates have risen with the rate of inflation, the real rate has not risen in conformity with nominal rates over the long term. Indeed, in recent years, the long rate – even ignoring the influence of income tax – has commonly been negative in real terms. In the very short run, however, fluctuations in the real rate tend to be dominated by fluctuations in the nominal rate. This is simply because nominal interest rates can, and do, change rapidly – while the rate of inflation tends to change relatively more slowly.

The allocation of output

In our outline of national income accounting, we defined:

$$\text{gross national expenditure} \equiv \text{consumption} + \text{gross investment} + \text{government expenditure} + \text{exports} - \text{imports}$$

and, as we know, gross national expenditure is, by definition, equal to gross domestic product. Since real GDP has, in general, a rising trend about which it exhibits cyclical movements, it is reasonable to ask what are the expenditure counterparts to these. In Figure 6.11 we set out *quarterly series* for the components of this identity and, in the process, disaggregate investment by first writing:

$$\text{gross private fixed investment} + \text{investment in stocks and work in progress} \equiv \text{gross private investment}$$

and second by aggregating public-sector fixed investment with government expenditure under the general heading 'public authority expenditure'.[1]

Quite a lot can be learned from Figure 6.11. For example:

(1) Real consumer expenditure has risen virtually continuously. Only in very few periods has it fallen absolutely. Moreover, by looking at the GDP series (also shown), we see that this item dominates expenditure, accounting for greater than 60 per cent of GDP.

(2) Gross fixed investment also exhibits an upward trend. Fluctuations about this trend are, however, relatively more severe than is the case with consumer expenditure. The series includes relatively long periods of little or no expansion and even of absolute decline. Finally, as you can check for yourself, the manufacturing component of private fixed investment (which we have not plotted) exhibits more severe fluctuations than the total.

(3) Public authority expenditure on goods and services exhibits an upward trend. Its fluctuations, however, are considerably more severe than those of consumers' expenditure, while absolute declines are more common.

(4) Our final series relates to investment in stocks (including work in progress). This series has little trend. On the other hand, its fluctuations are very severe. Moreover, it is also noticeable that the rate of stock-building tends to increase in periods in which GDP is

[1]This disaggregation is only possible from 1962 onwards.

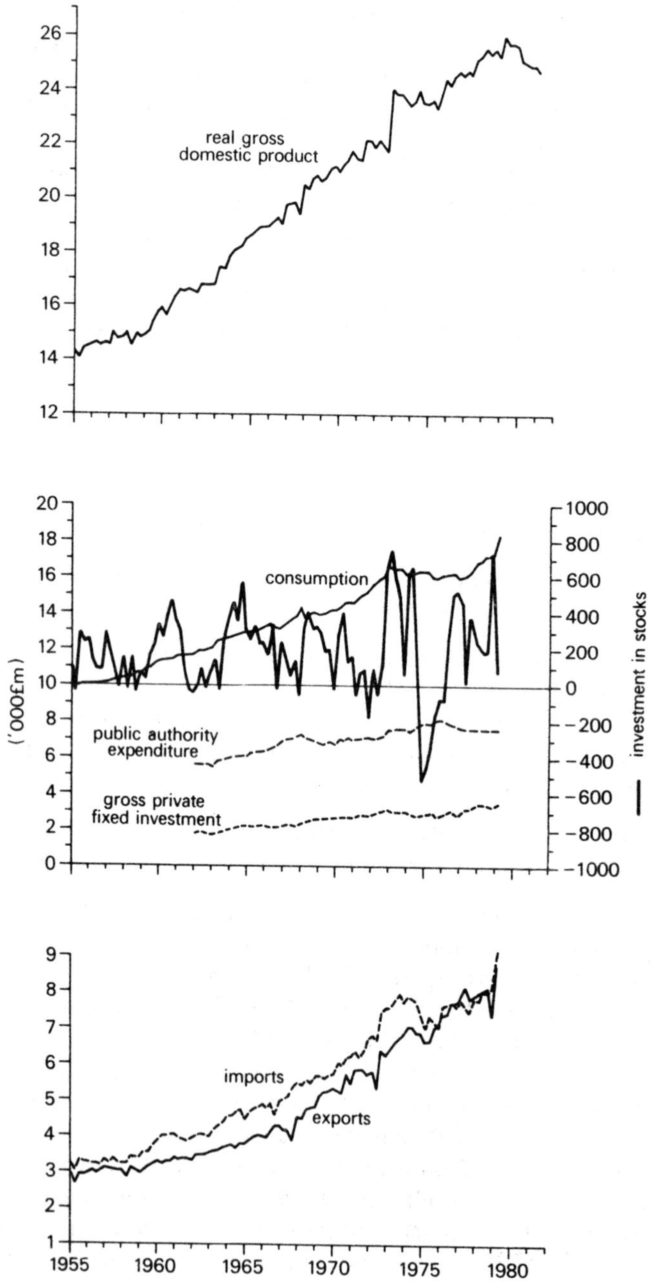

Source: *Economic Trends*, Annual Supplements.

Figure 6.11 The allocation of output

growing faster than its trend and decline to zero – or a substantial negative value – after output has reached its cyclical peak.

This kind of visual interpretation is helpful. However, it is desirable to have rather more precise indexes of the relative tendency of each form of expenditure series to fluctuate about its trend. Accordingly we define an index of each series' amplitude of fluctuations as:

$$\text{index of amplitude} \equiv \frac{\left[\text{maximum positive deviation from trend} \;\; \textit{minus} \;\; \text{maximum negative deviation from trend}\right]}{\text{average value over the period}}$$

Using this approximation, Table 6.1 demonstrates clearly the immensely greater variability of investment in stocks and the relative stability of consumers' expenditure. It should be noted, however, that a given percentage change in the latter has an impact on gross national expenditure many times that of a similar percentage change in investment in stocks.

Table 6.1 Approximate measures of amplitude: 1955–79*

Variable	Maximum deviations		Mean value	'Amplitude' index
	Positive	Negative		
	£1975	£1975	£1975	%
Consumers' expenditure	1,288	1,087	13,965	17.0
Gross private fixed investment†	395	361	2,698	28.0
Investment in stocks	556	725	187	685.6
Public authority expenditure†	627	629	7,122	17.6
Exports	624	819	5,400	26.7
Imports	1,064	657	5,891	29.2

*Based upon seasonally adjusted quarterly data and logarithmic trends.
†Based on data from 1962 onwards.
Note: For an alternative method of calculating 'amplitude', consult *NIESR Review*, no. 98 (November 1981) table 1, p. 7.

These calculations are illustrative, not definitive. The results depend upon the length of the time series we have chosen to employ and the form of trend we have imposed on each series. They should, however, serve to give the reader a broad picture of the orders of magnitude of the main domestic elements in gross national expenditure and their susceptibility to fluctuations. We now turn to examine exports and imports and the balance of payments.

The balance of payments on current account

The UK economy is what is called extremely 'open', in the sense that exports and imports, the remaining two elements in our gross national expenditure identity, each constitute a very significant element in the total, while, because London is a major financial centre, there are very considerable flows of funds to and from the rest of the world arising out of transactions not directly related to flows of goods. The balance-of-payments accounts of the UK provide a summary of all transactions with the rest of the world. In later chapters of this book we discuss the balance of payments – and the determination of its principal components – in greater detail. Here our concern is primarily with description.

The transactions entering the balance of payments are conveniently analysed under three heads. These are:

(1) The balance of transactions relating to our overseas purchases and sales of goods. This is called the *visible balance* and is defined as:

$$\text{exports} - \text{imports} \equiv \text{visible balance}$$

By convention, if exports exceed imports this balance is said to be positive or favourable – alternatively it is described as being in *surplus*; in the reverse case it is in *deficit*.

(2) If we add to this the balance of what is called *invisible trade* – that is, the payments and receipts arising out of trade in services such as freight, insurance, travel, and other financial services and the payment of interest and dividends – we arrive at what is defined as the *current-account balance*. In short,

$$\text{visible balance} + \text{invisible balance} \equiv \text{current-account balance}$$

(3) The third element in the balance of payments is known as the *balance on capital account*. This arises in part out of *long-term* investment transactions – for example, the purchase of factories overseas or foreign long-term financial obligations – and in part out of *short-term* transactions reflecting London's importance as a financial centre in the international economy. Taken together we have:

$$\begin{matrix}\text{balance on} \\ \text{capital account}\end{matrix} \equiv \begin{matrix}\text{balance of} \\ \text{long-term capital} \\ \text{movements}\end{matrix} + \begin{matrix}\text{balance of} \\ \text{short-term capital} \\ \text{movements}\end{matrix}$$

If we sum (1) – (3) in any period we arrive at the overall balance-of-payments position. There is, of course, no reason why the overall balance should be zero. Thus the overall balance may be in surplus or in deficit. If it is in surplus, payments *to* the UK from the transactions summarised in the three acounts *exceed* payments *from* the UK. If it is in deficit, the reverse applies.

Suppose a deficit exists. We have paid foreigners *more* than they have paid us. How was this accomplished? What additional item balances the position?

The additional item is known as *official financing* and consists in official borrowing from overseas institutions – foreign monetary authorities or the International Monetary Fund – and reductions in the UK's reserves: that is, the UK's holdings of foreign currency. Thus a deficit is financed by official borrowing and/or a reduction in UK reserves, while a surplus is financed by official lending and/or an increase in the UK's reserves. Accordingly we have:

$$\begin{matrix}\text{current-} \\ \text{account balance}\end{matrix} + \begin{matrix}\text{capital-} \\ \text{account balance}\end{matrix} + \begin{matrix}\text{official} \\ \text{financing}\end{matrix} \equiv \text{zero}$$

which is the form in which the summary of the UK's external transactions is typically presented.

From the end of the Second World War up to 1973, the rate of exchange between the pound sterling and other currencies was fixed – or 'pegged' – for long periods, for example from 1949 to 1967. Since 1972 the rate has been determined on the open market. It is thus said to be 'flexible' or to 'float', and typically changes, albeit by small amounts, from day to day. Because of these two different exchange-rate regimes, we subdivide the UK's postwar experience into two periods: 1946–73, and 1974–81.

During the former period, overall balance-of-payments surpluses or deficits are reflected entirely in official financing. During the latter period they are partly offset by exchange-rate movements. As we shall see later, under a *perfectly flexible* exchange-rate regime, official financing would be identically zero. It follows that from 1973 onwards any account of the balance of payments needs to be supplemented by an account of the behaviour of the exchange rate.

Now consider Figure 6.12 which presents a summary of the balance of payments out-turn on the basis of annual data from 1946 to 1973 and the definitions set out above.

In the upper part of the diagram are series for exports and imports and the visible balance. The latter was typically negative. The current-account balance, however, varies in sign. The invisible balance is typically positive, and in fact invisible trade is of a major importance to the UK.

Annual figures tend to obscure cyclical movements. But it seems clear that periods of rapid expansion in GDP are commonly associated with deterioration in the current account. Thus from 1958 to 1961 there was a tendency to deterioration which recurred with the shortlived expansion of 1963–5 and yet again in what is often called the Heath–Barber expansion of 1971–3. Again, a very severe swing occurred in the shortlived recovery in output in 1978–9. It is also plain that the deterioration is typically due to expansion in import demands rather than a deterioration in exports. In short, the data suggest that the behaviour of UK imports – and the current-account balance – is closely related to the behaviour of real GDP.

We cannot at this stage comment extensively on the behaviour of the *capital account*. The short-run changes in this account were often severe. Moreover, some of the major deteriorations in the *capital-account balance* not only coincided with 'sterling crises', as in 1948–9, 1955–6, 1960–1, 1964 and 1967, but *followed* deteriorations in the current account, as, for example, in 1960–1, 1964 and 1967. Finally, on two occasions, capital outflows may have anticipated sterling devaluations. Thus the explanation of the capital-account balance – changes in which exert considerable influence on the UK's external position – seems to be related to the current-account position (and thus output behaviour) and, on occasions, a strong 'speculative' element where funds move in the expectation of making a profit from exchange-rate changes or at least avoiding the risk of a loss.

In 1972 any notion of an officially 'pegged' rate was abandoned. Since 1973 the pound's value in terms of any foreign currency has been determined by 'market forces' with occasional intervention by the UK authorities (i.e. the Bank of England). Thus, in any given period, the pound can move differently in relation to different currencies. It may, for example, rise against the dollar and yen while falling against the mark or the franc. Measuring 'the' exchange rate thus involves a problem similar to measuring 'the' price level, and is solved in the same way by defining what is called the 'effective' rate of exchange. This exchange rate is plotted (in the form of an index number), together with the £/US dollar rate, in Figure 6.13, which also brings together series for the current-account and capital-account balances.

For the period 1973–9, the *current account* has, on average, been in deficit. In 1980 and 1981, however, exports of oil have grown considerably, while UK real GDP has fallen sharply from its early 1979 level, thus reducing the UK's import bill. As a result, the *current account* has moved into surplus. The *capital-account balance* has fluctuated sharply but until 1977 – a year in which the current balance was close to zero – did not permit either the

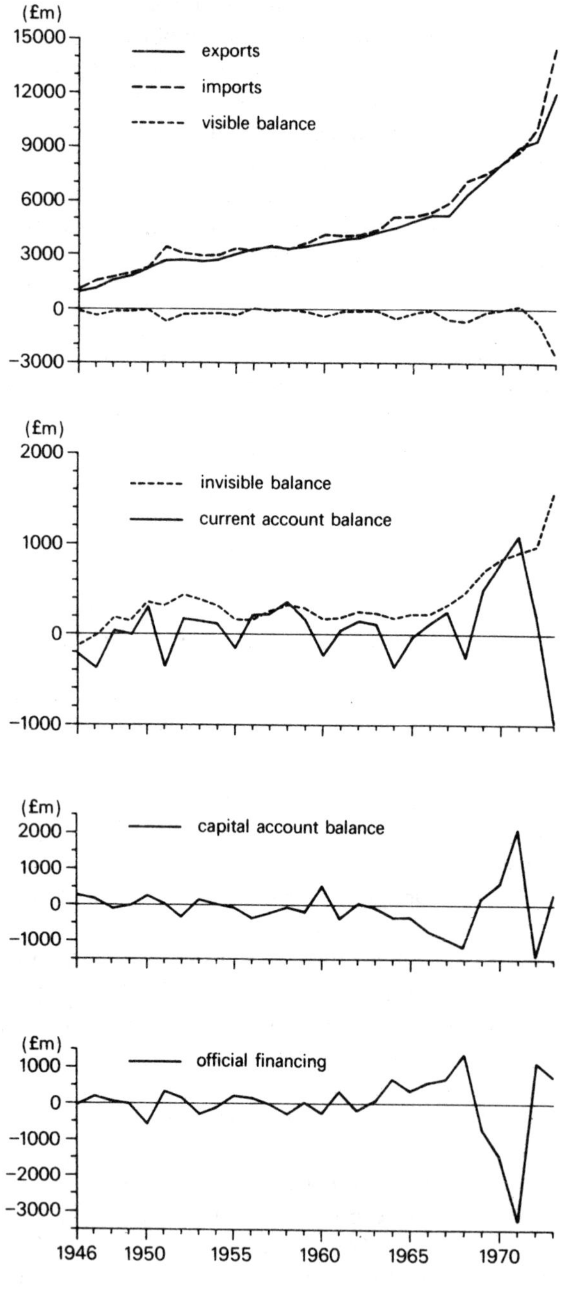

Note: all data in current prices.

Source: *Economic Trends*, Annual Supplement 1981.

Figure 6.12 The UK balance of payments

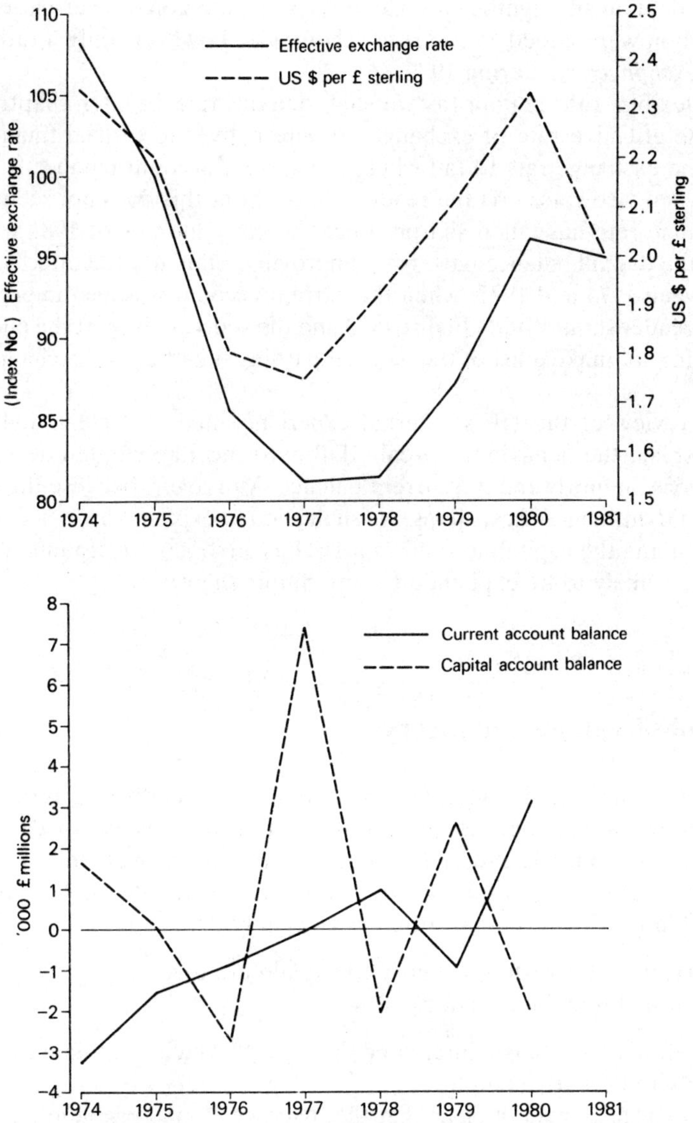

Note: Estimates of current and capital accounts for 1981 incomplete due to industrial dispute in the Civil Service.

Source: *NIESR Review*, various issues.

Figure 6.13 The exchange rate and the balance of payments

repayment of debt on any significant scale *or* the accumulation of overseas reserves. In 1977 some £9.5 billion were added to reserves. There was, however, only a rather small rise in the *effective exchange rate* during 1977.

Under a 'flexible' rate regime (as we shall demonstrate in later chapters) appropriate changes in the effective rate of exchange are alternatives to official financing. We might thus expect the exchange rate to fall where the current-account balance is negative and/or deteriorating and vice versa. As the reader can confirm, this does not seem to be the case, for the exchange rate has fallen sharply since the early months of 1981 when the current account and the overall balance have been improving. Similarly the effective exchange rate *declined* between 1974 and 1977, when the current account was also improving (though in deficit). The reader should study Figure 6.13 and the sources given at the end of this chapter and, after doing so, make a list of the issues regarding the effective exchange rate that they suggest.[1]

This brief review of the UK's external experience makes it clear that any theory we develop to explain the behaviour of real GDP must inevitably entail developing a related theory of exports, imports and the current balance. Moreover, because the exchange rate is almost certain to influence these items, we shall need to explain how it is determined, which involves explaining the capital-account items. Thus an 'open' or 'trading' economy such as the UK's is not likely to be explained by any simple theory.

Problems, observations and theory

In this chapter we have tried to give an account of the UK economy in terms of what may be called the principal macroeconomic variables. For reasons of space, as well as the complexity of our economic experience, this account has been skeletal in the extreme.

Nevertheless our survey, despite its brevity and the relatively small number of variables we have used in making it, demonstrates very plainly that:

(a) the observations we wish our theory to explain are diverse
(b) they are also closely interrelated

We shall therefore need a single integrated theory with which to explain them, and any such theory is likely to be fairly complex.

Our survey has also made it clear that the macroeconomic problems we have identified are real.

In the remaining chapters of this book we attempt to show what theoretical explanations economists have developed to explain macroeconomic observations. For pedagogic reasons, the theory is presented in parts. Nevertheless it constitutes an integrated whole. Necessarily, however, since this book is an introductory text, the theory has been somewhat simplified. It is therefore a valuable exercise for the reader to develop his own critique of the book as it is read, and the best way of doing this is by:

(a) asking, after each chapter, what problems and difficulties have been omitted and how far the analysis presented is capable of explaining them
(b) asking how far the theory developed in Chapters 8–25 can explain the experience recorded in this one.

[1]It will be a valuable exercise for the reader to reconstruct Figure 6.13 on the basis of quarterly data.

In an introductory text the theory presented should aim to do four things:

(a) throw some light on our economic experiences and give the reader some idea of the problems involved in formulating testable theories explaining them
(b) encourage the reader to be constructively sceptical of popular dogma, distrustful of panaceas and insistent on systematic evidence in support of arguments
(c) make it plain where the theory presented needs extension or modification or economists are in disagreement
(d) whet the reader's appetite for more advanced studies

The chance of doing these four successfully will be much enhanced if the reader keeps it in mind that these, and not the inculcation of some fashionable set of 'answers to problems', is the purpose of this book.

Questions and exercises

1. Write down a list of the problems suggested to you by the data and discussion in this chapter. Which seem the most urgent? Why?

2. What criticisms can you make of our method of calculating (i) 'capacity output', and (ii) its rate of growth? What method would you propose instead? Why?

3. Professor Paish's approximate formula was:

   proportion of productive capacity employed = 105 − 5 × percentage of the work-force unemployed

   Why do you think this formula applies (if at all) only to 'small' percentages of unemployment? What does it suggest about the present level of 'excess capacity'?

4. According to an eminent economist *full-employment* output in 1938 would have been 11 per cent higher than observed output. Accepting this estimate, can you suggest a way of calculating *full-employment* output for each year from 1920 to 1938? Give an approximate estimate of (i) the total loss in output due to unemployment over the period; (ii) the average annual loss.

5. According to *National Income Statistics: Sources and Methods* the estimates of gross national product at *current prices* are subject to an error which is ± 3 per cent. In real terms the range of error probably lies between ± 3 per cent to 10 per cent for relatively 'long' periods. How, in these circumstances, would you value the reliability of our calculated rates of growth in capacity? Between what upper and lower limits do the 'true' rates lie? Can we be *confident* that capacity really grew faster from 1948 to 1973 than in the interwar years? Give your reasons.

6. On the basis of Figures 6.1 and 6.2, what value judgement is implied in the statement that we have done 'better' in the postwar years than we did in the interwar years? Do you accept it?

7. How would you seek to measure the 'amplitude' of the fluctuations in either GDP or the percentage of unemployment? Use your measure to compare the experience of the interwar and postwar years. Discuss your results.

8. Assemble the evidence for and against the view that the current balance of payments deteriorates sharply in periods in which output grows faster than capacity because of the resultant increase in imports.

9. Prices rose from 1932 to 1938. They rose also from 1948 to 1972. It is nowadays common to speak of the price increases in the second period as constituting 'inflation'. Did we have 'inflation' from 1932 to 1938? If not, why not? What does your view imply for the definition of inflation?

10. Figure 6.2 suggests that 'capacity' grew steadily at about 3 per cent from 1955 to 1973. Make use of the concept of the production possibility curve, the determinants of its rate of movement and the data of Figure 6.6 and Table 6.1 to criticise this hypothesis.

11. Compare our dating of UK cycles with that of the Central Statistical Office (in *Economic Trends*) and the NIESR (in the *Review* of November 1981). How would you seek to establish which dating is the 'best'? What would 'best' mean?

12. From the charts given in *Economic Trends* examine critically the diagrams and discussion given in this chapter. What amendments would you make, and why?

13. Use Figure 6.7 to distinguish between the two concepts 'amplitude' and 'amplitude corrected for trend'. Which is the 'better' measure? Why?

14. Again using *Economic Trends*, examine critically our discussion of investment in stocks. Is there any reason to suppose a relationship between the rate of investment in stocks and the rate of imports? If so, why do you think that such a relationship might exist?

15. Compare our amplitude index with the measures used by the NIESR (*Review*, November 1981). Which do you prefer and why?

16. 'It is true that inventory investment fluctuates far more violently than consumption. But its effect on GDP is not simply dependent upon this but upon its relative importance as a component of GDP.' Elucidate. Express the main sub-aggregates as proportions of GDP and define for each an approximate index of 'effective amplitude'.

17. It is sometimes said that the rate of change of prices is explained by the percentage of the work-force unemployed. Do the data in this chapter support this hypothesis?

18. Is the British 'balance-of-payments problem' exclusively or even primarily one of the current account? Discuss carefully.

19. 'During the cycle some series lead and others lag. We can use the former to forecast the cycle itself.' Can we? Are there series which *consistently* lead the cycle? Which series lead real GDP? Use *Economic Trends* (March 1975 and May 1980) and HM Treasury *Economic Progress Report*, no. 149 (September 1982) as background.

20. Which sterling crises did *not* occur after sharp expansions in the UK output? How would you (i) describe, (ii) explain them?

21. 'Observed unemployment has *seasonal*, *structural* and *voluntary* components as well as *involuntary*.' Define these terms. How big do you think each component is likely to be at the present time? Does 'observed unemployment' measure 'unemployment' with reasonable accuracy? Comment on the contention that recorded unemployment in mid-1982 understated 'real' or 'true' unemployment by some 600–700,000.

Suggested reading

H. L. Beales and R. S. Lambert, *Memoirs of the Unemployed* (Gollancz, 1934).

Sir William Beveridge, *Full Employment in a Free Society* (Allen & Unwin, 1945) particularly pp. 40–88, 242–58.

F. T. Blackaby, 'British Economic Policy 1960–74: A General Appraisal', *NIESR Review*, no. 80 (May 1977).

S. Brooks, *The Economic Implications of North Sea Oil*, NIESR Discussion Paper no. 38.

J. C. R. Dow, *The Management of the British Economy 1946–60* (Cambridge University Press, 1964).

W. Greenwood, *Love on the Dole* (Jonathan Cape, 1934).

W. A. Lewis, *Economic Survey 1919–39* (Allen & Unwin, 1949) particularly chs 1–5.

P. Minford, 'The Four Ages of Post-War British Policy Debate', *NIESR Review*, no. 100 (May 1982).

G. Orwell, *The Road to Wigan Pier* (Penguin, 1962).

D.C. Paige, 'Economic Growth in the Last 100 Years', *NIESR Review*, no. 16 (1961).

F. W. Paish, 'The Management of British Economy', *Lloyds Bank Review*, no. 76 (1965).

F. W. Paish, *Studies in an Inflationary Economy* (Macmillan, 1966) ch. 17.

Chapter 7
Analytical and Expository Devices

Many students of economics find the analytical and expository devices used by economists forbidding or even frightening. This is particularly the case where the devices employ – or look as if they employ – mathematical modes of expression and mathematical methods of reasoning.

Those who read this book are therefore reassured at this stage that, in the pages which follow, no mathematical knowledge or manipulatory skill above that demanded at GCE 'O' Level is assumed. If readers have reached this level, *and resolutely refuse to be upset by the use of symbols* – however terrifying they look – they have nothing to worry about at all. If they have passed this level and studied, let us say, 'A' Level Mathematics,[1] so much the better for them. But 'O' Level plus a little determination is all that is required.

After this reassurance readers are now asked to study carefully the following short notes on particular concepts and devices and to work through the Questions and Exercises at the end of the chapter.

The concept of a function

In later chapters we shall frequently have to make assumptions about human behaviour which imply that some variable (call it X) depends systematically upon some other variable (call it Y). In this case we shall say that

X is a function of Y

and write this:

$$X = f(Y) \tag{7.1}$$

where the notation f can be translated 'is a function of' or 'depends systematically upon'.

[1]The advantage of mathematical knowledge in studying economics is immense. The fact that such knowledge is *not* necessary for this book should not obscure from the reader the immense gains to be derived from access to this principal technique of analytical thinking.

The notation $X = f(Y)$ is used because of its convenience. It is obviously nothing to worry about since it merely states a general dependence of X (the *dependent* variable) on Y (the *independent* variable) and this is not of itself a very difficult idea.

Now $X = f(Y)$ is a general statement. It tells us nothing about *the way* X depends upon Y. If we want to know this, we must know the *form* of the function. Three simple forms are as follows:

$$\left.\begin{aligned} X &= A + bY \\ X &= F + cY^2 \\ X &= H + dY^{-2} \end{aligned}\right\} \qquad (7.2)$$

$$\left.\begin{aligned} X &= 100 + 0.8Y \\ X &= 80 + 2Y^2 \\ X &= 50 + 11Y^{-2} \end{aligned}\right\} \qquad (7.2n)$$

where A, F and H are constants independent of Y and thus give the value of X where Y is zero.

All of these are special cases of the general statement $X = f(Y)$. They tell us *generally* that a particular value of Y implies a particular value of X and *specifically* how to *calculate* X given Y, the constant term (A, F, H) and the coefficient (b, c, d).

Obviously it is possible for one variable (X) to depend systematically upon (be a function of) more than one variable. Thus we could write:

$$X = f(Y, Z, Q, L, M) \qquad (7.3)$$

which is simply translated as:

X depends systematically upon the variables Y, Z, Q, L and M

A particular and simple example is:

$$X = A + aY + bZ + cQ + dL + eM \qquad (7.4)$$

or, to give a numerical version:

$$X = 0.79 + 0.2Y + 4.7Z + 6.23Q + 8L + 0.0001M \qquad (7.4n)$$

This tells us that, to calculate X, we now need to know the values of the constant A and of the five independent variables Y, Z, Q, L and M. Once we know these, and the values of the coefficients a, b, c, d, e, it is a simple matter to calculate X.

In Chapter 2 we have developed a rather crude behaviour hypothesis to explain the monthly consumption of beer. This was to the effect that the monthly consumption of beer (the dependent variable) depended systematically upon, *or* was a function of:

(a) the weather (defined as the average monthly temperature)
(b) the level of general prosperity (defined as the reciprocal of the percentage of unemployment)
(c) the ratio of the price of whisky to the price of beer

Written in general functional form this would appear:

$$B_c = f(T, U, P_w/P_b) \qquad (7.5)$$

where

$B_c \equiv$ monthly beer consumption
$T \equiv$ average monthly temperature

U ≡ average percentage of the work-force unemployed in each month
P_w ≡ average price of whisky in each month
P_b ≡ average price of beer in each month

Let us take the 'beer' example a little further. In Chapter 2 we argued that *if*, with U and P_w/P_B constant, T increased, *then* B_c would increase.

We now define a symbol to indicate this *marginal response* of the *dependent* variable (beer consumption) to a change in *one* of the *independent* variables, *the remaining independent variables being held constant*, as:

$\frac{\partial B_c}{\partial T}$ ≡ marginal response of beer consumption to a change in T (temperature) [U and $\frac{P_w}{P_b}$ constant]

$\frac{\partial B_c}{\partial U}$ ≡ marginal response of beer consumption to a change in U (unemployment) [T and $\frac{P_w}{P_b}$ constant]

$\frac{\partial B_c}{\partial (P_w/P_b)}$ ≡ marginal response of beer consumption to a change in $\frac{P_w}{P_b}$ (the ratio of the price of whisky to the price of beer) [T and U constant]

Our behaviour hypothesis did not specify numerical values for these *marginal response coefficients*. That is, it did not set out either the *form* of the function or the *numerical value of the marginal response coefficient* as, for example, we did at 7.4n. It did, however, specify the *sign* of the coefficients, as the reader can easily see by looking back. We argued that

$$\frac{\partial B_c}{\partial T} > 0 \quad \frac{\partial B_c}{\partial U} < 0 \text{ and } \frac{\partial B_c}{\partial (P_w/P_b)} > 0.$$

To fix our ideas let us now give an (assumed) *form* and *set of numerical values* to (7.5) and write:

$$B_c = aT + b\left(\frac{1}{U}\right) + c\left(\frac{P_w}{P_b}\right) \tag{7.6}$$

$$B_c = 0.7T + 6.71\left(\frac{1}{U}\right) + 32\left(\frac{P_w}{P_b}\right) \tag{7.6n}$$

If we now assume values for T, U and (P_w/P_b) we can calculate the resulting values for B_c by (fairly) simple arithmetic. A few such calculations are given in Table 7.1. In this table a number of values of B_c have been left blank for you to calculate for yourself.

A lot can be learned from this table. For example, between months 4 and 5 all three independent variables changed. What was the resultant *change* in beer consumption? If we look carefully we see that it was:

$$15.7 = 0.7 \times (4.0) + 6.71 \times (0.02) + 32 \times (0.4) \tag{7.7n}$$

or, to forget our numbers for a moment:[1]

[1]Those readers familiar with the calculus will be aware of the special nature of this case.

Table 7.1 The monthly consumption of beer varying with the weather, the level of general prosperity and the price ratio of whisky and beer (hypothetical values of T, U, P_w/P_B)

Month	$\frac{\partial B_c}{\partial T}$	T	$\frac{\partial B_c}{\partial (1/U)}$	$\frac{1}{U}$	$\frac{\partial B_c}{\partial (P_w/P_b)}$	$\frac{P_w}{P_b}$	B_c
1	0.7	(40)	+6.71	($\frac{1}{3}$)	+32	(1.2)	= 68.6
2	0.7	(44)	+6.71	($\frac{1}{3}$)	+32	(1.2)	= 71.4
3	0.7	(48)	+6.71	(1/3.2)	+32	(1.5)	= 83.7
4	0.7	(52)	+6.71	(1/3.2)	+32	(1.5)	= 86.5
5	0.7	(56)	+6.71	($\frac{1}{3}$)	+32	(1.9)	= 102.2
6	0.7	(60)	+6.71	($\frac{1}{3}$)	+32	(1.9)	= 105.0
7	0.7	(64)	+6.71	($\frac{1}{3}$)	+32	(2.0)	= 111.0
8	0.7	(70)	+6.71	($\frac{1}{3}$)	+32	(1.9)	= 112.0
9	0.7	(64)	+6.71	($\frac{1}{3}$)	+32	(1.9)	=
10	0.7	(55)	+6.71	(1/3.4)	+32	(1.3)	=
11	0.7	(45)	+6.71	(1/3.4)	+32	(1.3)	=
12	0.7	(40)	+6.71	(1/3.2)	+32	(1.3)	=

$$\Delta B_c = \frac{\partial B_c}{\partial T} . \Delta T + \frac{\partial B_c}{\partial (1/U)} . \Delta\left(\frac{1}{U}\right) + \frac{\partial B_c}{\partial (P_w/P_b)} . \Delta\left(\frac{P_w}{P_b}\right) \tag{7.7}$$

where the notation Δ indicates 'the change in' the variable to which it is applied. It all looks very complicated at first sight but a little patience – and a little practice – will soon convince the reader that it is not complicated at all.

Let us now take one more example of the use of functions. In Chapter 5 we argued that real output depended upon (or was a function of): (i) the quantity of capital employed; (ii) the input of labour services; and (iii) the state of technique. This hypothesis can be, and often is, written in the form of a *production function* which would appear thus:

$$Y = f(K, N, T)$$

where

$Y \equiv$ real output
$K \equiv$ real capital stock employed in production
$N \equiv$ labour employed
$T \equiv$ state of technique

For this function we would expect $\partial Y/\partial K > 0$, $\partial Y/\partial N > 0$, $\partial Y/\partial T > 0$, since it is reasonable to suppose that an increase in any input (the quantity of the other input(s) and the state of technique remaining constant) would raise output, as would an improvement in technique (with both inputs constant).

A particular production function, commonly met in macroeconomics, is:

$$Y = TK^{\alpha} N^{1-\alpha}$$

This, too, is an awkward looking expression at first sight but again there is really nothing to be afraid of. Suppose $\alpha = 0.5$ so that $1 - \alpha$ also is 0.5. For simplicity assume $T = 10$. Then since any number raised to the power of 0.5 is merely the square root of the number we can calculate Y from the values of the two independent variables K and N either by using logarithms or, simpler still, by employing a table of square roots. This is done for assumed values of K and N in Table 7.2. As before, you should complete the table for yourself.

Table 7.2 Production function relating output to varying combinations of inputs

Number of units of labour	Number of units of capital 25	50	75	100	125	150	175	200	225	250	275
5	**112**	158	194		250	274	296	317	336	354	371
10	158	**224**	274	316	353		418	447	474	500	524
15	194	274	**336**	387	432	474	512	547	581	612	642
20	224	316	387	**448**	500	548	592	632	671	707	
25		353	432	500	**560**	613	662	707		791	829
30	274	387	474	548	613	**672**	725		822	866	909
35	296	418		592	662	725	**784**	836	888	936	982
40	317		547	632	707	775		**896**	948	1,000	1,049
45	336	474	581	671		822	888	949	**1,008**	1,060	1,113
50	354	500	612	707	791	866	936	1,000	1,060	**1,120**	1,173
55	371	524	642	742	829	909	982	1,049	1,113	1,173	**1,232**

$Y = TK^{\alpha}N^{1-\alpha}$, where $\alpha = 0.5$, $T = 10$.

If we read *down* any colum of Table 7.2 we find what happens to output when the input of *labour* increases with *capital* and *technique* constant. If we read *across* any row we find what happens to output when the input of *capital* increases with labour *input* and *technique* constant. If we read down a *diagonal* we discover what happens to output when both labour and capital inputs experience *equiproportional* increases.

We now give the names to the *marginal response coefficients* of the *production function* employed by economists. These are:

$$\frac{\partial Y}{\partial K} \equiv \text{marginal product of capital} \equiv \text{the increase in output produced by a unit increase in } K \text{ with } N, T \text{ constant}$$

$$\frac{\partial Y}{\partial N} \equiv \text{marginal product of labour} \equiv \text{the increase in output produced by a unit increase in } N \text{ with } K, T \text{ constant}$$

The reader should now check, from the table, that the following propositions are correct for this particular production function:

1. Doubling (trebling) both capital and labour always doubles (trebles) output.
2. The marginal product of both factors is always positive.
3. The marginal product of either factor tends to fall as more of it is employed with the other factor constant.
4. The marginal product of either factor is greater, the smaller is the ratio of the quantity of it employed to the quantity employed of the other factor.

This particular function has a number of other important and interesting properties which we shall have to discuss in detail when we turn to consider economic growth. At this stage, however, they do not concern us for our aims are merely:

(a) to explain what is meant by a function
(b) to show that the functional notation is nothing to worry about
(c) to explain what is meant by *marginal response coefficients*

Graphs

Economists make considerable use of graphs (or diagrams) to represent functional relations. A graph expresses a relationship between two variables, one of which is the dependent variable and the other the independent variable. Graphs are useful but, since they are limited to two dimensions, less powerful than the analytical methods discussed under the heading of *marginal response coefficients* which, obviously enough, can handle any number of 'systematic dependencies' we care to postulate. To illustrate we can draw a graph derived from our *production function*:

$$Y = f(K, N, T) \tag{7.8}$$

This graph measures Y on the vertical axis and N on the horizontal. To construct the graph we then take K and T to be constant. The resulting relationship gives Y as a function of N (output as a function of labour input) with both the stock of capital (K) and the state of technique (T) given. It is thus a *short-run production function*. The slope of this curve relating Y and N is easily seen to be the *marginal response coefficient* $\partial Y/\partial N$ – that is, the marginal product of labour – or the increment in output brought about by a unit increase in labour (N) with both capital (K) and technique (T) constant.

We have drawn the curve to illustrate the propositions that:

(a) the marginal product of labour is always positive
(b) the marginal product of labour diminishes as labour input increases

If K and/or T changes, the curve itself will shift. Suppose, for example, we were to draw a second curve on the basis of a greater capital stock. This curve would lie above the old.

The points to notice about graphs are:

(a) a graph only shows the relationship between a dependent variable and *one* independent variable, of which the former is a function; *given*
(b) the values of any other independent variables on which the dependent variable systematically depends (i.e. of which it is a function)

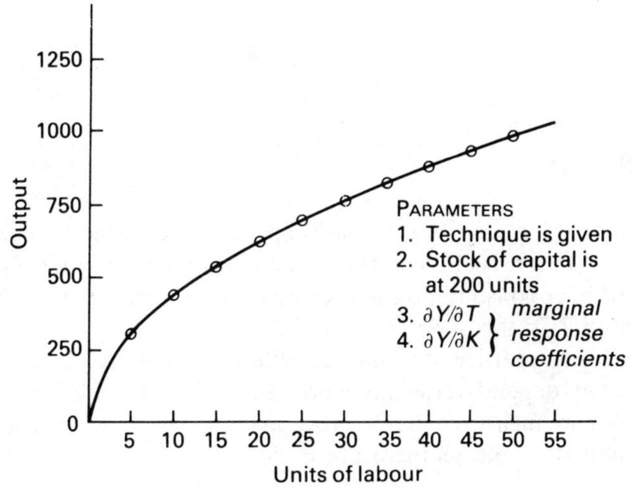

Figure 7.1 The relationship between total product and varying units of labour output

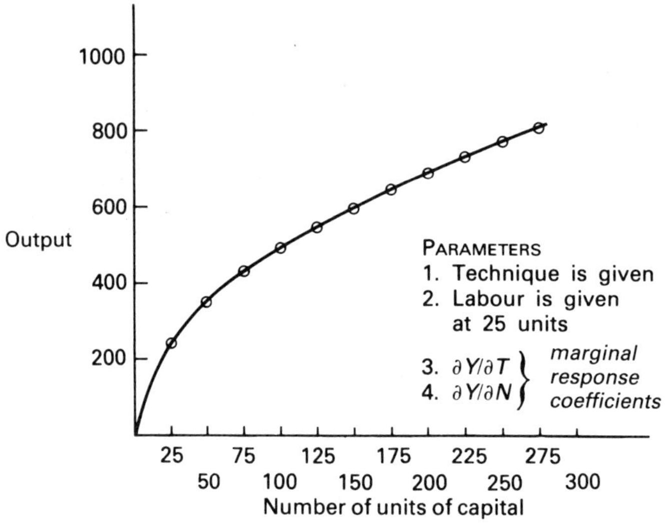

Figure 7.2 The relationship between total product and varying units of capital input

(c) the slope of the graph is the *marginal response coefficient* relating the dependent variable to the independent variable.

The independent variables not measured on either axis and their marginal response coefficients, taken as given in drawing a graph (i.e. in our example K, $\partial Y/\partial K$, T and $\partial Y/\partial T$) are termed the *parameters* of the curve. Hence whenever you are confronted with a curve relating two variables you should *always* ask yourself two questions:

1. What are the parameters of this curve?
2. Which way would the curve shift if one of the parameters changed?

The concept of elasticity

So far we have discussed the response of one (dependent) variable to a change in another (independent) variable in terms of the concept of a marginal response coefficient. Thus the marginal response of beer consumption to a change in temperature was defined as $\partial B_c/\partial T$ and given, in equation 7.7n the hypothetical value of 0.7.

The marginal response coefficient is an important concept. Nevertheless it is not free from ambiguity, for it depends crucially upon the units in which the dependent and independent variables are measured. To see this, assume beer to be measured in thousands of barrels (of standard size) and temperature in degrees of Fahrenheit. Then:

$$\frac{\partial B_c \text{ (in thousands of barrels)}}{\partial T \text{ (in degrees Fahrenheit)}} = 0.7$$

So a *one* degree rise in temperature increases beer consumption by 700 barrels, for, holding all other variables in equation 7.7 constant:

$$\Delta B_c = \frac{\partial B_c}{\partial T} . \Delta T$$
$$= \textit{0.7 thousand barrels per degree} \times \textit{1.0}$$
$$= \textit{700 barrels}$$

If we now measured beer in units of 100 barrels we should have $\partial B_c/\partial T = 7.0$ and, if we measured in single barrels, $\partial B_c/\partial T = 700$. Behaviouristically speaking nothing has changed: only the units of measurement have altered and with them $\partial B_c/\partial T$.

This dependence of marginal response coefficients, the constants of human behaviour in linear functions like 7.6, on the units in which the variables are measured is awkward, for it makes it hard to estimate their importance – and thus compare two or more marginal response coefficients. Hence economists tend to use a measure which is independent of the units in which the variables are measured. This measure is known as *elasticity* and defined as:

the proportionate change in the dependent variable $\equiv \dfrac{\Delta B_c}{B_c}$

divided by

the proportionate change in the independent variable bringing it about $\equiv \dfrac{\Delta T}{T}$

So that the elasticity of beer consumption with respect to temperature alone is:

$$\frac{\Delta B_c}{B_c} \div \frac{\Delta T}{T} \equiv \frac{\Delta B_c}{\Delta T} \cdot \frac{T}{B_c}$$
$$\equiv \frac{\frac{\partial B_c}{\partial T} \cdot \Delta T}{\Delta T} \cdot \frac{T}{B_c}$$
$$\equiv \frac{\partial B_c}{\partial T} \cdot \frac{T}{B_c} \equiv \frac{\partial B_c}{\partial T} \div \frac{B_c}{T}$$

In short, the elasticity is the marginal response coefficient relating B_c to T *divided by* the ratio B_c/T. Since the latter expression is measured in the same units as the former, the choice of units has no influence on the elasticity which is a pure number. For example, using equation 7.7n and taking two hypothetical values of T, we have:

$$B_c = 0.7 \times (40) + 6.71(\tfrac{1}{3}) + 32\ (1.2) = 68.6 \qquad (7.9na)$$
$$B_c = 0.7 \times (44) + 6.71(\tfrac{1}{3}) + 32\ (1.2) = 71.4 \qquad (7.9nb)$$

Therefore:

$$\Delta B_c = 0.7\ \Delta T$$
$$= 0.7 \times 4.0$$
$$= 2.8$$

and the elasticity is:

$$\text{elasticity}_{(1)} \equiv \frac{\partial B_c}{\partial T} \div \frac{B_c}{T} \simeq 0.7 \div \frac{68.6}{40} = 0.7 \div 1.715 = 0.408$$

Why do we use the sign $\simeq$ signifying *approximate* equality? Simply because we *could* have written, by using (7.9nb) to give us the values of B_c and T:

$$\text{elasticity}_{(2)} \equiv \frac{\partial B_c}{\partial T} \div \frac{B_c}{T} \simeq 0.7 \div \frac{71.4}{44.0} = 0.7 \div 1.623 = 0.431$$

Hence the numerical value of the elasticity over a *range* of change in the independent variable is not unambiguous. If we began with 7.9na and moved to 7.9nb we estimated the elasticity as 0.408. Reversing the procedure we found a different value. A diagram may make the point clearer (see Figure 7.3).

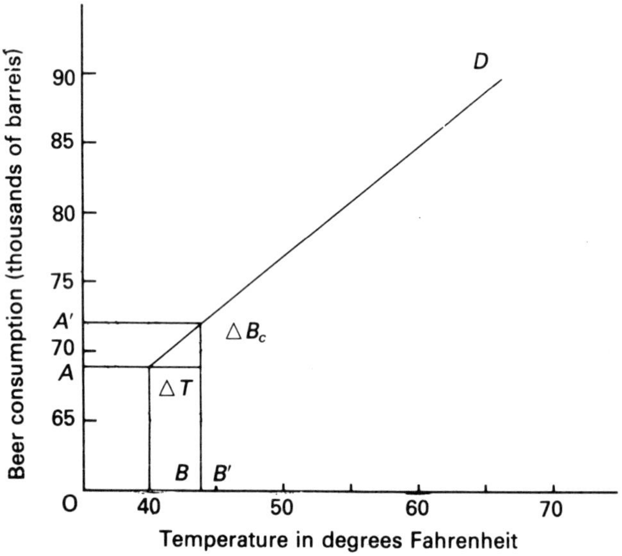

Figure 7.3 Beer consumption function

At 40° F the ratio

$$\frac{B_c}{T} = \frac{OA}{OB} = \frac{68.6}{40.0}$$

At 44° F the ratio

$$\frac{B_c}{T} = \frac{OA'}{OB'} = \frac{71.4}{44.0}$$

The marginal response coefficient

$$= \frac{\partial B_c}{\partial T} = \frac{\frac{\partial B_c}{\partial T} \cdot \Delta T}{\Delta T} = \frac{\Delta B_c}{\Delta T}$$

Suppose we now make the temperature change, not four degrees, but 0.004 degrees: that is, one-thousandth part of our first example. We have for our two measures:

$$\text{elasticity}_{(1)} \simeq 0.7 \div 1.715 = 0.408163$$

and

$$\text{elasticity}_{(2)} \simeq 0.7 \div 1.71505 = 0.408151$$

Clearly the *smaller* we make the temperature change (and thus the resultant beer consumption change) the nearer our two elasticity measures approach. As the temperature change tends to zero – that is becomes smaller and smaller – the elasticity becomes closer to $0.7 \div 68.6/40.0$. In the limit – that is, when ΔT is indefinitely small – we can say that the elasticity *at temperature 40* is given by:

$$\text{elasticity (at } T = 40) = 0.7 \div \frac{68.6}{40.0}$$

This last concept, the elasticity of a schedule (in this case the beer consumption schedule) *at a particular point upon it*, is the concept usually employed in economics. It is safe to use it only when the change in the independent variable is small. Where this is not the case, we generally need to use the concept of elasticity over a range – in our example over the range of 40–44 degrees of temperature.

The reader should notice that the elasticity depends upon two factors:

(a) the slope of the schedule (the marginal response coefficient) at the point at which elasticity is being measured
(b) the *ratio* of the values of the dependent and independent variables at the same point

For the special case of a straight-line schedule the slope is constant, as the figure makes clear. But the ratio between the values of the variables is not (in general) constant. Hence the elasticity will vary along the curve. The reader should make sure that he understands this point by working a few examples in addition to those given in the Questions and Exercises at the end of this chapter.

Although in general straight-line curves do *not* exhibit constant elasticity some straight-line curves exhibit this property.

There are in fact two special straight-line curves commonly used to illustrate elasticity. They are shown in Figure 7.4.

The first of these curves has zero elasticity of demand for butter over the price range $p_A - p_B$. The second has infinite elasticity at the price p_x. The reader should be satisfied that these statements are consistent with our earlier discussion of elasticity.

Apart from its freedom from the problem of units, the concept of elasticity has other uses. Suppose that the community's demand for peanuts (X) depends only on their price (p). Suppose now that producers lower price by, say, 1 per cent. If the elasticity of demand is -1, then the proportionate change in quantity will be equal (in absolute value) but opposite in sign to the price change. The quantity sold will *increase* by 1 per cent. Hence the

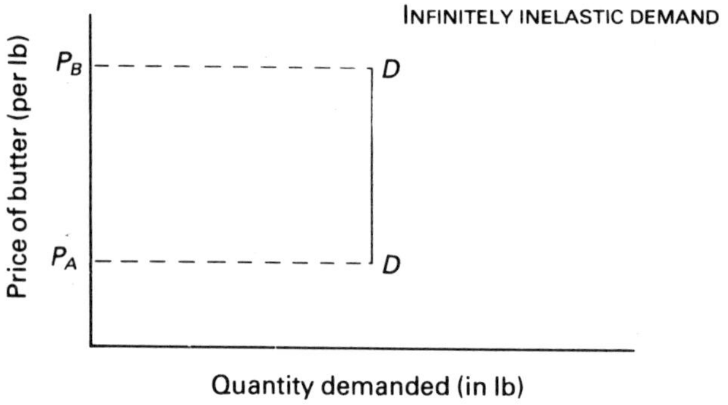

Zero elasticity of demand over the price range P_A–P_B

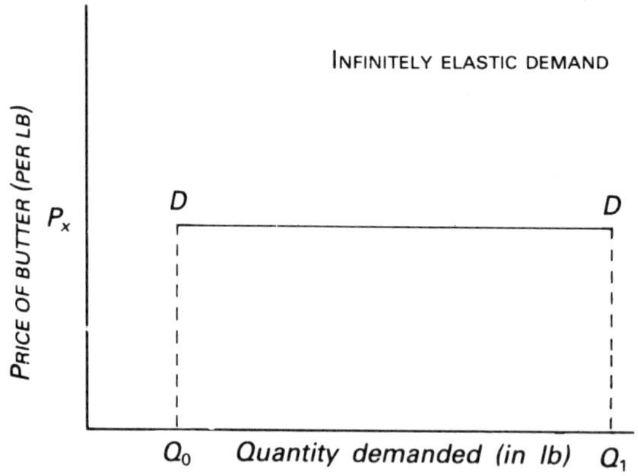

Infinite elasticity at the price P_x over the range $Q_0 - Q_1$

Figure 7.4 Hypothetical demand curves for butter

value of total sales will be constant. If the elasticity is algebraically less then -1 (say -3) a 1 per cent *cut* in prices will be associated with a 3 per cent *increase* in sales. Conversely, if the price elasticity were algebraically greater than -1 (say equal to zero) the quantity sold would not change. Hence the effect of a price cut on total revenue ($\equiv$ price $\times$ quantity sold) depends upon the elasticity of demand, which is for peanuts in this case.

The term 'elasticity' is frequently used with reference to the absolute value of the elasticity rather than its algebraic value. The *sign* of the elasticity is usually clear from the context. Adopting this convention we may summarise the peanut example by saying that if the price of peanuts is reduced by a *small* percentage, then the value of sales will

(a) *increase* if the elasticity of demand > 1
(b) *decrease* if the elasticity of demand < 1
(c) *remain unchanged* if the elasticity of demand $= 1$

We call case (a) *elastic* demand and case (b) *inelastic* demand. Why do we say a *small* percentage? To see this denote:

$$
\begin{aligned}
p &\equiv \text{price of peanuts} \\
\Delta p &\equiv \text{change in price of peanuts} \\
X &\equiv \text{quantity purchased} \\
\Delta X &\equiv \text{change in quantity purchased}
\end{aligned}
$$

Then *before* the price change, total revenue = pX. After the price change we have:

$$\text{total revenue} = (p + \Delta p)\,(X + \Delta X) = pX + p\Delta X + X\Delta p + \Delta p\Delta X$$

Hence the change in revenue is given by:

$$\begin{aligned}\Delta\,(\text{total revenue}) &= pX + p\Delta X + X\Delta p + \Delta X\Delta p - pX \\ &= p\,\Delta X + X\Delta p + \Delta X\Delta p\end{aligned}$$

Now this expression can be written as:

$$\begin{aligned}\Delta\,(\text{total revenue}) &= pX\left(\frac{\Delta X}{X} + \frac{\Delta p}{p} + \left[\frac{\Delta X}{X}\,\frac{\Delta p}{p}\right]\right) \\ &= pX\left\{\begin{matrix}\text{prop.}\\ \text{change}\\ \text{in}\\ \text{quantity}\end{matrix} + \begin{matrix}\text{prop.}\\ \text{change}\\ \text{in}\\ \text{price}\end{matrix} + \left[\begin{matrix}\text{prop.}\\ \text{change}\\ \text{in}\\ \text{quantity}\end{matrix} \times \begin{matrix}\text{prop.}\\ \text{change}\\ \text{in}\\ \text{price}\end{matrix}\right]\right\}\end{aligned}$$

Suppose the last term is sufficiently small to be neglected. Then:

$$\Delta\begin{pmatrix}\text{total}\\ \text{revenue}\end{pmatrix} \gtrless 0$$

$$pX\left\{\begin{matrix}\text{prop.}\\ \text{change}\\ \text{in}\\ \text{quantity}\end{matrix} + \begin{matrix}\text{prop.}\\ \text{change}\\ \text{in}\\ \text{price}\end{matrix}\right\} \gtrless 0$$

Clearly, since the proportionate change in price is *negative*, the second inequality can be written:

$$pX\left\{\frac{\text{prop. change in quantity}}{\text{prop. change in price}} + 1\right\} \gtrless 0$$

That is:

$$pX\ \{\text{elasticity of demand} + 1\} \gtrless 0$$

Hence revenue will increase if the elasticity is < -1: which is the result that we reached verbally above. To reach this result we have, however, had to set $\Delta p/p \times \Delta X/X$ (the product of the proportionate changes) to zero. This is permissible if Δp is close to zero. Hence our elasticity *result*, not very surprisingly in view of our *definition* of point elasticity, holds strictly only where Δp is indefinitely small. *In all other cases it is an approximation which involves an error dependent on* $\Delta p/\Delta p \times \Delta X/X$. The reader should calculate how good this approximation is by assuming a variety of values for $\Delta p/p$ and $\Delta X/X$.

Functions and schedules

In our beer consumption example we wrote quite generally:

$$B_c = f\left(T,\ U,\ \frac{P_w}{P_b}\right) \qquad (7.5)$$

and specifically:

$$B_c = aT + b\left(\frac{1}{U}\right) + c\left(\frac{P_w}{P_b}\right) \tag{7.6}$$

This specific function (7.6) is said to be *linear* in the independent variables because it involves no powers of these variables other than unity. Had we written:

$$B_c = a_1 T + aT^2 + b\left(\frac{1}{U}\right) + c\left(\frac{P_w}{P_b}\right)^2 + d\left(\frac{P_w}{P_b}\right)$$

the function would have been *quadratic* in T and P_w/P_b and *linear* in $1/U$.

In general, in economics, we must expect non-linear relationships to occur. Nevertheless, in most of this book, we shall only use functions which are *linear* – that is, of the form:

$$Y = a + b\,x + c\,z + d\,w$$

or *logarithmically linear* – that is, of the form:

$$\log Y = \log a' + b' \log x + c' \log z \tag{7.6}$$

The latter function, since multiplying the logarithm of a variable means raising the variable to the power of its multiplier, can be written:

$$Y = a'x^{b'}z^{c'}$$

a form we have already met in the production function discussed earlier.

The justification for restricting ourselves to linear or log-linear functions is twofold. The first point is that these functions are algebraically convenient. Thus the linear function 7.6 has the constant marginal response coefficients $\partial B_c/\partial T = a$, $\partial B_c/\partial(1/U) = b$ and $\partial B_c/\partial(P_w/P_B) = c$, while the log-linear function also has the constant marginal response coefficients $\partial \log y/\partial \log x = b'$ and $\partial \log y/\partial \log z = c'$.

There is also the second point that *any function, over a sufficiently small range of values of the independent variable, can be approximated by a linear function*. This is illustrated in Figure 7.5 which shows how two functions which are certainly not linear can be approximated in this way.

Thus in Figure 7.5a for values of the independent variable close to x_1 we can approximate the function by the line aa', for values around x_2 by the line bb', and so on. In the same way the function in Figure 7.5b can be approximated reasonably well by the four straight lines aa', bb', cc' and dd', each of which is applicable only over a range of values (or a particular value) of the independent variable.

To visualise the properties of the logarithmic function 7.7 consider some variable Y which is growing through time as follows:

Time	0	1	2	3	4
Value of Y	10	15	22.5	33.75	50.625

It is easy to see that the law of growth in this case is a 50 per cent increase in Y per period of time. If we graph this function using a *logarithmic scale* for Y and a natural scale for time we have the values:

Time	0	1	2	3	4
log Y	1.0	1.1761	1.3522	1.5281	1.7042
Y	10.0	15	22.5	33.57	50.625

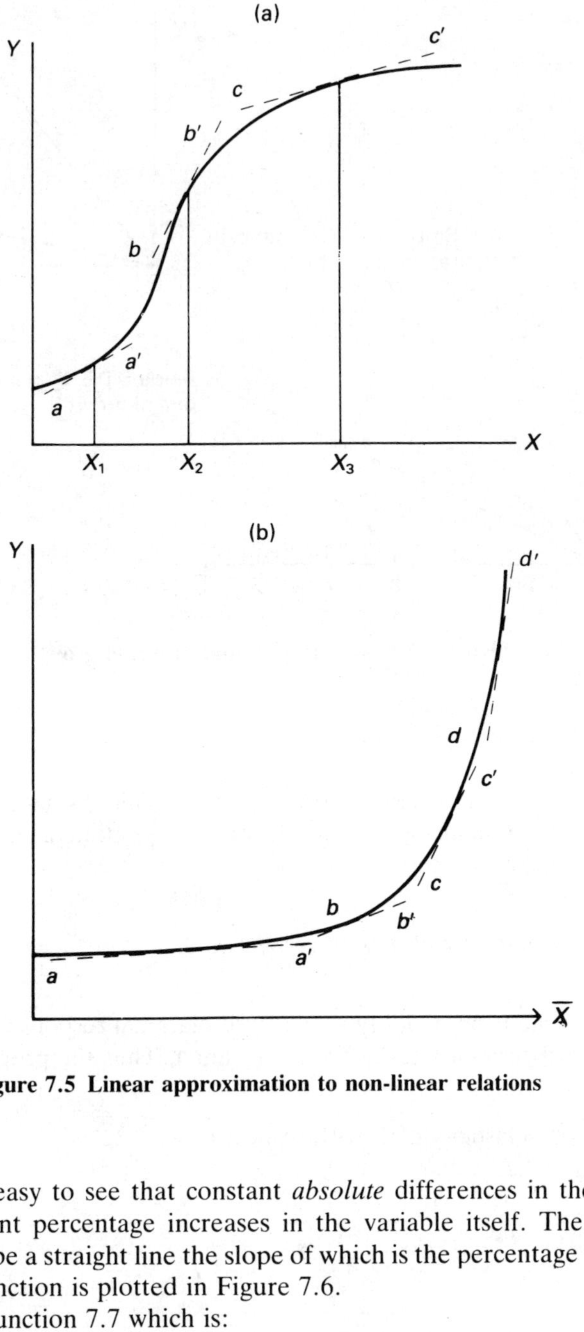

Figure 7.5 Linear approximation to non-linear relations

From this table it is easy to see that constant *absolute* differences in the logarithm of a variable imply constant percentage increases in the variable itself. The graph of log Y against time will thus be a straight line the slope of which is the percentage rate of growth in Y per period. This function is plotted in Figure 7.6.

Now consider the function 7.7 which is:

$$\log Y = \log a' + b' \log X + c' \log Z$$

If we use this relationship to plot log Y against log X holding log Z constant at some fixed value log $\bar{Z}$ and using a log scale for *both* the x and y axes, we shall get a straight-line function relating log X and log Y. The slope of this function will be the marginal response coefficient $\partial \log Y / \partial \log X = \underline{b}'$. The constant will define the origin of the curve at the point $\log X = 0$ and $\log Z = \log \bar{Z}$. This curve is plotted in Figure 7.7.

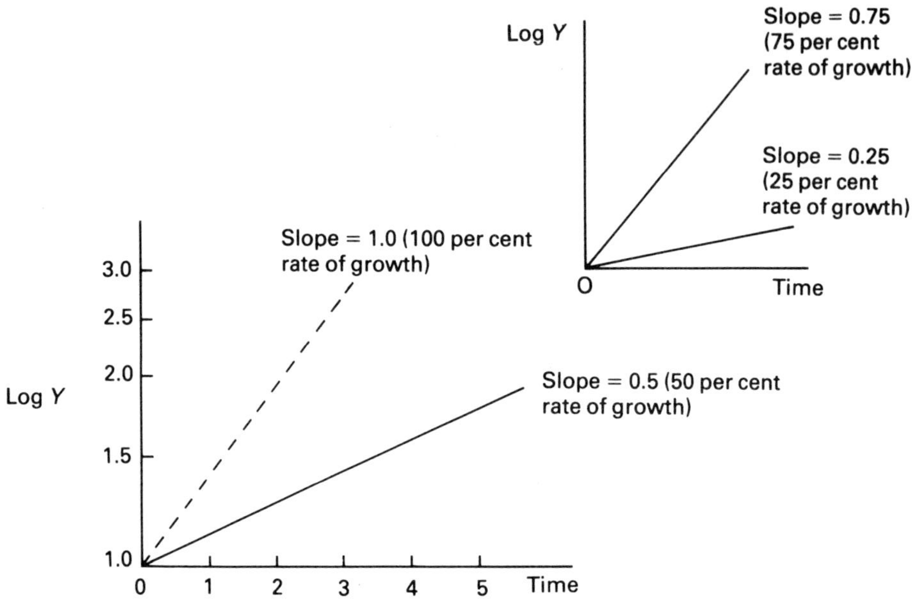

Figure 7.6 Constant percentage rates of growth

Suppose now that log X increases from x_1 to x_2. This distance defines a percentage increase in X. The resultant change in log Y from y_1 to y_2 defines a percentage increase in Y. The slope of the function is thus:

$$\frac{\Delta Y}{Y} \div \frac{\Delta X}{X} \equiv \text{elasticity of } Y \text{ with respect to } X$$

Hence functions of the form of 7.7 have constant marginal response coefficients which are elasticities (slopes of straight lines in the logarithms). Thus the properties of 7.7 are:

$$\frac{\Delta Y}{Y} \div \frac{\Delta X}{X} \equiv \text{elasticity of } Y \text{ with respect to } X$$

$$\equiv \frac{\frac{\partial Y}{\partial Z} \,.\, \Delta X}{Y} \div \frac{\Delta X}{X} \equiv b$$

$$\frac{\Delta Y}{Y} \div \frac{\Delta Z}{Z} \equiv \text{elasticity of } Y \text{ with respect to } Z$$

$$\equiv \frac{\frac{\partial Y}{\partial Z} \,.\, \Delta Z}{Y} \div \frac{\Delta Z}{Z} \equiv c$$

These relationships are useful to remember when interpreting graphs and functions.

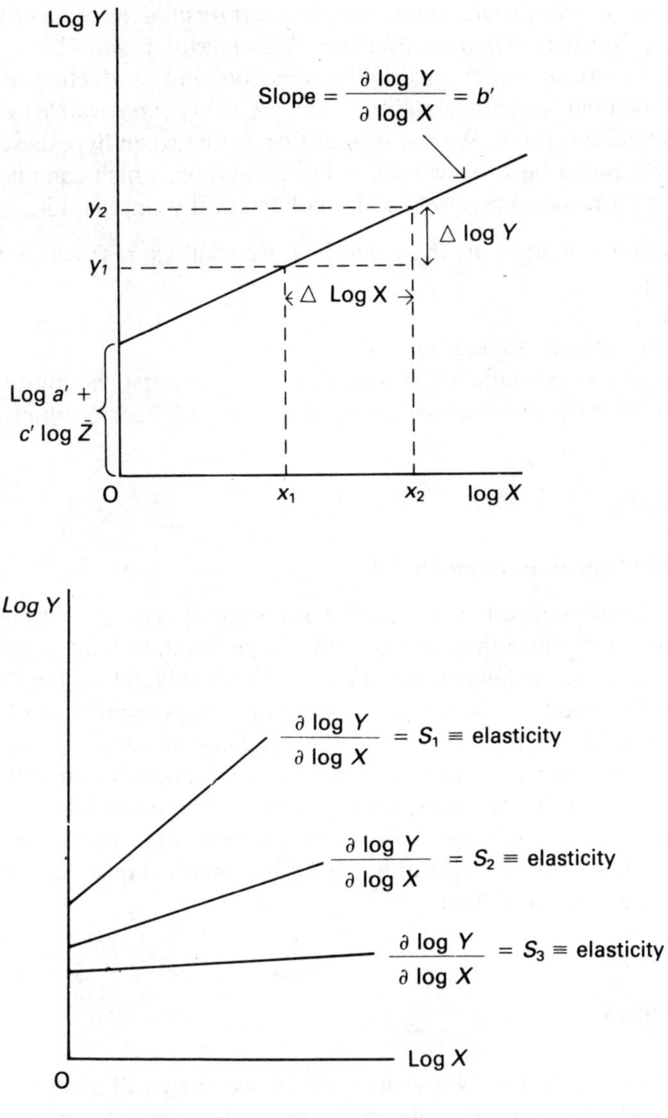

Figure 7.7 Elasticities and logarithmic relationships; and three different marginal response coefficients

Equations and identities

In Chapters 3 and 4 we set out the framework of definitions which we used in national income accounting. In these chapters we always wrote equally with the sign ≡ rather than the more familiar =. Thus we wrote:

$$Y \equiv C + S$$
$$Y \equiv C + I$$
$$\therefore \quad S \equiv I$$

This was done to emphasise the point that these expressions were identities which held by definition of the concepts employed whatever the values of Y and C.

By contrast, in writing our 'beer-drinking function' and production fuction we used the more familiar two-bar sign for equality. *This is a convention which we shall consistently employ throughout this book*. We use it to distinguish between hypotheses about economic behaviour – which can be true or false – and definitions which cannot. Our convention, which does not correspond precisely with mathematical usage, is this:

1. *Definitions* and equalities arising from them we shall express with a three-bar sign for equality, e.g.

   $Y \equiv C + I$

   These will be referred to as *identities*.
2. *Hypotheses* about economic behaviour, including, of course, equilibrium conditions, we shall express with the two-bar sign for equality, e.g. our 'beer-drinking hypothesis' which we write:

   $$B_c = f\left(T,\ U,\ \frac{P_w}{P_b}\right)$$

   These we shall speak of as *equations*.

In short, meaningful (because conceivably testable) propositions will always be expressed as *equations* simply because they may or may not be found to hold in the real world. Such relations are often called *behaviour equations*. Definitional relationships, which *always* hold irrespective of the values of the variables, we shall always express as *identities*.

This distinction we employ between identities and equations is of great importance and is commonly found in economics writing. The significant point is that identities, which hold whatever the values of the variables, tell us nothing about economic behaviour and cannot be tested by empirical observation. Equations, on the other hand, embody propositions about economic behaviour which can be tested by empirical observation either directly or via predictions derived from them.

Stocks and flows

Economic variables fall into two groups which we shall call *stocks* and *flows*: a *stock* variable is one which has no time dimension but is described at a moment of time; a *flow* variable necessarily involves a time dimension.

To give an example of a flow variable we may take income. To say that a man's income is £1,000 is meaningless *unless* we know the *time period of measurement*. An income of £1,000 *per year* is very different from an income of £1,000 *per decade* or £1,000 *per week*. All flow variables are thus rates (of flow) over some defined time period. This applies, as a little reflection will make clear, to all the national income accounting concepts we discussed in Chapters 3 and 4.

Stock variables, on the other hand, do not require a time dimension to have meaning. It makes sense to say that on 1 January 1983 a man's height is 5 feet 11 inches or his wealth £100,027 without specifying a period of time. We may conclude that

(a) *flow* variables are necessarily defined with reference to a period of time, i.e. a year, month, decade or quarter, and can be measured and given meaning only in terms of this (or some other) period

(b) *stock* variables are measured at a moment of time and have meaning independently of any period.

It should also be clear that many flow variables are simply the change in some stock variable *over a given period*. For example, if at the end of December 1980 real capital (or stock variable) is £10 million and at the end of December 1981 it is £14 million then the increment in real capital *over the year* is £4 million. We have already defined the increase in real capital as real net *investment*. Hence the *rate* of real *net* investment (a flow variable) is £4 million *a year* for the year 1981.

Much confusion arises from a failure to distinguish between *stocks* and *flows*. The reader is strongly recommended to ask, on meeting any economic variable for the first time: is this a *stock* variable or is it a *flow*?

The concept of equilibrium

Economists constantly speak of the 'economic system' or the 'market for some commodity' as being in 'equilibrium'. By this they imply no more than that the system or market has reached a position from which it has no tendency to depart – in short a position of rest. Such a position will occur only if the forces making for movement in one direction are exactly counterbalanced by the forces making for movement in the opposite direction. The *equilibrium* value of any variable is thus simply the value of the variable which, if reached, will tend to persist unchanged.

Since, as we have seen, economics is a social science and thus concerned with human behaviour, we may now ask what this concept of equilibrium implies *in terms of human behaviour*. To see this let us take an example and enquire what is meant by, let us say, the market for peanuts, being in *equilibrium* at a price of 50p per packet and a monthly volume of sales of 2 million packets. Clearly the market will only be in equilibrium if *both* buyers and sellers are 'satisfied' with the ruling price and quantity sold. If they are not, one group or the other will, in future periods, modify its behaviour which will *change* the price and quantity sold. Thus we may enunciate the general proposition that, for *equilibrium* to exist in any period, people must be 'satisfied' with the actual price ruling in the market and the actual quantities sold in any period. When they are *not* 'satisfied' *disequilibrium* exists *and some persons will modify their behaviour*.

What is meant by being 'satisfied'? All we mean by this expression is that what people *plan* to do is in conformity with what *actually* occurs, for where this is not so, *those people whose plans are not satisfied will, in the next period of time, modify their plans*. Equilibrium thus requires *all plans to be satisfied*, which again requires all *plans to be consistent*.

A table depicting hypothetical situations in the market for peanuts will serve to illustrate the point (see Table 7.3).

Suppose that, in some period, producers plan to make and sell 2 million packets of peanuts at a price of 50p per packet and that, in the same month, consumers plan to purchase 2 million packets at 50p per packet. In this case:

(a) all plans are consistent
(b) the actual price and quantity sold (and purchased) will correspond with the plans of both groups
(c) the market is in equilibrium

Table 7.3 Equilibrium and the peanut market

	Price (per packet)	Planned sales of producers (m.)	Planned purchases of consumers (m.)	Remarks
Position 1	50p	2.0	2.0	Consistent plans – *equilibrium*
2	50p	2.0	1.5	Inconsistent plans – *disequilibrium*
3	40p	1.75	1.75	Consistent plans – *equilibrium*

Suppose now that in period two producers' plans are the same as in period one but, because of a change in consumers' tastes, consumers now plan to purchase only 1.5 million packets at the price of 50p. In this case:

(a) all plans are *not* consistent
(b) the *actual* price and/or quantity sold (and purchased) can *not* and hence will *not* correspond with the *plans* of *both* groups
(c) the market is in *disequilibrium* and, in the next period, producers will obviously wish to modify their plans.

We may sum up the discussion so far by the following statements:

(a) to say that a system is in *equilibrium* means that it has reached a position of rest from which it has no tendency to depart
(b) where an economic system is in equilibrium then
 (i) the *actual* values of the variables it contains must correspond with
 (ii) the values of the same variables which people *planned* or *expected*
(c) this can only occur when *all plans* are consistent
(d) where plans are *not* consistent, *disequilibrium* exists
(e) the sign of existence of disequilibrium is that, for some persons or groups, *planned* and *actual* values of variables do not coincide
(f) the outcome of *disequilibrium* is a *change* in *plans* by the persons or groups from whom *actual* and *planned* variables do not coincide.

It is obviously a simple matter to extend this argument one stage further. Suppose our peanut market reaches position 2 – a position of disequilibrium. Then producers will modify their *plans* until a new position (say position 3) is reached. At this position we have once again a situation in which:

(a) *all* plans are consistent
(b) the *actual* price and quantity sold (and purchased) corresponds with the plans of both producers and consumers
(c) neither group has any need to modify its behaviour
(d) the peanut market is in *equilibrium* once again

Statics and dynamics

In Chapter 5 we drew a distinction between *static* and *dynamic* analysis. This distinction can now be illustrated in terms of our 'peanut' example.

In *static* analysis – commonly called *comparative statics* – we compare only positions of equilibrium: that is, we compare positions 1 and 3 and note that, as a consequence of a change in consumers' tastes *both* the *equilibrium price* of a packet of peanuts and the *equilibrium quantity* sold (and purchased) is lower than it was in the initial equilibrium position.

We do not, however, seek to explain either *how long* (i.e. how many months) it takes to get from position 1 to position 3 or the *path* by which *price* and *quantity* adjust to the new *equilibrium* position, for these questions, though important, form part of *dynamic* analysis.

Comparative statics thus simplifies reality by ignoring the *process* of change. Hence in comparative statics the rates at which variables change are ignored. At one period we are at position 1. At another we are position 3. Our sole aim is to compare these two positions. Perhaps the simplest way of moving in this somewhat unreal world is to regard all changes as taking place instantaneously.

Questions and exercises

1. The 'beer-consumption' hypothesis of 7.6n is:

$$B_c = 0.7\,T + 6.71\left(\frac{1}{U}\right) + 32\left(\frac{P_w}{P_b}\right)$$

Assume U to be constant at 2 per cent (i.e. $1/U = ½$), P_w/P_b to be constant at 1.5. Then calculate the values of B_c for the following values of T:

$T = 40, 45, 50, 55, 60, 65, 70, 75, 80$

Draw a graph with B_c on the vertical axis and T on the horizontal. From this curve identify (i) the marginal response coefficient $\partial B_c/\partial T$, (ii) the quantity $6.71(½) + 32(1.5)$.

On what does the position of the curve depend? In what way would the curve shift if the public's taste for beer suddenly increased?

What is the (theoretical) value of beer consumption when T is zero?

2. From the following data, again using 7.6n, plot a graph with B_c on the vertical axis and T on the horizontal:

T	U	P_w/P_b
40	2	1.5
45	2	1.5
50	3	1.8
55	3	1.8
60	2	1.8
65	4	2.0
70	1	1.1

(a) What meaning, if any, can be given to the *slope* of this curve?
(b) What is the relation between the slope of this curve and the slope of the curve constructed in question 1?

(c) In what circumstances, if any, could the slope of a curve which simply plots observed values of a dependent variable (in this case B_c) and one independent variable (in this case T) give a good estimate of the marginal response coefficient $\partial B_c/\partial T$?

3. Plot the following graphs putting X on the vertical axis and Y on the horizontal:

$$X = A + bY \quad \text{(where } A = 100;\ b = 0.8)$$

$$X = F + cY^2 \quad \text{(where } F = 100;\ c = 0.2)$$

and Y takes the following values:

$$Y = 0, 2, 10, 12, 20, 40, 50$$

In each case find the value of $\partial X/\partial Y$ (the marginal response coefficient) when $Y = 2$ and $Y = 10$. What difficulties arise with the second function?

Show that, for one curve, $\partial X/\partial Y$ is a constant, while for the other $\partial X/\partial Y$ depends upon (is a function of) Y.

At what value of Y do the two curves cut? What is the corresponding value of X?

4. In economics the elasticity of any dependent variable (X) with respect to some other independent variable (Y), of which it is a function, is defined as follows:

$$\text{elasticity} \equiv \text{proportionate change in } X \div \text{proportionate change in } Y$$

$$\equiv \frac{\Delta X}{X} \Big/ \frac{\Delta Y}{Y}$$

$$= \frac{\frac{\partial X}{\partial Y} \times \Delta Y}{X} \Big/ \frac{\Delta Y}{Y}$$

Using this formula find the approximate elasticity of both curves in question 3 when Y changes from 50 to 51 and 100 to 101.

Can you find the elasticity of output (Y) with respect to labour (N) from the production function $Y = TK^{\alpha}N^{1-\alpha}$? Put $T = 10$, $K = 10\,000$, $N = 100$, $\alpha = 0.5$. Is there a relationship between this elasticity and $1 - \alpha$? (*Hint*: use the logarithmic formulation.)

5. Figure 7.1 is drawn on the assumption that the production function is:

$$Y = TK^{\alpha}N^{1-\alpha}$$

where $T = 10$, $K = 200$, and $\alpha = 0.5$. What would happen to the curve if K became 100? Would the slope of the curve $\partial Y/\partial N$ be greater, less or the same at any given value of N? What does your answer mean in terms of economics? Suppose alternatively that with $K = 200$, T became 20. Plot the new curve and explain your result.

6. Using the same production function $Y = TK^{\alpha}N^{1-\alpha}$, put $T = 1$ and $\alpha = 0.5$, and show that the following tables gives numerical values of K and N which produce a given constant output:

K *Capital stock units*	N *Labour input units*
8	1,250
10	1,000
20	500
25	400
40	250
50	200
100	100

(a) What is the constant value of Y?
(b) What is the cheapest method of those shown of producing the given output when
  (i) labour costs £1 per unit per year; capital £25 per unit per year?
  (ii) labour costs £1 per unit per year; capital £4 per unit per year?
  (iii) labour costs £2 per unit per year; capital £50 per unit per year?
(c) What can you learn by comparing (i) and (iii)?
(d) What can you learn be comparing (ii) and (i)?

Explain your results and the lessons you draw from them.

7. Using the same function as question 6, the marginal physical products of labour and capital respectively are:[1]

$$\frac{\partial Y}{\partial K} \equiv \text{marginal physical product of capital} = T\alpha\left(\frac{N}{K}\right)^{1-\alpha} = 0.5\left(\frac{N}{K}\right)^{\frac{1}{2}}$$

$$\frac{\partial Y}{\partial N} \equiv \text{marginal physical product of labour} = T(1-\alpha)\left(\frac{K}{N}\right)^{\alpha} = 0.5\left(\frac{K}{N}\right)^{\frac{1}{2}}$$

Find numerical values for these marginal physical products for your answer to question 6bi. What do you notice about the relationships of marginal physical products to factor prices? Can you find a simple formula expressing minimum cost conditions?

8. Re-read and reformulate in the light of your answers to these two questions the discussion of the shape of the production possibility curve in Chapter 5. What kinds of production possibility curve would you expect to derive from the following pairs of production functions? Give your reasons.

(a) SITUATION A

agricultural output $= T_A K_A^{\alpha_A} N_A^{1-\alpha_A}$, where $\alpha_A = \alpha_M$

manufacturing output $= T_M K_M^{\alpha_M} N_M^{1-\alpha_M}$, where $T_M \gtrless T_A$

(b) SITUATION B

agricultural output $= T_A K_A^{1-\alpha_A} N_A^{1-\alpha_A}$, where $\alpha_A \neq \alpha_M$
manufacturing output $= T_M K_M^{\alpha_M} N_M^{1-\alpha_M}$, where $T_A \lesseqgtr T_M$

9. Suppose the production function is:
$Y = TK^{\alpha} N^{1-\alpha}$ (where $T = 1$; $\alpha = \frac{1}{3}$)
Show (as in question 6) that the following table gives numerical values of K and N which produce a given constant output:

K Capital stock	N Labour input
1	1,000
4	500
6.25	400
16	250
25	200
100	100

Show that, of the possibilites depicted in this table, the combination $K = 25$, $N = 200$ is the cheapest when labour costs £1 per unit per year and capital costs £4 per unit per year. Compare this result with that of question 6. What is its relationship to the argument by which we justified the increasing cost production possibility curve of Chapter 5?

[1]Readers familiar with the calculus will readily accept these results. Those not so familiar are asked to take them on trust.

10. The elasticity of output with respect to labour asked for in question 4 is given by:

$$\frac{\Delta Y}{Y} \Big/ \frac{\Delta N}{N} \equiv \frac{\frac{\partial Y}{\partial N} \times \Delta N}{Y} \Big/ \frac{\Delta N}{N}$$

$$\equiv \frac{\frac{\partial Y}{\partial N} \times \Delta N}{\Delta N} \times \frac{Y}{N}$$

$$\equiv \frac{\partial Y}{\partial N} \times \frac{Y}{N}$$

Using the information given in question 7 express this in terms of α.

11. Suppose labour is paid its marginal product. Then:

$$\frac{\text{wages bill}}{\text{output}} \equiv \text{share of wages}$$

$$\equiv \frac{\text{no. of workers} \times \text{marginal product of labour}}{\text{output}}$$

Calculate this for the production function of question 4 using the information given in question 7. What is its relation to α? What is the share of capital? Is capital paid its marginal product?

12. The production function $Y = TK^{\alpha}N^{\beta}$ has constant returns to scale of $\beta = 1 - \alpha$. Show that it has increasing returns if $\alpha + \beta > 1$ by two arithmetic examples. If either α or β are < 0, the function does not make economic sense. Why?

13. Suppose the production function is $Y = TK^{\alpha}N^{\beta}$ when $\alpha = 0.5$, $\beta = 0.6$. Find the share of labour. If labour receives this, can capital also receive its marginal product? If not, why not? Can you give an economic interpretation to your results?

14. The demand for peanuts is written:

$$Q^D \equiv \text{number of packets demanded in millions} = f(P_p, P_c, Y) = aP_c + bP_p + cY$$

where $P_p \equiv$ price of peanuts; $P_c \equiv$ price of potato crisps; $Y \equiv$ consumers' money income. The quantity supplied is:

$$Q^s = f(P_p, P_c) = A + dP_c + eP_p$$

Equate Q^D and Q^s to find the equilibrium values of P_p in terms of *a, b, c, d, e, A*, P_c and *Y*. Put

$a = 10$	$d = -10$
$b = -2$	$e = 13$
$c = 0.1$	$A = 0$
$Y = 100$	$P_c = 1$

and calculate the equilibrium values of P_p, Q^S and Q^D. How would you justify the signs of marginal response coefficients? Assume *Y* rises to 200. What are the new equilibrium values of P_p, Q^S and Q^D? Illustrate your calculations on a simple diagram.

15. The elasticity of any dependent variable (X) with respect to any independent variable (Y) of which it is a function is given by:

$$\frac{\Delta X}{X} \Big/ \frac{\Delta Y}{Y} \equiv \frac{\frac{\partial X}{\partial Y} \times \Delta Y}{X} \Big/ \frac{\Delta Y}{Y}$$

$$\equiv \frac{\frac{\partial X}{\partial Y} \times \Delta Y}{\Delta Y} \times \frac{Y}{X} \equiv \frac{\partial X}{\partial Y} \times \frac{Y}{X}$$

If $X = A + bY$, show that (i) elasticity is not in general a constant; (ii) that it will be constant if $A = 0$.

Illustrate your conclusions by a graph identifying both $\partial X/\partial Y$ and Y/X. What general conclusion can you reach regarding the relationship between constant marginal response coefficients and constant elasticities? Show, by a numerical example of your own choice, that while the elasticity is independent of the *units* in which X and Y are measured, the marginal response coefficient is not.

16. Suppose the *observed* change in some dependent variable (X) is ΔX and the *observed* change in some independent variable (Y) on which X depends is ΔY. In what circumstances will be the observed ratios

$$\frac{\Delta X}{X} \Big/ \frac{\Delta Y}{Y}$$

be a good measure of the elasticity

$$\frac{\partial X}{\partial Y} \cdot \frac{Y}{X}?$$

Check your answer with the data in question 7.

Suggested reading

As a supplement to this chapter readers should consult:

R. G. D. Allen, *Mathematical Analysis for Economists* (Macmillan, 1953) chs 1–3, 9.

G. C. Archibald and R. G. Lipsey, *An Introduction to a Mathematical Treatment of Economics* (Weidenfeld & Nicolson, 1967) chs 1–5, 9, 10.

Those who wish to proceed further with mathematics should continue with:

R. G. D. Allen, *Mathematical Analysis for Economists.*

W. J. Baumol, *Economic Dynamics* (Collier-Macmillan, 1959).

R. J. O'Brien and G. G. Garcia, *Mathematics for Economists and Social Scientists* (Macmillan, 1972).

Part II
Neo-Keynesian Economics

Chapter 8
The Determination of Equilibrium Output

In this chapter we begin our main job of constructing an economic theory which can be used to explain *why* the economic system behaves as we saw that it did in Chapter 6. We approach this task by developing a *model* of the economic system. Since the economic system is complicated, the model, to be useful, must necessarily also be complicated. We shall begin, however, by constructing a model of extreme simplicity and introduce complexities later only when the properties of the simple model have been thoroughly understood. Accordingly we start with a system in which (i) there is no government (i.e. no public-sector) economic activity, and (ii) there is no international trade. We also make one additional assumption, namely that the price of a unit of output is constant. This enables us to identify changes in the money values of variables with changes in their 'real' values and postpone discussion of the determination of prices. Each of these assumptions is removed later.

Output, employment and business decisions

In any period of time it is *enterprises* which determine how much output shall be produced. Since our theory is a *short-run* theory which takes as given both the real stock of capital (K) and the state of technique (T), then our production function tells us that $Y = f(N)$ with K and T given, or that the level of output (Y) per period depends only on the input of labour (N). Assuming hours per period per worker to be unchanged, this tells us that a given level of output determines a given level of employment in terms of workers. Hence if we can explain the level of output which enterprises produce we can also explain, in the *short run*, the level of employment.

The full study of the behaviour of enterprises belongs to *microeconomics*. We can, however, make considerable progress by assuming, as a first approximation, that the *behaviour of enterprises* is, in general, *governed by the aim of maximising profits*. Since profits can only be earned by the sale of products, we can argue that (i) what enterprises will plan to produce in any period is what they think they can sell in that period, (ii) what they think they can sell depends upon their expectations regarding demands. We can indeed go a little further than this by arguing that the planned level of output not only depends upon *expected* demand but will adjust itself to *actual* demand so that, if actual demand in any period is *less* than expected, output will tend to be reduced, in later periods, to the level of actual demand. Only when *expected* and *actual demand* and so *planned* and *actual sales*, coincide will the enterprise be in equilibrium.

Table 8.1

Example (1)	Price per unit of output (2)	Planned output = actual output (3)	Planned value of output (4)	Wage cost (5)	Planned profit (6)	Actual sales (7)	Unsold output added to stocks (8)	Realised distributable profit (9)	Result (10)
1	£1	15,000	£15,000	£12,000	£3,000	£10,000	£5,000	£2,000	Contraction
2	£1	15,000	£15,000	£12,000	£3,000	£17,000	−£2,000	£3,400	Expansion
3	£1	15,000	£15,000	£12,000	£3,000	£15,000	nil	£3,000	Equilibrium

The arithmetical example shown in Table 8.1 should make the point clear. This statement tells us that, in some period, which we have called 1, the *XYZ* Co. expected demand for its products to be, at given prices, equal to £15,000. It therefore *planned* to produce, and did produce[1] this value of output. At the ruling level of money wages this involved a wage bill of £12,000. To this wage cost the firm added a 25 per cent 'mark-up' which gave it an *expected* profit of £3,000. In the event, however, *actual* sales were only £10,000 as against the *planned* value of £15,000. As a result the *XYZ* Co. would certainly contract output (and employment) in future periods.

The position depicted is clearly one of *disequilibrium* in that we have:

(a) planned sales ≠ actual sales, *but* planned sales > actual sales
(b) planned profits ≠ actual profits, *but* planned profits > actual profits

and our argument tells us that, in a disequilibrium of this particular kind, the result would be *contraction* in output and employment.

How are the figures in Table 8.1 to be interpreted? The first eight columns give no trouble. The ninth, however, requires a word of explanation.

The realised distributable profit of an enterprise will be estimated by an accountant as:

$$\begin{array}{c}\text{sales } \textit{plus} \text{ value of}\\ \text{increase in stocks}\end{array} - \text{costs} \equiv \begin{array}{c}\text{realised distributable}\\ \text{profit}\end{array}$$

Accountants, however, will value the increase in stocks not at the price at which the enterprise would *sell* from stocks but at the cost it incurs in increasing its stocks. That is, the profit element is not included in the valuation of stock increase. Now in our example the planned profit margin is £3,000/£15,000, which, in percentage terms, is 20 per cent. We thus have, in the first case:

$$\text{realised distributable profit} \equiv \begin{array}{c}\text{sales + increase in stocks}\\ \text{(valued at cost)}\end{array} - \text{total costs}$$

[1]We shall assume that producers' plans are always realised in that planned output *equals* actual output.

$$\equiv \text{£}10{,}000 + \text{£}5{,}000[1 - {}^{20}\!/_{100}] - \text{£}12{,}000$$
$$\equiv \text{£}10{,}000 + \text{£}4{,}000 - \text{£}12{,}000$$
$$\equiv \text{£}2{,}000$$

This is the figure shown in the ninth column of the table.

Now take the second case. We have, since inventories *fall*:

$$\text{realised distributable profit} \equiv \begin{matrix}\text{sales + increase in stocks}\\ \text{(valued at cost)}\end{matrix} - \text{total costs}$$
$$\equiv \text{£}17{,}000 + (-\text{£}2{,}000[1 - {}^{20}\!/_{100}]) - \text{£}12{,}000$$
$$\equiv \text{£}17{,}000 - \text{£}1{,}600 - \text{£}12{,}000$$
$$\equiv \text{£}3{,}400$$

Finally in the third case we have:

$$\text{realised distributable profit} \equiv \begin{matrix}\text{sales + increase in stocks}\\ \text{(valued at cost)}\end{matrix} - \text{total costs}$$
$$\equiv \text{£}15{,}000 + \text{nil} - \text{£}12{,}000$$
$$\equiv \text{£}3{,}000$$

Obviously, as Table 8.1 shows:

IN CASE 1 planned profit > realised distributable profit
IN CASE 2 planned profit < realised distributable profit
IN CASE 3 planned profit = realised distributable profit

Notice that in cases 1 and 2 – the disequilibrium situations – the *XYZ* Co. experienced *unplanned* stock changes. Only in case 3 – the equilibrium situation – is there *no unplanned* change in stocks.

It follows from this example that only if *actual* sales turn out to be exactly £15,000 – as the *XYZ* Co. *planned* – is there *equilibrium*, for then planned sales = actual sales, planned profits = realised distributable profits, and the firm has no reason to change its *plans*.

Let us now generalise this example to all firms and define:

total value of planned output ≡ aggregate supply

We may, on the demand side, also write:

total value of planned expenditure ≡ aggregate demand

Then utilising the *assumption* that

$$\begin{matrix}\text{total value of planned}\\ \text{expenditure}\end{matrix} = \begin{matrix}\text{total value of actual}\\ \text{expenditure}\end{matrix}$$

that is, the *assumption* that consumers' plans are always realised, we can argue that:

(a) for *output* to be in equilibrium we required aggregate demand = aggregate supply

and predict that if:

(b) aggregate demand > aggregate supply, output will expand

while if:

(c) aggregate demand < aggregate supply, output will contract

These three possibilites are depicted in Table 8.2.

In each situation enterprises pay out £150m in wages and rents. They *plan* a profit of £50m. Aggregate supply is therefore £200m.

In situation 3 planned expenditure (and hence by assumption actual expenditure) equals £180m. The result is: planned profits > realised distributable profits and output *contracts*.

We thus have the following propositions:

1. If aggregate demand > aggregate supply, *planned* profits will be less than realised distributable profits. Result: *expansion of output.*
2. If aggregate demand < aggregate supply, *planned* profits will be greater than realised distributable profits. Result: *contraction of output.*
3. If aggregate demand = aggregate supply, planned profits will equal realised distributable profits. Result: *equilibrium.*

We can now take our analysis a little further and show its relationship with our national income accounting concepts.

It will be remembered that we have assumed prices to be constant throughout the discussion. Hence *planned* output (which we have assumed to be that actually produced) is equal in value to the national product. This, *in each situation*, is equal to £200m.

In situation 1 of Table 8.3 only £180m is sold on the market to consumers. It follows that the remaining £20m of output must be added to stocks. But this, by definition, *is investment whether firms planned to make the addition or not.* Accordingly, we can rearrange the data of Table 8.3 as shown.

On looking at this table we have:

$$\text{national product} \equiv \text{sum of cols (2), (3) and (4)} \equiv \pounds 200\text{m}$$

On the expenditure side we have:

$$\begin{aligned}\text{national expenditure} &\equiv \text{consumption} + \text{investment}\\ &\equiv \pounds 180\text{m} + \pounds 20\text{m}\\ &\equiv \pounds 200\text{m}\end{aligned}$$

Turning to the earnings side matters are a little more complicated. We know that:

$$\begin{aligned}\text{national income} &\equiv \text{wages} + \text{rents} + \text{profits}\\ &\equiv \pounds 100\text{m} + \pounds 50\text{m} + \pounds 50\text{m}\\ &\equiv \pounds 200\text{m}\end{aligned}$$

This, however, appears to show that, at £50m, actual profit equals planned profit – a situation we have learned to think of as one of equilibrium. This is awkward since we know that the situation we are depicting is one of disequilibrium. How do we reconcile this apparent contradiction? We have:

$$\begin{aligned}\text{national income} &\equiv \text{wages} + \text{rents} + \text{profits}\\ &\equiv \text{wages} + \text{rents} + \begin{matrix}\text{realised}\\ \text{distributable}\\ \text{profits}\end{matrix} + \text{unrealised profits}\\ &\equiv \pounds 100\text{m} + \pounds 50\text{m} + \pounds 45\text{m} + \pounds 5\text{m}\\ &\equiv \pounds 200\text{m}\end{aligned}$$

Table 8.2 Aggregate demand and supply

Situation	Value of planned and actual output: Wages £m	Rents £m	Planned profit £m	Value of aggregate supply £m	Aggregate demand: Planned expenditure £m	Actual expenditure £m	Realised profits £m	Unsold output added to stocks £m	Result
1	100	50	50	200	200	200	50	nil	Equilibrium
2	100	50	50	200	220	220	55	−20	Expansion
3	100	50	50	200	180	180	45	20	Contraction

Table 8.3

Situation	Value of output	Wages	Rents	Planned distributable profits	Expenditure: Consumption	Investment in inventories	Earnings side: Wages	Rents	Profits: Realised distributable profit	Unrealised profit
	(1)	(2)	(3)	(4)	(5)	(6)	(7)	(8)	(9)	(10)
1	£200	£100	£50	£50	£180	£20	£100	£50	£45	£5
2	£200	£100	£50	£50	£200	nil	£100	£50	£50	nil
3	£200	£100	£50	£50	£220	−£20	£100	£50	£55	−£5

Values in £m.

Disequilibrium manifests itself in the discrepancy between actual profits, as measured by the national income statistician (£50m) and the realised distributable profits accruing to the enterprise (£45m). The difference arises from the mark-up hypothesis.

In situation 2 we have

$$
\begin{aligned}
\text{national product} &\equiv \text{£200m}\\
\text{national expenditure} &\equiv \text{consumption} + \text{investment}\\
&\equiv \text{£200m} + \text{nil}\\
&\equiv \text{£200m}\\
\text{national income} &\equiv \text{wages} + \text{rent} + \text{profits}\\
&\equiv \text{wages} + \text{rents} + \begin{matrix}\text{realised}\\ \text{distributable}\\ \text{profits}\end{matrix} + \begin{matrix}\text{unrealised}\\ \text{profits}\end{matrix}\\
&\equiv \text{£100m} + \text{£50m} + \text{£50m} + \text{nil}\\
&\equiv \text{£200m}
\end{aligned}
$$

In situation 3:

$$
\begin{aligned}
\text{national product} &\equiv \text{£200m}\\
\text{national expenditure} &\equiv \text{consumption} + \text{investment}\\
&\equiv \text{£220m} - \text{£20m}\\
&\equiv \text{£200m}\\
\text{national income} &\equiv \text{wages} + \text{rents} + \text{profits}\\
&\equiv \text{£100m} + \text{£50m} + \begin{matrix}\text{realised}\\ \text{distributable}\\ \text{profits}\end{matrix} + \begin{matrix}\text{unrealised}\\ \text{profits}\end{matrix}\\
&\equiv \text{£100m} + \text{£50m} + \text{£55m} - \text{£5m}\\
&\equiv \text{£200m}
\end{aligned}
$$

In short, we can say that unless the situation is one of equilibrium then (i) there will be *unplanned* increases/decreases in stocks, and (ii) realised distributable profits will not be equal to planned profits. Only in equilibrium will there be *no unplanned* increase/decrease in stocks and no discrepancy between planned profits and realised distributable profits.

Notice that though in each situation we have our familiar identity of:

$$\text{national product} \equiv \text{national expenditure} \equiv \text{national income}$$

each situation is, *from the point of view of behaviour*, very different from the others.

To say that disequilibrium manifests itself in a discrepancy between actual profits as measured by the national income statisticians and realised distributable profits is, on our definitions and assumptions, correct. Some explanation of what this implies is nevertheless necessary.

In our table we have taken the value of output, as measured by the statistician, to be £200m. Of this sum wages are £100m, rents £50m, and profits £50m. If the national income statistician adopts this definition, he must value the increase in stocks at £20m to preserve the definitional relationship: output ≡ consumption *plus* investment. This means that he values the increase in stocks *inclusive* of the profit element. On this basis the income accruing to households in the form of wages, rents and profits is £200m, but the statistician is including, in the profits of the current period, an element which will not be *realised* until the goods added to inventory are actually sold.

As we have seen, in situation 1, the realised distributable profit of firms, as calculated by their accountants, will be £45m and not the £50m taken (on this convention) by the national income statistician. If the whole of this £45m is paid out to households, the income received by households, £195m, will be *less* than the income which the statisticians attribute to them. Conversely in situation 3 it will be more.

If, on the other hand, the statistician adopts the accountant's definition of realised profit he must value the change in stocks at cost, in which case each of our hypothetical situations yields a different total for national income thus:

SITUATION 1 national income ≡ wage + rents + realised distributable profits
≡ £100m + £50m + £45m
≡ £195m

SITUATION 3 national income ≡ wages + rents + realised distributable profits
≡ £100m + £50m + £55m
≡ £205m

SITUATION 2 national income ≡ £100m + £50m + £50m
≡ £200m

In each case, by assumption, the flow of output is the same. The second way of defining profit therefore leads to a contradiction worse than the first, for the main purpose of national income accounting is to measure the flow of goods and services produced in the current period. A system of definitions which describes an identical flow by three different totals is obviously awkward. Accordingly the first definition of profit – arrived at by valuing the increase in stocks at market prices – seems preferable.[1]

Notice that, in all this, there is no dispute as to what has occurred. This was assumed at the start. What matters is to find a consistent and convenient way of *describing what has occurred*.

The fundamental lessons of this example are, however, clear enough:

1. Although actual *expenditure* and actual *output as defined* in *national income accounting are always* identically *equal it makes sense to speak of* planned *expenditure being equal* to, *greater or less than*, planned output.
2. *The national income accounting concepts can tell us nothing about economic behaviour, for though each of our three situations is, from the behaviour aspect, entirely different, from the national income accounting point of view they exhibit no essential differences.*

The general point is a simple one:

(a) *national income* accounting is concerned with *actual* magnitudes
(b) *economic behaviour* is determined by the relationship between *planned* magnitudes about which national income accounting, *of itself*, has nothing whatsoever to say.

This reflects the important points we made in discussing the concept of equilibrium in Chapter 7. *Plans to purchase, sell and produce may not be realised.* They will, in fact, only be realised when they are consistent: that is, when equilibrium exists. In this situation, and only in this situation, will *all actual* magnitudes correspond with planned magnitudes.

[1]See *National Accounts Statistics: Sources and Methods*, ch. 13.

Of course, in any given period there will only be one set of actual magnitudes in terms of national accounting definitions, and these are what the statisticians will record. But in disequilibrium situations these *actual* magnitudes *result* from the interaction of *inconsistent plans*. The statisticians' estimates do not record the existence of inconsistent plans, though, as we have shown, plans may well be inconsistent. They merely record *what happens whether it is planned or unplanned*. This is why they are identities and not equations and, by the same token, why they can tell us nothing about economic behaviour except its results. It is, indeed, precisely because they give a measure of these results that the statisticians' estimates are important.

This section contains propositions of such fundamental importance that a summary of them is essential. The propositions are as follows:

1. Output and employment are only in equilibrium when aggregate (planned) demand = aggregate (planned) supply.
2. Where aggregate demand > aggregate supply the resultant disequilibrium will manifest itself as:
   (a) an *unintended* decumulation in inventories: that is, *unplanned* disinvestment in stocks
   (b) an excess of realised distributable profits over *planned* profits

   The *result* will be an expansion in output and employment.
3. These propositions are simply reversed for the situation where aggregate demand < aggregate supply.
4. Despite the fact that, in national income accounting,
   actual expenditure ≡ actual output
   it is perfectly possible, provided *plans* are inconsistent, for
   aggregate demand ≠ aggregate supply
5. Without additional assumptions relating *planned* to *actual* magnitudes, national income concepts can tell us nothing about *plans* and therefore do not register any inconsistency in them.

The saving and investment analysis

We now know that output is in equilibrium only when aggregate demand = aggregate supply. In our present simple model we can divide aggregate demand into two components thus:

aggregate demand = *planned* consumption *plus planned* net investment

If we assume, as we have so far, that producers' *plans* for output are always realised, then:

$$\text{aggregate supply} \equiv \text{planned value of output} \equiv \text{national product} \equiv \text{national income}$$

Hence our *equilibrium* condition can be rewritten:

national income = *planned* consumption + *planned* net investment

or, using the notation which is now fashionable:

$$Y = C_p + I_p, \tag{8.1}$$

where the suffix *p* denotes *planned* magnitude and *Y* denotes national income. *Planned* net saving is now defined as income *minus planned* consumption, i.e.

$$S_p \equiv Y - C_p. \tag{8.2}$$

Hence, combining (8.1) and (8.2), our equilibrium condition becomes:

$$\left.\begin{array}{ccc} S_p & = & I_p \\ \textit{planned}\text{ saving} & = & \textit{planned}\text{ investment} \end{array}\right\} \tag{8.3}$$

Thus the propositions:

aggregate demand $\gtreqless$ aggregate supply

and

planned investment $\gtreqless$ *planned* saving

are simply alternative ways of saying the same thing.

We have already shown that, despite the fact that, by definition, national expenditure is always equal to national product, it makes sense to speak of aggregate demand being equal to, greater or less than aggregate supply. We now show that despite the fact that, by definition, *actual* saving is always identically equal to *actual* investment, it makes sense to speak of *planned* saving being equal to, greater or less than *planned* investment.

Obviously when we write:

$$S_p \gtreqless I_p$$
$$S \equiv I$$

we are using the terms in different senses. This is the crucial point and must be understood. It looks and is simple. But in the past failure to understand the distinction has caused great trouble not only to students but also to professional economists.

The former *equation* refers to *planned* saving and investment and the expression is a genuine equation which may or may not be satisfied: the latter *identity* refers to *actual* saving and investment which *by definition are always equal* since they are, in fact, alternative ways of describing the same thing.

Since economic terminology is not uniform, the student is certain to meet many expressions which are, broadly speaking, synonyms for our terms 'planned' and 'actual'.

For convenience they may be tabulated as follows:

$$S_p \gtrless I_p$$

$$\left\{\begin{array}{l}\text{planned}\\ \textit{ex ante}\\ \text{scheduled}\\ \text{intended}\end{array}\right\} \text{ saving } \gtrless \left\{\begin{array}{l}\text{planned}\\ \textit{ex ante}\\ \text{scheduled}\\ \text{intended}\end{array}\right\} \text{ investment}$$

while:

$$S \equiv I$$

$$\left\{\begin{array}{l}\text{actual}\\ \textit{ex post}\\ \text{observable}\\ \text{realised}\end{array}\right\} \text{ saving } \equiv \left\{\begin{array}{l}\text{actual}\\ \textit{ex post}\\ \text{observable}\\ \text{realised}\end{array}\right\} \text{ investment}$$

Although we may now be satisfied that, since we are using the terms 'saving' and 'investment' in two senses, we are not involved in a logical contradiction, it is nevertheless interesting to enquire how it is that actual saving and investment can be equal when planned saving and investment are not equal: that is, when the system is in disequilibrium. This may be made clear by taking a further look at our earlier examples (see Table 8.4).

Table 8.4

Case	Aggregate supply Y_p	Planned consumption C_p	Actual consumption C	Planned saving S_p	Actual saving S	Planned investment I_p	Actual investment I	Unplanned investment I_u	Overall situation
1	£200m	£180m	£180m	£20m	£20m	zero	£20m	£20m	$S_p > I_p$
2	£200m	£220m	£220	−£20m	−£20m	zero	−£20m	−£20m	$I_p > S_p$
3	£200m	£200m	£200	nil	nil	zero	zero	zero	$S_p = I_p$

Consider case 1. The value of output is £200m. But aggregate demand ($C_p + I_p$) is equal to only £180m. It follows, therefore, that output unsold during this period will be £200m − £180m = £20m. This unsold output (saving) must be added to stocks existing at the beginning of the period. It therefore constitutes *actual* investment. But it *does not constitute planned investment*, which, by assumption, is zero. In case 1, therefore, actual saving (output which is not consumed) is, as it must be, equal to actual investment. Actual investment, however, exceeds planned investment by an amount we shall speak of as *unplanned investment*. It follows, therefore, that when planned saving exceeds planned investment, actual investment also exceeds planned investment by the value of unplanned investment. This unplanned investment, taking the form of an unexpected (and unwelcome) accumulation of stocks, is a signal to firms to *contract* output. Nevertheless, despite the assumed discrepancy between planned saving and investment and the resultant disequilibrium, it is clear that actual saving and investment, as measured by the national income statistician, are necessarily equal.

Case 2 illustrates the alternative form of disequilibrium; in that case planned investment exceeds planned saving, which means that aggregate demand ($C_p + I_p$) exceeds aggregate supply. Clearly this is so, for the table shows aggregate demand of £220m and the aggregate supply of £200m. To meet this excess demand of £20m producers must decumulate stocks.

Now the decumulation of stocks constitutes *disinvestment*. Hence actual investment, which we know to be equal to planned investment *plus* unplanned investment, is given by:

$$\begin{aligned} I &\equiv I_p + I_u \\ &\equiv \text{nil} - £20\text{m} \\ &\equiv -£20\text{m} \end{aligned}$$

In this case an unexpected *decumulation* of stocks is a signal to producers to *expand* production and thus employment and incomes.

In case 3 we have assumed equilibrium. In this situation planned and actual investment coincide at zero. Unplanned investment is therefore also zero. Hence producers' expectations are realised. They therefore have no incentive to expand or contract production, employment and incomes.

From this account of matters we may draw the following conclusions:

1. There is no contradiction in the statements
   (a) planned saving and investment are equal only when incomes are in equilibrium
   (b) actual (accounting) saving and investment are always equal by definition
2. Where planned saving is not equal to planned investment the resulting disequilibrium will show itself in the form of a discrepancy between planned and actual investment.
3. We define:

   unplanned investment ≡ actual investment − planned investment

   $$I_u \equiv I - I_p$$
4. Where $S_p > I_p$ then $I_u > 0$, i.e. there is unintended inventory accumulation

   Where $I_p > S_p$ then $I_u < 0$, i.e. there is unintended inventory decumulation

   Where $I_p = S_p$ then $I_p = 0$, i.e. no unintended change in inventories.
5. It is the presence of unintended investment (positive or negative) which provides the signal to firms to contract or expand output. This is merely another aspect of the discrepancy between planned and actual (sales) and planned and realised distributable profits illustrated earlier.

The basic postulate of the saving and investment analysis

The analysis of the earlier sections of this chapter has made it plain that:

1. Any inconsistency between the rates at which the community *plans* to invest and to save will involve discrepancies between:
   (a) firms' *expected* and *realised* distributable profits
   (b) firms' *planned* and *actual* investment.
2. Such discrepancies will cause firms to modify their production plans in the light of experience, thus bringing about changes in output (income) and employment.
3. There is no contradiction between speaking about the possible inequality of *planned* saving and *planned* investment while at the same time insisting upon the definitional identity of actual savings and investment as measured in national income accounts.

So far so good. But this analysis, though logically consistent, would be of little interest if, as a matter of experience, planned saving and investment tended automatically (in the sense of without any need for changes in the level of output) to achieve and maintain equality. In that case the saving and investment analysis and the theory of income determination which we develop in later chapters would be a theoretical curiosity of no empirical significance whatsoever. Clearly if a theory based upon the saving/investment analysis is to have any practical importance it can only be because, as a matter of fact, there is no mechanism tending to ensure that any plan to save (or invest) will automatically be matched by a corresponding plan to invest (or save).

Now there are two important facts concerning saving and investment decisions in the modern developed 'mixed economy' which make it reasonable to accept the view that there is no 'automatic' correspondence between the amount per period that the community plans to save and invest. They are that:

(a) saving and investment plans tend to be made by different groups in the community, i.e. broadly speaking households save, firms invest
(b) decisions to save and invest are undertaken for very different reasons.

Admittedly enterprises (firms) do undertake saving in the form of depreciation allowances and undistributed profits. But a considerable part of saving is still performed by persons. Again it is true that households and persons do undertake investment expenditure.

Nevertheless the overwhelming share of private investment is undertaken by firms. It is thus in accordance with experience and acceptable to common sense to admit that saving and investment decisions are carried out to a significant extent by different groups. As a first approximation we might assume that *only* households save and *only* enterprises invest. This indeed will be a convenient assumption on which to build the model from Chapter 9 onwards. The reader should remember its limited correspondence with the facts.

The second assertion, that saving and investment decisions are undertaken for different reasons, is also in accordance with common observation once the precise economic meaning of the term *investment* is recalled. People save, after all, for a bewildering variety of reasons. The more obvious are: to provide for old age; to provide a contingency fund against any sudden loss in earning power; because they were brought up to believe that to save was a 'proper' mode of behaviour; because they were in the past unable to resist the appeals of life-assurance salespeople; because they are compelled to do so through a legal obligation to join a superannuation scheme; or merely because of habit. None of these has much (if anything) to do with the wish to undertake investment, which, as we know, is defined as making an addition to the *real* stock of capital. Most of the things savers do with their saving, and therefore which presumably provide much of the motive for saving, do *not* constitute investment. Many savers, for example, buy government bonds. If Brown buys a bond and Smith sells it Brown's 'investment' is cancelled by Smith's 'disinvestment'. In any case the transaction does not directly increase the real capital stock and so, by definition, is not investment. This argument can be extended to cover nearly all the transactions undertaken by persons who save, most of whom use their saving to carry out what economists call *capital transfers. Once it is realised that purchases of bonds, shares, life policies, mortgages, debentures, old houses and so on, though commonly called investment, do not constitute investment as economists define the term but are merely transfers*, the very remote relation between personal planned saving and planned investment becomes clear.

If we accept that plans to save and plans to invest are made independently of one another, then the economic system must contain some mechanism to bring the different plans into equality. The central tenet of macroeconomics derived from the work of Lord Keynes is that the price mechanism does not effectively perform this task, and in particular that the rate of interest does not do so. Consequently adjustment requires a change in the level of income (output). To put the same point rather differently we can, given the independence of the plans to save and invest, develop a model of the economy that uses the saving and investment analysis to explain the determination of output (income) and employment.

It is important, however, for the student to notice that, while it is reasonable to accept the postulated dichotomy between savers and investors in a modern developed 'mixed economy', it is not a reasonable assumption in all economies or in the same economy at all times. This is obvious even if we neglect the special case so thoughtfully provided by Defoe. Robinson Crusoe clearly saved (refrained from consumption) *only in order to invest* (add to his real capital stock). Neglecting Robinson, however, broadly similar conditions prevail in the subsistence economies of some underdeveloped territories in which peasant farmers, in general, save only in order to invest; indeed, to put the matter more concisely, a plan to save *is* a plan to invest. Hence, though the dichotomy certainly holds with respect to, say, Britain, America and Australia today, it would probably not have held in Britain during the eighteenth century and it may not hold in any of the three countries during the twenty-first.

This is an important point. A theory which seeks to explain the level of output by requiring it to adjust in order to bring the community's plans to save and invest into equality will always be logically consistent. It may not, however, be a useful theory in the sense that the community may have another mechanism for adjusting saving and investment plans or, alternatively, may be organised institutionally in such a way that automatic correspondence between saving and investment plans is assured.

'Keynesian' theory is of contemporary relevance only in so far as, under present conditions in 'Western mixed economies', the financial system typically does *not* ensure that investment and saving plans are brought into equality *without* the need for output adjustments. We do, in fact, observe fluctuations in real aggregate demand in relation to aggregate supply, unplanned increases in stocks and consequential reductions in planned output and employment. Indeed, as we shall see in Chapter 20, the explanation we offer of 'cyclical' fluctuations relies essentially upon this type of adjustment process.

Finally, as we saw in Chapter 6, there are fairly well-marked fluctuations in real GDP in relation to capacity in the UK which can be called 'cyclical'.

Summary

This is an important chapter outlining a number of ideas fundamental to the whole theory of income determination. The *basic* ideas underlying the theory and sketched in the earlier sections are summarised below:

1. A firm will adjust output in accordance with its experience of demand. This proposition, which is of course empirical and not logical in nature, may be regarded as either
   (a) derived from the study of business behaviour, or
   (b) deduced from the assumption that firms seek to maximise profits – which is itself an assumption derived from observing business behaviour; this assumption about business behaviour, when generalised for all firms, enables us to derive the equilibrium condition for output as a whole ($S_p = I_p$) and the conditions in which output will tend to expand ($I_p > S_p$) or contract ($S_p > I_p$).
2. In a modern 'mixed' capitalist economy saving and investment decisions are taken by different groups for dissimilar reasons. This fact enables us to argue that the consequ-

ences which must logically follow if, in any period, $S_p \neq I_p$ are of great practical interest since there is no reason to suppose that S_p will automatically tend to equal I_p.

3. In the short run the quantity of employment is uniquely related to the quantity of output firms plan to produce.

These three propositions form the basis for the whole of the analysis contained in this part of the book. The remaining assumptions, namely the absence of government activity, the absence of international trade and the constancy of the price level, are made for expositional convenience only and are related later. Beyond stating and examining the implications of the ideas listed above, the chapter is also concerned to explain and emphasise the distinction between *planned* saving (investment) on the one hand and *actual* saving (investment) on the other. The comprehension of this distinction is fundamental and you are recommended to re-read it very carefully and to work out some arithmetic examples for yourself.

Questions and exercises

1. 'The aim of the government's policy is to equate saving and investment at a level of output corresponding to full employment. Their success is demonstrated by this year's national income estimates which show saving equal to investment.' Discuss.

2. 'If saving increases, then, since saving equals investment, investment increases. It follows that aggregate demand and supply always increase together and are always equal.' Discuss.

3. Assuming

$$C_p = C_A = £1{,}000\text{m per period}$$
$$I_p = £500\text{m per period,}$$

what is the *equilibrium* level of output?

If planned output is £1,700m per period and planned output *equals* actual output find (i) gross national product; (ii) gross national expenditure; (iii) actual investment; (iv) unintended investment.

In future periods would you expect output to expand or contract? Why?

In what forms does the disequilibrium in the system show itself?

4. 'People spend with that part of their income that they save just as surely as with that part of their income they consume.' Do you agree? If so, why? If not, why not? What, in terms of this chapter, is the assumption implicit in the statement?

5. The national income estimates of a hypothetical economy reveal the following data for the first half of 1965:

GNP	£4,000m
Consumption	£3,000m
Gross investment in:	
(a) fixed capital	£900m
(b) inventories	£100m

Do these figures throw any light upon whether the economy was in equilibrium or not? If so, how?

6. Suppose that, contrary to our assumptions, an act of saving was undertaken only in order to make investment. How would the level of output in an economy of this kind be determined? Would 'full-capacity' output be automatic? If so, where would the equilibrium of the economy appear on the 'production possibility curve'?

7. According to a Liberal MP the £600m the 1967 (Labour) government expended on the purchase of steel companies (as part of nationalisation) would have been better spent on the construction of roads. Is his statement sense or nonsense? Does the purchase of steel companies increase aggregate demand? If so, how? If not, why not?

8. Assume

$$C_p = C_A = £2{,}000\text{m per period}$$

$$I_p \equiv I_{fp} + I_{sp}$$

$$\equiv \underset{\text{in fixed capital}}{\text{planned investment}} + \underset{\text{in inventories}}{\text{planned investment}}$$

If $I_{fp} = £250\text{m}$ per period; $I_{sp} = £400\text{m}$ per period
what is the equilibrium level of output?
If planned output = actual output is £3,000m then

   (a) How much is actual investment in inventories?
   (b) How much is unplanned investment in inventories?
   (c) How much are actual saving and investment?

9. Reconstruct the example of Table 8.1 and the subsequent discussion on the assumption that the 'mark-up' of firms is 5⁄12, *not* 3⁄12. Show that the basic analysis is unaffected by this change.

10. Reformulate the discussion of Table 8.1 *et seq* on the assumption that firms adjust their 'mark-up' percentage to the level of output. Assume that planned profit (P^*) is given by $P^* = A + bY$, where $b = 0.1$ and $Y \equiv$ actual = planned output. What is the value of A assumed in Table 8.1? Does the new assumption *significantly* affect the analysis? What do you mean by *significantly*?

11. 'The function of what is called the capital market – that is the Stock Exchange and related financial institutions – is to facilitate capital transfers.' Discuss.

12. Use the Blue Book to construct a table of personal and business savings for the years 1960–80. What is the average share of each source in total private saving?

Suggested reading

F. S. Brooman, *Macroeconomics* (Allen & Unwin, 1962) chs 1, 3.

P. Davidson and E. Smolensky, *Aggregate Supply and Demand Analysis* (Harper & Row, 1965) ch. 1.

P. A. Samuelson, *Economics*, 11th edn (McGraw-Hill, 1979) chs 11–13.

Chapter 9

The Consumption Function and the Multiplier

In the last chapter we argued that enterprises would adjust their output per period until *planned* sales and *actual* sales were equal. At this level of output enterprises would be in equilibrium: that is, they would have no reason to adjust their output *plans* in any way.

Examining this condition a little further we discovered that output (income) would be in equilibrium when aggregate supply = aggregate demand, or, what is the same thing, $S_p = I_p$. Where this condition prevailed all planned and actual magnitudes would coincide: both sectors of the economy – that is, enterprises and households – would then have no reason to modify their behaviour.

Retaining our assumption that production plans are always realised so that actual and planned production coincide, and using the notation of chapter 8, we can write our equilibrium condition as:

$$\begin{array}{ccc} Y & = & C_p + I_p \\ \text{aggregate supply} & = & \text{aggregate demand} \end{array}$$

Hence, to explain the equilibrium value of Y, we need to develop theories which explain the determination of C_p and I_p. These theories will, obviously enough, contain hypotheses about human behaviour, for what we are trying to explain is, first, the rate at which households (in general) will plan to spend upon consumption and, second, the rate at which enterprises (in general) will plan to spend upon investment.

In this chapter we concentrate on the first problem and seek to develop a theory of consumption. Accordingly we shall assume, without either explanation or justification, that enterprises plan to spend upon investment at some fixed rate. This assumption, which is obviously artificial and made merely for convenience, will be relaxed in the next chapter. It amounts to treating planned investment expenditure as an *exogenous* variable – that is, one determined (like the weather) outside our model. Formally it may be expressed as follows:

$$I_p = \bar{I} \qquad (9.1)$$
$$I_p = \text{£500m per year} \qquad (9.1n)$$

This leaves us free to concentrate on the determination of planned consumption.

The aggregate consumption function

The aim of our consumption hypothesis is to explain the determination of 'real' *aggregate* planned consumption expenditure – that is, the total 'real' expenditure of all households together. On what variables is it reasonable to argue that aggregate 'real' planned consumption would depend?

The first (and most important variable) is clearly the *level of real income*. Statistical studies of household expenditure confirm that the simple hypothesis that the real expenditure of households is related to their real income levels is well grounded. Moreover, the same studies show that households with 'high' real incomes (say those in the top 10 per cent) save more, proportionately to income as well as absolutely, than those in 'low' real income groups (say the bottom 10 per cent). Since any given total of *household* incomes may be distributed more (or less) equally and since the *more equally* any given total household income is distributed the *greater* will be the level of planned consumption associated with it, we know, from these studies, *two* variables that influence real planned consumption. They are:

(a) the level of real income (Y)
(b) the distribution of real income (α)[1]

Of these the first, the level of real income, is of primary importance, in the sense that variations in planned consumption are due largely to changes in income.

It also seems plausible to argue, and there is empirical evidence to support the hypothesis that in general any individual with a given real income will plan to consume *more* the greater is his or her real *wealth*. We thus have a third variable to consider: the real value of assets.

The real value of assets is a *stock* concept which relates to the capital account or balance-sheet of the household and not its income account. Our hypothesis states that, in general, if we look at two households which are otherwise identical and which each enjoy an income of (say) £20,000 per year one of which holds, say, bank deposits, government bonds, equity shares and real property to the value of £100,000 and the other which holds only bank deposits to the value of £1,000, the former type of household will in general plan the higher rate of consumption. Extending this hypothesis to the community as a whole gives us a third variable influencing the value of real planned consumption namely:

(c) the real value of household asset holding (A)

A fourth variable which *may* influence consumption expenditure is the rate of interest, which we defined in Chapter 6 as:

> the rate of return (per cent per annum) obtainable in the market on long-term government securities

As everyone knows, the act of saving – this is, of abstaining from consumption – does not, of itself, entitle the saver to receive interest. If, for example, accumulated savings (wealth) are held in the form of banknotes, no interest accrues. Nevertheless accumulated savings (wealth) *can* be held in a form which provides their owner with an income in the form of interest (for example, as bonds or building society deposits). Hence it is reasonable to believe that some people would plan to save more out of their incomes if the rate of interest

[1]We use the term α to describe the distribution of income so that the *greater* is α the *more equally* income is distributed. The parameter α thus refers to income distribution in this sense and *not* to the *functional* distribution between *wages* and *profits*.

were (say) 20 per cent rather than 5 per cent. Moreover, some people who now tend to consume more than their incomes (that is, to *dissave*) by making use of hire-purchase finance would probably be less willing to do so if the rate charged by hire-purchase companies (which is related to the rate of interest) was 40 rather than 16 per cent.

In short there are some reasons to suppose that, the *higher* the rate of interest, the *more* willing some people will be to save and the *less* willing some other people will be to dissave.

Against this, some people save, in the main, to provide an income on retirement. The higher is the rate of interest, the smaller the accumulated savings necessary to provide any *given* income on retirement. Those who save primarily to provide for retirement and who aim at a fixed income at a certain age (say 60) may thus save *less* if the rate of interest is (say) 20 per cent than they would if it were (say) 5 per cent. It follows that though there are some reasons for thinking that the rate of interest is a variable which influences consumption out of any given income we cannot, on *a priori* grounds, be any too confident about either the *direction* or *magnitude* of its influence. Nevertheless it is clearly a variable which needs to be included in any hypothesis designed to explain aggregate consumption. Hence our fourth variable is:

(d) the rate of interest (r)

A fifth variable is the psychological attitude of members of households (consumers) as conditioned by the 'accepted' behaviour of the society in which they live and have their upbringing. Some people are brought up to believe that to save is a virtue which, if not rewarded in this world, will be in the next. Others believe that income is for spending. Hence these psychological attitudes – which we shall call *preferences* – are an important determinant of aggregate consumption.

There are a whole host of other variables which have some claim to be considered as factors influencing consumption plans. The age composition of society, for example, might well be an influence. So might expectations with regard to future incomes and expectations with regard to future prices. The problem in economics is not, however, to find the *longest* possible list of independent variables which might, in general, be thought to exert some influence on the dependent variable, aggregate consumption, but to find the *smallest* number of variables which permits us to make useful predictions of the dependent variable. *Which these variables are is a question of fact.* It is thus always wise to begin with a simple hypothesis and modify it only when tests show it to be inadequate. Accordingly we shall put forward the following hypothesis to explain real aggregate planned consumption:

aggregate real planned consumption	*depends upon*	real income real value of assets rate of interest distribution of income preferences

In our functional notation this may be conveniently written as a *consumption function* thus:

$$C_p = f(Y, A, r, \alpha) \tag{9.2}$$

where the last influence, households' preferences, is expressed in the form of the functional relationship (systematic dependence) betwen C_p (the dependent variable) and Y, A, r and α (the independent variables).

At this point the reader should notice the obvious analogy between the *consumption function* of 9.2 and our 'beer-drinking' function of earlier chapters. The new function, like the earlier one, expresses an hypothesis about economic behaviour which may be true or false. Moreover since Y, A, r, α and (assuming that consumption plans are always realised) C_p are all conceptually measurable, our consumption function hypothesis is meaningful: that is, it can be tested.

What properties is this consumption function likely to have? If we refer back to Chapter 7, we see that this question first requires us to say what *signs* we expect the marginal response coefficients to possess. Our discussion has already given us expectations about these, so we can immediately write down the signs of the marginal response coefficients as follows:

$$\frac{\partial C_p}{\partial Y} \equiv \text{the increase in real planned consumption resulting from a unit increase in real income } \textit{alone} \quad > \quad 0$$

$$\frac{\partial C_p}{\partial A} \equiv \text{the increase in real planned consumption resulting from a unit increase in the real value of assets } \textit{alone} \quad > \quad 0$$

$$\frac{\partial C_p}{\partial \alpha} \equiv \text{the increase in real planned consumption resulting from a unit increase in the equality of income distribution } \textit{alone} \quad > \quad 0$$

$$\frac{\partial C_p}{\partial r} \equiv \text{the increase in real planned consumption resulting from a unit increase in the rate of interest } \textit{alone} \quad ? \tag{9.3}$$

Notice that these marginal response coefficients are descriptive of human behaviour.

This information, which simply restates the results of our earlier discussion, tells us something about the consumption function. We now ask what is the *form* of the function?

On empirical grounds there are good reasons for writing the function in the following form:

$$C_p = Q + cY + dA + e\alpha + fr \tag{9.4}$$

which is the form illustrated in Chapter 7. In this notation Q is *autonomous* consumption – that is, consumption which is independent of Y, A, α and r. The form chosen, in addition to being plausible on empirical grounds, is also convenient, for with it each of the marginal response coefficients is a constant. Thus:

$$\frac{\partial C_p}{\partial Y} \equiv c > 0, \quad \frac{\partial C_p}{\partial A} \equiv d > 0, \quad \frac{\partial C_p}{\partial \alpha} \equiv e > 0, \quad \frac{\partial C_p}{\partial r} \equiv f \gtrless 0$$

These are the properties which, in what follows, we shall assume our consumption function to possess. We now proceed to illustrate by means of a numerical example.

The propensity to consume and its formal properties

Our consumption hypothesis is that real planned consumption is a function of four variables. Of these real income Y is by far the most important. Hence, if we take the values of Q, A, α and r as given together with the values of their marginal response coefficients, we can draw, on the graph, the relation between C_p and the remaining independent variable Y.

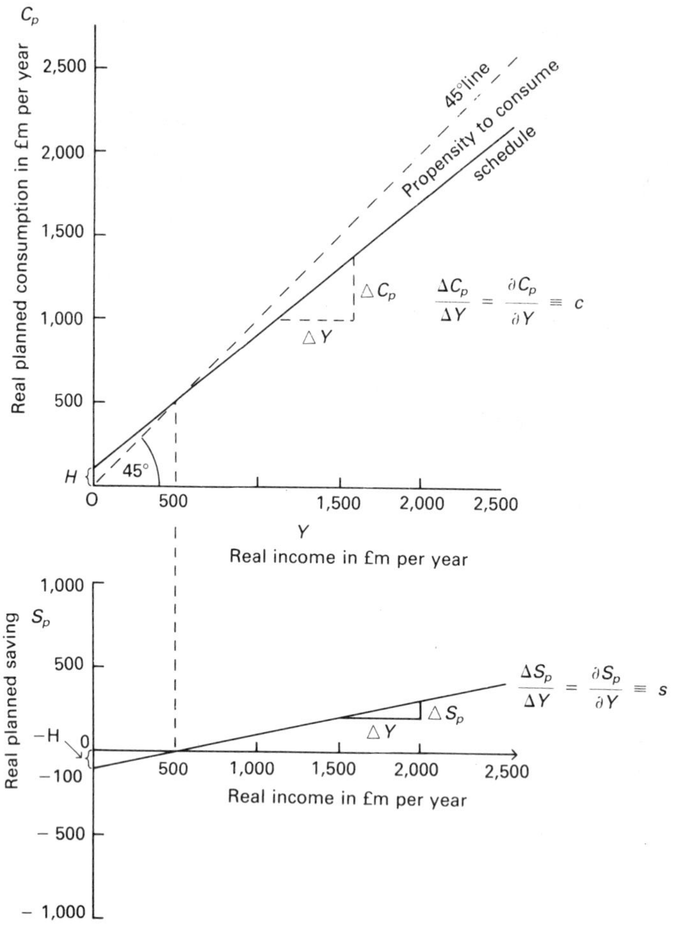

Figure 9.1 Propensity to consume and save schedules

This is done in Figure 9.1 using data set out in Table 9.1. The resultant curve or schedule is called the *propensity to consume schedule*. It shows (for given values of Q, A, α, r, d, e and f) the rate of real planned consumption at each real income level. Since real planned saving is equal, by definition, to real income *minus* real planned consumption, the same information can be used to draw a schedule relating real planned saving to real income. This too is done in the diagram. The resultant curve is called the *propensity to save schedule*.

The position of the propensity to consume (save) schedule depends upon households' preferences, the values of A, α, r, and their marginal response coefficients, and the value of Q. Hence the two curves, given these values, can be written:

$$C_p = H + cY \tag{9.5}$$
$$C_p = 100 + 0.8Y \tag{9.5n}$$
$$S_p = -H + (1 - c)Y \tag{9.6}$$
$$S_p = -100 + 0.2Y \tag{9.6n}$$

The *slope* of the propensity to consume schedule is $\partial C_p/\partial Y \equiv c$: the marginal response of real planned consumption to real income. This has a special name in economics which is the

Table 9.1 Determination of real planned consumption

(annual rates)

Aggregate real planned consumption C_p £m	Autonomous real planned consumption Q £m	$\frac{\partial C_p}{\partial Y}$ c	Real income Y £m	$\frac{\partial C_p}{\partial A}$ d	Real value of assets A £m	$\frac{\partial C_p}{\partial \alpha}$ e	Income distribution α Index	$\frac{\partial C_p}{\partial r}$ f	Rate of interest r %	Real planned saving $Y - Cp$ £m
100	52	0.8	0	0.01	1,000	1.0	50	−3.0	4.0	−100
500	52	0.8	500	0.01	1,000	1.0	50	−3.0	4.0	0
900	52	0.8	1,000	0.01	1,000	1.0	50	−3.0	4.0	100
1,060	52	0.8	1,200	0.01	1,000	1.0	50	−3.0	4.0	140
1,220	52	0.8	1,400	0.01	1,000	1.0	50	−3.0	4.0	180
1,380	52	0.8	1,600	0.01	1,000	1.0	50	−3.0	4.0	220
1,700	52	0.8	2,000	0.01	1,000	1.0	50	−3.0	4.0	300
2,100	52	0.8	2,500	0.01	1,000	1.0	50	−3.0	4.0	400
2,500	52	0.8	3,000	0.01	1,000	1.0	50	−3.0	4.0	500
2,900	52	0.8	3,500	0.01	1,000	1.0	50	−3.0	4.0	600
3,300	52	0.8	4,000	0.01	1,000	1.0	50	−3.0	4.0	700
?	52	0.8	4,200	0.01	1,000	1.0	50	−3.0	4.0	?
?	52	0.8	4,400	0.01	1,000	1.0	50	−3.0	4.0	?
?	52	0.8	4,700	0.01	1,000	1.0	50	−3.0	4.0	?
4,100	52	0.8	5,000	0.01	1,000	1.0	50	−3.0	4.0	900

Table based on the hypothesis that:

$$C_p = Q + cY + dA + e\alpha + fr \qquad (9.4)$$

$$C_p = 52 + 0.8Y + 0.01A + 1.0\alpha - 3.0r \qquad (9.4n)$$

marginal propensity to consume. It is the increment in real planned consumption resulting from a unit increase in real income alone. Analogously the *slope* of the propensity to save schedule is known as the *marginal propensity to save*: $\partial S_p/\partial Y \equiv s$. Since, by definition, households must plan to save (or consume) the whole of any increase in income then:

$$\frac{\partial C_p}{\partial Y} + \frac{\partial S_p}{\partial Y} \equiv 1 \quad \text{or} \quad c + s \equiv 1$$

so that

$$\frac{\partial S_p}{\partial Y} \equiv 1 - \frac{\partial C_p}{\partial Y} \quad \text{or} \quad s = 1 - c$$

The consumption schedule, as plotted, shows that, when real income is zero, real planned consumption is H or, in numerical terms, £100m per annum. *This is the value of consumption which is autonomous with respect to income*. Notice that it depends on Q, A, α, r as well as d, e and f. Analogously autonomous saving is −£100m – which, of course, is simply *dissaving*, for when Y = zero:

$$S_p \equiv Y - C_p \equiv 0 - £100\text{m} \equiv -£100\text{m}$$

Finally, we define the *average propensity to consume* as:

$$\frac{C_p}{Y} \equiv \frac{\text{real planned consumption}}{\text{real income}}$$

and the *average propensity to save* as S_p/Y. Clearly since all income must be consumed or saved we have:

$$C_p + S_p \equiv Y$$

or

$$\frac{C_p}{Y} + \frac{S_p}{Y} \equiv 1$$

that is, the average propensities to save and consume add to unity. Notice that if autonomous consumption (H) is positive, the average propensity to consume exceeds the marginal. If autonomous consumption is zero, the two are equal. If autonomous consumption is negative, the marginal propensity exceeds the average.

This is easily established from 9.5, where we wrote:

$$C_p = H + cY$$

so:

$$\frac{C_p}{Y} = \frac{H}{Y} + c$$

which tells us that the average propensity to consume, C_p/Y, is equal to the marginal propensity (c) *plus* the term H/Y. Clearly if H is negative $c > C_p/Y$ and conversely if H is positive.

We have now listed the formal properties of the propensity to consume schedule. But formal properties are not of themselves economics. We now look at the economics.

The *position* of the schedule depends upon

(a) households' preferences
(b) the values of Q, and A, α, r – the three dependent variables not shown in the figure
(c) the marginal response coefficients, d, e and f

A change in any one of these will shift the whole schedule – upwards or downwards – leaving its slope unaltered. Suppose, for example, α increases (income becomes more equally distributed). The schedule shifts upwards and we say that the propensity to consume has increased, for now at *each* level of real income real planned consumption is greater.

The *slope* of the schedule – the marginal propensity to consume – describes the reaction of real planned consumption to an increase in real income, *everything else held constant. It is an important proposition of economics that, when real income increases real consumption also increases but by less than the increase in real income*. That is, the marginal propensity to consume, $\partial C_p/\partial Y$, is greater than zero but less than unity – a proposition which also applies to the marginal propensity to save. Thus we have the hypothesis:

$$0 < c \equiv \frac{\partial C_p}{\partial Y} < 1$$

$$0 < s \equiv \frac{\partial S_p}{\partial Y} < 1$$

An increase in the propensity to consume must be sharply distinguished from an increase in consumption. The former, as we have seen, means an upward shift of the whole schedule indicating that, *because of a change in one of the parameters of the schedule*, households now plan a higher rate or real consumption at *each* level of real income. This is called an autonomous increase in consumption since it is autonomous with respect to income.

By contrast an increase in real planned consumption may occur simply because real income rises and, as a result, we move *along* an *unchanged* propensity to consume schedule. Consumption then rises because, we have already seen, the marginal propensity to consume is positive. This is called an *induced* increase in consumption because it is brought about (induced) by an increase in real income.

It is extremely important for the reader to bear these distinctions clearly in mind. Words are often used loosely in the belief that their precise meaning can be distinguished in the context. Thus 'an increase in consumption' is a potentially misleading phrase since, of itself, it does not make it clear whether there has been a *shift* in the consumption function (propensity to consume schedule), or movement along it, or some combination of the two. The same confusion can occur with the phrase 'an increase in demand' referred to some commodity – say peanuts. Does this mean a shift in the demand schedule, a movement along it or some combination of the two?

In practice, though for pedagogic reasons we discuss shifts in the consumption function (and hence the propensity to consume schedule), this function is believed to be relatively stable: that is, to shift rather rarely. Hence most increases in consumption which are observed are probably induced: that is, are due to movements along an unchanged function.

The determination of the equilibrium level of output

At the beginning of this chapter we wrote our equilibrium condition in two equivalent ways: $Y = C_p + I_p$, and $S_p = I_p$. We also assumed that $I_p = \bar{I}$ and took, as a numerical illustration, the value of $\bar{I}$ to be £500m a year. This value we treated as *exogenous* – that is, determined outside our model – and hence independent of income (output). We shall continue to treat r, A and α also as *exogenous* and assume them to take the special values $\bar{r}$, $\bar{A}$, $\bar{\alpha}$, shown in Table 9.1. Obviously from Table 9.1, simply by adding the rate of planned investment (I_p) to the rate of planned consumption, we can draw up a new table showing aggregate demand ($C_p + I_p$) *at each level of real income*. This is done in Table 9.2. Plainly the equilibrium level of income, defined by the condition $Y = C_p + I_p$, is £3,000m.

By the same token we can use Table 9.1 to give the rates of real planned saving at each level of real income. Our second version of the equilibrium condition tells us that income will be in equilibrium when real planned saving is £500m – that is, equal to the fixed rate of real planned investment. The reader can easily verify that this gives the same result.

Precisely the same result can be arrived at by elementary algebra. We have in fact a simple problem which can be set out and solved as follows: First we write the equilibrium condition:

$$Y = C_p + I_p$$

Our consumption hypothesis tells us that:

$$C_p = Q + cY + d\bar{A} + e\bar{\alpha} + f\bar{r} \qquad (9.7)$$
$$C_p = 52 + 0.8Y + 0.01\bar{A} + 1\ \ 0\bar{\alpha} - 3.0\bar{r} \qquad (9.7n)$$

Our investment assumption gives:

$$I_p = \bar{I} \qquad (9.8)$$
$$I_p = £500\text{m} \qquad (9.8n)$$

Table 9.2 Aggregate demand at each level of real income (in £m.)

Real income (aggregate supply)	Real planned consumption C_p	Real planned investments I_p	Real aggregate demand $(C_p + I_p)$
0	100	500	600
500	500	500	1,000
1,000	900	500	1,400
1,200	1,060	500	1,560
1,400	1,220	500	1,720
1,600	1,380	500	1,880
2,000	1,700	500	2,200
2,500	2,100	500	2,600
3,000	2,500	500	**3,000**
3,500	2,900	500	3,400
4,000	3,300	500	3,800
4,200	?	500	?
4,400	?	500	?
4,700	?	500	?
5,000	?	500	4,600

Assumptions:
1. $I_p = \bar{I} =$ £500m.
2. $C_p = Q + cY + dA + e\alpha + fr$, with the value of the parameters as in Table 8.1.

If we now substitute 9.7 and 9.8 into the equilibrium condition, we obtain a single equation in Y – which is equilibrium income – which can easily be solved in terms of $\bar{I}$, the given rate of investment, and the parameters of the consumption function. The manipulation is extremely simple. We have, on substitution,

$$Y = Q + cY\ d\bar{A} + e\bar{\alpha} + f\bar{r} + \bar{I} \tag{9.9}$$
$$Y = 52 + 0.8Y + [0.01 \times 1{,}000] + [1.0 \times 50] - [3.0 \times 4] + 500 \tag{9.9n}$$

Therefore:

$$Y - cY = Q + d\bar{A} + e\bar{\alpha} + f\bar{r} + \bar{I}$$
$$Y - 0.8Y = 52 + [0.01 \times 1{,}000] + [1.0 \times 50] - [3.0 \times 4] + 500$$

so that:

$$Y = [\{Q + d\bar{A} + e\bar{\alpha} + f\bar{r}\} + \bar{I}]\frac{1}{1 - c} \tag{9.10}$$

$$Y = [\{52 + 10 + 50 - 12\} + 500]\frac{1}{1 - 0.8} \tag{9.10n}$$

The elementary algebra yields, as it must, the same result as elementary arithmetic. Equilibrium real income is £3,000m per year. The algebraic formulation of 9.10, however, brings out explicitly three points which the arithmetic formulation obscures.

First, the expression in the *curly* brackets is that rate of consumption which is independent of (autonomous with respect to) income. It is, in fact, the constant (H) of equation 9.5. Equation 9.10 therefore confirms *explicitly* that H depends on the values of A, α, r and their marginal response coefficients as well as on Q. It, in short, depends on *all* the parameters of the propensity to consume schedule – a point which we earlier stated without full demonstration.

Second, the result for equilibrium Y takes the form of one expression (in the square brackets) *multiplied* by a second expression which is $1/(1 - c)$. What is the expression in the square brackets? A moment's thought shows that it is the sum of all those planned expenditures – whether consumption or investment – which are independent of income. This tells us that the equilibrium level of income is given by the sum of those expenditures which are independent of income multiplied by the expression $1/(1 - c)$.

Third, what can we say about the expression $1/(1 - c)$? This is simply 1/(1 – marginal propensity to consume). Since the marginal propensity to consume is positive – but less than unity – the denominator of this expression must be less than 1. Hence $1/(1 - c)$ must be greater than 1. Indeed in our example it is 5. We should also remind ourselves that, since $1 - c \equiv s$, this 'multiplier' can also be written as $1/s$. The precise significance of this 'multiplier' will be explained later. It is, however, obvious that the 'multiplier' will be greater the greater is c – that is, the more nearly c approaches unity.

We have now shown that either via arithmetic or algebra we can, if we are given (i) the consumption function, and (ii) the rate of planned investment, determine the equilibrium level of income (output) and hence the equilibrium level of employment.

This is the crucial result of the modern theory of the short-run determination of output and employment. Its meaning is simply that, given the rate of planned investment, income will adjust (upwards or downwards) until it reaches a level at which households will plan to save at the same rate as enterprises plan to invest. In short, income (and hence employment) is the variable which moves to equate the saving and investment plans of the community.

These important results which we have reached by arithmetic and algebra are commonly presented geometrically. Since arithmetic is tedious while some people dislike algebra we now perform the same exercise, using the same data, geometrically.

On the vertical axis of Figure 9.2 we measure real planned expenditures (C_p and I_p), and on the horizontal axis real income. The line marked C_p is thus the propensity to consume schedule of Figure 9.1. Its *slope*, as before, is the marginal propensity to consume. Its *position* is determined by OA – the rate of planned consumption which is independent of income. The distance OA is therefore given by:

$$\begin{aligned} OA &\equiv Q + d\bar{A} + e\bar{\alpha} + f\bar{r} \equiv H \\ &\equiv \text{£100m per year} \end{aligned}$$

From the origin of the diagram we draw a line *00* at an angle of 45°. Geometrically this line has the property that any point on it subtends equal distances along the horizontal and vertical axes. It follows that at any point on *00*:

aggregate real planned expenditure = aggregate real income (output)

that is:

$$C_p + I_p = Y$$

or

$$I_p = S_p$$

The line 00 thus defines all possible positions of equilibrium.

To this diagram we now add a third line showing the rate of real planned investment (I_p). Since this is independent of income ($I_p = \bar{I}$) the line is horizontal and drawn showing a rate of £500m per year. We now add this rate of planned investment to the rates of consumption shown by the consumption schedule. This gives us the $C_p + I_p$ schedule or the *schedule of aggregate demand*. The schedule cuts OO at the point X. At X income is Y_0, which is the

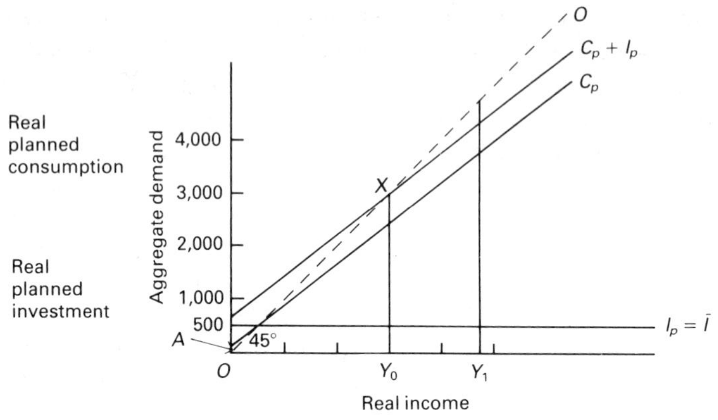

Figure 9.2 Income determined by the aggregate demand schedule

equilibrium level of income, for, since X lies on OO, it is a point at which aggregate demand is equal to aggregate supply (income). It is indeed the only point at which, with our given consumption and investment schedules, aggregate demand does equal aggregate supply.

The same result is depicted on Figure 9.3, where we have drawn, instead of the consumption schedule, the saving schedule. On this we have superimposed the investment schedule. Where these two curves cut – that is, where $I_p = S_p$ – determines the equilibrium level of income. Again this is $Y_0 =$ £3,000 per year.

Both diagrams thus depict the determination of equilibrium output (income) either (as in Figure 9.2) by the condition that $Y = C_p + I_p$ or (as in Figure 9.3) by the equivalent condition that $S_p = I_p$.

Suppose income is not at Y_0 but at some higher level Y_1. Will it tend to move towards Y_0? At Y_1 we can see from Figure 9.2 that $C_p + I_p$ (aggregate demand) is less than Y (aggregate supply). Hence some part of output will be unsold so that there will be *unintended* investment in inventories. In short, *actual* investment ($Y_1 - C_p$) will exceed *planned* investment (I_p). In this situation, as we have already shown, enterprises will *reduce* output and employment. Hence income will move *towards* Y_0. This argument is readily

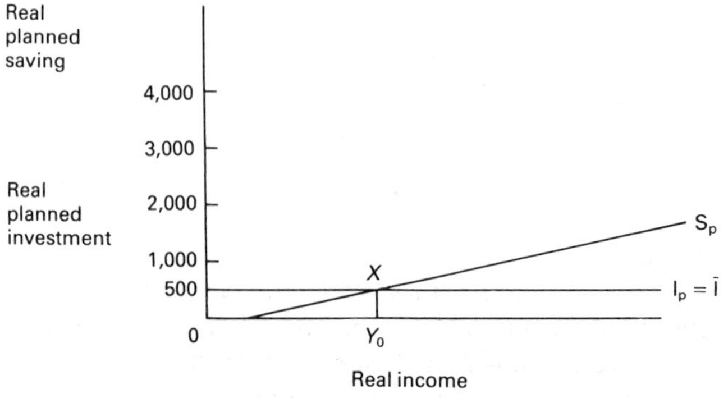

Figure 9.3 Income determined by saving and investment schedules

reversible for income levels less than that of Y_0. It follows that Y_0 is not only the *equilibrium level of income* but is a *stable*[1] equilibrium, in the sense that, if income departs from it, forces will be set up which tend to compel it to return to Y_0.

We have now shown, by arithmetic, algebra and geometry, that if we know (i) the consumption function, and (ii) the rate of planned investment, we can determine the equilibrium level of income (output) and employment. We have also shown that, provided the marginal propensity to consume is less than unity, the equilibrium level of income is *stable*.

The meaning of this analysis can be summed up as follows: Assuming:

(a) constant prices
(b) a given level of the interest rate

then:

1. The variable which adjusts to equate aggregate demand with aggregate supply – that is, to reconcile the saving plans of households with the investment plans of enterprises – is income.
2. The equilibrium level of income which reconciles these plans need not be – and in general will not be – a level of income corresponding to full employment.

The multiplier and the marginal propensity to consume

Our analysis so far tells us that, given the rate of real planned consumption which is independent of income (H in equation 9.5) and the rate of real planned investment, we can determine the equilibrium level of real income. It follows that if either of these determinants changes, so will the equilibrium level of income. What determines the extent of the change?

Originally we assumed I_p to be £500m per year. Suppose this rises to £900m. What will be the new equilibrium level of income?

A glance back at Table 9.1 tells us that, to generate a rate of planned saving of £900m a year, incomes will need to be £5,000m. Hence:

$$\begin{aligned}\Delta Y &\equiv \text{the change in equilibrium real income}\\ &= £5{,}000\text{m} - £3{,}000\text{m} = £2{,}000\text{m}\end{aligned}$$

while

$$\begin{aligned}\Delta I_p &\equiv \text{the change in real planned investment}\\ &= £900\text{m} - £500\text{m} = £400\text{m}\end{aligned}$$

Hence

$$\frac{\Delta Y}{\Delta I_p} = \frac{£2{,}000\text{m}}{£400\text{m}} = 5$$

We now define $\Delta Y/\Delta I_p$ as the 'multiplier': that is, *the coefficient relating the change in real income to the change in real autonomous expenditure bringing it about.* We use 'real

[1]Strictly, *stability* is a dynamic concept.

autonomous expenditure' rather than 'real investment' because *the same multiplier applies to changes in autonomous consumption*. If we refer back to equation 9.10 or Figure 9.2 this is obvious enough. Using this equation we have, for the initial equilibrium level which we now call Y_0:

$$Y_0 = [H + \bar{I}]\frac{1}{1 - c} \quad (\text{where } H = Q + \ d\bar{A} + e\bar{\alpha} + f\bar{r}) \tag{9.11}$$

If $\bar{I}$ increases by $\Delta\bar{I}$ the new equilibrium level Y_1 is given by:

$$Y_1 = [H + \bar{I} + \Delta\bar{I}]\frac{1}{1 - c} \tag{9.12}$$

so that:

$$\Delta Y = Y_1 - Y_0 = \Delta I\frac{1}{1 - c}$$

and

$$\frac{\Delta Y}{\Delta\bar{I}} \ \Delta\bar{I} = \frac{1}{1 - c} = \frac{1}{1 - 0.8} = 5$$

Obviously had the change been in the propensity to consume so that H increased by ΔH we should have had:

$$\frac{\Delta Y}{\Delta H} = \frac{1}{1 - c} = \frac{1}{1 - 0.8} = 5 \tag{9.13}$$

In the short run, therefore, *any* change in autonomous real expenditure has a multiplied effect on income whether (in terms of Figure 9.3) it shifts the consumption schedule upwards or the investment schedule.

The multiplier is given by the formula:

$$\frac{1}{1 - c} \equiv \frac{1}{s}$$

where $c \equiv$ marginal propensity to consume, and $s \equiv 1 \ - c \equiv$ marginal propensity to save.

So far this, though obvious enough, is merely algebra. What does it mean in economic terms?

Suppose autonomous consumption increases by £100m per year, i.e. ΔH = £100m. Additional income is thus created for those who produce the additional output. From this income they spend $c \times$ £100m = 0.8 $\times$ £100m = £80m. This generates further output and incomes which cause a further induced increase in consumption. This in turn generates further income for those who produce the additional consumption goods, and so the process continues.

We have, indeed, the following series for the increase in income:

$$\Delta Y = £100\text{m} + c \times £100\text{m} + c^2 \times £100\text{m} + c^3 \times £100\text{m} + \ldots + c^n \times £100\text{m}$$

or

$$\Delta Y = £100\text{m} + 0.8 \times £100\text{m} + (0.8)^2 \times £100\text{m} + (0.8)^3 \times £100\text{m} + \ldots + (0.8)^n \times £100\text{m}$$

This series is easily summed to give:

$$\Delta Y = £100\text{m} \times \frac{1 - c^{n+1}}{1 - c} = £100\text{m} \times \frac{1 - (0.8)^{n+1}}{1 - 0.8} \quad (9.14)$$

As n, the number of income 'rounds', approaches infinity, c^{n+1}, since c is less than unity, approaches zero. Hence the *limit* of (9.14) as $n \rightarrow$ infinity is:

$$\Delta Y = £100\text{m} \frac{1}{1 - c}$$

which is, clearly enough, our formula at (9.13), for we have simply taken ΔH to be £100m.

In other words the new equilibrium level of income, reached after an infinitely large number of income 'rounds', is greater than the original level by:

$$\begin{aligned} \Delta Y &= £100\text{m} \frac{1}{1 - c} \\ &= £100\text{m} \times 5 \\ &= £500\text{m} \end{aligned}$$

The change in income is greater than the change in autonomous expenditure which causes it because as long as $c > 0$ the multiplier, $1/(1 - c)$, must be > 1. Notice that if $c = 0$ the multiplier is unity. This, however, is economically quite implausible.

The common sense proposition underlying this result is that one person's income is another person's expenditure – which is obviously correct – and, as a result, the more the latter spends the more the former will receive and spend in turn.

The multiplier is thus a *leverage coefficient* and, as such, works in either direction. To see this suppose ΔH to be negative and equal to $-£100\text{m}$. We should then have:

$$\begin{aligned} \Delta Y &= -£100\text{m} \frac{1}{1 - c} \\ &= -£500\text{m} \end{aligned}$$

so that, in this case, equilibrium income would *fall* by £500m.

To know that, after an infinite passage of time ($n \rightarrow$ infinity), equilibrium income will rise (or fall) by an amount determined by the multiplier and the increase (decrease) in the rate of autonomous expenditure is interesting. We are, however, not primarily concerned with what will *eventually* occur but only with *what will occur after the lapse of a finite period of time*. To see this we must engage in some elementary dynamics. Accordingly in Table 9.3

Table 9.3 The multiplier process (£m. at quarterly rates)

Period	Income (1)	Planned consumption (2)	Actual consumption (3)	Planned saving (4)	Actual saving (5)	Planned investment (6)	Actual investment (7)	Unintended investment (8)
0	750	625	625	125	125	125	125	nil
1	750	625	625	125	125	225	125	−100
2	850	705	705	145	145	225	145	− 80
3	930	769	769	161	161	225	161	− 64
4	994	820.2	802.2	173.8	173.8	225	173.8	− 51.2
5						225		
6						225		
.								
.								
.								
n	1,250	1,025	1,025	225	225	225	225	nil

Note: This table is based on the consumption function of Table 9.1.

we (i) *express* all flows at quarterly and *not* annual rates; (ii) *divide* time into periods of three calendar months' duration; (iii) *assume* that output takes one period (three months) to adjust to a change in demand. On these assumptions, making use of the consumption function specified in Table 9.1 – that is, holding the variables A, α and r constant – we can set out the following multiplier process.

We begin in period 0 with income in equilibrium at £750m. In period 1, I_p increases to £225m. Output, however, does not increase until period 2, since, by assumption, it takes one period to adjust. Hence in period 1 aggregate demand ($C_p + I_p$) exceeds aggregate supply and there is involuntary decumulation of stocks to the extent of £100m.

In period 2 output adjusts upwards by £100m. Since the marginal propensity to consume is 0.8, this raises consumption by £80m. Again aggregate demand exceeds supply – this time by £80m – and there is a second involuntary decumulation of stocks.

In period 3 output expands again – this time by £80m. Hence consumption rises by $0.8 \times$ £80m = £64m, and in this way the process continues with enterprises always adjusting output upwards in an endeavour to catch up with expanding aggregate demand.

Table 9.3, which gives a somewhat oversimplified account of a dynamic multiplier process, conveys some interesting information. This can be summarised as follows:

1. The *ultimate* change in the *quarterly* rate of income is given by:

$$\Delta Y = \Delta I_p \times \frac{1}{1 - c}$$

$$= \text{£}100\text{m} \times 5$$

$$= \text{£}500\text{m}$$

   By the fourth period – that is, after one year – 48.8 per cent of this change has occurred.

2. From period 1 to period $n - 1$ the system is in disequilibrium. Hence:

$$Y < C_p + I_p$$

   and

$$I_p > I$$

and so periods 1 to $n - 1$ are characterised by unintended disinvestment in stocks which diminishes as the system moves towards its new equilibrium.

3. In *all* periods – that is, whether equilibrium exists or not:

$$S \equiv I$$

and

$$Y \equiv C + I$$

where S, I and C denote saving, investment and consumption in their national accounting sense.

These points you should check for yourself. You should also calculate the values for columns 1, 2, 3, 4, 5, 7 and 8 for periods 5 and 6.

Questions and exercises

1. The following observations are generated by a consumption function of the form: $C_p = Q + cY + dA + e\alpha + fr$.

Year	C_p	Y	A	α	r
1	662.4	1,000	1,000	0.5	4
2	762.4	1,200	1,000	0.5	4
3	767.4	1,200	1,500	0.5	4
4	817.4	1,200	1,500	1.0	4
5	766.2	1,200	1,500	0.5	2

Calculate the numerical values of the marginal response coefficients c, d, e, f and the constant Q. Next, taking $A = 1{,}000$, $\alpha = 0.5$ and $r = 4.0$ per cent, plot the propensity to consume schedule. What is the value of consumption when income is zero? Draw a second schedule for the value $A = 1{,}000$, $\alpha = 1.0$, $r = 4$ per cent.

2. The elasticity of consumption with respect to income is defined as:

$$\frac{\Delta C_p}{C_p} \Big/ \frac{\Delta Y}{Y}$$

when Y is the only independent variable to change. This can be rewritten:

$$\frac{\Delta C_p}{\Delta Y} \times \frac{Y}{C_p}$$

Since $\Delta C_p = (\partial C_p/\partial Y) \times \Delta Y$ calculate from *both* the propensity to consume schedules the elasticity of consumption with respect to income. Show that the elasticity will be unity if autonomous consumption is zero. Why is this? What general relationship does it reflect between the average and marginal propensities and the elasticity? In what circumstances will the elasticity be independent of the level of income?

3. Use the UK national income estimates to obtain figures for real consumption and real income on a quarterly basis for the years 1969–82. Draw (freehand) a straight line through these observations when plotted on a graph. Measure consumption on the vertical axis and income on the horizontal axis.
   (a) Explain and justify your choice of data.
   (b) What is the slope of your straight line?

(c) In what circumstances, if any, would the slope of your line be a 'reasonable' estimate of the marginal propensity to consume?
(d) Assuming that it is a 'reasonable' estimate, what is the value of the multiplier?
(e) What do you think is meant by 'reasonable'?

4. Using the data of question 1 plot C_p and Y as for question 3. Again draw (freehand) a straight line through the observed points. Why is the slope of this line not a good estimate of $\partial C_p/\partial Y$?

5. *Ceteris paribus* according to Table 9.1 a 10-unit increase in income 'induces' an 8-unit increase in consumption. Give a precise statement of what is meant by *ceteris paribus.* Explain the meaning of 'induced'.

6. For the multiplier of Table 9.3 what proportion of the ultimate change in income is completed after (i) two quarters; (ii) four quarters; (iii) eight quarters.

7. Discuss critically the assumptions about human behaviour underlying the consumption function of question 1. Are all the variables measurable (i) in principle, (ii) in practice? How would you attempt to measure A, α and r?

8. The multiplier model of Table 9.3 can be written formally as follows:

$$C_p(t) = H + cY(t) \qquad \text{(with } H = 25,\ c = 0.8)$$
$$I_p(t) = \bar{I} \qquad (\bar{I} = 125)$$
$$Y(t) = C_p(t-1) + I_p(t-1)$$

where the suffixes in brackets indicate the period (t, $t - 1$, etc.) of the variable and the last equation indicates that it takes one period for output to adjust to demand.

An alternative model can be written:

$$C_p(t) = H + cY(t-1)$$
$$I_p(t) = \bar{I}$$
$$Y(t) = C_p(t) + \bar{I}_p(t)$$

where the lag of output behind demand no longer exists and, in its place, we have put the hypothesis that this period's consumption depends upon last period's income.

Construct a table similar to Table 9.3 showing the multiplier process for this model. How does disequilibrium manifest itself? Why are there no unplanned stock changes? Is the equilibrium result of the two processes the same? Which model do you consider the more realistic?

9. Plot the following data on an appropriate graph:

Per cent of income recipients	*Per cent of income received*
10	3
20	7
30	11
40	16
50	22
60	29
70	36
80	47
90	59
100	100

What would a graph showing equal distribution of income look like? Construct one and compare it with the graph of the data. From your comparison suggest a way of measuring α (the parameter of income distribution). What would graphs of $\alpha = 0$ (perfect inequality of income distribution) and $\alpha = 1$ look like?

10. The multiplier model of Table 9.3 yields the following equilibrium results.

Period	Y	$C_p = C_A$	I_A	I_p	S_p	S_A
t	750	625	125	125	125	125
$t + n$	875	750	125	125	125	125

How much of the increase in consumption is due to: (i) a shift in the consumption function; and (ii) a movement along it?

11. The multiplier process of Table 9.3 can be written as follows:

Period	*Change in income*
2	ΔI_p
3	$c\Delta I_p$
4	$c^2\Delta I_p$
5	$c^3\Delta I_p$
⋮	⋮
$n + 2$	$c^n\Delta I_p$

So the total change in income is:

$$\Delta Y = \Delta I_p\,[1 + c + c^2 + \ldots + c^n]$$
$$= \Delta I_p \left[\frac{1 - c^{n+1}}{1 - c}\right]$$

Use this formula to calculate the proportion of the total change which will have occurred by the end of (i) period 2, (ii) period 4, (iii) period 10. Would your results have been different if c had been 0.5 and not 0.8? Do your results imply that the greater the multiplier, the greater the number of periods required to achieve any given proportion (say 50 per cent) of its equilibrium result?

12. How would you characterise the business behaviour assumed in Table 9.3?

13. From national income estimates obtain figures for the quarterly expenditure on (i) consumption of non-durables, (ii) consumption of durables, for the years 1969–82. Graph them against income. Compare these graphs with that you prepared for question 3. What does the comparison suggest to you? What additional variables (if any) would you introduce into the consumption function hypothesis to obtain a better explanation of expenditure on durables? How would you seek to measure them?

14. The function $C_p = Q + cY + dA + e\alpha + fr$ used in this chapter has, in our numerical examples, $Q = 52$. Has Q any economic meaning? Is $Q \neq$ zero possible? Discuss carefully in the light of (i) your answer to question 3, and (ii) the fact that the equation of a straight line is $Y = A + bX$.

Suggested reading

K. Cuthbertson, 'The Determination of Expenditure on Consumer Durables', *NIESR Review*, no. 94 (November 1980).

K. Cuthbertson, 'The Measurement and Behaviour of the UK Savings Ratio in the 1970s', *NIESR Review*, no. 99 (February 1982).

J. C. R. Dow, *The Management of the British Economy, 1945–60* (Cambridge, 1964) ch. 11.

*M. Evans, *Macroeconomic Activity* (Harper & Row, 1969) chs 2, 3.
J. M. Keynes, *The General Theory of Employment, Interest and Money* (Macmillan, 1936) chs 8–10.
*L. R. Klein and A. S. Goldberger, *An Econometric Model of the United States, 1929–52* (North-Holland, 1955) chs 2, 4.
L. Metzler in *Incomes, Employment and Public Policy* (Norton, 1948).

*More advanced references.

Chapter 10
The Investment Function

In Chapter 9 we showed that if we knew:

(a) the propensity to consume schedule
(b) the rate of real planned investment

we could determine the equilibrium level of output and hence, via the production function, the equilibrium level of employment. We also demonstrated that the equilibrium level of output (= income) was stable.[1]

These are important conditions. We established them, however, on the pedagogically convenient assumption that the rate of real planned investment was exogenously determined by, say, some hypothetical 'planning authority'. In a market economy there is no such authority. It follows that, to develop our theory, we must now put forward an explanation of how real planned investment is determined.

The purpose of this chapter is therefore to develop a theory of how investment is determined: or, as we shall call it, by analogy with the consumption function already discussed, the theory of the investment function.

At this stage the reader should recall our definition of the term 'investment'. This must be carefully distinguished from colloquial usage in which it is common to speak of 'investment' in financial assets such as bonds, shares or deposits. There are three fundamental points:

(a) real net investment is the process of increasing the real capital stock of the community
(b) an investment decision is a decision to bring about such an increase
(c) real gross investment is defined as real net investment *plus* real depreciation.

In practice, net investment expenditure by the private sector takes three forms which it is useful to distinguish:

$I_f \equiv$ real planned net investment in fixed capital (other than dwellings)
$I_d \equiv$ real planned net investment in dwellings
$I_s \equiv$ real planned net investment in inventories

so that:

$$I_p \equiv \text{real planned net investment} \equiv I_f + I_d + I_s$$

[1]We return to this issue – in a dynamic context – in Chapter 20.

There are certain features of investment in inventories which need special consideration. Accordingly discussion of I_s is postponed until Chapter 20. Hence the theory of this chapter should be regarded as primarily applicable to investment in fixed capital and dwellings.

We begin by asking: who takes investment decisions and why?

Investment decisions

In our simple model, by assumption, all investment decisions are taken by enterprises or, more strictly, by the business people who run them. We have assumed that the aim of businesses is to maximise profits; our problem is therefore to explain in what circumstances a profit-maximising business will plan to invest.

In outline, the explanation is not far to seek or difficult to comprehend. It states that a profit-maximising business will purchase an additional real capital asset (i.e. invest) if:

the rate of return (per cent per period) he expects to derive from the asset over its life	>	the rate of cost (per cent per period) he must pay for borrowing the funds with which to finance the investment

The remainder of this chapter is concerned to make this simple proposition rather more precise and derive from it a theory of aggregate real planned investment.

The easiest approach to this problem is to consider a simple hypothetical example. Let us assume, therefore, that a businessman is considering whether (or not) to invest by adding a new machine costing £10,000 to his shoe-manufacturing factory. He *knows* the cost of the machine. Is it worth his while to purchase it?

In buying the machine the businessman can be thought of as purchasing the right to the net returns produced by the machine over its *useful economic life*. Since these returns lie in the future, he cannot *know* them. He must *forecast* them. Equally he cannot *know* the economic life of the machine since this too depends on future events – for example, the development of economically superior machines. This too must be *forecast*. However, making such forecasts and taking decisions under uncertainty is precisely the job of the creative entrepreneur. How, then, does he go about it?

His first step is to *forecast* the economic life of the machine. This is *not* the same as its technical life. The machine may be operating efficiently, from a *technical* point of view, long after it has become economically inefficient because of the development of superior machines. This is one consideration. A second is that, since he cannot know the future, he may feel unable to make forecasts for more than a few years ahead simply because the future is economically – and perhaps politically – uncertain. Let us suppose that after weighing (what he believes are) the relevant factors, he forecasts the economic life of the machine as five years.

We shall assume that no second-hand market in capital assets exists. The machine, once purchased, must be held for five years and then sold as scrap. Our businessman forecasts the scrap value as £1,900. This gives our businessman the following data:

(a) he *knows* the cost of the machine to be £10,000
(b) he *estimates* its useful economic life at five years
(c) he *estimates* its scrap value at £1,900

He must now make estimates of the net returns from the asset in each year of its useful life.

This is not simple – for to obtain estimates he must calculate:

(a) the output of shoes in each year and the prices in each year at which the output can be sold
(b) the raw materials required in each year and their prices in each year
(c) the labour required to work the machine in each year and its wage cost in each year

To do this he has information on the technical capacity of the machine to produce shoes, its technical requirement for raw materials, the present and past costs of raw materials and labour and present and past shoe prices. He can only do the best he can with the information he has. Let us suppose that he does this and produces the following *estimates* of returns net of raw material and labour costs:

Year 1 £2,500 *Year 2* £2,500 *Year 3* £2,500 *Year 4* £2,000 *Year 5* £2,000

Given these (obviously uncertain) estimates, how can the entrepreneur decide whether to invest or not? There are two possible methods of proceeding.

In the first method he asks: What is the *present value* of this stream of prospective returns: that is, what sum, if held in a form which yielded the current interest rate, would provide an equivalent income stream? If this calculated present value *exceeds* £10,000 – the known cost of the capital asset – the investment is worth while: if it is less, it is not worth while.

An elementary example may make this clearer. Suppose a man is asked: What sum would you pay *today* for £105 receivable in *one year's time*? He can answer this question by asking himself:

> What sum accumulated for one year at the existing rate of interest would provide £105 in one year's time?

This sum is the *present value* of £105 in one year's time.

If we call the present value ($\equiv$ PV) x we have the equation:

$$x(1 + r) = £105$$

where r is the market rate of interest. Obviously if $r = 5$ per cent (that is 0.05) we have

$$x(1.05) = £105$$

so that

$$x = £100$$

that is, the PV of £105 in one year's time is £100 if $r = 5$ per cent.

Suppose instead the man had been offered £105 in *two* years' time. Interest would then have accumulated twice and the expression for the PV would be

$$x(1.05)^2 = £105$$

which gives

$$x = £95.45$$

In general, the PV of a stream of prospective returns over the life of an asset can be written:

$$\text{PV} = \frac{Q_1}{1 + r} + \frac{Q_2}{(1 + r)^2} + \ldots + \frac{Q_n}{(1 + r)^n} \qquad (10.1)$$

where $Q_1, \ldots, Q_n$ are the returns expected in each year, n is the number of years, r is, as before, the rate of interest.

Notice that this formula somewhat simplifies matters by assuming a constant value of r over the life of the asset.

Applying this formula to our example we have:

$$\text{PV} = \frac{£2{,}500}{(1+r)} + \frac{£2{,}500}{(1+r)^2} + \frac{£2{,}500}{(1+r)^3} + \frac{£2{,}000}{(1+r)^4} + \frac{£2{,}000 + £1{,}900}{(1+r)^5} \tag{10.2}$$

which for three assumed values of r yields, to a close approximation:

	$r = 0.05$	$r = 0.10$	$r = 0.15$
PV	£11,511	£10,000	£8,791

Notice that if $r < 0.10$ (10 per cent) the present value exceeds the cost; conversely if $r > 0.10$ the cost exceeds the present value. In the former case the investment is profitable since the businessman expects a higher return on the project than the interest cost; in the latter it is not.

An alternative approach is not to use the present value method but to calculate directly the rate of return which the businessman expects to obtain by purchasing the asset. In this case we replace PV (the unknown) in equation 10.2 by the *known* cost of the asset (£10,000). The unknown is now the rate of return which we shall call i. We thus obtain:

$$£10{,}000 = \frac{£2{,}500}{1+i} + \frac{£2{,}500}{(1+i)^2} + \frac{£2{,}500}{(1+i)^3} + \frac{£2{,}000}{(1+i)^4} + \frac{£2{,}000 + £1{,}900}{(1+i)^5} \tag{10.3}$$

which we solve for i.

Clearly i is the rate of return which makes the present value of the stream of prospective returns expected over the life of the asset exactly equal to its supply price (cost). This rate is known as the *marginal efficiency of the capital asset*.[1] As one of our PV calculations has already shown, it is equal to 0.10 (10 per cent). The decision rule is now: if $i > r$, the project is worth while; if $i < r$ it is not. Obviously this is a nasty-looking problem since the unknown (i) appears in the equation raised to the power of 5. How then do we find it? The practical answer is by successive approximations. This is illustrated in Table 10.1.

In cols 2 and 3 of Table 10.1 we set out the data of our example and try the experiment of putting i = 9 per cent. On this basis we require to earn 9 per cent on the capital employed in each year. For example, in year 1 the capital employed is £10,000. Hence, given i = 9 per cent, we require to earn £900. This figure is shown in col. 4 of the table.

In year 1, however, the estimated return is £2,500. Hence £1,600 (i.e. £2,500 *minus* £900) is available for depreciation. Alternatively we may write:

$$\text{depreciation} \equiv \text{return} - i \times \text{capital employed}$$

which gives us the figure of £1,600 entered in col. 5.

[1]This is substantially identical to the definition given by Keynes: J. M. Keynes, *The General Theory of Employment, Interest and Money* (Macmillan, 1936) p. 135.

Table 10.1 Hypothetical estimation of the marginal efficiency of capital: trial with i = 9 per cent

(1) Year	(2) Capital employed £	(3) Return £	(4) $i \times$ capital employed £	(5) Depreciation £
1	10,000	2,500	900	1,600
2	8,400	2,500	756	1,744
3	6,656	2,500	599	1,901
4	4,755	2,000	428	1,572
5	3,183	2,000 1,900	286	3,614
			Accumulated depreciation =	£10,431

In year 2 capital employed is £8,400 – the original £10,000 *minus* the depreciation in year 1. Hence with i = 9 per cent the required return is £756 and the depreciation (£2,500 – £756) is £1,744.

This process is continued for each year until the fifth, when the receipts are:

return (£2,000) *plus* scrap value (£1,900)

Given the value of the capital employed in year 5 and i = 9 per cent this gives a final depreciation figure of £3,614.

If we now add col. 5, which is the depreciation including the accumulated scrap value, we find that this comes to £10,431. We require, of course, that it should come to £10,000 for if we calculate our available income ($i \times$ capital employed) correctly the accumulated depreciation including the scrap value should just suffice to maintain our capital intact. In short we have depreciated too fast or, what is clearly the same thing, *underestimated* the marginal efficiency of capital.

Table 10.2 Hypothetical estimation of the marginal efficiency of capital: trial with i = 11 per cent

Year	Capital employed £	Return £	$i \times$ capital employed £	Depreciation £
1	10,000	2,500	1,100	1,400
2	8,600	2,500	946	1,554
3	7,046	2,500	775	1,725
4	5,321	2,000	585	1,415
5	3,906	2,000 1,900	430	3,470
			Accumulated depreciation =	£9,564

Accordingly we try a higher value – say i = 11 per cent. This gives us Table 10.2. Here the sum of the depreciation allowances – plus the scrap value – is *less* than the original investment. We have not recovered the whole of our investment because we have depreciated too *slowly*. In short i = 11 per cent is *too large*.

Table 10.3 Hypothetical estimation of the marginal efficiency of capital: trial with i = 10 per cent

Year	Capital employed £	Return £	$i \times$ capital employed £	Depreciation £
1	10,000	2,500	1,000	1,500
2	8,500	2,500	850	1,650
3	6,850	2,500	685	1,815
4	5,035	2,000	504	1,496
5	3,539	2,000 1,900	354	3,546
			Accumulated depreciation =	£10,007

We now know that 9 per cent < i < 11 per cent. Accordingly we try 10 per cent and obtain Table 10.3. Here the sum of depreciation allowances – plus the scrap value – is £10,007. This is close enough to £10,000 for our purposes, for, since all the figures in the table – apart from the initial £10,000 – are *estimates* of the future, which are obviously *uncertain*, there is no point in straining after arithmetic precision. To a quite satisfactory degree of approximation we have found that:

$$\text{marginal efficiency of the capital asset} \equiv i = 10 \text{ per cent}$$

We now know, in principle and in practice, how to calculate the marginal efficiency of a capital asset. *We also know, since the calculation depends upon estimates of the future, what a subjective and uncertain quantity the marginal efficiency of a capital asset is.*

The demand for capital and the marginal efficiency of investment schedules

We have now seen how our hypothetical businessman can calculate the marginal efficiency of a particular capital asset and, by comparing the estimated MEC with the rate of interest, make a rational (profit-maximising) decision to purchase the asset or not.

At any time the typical businessman will be faced with a number of possible capital asset purchases. Since the estimation of the MEC can be applied to any type of capital asset, the MEC can be calculated for each and the projects ranked in descending order. This is done in Figure 10.1 with K', defined as the real quantity of additional capital, measured along the horizontal axis, and the marginal efficiency of capital (i) and the interest rate (r) measured on the vertical axis. Because of our ranking the resultant schedule is downward-sloping from left to right.[1]

If we now superimpose the rate of interest (assumed to be constant) on the figure it is easy to see that this determines an optimum value for K' – in the sense of that value of K' which the businessman estimates will maximise his profits at the given value of r. For example, if $r = r_1$ then $K' = K'_1$, and so on. We see at once that the value of K' will be greater the *lower* is r.

[1]In long-run equilibrium this slope can be explained by the fall in the marginal product of capital as K increases.

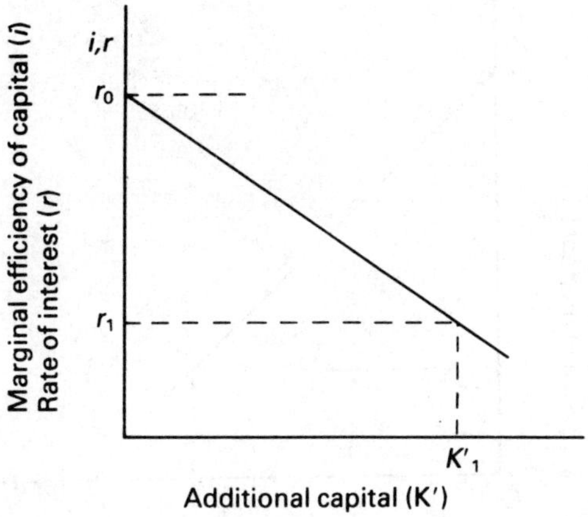

Figure 10.1 The marginal efficiency of capital schedule

Suppose $r = r_0$. Then according to our figure $K' = K_0' =$ zero. Does this mean that the optimal capital stock is zero? Certainly not. It simply means that at r_0 it is not worth the businessman's while to purchase any of the *additional* capital assets he has in contemplation. But if this is so then, at r_0, the capital he actually possesses, which we denote by $\bar{K}$, must coincide with the optimal[1] value. This enables us to re-label the horizontal axis of Figure 10.1 in a way which makes clear precisely what we meant when we defined it earlier as additional capital. We now define:

$\hat{K} \equiv$ optimal real capital stock
$\bar{K} \equiv$ the existing real capital stock

Hence the horizontal axis of Figure 10.1 can now be labelled $\hat{K} - \bar{K}$ where we earlier used the notation K' (see Figure 10.2). We now see that, given schedule:

(a) any value of r determines a value of $\hat{K} - \bar{K}$
(b) this value will be greater the *lower* is r
(c) $\hat{K} - \bar{K} = 0$ for $r = r_0$

These conditions may be written formally as:

$$\begin{aligned} \hat{K} - \bar{K} &= f(r) \\ \frac{\partial(\hat{K} - \bar{K})}{\partial r} &< 0 \qquad (10.4) \\ \hat{K} - \bar{K} &= 0 \text{ (for } r = r_0) \end{aligned}$$

What would happen if $r > r_0$? Theoretically we should have $\hat{K} - \bar{K} < 0$ – which simply states that, if $r > r_0$, our businessman's optimal capital stock is *less* then he presently possesses.

[1]In the sense of profit-maximising.

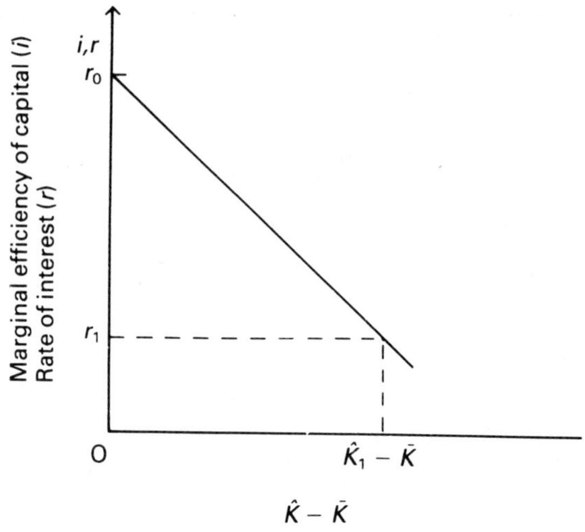

Figure 10.2 The marginal efficiency of capital schedule and the optimal capital stock

Hence it would be optimal to *decumulate* capital, whereas if $\hat{K} - K > 0$ it is optimal to *accumulate* capital. We shall confine ourselves to situations in which $\hat{K} - K \geqslant 0$: that is, situations depicted in Figure 10.2.

What determines the position of this schedule? Clearly all the elements which we have already found to enter into the estimation of the marginal efficiency of capital. In particular these are:

(a) the cost of capital assets
(b) the wage rate
(c) the state of technique
(d) the existing capital stock ($\bar{K}$)
(e) the state of expectations
(f) the degree of uncertainty attaching to (e)

How changes in these parameters of the schedule will shift it to the left or right should be clear from our earlier calculations. In the long run, of course, all are variables. It seems likely, however, that, over relatively short periods of time, shifts in the position of the schedule, if they occur, will be due mainly to changes in expectations and the uncertainty attaching to them. An increase in business optimism will shift the curve to the right; a leftward shift would occur if optimism declined. The reader should work out further possibilities for himself.

Conceptually, we can construct such a curve for each and every businessman and, by adding the individual values of $\hat{K} - \bar{K}$ for any given interest rate, obtain an aggregate curve for the private sector as a whole.

The resultant curve we define as the *marginal efficiency of investment schedule*. For formal completeness we redefine the marginal efficiency of capital as the marginal

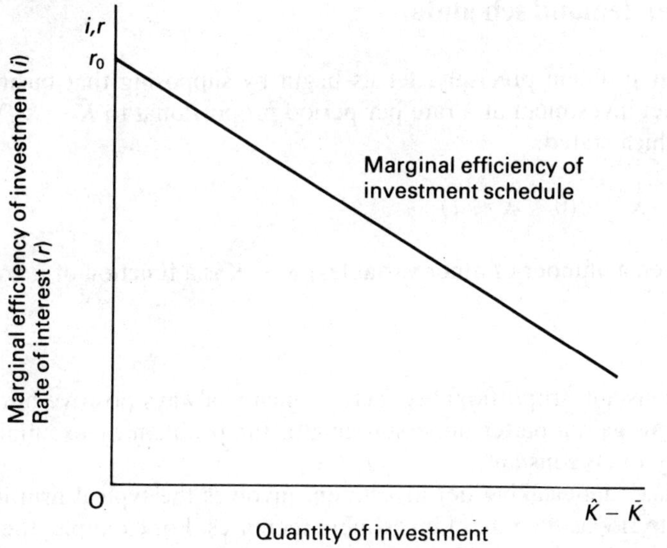

Figure 10.3 The marginal efficiency of investment schedule

efficiency of investment (MEI), Why do we do this? Simply because the quantity $\hat{K} - \bar{K}$ is the optimal amount of capital accumulation at any given interest rate. Since additions to the real capital stock are, by definition, real net investment, $\hat{K} - \bar{K}$ defines the optimum *quantity* of real net investment at any given value of r. For this reason the aggregate schedule, depicted in Figure 10.3, can properly be called the marginal efficiency of investment schedule.

In the opening section of this chapter we were careful to define $I_p \equiv$ real planned investment as a rate per period of time. The quantity $\hat{K} - \bar{K}$ does not enable us to determine the *rate* of real planned investment, for this depends on how *quickly* businessmen undertake expenditure to eliminate the gap between $\hat{K} - \bar{K}$. For example, if they planned to eliminate it within one quarter, the quarterly rate of net investment would be $\hat{K} - \bar{K}$. Alternatively, if they planned to eliminate it within a year the (average) quarterly rate would be:

$$\frac{\hat{K} - \bar{K}}{4}$$

In short, additional analysis is required to move from:

(a) the existence of a positive value of $\hat{K} - \bar{K}$ to
(b) a *rate* of real planned net investment (I_p)

All we can say at this moment is that I_p will be functionally related to $\hat{K} - \bar{K}$ and thus to r. We now seek, by analysis of the problems involved, to develop a relationship between I_p and r – given the values of certain other variables. The resultant schedule we shall call the *investment demand schedule*.

The investment demand schedule

Simply to fix our problem precisely, let us begin by supposing that businessmen always undertake real net investment at a rate per period proportional to $\hat{K} - \bar{K}$. We should then have a theory which stated:

$$I_p = (\hat{K} - \bar{K} \qquad (0 < \lambda \leqslant 1) \tag{10.5}$$

which, since (given a number of other variables) $\hat{K} - \bar{K}$ is a function of r, could be written:

$$I_p = \lambda f(r) \tag{10.6}$$

where λ is the constant proportionality factor which is always positive but cannot exceed unity. We can now gain a better understanding of the problem by examining why λ is, in practice, unlikely to be constant.

In the first place, undertaking net investment involves the typical firm in internal costs which are likely to rise as the rate of investment increases. For example, the higher the rate of investment, the more time the firm's executives will have to devote to the organisation and planning connected with it. To do this they have to be diverted from more and more important work connected with the firm's existing operations – a process which is certain to result in rising internal costs. Hence, unless $\hat{K} - \bar{K}$ is very small, we may reasonably expect λ to be less than 1. Moreover, as $\hat{K} - \bar{K}$ increases, we may, on this account, expect λ to decline.

So far, we have assumed that, whatever the rate at which net investment is undertaken, i.e., whatever the rate at which the capital goods industries are required to produce, the price of such goods (in terms of the output they will generate) is constant. This assumption, though convenient, is unrealistic. As the rate of net investment increases, we must expect the supply price of capital goods (relative to the price of their output) to rise. Hence, if we refer back to our formula for calculating the marginal efficiency of capital, we must expect the estimated rate of return per pound of investment to decline. Hence the return per pound on investment will tend to fall as the rate of investment increases for reasons which are external to the firm.

If we now incorporate these modifications into our marginal efficiency of investment schedule and (recalling that profit maximisation implies that businessmen will equate the MEI with r) plot r on the vertical axis and I_p on the horizontal, we obtain a curve we shall call the *investment demand schedule* (see Figure 10.4).

Note that because of the internal and external factors this curve is more steeply sloped than our original MEI schedule. Note also that it expresses the rate of real net investment (I_p) as a function of r and suggests that the slope of the schedule becomes steeper as r declines.

As we have constructed it, the curve reflects the following hypothesis:

1. $\hat{K} - \bar{K}$ is a function of r with $\partial(\hat{K} - \bar{K})/\partial r < 0$.
2. At r_0, $\hat{K} - \bar{K} = 0$; hence at r_0, I_p will be zero.
3. The supply price of capital assets (in terms of the prices of their output) rises as I_p increases.
4. The internal costs associated with I_p rise with I_p so that λ will be unity only if $\hat{K} - \bar{K}$ is small and will decline after $\hat{K} - \bar{K}$ reaches some critical value.

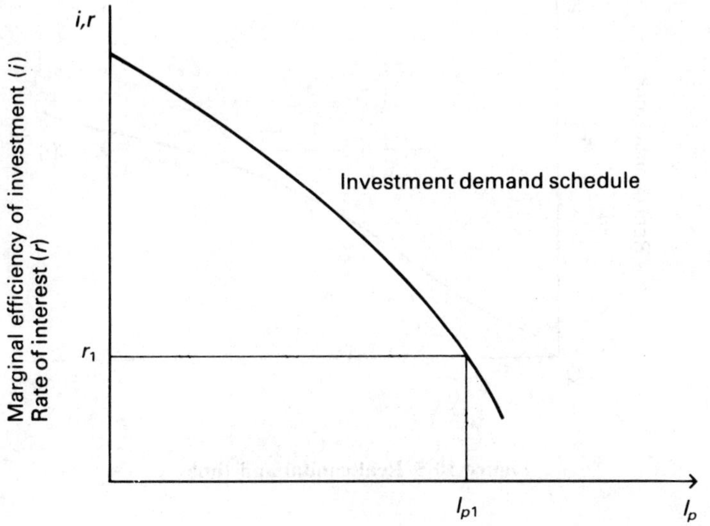

Figure 10.4 The investment demand schedule

Given this investment demand schedule we can now determine I_p for any given value of r. For example, at r_1 the rate of net investment is I_{p1}.

It may now be helpful if we bring together the elements of our theory. These are as follows:

1. The optimum capital *stock* ($\hat{K}$) is determined by the condition that the rate of interest is equal to the marginal efficiency of capital.
2. The optimum *quantity* of real net investment is determined by $\hat{K}$ and the existing quantity of real capital ($\hat{K}$).
3. The *rate* at which businessmen will plan to undertake net investment – eliminate the gap between $\hat{K}$ and $\bar{K}$ – depends upon:
   (a) the internal costs of net investment
   (b) the supply conditions of capital goods.

It follows that if we take as given the items 3a and 3b *and* the parameters of our marginal efficiency of investment schedule, we may write

$$I_p = f(r) \quad (\text{with } \frac{\partial I_p}{\partial r} < 0) \tag{10.6}$$

This theory is commonly simplified by saying that the rate of real planned net investment is determined by the rate of interest and the marginal efficiency of investment schedule.

Since the investment demand schedule depends upon all the parameters of the marginal efficiency of investment, it clearly incorporates the assumption of a given capital stock ($\bar{K}$). But net investment is simply the rate of increase of the capital stock. It appears, therefore, that we are seeking to determine the rate of increase in K on the assumption that K is constant at $\bar{K}$. This looks like an internal contradiction. Can we rationalise it?

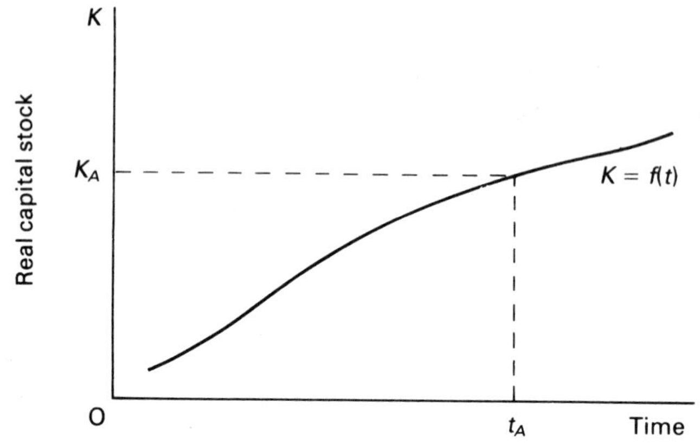

Figure 10.5 Real capital and time

There are two ways of doing this. The first, which is imprecise, consists in saying that, in the period of time in which we are interested, the rate of net investment makes so small an addition to the capital stock that we can neglect it – at least as a first approximation.

The second, which is precise, is to relate our procedure to that of the differential calculus. Suppose, for example, we described K, the real capital stock, as a function of time as depicted in Figure 10.5, which plots $K = f(t)$, where t is time.

Now, by definition, dK/dt is the rate of increase of the capital stock: that is, the rate of net investment. Graphically, it is also the slope of the curve. If we evaluate this slope at a point on the curve, say point A, we obtain the rate of net investment at a particular point in time (t_A) or, alternatively, at a particular value of $K = K_A$. Thus, for those who are familiar with the differential calculus – which is generally not necessary for comprehension of this book – I_p need only be identified with dK/dt for a rationalisation of our assumption that K is held constant at $\bar{K}$.

A final difficulty relates to the objection that, given r, sooner or later continuing net investment must eliminate the gap $\hat{K} - \bar{K}$. When this occurs, provided r is unaltered, net investment must cease. As a matter of observation, however, net investment is typically positive. Is there, then, some contradiction between our theory and observation?

There is no contradiction once we recall that, in the dynamic real world, the MEI schedule will typically be moving to the right because of expected increases in the demand for output and technical innovations. Thus, though our theory is essentially a capital *stock* adjustment theory, there is no presumption that we shall ever observe a situation in which, for all firms, $\hat{K} = \bar{K}$ and hence I_p is zero: that is, a situation in which the actual capital stock is precisely adjusted to the optimal capital stock for all firms in the economy.

The investment function

Our investment demand schedule is essentially a *two*-dimensional representation of a function which involves *more* independent variables than r. These variables are treated as parameters in constructing the MEI schedule. Can we now develop, from our earlier analysis, an investment function analogous to our consumption function?

An important parameter of the MEI schedule (and thus the investment demand schedule) was the state of business expectations. Essentially this refers to the demand for output which businessmen expect in the future. Since demand depends upon income, we might make our notion of expectations more precise by relating it to the income expected when the new capital goods begin to produce output. Let us call this Y^*.

Clearly a wide variety of factors will influence Y^*. Perhaps the most important, however, will be the present level of income (Y). On this assumption we might write our investment function provisionally as:

$$I_p = f_1(r, Y^*, u_{y^*}, \bar{K}) \tag{10.7}$$

where u_{y^*} is an index of the uncertainty attaching to the expectation Y^*.

Then, introducing the assumption that Y^* is a function of Y, we obtain:

$$I_p = f_2(r, Y, u_{y^*}, \bar{K}) \tag{10.8}$$

with

$$\frac{\partial I_p}{\partial r} < 0 \; ; \quad \frac{\partial I_p}{\partial Y} > 0 \; ; \quad \frac{\partial I_p}{\partial u_{y^*}} < 0 \; ; \quad \frac{\partial I_p}{\partial \bar{K}} < 0$$

In this relation the state of technique, the supply conditions for capital goods and the internal investment cost schedules of the individual firms are subsumed in the function itself.

The expression in 10.8 relates only to the rate of net investment. If we wish – as we usually do – to explain the rate of gross investment we recall:

$$\begin{aligned} I_{pg} &\equiv \text{rate of real planned gross investment} \\ &\equiv I_p + D = f_2(r, Y, u_{y^*}, \bar{K}) + D \end{aligned} \tag{10.9}$$

where D is real depreciation.

What explains depreciation? A simple hypothesis is that $D = \delta\bar{K}$ with $0 < \delta < 1$: that is, depreciation is a constant proportion of the existing capital stock. Since 10.7 already contains $\bar{K}$, we may now write:

$$I_{pg} = f_3(r, Y, \bar{K}, u_{y^*}) \tag{10.10}$$

Unfortunately, we can now say nothing definite regarding the sign of $\partial I_{pg}/\partial \bar{K}$ since it consists in two elements: the negative marginal response coefficient $\partial I_p/\partial \bar{K}$ and the positive marginal response coefficient $\partial D/\partial \bar{K}$ ($\equiv \delta$). Clearly their sum could be positive, negative or zero.

If we now set out a linear version of 10.8 – which in view of our earlier analysis of the investment demand schedule is not very plausible – we obtain:

$$I_{pg} = a_1 r + a_2 Y + (a_3 + \delta)\bar{K} + a_4 u_{y^*}. \tag{10.11}$$

with the theoretical expectation that a_1, a_3, $a_4 < 0$ and a_2, $\delta > 0$.

This is a simple formal representation of our basic theory of the rate of real planned gross investment.

The rate of interest and the cost of funds

Thus far we have identified the cost of borrowed funds to the firm with the rate of interest, which we have already defined as the rate of return on government bonds. This approximation obviously requires consideration since typically firms cannot borrow as cheaply as the UK government.

In addition we have implicitly assumed that each firm can borrow as much as it likes at the going rate of interest: that is, that the cost of funds to the firm does *not* rise as the amount borrowed increases. If this is not correct, the marginal cost of funds will exceed the average cost and this needs to be allowed for in our formulation.

Lending to the UK government is riskless in the sense that the nominal capital and interest are fully secured. Lending to any business, however, involves *some* risk. Any business may fail – through incompetence, dishonesty, or the occurrence of events which no reasonable degree of competence could have foreseen. Hence lenders will typically require from firms a premium over the interest rate to compensate them for assuming these risks. We may call this the lender's risk premium. Thus the cost of borrowing may be thought of as:

rate of interest *plus* a lender's risk premium

In general it is also likely to be the case that individual firms cannot borrow as much as they like at a constant cost. As firms borrow – and the debt/equity ratio rises – bond-holders tend to feel increasingly vulnerable in the face of any shortfall in profits. Hence they will supply additional funds only at higher rates. Thus the marginal cost of borrowing to the firm will differ from the average cost and must be regarded as the relevant concept in determining investment.

Accordingly, in so far as firms invest with borrowed funds, the rising average cost of borrowing will consist of the rate of interest (as defined) plus a rising lender's premium.

In practice, of course, some net investment is undertaken from firms' own saving in the form of undistributed profits. If the alternative to employing this net cash flow to finance net investment is for the firm to hold government bonds, then for the rate of net investment which this flow could finance, the rate of interest is the opportunity cost and is constant over the relevant range.

Taking all these considerations into account the determination of real planned net investment is shown on Figure 10.6, which superimposes the investment demand schedule on a schedule showing the marginal cost of borrowing.

On this slightly more complete formulation the rate of real planned investment is now determined by the condition:

$$\text{marginal efficiency of investment} = \text{marginal borrowing cost}$$

where the average cost of borrowing is equal to the rate of interest *plus* a lender's risk premium. That is, the rate of investment is I_{p1} determined by the intersection of the investment demand schedule and marginal cost of borrowing schedules at Z.

Since borrowers also assume risks, while we have made no mention of a borrower's risk premium (which clearly reduces the MEI associated with any given value of I_p), we have in Figure 10.6 emphasised that the investment demand schedule, as we have defined it,

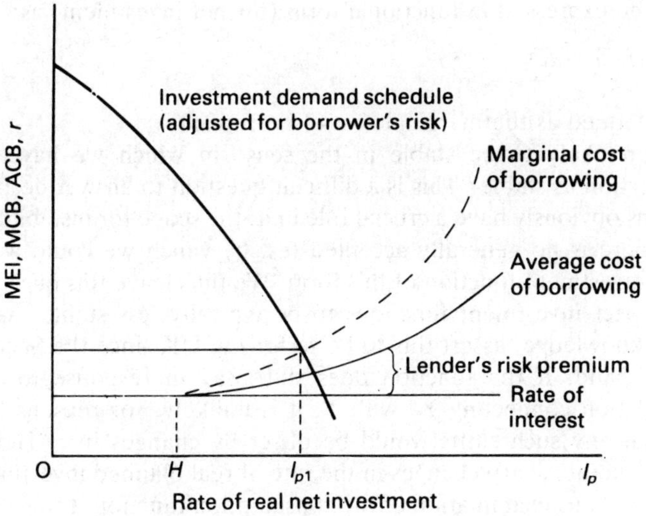

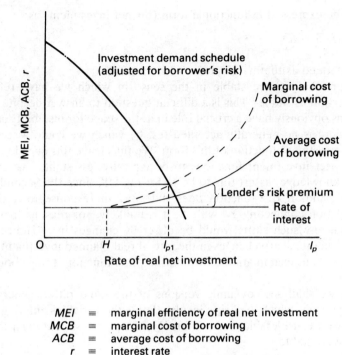

MEI ≡ marginal efficiency of real net investment
MCB ≡ marginal cost of borrowing
ACB ≡ average cost of borrowing
r ≡ interest rate
OH ≡ rate of undistributed profit

Figure 10.6 Real net investment and cost of borrowing

already allows for the risk arising from uncertainty of expectations. In our formal presentation in 10.9 we symbolised this adjustment by the inclusion of the variable u_{y^*} – defined as an index of uncertainty.

Some final problems

We can now summarise our rather simple theory of the determination of the rate of real planned investment. It consists of the following propositions:

1. The equilibrium rate of real planned investment is determined where the investment demand schedule (incorporating an allowance for borrower's risk) cuts the schedule of the marginal cost of borrowing.
2. The average cost of borrowing is the rate of interest *plus* an allowance for lender's risk which probably rises with the rate of borrowing.
3. The higher the marginal cost of borrowing, the lower, given the investment demand schedule, will be the equilibrium rate of real planned investment.

This theory can be expressed in functional form (for net investment) as:

$$I_p = f_2(Y, \tilde{r}, u_{y^*}, \bar{K}) \tag{10.8}$$

where $\tilde{r}$ is now defined as the marginal cost of borrowing.

Is this function likely to be stable in the sense in which we have referred to the consumption function as stable? This is a difficult question to answer despite the fact that, since expectations obviously have a crucial role in it, the scope for instability seems greater. Unfortunately there is no generally accepted test by which we could assert the relative instability of an investment function of this form. We thus leave this question unanswered. Although we expect investment functions to be typically less stable, we cannot, in the present state of knowledge, assert this to be so for the UK since the Second World War.

On the other hand, if the function does shift, say in response to a change in the expectational relation connecting Y^* with Y, it is unlikely, for reasons that will become clearer later, that any such shifts would be offset by changes in r. Hence shifts in the function would generate sharp changes in the rate of real planned investment which, as we know from our previous examination of the consumption function, bring about 'multiplied' changes in real income.

Moreover, as we shall see, dynamic versions of the same rather general investment hypothesis, i.e. versions which explicitly involve dating the variables entering the function, are compatible with considerable fluctuations in real net investment even if the dynamic function is relatively stable.

Can we make our investment function operational in the way we made our earlier consumption hypothesis operational? In its linear version, for gross investment, we wrote:

$$I_{pg} = a_1 r + a_2 Y + (a_3 + \delta)\bar{K} + a_4 u_{y^*} \tag{10.11}$$

Y is directly observable and we can use estimates of K (which exist) at the beginning of any period as a measure of $\bar{K}$. Difficulty arises, however, with u_{y^*} and with $\tilde{r}$, which we now know should replace r. No obvious measure of u_{y^*} can be defined or approximated. We therefore truncate our theory, replace r by $\tilde{r}$, and concentrate upon

$$I_{pg} = a_1\tilde{r} + a_2 Y + (a_3 + \delta)K_{-1},$$

where $K_{-1} \equiv$ the real capital stock at the end of the previous period, and, in particular, concentrate upon the meaning of $\tilde{r}$.

Strictly $\tilde{r}$ is the marginal cost of borrowing. Typically we have no means of measuring this, so we are generally content to use the average cost of borrowing and measure this by, say, the rate of return on firms' debentures.

This use of the average rate as a proxy for the marginal will involve an error; but a more important source of error may arise from the use of a *nominal* rate rather than a *real* rate. To see the distinction – and its importance – consider the following example.

Suppose today (at time t) we lend £100 for one year on the promise of £106 at the end of the period. The nominal rate of interest (r) is 6 per cent. In real terms, however, the gain from the transaction appear thus:

$$\frac{£106}{p(t+1)} - \frac{£100}{p(t)} = £100\left[\frac{1+r}{p(t+1)} - \frac{1}{p(t)}\right]$$

where:

$p(t) \equiv$ price level ruling now

$p(t+1) \equiv$ price level *expected* to rule at the time of repayment

Assume:

$$p(t + 1) = p(t)[1 + \alpha]$$

where $\alpha \equiv$ *expected* percentage price change. Therefore, the real rate of return (r_r) is (putting $p(t) = 1$) given by:

$$r_r = \frac{1 + r}{1 + \alpha} - 1 = \frac{r - \alpha}{1 + \alpha}$$

Hence:

$$r_r - r = \frac{r - \alpha}{1 + \alpha} - r = \frac{-\alpha - \alpha r}{1 + \alpha}$$

which is the measure of the difference between the real rate (r_r) and the nominal rate (r) valued at the prices of period $t + 1$. Revaluing in terms of prices at time t gives:

$$r_r - r = - \alpha - \alpha r$$

whence:

$$r_r = r - \alpha - \alpha r$$

Typically the term in αr is neglected, since for plausible values of α and r it is small compared with either.[1] Hence the usual approximation is:

$$r_r \approx r - \alpha$$

where $\alpha \equiv$ expected percentage change in prices. The obvious conclusion is that we must distinguish between nominal and real rates whenever, as is currently the case, there is a general expectation of price changes.

We have no theory to explain satisfactorily how people form their expectations concerning $1/p \times dp/dt$ – that is, select α. This being so, we cannot exclude the possibility that r and r_r may not always move together in the relatively short run. Hence it may matter very much whether we interpret $\tilde{r}$ in equation 10.11 as appropriately measured by:

(a) the debenture rate (a nominal rate)
(b) the dividend yield on equities (a rough proxy for r_r)
(c) a weighted average of the two (which is an increasingly common proceeding)

Although we would expect the real rather than the nominal rate to be relevant, much empirical work has employed a nominal rate. But clearly this is an important issue requiring further investigation.

Given a definition of $\tilde{r}$, equation 10.11 is now operational and we may – by appropriate econometric means – hope to estimate a_1, a_2 and $a_3 + \delta$. From our estimate of a_2 ($\equiv \partial I_p/\partial \tilde{r}$) we can obtain an estimate of:

$$\frac{\partial I_p}{\partial \tilde{r}} \frac{\tilde{r}}{I_p} \equiv \text{the borrowing cost elasticity of gross investment}$$

Considerable controversy has been waged over this partial elasticity and much early work yielded very low estimates. Later studies suggest, however, a value in the neighbourhood of −0.4. This is certainly not a negligible elasticity and clearly has important implications, if it

[1]In our example, $r = 0.06$. Suppose $\alpha \equiv$ the expected rate of inflation = 5 per cent, i.e. $\alpha = 0.05$. Then $\alpha r = 0.06 \times 0.05 = 0.003$, which is small compared with r or α.

is correct, regarding the possibility of influencing I_p through variations in the cost of borrowing.

Finally, a word of warning to the reader. In many formal expositions later in this book we shall continue, in the interests of pedagogic simplicity, to make use of investment functions written:

$$I_p = f(r)$$

or in more explicit linear form:

$$I_p = Z + hr \quad (h < 0)$$

where r denotes that cost of borrowing. Since our original function, in linear form, would have been written:

$$I_p = a_1 r + a_2 Y^* + a_3 \bar{K} + a_4 u_{y^*}$$

we must have:

$$\begin{aligned} Z &= a_2 Y^* + a_3 \bar{K} + a_4 u_{y^*} \\ h &= a_1 \end{aligned}$$

Hence, for simplicity, treating Z as constant involves treating Y^* as constant. This means, in models in which we seek to determine Y, that we are ignoring the (empirically plausible) link between Y and Y^* – otherwise changes in Y, by changing Y^*, would change Z.

This procedure is followed *only* to simplify exposition. It would readily be possible to work with:

$$I_p = Z' + a_1 r + a_2 Y$$

with:

$$Z' \equiv a_3 \bar{K} + a_4 u_{y^*}$$

but the gain in generality does not seem sufficient compensation, in elementary comparative statics, to justify the resulting complication.

Additionally, for most purposes, we shall continue to interpret r as the *nominal* interest rate on long-term government bonds. The logical justification for this is that, until Chapter 21 we present no account of the theory of inflation as an essentially dynamic process – and confine ourselves in the main to constructing a *static* model of the macroeconomic system. This is, of course, a simplification for pedagogic purposes which imposes a limitation upon our analysis. This limitation, however, may not be too serious if we can assume that changes in the nominal interest rate brought about by government action (as explained in Chapters 11, 15 and 16) do not, over a period such as, say, one year, significantly change α. For if this is so, changes in the nominal rate ($\equiv r$) will involve equivalent changes in the real rate (r_r).

Questions and exercises

1. If the market rate of interest is 5 per cent, what is the present value of the following two prospects?

	Return at end of Year 1	Return at end of Year 2
Prospect 1	£105	£110.25
Prospect 2	£110.25	£105

Which would you prefer? Would you purchase either at £200? Give your reasons. Why are the present values not identical?

2. From the following data calculate, by trial and error, the marginal efficiency of capital. Would you invest if the market rate of interest (= cost of borrowing) was 7 per cent?

Year	*Capital cost* £	*Estimated return* £
1	10,000	2,800
2		2,800
3		2,800
4		2,800

At the end of year 4 the asset is expected to have a disposal value of £990.

3. What do you think would happen to the marginal efficiency of investment schedule if a threat of war arose in Europe? Why?

4. You are asked to construct an investment hypothesis which gives the rate of real planned investment in fixed capital as a function of observable quantities. What function would you propose, and why? What variables, other than those discussed in the text, would you include in the function?

5. From the national income estimates of the UK obtain quarterly figures for real gross private investment in manufacturing for the years 1957–80 and plot them on a graph measuring (i) the quarterly rate of investment on the vertical axis, and (ii) time on the horizontal axis.

   Do these observations tend to support our judgement that the marginal efficiency of investment schedule is likely to be volatile? How would you explain the observed fluctuations in investment in fixed capital?

6. Perform the same exercise for investment in stocks. Are there any special theoretical difficulties in interpreting this series?

7. Using the data of question 2 assume that a company tax of £0.1 in the pound is levied on the net annual return *after* charging depreciation. Recalculate the marginal efficiency of capital. Is the investment still worth while if the cost of borrowing is 7 per cent? Use your answer to show the effect on the marginal efficiency of investment schedule of (i) raising the rate (per pound) of taxation on company profits, and (ii) increasing the tax allowance for depreciation.

8. Suppose that the relationship between planned investment and the rate of interest is given by:

   $$I_p = Z - gr$$

   where $Z = 1{,}000$, $-g = \partial I_p/\partial r = -10$.

   Plot the resulting *investment function* for all integral values of r up to 20 per cent.

   If the propensity to consume schedule is given by:

   $$C_p = A + bY$$

where $A = 100$ and $b \equiv \partial C_p/\partial Y = 0.8$,

then:

$$\text{aggregate demand} \equiv C_p + I_p = A + bY + Z - gr.$$

In equilibrium we require, assuming planned total output to be equal:

$$Y = A + bY + Z - gr$$

Find:

(a) all the pairs of values of Y, r which satisfy this equation
(b) plot the resulting values on a graph with r on the vertical axis and Y on the horizontal
(c) interpret the curve traced out by these pairs of values

Show:

(d) which way the curve would move if
    (i) business expectations became more optimistic
    (ii) incomes were redistributed from 'rich' to 'poor'
(e) interpret these changes in terms of the equations describing the investment and consumption hypotheses.

9. Using the investment function of question 8 find the *interest elasticity of investment* when $r = 10$ per cent and $r = 4$ per cent. At what rate of interest will the elasticity be -1?
   Why is the elasticity not a constant? Is the marginal response coefficient $\partial I_p/\partial r$ a constant? What can you recall about the elasticity of any straight-line schedule?

10. In the text we proceed on the assumption of constant prices. What sense (if any) do you therefore find in the explanation of the downward slope of the investment demand schedule? What is meant by a 'rise in the price of capital goods'?

11. Superimpose on your graph for question 5 a second graph plotting quarterly values for the rate of interest (represented by the rate of return on Consols). Can you reconcile your observations with the theory of this chapter? What are your difficulties?

12. An alternative simple investment hypothesis could be written:

$$I_p = Z + g\pi + h\mu$$

where

$\pi \equiv$ ruling percentage rate of profits
$\mu \equiv$ rate of interest on debentures
$Z \equiv$ autonomous real net investment

putting:

$$g \equiv \frac{\partial I_p}{\partial \pi} = 100 \quad \text{and} \quad h \equiv \frac{\partial I_p}{\partial \mu} = -200$$

Complete the following table and explain the values of I_p. How far is the behaviour of I_p explained by movements *along* the function and how far by *shifts* in its position?

Period	Observed values		
	I_p	π	μ
1	1,000	12	4
2	1,000	12	4
3	1,200	14	5
4	1,400	16	8
5	1,900	20	8
6	1,500	18	8
7	1,100	15	8
8	1,100	12	6
9	1,100	12	6
10	1,200	10	4

Clearly π enters the function as a proxy for the expected rate of profits. Is this, in your view, compatible with the data?

13. Consider the view that the theory of investment put forward in this chapter fails because its central hypothesis is that investment behaviour is rational – that is, dictated by the aim to maximise profits.

14. Examine critically the suggestion that the dividend yield on equities is a good proxy for the 'real' rate of interest.

15. Construct a graph of (i) the dividend yield on equities, and (ii) the rate of return on Consols using annual data for 1955–80. How do you explain the changing relations between the yields?

Suggested reading

Bank of England, 'Trends in Company Profitability', *BEQB* (March 1976).

Bank of England, 'The Cost of Capital, Finance and Investment', *BEQB* (June 1976). See also articles in June 1977 through to 1982.

J. C. R. Dow, *The Management of the British Economy, 1945–1960* (Cambridge University Press, 1964) ch. 11.

*M. Evans, *Macroeconomic Activity* (Harper & Row, 1969) chs 4, 5.

C. J. Hawkins and D. W. Pearce, *Capital Investment Appraisal* (Macmillan, 1971).

*P. N. Junankar, *Investment: Theories and Evidence* (Macmillan, 1972).

J. M. Keynes, *The General Theory of Employment, Interest and Money* (Macmillan, 1936) chs 11, 12.

A. R. Nobay, 'Short-term Forecasting of Housing Investment', *NIESR Review*, no. 41 (August 1967).

A. R. Nobay, 'Forecasting Manufacturing Investment', *NIESR Review*, no. 52 (May 1970).

D. Savage, 'Interpreting the Investment Intentions Data', *NIESR Review*, no. 75 (August 1975).

*More advanced references.

Chapter 11

Liquidity Preference and the Theory of Interest

In Chapter 10 we developed a theory of investment and found that, given (i) the marginal efficiency of capital schedule adjusted for borrower's risk, and (ii) the cost of borrowing, we could determine the equilibrium rate of real planned investment. Given the rate of real planned investment (determined in this way) we could then, from the schedule of the propensity to consume (itself derived from the consumption function) determine the equilibrium level of output and employment from the condition that, in equilibrium, planned saving must be equal to planned investment.

Moreover our analysis of the determinants of investment – in particular of the marginal efficiency of capital schedule – showed that the rate of real planned investment depended crucially upon (i) business expectations, and (ii) business uncertainty. Hence, even in the short run, investment seemed likely to fluctuate sharply (thus bringing about fluctuations in the equilibrium levels of output and employment) since both business expectations and uncertainty were liable to change in response to the 'state of the news'.

Our theory has thus become closer to completion, for we are now able to abandon the artificial assumption that the rate of real planned investment is determined by some hypothetical (and mythical) planning authority.

In formal terms our theory now stands as follows:

$$Y = C_p + I_p \tag{11.1}$$
$$C_p = f(Y, r) \tag{11.2}$$
$$I_p = f(r) \tag{11.3}$$

We thus have three equations to determine the four unknown variables Y, C_p, I_p and r. Such a system cannot give us a solution. This reflects the fact that, so far, we have no theory to explain the determination of the rate of interest. To provide a theory of interest determination is the task of this chapter.

Assumptions and definitions

To simplify our exposition we need to speak of 'the rate of interest'. A glance at the financial page of any reputable paper, however, make it clear that there is not one rate of interest but many. Accordingly our first assumption is that:

> all rates of interest in the market move together, so that any one rate can stand as an index of all rates

On this assumption we then continue to define *the* rate of interest as:

> the rate of return per cent per annum obtainable in the market on long-term government securities

Defined in this way the rate of interest must be carefully distinguished from the *coupon rate* on long-term government securities. An example should make this distinction clear.

In 1982, looking in the *Financial Times*, we find the following information:

	Price	Rate of interest per cent
8¾ per cent Treasury Stock 1997	£83	11.10

This tells us that:

(a) the market price of £100 nominal value of 8¾ per cent Treasury Stock is £83,
(b) at this price the rate of interest obtainable until 1997 – when the government will repay £100 – is 11.10 per cent,
(c) the *coupon rate* is 8¾ per cent

The method of calculation is essentially the same as that we have already employed to find the 'marginal efficiency of real capital assets'. Each year that we hold £100 *nominal* of this security we receive as income the *coupon rate* on the *nominal* value of the security:

$$8.75 \times £100 = £8.75$$

In 1997 we shall be repaid in full: that is, the government will redeem its bond by paying us £100 in cash. We thus have (in 1982) an asset with:

(a) a price of £83
(b) a life of fifteen years
(c) fourteen annual returns of £8.75
(d) one return (the last) of £108.75.

We find the rate of interest r from the formula:[1]

$$S = \frac{Q_1}{(1 + r)} + \frac{Q_2}{(1 + r)^2} + \ldots + \frac{Q_n}{(1 + r)^n}$$

or:

$$£83 = \frac{£8.75}{(1 + r)} + \frac{£8.75}{(1 + r)^2} + \ldots + \frac{£8.75}{(1 + r)^{13}} + \frac{£108.75}{(1 + r)^{14}}$$

[1]In practice, since interest is paid half-yearly, this formula is only an approximation.

We do not need to go to the trouble of calculating r since the *Financial Times* has already done so. The formula reminds us, however, that (i) the *coupon rate* (8¾ per cent) is *not* the rate of interest, and (ii) the rate of interest (on any bond) is *lower* the *higher* is the *market price* of the bond.

In short, the rate of interest depends upon three factors:

(a) the price of the bond
(b) the coupon yield
(c) the length of time which must elapse before the bond is redeemed

and the rate of interest will be *lower* the *higher* is the price of bonds.

In the discussion which follows we shall take the last two factors as given. Hence the rate of interest will be determined simply by the price of bonds and is inversely related to it.

We now know not only what we *mean* by the rate of interest but also *how to calculate it*. In the theory we shall shortly develop to explain the determination of the rate of interest (i.e. bond prices) we need to make use of a second concept. This is the *quantity of money*. We *define* this to be:

> the quantity (measured in pounds and pence) of *legal tender notes and coin* and *demand deposits with the commercial banks* in the possession of the *non-bank public*.[1]

Precisely *why* we use this definition, and *how* the *quantity of money* so defined gets determined, we shall explain later. Throughout this chapter we assume, for simplicity, that the *quantity of money* – often called the *money supply* – is fixed and invariant with respect to all other variables in the system. Readers are also asked to notice that, *unlike* consumption, saving and investment, the money supply is a *stock* variable. On our present assumption it is also an *exogenous* variable independent of every other variable in the system.

An outline of the liquidity preference theory of interest

The first problem which arises in developing any interest theory is why is interest paid at all? At first sight it seems natural to answer that interest is the reward for saving. A moment's reflection shows that this view is untenable. Saving is the act of refraining from consumption. If an individual saves (i.e. refrains from consumption) *and holds his accumulated savings in the form of money* (say as notes and coin) he receives no interest. Interest is only received if the saver is prepared to *hold his accumulated savings in the form of bonds*.[2] This tells us two things: first, interest is paid to induce wealth-owners to hold their accumulated wealth in the form of bonds rather than money; hence, second, the determination of the rate of interest is intimately connected with the decisions of wealth-owners as to how to hold their wealth – or, more precisely, how they should allocate their wealth between money (which provides no interest) and bonds (which do).

Why is an inducement necessary to persuade wealth-owners to hold their assets in the form of bonds rather than money?

[1]This definition corresponds closely with what is called M_1 or 'narrow money'. For details consult the *Bank of England Quarterly Bulletin*.

[2]Bonds stand here for all interest-bearing financial assets.

As an asset money has a number of obvious attractions. These are:

1. It is *perfectly liquid* in the sense that it can readily be converted into anything (goods or service) which is sold on a market.
2. It can be held, either as legal tender or better still as demand deposits, without incurring either
   (a) significant storage costs *or*
   (b) risks of loss.
3. If *the price level is constant* (as we are at present assuming) money is an asset which does not deteriorate over time.

Hence to hold accumulated wealth in the form of money is to obtain a subjective *convenience yield* (due to (1) and (3) above) at virtually zero costs (due to (2)).

To sacrifice this convenience yield wealth-owners must be offered an inducement. This inducement is the rate of interest.

Approaching the problem in this way we can think of the rate of interest as the price of money: for (i) *interest* is what wealth-owners must *forgo* if they wish to hold *wealth* in the form of *money* rather than bonds; (ii) *interest* is what an individual who wishes to hold money must *pay* to some other individual to induce him or her to *part with it*.

If the rate of interest is the price of money, how is it determined? Economists are accustomed to argue that equilibrium prices are determined by the equality of demand and supply. There is a simple analogy here with our theory of income determination. In this we argued that the equilibrium level of income was determined by the equality of aggregate demand and aggregate supply. In a commodity market we argue that the equilibrium *price* is determined by the equality of planned purchases (demand) and planned sales (supply). Putting the interest problem in these terms we may say that:

> *the rate of interest is the price which equates the community's planned money holdings (demand for money) with the quantity of money (supply of money) in existence*

To illustrate this argument consider the following example.

Suppose we construct a schedule showing the quantity of money the community will *plan* to hold at any given rate of interest. We assume (what we shall later defend and elaborate) that the quantity of *planned* money holdings *is less the higher is the rate of interest*. Formally we have the *general* proposition:

$$M_p^D = f(r) \quad \text{and} \quad \frac{\partial M_p^D}{\partial r} < 0 \tag{11.4}$$

and the *specific* proposition:

$$M_p^D = R + qr \qquad M_p^D = £1{,}000\text{m} - £100\text{m}\ r \tag{11.5}$$

where:

$$M_p^D \equiv \text{planned money holdings}$$
$$r \equiv \text{rate of interest}$$
$$q \equiv \frac{\partial M_p^D}{\partial r} \equiv -\ £100\text{m}$$

We plot the curve defined by 11.5 as the *LL* schedule of Figure 11.1.

For equilibrium in the money market – that is, for the rate of interest to be in equilibrium – we require:

$$M_p^D = M_p{}^S \tag{11.6}$$

which is simply the statement that *planned* holdings must equal *planned* supplies.

We assume that *actual* supplies (M_A^S) = M_p^S. That is, whoever, (which we have yet to explain) *plans* the supply of money always carries out his plans. Since we have already assumed that the quantity supplied is fixed (say equal to M_0) we have:

$$M_p^S = M_A^S \tag{11.7}$$

$$M_A^S = M_0 \quad (M_0 = £600\text{m}) \tag{11.8}$$

Hence equilibrium requires:

$$M_p^D = M_0$$

To illustrate this we construct a line *SS* on Figure 11.1 at a distance along the horizontal axis equal to £600m. This line is vertical, reflecting the assumption that M_p^S *is independent of r.*

Equilibrium is determined where the LL curve cuts the SS curve. At this point the rate of interest is 4 per cent and the planned money holdings are £600m, exactly equal to actual money supplies. All actual and planned magnitudes coincide.

Suppose the rate of interest was not 4 per cent but 3 per cent. Then, from 11.1 we should have:

$$M_p^D = £700\text{m}$$

This is greater than M_p^S. Planned holdings in short *exceed* planned supplies. Hence some persons, *who hold less money than they plan*, offer bonds for sale. Hence bond prices *fall* and the *interest rate rises*. The rise in the interest rate reduces M_p^D until, when it has reached 4 per cent, the demand for money equals the supply.

This example can easily be reversed for an initial interest rate greater than 4 per cent.

Taken together the two examples show that, as we have drawn Figure 11.1, the money market is *stable* and that there is a simple explanation of how the rate of interest reaches its equilibrium level.

Suppose the *LL* curve *shifts* so that planned money holdings *are greater at each interest rate* (i.e. the demand for money increases). We have a new curve *L'L'* and a new equilibrium rate of interest, 8 per cent. How do we get it? An increased demand for money means that some persons who at 4 per cent *were* happy to hold bonds *now* wish to hold money. They offer bonds for sale. Bond prices *fall*. The rate of interest *rises* until, at the new rate of 8 per cent, we have once again:

$$M_p^D = M_A^S$$

planned money holdings = actual (= planned) money supplies

Notice that, unless M_A^S *changes*, the community *cannot* hold more (or less) money than £600m. *All that it can determine is the price at which it will hold the given supply.*

The demand for money (represented by *LL* and *L'L'*) depends, among other things, on wealth-owners' preferences for holding accumulated wealth in the form of money. This, for reasons which should be obvious, we call 'liquidity preference'. Hence the essentials of what is called the liquidity preference theory of interest can be summarised as follows:

1. Interest is paid to induce persons to sacrifice the convenience of holding wealth in liquid form: that is, to overcome liquidity preference.
2. The determination of the rate of interest is thus bound up with decisions of wealth-owners as to how to distribute their assets between money and bonds.
3. The rate of interest is the price of opportunity cost of holding money.
4. It is determined by the relationship between the demand for money (planned money holdings) and the supply of money (planned quantity of money supply).
5. The greater (smaller) is the demand for money then, with a given money supply, the higher (lower) is the equilibrium rate of interest.
6. The greater (smaller) is the money supply then, with any given demand for money, the lower (higher) is the rate of interest.
7. The higher (lower) is the price of bonds, the lower (higher) is the rate of interest.

These propositions should be carefully studied. We now seek to develop this skeletal interest theory by examining, in greater detail, the determinants of the demand for money – that is, the *LL* curve of Figure 11.1.

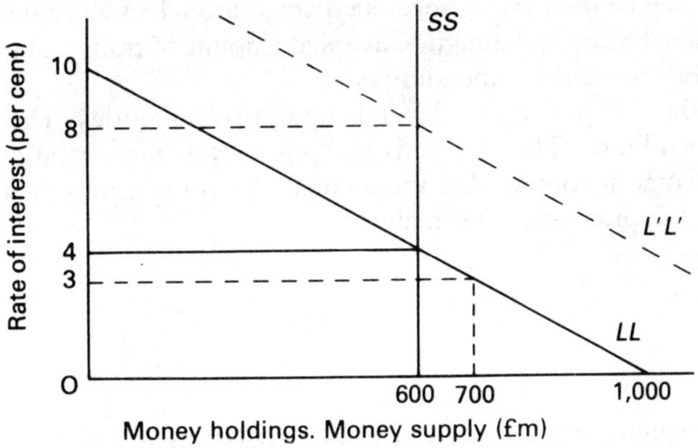

Figure 11.1 The rate of interest and the demand for and supply of money

The four demands for money

To analyse the demand for money we break it down into four components:

1. The *transactions demand.*
2. The *precautionary demand.*
3. The *asset demand.*
4. The *speculative demand.*

Aggregated together these constitute the total demand for money. We begin with the *transactions demand.*

Transactions demand

Households and enterprises are continually receiving money and making money payments. A certain money holding is, on average, required over any period of time, to avoid the difficulties which can arise from running completely out of money and thus being unable to make necessary payments. How much is required depends upon (i) the value of receipts and payments in the period, (ii) the time correspondence btween receipts and payments. To see this, picture an individual whose annual income is £365 and who spends it all at the regular rate of £1 per day.

If this income is received at the rate of £1 per day the average balance over the year would be 50 pence. If, alternatively, income was received as a single payment on 1 January the average balance would be £182.50. In practice some incomes are received daily, some weekly, some monthly, some quarterly, some half-yearly and some at varying intervals throughout the year. However, in modern financially developed communities the ways in which most people receive their incomes change only very slowly. *There is, in short, an institutional pattern of income receipts which, though it does change, can in a short-run analysis such as ours be taken as given and invariant.*

In the same way conventions exist regarding a whole host of payments from rent, building society repayments and car licence fees to tradespeople's accounts.

We may thus argue that where the time correspondence pattern of receipts and expenditures is determined by a developed institutional environment, households and enterprises will need a certain minimum average amount of transaction balances to finance any given level of *foreseeable* expenditures.

The value of these expenditures depends upon two quantities. The first is the planned level of *real* expenditure. The second is the price level. Since real expenditure depends upon the real income it follows that the demand for transactions balances depends upon real income and the price level. Formally:

$$M_p^D\ _{\text{(transactions)}} = f(Y, p) \qquad (11.9)$$

where:

$M_p^D \equiv$ planned holdings of transactions balances
$Y \equiv$ real income (= output)
$p \equiv$ price of a unit of output

and both marginal response coefficients are positive, that is:

$$\frac{\partial M^D}{\partial Y} \text{ and } \frac{\partial M^D}{\partial p} > 0$$

What form is this function likely to take? If money income is zero it is reasonable, as a first approximation, to expect the transactions demand to be zero. In addition we have, at this stage, developed no theory to suggest that, as income increases, the transactions demand will increase other than proportionately. A plausible first approximation would thus be a linear and proportional relationship between transactions demand and money income of the form:

$$M_p^D\ _{\text{(transactions)}} = KYp \qquad (11.10)$$

or, in numerical form:

$$M_p^D\ _{\text{(transactions)}} = 0.15\ Yp \qquad (11.10n)$$

with $K = 0.15$.

At the moment we are taking the price level p as given and invariant. Hence any change in Y will bring about an equal proportionate change in Yp – which is money income. Moreover, since p is constant, money income can change only if Y – real income – changes. Hence we can, for the time being, simplify 11.10 by writing:

$$M_p^D{}_{\text{(transactions)}} = KY \text{ (with } p \text{ given and taken equal to unity)} \qquad (11.10^*)$$

where K is the planned ratio of transactions balances to real income at the given constant price level $p = 1$. To give a numerical illustration we write:

$$M_p^D{}_{\text{(transactions)}} = 0.15Y \text{ (with } p = 1) \qquad (11.10\text{n})$$

The demand curve for transactions balances is now depicted in Figure 11.2 as the L_r function. Its parameters are:

(a) institutional arrangements regarding receipts and payments
(b) the given level of prices

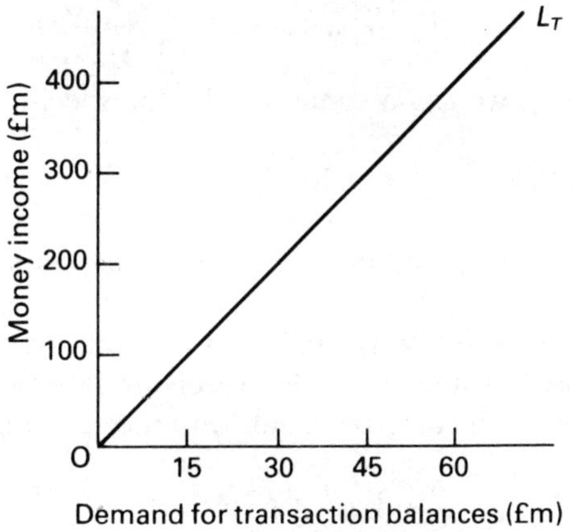

Figure 11.2 The transactions demand for money holdings

Precautionary demands

Not all income receipts or payments can be *foreseen with certainty*. Hence, in practice, households and enterprises will need to hold rather more than the minimum amount of transaction balances to guard against the risks arising out of the uncertainty of future receipts and payments. Consider, for example, a sales representative setting out to drive from London to Glasgow to negotiate an important contract. He calculates his expenditure on petrol, oil, food, drink and accommodation and, in accordance with equation 11.10, sets off with the minimum amount of transaction balances necessary to finance these foreseeable expenditures. En route his car breaks down and he has to pay a garage £20 for repairs.

He must now either (i) go without food, drink or accommodation and/or (ii) incur the expense and delay of telephoning his London bank for funds. If he does (i) he will suffer discomfort. If he does (ii) he may lose his contract and suffer serious loss. Had he started on his journey with sufficient *precautionary* balances over and above his *minimum transactions* requirements, he could have avoided both.

It is easy to see that this illustration applies with particular force to enterprises who may suffer severe losses due to an *unforeseen* shortage of money holdings arising from the need to make an unforeseen payment or the unforeseen postponement of an expected receipt.

The demand for *precautionary* balances is thus readily explicable in terms of uncertainty about the timing of future expenditures and receipts and their expected values. We thus regard this demand as a function of real income, the price level and uncertainty of this particular type. Formally, again taking p as given:

$$M_p^D\ _{\text{(precautionary)}} = f(Y,\ u_y) \tag{11.11}$$

where u_y is an index of uncertainty regarding future receipts and payments.

This demand is now added to the transactions demand to get what is called the *demand for active balances*. Thus:

$$M_p^D\ _{\text{(active)}} \equiv M_p^D\ _{\text{(transactions)}} + M_p^D\ _{\text{(precautionary)}} = \text{f}(Y,\ u_y) \tag{11.12}$$

which, *for a given value of* u_y, we can assume to take the specific form:

$$M_p^D\ _{\text{(active)}} = k'Y \text{ or } M_p^D\ _{\text{(active)}} = 0.20Y \tag{11.13}$$

again taking $p \equiv$ price level $= 1$, and to be represented diagrammatically in Figure 11.3 as the L_1 function.

This curve, the demand curve for active balances, we call the L_1 function. Its position depends upon (i) institutional arrangements for receiving income and making payments, (ii) uncertainty regarding future income payments and receipts, and (iii) the given level of prices.

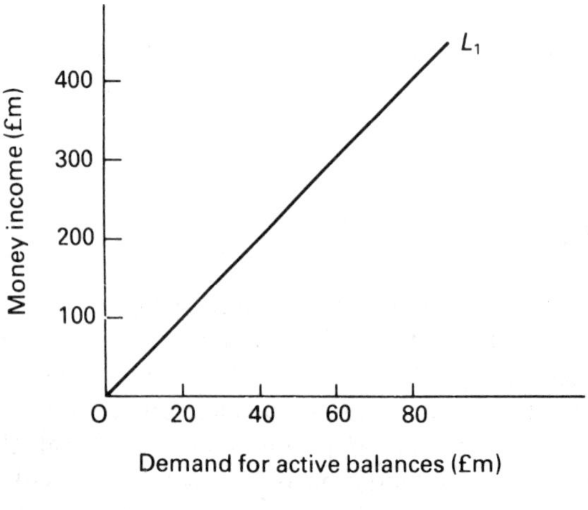

Figure 11.3 The demand curve for active balances

The demand and idle balances: asset demand

Some households and enterprises will plan to hold money in excess of their planned holdings of active balances. These additional balances we call *idle*. Hence in addition to the demand for active balances (analysed above) there is a demand for idle balances which requires analysis. To facilitate this analysis we divide idle balances into two classes: *asset* balances and *speculative* balances. The three concepts are related by the identity:

$$M^D_{\text{idle}} \equiv M^D_{\text{asset}} + M^D_{\text{speculative}}$$

Consider now the demand for asset balances. This is related to money's ability to act as a store of wealth. Money, to put the same point rather differently, *is one form of asset in which an individual may hold his accumulated savings (wealth)*. The demand for asset balances is thus related to an individual's capital account and reflects what is called a *portfolio decision*: that is, a decision regarding the assets over which an individual chooses to distribute his accumulated savings.

In the simple macroeconomic model we are constructing there are, by assumption, only three forms of asset: money, bonds and goods. In our examination of the consumption and investment functions we have already discussed the factors influencing planned expenditure on goods. Hence the demand for idle balances (in general) and asset balances (in particular) is concerned essentially with the decision as to how to distribute a given value of accumulated savings (wealth) over money and bonds: that is, the portfolio decision. In what circumstances, then, will an individual plan to hold some part of his accumulated savings in the form of idle balances: that is, hold money as part of his chosen portfolio?

Suppose the rate of interest on bonds is 4 per cent and is expected to remain 4 per cent for ever. Suppose further, though this is in practice impossible, that the expectation that 4 per cent will remain the rate of interest is held with complete certainty. In these circumstances no individual will wish to hold idle balances since, by holding bonds rather than money, he can obtain 4 per cent per annum on his accumulated savings *without risk*. Admittedly converting money into bonds or bonds into money costs something in time, trouble and brokerage fees. It is therefore possible that some persons whose accumulated savings are small or who plan to dissave in the near future many consider it not worth while to purchase bonds. But if we neglect these cases, which are probably rather rare and quantitatively unimportant, our general proposition holds. In the postulated circumstances no individual wealth-owner would wish to hold any part of his wealth in money, for money earns no interest and bonds, by assumption, earn 4 per cent. Thus the portfolio of, say, John Smith who has, say, accumulated savings of £10,000 would look like this:

Accumulated savings	10,000	Money (asset balances)	Nil
		Bonds	10,000
Total wealth	10,000	Total assets	10,000

This example, though unrealistic, is nevertheless instructive, for in demonstrating that, in our assumed conditions, John Smith will *not* plan to hold any asset balances we have provided ourselves with a clue to the explanation of why, in general, people will choose to hold such balances. This is so because the implausibility of our hypothetical example lies in the assumption that John Smith's expectations were held with perfect certainty. In such a situation Smith clearly, because the future rate of interest was expected with complete certainty, ran no risk of a fall in bond prices (rise in interest rates) or rise in bond prices (fall in interest rates). The portfolio of 'bonds only' thus emerges in a situation in which there is *no uncertainty* about the future interest rate and thus *no risk* of changes in the value of the bond holding. As we know, complete certainty about the future of the interest rate or anything else is impossible. However confident Smith may feel about his expectation of an unchanged rate, the rate *may* change. Hence, in practice, uncertainty (and thus risk) will always be present in some degree. What happens to the portfolio choice when the existence of uncertainty is admitted? Before examining this problem let us see first the consequences of interest-rate changes.

Suppose Smith holds his whole wealth in bonds purchased when the ruling rate of interest is 4 per cent; then if the rate rises to 5 per cent, each £100 worth of bonds he holds will be valued in the market at £80. He will have incurred a £2,000 capital loss – a capital loss sufficient to reduce the market value of his wealth by 20 per cent. Conversely, if the rate *falls* to, say, 2 per cent, the market value of his bond holding, and thus his accumulated savings, will have doubled, for each £100 of bonds purchased at 4 per cent which he holds will now be worth £200. We may thus conclude that where there is, as there always will be, uncertainty about the rate of interest ruling in the future, to hold accumulated savings in the form of bonds (i) provides a money income, but (ii) involves the acceptance of uncertainty and hence the risk of capital gain or loss.

Most individuals seek money income but try to avoid risk. It is therefore likely that Smith will distribute his portfolio between money (asset balances) and bonds in such a way as to give him his preferred combination of interest income and risk. This means that he will tend to hold a *mixed portfolio* – reducing his risk (at the cost of sacrificing some interest income) by holding some of his wealth in the form of money. In short he will heed the ancient adage on the unwisdom of 'putting all his eggs in one basket' and distribute them over two: bonds *and* money.

We can perhaps make the argument slightly clearer by a table illustrating three possible portfolio positions:

	£		£	*Portfolio characteristics*
		Portfolio 1		
Accumulated savings	10,000	Money	Nil	Maximum money income
		Bonds	10,000	Maximum risk
		Portfolio 2		
Accumulated savings	10,000	Money	10,000	Zero income
		Bonds	Nil	Zero risk
		Portfolio 3		
Accumulated savings	10,000	Money	2,000	*Less* than maximum income
		Bonds	8,000	*Less* than maximum risk

Portfolio 1 provides maximum income *and* maximum risk. It will be selected only by those who are either indifferent to risk or who positively relish it. Portfolio 2 provides zero income and zero risk. It is unlikely to be selected. Portfolio 3 represents a mixed portfolio strategy – an attempt to find the optimal income/risk combination.

We may thus argue that where individuals seek, as we have assumed John Smith to do, to avoid risk: (i) they will in general hold mixed portfolios of assets, and thus (ii) hold some of their wealth in the form of idle (asset) balances.

Hence the demand for asset balances arises because:

(a) the future rate of interest cannot be known with certainty; and
(b) individuals are, in general, risk-avoiders; though
(c) they have no reason to expect the rate of interest to be higher or lower in the future.

Assumption (c) is worth spelling out in slightly greater detail. It is, clearly enough, an alternative way of expressing an assumption that the rate of interest is expected to remain unchanged at 4 per cent. Where expectations are of this form – sometimes called *neutral* – the demand for idle balances is, by definition, purely an asset demand. Money is held as an asset simply to reduce risk.

Suppose, however, that with the rate of interest at 4 per cent some individual, say Henry Snodgrass, though uncertain of the future rate of interest (as he must be), expects *not that it will remain unchanged but that it will fall to 3 per cent*. Then, by buying bonds now (at 4 per cent) and holding them until the rate falls to 3 per cent, Snodgrass can obtain not only his interest income but also a capital gain equal to 33⅓ per cent of his bond holding. In short Snodgrass can make a speculative gain from 'knowing better than the market what the future will bring forth'. As we shall see shortly it is from considerations of this kind that the *speculative* demand for idle balances arises. In such a case we say that expectations are non-neutral.

The demand for *asset balances* thus gives rise to planned money holdings in excess of planned active balances and arises fundamentally because the future of the rate of interest is uncertain. *It contains no speculative element whatever*. Its basic assumption is that whatever the ruling rate of interest happens to be, so it is expected to remain.

Now for a given degree of risk, i.e. a given amount of uncertainty, it is reasonable to argue that the higher is the rate of interest – and thus the stronger the reason for accepting risk – the greater the proportion of accumulated wealth which will be held in the form of bonds and, what is the same thing, the smaller the proportion of accumulated wealth which will be held in the form of money. Hence the planned holdings of asset balances will depend upon:

(a) the value of wealth (W) or accumulated savings
(b) the rate of interest (r)
(c) uncertainty regarding the future value of r (u_r)
(d) people's attitudes towards risk and income

In our usual functional notation we may write:

$$M^D_{p\,(\text{asset})} = L'_2\,(r,\ u_r,\ W) \tag{11.14}$$

and expect the marginal response coefficients to have the following signs:

$$\frac{\partial M^D_{p\,(\text{asset})}}{\partial r} < 0; \quad \frac{\partial M^D_{p\,(\text{asset})}}{\partial u_r} > 0; \quad \frac{\partial M^D_{p\,(\text{asset})}}{\partial W} > 0$$

This, of course, is a very general statement. Since our theory is short run we may regard wealth as a constant. Then, given the (constant) value of wealth, we might postulate a familiar linear function thus:

$$M^D_{p\,(\text{asset})} = T + nr + ou_r \qquad (11.15)$$
$$M^D_{p\,(\text{asset})} = £100\text{m} - £6\text{m}\,r + £1\text{m}\,u_r \qquad (11.15\text{n})$$

This formulation presupposes that we can define, and measure, an appropriate index of uncertainty (u_r). Taking a given value for this index (say $u_r = 20$) we can plot the resultant demand curve in Figure 11.4.

Notice that, at rates of interest above 20 per cent, this function makes no economic sense. This is a limitation not of theory but of the functional form which is only an approximation and a very simple one at that.

What are the parameters of the function? Apart from wealth which we have suppressed, they are as usual the value of the constant (T), the value of the marginal response coefficients n and o and the value of u_r (the uncertainty index). T, n and o reflect the public's preference for holding wealth in money rather than bonds; they thus reflect its preference for liquidity or its liquidity preference. Hence *demand schedules* of this type are frequently referred to as *liquidity preference schedules*.

Suppose the public becomes more anxious to avoid risk. The curve will move to the right. Alternatively, suppose, with unchanged preference on the part of the public, the index of risk u_r increases; the curve will move to the right. Similarly if wealth were greater the curve would lie further to the right.

In interpreting this curve it is important to remember that it reflects the assumption that, whatever the rate of interest is, it is expected to remain unchanged. Put another way, the curve shows the demand for idle balances when the expected capital gain or loss from holding bonds is zero: that is, gains and losses are equally probable. It supposes a zero speculative demand for idle balances. Hence the L_2' schedule as we have called it is *not* the

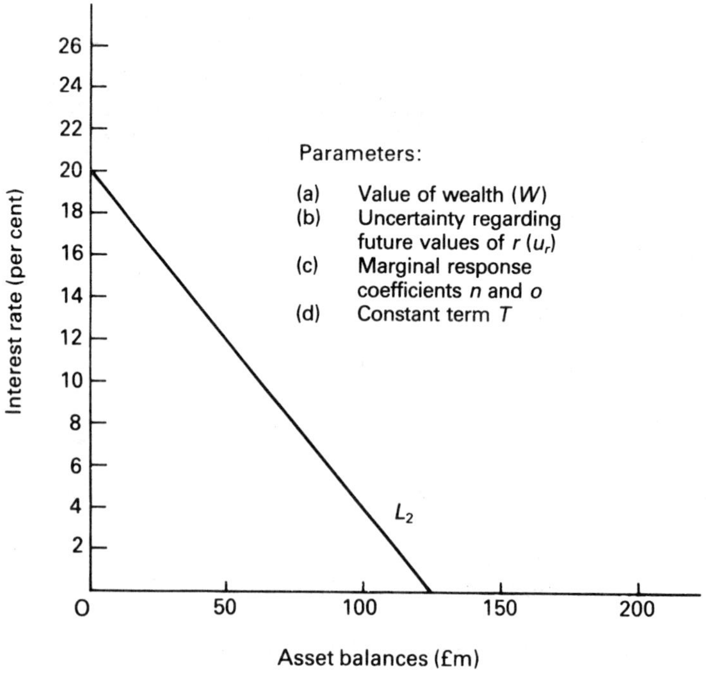

Figure 11.4 The asset demand for money (from 11.15n)

demand for idle balances but simply a component of it. It is identical with the total demand for idle balances only in the special case in which the public expects no gains from speculation. If it were empirically the case, as the L_2' curve assumes, that whatever the rate of interest ruling the expected capital gain or loss was zero, then the L_2' curve would be identical with the total demand for idle balances. However, as we shall now demonstrate, this is not likely to be the case and the demand for idle balances, when account is taken of the speculative element, differs very significantly from the asset demand which assumes neutral expectations.

The demand for idle balances: speculative demand

As we have seen, the asset demand for idle balances arises because:

(a) future interest rates (bond prices) are not known with certainty
(b) wealth-owners in seeking to reduce the risk of capital losses which then arise will, in general, adopt a mixed portfolio, selecting it so that
(c) the quantity of idle balances demanded for asset reasons will be greater the smaller is the interest rate

The fundamental assumption of the asset demand as we have defined it is that whatever the rate of interest ruling in the market is, it is expected to remain unchanged in the future. Expectations in this case are neutral.

The *speculative demand* arises where future interest rates are uncertain, as is always the case, and some people think they know better than the market what the future will bring forth. Thus, for some people at least, *expectations are not neutral*. Accordingly they will buy bonds, if they expect rates to fall (and thus anticipate a capital gain) and sell bonds if they expect interest rates to rise (thus avoiding an anticipated capital loss).

In short, where the ruling market rate is above (below) the rate of interest expected to rule in the future people will, *for speculative reasons*, wish to hold more bonds (money) than the analysis of the asset demand would suggest. Or, to put the same point another way, when the rate of interest is expected to rise (bond prices to fall) wealth-owners have a *positive* demand for idle money balances on speculative account; when the rate of interest is expected to fall (bond prices to rise) wealth-owners have a *negative* demand for idle money balances on speculative account.

This second proposition does not imply a negative demand for idle balances as a whole. This demand cannot be less than zero. Recalling our basic identity, which was:

$$M^D_{(\text{idle})} \equiv M^D_{(\text{asset})} + M^D_{(\text{speculative})}$$

shows that all it implies is that $M^D_{(\text{idle})} < M^D_{(\text{asset})}$.

We may thus argue that the speculative demand for money depends upon:

(a) the market rate of interest (r)
(b) uncertainty about the rate of interest (u_r)
(c) the rate of interest which is expected to rule in the future ($\hat{r}$)
(d) the general attitude of wealth-owners towards speculation

The reader can now see that, in formulating the asset demand, we made the special assumption that, whatever the value of r, the general expectation was that $r = \hat{r}$: that is, expectations were neutral. The speculative demand arises once this assumption is relaxed so that $r \lesseqgtr \hat{r}$: that is, expectations can be non-neutral.

Suppose now wealth-owners possess a unanimous and firmly held expectation that the 'safe' or 'normal' rate of interest in the long term is 5 per cent. The expectation can be regarded as being based on historical experience of interest rates and the current state of the news. Two conclusions emerge immediately:

1. If the ruling rate in the market is 5 per cent, the speculative demand for money will be zero. Hence:

$$M^D_{(\text{idle})} = M^D_{(\text{asset})}$$

2. If the ruling rate is 6 per cent, capital gains will be expected from bond holding and the speculative demand for money will be *negative*. Hence:

$$M^D_{(\text{idle})} < M^D_{(\text{asset})}$$

Figure 11.5 depicts the demand curve for speculative balances in such a case.

How is this figure to be interpreted? At $r = 5$ per cent we have $r = \hat{r}$ and $M^D{}_{(\text{speculative})}$ is consequently zero. Immediately the rate of interest rises *above* 5 per cent we have $r > \hat{r}$.

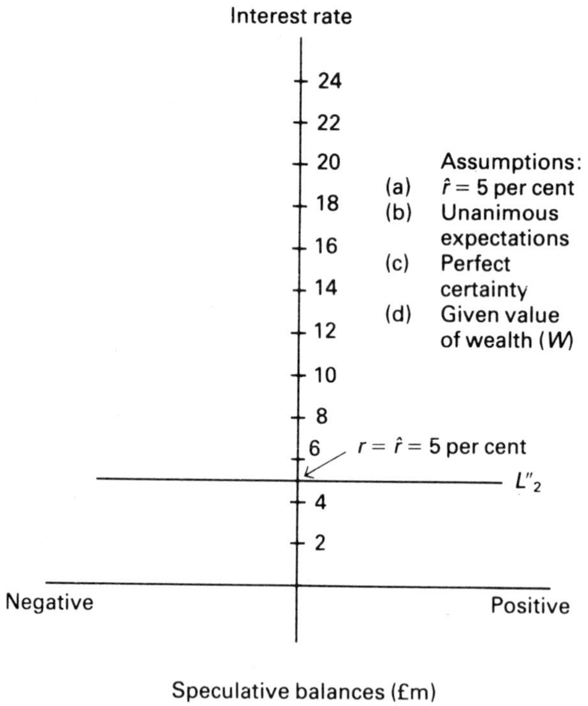

Figure 11.5 The speculative demand for money

Since we have assumed that expectations are unanimous and firmly held, speculators will move out of asset balances into bonds in order to make a capital gain when r returns to $\hat{r}$. Conversely if r is *below* 5 per cent we have $r < \hat{r}$ and the prospect of a capital loss, speculators would move out of bonds and into idle (speculative) balances.

Clearly if expectations were unanimous (as we have assumed) and held with perfect certainty (as in practice they cannot be) we should have the curve shown in Figure 11.5 –

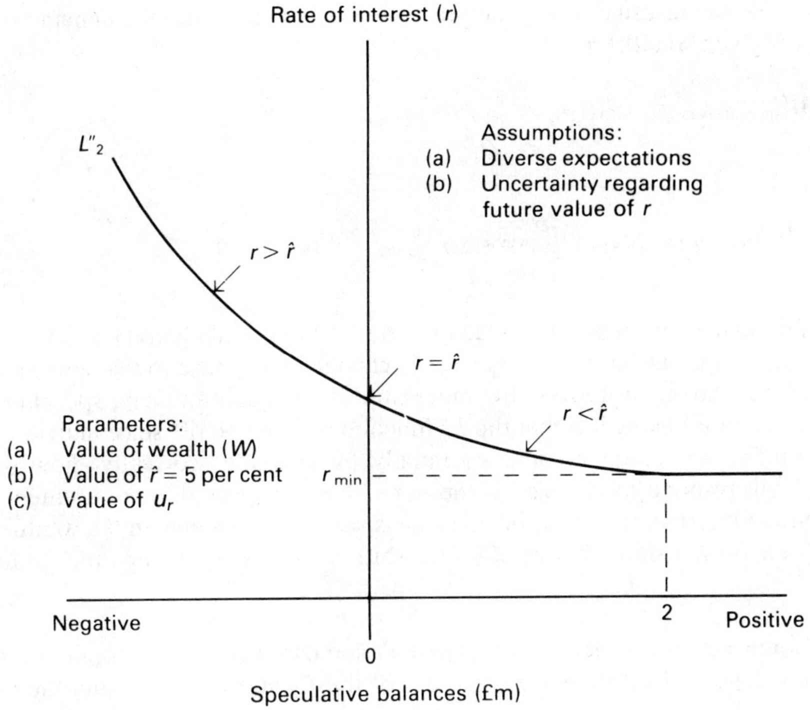

Figure 11.6 The speculative demand for money assumption: (i) diverse expectations, (ii) uncertainty regarding future value of r

simply a straight line with $r = \hat{r}$. The demand for speculative balances would be infinitely elastic at the rate $r = 5$ per cent and the rate of interest would never depart from this value for if r rose *above* $\hat{r}$ (i.e. above 5 per cent) speculators would rush to buy bonds and drive up their price until r fell to 5 per cent. Conversely if r were *below* $\hat{r}$ speculators would rush to sell bonds and their price would fall until r rose to 5 per cent.

The case depicted in Figure 11.5, though useful expositionally, is extremely artificial, for (i) expectations are not likely to be unanimous, and (ii) expectations cannot be held with complete certainty.

These two considerations lead us to construct a new curve as in Figure 11.6. This assumes (i) diversity in expectations, and (ii) incomplete certainty. As a result it shows the speculative demand increasing (negatively) as r rises *above* $\hat{r}$ (which must now be interpreted as an average of the diverse expectations of wealth-owners) and increasing (positively) as r falls *below* $\hat{r}$.

This curve also incorporates a further hypothesis to the effect that at some interest rate, which we have called r_{min}, the L_2'' curve becomes completely horizontal. This is the lowest rate of interest acceptable to the community. At this rate, provided speculative balance holdings are greater than or equal to OZ, the community is indifferent between money and bonds. In short, because expectations are diverse, the horizontal part of the L_2'' function indicates a range along which even the most sanguine speculators expect the capital losses from bond holding to offset so much of the income derived from interest that, allowing for the uncertainty which always attaches to holding bonds, the marginal advantages of holding bonds and money are equal.

Reverting to our usual functional presentation, we may write the demand for speculative balances (given wealth) as:

$$M^D_{(\text{speculative})} = L_2''(r, \hat{r}, u_r) \tag{11.16}$$

with

$$\frac{\partial M^D_{(\text{speculative})}}{\partial r} < 0 \quad \frac{\partial M^D_{(\text{speculative})}}{\partial \hat{r}} > 0 \quad \frac{\partial M^D_{(\text{speculative})}}{\partial u_r} > 0$$

From this analysis we may also argue that the L_2'' curve is likely to be volatile. Expectations concerning r (i.e. the value of $\hat{r}$) may easily change in response to the news and changes in $\hat{r}$ will shift the curve. Moreover, the more important, quantitatively, speculators are in the market, the more likely it is that the L_2'' function will be volatile since individual speculators make profits on capital account essentially by guessing (correctly) how speculators in general will respond to changes in the news. An unexpected announcement of a general election, an international crisis or, in some cases, even a change in the weather, may cause the L_2'' function to shift, though any such shift is unlikely to change the value of $r_{\min}$.

We can now add the asset and speculative demands for money to obtain the total demand for idle balances. To do this we make use of the L_2' and L_2'' curves and the identity:

$$\begin{aligned} M^D_{(\text{idle})} &\equiv M^D_{(\text{asset})} + M^D_{(\text{speculative})} \\ &= L_2''(r, u_r) + L_2'(r, \hat{r}, u_r) \\ &= L_2(r, \hat{r}, u_r) \end{aligned}$$

Thus our hypotheses are that the demand for idle balances is dependent upon liquidity preference (reflected in the L_2 function itself) and the values of the rate of interest (r), the expected 'safe' rate of interest ($\hat{r}$) and the uncertainty of the expectation (u_r). This formulation is, of course, essentially short run in that it takes as given and constant the value of wealth.

The addition to the asset and speculative demands to obtain the total demand for idle balances is carried out geometrically in Figure 11.7. Interpretation of the figure is simple enough, for it is constructed to reflect the hypothesis that:

(a) with $r > \hat{r}$, $M^D_{(\text{speculative})}$ is negative

(b) with $r = \hat{r}$, $M^D_{(\text{speculative})}$ is zero

(c) with $r < \hat{r}$. $M^D_{(\text{speculative})}$ is positive

and the constraint that $M^D_{p(\text{idle})}$ cannot be less than zero.

Obviously, from the shape of the L_2 curve, no simple linear function can be used to represent it, though if the speculative motive were absent a linear relationship might be a plausible approximation (as we have assumed).

Consider now the L_2 curve shown in Figure 11.7. At some interest rate r^*, the sum of the asset and speculative demands is zero: that is, the public would plan to hold no idle balances whatever. As the rate (r) falls below r^*, the demand for idle balances increases until at $r = \hat{r}$ it is equal to the demand shown by the L_2' function. As r falls below $\hat{r}$ the planned holdings of idle balances increase and with $r = r_{\min}$ the L_2 curve (like the L_2'' curve and for the same reason) becomes horizontal – that is, infinitely interest elastic.

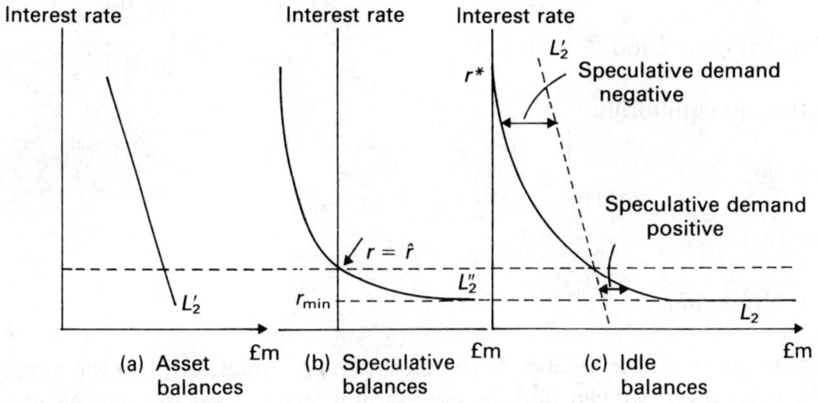

Figure 11.7 The demand for idle balances

What are the parameters of the L_2 function? Since the L_2 function depends upon both the L_2' and L_2'' functions, the reader may work out the answer to this problem and use the answer to explain the circumstances in which an increase or decrease in liquidity preference might be expected. Both changes are illustrated in Figure 11.8.

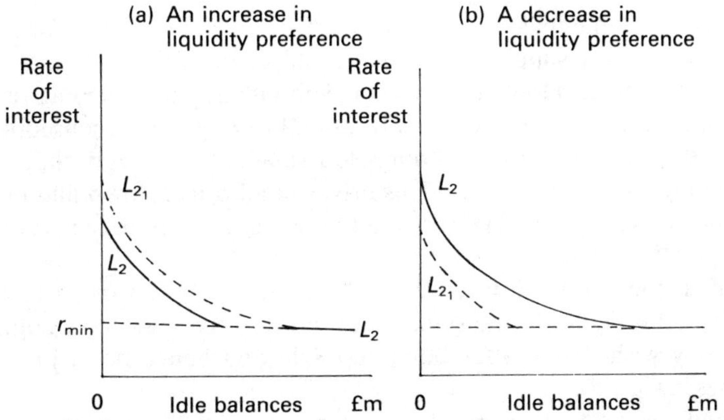

Figure 11.8 The demand for idle balances

The demand for money and the interest rate

We can now write the total demand for money, given the price level, as:

$$
\begin{aligned}
M_p^D &\equiv M_{p(\text{active})}^D + M_{p(\text{idle})}^D \\
&\equiv L_1(Y, u_y) + L_2(r, \hat{r}, u_r)
\end{aligned}
$$

which, taking u_y, $\hat{r}$ and u_r as given, is more commonly written as:

$$M_p^D = L_1(Y) + L_2(r) \tag{11.17}$$

We know that, in equilibrium:

$$M_p^D = M_p^S$$

and assume that:

$$M_a^S = M_p^S = M_0$$

Hence if we are given (i) the level of Y, (ii) the L_1 and L_2 functions, (iii) the money supply, and (iv) the price level, we can find the equilibrium value of r – the rate of interest.

To see this look at Figure 11.9. From Figure 11.9a if $Y = Y_0$ then $M^D_{p(\text{active})} = OQ =$ £100m. It follows that the supply of idle balances is:

$$M_0 - M^D_{p(\text{active})} = £600\text{m} - £100\text{m} = £500\text{m}$$

The supply of idle balances can now be inserted into Figure 11.9b as the dotted line $S'S'$. Where this line cuts the L_2 curve determines the rate of interest at r_0. This is easy to see since when income is Y_0 and the rate of interest r_0 we have:

$$M_p^D \equiv M^D_{p(\text{active})} + M^D_{p(\text{idle})} = M_0 = £600\text{m}$$

Notice that levels of income higher than Y_0 involve (i) *greater* demands for active balances, and so with a fixed money supply (ii) a *smaller* supply of idle balances and (iii) a *higher* equilibrium rate of interest. How does this come about? Suppose income rises to Y_1. As a result the demand for active balances rises from OQ to OQ'. As a consequence firms and households find their active money holdings too small. Accordingly they try to increase their money holdings by selling bonds. This drives bond prices down and interest rates up until the interest rate reaches r_1. At this rate the demand for money is again equal to the supply.

What happens if the community revises its estimate of $\hat{r}$ upwards? The L_2 curve shifts upwards: that is, to the right. At the ruling interest rate people are now holding less as idle balances than they wish. They offer bonds for sale and hence bond prices fall and the interest rate rises.

We can now give a short summary of our interest theory as follows:

1. The rate of interest is determined by the supply and demand for money.
2. The demand for money can be written:

$$M_p^D = L_1(Y) + L_2(r)$$

taking u_y, $\hat{r}$, p, u_r as given and the value of wealth as given.

3. An increase in liquidity preference (upward shift in L_2 function), given the money supply, raises r; a decrease lowers r.
4. An increase in Y raises r; a decrease lowers r.
5. An increase in the money supply (given L_2, L_2) lowers r.
6. The L_2 function is likely to be volatile and respond quickly to changes in the 'state of the news'.

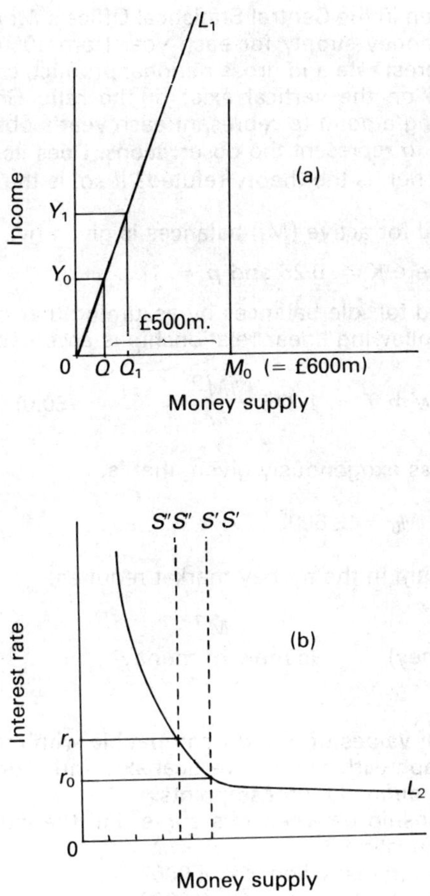

Figure 11.9 The determination of the equilibrium rate of interest

The reader should now verify that all these propositions are compatible with our introduction to the theory of interest on pages 164–7.

Questions and exercises

1. 'The essence of the liquidity preference theory of interest is that the rate of interest is the price which brings about equality between the demand for and supply of money.' Explain.

2. If the quotation in question 1 is correct, what relationship would you expect to observe between the ratio of gross national product/money supply and the rate of interest? Give your reasons and construct a rough graph of the relationship you predict.

3. Construct, from data given in the Central Statistical Office's *Monthly Digest of Statistics* a series for the average money supply for each year from 1950 to 1981. Selecting other series for the annual interest rate and gross national product, construct a scatter diagram with (i) the interest rate on the vertical axis; (ii) the ratio GNP/money supply on the horizontal axis, by plotting a point to represent each year's observation.
   Draw freehand a curve to represent the observations. Does its shape conform with your answer to question 2? If not, is the theory refuted? If so, is the theory proved?

4. Assume that the demand for active (M_1) balances is given by:

$$M_1^D = KYp \quad (\text{where } K = 0.25 \text{ and } p = 1)$$

Approximate the demand for idle balances by assuming that $r_{min} = 2$ per cent, and that with $r > 2$ per cent the following linear relationship is acceptable:

$$M_2^D = T + nr \quad \left(\text{with } T = 1{,}375;\ \frac{\partial M_2^D}{\partial r} = n = -50.0\right)$$

Take the money supply as exogenously given, that is:

$$M^S = M_0 \quad (\text{with } M_0 = 2{,}500)$$

Remember that equilibrium in the money market requires:

$$\underset{\text{(demand for money)}}{M^D} = \underset{\text{(supply of money)}}{M^S}$$

Applying this condition:
   (a) Find all the pairs of values of Y and r compatible with money market equilibrium.
   (b) Plot these on a graph with r on the vertical axis and Y on the horizontal.
   (c) Interpret the curve defined by these points.
   (d) Explain the relationship between this curve and the curve you constructed from observed data in question 3.
   (e) What is the rate of interest when $Y < 4{,}900$?
   (f) What is the rate of interest when $Y = 6{,}500$?
   (g) What is the maximum level of Y that the money supply can finance?

5. Using the model of question 4 show the consequences of (i) an increase of 100 in the money supply; (ii) an increase of 100 in the demand for idle balances; (iii) a rise in p from 1 to 2. Treat each problem separately and specify clearly the conditions under which your prediction holds.

6. 'It is possible to control *either* the money supply *or* the rate of interest but not both.' Use the analysis of Chapter 11 to discuss this contention.

7. 'It is well known that the prospect of a socialist government can only raise interest rates.' 'The Labour Party is, because of its detestation of rentiers, traditionally the party of low interest rates and cheap money.' Are these statements compatible? How do they relate to our theory?

8. Using the data of question 4, what is the interest elasticity of the demand for money when:
   (a) $r = 2.0$ per cent
   (b) $r = 5.0$ per cent
   (c) $r = 27.5$ per cent?

9. If the rate of interest is 5 per cent and expected to fall to 4 per cent, a speculator stands to make a capital gain by holding bonds rather than money. Would he hold *all* his wealth in

the form of bonds rather than money? Or would he hold some bonds and some money – a mixed portfolio? Give your reasons.

10. 'As long as a wealth-owner holds some bonds, the value of his wealth must be inversely related to the rate of interest.' Explain. Does this complication modify significantly or even invalidate the analysis given on pages 167–81? Give your reasons.

11. The accounts of John Hawgood on two dates gave the following information:

Date: 31 Dec 1980 *Assets*		*Date: 31 Dec 1981* *Assets*	
Money	1,500	Money	4,000
Bonds	4,000	Bonds	1,500
House	15,000	House	15,000

(a) Did Hawgood save or dissave in 1981? By how much?
(b) Did he invest in 1981? If so, how much?
(c) Did his liquidity preference increase/decrease in 1981?
(d) What was his demand for money on 31 December 1980 and 31 December 1981?
(e) On what assumptions and definitions are your answers based?

12. 'If there were no speculation, there would be no demand for idle balances.' Do you agree? If not why not?

13. Compare the graph you constructed to answer question 3 with that given by Artis and Lewis, p. 28 (see suggested reading). If income velocity is defined as

$$\frac{\text{nominal GNP}}{\text{nominal money supply}}$$

show that our theory predicts that velocity is a function of the interest rate.

14. 'In the short run, wealth is constant.' Elucidate. Does this simply reflect the definition of the short run? If it does not, is it correct?

15. 'Ultimately it is a question of fact whether it is the speculative or asset motive which dominates the demand curve for idle balances.' Elucidate. In what institutional environments would you expect the asset motive to be dominant? Can you suggest a way of testing whether the speculative motive is present?

16. The discussion of the speculative motive runs in terms of *both* diverse expectations and uncertainty. What would the speculative demand curve look like if expectations were diverse and uncertainty *absent*? Give your reasoning fully.

17. What do you think would be the consequences for (i) the L_2 function, and (ii) the rate of interest, of a statement by the Prime Minister that 'Her Majesty's Government is actively considering ways and means of reducing the rate of interest'? Why?

18. 'Even with the liquidity preference theory an increase in the propensity to save will reduce the interest rate – through its effect upon income.' Elucidate. Are there any limitations to this proposition?

19. In the text we have assumed a constant price level so that real and nominal interest rates coincide. How would the expectation of a rise in prices modify the analysis?

20. Can you suggest a method of defining and constructing a measurable index of 'uncertainty regarding interest rates (u_r)'?

21. The following hypothetical data relate to John Smith's expectations regarding the future interest rate on two different dates:

31 Dec 1976		*31 Dec 1977*	
Interest rate %	*Expected with probability of*	*Interest rate %*	*Expected with probability of*
3.0	0.10	3.0	0.00
4.0	0.20	4.0	0.10
5.0	0.40	5.0	0.80
6.0	0.20	6.0	0.10
7.0	0.10	7.0	0.00

At each date the ruling rate in the market is 5 per cent.

(a) At each date what is the value of $\hat{r}$?
(b) At either date will Smith have a speculative demand for money?
(c) Which set of expectations implies the greater value of u_r?
(d) Assuming no change in Smith's wealth between the two dates, in which situation will Smith have the greater demand for idle balances? Why?
(e) Can you *now* define a measurable index of u_r?

22. Use the current *Financial Times* to obtain the ruling rate of interest on UK government 2½% Consols. Then:

(a) write down the highest rate which you think might rule in a year's time
(b) the lowest rate you think might rule in a year's time
(c) the rate you think most likely to rule in a year's time

Identify $\hat{r}$. Have you a speculative demand for money? How would you estimate the value of u_r attaching to your expectations.

23. How far do you think the estimates of money demand functions given in Artis and Lewis, table 2.1, p. 18, support or refute the theory of money demand?

Suggested reading

M. J. Artis and M. K. Lewis, *Monetary Control in the United Kingdom* (Philip Allan, 1981) ch. 2.
G. E. J. Dennis, *Monetary Economics* (Longman, 1981) chs 4, 6.
Miles Fleming, *Monetary Theory* (Macmillan, 1971).
*H. G. Johnson (ed.), *Readings in British Monetary Economics* (Oxford University Press, 1972) pp. 138–50.
J. M. Keynes, *The General Theory of Employment, Interest and Money* (Macmillan, 1936) ch. 15.
A. M. Khusro, 'An Investigation of Liquidity Preference', *Yorkshire Bulletin of Economic and Social Research* (January 1952).
*D. W. Laidler, *The Demand for Money* (Scranton, 1969).

*More advanced references.

Chapter 12
The Theory of Income Determination

As a result of our work in Chapter 11 we now have a theory of the determination of the equilibrium rate of interest. Our elementary model is thus complete. It is therefore convenient at this point to summarise our argument: that is, to display in full the characteristics of the model at this stage. Once this is done we can proceed (i) to see where the model needs further extensions, and (ii) to see what predictions it yields.

How, then, can we conveniently summarise the model we have developed?

Characteristics of the model: goods market

As we have developed it our model consists of *two* markets: one for goods and services (the *goods market*), and one for money (the *money market*). For the *whole system* to be in equilibrium, *both* these markets must *simultaneously* be in equilibrium. What does this imply?

Consider the market for goods and services. Equilibrium here requires that aggregate demand is equal to aggregate supply: in short, that $C_p + I_p = Y$. To explain C_p and I_p we have a theory of aggregate consumption (developed in Chapter 9) and a theory of investment (developed in Chapter 10). These two theories may be written:

$$\begin{aligned} C_p &= f(Y, r, A, \alpha) \\ I_p &= f(\lambda, r) \end{aligned}$$

We take the values of $A \equiv$ real value of households' assets, $\alpha \equiv$ the distribution of income, and $\lambda \equiv$ schedule of marginal efficiency of investment as *given*. This enables us to write:

$$\begin{aligned} C_p &= f(Y, r) \\ I_p &= f(r) \end{aligned}$$

From this it follows that for any given value of r we can determine the rate of real planned investment I_p. Once we know this, since we know the schedule of the propensity to consume, we can determine the equilibrium level of real income (Y). In other words, for any given rate of interest there will be (i) a determinate rate of real planned investment which, *given* (ii) the schedule of the propensity to consume, *determines* (iii) an equilibrium level of real output.

To see this consider Figure 12.1. On the left we have the familiar 45° diagram of Chapter 9. In the centre the theory of investment of Chapter 10. On the right we have a new graph with the rate of interest plotted on the vertical axis and the level of real income on the horizontal.

Take any rate of interest r_0. This determines, *from the MEI schedule*, a rate of real planned investment I_p. This rate can now be transferred to the 45° diagram yielding an aggregate demand schedule $C_p + I_{p0}$. This cuts the 45° line at Z_0 and determines the equilibrium level of income Y_0. The pair of values r_0, Y_0 now define a point (P_0) on the third diagram.

Repeat the process with rate of interest r_1 and rate of planned investment I_{p1} to obtain the equilibrium income Y_1. This yields a second point (r_1, Y_1) in the third figure. Obviously for *any* value of r we can find *that* level of Y at which the *goods market is in equilibrium*, and these pairs of values, plotted on the third diagram, will trace out a curve – called the *IS* curve – *which shows all the pairs of values of r and Y at which the goods market is in equilibrium.*

The slope of this IS curve is downwards because the higher is r the lower is I_p and the lower is I_p the lower is the value of Y at which the goods market is in equilibrium.

The position of the IS curve depends upon (i) the marginal efficiency of investment schedule, and (ii) the schedule of the propensity to consume.

The reader is invited to work out for himself the direction in which the *IS* curve will shift in response to shifts in either the propensity to consume schedule or the MEI schedule and to refresh his memory as to why either of these schedules may shift.

Characteristics of the model: the money market

This *IS* curve is not, by itself, sufficient to tell us the equilibrium level of income. All it can say is that *if* the rate of interest is, say, r_0, *then* the level of income at which aggregate

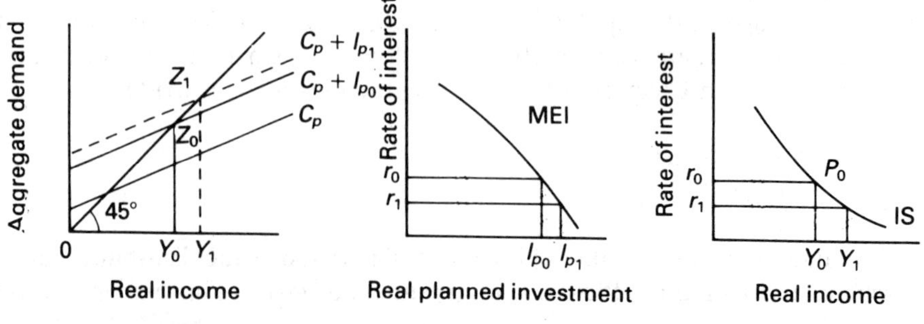

Figure 12.1 The determination of the equilibrium level of income, given the rate of interest, the marginal efficiency of investment schedule and the consumption function

demand equals aggregate supply will be Y_0. To find *the* equilibrium level of income we must find the value of r. To do this we turn to the money market.

The equilibrium condition in the money market is:

$$M_p^D = M_p^S$$
$$\text{demand for money} = \text{supply of money}$$

As in Chapter 11, we assume a fixed and invariant supply of money M_0. Hence we require $M_p^D = M_0$. The demand for money, M_p^D, we already know can be written:

$$M_p^D = L_1(Yp) + L_2(r)$$

Our model takes the value of p ($\equiv$ the price level) as given and constant. Hence real income (Y) and money income (Yp) move together in the sense that any given value of Y implies a single value of Yp. This being so we can think of the demand for money as:

$$M_p^D = L_1(Y) + L_2(r) \quad (given\ p)$$

Now look at Figure 12.2 . As before this is divided into three sections. On the left we have the demand curve for *active balances* (the L_1 function). In the centre we have the demand curve for *idle balances* (L_2 function). On the right we have a diagram with the same axes as we had on the right of Figure 12.1. On the left-hand figure the vertical line SS is drawn at a distance along the horizontal axis equal to the given money supply M_0.

Suppose income is Y_0. Then the demand for *active* balances is $M^D_{p(\text{active})0}$. Hence the supply of the idle balances is $M_0 - M^D_{p(\text{active})0}$. This is shown by the curve QQ_0. The equilibrium rate of interest is r_0. Thus (Y_0, r_0) are a pair of values which equate the community's planned holdings of money balances with the money supply.

Now assume income to be Y_1. The new supply curve of *idle* balances is QQ_1. The new equilibrium rate of interest is r_1. Hence (Y_1, r_1) is a second pair of values at which the demand for money equals the supply. Clearly by running through all possible levels of Y – and finding the associated equilibrium values of r – we can trace out a curve, which we call the LM curve, showing *all the pairs of values of r and Y at which the money market is in equilibrium*.

The *position* of the LM curve depends upon:

(a) the L_1 and L_2 functions – the two liquidity functions as they are often called
(b) the quantity of money (M_0)
(c) the assumed level of prices (p)

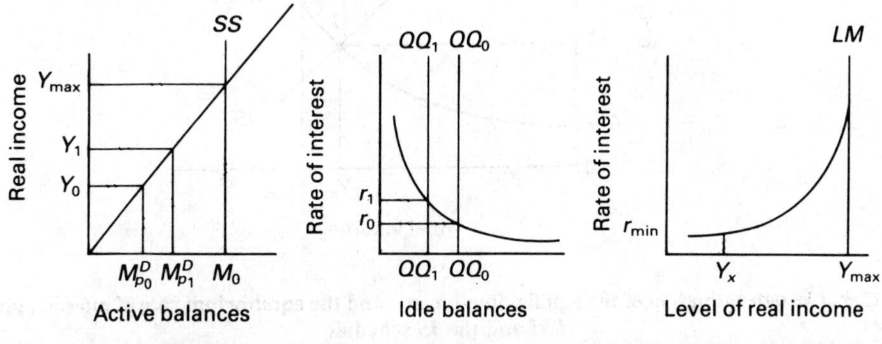

Figure 12.2 The *LM* schedule establishing a relation between real income and the rate of interest, given the liquidity preference function, the money supply and the price level

The *shape* of the curve is dominated, as the diagram shows, by the L_2 function. Over a range this curve is horizontal at the rate of interest r_{min}. This tells us that so long as income is equal to or less than Y_x the *demand* for active balances is such that the *supply* of idle balances (the money supply *less* the quantity demanded for active balances) is sufficient to keep interest at the minimum level acceptable to the community.

As income rises above Y_x, and thus the quantity of money demanded for active balances also rises, so does the equilibrium interest rate. This reflects the fact that, to obtain additional active balances, bonds must be sold, and to do this their price must now fall since, with the prevailing holding of idle balances, wealth-owners are no longer indifferent – as they were to the left of Y_x – between holding money and bonds. At income Y_{max} the *LM* curve becomes vertical. At this income level the whole of the existing money supply is required as active balances. Hence, so long as the L_1 function is unaltered, Y_{max} (given the value of p) is the highest level of *real income* which the community can finance with the given money supply. Attempts to obtain additional active balances, by offering bonds for sale, cannot succeed. They can only drive up interest rates by lowering bond prices.

The complete model

Now that we have constructed both the *IS* and *LM* curves we can put them on a single diagram. This is done in Figure 12.3. The curves cut at the point O, which has co-ordinates Y_e and r_e. The significance of this point is clear from the definition of *IS* and *LM*:

1. Because O lies on *IS*, *then* Y_e and r_e are a pair of values at which:

$$C_p + I_p = Y$$

and the *goods market is in equilibrium*.

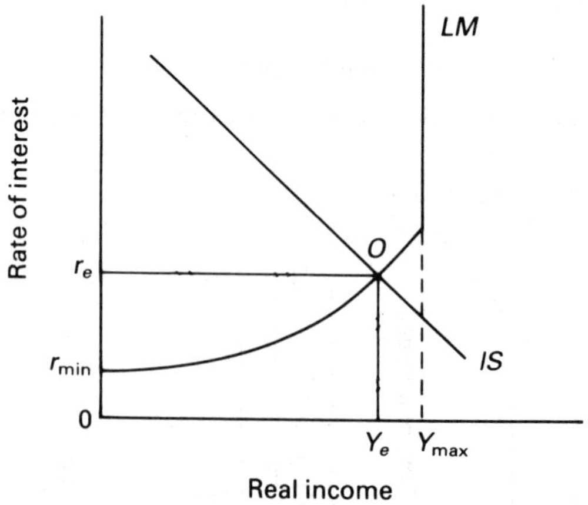

Figure 12.3 The determination of the equilibrium income and the equilibrium rate of interest, given the *LM* and the *IS* schedule

2. Because O lies on LM, *then* Y_e and r_e are a pair of values at which:

$$M_p^D = M_p^S$$

and the *money market is in equilibrium.*

It follows that Figure 12.3 describes the full equilibrium of the system, in short it shows how the equilibrium values of the *two* dependent variables, income and the rate of interest, are simultaneously determined by the independent variables which are, *as a first approximation*:

(a) the propensity to consume schedule
(b) the marginal efficiency of investment schedule
(c) the liquidity preference (L_1 and L_2) functions
(d) the money supply
(e) the given level of prices

Why do we say 'as a first approximation'? Simply because in depicting our system in these terms we need to remember that the first three independent variables – as we are here defining them – are themselves simplifications. For example, our propensity to consume schedule is a relationship between:

C_p		Y		r
real planned consumption	*and*	real income	*and*	interest rate

We derived it from a consumption function hypothesis of the form:[1]

$$C_p = Q + cY + dA + e\alpha$$

by taking as given the value of Q, d, A, e and thus obtaining:

$$C_p = (\bar{Q} + \bar{d}\bar{A} + \bar{e}\bar{\alpha}) + cY$$

Analogously to write the demand for active balances as a function of Y we not only have to take p (the price level) as given, but also u_y, the degree of uncertainty with regard to future income receipts and payments, while to draw the L_2 function we need to take as given the expected ('safe') rate of interest ($\hat{r}$) and the degree of uncertainty with respect to r which we called u_r.

In short, in interpreting Figure 12.3 the reader needs to keep constantly in mind not only that the IS and LM curves depend on the four independent variables listed above but that these themselves are but convenient simplifications of relatively complicated theories. Provided this is done Figure 12.3 is a convenient and useful device for thinking about problems in the theory of income determination.

In Figure 12.3 we do not show *directly* the determination of employment. However, since we can from the figure determine Y_e – the equilibrium level of real output (income) – we need only to refer back to our short-run production function (Chapter 7) to find the equilibrium level of employment.

[1] In this form we have omitted the rate of interest, for reasons given earlier.

What the model predicts

Now that we have got our model, what predictions does it yield? A prediction, we must recall, is a statement of the form:

if X occurs in context *Y, then Z* will occur

Our model is not specified quantitatively. Hence our predictions can only be qualitative. Let us generate a few to show how the model operates.

An increase in the marginal efficiency of capital

This means a *rightward* shift of the MEI schedule. From Figure 12.1 we see that this shifts the *IS* curve to the *right*. In *general* the new equilibrium will give (i) a higher level of income, and (ii) a higher rate of interest than the initial level. The precise result, however, will depend upon the nature of the initial equilibrium. The geometry of this is shown in Figure 12.4 where *IS'* is the position of the *IS* curve after the MEI has increased.

What lies behind the geometry?

The rightward shift in the MEI raises the level of planned investment at each interest rate. Hence the multiplier comes into operation to raise income. However, as income rises, the quantity of active balances demanded increases. To satisfy this demand, bonds are offered for sale and bond prices fall (the interest rate rises). This rise in the interest rate brings about an *induced* decline in investment, which thus increases by less than the *autonomous* increase brought about by the shift in the MEI schedule. Our prediction is therefore that an increase in the MEI schedule will in general raise *income* and the rate of interest.

The conditions we assume for this result are:

(a) *given* and *invariant* nominal money supply and price level
(b) *given* and *invariant* propensity to consume schedule
(c) *given* and *invariant* liquidity functions

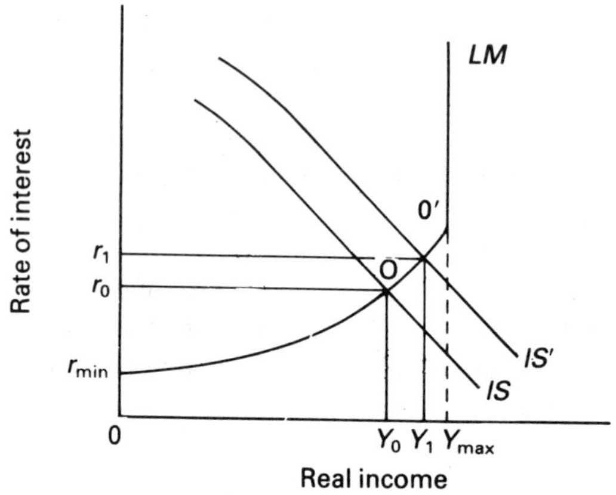

Figure 12.4 A shift in the *IS* curve and the changes in the level of income and the rate of interest

An increase in liquidity preference

This is usually interpreted, as a matter of geometry, as an upward shift in the L_2 function which leaves unchanged the level of the minimum acceptable interest rate and, of course, the maximum money income which, given the price level, the given money supply can finance.

How can such a shift come about? The reader can refer back to Chapter 11 for the full range of possibilities but two obvious reasons for such a shift are (i) an upward revision in $\hat{r}$ (the expected rate of interest), and (ii) an increase in u_r (uncertainty about the future of r). Either can occur separately; alternatively they may occur together. What are the consequences of such an increase in liquidity preference?

As a result of this increased demand for idle balances the *LM* curve shifts to the *left*. The result, as is shown in Figure 12.5, is, in general, a new equilibrium with (i) a higher rate of interest, and (ii) a lower level of income.

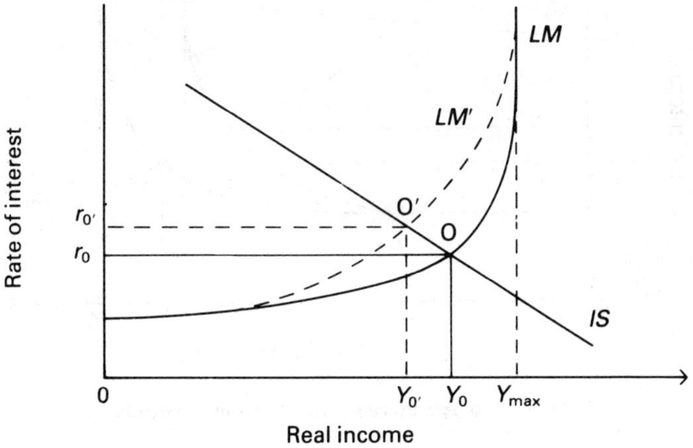

Figure 12.5 An increase in liquidity preference

What is the economic mechanism underlying this result?

The increase in the demand for *idle* balances means that at the initial rate of interest and income the community's actual holding of idle balances is now less than their planned holding. Accordingly bonds are offered on the market as some people seek to move out of bonds and into money. As a result bond prices fall (interest rates rise). This rise in the rate of interest reduces real planned investment. Hence the multiplier comes into operation and incomes fall. This reduces the quantity of active balances demanded and so increases the supply of idle balances. This rise in the supply of idle balances somewhat reduces the extent to which the rate of interest increase. This is now less than it would have been had income remained constant.

What conditions are we assuming to reach this result? They are:

(a) *given* and *invariant* propensity to consume schedule
(b) *given* and *invariant* MEI schedule
(c) *given* and *invariant* money supply and price level

An increase in the nominal money supply

Suppose the money supply increases because of, let us say, the purchase of bonds from the general public by the government. In this case the additional money (created by the central bank by methods explained more fully in Chapter 16) enters the system as a result of a capital-account transaction. The new money does not enter the system as anyone's income but simply as an asset received for the transfer of another asset (bonds). What happens?

In terms of our diagram the *LM* curve moves to the *right*. Hence the new equilibrium is characterised by (i) a higher level of income, and (ii) a lower rate of interest than the old. This is shown in Figure 12.6.

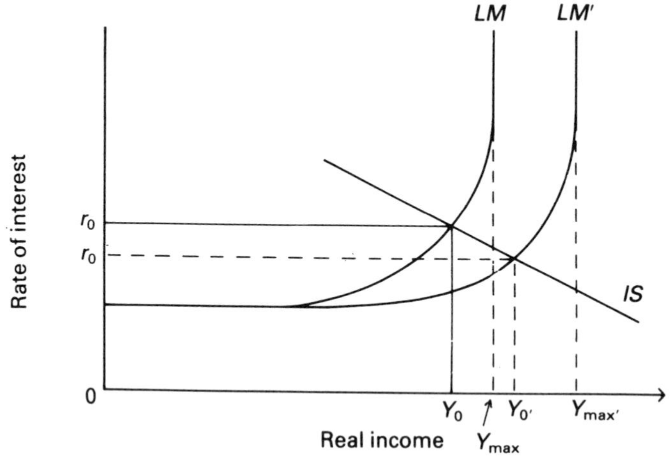

Figure 12.6 An increase in the money supply

What is the mechanism?

By hypothesis the government is purchasing bonds from the public and giving money in exchange. At the initial equilibrium the public was holding its preferred ratio of money/bonds. To persuade it to *raise* this ratio, the interest rate must fall. Hence as the government seeks to purchase bonds, bond prices rise to persuade those who at the initial prices preferred bonds to money to move *out of* bonds and *into* money. A rise in bond prices is a fall in interest rates. The mechanism is thus straightforward.

The fall in the rate of interest induces an increase in investment. This brings the multiplier into operation and raises income. The rise in income increases the quantity of active balances demanded. Hence the final increase in the supply of idle balances is *less* than the increase in the money supply and the fall in the rate of interest *less* than it would have been if income had not changed.

The conditions we assume to reach this should be worked out by the reader.

The qualitative predictions set out above have been reached by a highly formal process of reasoning in which the assumed conditions under which they will be valid are stated in some detail. This is a necessary step in economic analysis. But it is very far from being the whole of economics. We must always remember that a shift in one schedule may itself induce changes in others. According to our model, such induced changes need not occur. Whether they do so or not is a question of fact. It follows that, after making a prediction from the model and specifying the conditions under which it is valid, it is essential to consider whether, in practice, these conditions are likely to hold or not and, if they are not, in what way we should modify our initial prediction.

To give an example: we predicted that *if* the MEI schedule shifted upwards, then *both* income *and* the rate of interest would tend to rise. We reached this result by assuming, among other things, unchanged L_1 and L_2 functions.

Suppose that the MEI schedule shifted upwards because of a decline in business uncertainty. Might the factors which brought this about not also lead to a decline in the uncertainty regarding future income payments and receipts (thus shifting the L_1 function) or the uncertainty regarding the future expected interest rate (thus shifting the L_2 function)? If so, can we be very confident in our prediction that the rate of interest would rise?

This sort of consideration is important. Formal theoretical analysis is the first step in economic analysis. And it is essential. Failure to specify our model, and its properties, carefully and precisely is simply to invite confusion. The second step, however, must always be to review the assumptions underlying any given prediction. Failure to do this is to risk irrelevance.

Weakness of the model

In its present form the model has four principal weaknesses which we must try to remove in later chapters.

In the first place it is entirely static. This means that we can use it only to compare positions of (short-period) equilibrium and *not* to discuss how the system *moves* from one equilibrium position to another. For many problems, for example, the *stability* of the model and for the theory of investment, *dynamics* are of crucial importance. In short we need at least some elementary dynamic developments.

In the second place the model admits no government activity and assumes that there is no international trade. This reduces its usefulness for the study of policy problems. We need extensions here.

In the third place the model treats the price level as given and invariant: that is, as an *exogenous* variable. This is convenient but no more than that. We need a theory of prices.

Finally, we need to explain the workings of the monetary system.

All these weaknesses are removed in later chapters.

Questions and exercises

1. 'If the rate of investment is greater the *lower* is the rate of interest, why is it that, as a matter of observation, the rate of interest is high when investment is high?' Explain.

2. From the following information construct the *IS* and *LM* curves and graph them. Then find the equilibrium value of (i) income (Y), (ii) the rate of interest (r).

$$
\begin{aligned}
C_p &= A + cY && \text{(when } A = 100,\ \ c = 0.8\text{)} \\
I_p &= Z - gr && \text{(when } Z = 1{,}000,\ g = 10\text{)} \\
M_1^D &= kYp && \text{(when } k = 0.25,\ p = 1\text{)} \\
M_2^D &= R - hr && \text{(when } R = 1{,}375,\ h = 50\text{)} \\
M^S &= M_0 && \text{(when } M_0 = 2{,}500\text{)} \\
r_{\min} &= 2.0 \text{ per cent}
\end{aligned}
$$

One way of increasing the equilibrium level of Y is to reduce r to its minimum level. Suppose this is done.

(a) What is the new equilibrium level of Y?
(b) What is the minimum value of the money supply necessary to equate r to $r_{\min}$ at the new equilibrium level of Y?
(c) What are the consequences of a shift in the consumption schedule raising A to 200?

3. Using the model of question 2 assume the investment function to shift upwards so that, in the new situation:

$$I_p = Z + \Delta Z - gr$$

where Z and g are as before but $\Delta Z = 100$. Calculate the new equilibrium level of: (i) income Y; (ii) interest r; (iii) planned investment I_p.
What is the value of the multiplier? And what is the *induced* change in I_p.

4. Write down as fully as possible the assumptions underlying the consumption and investment function of question 2. What is

(a) the interest elasticity of M_2^D when $r = 4$ per cent?
(b) the income elasticity of C_p when income is 5,300?
(c) the interest elasticity of investment when $r = 4$ per cent?

5. Using the data of question 2 suppose the price level to double so that $p = 2$. Which curve (*IS* or *LM*) is affected? Why? Calculate the new equilibrium values of income and interest.

6. 'An increase in the propensity to save does not lower the rate of interest. One the contrary it lowers income.' 'An increase in the propensity to save always lowers the rate of interest. In some cases it may also lower income.' Discuss these two statements in the light of the analysis of this chapter.

7. In question 3 the autonomous change in $I_p \equiv \Delta Z = 100$. According to the simple multiplier theory, the change in equilibrium income should be given by:

$$\Delta Y = \Delta Z \frac{1}{1 - c} \quad \left(\text{where } c \equiv \frac{\partial C_p}{\partial Y}\right)$$

From question 2 the value of c is 0.8. Hence we should find:

$$\Delta Y = \Delta Z \frac{1}{1 - 0.8} = 5\Delta Z$$

Reconcile this result with your answer to question 3. What are the *ceteris paribus* assumptions of the simple multiplier which are not satisfied in the more general model? Illustrate the simple multiplier on the *IS*/*LM* diagram. Is there any part of the diagram to which simple multiplier theory is applicable?

8. Suppose the money supply were increased not by purchases of bonds from the general public but by a single payment to all persons reaching their eighteenth birthday in a given year. How would your analysis differ from the analysis in the text? Why would it differ? Can you predict the change in the interest rate?

9. If the MEI schedule is volatile, how will income and the rate of interest behave? Do your conclusions throw any light on question 1?

10. On what behaviour hypotheses would the *IS* curve be a horizontal straight line? Do they seem plausible to you? On what hypotheses would it be vertical?

11. Analyse the consequences for income, employment and the interest rate of an increase in the equality of income distribution. Illustrate your analysis on the *IS*/*LM* diagram.

12. 'A movement *along* one function may in practice cause a *shift* in another function.' Do you agree? Suggest plausible examples.

13. From Figure 12.6 it is clear that output will fluctuate if the position of the *IS* and/or *LM* curves fluctuates. Show that if all the fluctuation is in the *IS* curve, the fluctuations in income will be greater the smaller is the response of the interest rate. Use this result to show that if the authorities seek to control the economy by controlling *either* the nominal money supply *or* the interest rate, it is the former they should control. Explain your results.

14. Use a similar analysis on the assumption that only the *LM* curve shifts about. Which should be controlled now? Is it the nominal money stock or the interest rate? Explain your result.

15. How should control be carried out if *both IS and LM* curves fluctuated?

16. Assume that the money demand function is of the form:

$$M^D = kY_p \quad (k = \text{a positive constant})$$

Show that, for a given value of $M^S = M_0$, then:

(a) the LM curve is a vertical line, *and*
(b) the multiplier of the full system is zero whatever the value of the 'simple' multiplier.

Explain your results.

Suggested reading

Miles Fleming, *Monetary Theory* (Macmillan, 1971).

*J. R. Hicks, 'Mr Keynes and the Classics', in *Readings in the Theory of Income Distribution*, ed. W. Fellner and B. Haley (Allen & Unwin, 1950).

J. M. Keynes, *The General Theory of Employment, Interest and Money* (Macmillan, 1936) ch. 18.

D. W. Laidler, *The Demand for Money* (Scranton, 1969).

W. T. Newlyn, *The Theory of Money* (Oxford University Press, 1971) ch. 8.

*More advanced reference.

Chapter 13
The Public Sector

Introduction

Thus far our analysis has proceeded on the convenient, but highly unrealistic, assumptions that the economy *does not* engage in international trade and *does not* contain a public sector. In this chapter we relax the second of these assumptions: that is, we seek to introduce a *public sector*. In the chapter which follows we shall take account of international trade: that is, we shall introduce the *international sector*.

Both modifications are of major importance to the development of a 'model' relevant to the UK economy since, as we know from Chapter 6, both the international and public sectors constitute major elements of the UK economy.

We begin our task by recalling that the *public sector* in the UK consists in:

(a) central government
(b) local government
(c) the so-called 'public corporations'

The third of these consists essentially of industrial and commercial undertakings owned by the state and managed by some state-controlled organisation such as, for example, the National Coal Board. Just why these enterprises are state-owned in the UK need not detain us, though, in general, industries do not become state-owned unless they are difficult to operate at a profit. However, profitable or otherwise, these public corporations typically perform functions which are not, in any essential way, those of government and which do not differ in any essential way from those performed by private enterprises. We therefore concentrate on the activities of central and local government and, in discussing the public sector, it is primarily these that we have in mind.

The function of central and local governments is to provide public services such as defence, justice, health, etc., and to make transfers of income. They finance the expenditure so incurred by levying taxes and by borrowing. To put matters rather more precisely, if we define:

G_p ≡ government's planned expenditures on goods and services
R_p ≡ government's planned expenditures on transfer payments to households
T_p ≡ government's planned tax receipts

then the public sector's accounting identity is:

$$G_p + R_p - T_p \equiv B_p \tag{13.1}$$

where $B_p \equiv$ government's planned borrowing, which in this simple model can be taken as a first approximation to the planned public sector borrowing requirement (PSBR).

Notice that B_p *is very much of an approximation to the PSBR* since it ignores the borrowing plans of public corporations. However, since we are dealing in rough approximations, let us go further and interpret T_p as consisting in the receipts from *direct* taxes on persons.

The identity 13.1 does no more than reflect the fact that G_p and R_p have to be financed *either* from tax receipts *or* by borrowing from the private sector. The *public sector* faces a budget restriction just like any other transactor or group of transactors.

How are we to integrate G_p, R_p, T_p into our theory of aggregate demand?

The public sector and aggregate demand

Clearly government expenditure on goods and services (G_p) is an element in the aggregate demand for domestic output. Equilibrium in the goods market now requires:

$$Y = C_p + I_p + G_p \tag{13.2}$$

How do taxes (T_p) and transfers (R_p) influence aggregate demand? Direct taxes reduce the incomes available to persons *below* the income they obtain from the productive process. Conversely transfers act like negative direct taxes and increase available income. Thus, ignoring undistributed profits, we can define:

$$\text{personal disposable income} \equiv Y - T_p + R_p \tag{13.3}$$

What behaviour assumptions are we to make? It seems sensible to relate planned consumption to personal disposable income, i.e. to write:

$$C_p = Q + c(Y - T_p + R_p) \quad (0 < c < 1) \tag{13.4}$$

For simplicity, we retain our earlier investment hypothesis and write:

$$I_p = H - br \quad (b > 0) \tag{13.5}$$

We now assume that the government determines G_p independently of the levels of all other variables in the system. This, in effect, makes G_p *exogenous*. We write:

$$G_p = \bar{G} \tag{13.6}$$

How are T_p and R_p to be determined? In general, for perfectly obvious reasons, we must expect T_p ($\equiv$ planned receipts from direct taxes) to rise with income. Thus we should expect $T_p = f(Y)$, with $\partial T_p/\partial Y > 0$.

Many transfer payments arise from social security payments such as unemployment benefit. These tend to be *inversely* related to income. We should therefore expect $R_p = f(Y)$ with $\partial R_p/\partial Y < 0$.

Despite these general considerations, we shall *for the moment* assume *both* T_p *and* R_p to be determined like G_p: that is, to be *exogenous*. Hence:

$$\left.\begin{aligned} T_p &= \bar{T} \\ R_p &= \bar{R} \end{aligned}\right\} \tag{13.7}$$

Substituting 13.3 – 13.7 into 13.2 yields the *IS* curve for our model with a public sector. This is:

$$Y = [Q + H + \bar{G} + c(\bar{R} - \bar{T}) - br]\frac{1}{1-c} \tag{13.8}$$

From 13.8 it is easy to obtain the 'simple' (constant interest rate) multipliers for fiscal changes (i.e. changes in G_p, T_p, R_p). These are:

$$\begin{aligned} \frac{\Delta Y}{\Delta \bar{G}} &= \frac{1}{1-c} \\ \frac{\Delta Y}{\Delta \bar{T}} &= \frac{-c}{1-c} \\ \frac{\Delta Y}{\Delta \bar{R}} &= \frac{c}{1-c} \end{aligned} \tag{13.9}$$

What is the meaning of these 'multipliers'? Take $\Delta Y/\Delta \bar{G}$. The expression $\Delta Y/\Delta \bar{G}$ tells us that if the government:

(a) increases $\bar{G}$ by $\Delta \bar{G}$
(b) finances the increase by *borrowing*
(c) the rate of interest remains invariant

then incomes will rise by:

$$\Delta Y = \Delta \bar{G} \times \frac{1}{1-c}$$

Why do we say 'financed by borrowing'? Recall the government's budget identity in 13.1. In our example we have increased G_p (= $\bar{G}$). But T_p and R_p are, on our assumptions, unaltered. Hence $\Delta B_p = \Delta G_p = \Delta \bar{G}$: *that is, the finance for the additional expenditure must be borrowed.*

Notice that the 'simple' multiplier for an increase in taxation is $-c/1-c$: that is, it *reduces* income but by a multiplier which is *less* than that applicable to $\Delta \bar{G}$. It is therefore obvious that *equal* increases in $\bar{G}$ and $\bar{T}$ – that is, an increase in $\bar{G}$ financed by taxation – have a multiplier of unity. For example, we have:

$$\Delta Y = \Delta \bar{G}\,\frac{1}{1-c} - \Delta \bar{T}\,\frac{c}{1-c}$$

but $\Delta \bar{T} = \Delta \bar{G}$, so that:

$$\Delta Y = \Delta\bar{G}\left[\frac{1}{1-c} - \frac{c}{1-c}\right]$$
$$= \Delta\bar{G} \qquad (13.10)$$

This result looks a little surprising but is not hard to understand. Using the method of Chapter 9 the multiplier series for an increase in $\bar{G}$ is:

$$\Delta Y_1 = \Delta\bar{G}(1 + c + c^2 + c^3 + c^4 + \ldots + c^n) \qquad (13.11)$$

The corresponding series for the increase in taxation is:

$$\Delta Y_2 = -\Delta\bar{T}(c + c^2 + c^2 + c^3 + c^4 + \ldots + c^n) \qquad (13.12)$$

The second series lacks the first term in the former. This reflects the fact that an increase in taxation does not reduce household consumption by its full amount but only by that part of the additional tax which would have been consumed i.e. $c\Delta\bar{T}$. As against this, any change in government expenditure on goods and services changes aggregate demand by the same amount.

Summing (13.11) and (13.12) when, by assumption, $\Delta\bar{G} = \Delta\bar{T}$ we have:

$$\Delta Y \equiv \Delta Y_1 + \Delta Y_2 = \Delta\bar{G}[1 + (c - c) + (c^2 - c^2) + \ldots + (c^n - c^n)]$$
$$= \Delta\bar{G} \qquad (13.13)$$

All these results are 'simple multiplier' results in that they assume an invariant rate of interest. As we know, the *LM* curve will typically *not* be horizontal, so that any increase in income (with a given nominal money supply) will raise r, thus *reducing* the multiplier by generating an *induced* reduction in real planned investment (I_p).

We can show this formally by writing:

$$M^D = M^S \qquad (13.14)$$
$$M^D = kpY + Z + mr \quad (m < 0\ k > 0) \qquad (13.15)$$
$$M^S = \bar{M}^S \qquad (13.16)$$

where 13.14 defines money market equilibrium, 13.15 gives a highly simplified version of a money demand function, and 13.16 states that the nominal money supply is held constant at $\bar{M}^S$.

Now p ($\equiv$ price level) is taken to be constant (say at $\bar{p}$). Hence combining 13.14 – 13.16 we can find r, which is:

$$r = \frac{\bar{M}^S - k\bar{p}Y - Z}{m} \quad (\text{m} < 0) \qquad (13.17)$$

This expression can be substituted into 13.8 to give the 'full' solution for Y from which we can derive the 'full multiplier' which does *not* assume an invariant interest rate. This is:

$$y = \frac{Q + H + \bar{G} + c(\bar{R} - \bar{T}) - b/m\,[\bar{M}^s - Z]}{1 - c - kb\bar{p}/m} \qquad (13.18)$$

The new term in the multiplier, $kb\bar{p}/m$, is less than 0 so that *minus* $kb\bar{p}/m$ is positive. As $m \to$ zero, i.e. as the *LM* curve becomes *vertical, minus* $kb\bar{p}/m$ tends to infinity and the 'full' multiplier to zero. Conversely as $m \to \infty$, the *LM* curve tends to the horizontal. In this case *minus* $kb\bar{p}/m$ tends to zero and the multiplier to $1/1-c$, that is, the 'simple' multiplier.

In short, the term *minus* $kb\bar{p}/m$ summarises the induced response of aggregate demand to the change in the demand for money and its impact on the rate of interest. We can now tabulate these results (see Table 13.1).

Table 13.1

Action	Method of finance	'Simple' multiplier	'Full' or 'total' multiplier		
			General	Maximum value	Minimum value
ΔG_p	Borrowing	$\frac{1}{1-c}$	$\frac{1}{1-c-kb\bar{p}/m}$	$\frac{1}{1-c}$	Zero
	Taxation	Unity	$\frac{1-c}{1-c-kb\bar{p}/m}$	Unity	Zero
	Reduction in transfer payments	Unity	$\frac{1-c}{1-c-kb\bar{p}/m}$	Unity	Zero
$\Delta\bar{T}$	—	$\frac{-c}{1-c}$	$\frac{-c}{1-c-kb\bar{p}/m}$	$\frac{-c}{1-c}$	Zero
$\Delta\bar{R}$	Borrowing	$\frac{c}{1-c}$	$\frac{c}{1-c-kb\bar{p}/m}$	$\frac{c}{1-c}$	Zero

For those who prefer geometry to 'algebra', Figure 13.1 illustrates a shift in the *IS* curve of 13.8 due to $\Delta\bar{G}$ in a situation in which the *LM* curve is approximated by *three* straight-line segments. In the first of these we have:

$$m_1 \equiv \frac{\partial M^D}{\partial r} = -\infty$$

In the second and third we have:

$$m_2 \equiv \frac{\partial M^D}{\partial r} > -\infty < 0$$

$$m_3 \equiv \frac{\partial M^D}{\partial r} = 0$$

In each of the three panels the *IS* curve is shown shifting to the right by $\Delta\bar{G}$. In each case the *simple* multiplier is the same, the 'full' multiplier by contrast, clearly depends on the initial position and thus whether $m = m_1$ or m_2 or m_3, which governs the slope of the *LM* curve.

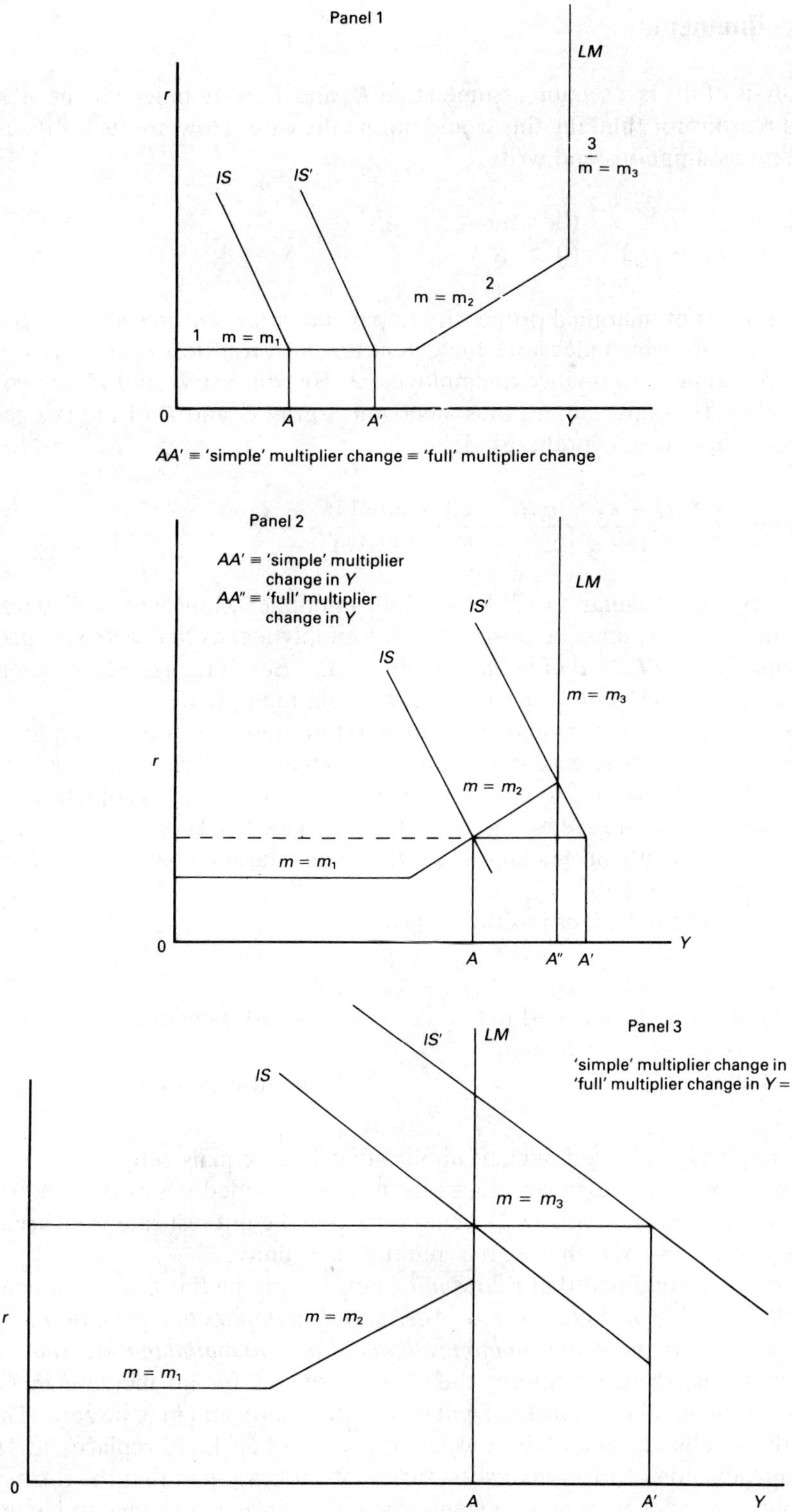

Figure 13.1 Fiscal policy multipliers

Some refinements

The analysis of the last section assumed that R_p and T_p were independent of Y even though we gave reasons for thinking this would not be the case. How are its results modified if we relax these assumptions and write:

$$\begin{aligned} T_p &= t_0 + t_1 Y \quad (0 < t_1 < 1) \\ R_p &= R_0 + R_1 Y \quad (0 > R_1) \end{aligned} \tag{13.19}$$

Here t_1 is a sort of 'marginal propensity to pay direct tax' enforced by the government and R_1 is a parameter which measures the extent to which transfers decline as Y rises due, say, to the reduced need to finance unemployment. By contrast T_0 and R_0 are constants which reflect policy decisions and are thus analogous to the $\bar{G}$ and $\bar{R}$ of the last section.

Inserting these new hypotheses yields:

$$Y = \frac{Q + H + \bar{G} + c(R_0 - t_0) - b/m\,[M^S - Z]}{1 - c + c(t_1 - R_1) - kb\bar{p}/m} \tag{13.20}$$

This expression is similar to 13.8. The 'full multiplier', however, will tend to be rather smaller since $t_1 - R_1$ must be positive, which simply means that a rise in income increases tax revenue (T_p) by $t_1\Delta Y$ *and reduces* R_p by $R_1\Delta Y$. Both factors reduce demand. They are thus 'leakages' which reduce the value of the 'full multiplier'.

In the case in which we assumed an invariant interest rate (i.e. a 'simple' multiplier) we noted that a marginal increase in $\bar{G}$ financed by an identical increase in $\bar{T}$, i.e. a marginally balanced budget, gave rise to a multiplier of unity. This result is sometimes referred to as the 'balanced budget theorem', though since the condition $\Delta\bar{G} = \Delta\bar{T}$ does *not* entail $\bar{G} + \bar{R} - \bar{T} = 0$, this is slightly misleading. Does the same 'marginal balanced budget theory' hold when we introduce 13.19?

The *change* in the budget position is given by:

Δt_0	+	$\Delta Y(t_1 - R_1)$	−	$\Delta\bar{G}$	
autonomous tax change	+	induced net change in revenue	−	autonomous change in government expenditure	(13.21)

and a 'marginally balanced budget' implies that 13.21 equals zero.

Suppose now that the government selects $\Delta\bar{G}$. Provided it sets Δt_0 (the shift in the tax function) in accordance with 13.21 being zero, *and* the interest rate is invariant, it is simple to show that $\Delta Y = \Delta G$: that is, the 'multiplier' is unity.

Note that the condition that r does *not* change implies a flat LM curve over the relevant range: that is, $-kb\bar{p}/m$ equal to zero. *Alternatively it implies that the nominal money stock is allowed to adjust to the change in money demand so as to maintain r invariant.* When neither condition holds, then, as before, the 'full multiplier' for an increase in $\bar{G}$ financed by taxation (or reduction in transfers) will be *less* than unity and may be zero. Thus, in general terms, the results of our earlier analysis still holds when 13.20 replaces 13.18.

The introduction of 13.19 involves a further complication in that the financial position of the public sector becomes an endogenous variable since any change in income changes T_p (via t_1) and R_p (via R_1). Thus, for example, an increase in $\bar{G}$ of, say, £100 million per period will, at the new equilibrium level of income, be partly financed by the additional tax revenue ($t_1 \Delta Y$) and fall in transfers ($R_1 \Delta Y$) induced by the multiplier process. In the static model presented here, the induced changes will not be sufficient to finance the full £100m per period even if the interest rate is invariant and the multiplier 'simple'. If m does *not* tend to infinity (so that the LM curve is flat) and, as a consequence r rises as Y increases, this result is strengthened (i.e. the revenue shortfall per period is increased) and, obviously enough, as m tends to zero and the LM curve to the vertical, the shortfall per period tends to £100m.

Thus, although an increase in taxation ($\Delta t_0 > 0$) or a reduction in expenditure on transfers ($\Delta R_0 < 0$) or goods and services ($\Delta \bar{G} < 0$) will *reduce* government borrowing (B_p) it will *not* reduce it by as much as the autonomous change except in the case in which the 'full multiplier' is zero. Conversely an increase in $\bar{G}$ ($\Delta \bar{G} > 0$) will *increase* the PSBR but by less than $\Delta \bar{G}$.

Our model therefore typically yields a 'full multiplier' of something between zero (the result when m ($\equiv \partial M^D / \partial r = 0$)) and the value of the 'simple multiplier' (the result when $\partial M^D / \partial r = -\infty$). In the former situation an increase in government expenditure has no effect on total output because its expansionary impetus is offset by the induced fall in real planned investment brought about by the rise in the interest rate. The offsetting induced decline in $C_p + I_p$ is, in our model, restricted to investment, though in practice there might also be an induced fall in consumption. In recent years this process has come to be called 'crowding out', for the expansion of public-sector expenditure, even when financed by borrowing, is said to 'crowd out' – via the interest-rate mechanism – expenditure by the private sector.

Notice that:

1. *Some* element of private-sector expenditure must always be 'crowded out' as long as:
   (a) the IS curve is *not* vertical
   (b) m ($\equiv \partial M^D / \partial r$) is greater than $-\infty$
2. 'Crowding out' will be complete (i.e. there will be no change in aggregate demand) if:
   (a) $m = 0$ (the demand for money exhibits zero interest elasticity) *or*
   (b) the IS curve is horizontal

We must of course recall, at this stage, the limitations of our very short-run analysis in which, in particular, the price level is assumed to be invariant ($p = \bar{p}$) and private-sector wealth (consisting in real capital goods and the stock of bonds) is also invariant. Relaxing these assumptions, as we shall see in a later chapter, introduces additional mechanisms by which 'crowding out' may occur. Moreover, once we eliminate the assumption that p is invariant, we shall need to distinguish between 'real crowding out' ($\Delta Y = 0$) and 'nominal crowding out' ($\Delta pY = 0$) which, at present, we do not need to do.

We can summarise our analysis thus far by arguing that:

1. Increases in government expenditure on goods and services or on transfers (or reductions in taxation) will typically have some (net) expansionary effect upon income when they are financed by borrowing.
2. They will, in general, also raise the rate of interest.
3. In general, via the rise in the interest rate, they will 'crowd out' some elements of private-sector expenditures.
4. 'Crowding out', however, is unlikely to be complete. Thus
5. An increase/decrease in government expenditures does not entail an equivalent increase/decrease in B_p ($\approx$ PSBR).

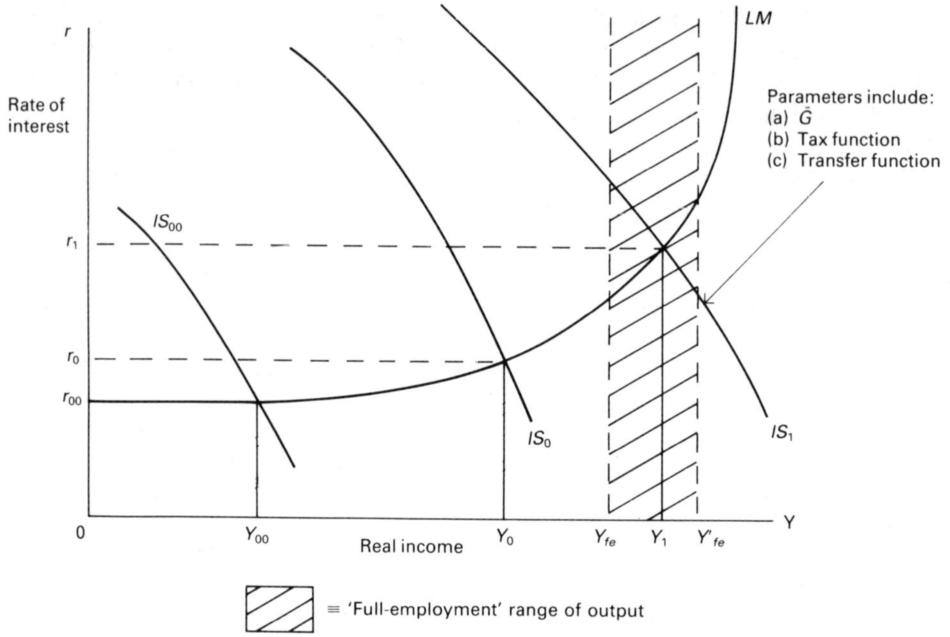

Figure 13.2 Fiscal policy and aggregate demand

Elements of 'neo-Keynesian' fiscal policy

The analysis in the last two sections immediately makes it clear why many economists regard discretionary changes in G_p and the functions explaining T_p and R_p – that is, changes in fiscal policy – as potentially very powerful instruments of macroeconomic management.

Consider, for example, the period 1948–73, during which Labour and Conservative governments sought to maintain 'full employment' and interpreted this to mean restricting the percentage of the work-force unemployed within the range of, say, 1½–3 per cent. Given the production function, then, in any short period for which productive capacity is given, this defines a range of output levels ($Y_{fe} - Y'_{fe}$) compatible with this objective. We can depict this geometrically on our usual *IS/LM* construct (see Figure 13.2).

Clearly, by changing G_p, R_p or T_p – or some combination – the authorities can manipulate the *IS* schedule so that it cuts the *LM* schedule within the range $Y_{fe} - Y'_{fe}$. This means that *if private-sector* expenditure fluctuates (typically through shifts in the investment function) the *public sector* can be used to stabilise (or 'tune') aggregate demand. The narrower the range of $Y_{fe} - Y'_{fe}$ defined by the authorities, the 'finer' the degree of 'tuning' which the authorities believe they can attain.

All this looks extremely simple. But even at the very much simplified level of our analysis, there are no simple rules for the operation of fiscal policy. Suppose, for example, income is at Y_0 with, say, unemployment at 5 per cent. An expansionary fiscal policy is required. But the form it takes is still at choice and is no easy matter to decide.

This is because *IS_0 can be shifted to, say, IS_1* by:

(a) increasing G_p and financing the increase by raising T_p and/or reducing R_p

(b) increasing G_p and financing the increase by borrowing
(c) reducing T_p and financing the reduction by borrowing
(d) increasing R_p and financing the increase by borrowing
(e) making use of some combination of (a)–(d)

This is so because, as we have demonstrated, each of (a) – (e) will, provided 'crowding out' is not complete (the *LM* curve is *not* vertical), raise Y. In short, there is an infinite number of possible 'fiscal policy' changes which will shift IS_0 to IS_1 and our analysis provides no criteria for choosing between them.

On the other hand, if the analysis is correct, and it is the objective of the authorities to restore 'full employment' in some meaningful sense, we can and should examine each budget to see how far the changes in G_p, T_p and R_p contained in it are consistent with the authorities' assumed objective. For example, it would be entirely inconsistent with our analysis if, with output at Y_0, the authorities attempted to return to $Y_{fe} - Y'_{fe}$ by *reducing* government expenditures and *raising* taxes.

That governments might act in this way is entirely conceivable. Suppose, for example, the economy was initially at IS_1 but that, because of a sharp fall in business optimism, the I_p function shifts and takes the *IS* curve to IS_0. Since Y has fallen, so has tax revenue. For the same reason R_p has increased since the numbers on unemployment benefit have roughly doubled. There has therefore been a sharp increase in the *public sector*'s deficit (or reduction in its surplus) due to these *induced* changes which are not themselves the results of discretionary policy. In such a situation the authorities may seek to eliminate or reduce the deficit by cutting expenditure (for example, on schools or universities) or seeking to reduce transfers (by reducing the scope and/or scale of social security benefits). Alternatively they may seek to raise taxes. On our analysis, the result is likely to be a further leftward shift of the *IS* curve, say to IS_{00}, and an *increase* in unemployment. Moreover, since there will be a further element of induced increase in the fiscal deficit as Y declines to Y_{00}, a cumulative programme of 'fiscal restraint' is quite conceivable.

Many countries experienced this kind of fiscal response during the Great Depression of the 1930s. And from some points of view the fiscal policies of the Thatcher–Howe administration have exhibited similar characteristics. It is therefore not entirely surprising that these policies have been accompanied by a very sharp increase in unemployment and an unusually severe fall in real GDP and industrial production.

Later in this book we shall examine the theoretical rationale of the Thatcher–Howe policies. We can note here, however, that one common explanation of such policies is plainly absurd. This is the argument that a nation is like an individual household in that, faced by a fall in national income, it must reduce expenditure just as must a household faced by a fall in *its* income. This is an example of the fallacy of composition which asserts that what is true for an individual is true for the sum of individuals in a community. Any individual, for example, can make himself better off by stealing from others. But all individuals cannot do this and no one would argue that they should. However, the nation–household analogy is scarcely less absurd and forces otherwise quite sensible people to assert that we cannot have more output 'because resources are scarce' when (as I write this) recorded unemployment is over 10 per cent and excess capacity in industry of the order of 20 per cent. In these circumstances 'resources', in the economic sense, are anything but scarce.

Our analysis also makes plain that there is no particular virtue, from the point of view of controlling output via demand, in maintaining a 'balanced budget' or even a 'marginally balanced budget'. This does *not* mean that there may not be arguments in favour of a 'balanced budget'. Such arguments are not hard to find. But the issue of whether to budget for a surplus, deficit or balance is a complex one which cannot be settled by appeal to some simple fiscal 'rule' – let alone a 'rule' derived from a fallacious analogy between a nation and a household.

Finally, let us recall once again the limitations of our analysis: namely, its short-run character; its assumption of a constant price level ($p = \bar{p}$); and its assumption that M^S ($\equiv$ the nominal money stock) can be treated as an exogenous variable and thus independent of *all* other variables in the system including, *inter alia*, the size of the public sector borrowing requirement (PSBR). Later we shall have to ask how much of our analysis remains valid when these assumptions are relaxed.

Questions and exercises

1. Compare the *NIESR Review* presentation of the public sector borrowing requirement (in table 13 of the issue for May 1982) with the representation in the Central Statistical Office's *Financial Statistics*, tables 2.3 and 2.7. On the basis of this comparison, re-examine the approximation employed in the text. Is it a helpful simplification or a potentially misleading oversimplification?

2. In 1967 the PSBR was £1,860 million. By 1969 the PSBR was a *negative* figure of £424 million. How would you explain the change? Use the relevant data from *Financial Statistics* or *Economic Trends* to support your explanation.

3. 'Taxes on income raise just about as much as taxes on expenditure.' Is this so? Use official data for 1970–80 to check this assertion.

4. The models of Chapter 13 include only taxes on income. What problem arises in introducing taxes on commodities and services (i.e. indirect taxes)? How would you analyse the consequences of an increase in the rate of indirect taxes?

5. 'The so-called "crowding-out" argument applies to autonomous increases in investment and consumption just as much as it does to an increase in government expenditure. Consumption (or investment) crowds out investment (or consumption); the private sector "crowds out" itself.' Is this so? Discuss critically.

6. 'Tax evasion for the well to do has become institutionalised and is now known as "avoidance". For the less well to do it remains evasion, attracts moral disapprobation and is subject to legal penalties.' Discuss critically.

7. 'All the revenue we raise by subjecting ourselves to the horrors of VAT goes to the EEC.' Does it? Show, using data from central government accounts, the proportion of payments to the EEC of VAT receipts. What difficulties do you meet in measuring this ratio?

8. 'A change in fiscal policy may be defined as a shift in the tax and/or transfer functions (i.e. a change in t_0 and/or R_0) and/or a change in government expenditure on goods and services which is taken to be exogenous. Thus an *expansionary* fiscal policy is usually defined by the condition:

$$\Delta\bar{G} - (\Delta t_0 - \Delta R_0) > 0$$

This is a very different quantity from the change in the observed budget position which is $\Delta\bar{G} = (\Delta t_0 + t_1\,\Delta Y - \Delta R_0 - R_1\Delta Y)$.' Elucidate.

9. Given your answer to question 8, would you use actual data to estimate whether fiscal changes have been 'expansionary' or 'contractionary'?

10. What do you understand by the expression 'cyclically adjusted public sector borrowing requirement', and how would you measure it?

Suggested reading

J. C. R. Dow, *The Management of the British Economy: 1945–1960* (Cambridge University Press, 1964) chs 7–8.

J. C. R. Dow, 'Fiscal Policy and Monetary Policy as Instruments of Control', *Westminister Bank Review* (May, August, November 1960).

HM Treasury, *Economic Progress Report*, no. 118 (February 1980); no. 126 (October 1980); no. 130 (February 1981); no. 135 (July 1981); no. 144 (April 1982).

D. Savage, 'Fiscal Policy 1974/5–1980/1: Description and Measurement', *NIESR Review*, no. 99 (February 1982).

G. K. Shaw, *Fiscal Policy* (Macmillan, 1972).

*R. W. Spencer, in *Current Issues in Monetary Theory and Policy*, ed. T. M. Havrilevsky and J. T. Boorman. (AHM Publishing Co., 1976).

*More advanced reference.

Chapter 14
The International Sector

Introduction

So far we have proceeded on the convenient – but entirely unrealistic – assumption that the economy we are studying does *not* engage in international trade. We now eliminate this assumption and ask in what ways our earlier analysis has to be modified to take account of external transactions.

In examining this problem the reader should notice that we do *not* seek to explain *either* why international trade occurs on the existing scale *or* how its existence adds to economic welfare. We are concerned only with how the existence of international trade (on a scale in relation to GDP which we described in Chapter 6) modifies the analysis we have developed in the previous chapters.

We now begin this limited enquiry by asking:

> How does the existence of international trade modify our analysis of aggregate demand?

The international sector and aggregate demand

As we saw in our discussion of national income accounting:

(a) some part (and in the UK a significant part) of expenditure on GDP arises out of the expenditure of foreign residents on our exports
(b) some part (again a significant part) of the expenditure of domestic residents is devoted to purchasing foreign output (our imports).

Clearly exports constitute a positive expenditure on GDP and imports a negative expenditure. Thus, *in nominal terms*, expenditure on GDP – gross domestic expenditure – is given by:

$$Yp_d \equiv C_p p_d + I_p p_d + I_p p_d + G_p p_d + Ep_d - Zp_w q \qquad (14.1)$$

where:

E	$\equiv$	real exports
p_d	$\equiv$	domestic price level
p_w	$\equiv$	foreign price of a unit of foreign output measured in foreign currency
q	$\equiv$	cost of a unit of foreign currency in terms of domestic currency
qp_w	$\equiv$	cost of a unit of foreign output in domestic currency
Z	$\equiv$	quantity of units of foreign output imported

Notice that q is simply the reciprocal of the rate of exchange as this is usually quoted in the UK. A *rise* in q is thus a *fall* in the exchange rate: that is, a devaluation or a depreciation. A fall in q is thus an appreciation.

We are accustomed to working in 'real' terms. Hence we rewrite this relation in 'real' terms by dividing each item by p_d to give:

$$Y \equiv C_p + I_p + G_p + E - Z\left\{\frac{p_w}{p_d}\right\}q \tag{14.2}$$

so that our equilibrium condition in the goods market becomes:

$$Y = C_p + I_p + G_p + E - Z\left\{\frac{p_w}{p_d}\right\}q \tag{14.3}$$

Thus, in order to explain equilibrium output, we must develop theories to explain real exports ($\equiv E$) and real imports ($\equiv Z[p_w/p_d] \times q$).

Notice that, if p_w, p_d and q are assumed to be constant, we can rewrite $Zp_w \times q/p_d$ as, say, $Z\phi$, *where* $\phi \equiv [p_w/p_d] \times q$. Moreover, by redefining the units in which Z is measured, ϕ can be set equal to unity, i.e. $p_w q = p_d$. In these circumstances we can simplify by writing:

$$Y = C_p + I_p + G_p + E - Z \tag{14.4}$$

so that we now need theories to explain E and Z.

Consider exports first. The exports of the UK are part of the imports of the rest of the world. In a short-run analysis such as we are now developing we can take the 'institutional' framework of commercial transactions – such matters as our membership of the EEC, its rules and the rules of such bodies as GATT – as given. In these circumstances we may, as a useful approximation, regard the rest of the world's expenditures on our products (i.e. our exports) as being primarily determined by:

(a) the level of real income in the rest of the world (Y_w)
(b) the relative 'competitiveness' of UK goods and services

'Competitiveness' is not a simple concept to define. It involves such matters as design, reliability in delivery and performance, and marketing skill, as well as the *price* of UK goods in relation to competing overseas products. Apart from relative prices (or relative costs) these elements are hard to identify and quantify. We shall therefore follow traditional practice and interpret 'competitiveness' simply as relative prices.

Our export hypothesis – which is very much an approximation – is:

$$E = f\left\{Y_w, \left[\frac{p_w}{p_d}\right]q\right\} \tag{14.5}$$

where

p_w	$\equiv$	price of foreign goods in foreign currencies
q	$\equiv$	number of pounds sterling for which a unit of foreign currency exchanges
p_d	$\equiv$	price of UK goods and services in pounds sterling

What general characteristics do we expect this export function to possess?

Suppose real incomes rise in the rest of the world, *ceteris paribus* – which means with p_w, p_d and q constant. We would expect exports to rise. Thus we expect $\partial E/\partial Y_w > 0$. We would also expect $\partial E/\partial Y_w < 1$, since it seems highly unlikely that the whole of any increase in Y_w would be devoted to purchasing UK output. In short:

$$0 < \frac{\partial E}{\partial Y_w} < 1$$

seems to be reasonable with the implication that $\partial E/\partial Y_w$ is likely to be very small.

Equally clearly we expect any *increase* in the ratio $p_w q/p_d$ to *increase* exports since it indicates a *deterioration* of the 'competitiveness' *of the rest of the world's output*. Thus:

$$\frac{\partial E}{\partial p_w}, \frac{\partial E}{\partial q} > 0; \frac{\partial E}{\partial p_d} < 0$$

Recall here that an *increase* in q is an increase in the number of units of domestic currency which will exchange for a unit of the currency of the rest of the world. *A rise in q is thus a devaluation or depreciation of sterling.*

Now that we have a (simple) theory of exports, what of imports? Symmetrically with 14.5 we write:

$$Z = f\left\{ Y, \left[\frac{p_w}{p_d} \right] q \right\} \tag{14.6}$$

with:

$$0 < \frac{\partial Z}{\partial Y} < 1; \frac{\partial Z}{\partial p_w}, \frac{\partial Z}{\partial q} < 0; \frac{\partial Z}{\partial p_d} > 0$$

Notice that we have used Y (i.e. GDP) as the appropriate income variable rather than $Y-T+R$ (i.e. personal disposable income). This is because, in the UK, imports consist in large measure of raw materials, which are inputs into the general productive process, rather than consumption goods expenditures, which might be argued to depend upon personal disposable income.

Thus, on the basis of the two approximations – 14.5 and 14.6 – we have sought to explain the current account of the balance of payments or, what is the same thing, the international transactions which enter *directly* into the determination of aggregate demand (as in 14.4). To do this, however, we were compelled to introduce three additional variables, Y_w, p_w and q. Unless these can be explained, we are little further forward.

With two of the variables, namely Y_w and p_w, useful approximate explanations are not hard to find. Both may plausibly be regarded as exogenous on the grounds that:

(a) neither is likely, in practice, to be significantly influenced by what occurs in the UK economy, *and*
(b) *both* can therefore be regarded as determined entirely in the rest of the world

Thus, in our usual notation:

$$\begin{aligned} Y_w &= \bar{Y}_w \\ p_w &= \bar{p}_w \end{aligned} \tag{14.7}$$

This leaves us with q – the rate of exchange. Clearly it would be absurd to treat q as exogenous in the same sense as Y_w and p_w since this would amount to assuming that q (≡ the sterling exchange rate) was independent of what occurred in the UK economy. We must therefore give rather fuller consideration to the rate of exchange before our analysis can proceed.

The rate of exchange and exchange regimes

The rate of exchange (q) is a price. It gives the value, in pounds sterling, of a representative unit of the rest of the world's currency. To illustrate: identify the latter with the US dollar. Then $q \equiv$ the sterling cost of 1 US dollar: that is, 50p if £1 = 2 US dollars; 55.5p if £1 = 1.80 US dollars; and so on.

Since q is a price it can be determined in one of two ways: that is, it can either be *fixed* as, in practice, exchange rates were fixed (in the short term) from roughly the end of the Second World War to 1973, when the Bretton Woods arrangements finally collapsed; or it can be determined in a market by the forces of demand and supply. Since, under the Bretton Woods arrangements, exchange rates were subject to infrequent adjustments between which they were said to be 'pegged', the former system is often described as that of the 'occasionally jumping peg', while the latter is referred to as that of a 'flexible exchange rate', or 'floating rate'.

Consider the former. Under it assume q is set at, say, £0.5 per US dollar by the UK government. By doing this the UK authorities (the Treasury and Bank of England) become obliged to maintain the officially fixed rate. *This means that they have to operate as residual buyers (or sellers) of US dollars in the sense that, when UK residents are demanding more dollars (to make payments to the rest of the world) than the rest of the world is supplying (because of its need to make payments to UK residents) the UK authorities must either supply the difference or abandon the 'pegged' rate.*

This process, which is illustrated in Figure 14.1, is, as the reader will appreciate, an example of the general proposition that, in any market, the authorities can set the price, *or* the quantity, *but not both*.

In Figure 14.1 *DD* is the demand for dollars by UK residents. It slopes downwards since a rise in q (a devaluation) means that the rest of the world's goods and services become relatively more expensive. *SS* is the supply of dollars arising from foreign residents and it slopes upwards since a rise in q makes UK goods and services less expensive to foreigners. As drawn, the two curves intersect at *H* so that, in the absence of any intervention by the authorities:

(a) the equilibrium exchange rate would be q_e
(b) the equilibrium quantity of dollars traded would be *OX*

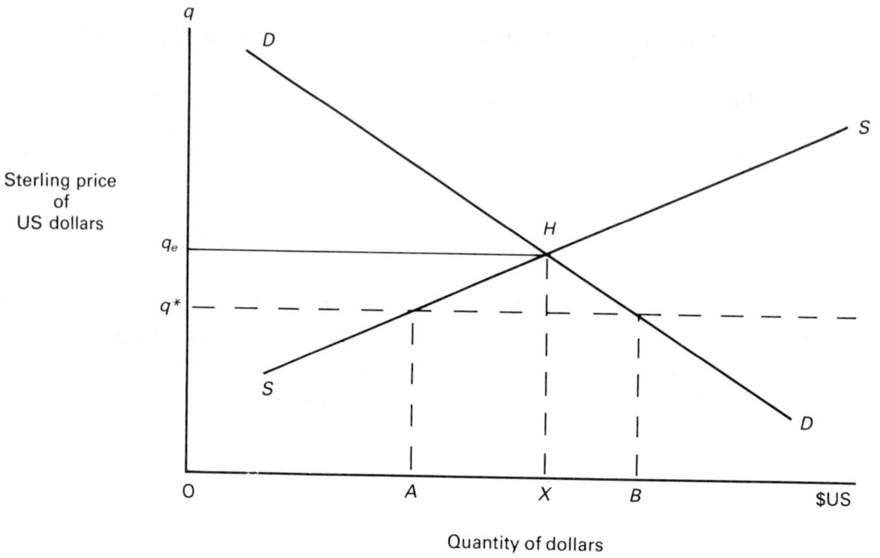

Figure 14.1 The occasionally jumping peg

Suppose, however, the authorities peg the rate at q^*. In this situation:

(c) the quantity of dollars demanded is OB
(d) the quantity of dollars supplied is OA

so that:

(e) the *excess demand* for dollars is AB

Thus, if the authorities wish to maintain $q = q^*$, they must act as residual sellers of dollars and provide AB dollars to equilibrate the market at q^*.

Conversely, if the rate is *not* pegged *and* the authorities do *not* intervene, the market will go to q_e: that is, the rate will be determined by the process of equating (non-official) demand and supply. With no 'peg' *and no intervention*, there is said to be a 'perfectly *clean* float'. This means only that the rate (q) is allowed to 'float' (i.e. be determined on the market) with no official intervention in the market. Where the rate is allowed to float but there *is* official intervention (say to limit the extent of day-to-day fluctuations) there is said to be a 'managed' or 'dirty' float. The greater the extent of official intervention, the 'dirtier' the float. Thus the 'occasionally jumping peg' can in a sense be thought of as the limiting case of a 'dirty' float plus an announced 'target' rate q^*.

To see what this means consider Figure 14.2.

In Figure 14.2 *DD* and *SS* are precisely as in Figure 14.1. The assumed objective of the authorities is now to maintain q within the band q_1q_2 shown by the shaded area. *There is no officially announced rate*. The authorities simply operate in the market to keep $q_1 \leqslant q$ and $q \leqslant q_2$. As the figure has been drawn the authorities must act as residual seller of *at least A′ B′* dollars and *no more than AB* dollars.

Clearly if the authorities narrow the band (i.e. the difference between q_1 and q_2), then it will, in the limit, converge to a single 'target' price q_T. The system will then conform, in its daily workings, to that of the 'occasionally jumping peg', though no official rate has been

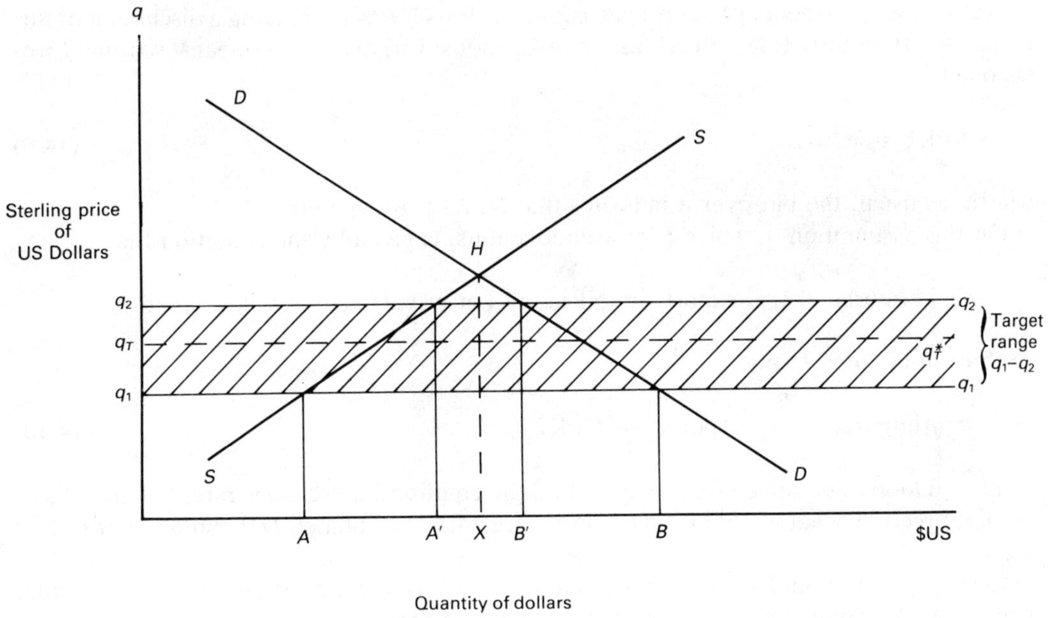

Figure 14.2 A managed float

formally announced and the authorities can, whenever they wish, change q_T or widen the range around it.

In practice, most floats are more or less 'dirty'. However, in order to avoid the problem of having to formulate a theory to explain the authorities' policy with regard to intervention in the market for foreign exchange, we shall assume *either* a fixed rate (an occasionally jumping peg) *or* a fully flexible rate (a perfectly clean float).

In the former case, we can write our assumption formally as:

$$q = q^* = \text{a constant set by the authorities}$$

In the latter case q is an *endogenous* variable determined by the condition:

$$\text{Demand for foreign exchange} = \text{supply of foreign exchange}$$

As we know from Chapter 6, both demand and supply arise on the capital as well as the current account of the balance of payments. Thus we have:

$$\text{supply of foreign exchange} \equiv \text{exports} + \text{private capital inflows}$$
$$\text{demand for foreign exchange} \equiv \text{imports} + \text{private capital outflows}$$

so that, for equilibrium in the foreign exchange market, we require:

$$\text{imports} - \text{exports} - \text{net private capital inflows} = \text{zero} \tag{14.8}$$

As yet we have no theory of net private capital inflows (NPKI). Pending a discussion of this issue, we therefore treat NPKI as an exogenous variable. This means writing (provisionally):

$$\text{NPKI} = \overline{\text{NPKI}} \tag{14.9}$$

where, as usual, the bar over it indicates that NPKI is *exogenous*.

On this assumption q, which is now endogenous, is given by the condition that:

$$\text{real imports} - \text{real exports} = \overline{\text{NPKI}} \equiv \text{net private capital inflow (real)}$$

so that, in nominal terms:

$$p_w q(\text{imports}) - p_d(\text{exports}) = \overline{\text{NPKI}}.p_d \tag{14.10}$$

is the equation to be solved for q so as to find the equilibrium exchange rate. Solving this is, in fact, precisely what was done when, in Figure 14.1, we equated *DD* and *SS* at *H* to find q_e.

Clearly a system under which q is fixed at q^* differs significantly from a system under which q is determined by a 'perfectly clean' float and must be analysed accordingly.

We shall therefore begin with the former.

External transactions and aggregate demand: occasionally jumping peg

We now have a system under which:

(a) p_d and p_w are assumed to be constant
(b) Y_w is regarded as exogenous
(c) q is 'pegged' at q^*

Inserting these assumptions into our export hypothesis makes it clear that E is independent of whatever occurs in the domestic economy provided output is less than full-capacity output. As a simplication, therefore, we can treat exports as exogenous and write:

$$E = \bar{E} \tag{14.11}$$

The import function not only contains p_d, p_w and q as arguments but also Y. The three former are all invariant. The latter, however, is not. In these circumstances we can write a linear approximation to the import function as:

$$Z = F + zY \tag{14.12}$$

where

$$0 \leqslant \frac{\partial Z}{\partial Y} \equiv z \leqslant 1$$

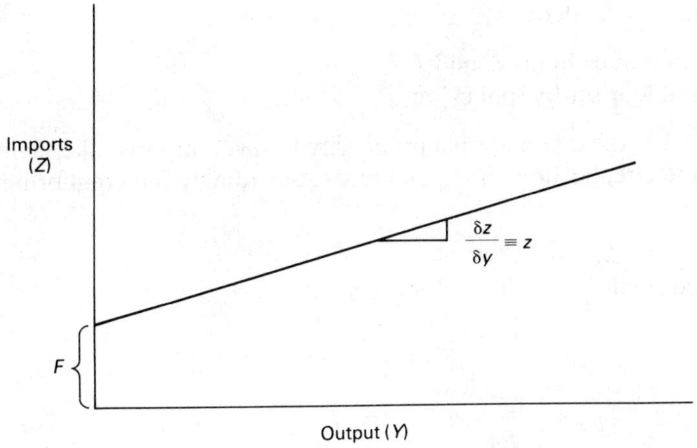

Note: This formulation assumes $\left[\dfrac{p_w}{p_d}\right] q^* = \text{constant} = \text{unity}$ and is derived from the general form:

$$z = F + zY\left[\frac{p_w}{p_d}\right]q^*$$

Figure 14.3 Linear import function

$F \equiv$ autonomous real imports and is dependent on the value of p_d, p_w and q
$z \equiv$ marginal propensity to import out of increases in Y, i.e. $\partial Z/\partial Y$
Z is defined so that $p_w q^* = p_d$

The approximation is illustrated in Figure 14.3. Substituting 14.11 and 14.12 as well as our earlier linear approximations to the consumption and investment functions into 14.4 gives:

$$Y = Q + c(Y - \bar{T} + \bar{R}) + H - br + \bar{G} + \bar{E} - (F + zY)\left[\frac{p_w}{p_d}\right]q^*$$

so that:

$$Y = \frac{Q + c(\bar{R} - \bar{T}) + H - br + \bar{G} + \bar{E} - F\left[\dfrac{p_w}{p_d}\right]q^*}{1 - c + z\left[\dfrac{p_w}{p_d}\right]q^*} \tag{14.13}$$

Since we are taking q^* as set by policy and *both* p_w and p_d as invariant, $[p_w/p_d]q^*$, by a suitable choice of units, can be taken as unity and 14.13 rewritten – along the lines of 14.12 – as:

$$Y = \frac{Q + c(\bar{R} - \bar{T}) + H - br + \bar{G} + \bar{E} - F}{1 - c + z} \tag{14.14}$$

Both 14.13 and 14.14 are equations of what we have called the *IS* schedule since they define pairs of values of Y, r which, *for a given value of* $q = q^*$, will equate aggregate demand with aggregate supply in the goods market. As usual this schedule depends upon:

(a) the autonomous elements Q, H and the 'policy' elements $\bar{G}$, $\bar{R}$, $\bar{T}$
(b) the constants of behaviour c ($\equiv \partial C_p/\partial Y$), b ($\equiv \partial I_p/\partial r$) and z ($\equiv \partial Z/\partial Y$)

to which must now be added:

(c) the new autonomous items $\bar{E}$ and F
(d) the new variable q set by 'policy' at q^*

Notice that since $1 - c \equiv s \equiv$ marginal propensity to save, imports, like saving, constitute a 'leakage' from the circular flow of expenditure. Accordingly the equilibrium condition for income:

$$\begin{array}{rcl} S_p & = & I_p \\ \text{planned saving} & = & \text{planned investment} \end{array} \tag{14.15}$$

becomes:

$$\begin{array}{ccccccc} S_p & + & \dfrac{Zp_w}{p_d}q & = & I_p & + & \bar{E} \\ \text{planned saving} & + & \text{imports} & = & \text{planned investment} & + & \text{exports} \end{array} \tag{14.16}$$

How will a change in q shift the *IS* curve? The external contribution to aggregate demand is:

$$E - \frac{Zp_w}{p_d}q \quad \equiv \text{real current-account balance (CAB)}$$

and if an increase in q^* ($\equiv$ a devaluation of the 'peg') increases this quantity (CAB) it will shift the *IS* current upwards. Now *both E and Z* are functions of q. We expect $\partial E/\partial q > 0$ and $\partial Z/\partial q < 0$. Hence it depends upon the marginal responsiveness of E and Z whether a change in q^* shifts the *IS* curve up or down. In fact the *IS* curve will shift upwards in response to a change in q if:

$$\frac{\partial E}{\partial q} \times \frac{q}{E} + \frac{\partial Z}{\partial q} \times \frac{q}{Z} > 1$$

which we shall assume to be the case.

Obtaining the 'multipliers' from 14.14 is straightforward, and these are given in col. 2 of Table 14.1. Notice that these are 'multipliers' which *assume* a constant interest rate: that is, what we have hitherto called the 'simple' multiplier.

We can now ask two questions. First, how do increases in exports or imports affect the level of income and the current-account balance? Second, how do fiscal policy changes or changes in private consumption or investment plans influence the current-account balance?

Consider an increase in exports by ΔE. As we can see, provided the rate of interest does not change, the increase in income is given by:

$$\Delta Y = \Delta\bar{E}\,\frac{1}{1 - c + z}$$

The change in the current-account balance is:

$$\text{change in exports} \quad - \quad \text{change in imports}$$

$$\Delta\bar{E} \quad - \quad z\Delta Y$$

$$\Delta\bar{E} \quad - \quad \frac{z\Delta\bar{E}}{1 - c + z}$$

so that the change in the current balance is:

$$\Delta\bar{E}\left\{\frac{1 - c}{1 - c + z}\right\} \quad \text{or} \quad \Delta\bar{E}\left\{\frac{s}{s + z}\right\}$$

This tells us that the improvement in the current balance will typically be less than $\Delta\bar{E}$ as long as ΔY is positive: for any increase in Y, via the marginal propensity to import (z) must bring about an induced (by ΔY) change in imports. Only if $z = 0$ can this result be avoided.

Table 14.1 'Simple' multipliers and the current-account balance (p_w, p_d, r_d are constant: $q = q^*$)

	Change	Income ΔY	Change in current account ΔCAB
1.	ΔQ	$\Delta Q \dfrac{1}{1 - c + [p_w/p_d]q^*z}$	$-z\Delta Y$
2.	$\Delta\bar{G}$	$\Delta\bar{G} \dfrac{1}{1 - c + [p_w/p_d]q^*z}$	$-z\Delta Y$
3.	$\Delta\bar{E}$	$\Delta\bar{E} \dfrac{1}{1 - c + [p_w/p_d]q^*z}$	$(1 - c)\Delta Y$
4.	ΔF	$-\Delta F \dfrac{1}{1 - c + [p_w/p_d]q^*z}$	$-(1 - c)\Delta Y$
5.	ΔH	$\Delta H \dfrac{1}{1 - c + [p_w/p_d]q^*z}$	$-z\Delta Y$
6.	$\Delta\bar{R}$	$\Delta\bar{R} \dfrac{c}{1 - c + [p_w/p_d]q^*z}$	$-z\Delta Y$
7.	ΔT	$-\Delta T \dfrac{c}{1 - c + [p_w/p_d]q^*z}$	$z\Delta Y$
8.	Δq^*	$\dfrac{\Delta q^* \, \partial\text{CAB}/\partial q^*}{1 - c + [p_w/p_d]q^*z}$	$(1 - c)\Delta Y$

NOTES

1. $$\frac{\partial \text{CAB}}{\partial q^*} = \frac{\partial E}{\partial q^*} - F\frac{p_w}{p_d} - \frac{\partial F}{\partial q^*}\left[\frac{p_w}{p_d}\right]q^* - zY\frac{p_w}{p_d}$$

where $\partial F/\partial q^*$ is the change in autonomous imports arising from devaluation and will typically be negative.

2. Simple multipliers set an upper limit for ΔY when ΔY is positive.

Suppose imports increase: that is, the linear import function drawn in Figure 14.3 rises so that, at any level of income, imports are now higher by ΔF. From Table 14.1 we can see that ΔY is given by

$$\Delta Y = \frac{-\Delta F}{1 - c + z\,[p_w/p_d]q^*}$$

which means that income falls – as we would expect – since imports are a 'leakage' in precisely the same sense as saving.

What happens to the current-account balance? We have:

$$\begin{aligned}
\Delta\text{current balance} &\equiv \Delta\text{exports} - \Delta\text{imports} \\
&\equiv \text{zero} - (\Delta F + z\Delta Y) \\
&\equiv \text{zero} - \Delta F + \frac{z\Delta F}{1 - c + z} \\
&\equiv -\Delta F\left(\frac{1 - c}{1 - c + z}\right) \\
&\equiv -\Delta F\,\frac{s}{s + z}
\end{aligned}$$

Here the autonomous element in Δcurrent balance is the autonomous increase in imports (ΔF). *The induced change in imports is, however, now negative since ΔF generates a fall in income.* In short, the current balance deteriorates but by less than the autonomous increase in imports.

What happens if some domestic demand element changes, for example government expenditure on goods and services ($\bar{G}$)? Plainly we have:

$$\Delta Y = \Delta\bar{G}\,\frac{1}{1 - c + z}$$

and

$$\Delta\text{current balance} = -\Delta\bar{G}\,\frac{z}{1 + c - z} \equiv \text{induced change in imports}$$

A formally identical pair of results holds for an autonomous increase in planned consumption (ΔQ) or planned investment (ΔH).

It would be possible but tedious to examine all other possible cases. Rather than do this, we summarise our results in col. 3 of Table 14.1. Table 14.1 looks rather formidable. Its implications are, however, readily summarised as follows:

1. Any changes in the determinants of domestic demand will:
   (a) entail a 'multiplied' change in income
   (b) an induced change in the current-account balance due to the change in imports resulting from the change in income and the marginal propensity to import
2. Any change in exports (treated as exogenous) or shift in the import function will:
   (a) change income
   (b) change the current balance in the same direction as the autonomous change in exports or imports, *but will*
   (c) typically do so by an amount less than the autonomous change because of the induced change in imports

3. The current balance will always change as set out above unless $1 - c = 0$ or, *alternatively*, $z = 0$.

What are the lessons provided by this analysis?

The first is the emphasis it places upon the interdependence of income and the current balance. Whatever influences the former will have an impact on the latter and vice versa. The importance of this was manifest from 1947 to 1973, when, broadly speaking, successive UK governments pursued with considerable success macroeconomic policies aimed at 'full employment'. For it was a common experience that expansionary fiscal policies aimed at stimulating demand and hence output and employment led to deterioration in the current balance and, on occasions, an emerging 'sterling crisis' which compelled a halt to the expansion.

The second, and closely related, point is that the equilibrium of income – that is, aggregate demand equal to aggregate supply – does not (unless $1 - c = 0$) entail equilibrium on the current account. There may be a deficit or a surplus at the fixed exchange rate q^*. And, if such an imbalance exists, the authorities must be prepared to act as residual buyer (surplus) or seller (deficit) of foreign exchange to maintain $q = q^*$. Will this lead to complications of which the analysis should take account?

We now turn to consider this and related issues.

The 'occasionally jumping peg': some qualifications

No analysis can be any more useful than the assumptions upon which it is based. And our present assumptions are quite stringent. In particular we are assuming:

(a) a *given* and *invariant* domestic price level (p_d)
(b) a *given* and *invariant* price level in the rest of the world (p_w)
(c) a *given* and *invariant* real income in the rest of the world (Y_w)

Assumptions (a) and (b) are relatively easily relaxed and we shall do so later in the book. Assumption (c) implies that the UK economy is 'small' with reference to the world as a whole so that a change in the UK's demand for imports has a negligible impact on the rest of the world's real income. This would certainly be true for a country as small as, say, Andorra. It would almost certainly be *untrue* for the USA. The UK lies between these extremes. Nevertheless the assumption is probably a reasonable – as well as convenient – first approximation.

Thus the three assumptions – though fairly stringent – are not in themselves reasons for rejecting our earlier analysis.

Two important qualifications do, however, arise.

The first occurs because, as we have seen, equilibrium in the goods market does *not*, except in special circumstances, entail equilibrium on the balance of payments. That is, it does *not* entail:

$$\bar{E} + \overline{\text{NPKI}} = Z$$

at the 'pegged' rate of exchange $q = q^*$. Moreover, where this condition does *not* hold, the authorities must, as we have also seen, act as residual buyers/sellers of foreign exchange.

Consider a situation in which:

$$\bar{E} + \overline{\text{NPKI}} - Z < 0 \equiv D \equiv \text{overall deficit}$$

that is, there is a deficit on the overall balance of payments. In each period, the authorities must *sell* foreign exchange equal to D. Such sales cannot continue indefinitely since, sooner or later, the authorities' stock of reserves will fall to zero. Thus any equilibrium in the goods and money markets which entails a deficit on external account *must* be shortlived.

This argument is also applicable, though probably after a much longer period than with a deficit, to an increase in which:

$$\bar{E} + \overline{\text{NPKI}} - Z > 0 \equiv S \equiv \text{overall surplus}$$

Our analysis has thus far assumed that the domestic nominal money supply is constant ($M^S = \bar{M}^S$). As we shall see in Chapter 24, it is generally the case that official sales (purchases) of foreign exchange (changes in the country's overseas reserves) tend to entail decreases (increases) in the domestic money supply. This is a second reason for arguing that any 'equilibrium' involving an overall deficit or surplus cannot be long-lived since, as we know, any change in M^S will modify the equilibrium.

Thus for *both* these reasons our analysis requires qualification.

A further need for qualification arises because we have assumed NPKI to be invariant. The capital account of the balance of payments is a complex problem which cannot be fully analysed in this book. At this stage it is sufficient for us to note that *if* both domestic and overseas portfolio owners seek to maximise the return they obtain from their asset portfolios *and* regard $q = q^*$ as a stable rate, overseas and foreign assets, whether in the form of real capital *or* financial claims, will be substitutes. In this case we must expect NPKI (which is the net flow of funds) into (NPKI > 0) or out of (NPKI < 0) domestic assets to (from) abroad to be related to the relation between the domestic interest rate (r_d) and 'the' rate ruling in the rest of the world (r_f). Formally we can hypothesise:

$$\text{NPKI} = f(r_d, r_f) \quad \text{with} \left(\frac{\partial \text{NPKI}}{\partial r_d} > 0; \frac{\partial \text{NPKI}}{\partial r_f} < 0 \right) \tag{14.17}$$

say as an approximation:

$$\text{NPKI} = Q_0 + f_1 r_d + f_2 r_f \quad (f_1 > 0; f_2 < 0) \tag{14.18}$$

Now r_d depends upon the nominal domestic demand for money (M^D) and the (assumed invariant) nominal money supply ($\bar{M}^S$). It follows that any change which increases (decreases) domestic money income (Y_{p_d}) and thus increases (decreases) M^D will raise (lower) r_d. If r_f, like p_w and Y_w, is unaffected (*as we shall assume*), then any such change must tend to increase (decrease) NPKI. The extent of the increase (decrease) will, of course, depend upon the numerical magnitude of the marginal response coefficient. In some cases this may prove to be very small. *Nevertheless, the qualitative conclusion holds.* Thus a change in, say, $\bar{G}$ (government expenditure on goods and services) which increases domestic income and thus imports will certainly bring about a deterioration in the current-account balance by $z\Delta Y$, as we have argued. But, since M^D increases, r_d will tend to rise, and with it the balance on capital account. Hence the change in the *overall balance will be less* – at least typically – than the change in the current account and, if $\partial \text{NPKI}/\partial r_d$ is large enough (domestic and overseas assets are very close substitutes) could be zero. This theoretically possible outcome need not, however, detain us. In general, despite the possible responsiveness of NPKI to changes in r_d, a domestic expansion typically leads to a deterioration in the overall balance of payments and hence, if initially $\bar{E} + \text{NPKI} - Z = 0$, to an overall deficit.

In an 'open economy' (i.e. one which engages in international transactions) it therefore seems sensible to think of 'full' equilibrium as existing only when *three* conditions are simultaneously satisfied. These are:

1. $Y = C_p + I_p + G_p + E - Z$ (aggregate demand = aggregate supply)
2. $M^D = M^S$ (demand for money = supply of money)
3. $E + \text{NPKI} - Z = 0$ (external receipts = external payments)

Notice also that the dependent variables of our system are still simply r_d and Y, as was the case with the 'closed' economy we discussed in Chapter 12 and analysed geometrically with *IS*/*LM* schedules. We now have *three* equations to be satisfied and only two variables to satisfy them with: a situation which typically involves a contradiction. Unless, by chance, the value of r_d determined by (2) *also* satisfies (3), this will be true of our system. *This is a formal way of stating what we have already shown: namely, that for income and the interest rate to be at the equilibrium levels defined by (1) and (2) does not entail that (3) is satisfied.*

Summary

The introduction of international trade into the system entails the introduction of a new variable: namely, the rate of exchange, here defined as q.

This variable is a price and can be *either* fixed (i.e. 'pegged') by the authorities ($q = q^*$) *or* 'flexible'. In the latter case it is said to 'float', and where the authorities do not intervene in the market the 'float' is said to be 'perfectly clean'.

Where the system is that of an 'occasionally jumping peg', the authorities must act as residual buyers or sellers of foreign exchange (i.e. gain or lose overseas reserves) since, in the foreign exchange market:

> exports + net private capital inflow − imports ≡ official financing ≡ change in overseas reserves

when $q = q^*$.

In the alternative case, i.e. a perfectly 'clean' float, the foreign exchange market is equilibrated by q so that q is determined by the equilibrium condition:

> exports + net private capital inflow − imports = 0

Since changes in reserves have a potential impact on the nominal money supply, which is explained in Chapter 24, control of the money supply by the authorities is weakened by the existence of an 'occasionally jumping peg'. It is complete (at least in theory) in the case of a 'perfectly clean float'.

In the case of $q = q^*$ fairly simple general assumptions about the determination of exports and imports allow our earlier *IS*/*LM* analysis to be extended to incorporate international trade. Notice that our earlier equilibrium conditions in the goods and money markets, if satisfied, *do not entail equilibrium on external account*. In the short run considerable overall surpluses/deficits may arise.

Such deficits/surpluses cannot, however, persist indefinitely, which limits the time period for which the analysis is applicable.

The central lesson of the analysis is the interdependence between the domestic and external position. Thus, with $q = q^*$, a domestic expansion may be halted by the emergence of an induced balance-of-payments deficit – a familiar UK experience in the 1960s and early 1970s.

Questions and exercises

1. Plot the *ratios* imports/GDP and exports/GDP for each year from 1960 to 1980. Is it correct to assert that:

   (a) the UK economy is becoming steadily more 'open'?
   (b) the UK economy is steadily more dependent on imports?

   If so, how would you explain these developments?

2. Between 1972 and 1980 UK imports of all manufactures by volume rose by 82 per cent and of finished manufactures by 111 per cent. In the same period real GDP rose by about 12 per cent. In terms of the theory in this chapter, how would you explain these observations?

3. The Annual Supplement to *Economic Trends* gives no less than *five* measures of UK trade 'competitiveness'. These are discussed in some detail in *Economic Trends* (February 1979). Which measure is closest to our definition? And which measure do you prefer, and why?

4. Plot your preferred 'competitiveness' measure for each quarter from 1973I to 1981IV (the Roman numerals refer to quarters). Compare your graph with one of the 'sterling effective exchange rate' for the same period. What does this comparison suggest?

5. How 'important' were fluctuations in the balance of payments on capital account in explaining fluctuations in the UK's overall balance between 1950–71 and 1972–81? Explain your definition of 'important'. Is there any significant difference between the two periods?

6. 'The days when the UK's imports were predominantly food and raw materials are long gone. Our main imports are now finished manufactures.' How would you check this statement? Do you agree with it? Support your answer by the data you believe to be relevant.

7. The pound was devalued in November 1967. How would you expect a devaluation to influence the current account (i) in the calendar quarter in which it occurs, and (ii) over a period of say, say, eight quarters? Give your reasons.

8. Exchange controls limit the range of capital-account payments domestic residents – households or firms – can make to foreigners. Such controls were removed in the UK in 1980. What results would you expect to see from *theory* on (i) the UK capital account, and (ii) the exchange rate? Do the data support your theory?

9. 'In a perfectly "clean" float, by definition, official financing is identically zero.' Explain. Given your explanation, comment on the UK balance-of-payments data. How 'clean' or 'dirty' was the UK 'float' between 1976 and 1981?

10. 'The year 1981 should show a considerable current-account surplus. But if the UK economy were to recover to anything like "full-capacity" operation then – at the existing exchange rate – the result could only be a massive current-account deficit.' What assumptions would lead you to this conclusion? Do you accept or reject them? Give your reasons. OR 'Provided you are prepared to throw enough people out of work – and keep them out of work – it is a relatively simple matter to maintain a surplus on current account.' What kind of model suggests this result? Do you accept it?

11. 'Until 1974, cyclical expansions in the UK economy were commonly checked by balance-of-payments problems. Hence what was called "stop–go". Under "flexible rates" these problems no longer exist. Curiously nor do the expansions.' Elucidate and appraise. Is the implied criticism justified ?

Suggested reading

F. R. Brechling and J. M. Wolfe, 'The End of Stop–Go', *Lloyds Bank Review* (January 1965).

R. N. Cooper, in *Britain's Economic Prospects*, ed. R. E. Caves (Allen & Unwin for the Brookings Institution, 1968).

L. B. Krause, in *Britain's Economic Prospects*, ed. Caves, *plus* the Epilogue (pp. 487–95) to the same volume.

HM Treasury, 'Overseas Investment and Capital Flows', *Economic Progress Report*, no. 142 (February 1982).

R. L. Major, 'Forecasting Exports and Imports', *NIESR Review*, no. 42 (November 1967).

R. L. Major, 'The Competitiveness of British Exports since Devaluation', *NIESR Review*, no. 48 (May 1969).

R. L. Major, 'Measures of Competitiveness in International Trade', *Bank of England Quarterly Bulletin*, (June 1978).

R. L. Major, 'Britain's Trade and Exchange Rate Policy', *NIESR Review*, no. 90 (November 1979).

NIESR, 'The British Economy in the Medium Term', *NIESR Review*, no. 98 (November 1981).

Chapter 14*

The International Sector and Flexible Rates

Introduction

In the previous chapter we looked at the consequences of introducing international trade into our model in the framework of a regime of 'pegged' exchange rates. However, since 1972, the UK exchange rate has *not* been pegged, but has been determined by a 'managed float': that is, by a foreign exchange market in which the authorities intervene, from time to time, as an additional buyer or seller of foreign exchange. At this stage we do not wish to discuss *why* the UK authorities chose to act in this way. We therefore consider only the limiting case of a 'perfectly clean' float even though, since the collapse of the Bretton Woods system (the 'occasionally jumping peg') most countries' floats have been more or less 'dirty'.

The significance of this assumption is, of course, that the rate of exchange ($\equiv q$) becomes an endogenous variable like the level of income (Y) and the interest rate (r_d). We now have *three* equilibrium conditions:

$$Y = C_p + I_p + G_p + E - Z \frac{\bar{p}_w}{p_d} q \tag{14*.1}$$

$$M^s = M^D = kY_{p_d} + l_1 r_d \quad (l_1 < 0) \tag{14*.2}$$

$$E + NPKI = Z \frac{\bar{p}_w}{p_d} q \quad (NPKI = Q_0 + f_1 r_d + f_2 r_f) \tag{14*.3}$$

where 14*.1 and 14*.2 as before, relate to the goods and money markets, and 14*.3 to the market in foreign exchange. Thus the equilibrium values of Y, r_d and q will be simultaneously determined just as, in our closed-economy model, Y and r (now denoted by r_d) were simultaneously determined.

How must our earlier analysis be modified when we permit q to be determined by a 'clean' float? We may simplify this problem by distinguishing two cases. The first of these –

which we can think of as the 'very short run' – is defined by the assumption that domestic prices (p_d) are independent of the exchange rate (q) in the sense that a rise (fall) in q leaves p_d unaltered.

Why do we call this the 'very short run'? The prices of imports in domestic currency ($p_w q$) will typically change proportionately to q. Some imports are inputs; others enter final consumption. In the former case producers' costs change; in the latter case there is a direct impact on the cost of living which, in general, is – sooner or later – likely to be reflected in money wage claims, and thence, in whole or in part, in money wage costs. Holding p_d constant thus implies a time period so short that none of these effects occurs or is sufficiently small to be neglected. It is a pedagogic device which is employed for its ability to simplify the analysis.

In the alternative analysis – the 'short run' – changes in q are permitted to influence domestic prices (p_d), and the marginal response coefficient ($\partial p_d/\partial q$) is assumed to be positive. This is the more relevant case. But, because of the 'feedback' represented by $\partial p_d/\partial q$ it is, unavoidably, the more complex.

Accordingly we begin by looking at the 'very short run'.

A flexible exchange rate: the very short run

To illustrate the modifications to the analysis made necessary by the existence of an endogenous q, it is simplest to begin by looking at the results of an expansion in government expenditure ($\bar{G}$).

We know that such an expansion tends to raise *both* Y and r_d. But what happens to q? We have *two* influences at work. As Y rises so do imports via the marginal propensity to import. Hence the current account deteriorates. But, since r_d rises, while r_f (by assumption) remains unaltered, the rate of net private capital inflow tends to increase, which has the reverse effect on the overall balance of payments. Will the new equilibrium value of q be higher or lower? We cannot say with any confidence since the result depends upon the relative magnitudes of certain parameters: that is, on numerical values which we have not specified. Notice, however, that if:

(a) *q rises* (i.e. the domestic currency depreciates), this will (on our earlier assumptions) improve the value of $[p_w/p_d]q$ (i.e. the current balance) so that the expansionary effect of a given increase in G on Y will be *greater* with a 'flexible rate' than a 'pegged' rate, *but*

(b) if *q falls* (because the interest-rate impact on NPKI dominates), the change in $\bar{G}$ will have a *smaller* expansionary impact than under a 'pegged' rate

Suppose now that the domestic expansion came from an increase in the nominal money stock ($\bar{M}$) rather than government expenditure. This lowers r_d – thus expanding planned investment and perhaps consumption – which increases Y and hence imports. Thus, as usual, the expansion entails a deterioration in the current account. But, since r_d *falls*, it also entails a deterioration in the capital account. In this case the impact on q is unambiguous. The exchange rate *depreciates*[1] and the expansion in output is, as a consequence *greater* than it would have been under a fixed rate.

[1]We speak of 'depreciation' when the rate is 'floating' and 'devaluation' when it is 'pegged'.

This argument is reversible if, instead of an increase in $\bar{M}$, we have assumed a *decrease*. Moreover, if $\bar{M}$ decreases, the resulting fall in domestic output may result *primarily* from the *appreciation* in the exchange rate (fall in q). This would, for example, be the case if *both* domestic planned investment and consumption responded very little to any *rise* in r_d or fall in 'real' money balance $\bar{M}/p_d$ induced by the *decrease* in $\bar{M}$. The experience of the UK from 1979 to 1981 may well be explained to a considerable extent by this sort of process: that is, a fall in demand resulting from an appreciation in the exchange rate and a consequential deterioration in the 'competitiveness' of UK exports and import-competing industries.

What of influences which operate *directly* on the balance of payments – say, for example, a shift in domestic tastes in favour of imports?

In this case imports are, *ceteris paribus*, higher at any level of output. Thus equilibrium output falls since the current balance deteriorates. The demand for money falls as Y falls so that r_d is lower. *Both* the lower r_d and the upward shift in the import function tends to raise q: that is, cause a depreciation in the rate of exchange. This tends to reduce imports and increase exports, thus offsetting the impact of the initial autonomous shift in the import function. It follows that, with the rate of exchange an endogenous variable, both the deterioration in the current balance *and* the fall in income (Y) resulting from the autonomous increase in imports are *less* then they would have been with a pegged exchange rate. In short the induced depreciation (rise in q) acts as a stabilising element in the case of a shift in the demand function for imports. And, as the reader can readily confirm, the same proposition holds for a shift (in either direction) in the export demand function.

By contrast, as we have seen, in the case of changes in the nominal money supply or, less certainly, changes in government expenditure, the induced responses of the exchange rate tend to increase rather than diminish the response of income in comparison with the 'pegged' rate result.

The final case worth considering is a shift in the function explaining net private capital flows. Such shifts are in practice not uncommon. This is because the yield on holding a foreign security for, say, three months consists in:

(a) the interest rate for three months, i.e. $\frac{1}{4} r_f$
(b) the percentage change in the exchange rate ($\equiv \dot{q}$).

Hence the *ex ante* or expected yield, which is what determines behaviour, is (ignoring tax complications) given by $\frac{1}{4} r_f + \hat{\dot{q}}$ where $\hat{\dot{q}} \equiv$ expected value of $\dot{q}$. Thus if the annual rate of interest were, say, 12 per cent, the expected yield for holding the foreign asset for three months would be:

$$0.25 r_f + \hat{\dot{q}} = 3\% + \hat{\dot{q}}$$

This is important since it suggests that the expected yield will often be dominated by expected changes in q. Since there are enormous stocks of funds on short-term deposit in all the main financial centres which can very easily be switched from one currency to another, it is only too likely that changes in expectations about exchange rates will generate large capital flows. This suggests that (i) the short-run behaviour of floating exchange rates tends to be dominated by the capital account rather than the current account, and (ii) that fluctuations in net private capital flows (*NPKI*) may themselves be dominated by shifts in short-term expectations resulting from, say, the revision of policy by some important central bank such as the Federal Reserve of the USA or the Bundesbank of West Germany, or some traumatic political event.

Formally such shifts in expectations are, in our model, to be regarded as changes in Q_0^- the autonomous elements in the linear equation for *NPKI*. Suppose now that Q_0 increases so that there is an autonomous expansion in *NPKI*. We must expect a *fall* in q, i.e. an *appreciation* of the exchange rate.

If q *falls*, exports tend to fall and imports to rise, and we expect the current-account balance to deteriorate. Hence output will fall. This will reduce imports, which will generate further pressure towards appreciation (further fall in q). There is, however, a mechanism offsetting this process. As output falls then with a given nominal money supply so will r_d, thus giving rise to an *induced* capital outflow or, more correctly, an induced reduction in NPKI. Nevertheless an increase in NPKI is, via the exchange rate, a factor which may exert very considerable downward leverage on output.

It may be helpful to the reader to put this analysis into a diagram showing the simultaneous determination of Y and q. Clearly, since our system also contains r_d as an endogenous variable, we cannot show Y, q and r_d on the same two-dimensional diagram. Thus, to give the full equilibrium of the system, any figure with Y and q on its axes must make use of schedules constructed on the condition that the money market is in equilibrium: that is, $M^D = M^S$. In this way we can represent in *two* dimensions the simultaneous satisfaction of *three* equations namely 14*.1, 14*.2 and 14*.3.

We begin by making use of the *IS*/*LM* apparatus to develop a schedule (which we call *GG*) showing all those combinations of Y and q at which:

(a) aggregate demand = aggregate supply (i.e. we are on the *IS* curve)
(b) money demand = money supply (i.e. we are on the *LM* curve)

Note that the *GG* curve therefore entails the simultaneous satisfaction of 14*.1 and 14*.2.

In the figure we have drawn the familiar *IS*/*LM* schedules for an open economy. The *IS* schedule depends upon the current-account balance, which is, in turn, a function of q. Since the greater is q (i.e. the lower is the exchange rate), the more favourable is the current balance and the greater, at any level of r_d, must be the equilibrium value of Y. IS_0 thus depends on a given q – say q_0. If q now *rises* from q_0 to q_1, the *IS* curve moves to IS_1 and equilibrium output rises from Y_0 to Y_1. Thus q_0, Y_0 and q_1, Y_1 are two combinations of Y and q which simultaneously satisfy 14*.1 and 14*.2. It is therefore clear that, in the right-hand figure, we can trace out an upward sloping *GG* curve showing that the higher is q (i.e. the *lower* is the rate of exchange) the higher is equilibrium Y. Note also that points to the *right* of *GG* indicate output levels for which aggregate supply *exceeds* aggregate demand, and points to the *left* indicate output levels at which aggregate demand exceeds aggregate supply.

We have constructed *GG* by shifting *IS*. *LM*, however, has not changed as q changes. Is this correct? For the 'very short run' it is, since, by definition of the 'very short-run', p_d (≡ domestic price) does not respond to changes in q. In the 'very short run' we are assuming $p_d = \bar{p}_d$ (a constant). If, however, we relaxed this assumption, p_d would rise (to some extent) as q rose. Hence the *LM* curve would shift to the left.

What are the parameters of the *GG* curve? Simply the parameters of the *LM* and *IS* schedules (other than q) with which we are now thoroughly familiar.

We now need to construct a second curve showing all combinations of Y and q at which $M^D = M^S$ (we are on the *LM* curve) and $E + NPKI - Zq.p_w/p_d = 0$ (i.e. the demand and supply for foreign exchange are equal). Accordingly we once more utilise the *LM* schedule and superimpose upon it a new schedule showing combinations of Y, r_d which satisfy 14*.3 at any given q. This is done in Figure 14*.2, where the second curve is labelled the *FP* schedule.

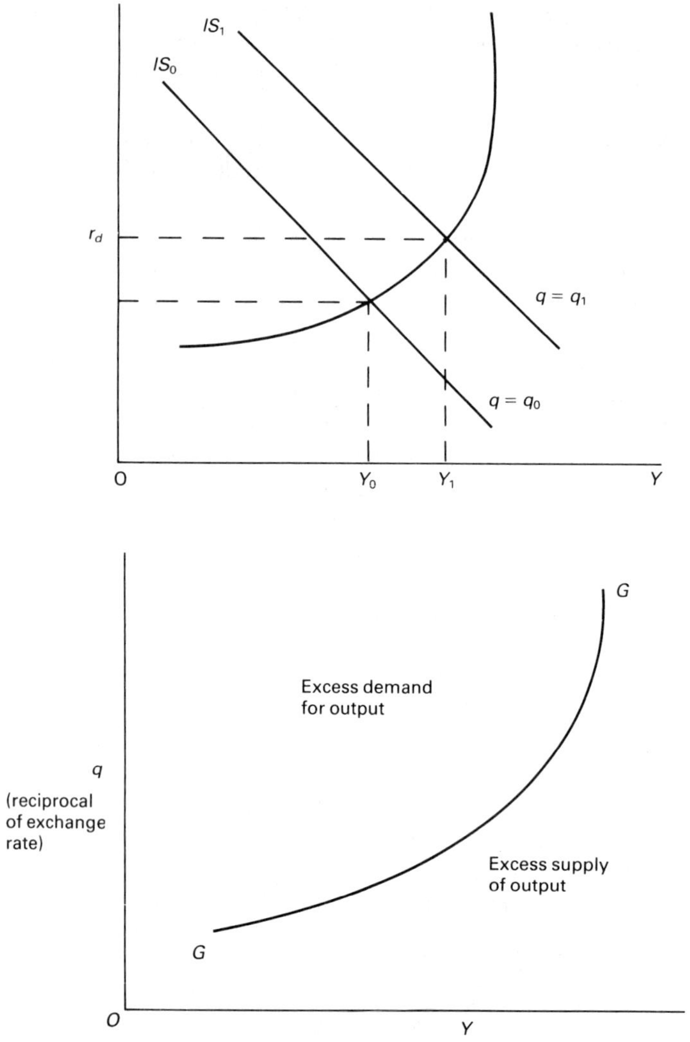

Figure 14*.1 The construction of the *GG* schedule

How is the *FP* curve obtained? Consider any increase in income at some given and invariant exchange rate – say denoted by q_0. Because the marginal propensity to import is positive, the increase in income brings about a deterioration in the current balance. It follows that, to maintain equilibrium in the foreign exchange market, capital inflows must be encouraged. Hence higher values of Y must be accompanied by higher values of r_d in order to generate an increase in *NPKI* (given by $f_1 \Delta r_d$ according to our *NPKI* funtion which is $NPKI = Q_0 + f_1 r_f + f_2 r_d$) which is sufficient to offset the increase in imports induced by the income change which is – given our linear import function – $z \Delta Y$. Thus any *FP* schedule must slope upwards to the right with its slope depending upon the parameters f_1 and z ($\equiv \partial Z/\partial Y \equiv$ marginal propensity to import).

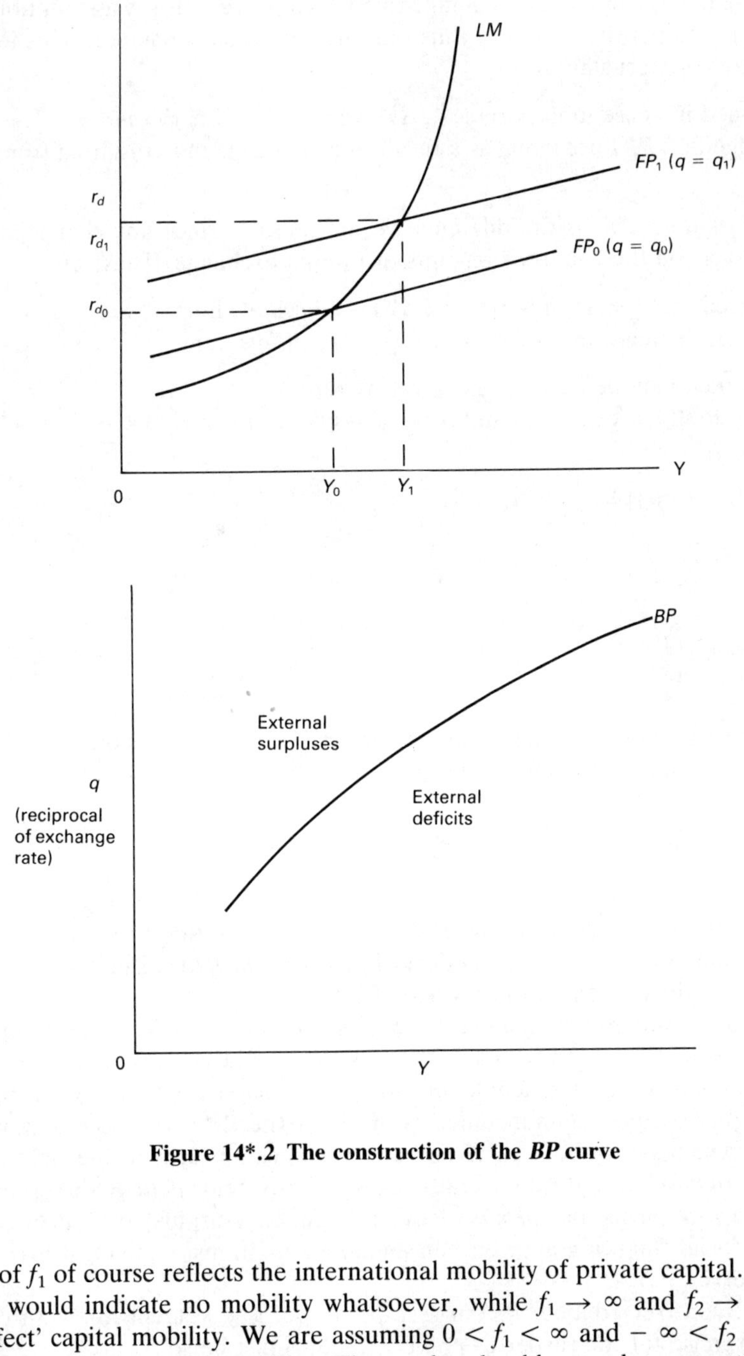

Figure 14*.2 The construction of the *BP* curve

The size of f_1 of course reflects the international mobility of private capital. Thus $f_1 = 0$ and $f_2 = 0$ would indicate no mobility whatsoever, while $f_1 \to \infty$ and $f_2 \to -\infty$ would define 'perfect' capital mobility. We are assuming $0 < f_1 < \infty$ and $-\infty < f_2 < 0$: that is, some, but not perfect, capital mobility. The reader should note, however, that with the increasing integration of national money and capital markets we are moving towards 'world financial markets' and the increasing international mobility of private capital.

The schedule FP_0 is drawn on the assumption that $q = q_0$. Thus Y_0, q_0 constitute a pair of values which simultaneously satisfy 14*.2 and 14*.3. What happens if we increase q_0 to q_1? Clearly the *FP* schedule shifts. But which way?

An increase in q is a fall in the exchange rate which, since p_d is (by assumption) invariant, improves our 'competitiveness' and thus our current-account balance. This improvement now has to be counterbalanced by:

(a) the induced increase in imports ($= z\Delta Y$, where $z = \partial Z/\partial Y$), *and*
(b) the change in *NPKI* occurring as a result of any change in r_d resulting from the change in Y

Must Y rise or fall? This is the dilemma we met before, since any change in Y has *two* opposed impacts on the country's receipts of foreign exchange. These are:

(a) the induced increase in imports ($= z\Delta Y$) – a *negative* item – *and*
(b) the induced increase in *NPKI* ($= f_1\ \Delta r_d$) – a *positive* item

the sum of which may be positive, negative or zero.

Now, if we look back at 14*.2 and solve it, as we can, for r_d, we obtain:

$$r_d = (M^S - kp_dY)\frac{1}{l_1} \quad (l_1 < 0)$$

so that:

$$\frac{\partial r_d}{\partial Y} = \frac{-k\bar{p}_d}{l_1}$$

which is, of course, positive: that is, an increase in Y *raises* r_d. Thus the impact of a change in income on receipts of foreign exchange is given by:

$$\Delta Y\left(-f_1\frac{k\bar{p}d}{l_1} - z\right) \qquad (14^*.4)$$

Plainly the term in brackets is of uncertain sign since ΔY *raises NPKI* and *raises* imports. We have assumed that the combined effect of the two is *negative*. But highly mobile capital (i.e. f_1 large) might well entail the reverse.

Retaining our assumption that an increase in income raises *NPKI* by *less* than it raises the import bill, i.e. that the term in brackets in 14*.4 is negative, a change in q from q_0 to a higher value q_1 shifts the *FP* schedule *upwards*. The greater is q (the lower is the exchange rate), the higher is equilibrium income. Accordingly the *BP* curve, which shows combinations of Y,q which satisfy both 14*.2 and 14*.3, slopes upwards to the right. Notice that points to the *right* of *BP* indicate overall balance-of-payments *deficits* and points to the *left* overall balance-of-payments *surplus*. Any such deficit (surplus) of course would imply equivalent official financing and, on our simple assumptions, equivalent losses (gains) in overseas reserves.

As we have constructed it our *BP* curve slopes upwards less steeply than our *GG* curve. It is a useful exercise for the reader to prove why this must be so.

What are the parameters of the *BP* curve? Clearly they are (i) those of the *LM* schedule – and are thus common with the *GG* curve; (ii) the export and import hypotheses, which are given determinants of the *GG* curve; and (iii) the net private capital inflow (*NPKI*) hypothesis which does *not* influence the *GG* curve. We must therefore be careful, in using the diagrams below to analyse parameter changes, to consider whether any change shifts *one* or *both* curves.

We can now use the GG and BP schedules to illustrate some of the matters we have discussed.

Consider, for example, an *expansionary fiscal policy*: that is, an increase in $\bar{G}$ (see Figure 14*.3). This shifts the GG curve to the right. Since the BP curve is not affected by the change in $\bar{G}$ and, on our assumptions, is upward-sloping, we have a new equilibrium in which both Y and q are higher. A rise in q is of course a depreciation in the exchange rate. The geometry thus illustrates our earlier analysis. Additionally it simplifies comparison with the 'pegged' rate situation.

On Figure 14*.3b a horizontal line drawn through q_0 indicates a pegged exchange rate. It is easy to see that the shift in GG to $G'G'$ now generates a smaller change in Y since there is no induced depreciation stimulating demand. Moreover, $G'G'$ cuts the 'pegged' rate

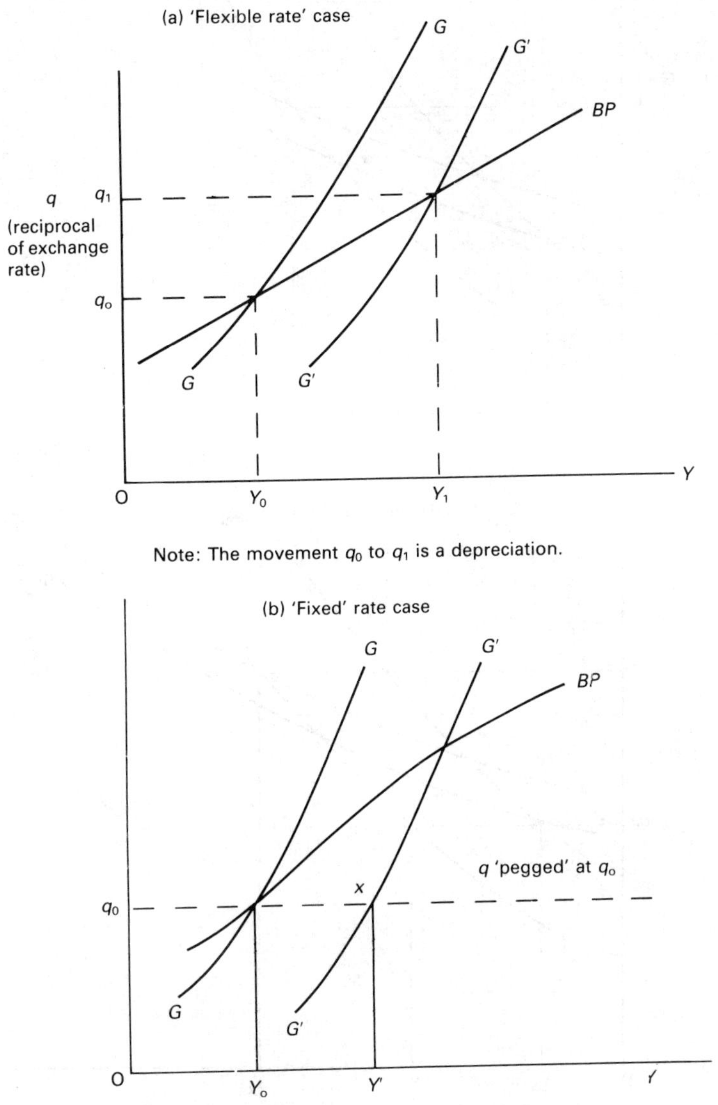

Figure 14*.3 An expansionary fiscal policy ($\Delta G > 0$)

schedule at X, which is *below* BP. This, as we know, entails an overall deficit on the balance of payments, equivalent official financing and, in our simple model, equivalent losses in overseas reserves.

The *monetary policy case* – defining monetary policy in terms of the money stock (M^S) – is illustrated in Figure 14*.4, where it is again compared with the 'pegged' rate case. Here we assume an expansionary monetary policy: that is, an increase in the exogenous nominal money supply. Since this has its impact via the money market – that is, via the LM schedule – *both* GG and BP will shift.

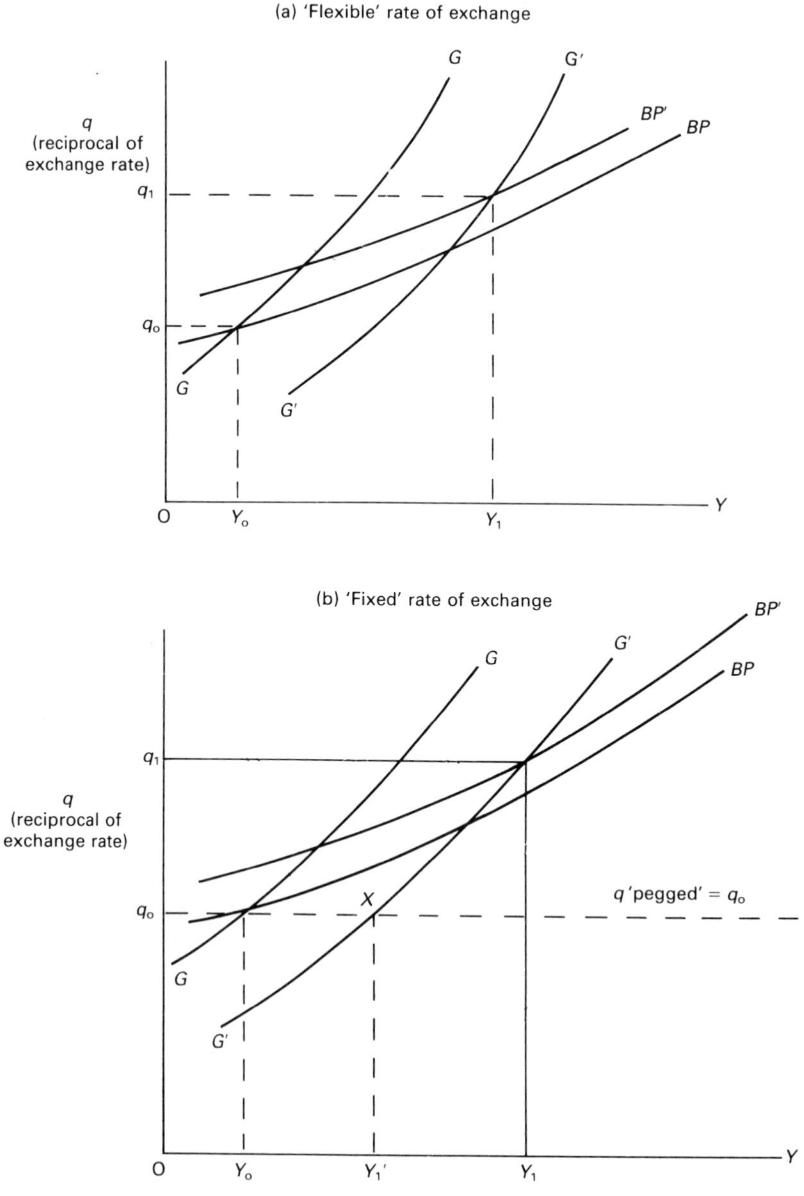

Figure 14*.4 An expansionary monetary policy ($\Delta M^S > 0$)

It is easy to see that the GG schedule shifts to the right to, say, $G'G'$. But what of the BP schedule? At any level of income, r_d will now be lower since M^S has increased. Hence *NPKI* will be smaller. To restore equilibrium on the external account, the current account must improve sufficiently to offset the induced (by the change in r_d) fall in the rate of capital inflow. Hence at any value of Y the rate of exchange must be *lower* (that is, q higher) in order to bring about the necessary improvement in the current account.

We can compare this with the 'pegged' rate case as we did before with the fiscal expansion. Plainly if q is fixed and held at q_0, then the expansionary monetary policy has a *smaller* impact on income. Moreover, since the point at which $G'G'$ cuts the horizontal line is *below* BP', we once again have an overall balance-of-payments deficit which must be financed by losses in overseas reserves.

The third case is that of an *autonomous increase in NPKI* due, let us say, to revised expectations about the UK economy. It is quite possible that some such revision has accompanied the growth in the output of North Sea oil and gas. In this case, as Figure 14*.5 shows, only the BP curve shifts and the shift is such that any level of Y now requires a higher exchange rate (lower value of q) to maintain external equilibrium. Thus the autonomous improvement in *NPKI* causes an exchange-rate appreciation which, via the current-account balance, *reduces* income. Of course, in the 'pegged' rate case income is unaffected. There is, however, an overall balance-of-payments surplus which must be 'financed' by a gain in reserves.

Our final case is an autonomous shift in the current balance due, let us say, to an increased desire by foreigners to consume UK products. *Exports rise by some positive* ΔE – the assumed shift in the export function. As we know, this change must shift both curves (see Figure 14*.6).

The GG schedule plainly shifts to the right since the autonomous increase in exports (ΔE) increases aggregate demand.

But what of the BP schedule? Since $\Delta \bar{E} > 0$, every level of Y will now require a higher value of the exchange rate (lower value of q) to maintain external equilibrium. Hence the BP curve also shifts to the right. Since both curve shifts in the same direction, it is clear that Y must rise. But what of q? Is q_1 higher, lower or identical with q_0? Clearly for $q_1 < q_0$ – that is, for the exchange rate to *appreciate* – the lateral shift in BP to BP' must *exceed* the lateral shift in GG to $G'G'$. Will it?

The relative size of the two shifts depends upon a number of parameters. These are z ($\equiv$ marginal propensity to import), f_1 ($\equiv \partial NPKI/\partial r_d$) c ($\equiv$ marginal propensity to consume), the parameters of the money demand function and the marginal response coefficients $\partial C_p/\partial r_d$ and $\partial I_p/\partial r_d$. On our assumptions about these, however, it can easily be proved that the lateral change in BP does exceed that of GG so that q' will be *below* q_0 and the exchange rate will appreciate. This is of course the result illustrated on Figure 14*.6. Notice that in the 'pegged' exchange-rate case the change in income is now *greater* than the 'flexible rate' case and that an overall *surplus* emerges.

The reader will find it a valuable exercise to prove the results given here and also to find the conditions – if any – under which $q_1 = q_0$, i.e. the GG and BP curves experience identical shifts in response to a given autonomous increase in export demand ($= \Delta \bar{E}$).

A similar analysis can be applied, *mutatis mutandis*, to an autonomous *decline* in export demand ($\Delta E < 0$) or increase in import demand.

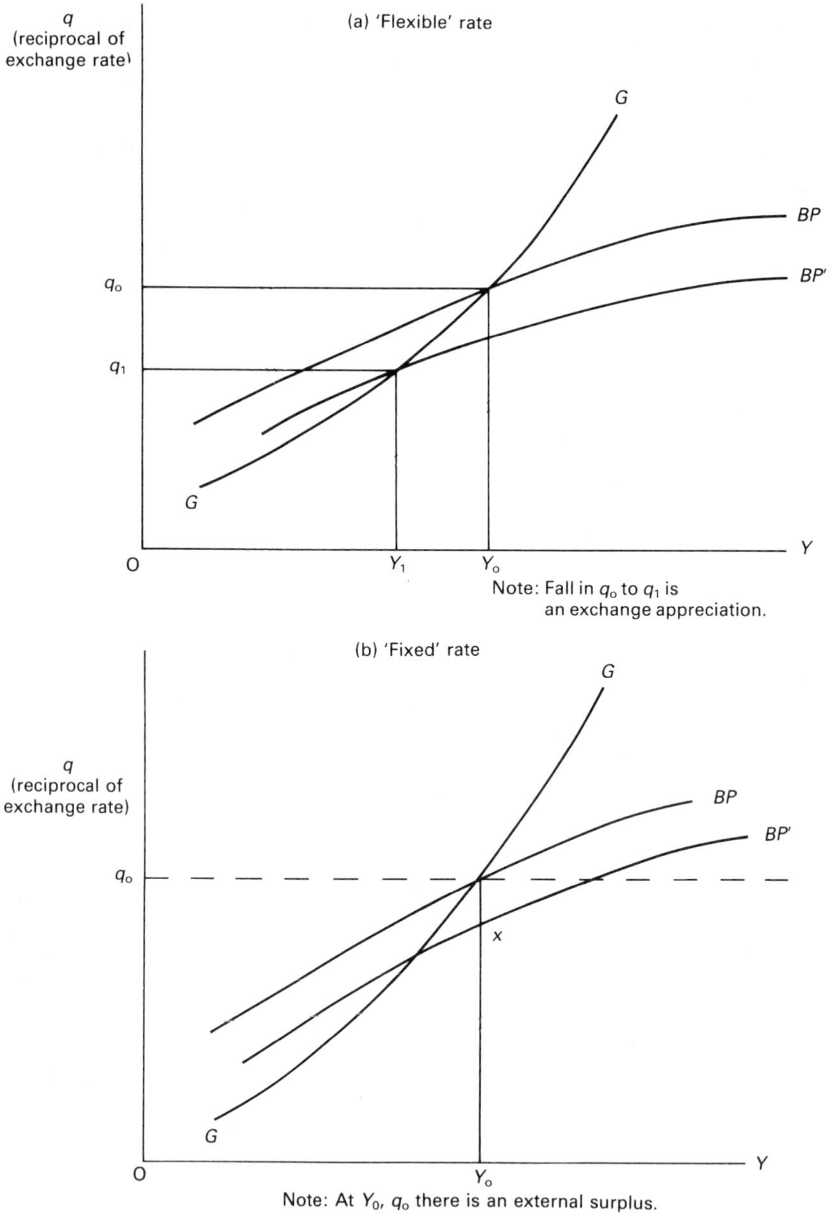

Figure 14*.5 An autonomous increase in net private capital inflow ($NPKI = Q_0 + f_1 r_d + f_2 r_f$: $\Delta Q_0 > 0$)

Flexible rates: the 'short-run' case

In the previous analysis we explicitly assumed that p_d was independent of q: that is, a rise (depreciation) or fall (appreciation) in q had no impact on domestic prices. If we think of the 'short-run' as, say, one to two years, this is probably an excessively strong assumption. What happens to our analysis if we relax it?

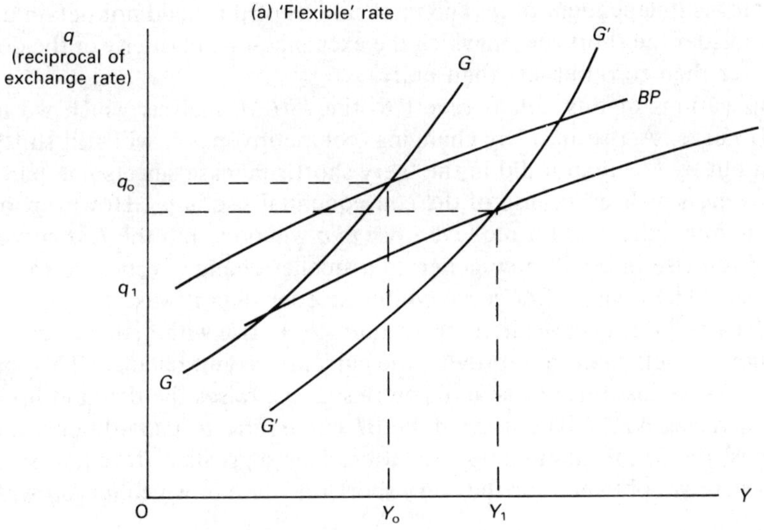

Note: The fall in q_0 to q_1 is an appreciation.

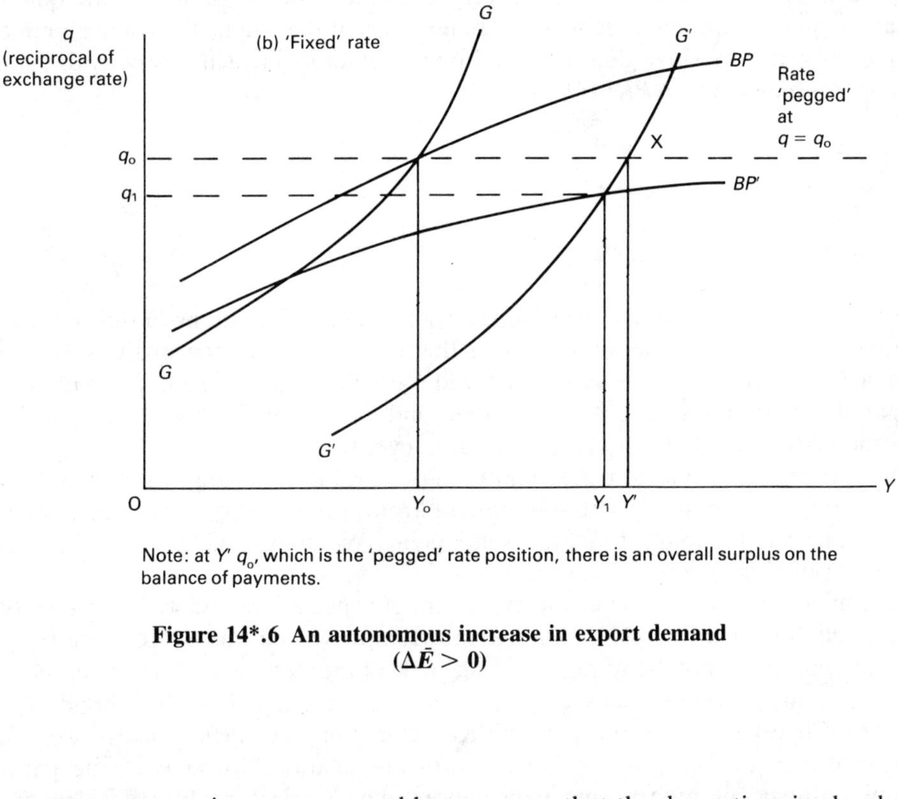

Note: at Y' q_o, which is the 'pegged' rate position, there is an overall surplus on the balance of payments.

Figure 14*.6 An autonomous increase in export demand ($\Delta \bar{E} > 0$)

Over one to two years it seems reasonable to assume that the domestic price level does react to the exchange rate but with an elasticity considerably less than unity. A depreciation now *raises* p_d but by *less*, proportionately, than the exchange rate has declined.

What happens if we now think in terms of some 'long period'? We may reasonably expect the proportionate response of p_d to exchange-rate change to approach unity. This implies that, in the *long run*, which may be very long indeed, 'competitiveness' (or the so-called 'real' exchange rate) is independent of q. The implications of this need not detain us here. We now turn to consider the short run, in which the exchange-rate elasticity of the domestic price level is greater than zero but less than unity.

To see the implications of this, let us revert to the *IS/LM* analysis which we used to construct the *GG* curve. A rise in q, by changing 'competitiveness', will still shift the *IS* curve to the right but by *less* than it did in the 'very short run' case since some part of the gain in 'competitiveness' is lost because of the consequential rise in p_d. However, because p_d influences the nominal demand for money, a rise in q will now shift the *LM* curve to the left. Hence any given rise in q will now generate a smaller change in income than in the 'very short-run' case. The revised *GG* curve will be steeper than it was.

What of the *BP* curve? Because we are now assuming p_d to rise with q, an increase in q (a depreciation) is now *less* efficient in improving the current-account balance. This implies a steeper *BP* curve. As against this, a rise in q, by raising p_d, raises the demand for money and the r_d which increases *NPKI*. The slope of the *BP* curve reflects *both* influences. On our earlier assumptions, the former dominates the latter. This suggests a *BP* curve somewhat steeper than the curve we obtained for the 'very short-run' case in which $\partial p_d/\partial q$ was taken to be zero.

On these arguments, the analysis of the 'very short run' asnd the 'short run' are qualitatively similar, though it is probably sensible to point out that this implicitly assumes that the fact that $\partial p_d/\partial q$ is now positive does not modify expectations in such a way as to change the autonomous element in *NPKI* (Q_0).

Limitations

As usual, we now ask readers to recall the rather severe limitations of our analysis.

Perhaps the most serious limitation in this context is that the analysis is *static*. For example, in the diagrams we have compared Y_0 with Y_1 and q_0 with q_1: that is, we have compared equilibrium levels of the variables and did not discuss the path by which, over time, the system moves from one equilibrium level to another.

This is a significant omission. As a matter of observation, exchange rates seem not only to fluctuate rather severely but also – in moving from, say, q_0 to q_1 – to overshoot the new equilibrium and only return to it after some delay. We discuss this problem of 'overshooting' in a brief appendix to this chapter.

A second limitation arises from our treatment of expectations. As we have seen, the yield of a foreign asset is not simply the foreign interest rate (r_f) but the interest rate (r_f) *plus* the *expected* appreciation of the foreign currency ($\hat{q}$). In the static equilibria of our analysis $\hat{q}$ is zero. But in the movement between equilibria, $\dot{q}$ – and hence, in all likelihood, $\hat{q}$ – will be non-zero. Clearly if we are to explain *NPKI* during the adjustment process, we must have some theory of $\hat{q}$. There is, in short, a two-way relationship between the path of the dynamic adjustment process and expectations which raises problems which our static approach ignores and is an integral part of exchange-rate 'overshooting'.

Finally, although our analysis emphasises the role of the capital account (i.e. *NPKI*) in determining the exchange rate, our discussion of the determinants of capital flows have been skeletal in the extreme. As we have noted, expectations have been treated extremely briefly and our linear hypothesis that:

$$NPKI = Q_0 + f_1 r_d + f_2 r_f \quad (f_1 > 0, f_2 < 0)$$

could hardly be simpler. This is important since it is almost certainly the case that the month-to-month and quarter-to-quarter behaviour of exchange rates predominantly reflect capital movements, which in turn reflect not only movements in relative interest rates but also shifts in expectations.

Summary

The existence of 'flexible' exchange rates modifies our earlier analysis in two important ways.

In the first place the exchange rate becomes an *endogenous* variable determined by demand and supply in the foreign exchange market, not an *exogenous* variable determined by the authorities and thus potentially a variable which they can change (as, for example, in 1949 and 1967) as a means of macroeconomic control.

In the second place this implies that the equilibrium of the system now entails three rather than two equilibrium conditions, since we must have simultaneous equilibrium in the three interdependent markets for goods, money and foreign exchange.

Notice that, where the 'flexible' rate is set by a 'perfectly clean float' – that is, there is no official intervention in the foreign exchange market – the change in overseas reserves is always zero. Hence there is no tendency for the balance-of-payments position to modify the domestic money supply. Hence control over the domestic money supply is theoretically complete, as it is not, save perhaps for relatively short periods, in the case of a 'pegged' rate.[1]

Causation in economics runs from exogenous variables to endogenous variables. The exogenous variables in our macroeconomic system are $\bar{G}$, $\bar{T}$ and $\bar{M}$ – which are controllable by the authorities – Y_w, r_f and p_w, which are determined in the rest of the world, and the autonomous elements in the consumption, investment and NPKI functions. Assumed changes in one or more of these can be analysed graphically by means of our *GG* and *BP* schedules, much as, with a closed economy, we employed the *IS/LM* analysis.

Empirically the 'short-run' behaviour of the exchange rate is, for the currencies of major financial centres, likely to be determined by the capital account of the balance of payments – itself strongly influenced by expectations regarding the future exchange rate. A major problem therefore arises in attempting to explain how such expectations are formed and, in particular, how far the position on current account influences expectations.

[1]These points are fully explained in Chapters 23–25.

Questions and exercises

1. 'If domestic prices rise proportionately to q, any change in the latter has no effect. In the *long term*, therefore, the value of q has no impact on real variables.' Do you agree? If so, why? And if not, why not? Does wealth vary with q? If so what are the consequences?

2. Analyse the behaviour of the sterling exchange rate between 1974 and 1982. What relative importance do you assign to the current and capital accounts?

3. Explain the construction of the *BP* curve if:

   (a) $f_1 \equiv \dfrac{\partial \text{NPKI}}{\partial r_d}$ approaches infinity (∞)

   and

   $f_2 \equiv \dfrac{\partial \text{NPKI}}{\partial r_f}$ approaches minus infinity ($-\infty$)

   or, in complete contrast:

   (b) $f_1 = f_2 = 0$

   In *both* situations analyse the consequence of an increase in the domestic money stock.

4. At the moment of writing in late 1982, the Thatcher–Howe administration is being pressed to stimulate industry by reducing interest rates. Use the model of the text to distinguish between the consequence of a fall in r_d and a fall in r_d/r_f. Which, in your view, is likely to be the greater stimulus? Why?

5. 'Under a "pegged" exchange rate, we cannot control our own money supply; with a perfectly "clean" float, control is – in theory – relatively simple.' Elucidate and appraise after reading Chapters 23 and 24.

6. 'Under perfectly "flexible" exchange rates, the rates of exchange cannot, except for very short periods, depart from "purchasing power parity".' Elucidate and evaluate in the light of the exchange-rate experience of (i) the UK, and (ii) Japan, between 1975 and 1982.

7. 'The UK recession of 1979–82 was primarily due to the decline in UK competitiveness – a process which largely reflected the behaviour of the exchange rate.' Examine the data and critically evaluate this statement.

8. 'Monetarism in Britain has so far (1982) meant high interest rates, a considerably overvalued exchange rate and, as a result, a recession which may yet become a major depression.' Elucidate and evaluate.

9. Explain what is meant by:

   (a) the interest differential betwen US and UK Treasury bills
   (b) the 'covered' interest differential

   In 1975 the US Treasury bill rate was 5.26 per cent, while the UK rate was 10.89 per cent, yet 'the differential' was given as 0.59 per cent. Why? And why is 'cover' important?

10. In the text the treatment of the capital account is both brief and formal. Develop a more comprehensive classification of capital transactions as described in official data and, on this basis, state how you would expand the text's treatment of the problem. How would you seek to develop a more comprehensive theory of net private capital flows?

11. Examine the UK's record, from 1967 onwards, as an exporter and importer of manufactures and semi-manufactures. What 'trends' do you find and how would you explain them?

12. 'The marginal propensity to import out of GDP is of the order of 0.35. But this is far smaller than the marginal propensity to import out of increases in stocks.' Discuss critically in the light of UK data.

13. 'At present (1982) we have a healthy current-account surplus. But this would become an unmanageable deficit if the economy was to approach – let alone attain – anything approximately like "full-capacity" working.' Elucidate and appraise.

14. 'Every person who is made unemployed improves the overall balance-of-payments position.' Do you agree? Elucidate and show how you would calculate the improvements on external account generated by an increase of 100,000 in registered unemployment. What is the unemployment cost of a £1 billion improvement in the overall balance? State your assumptions carefully.

15. 'With "flexible" exchange rates, when a rate starts to move towards its medium-term "equilibrium value", the behaviour of capital flows ensures that it will move too far.' Do you agree? What is the evidence? OR Set out, carefully and fully, how you would form an expectation of *next* year's sterling/dollar rate?

16. 'The Purchasing Power Parity Theory entails that the rate of depreciation (appreciation), in the pound, in relation to the dollar, is equal to the positive (negative) difference between the British and American "inflation" rates?' Elucidate.

17. Using data for the sterling/dollar rate and the UK and US rates of 'inflation' for 1973–82, evaluate the theory of Purchasing Power Parity as an explanation of the US/UK exchange rate.

18. 'If the *BP* curve was vertical, an expansionary fiscal policy ($\Delta \bar{G} > 0$) would leave income unaltered. *Crowding out* would be complete.' Is this correct? If so, give a clear account of the economic conditions for a vertical *BP* curve. If it is incorrect, explain why.

19. Examine carefully the impact of the following assumptions on the *GG* and *BP* schedule.

(i) $l_1 = \dfrac{\partial M^D}{\partial r_d} = 0$

or

(ii) $l_1 = \dfrac{\partial M^D}{\partial r_d} = -\infty$

(iii) $\left[- f_1 \left(\dfrac{kp_d}{l_1} \right) - z \right] > 0$

or

(iv) $\left[- f_1 \left(\dfrac{kp_d}{l_1} \right) - z \right] = 0$

Treat each possibility separately. What does (iii) imply about capital mobility?

20. 'An expansionary monetary policy *always* increases income. It will, indeed, do so even if both consumption and investment are entirely unresponsive to changes in r_d or M^S/p_d.' Do you agree? Set our your reasoning in full. OR 'Reducing the exchange rate as the CBI periodically demands will *not* increase output or employment. It will simply raise prices.' On what assumptions would this be correct? Do they, in your view, destroy the CBI's case?

Suggested reading

Bank of England, 'Evidence Presented to the Treasury and Civil Service Committee', *Memoranda on Monetary Policy*, series 1979–80 (HMSO, 1980).
Bank of England 'External and Foreign Currency Flows and the Money Supply', *Bank of England Quarterly Bulletin* (December 1978).
Bank of England, 'A Broad Look at Exchange Rate Changes for 8 Currencies: 1972–80', *Bank of England Quarterly Bulletin* (December 1981).
R. A. Batchelor, 'Sterling Exchange Rates, 1951–76: A Casselian Analysis', *NIESR Review*, no. 81 (August 1977).
*W. Buiter and M. H. Miller, 'Monetary Policy and International Competitiveness', *Oxford Economic Papers* (July 1981).
*R. Dornbusch, *Open Economy Macroeconomics* (Basic Books, 1980).
R. Dornbusch, Response to the Questionnaire on Monetary Policy, in Treasury and Civil Service Committee, *Memoranda on Monetary Policy*, (1980).
HM Treasury, 'Overseas Investments and Capital Flows', *Economic Progress Report*, no. 142 (February 1982).
NIESR, 'The European Monetary System', *NIESR Review* no. 87 (February, 1979).
R. Peters, 'Overseas Portfolio Investment Developments since the Abolition of Exchange Controls', *Westminister Bank Review* (May 1981).
H. Rose, 'The Strength of Sterling', *Barclays Bank Review* (February 1981).
J. Williamson, Response to the Questionnaire on Monetary Policy, in *Memoranda in Monetary Policy* (1980).

*More advanced references.

APPENDIX: A NOTE ON EXCHANGE-RATE DYNAMICS

In the previous two chapters our analysis has, in general, been *static*, in the sense that no variable has been dated and no variable has exhibited a *rate of change* with respect to time. In this appendix we offer a brief, informal and intuitive account of the *process* of adjustment over time which is necessarily dynamic.

A 'pegged' rate

It is useful to begin by examining how adjustment occurs in the 'pegged' rate case. To be specific we ask: What is the typical process by which the current balance adjusts to an autonomous change in the 'pegged' rate – let us say a devaluation (as occurred in the UK in November 1967)? In terms of our earlier notation this is, of course, an autonomous policy-determined increase in q from some initial 'pegged' level q_0.

The current balance is defined as:

$$E - Z \frac{p_w}{p_d} q \equiv \text{current balance} \equiv CAB \qquad \text{(A.1)}$$

and our underlying behaviour hypotheses are:

$$E = f(q) \quad \left(\text{such that } \frac{\partial E}{\partial q} > 0\right) \tag{A.2}$$

$$Z = f(q) \quad \left(\text{such that } \frac{\partial Z}{\partial q} < 0\right) \tag{A.3}$$

so that

$$CAB = f(q) \quad \left(\text{with } \frac{\partial CAB}{\partial q} > 0\right) \tag{A.4}$$

A.2 states that exports rise with q since our products become relatively cheaper; and A.3 that imports fall with an increase in q for the same reason. Moreover, both responses are assumed to be sufficiently great for A.4 to hold: that is, a rise in q to improve the current balance by improving our 'competitiveness'.

However, if we look at A.1, it is obvious that the *immediate* effect of a devaluation is simply to *raise* the sterling price of imports. With p_w and p_d invariant, therefore, the current balance must initially *deteriorate* by an amount, in nominal terms, given by $Zp_w \Delta q$. This is because it takes *time*, and empirically quite a lot of time, for foreign buyers to shift their purchases *towards* UK goods (which are now cheaper) and for domestic consumers and firms to shift their purchases *away* from imports, which are now dearer in relation to domestic output. As they make these substitutions E rises, Z falls and, when the substitutions are completed, the current balance will, in our assumptions, have improved.

In short, intuitive dynamic considerations tell us that, in response to an autonomous devaluation – that is, a downward shift in the 'pegged' rate – the current balance will initially deteriorate but subsequently begin to improve and that, when the short-run adjustment is complete, the effect on the current balance will be favourable.

We can plot this dynamic process on a diagram (Figure 14*.7) which measures the deviation of the current balance from its initial value on the vertical axis and time along the horizontal. At the beginning of the process ($t = 0$), a devaluation of Δq is imposed by the authorities. As a result, in nominal terms, the current balance deteriorates (assuming p_d and p_w are unaffected) by $-\Delta q p_w Z$.

Gradually, however, expenditure at home and abroad are adjusted to the new relative prices which – again assuming p_w invariant – are $[p_w/p_d]q\ (1 + \Delta q/q)$. Thus the negative initial impact is gradually eliminated and the current balance improves.

On these arguments the adjustment process traces out a curve which, for obvious reasons, is known as the *J*-curve.

The general form of this adjustment process is not modified, in the short run, by allowing $\partial p_d/\partial q$ to be greater than zero and foreign exporters to 'shade' their prices to offset some part of the exchange change (i.e. $\partial p_w/\partial q < 0$) – provided that the net result is still to increase the relative price of foreign output.

It is, of course, arguable that, in some 'long-run', $\partial p_d/\partial q \cdot q/p_d = 1$.

In this case devaluation does *not* improve our 'competitiveness' in the long run but simply raises domestic prices. This is a view held by many economists – and typically by 'monetarists'. We do not, however, discuss 'monetarism' until Chapter 17 and this last point should be noted for further consideration later.

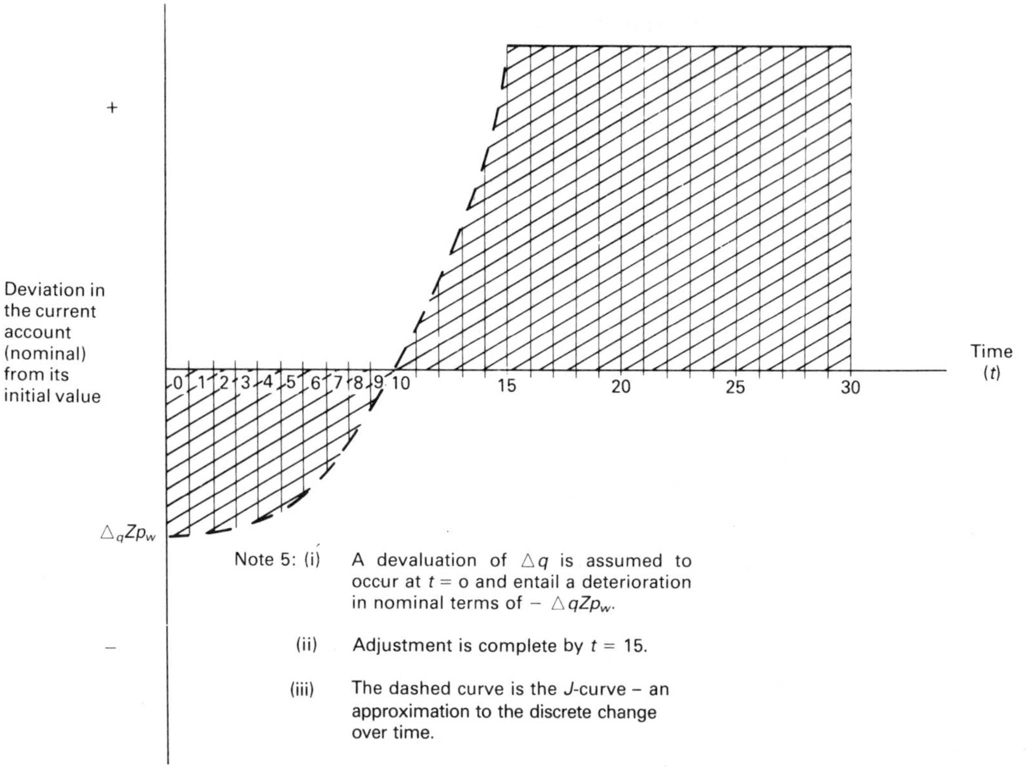
+
Deviation in the current account (nominal) from its initial value
0 1 2 3 4 5 6 7 8 9 10 15 20 25 30
Time (t)
$\triangle_q Zp_w$
Note 5: (i) A devaluation of $\triangle q$ is assumed to occur at t = o and entail a deterioration in nominal terms of $-\triangle qZp_w$.
(ii) Adjustment is complete by t = 15.
(iii) The dashed curve is the *J*-curve – an approximation to the discrete change over time.
–

Figure 14*.7 The adjustment of the current balance

A 'flexible' rate

What happens if we retain the behaviour hypothesis underlying the *J*-curve in the case of a perfectly 'clean' float?

Consider the case of an expansionary fiscal policy ($\Delta\bar{G} > 0$). According to our analysis, we shall move from q_0 to q_1 in Figure 14*.8. That is, the expansionary policy will induce a depreciation in the exchange rate. But by what path do we move from q_0 to q_1?

As income rises, the induced expansion in imports brings about a deterioration in the current account and the overall balance. But, according to our *J*-curve hypothesis, this depreciation *worsens* the current account still further in the early stages of adjustment.

This deterioration causes the exchange rate to fall (q to rise). If a fall in the exchange is *expected*, the rate of return on foreign assets rises to $r_f + \Delta\hat{q}/q$ when $\Delta\hat{q}/q \equiv$ the expected appreciation in foreign currency (that is, the expected domestic depreciation). Hence *NPKI falls*. Thus anticipated depreciation further weakens the external position and ensures further depreciation. Clearly this suggests that once the exchange rate starts to fall it *may* do so without apparent limit if wealth-owners' *expected* rate of exchange depreciation is derived by extrapolation from the *actual* current rate of depreciation.

It is probably the case that some wealth-owners do form expectations in this simple extrapolative manner. However, the foreign exchange market does contain professional

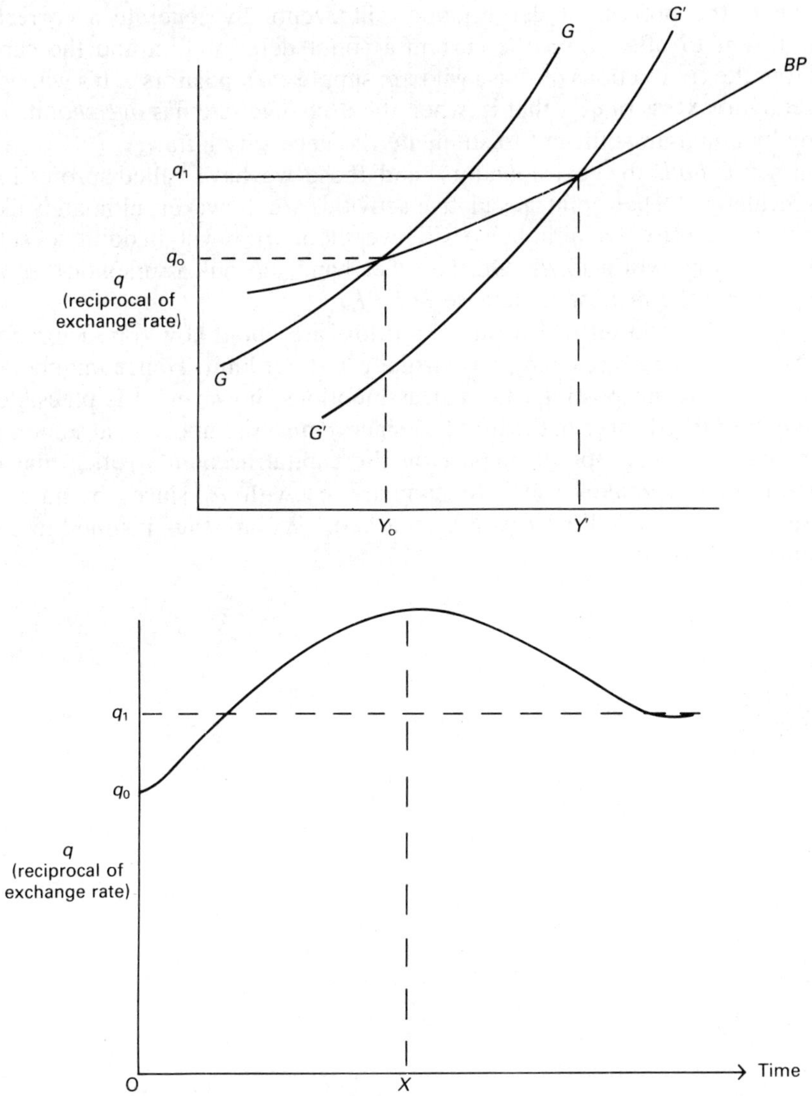

Note: at t = o GG shifts to $G'G'$
and equilibrium q becomes q_1
At $t = X$ $q > q_1$ by an amount sufficient to drive q towards q_1 due to its influence on *NPKI*.

Figure 14*.8 An expansionary fiscal policy: the adjustment of q

operators who are able to form an expectation of the new short-period equilibrium rate, which we know to be q_1.

When $q > q_1$, these operators will expect q to *fall*, thus moving towards q_1. They will thus expect an appreciation of the domestic currency if q is above q_1: that is, if the domestic currency has fallen below – or has 'overshot' – its new short-period equilibrium. It is likely that operators who form expectations in this way dominate the exchange market since, in practice, we do not observe currencies falling without apparent limit and at increasing rates of decline.

On this argument, the process of depreciation will eventually generate a corrective capital *inflow* sufficient to offset both the current-account deterioration and the capital outflow arising from the transactions of those who are simple extrapolators. This will occur when q is sufficiently in excess of q_1 – that is, when the exchange rate has *overshot* its new equilibrium value by a margin sufficient to stimulate the necessary inflow.

In the general sense *both* the 'extrapolators' and those we have called 'professional operators' are 'speculators'. Their joint speculative activities are, however, ultimately likely to be stabilising: that is, ensure that although q will 'overshoot' q_1, it will, in doing so, set up a process which ensures its return to q_1. On the other hand, on our assumptions, q *must* overshoot q_1 to generate the necessary increase in *NPKI*.

Clearly, the range of hypotheses which can be put forward about how transactors form their expectations of exchange-rate changes is virtually without limit. Hence innumerable dynamic paths for q_0 to q_1 are possible. On our assumptions, however, it is plausible to think of a path like the dashed curve in Figure 14*.7 since q must rise above q_1 at some stage in the process to have the appropriate impact on the capital account. Notice that our assumptions ensure that it makes sense to compare q_0 with q_1 since, because our assumptions ensure dynamic stability, q_1 will be reached.[1] We are thus justified in using 'comparative statics' in Chapter 14*.

[1]This issue of 'dynamic stability' is further discussed in Chapter 20. See also Chapter 7.

Chapter 15
The Theory of the Price Level

So far the whole of our analysis has proceeded on the simplifying assumption that the price level is given and invariant. This does not mean that the level of prices exerts no influence in our model. Indeed if we look back at Chapter 11 we see that the price level is a determinant of the demand for active (M_1) balances and thus of the rate of interest. Since the rate of interest, given the MEI schedule, determines (as explained in Chapter 10) the rate of real planned investment, which, in its turn, determines, via the multiplier, the equilibrium level of real income and, via the production function, the level of employment, it is clear that the level of prices exerts a considerable influence in our system. It is plain, therefore, that to complete our theory we need to consider how the price level itself gets determined. To explain this is the job of this chapter.

Price determination and profit maximisation

Our basic hypothesis concerning business behaviour is that businessmen seek to maximise profits. From this hypothesis we derive the *supply side* of our theory of prices.

Consider a businessman contemplating the production of an additional unit of output. If he produces it – and sells it at the price already established in the market – he will obtain additional revenue equal to the additional output multiplied by the price of a unit of output. The revenue so obtained we call the *marginal revenue* (MR) simply because it is the *additional revenue* derived from producing the additional unit. Call the additional units of output ΔO and write the price of a unit of output as p. Then if the marginal units can be sold *without* reducing prices[1] we have:

$$\text{Additional revenue} = p\,\Delta O$$

Obviously the businessman will only produce this output if it increases his profits. Since profits are the excess of revenue over costs, if we call the costs of producing the marginal units *marginal costs* (MC), then the hypothesis of profit maximisation tells us that:

[1]This implies that the goods market is one of 'pure' competition in which no single producer is sufficiently large for variation in his output to influence price.

(a) if MR $>$ MC the businessman will *expand* output
(b) if MR $<$ MC the businessman will *contract* output
(c) if MR $=$ MC the businessman will be in equilibrium: that is, he will have no incentive either to expand or contract his level of output.

If we now think of a closed economy, and of businessmen as a whole and not simply one individual businessman, and use a short-run analysis, then the cost of producing an additional unit of output, marginal cost, is the cost of employing the additional labour necessary to produce it. Write the money wage rate as W and the increase in employment, necessary to produce ΔO increase in output, as ΔN. Then:

$$\text{marginal cost of } \Delta O \text{ output} = W\,\Delta N$$

We have already found that, for businessmen to be in equilibrium, we require marginal revenue = marginal cost, that is:

$$p\,\Delta O = W\,\Delta N \tag{15.1}$$

or

$$p = W\frac{\Delta N}{\Delta O} \tag{15.2}$$

This tells us that p, the price at which the profit-maximising businessman would *plan* to produce ΔO additional unit of output, is determined by:

$$W \equiv \text{the money wage rate}$$

and

$\Delta N/\Delta O \equiv$ the amount of labour necessary to produce the additional units of out put

For the moment let us assume that W (the money wage rate) is given and constant: that is, it takes some special value W_h. Equation 15.2 then tells us that, if we know $\Delta N/\Delta O$, since we know that $W = W_h$, we can readily determine p. What, then, is the quantity $\Delta N/\Delta O$?

The production function and the marginal product of labour

The meaning of $\Delta N/\Delta O$ is plain enough. It is the (marginal) labour input required to produce the increase in output. We have not met this concept before. We are, however, familiar with its reciprocal form:

$$\frac{1}{(\Delta N/\Delta O)} \equiv \frac{\Delta O}{\Delta N} \equiv \text{marginal physical product of labour}$$

To see what this means divide both sides of 15.2 by $\Delta N/\Delta O$. We get:

$$p\frac{\Delta O}{\Delta N} = W \tag{15.3}$$

This tells us that businessmen will employ additional labour up to the point at which the marginal revenue product of labour (≡ marginal physical product × price of product) is equal to the marginal cost of doing so, i.e. the money wage rate. To give an example, suppose we produce cricket balls which sell at £1 each and that, by employing an additional man, we can make another forty cricket balls per week. Then p = £1, $\Delta O = 40$, $\Delta N = 1$, so that:

$$p\,\frac{\Delta O}{\Delta N} = \text{£40 per week}$$

If $W <$ £40 we shall gain by hiring an additional man. If $W >$ £40 we shall lose. Only if W = £40 per week shall we have no incentive to hire (or fire) an additional man.

It follows that, given that $W = W_h$, we can explain at what prices businessmen will be prepared to produce given levels of output, provided we can relate the marginal product to labour (and thus its reciprocal) to the level of output.

Earlier in this book, in Chapter 7, we introduced the notion of a *production function.* This stated quite generally that we could write a production function of the form:

$$Y = f(T, K, N)$$

showing that total output (Y) depended upon $T \equiv$ the state of technique; $K \equiv$ the quantity of real capital; $N \equiv$ the quantity of employment.

The particular function we made use of was $Y = TK^{\alpha}N^{1-\alpha}$. This function, and its properties, we discussed in some detail in Chapter 7 and the reader is now referred back to that earlier discussion. In the *short run* we take T and K as *given*. We can therefore plot the function on a diagram as a relationship between N and Y with K and T given. This is done in Figure 15.1.

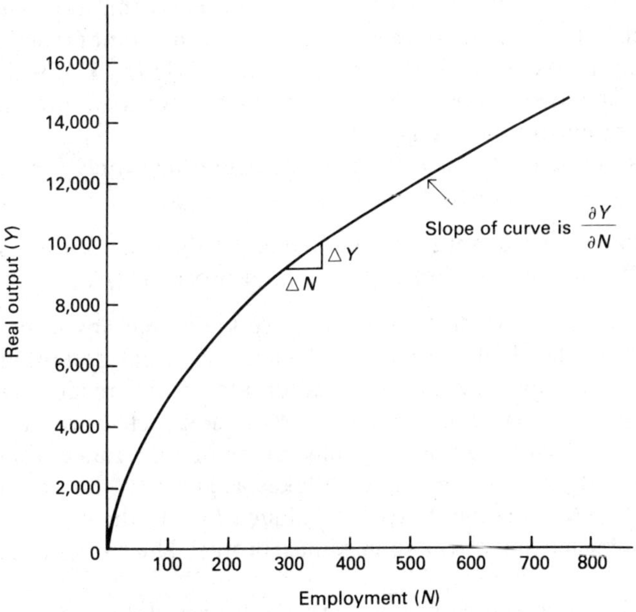

Figure 15.1 Short-run production function

Now the *slope* of the curve relating Y to N in this figure is the marginal response coefficient $\partial Y/\partial N$. This is the marginal physical product of labour. The curve thus tells us – and this is confirmed by Figure 7.1 (p. 80) – that:

(a) the marginal physical product of labour, $\partial Y/\partial N$, is always positive
(b) the marginal physical product of labour, $\partial Y/\partial N$, falls as Y (or N) increases
(c) for any level of Y (or N) there is a given value of $\partial Y/\partial N$, i.e. of the marginal physical product of labour

It follows that, for any given value of Y, there is a given value of $\partial N/\partial Y$, *the marginal labour cost of a unit of output,*[1] *and also that* $\partial N/\partial Y$ *increases as Y increases. This arises because of the operation of the principle of diminishing marginal physical productivity.*

We can now say that (i) for any level of real output there is a given marginal labour cost of a unit of output, hence, since $W = W_h$ by assumption, (ii) for any level of real output there will be a single determinate price level, while, since the marginal labour cost is higher, the higher the level of output, (iii) the higher the level of real output the higher the price level associated with it.

The aggregate supply function

We now know that, with a given money wage rate, businessmen will require, in order to maximise profits, a higher level of prices the higher the level of output simply because the *marginal labour cost of producing output* is higher the higher is the level of output. To see what this implies let us construct two curves.

The first of these curves relates the level of output (Y) to the price level (p) which will just induce businessmen to produce it. The second curve relates the level of output (Y) to the level of money proceeds (pY) which will just induce businessmen to produce it. The two curves are simply related. Any point on the first curve, say the point O, defines both a price level (p_0) and an output level (Y_0). It thus defines a rectangle ($p_0\ Y_0$), which is a point on our second curve. The two curves are thus alternative ways of presenting the same information. They are illustrated in Figure 15.2.

Both these curves can be regarded *as forms of the aggregate supply function*. Usually the aggregate supply function is defined as:

> a function relating the quantity of employment (N) which businessmen would be prepared to offer to each level of expected total proceeds (pY)

However, from the short-run production function we know that any level of employment (N) determines a given level of output (Y). Hence the usual definition can easily be converted into the form which we use here. Alternatively the reader can construct the traditional curve from our curve relating output (Y) and expected proceeds (pY).

Let us look at these two curves rather carefully taking first the range from zero output to the point of discontinuity $Y = Y_{fe}$. Each curve takes as given (i) the production function, (ii) the stock of capital (K), (iii) the state of technique (T), (iv) the money wage rate (W_h), and (v) *assumes* that businessmen seek to maximise profits. The curves both slope upwards

[1]That is, the additional labour input required, given the production function, the state of technique and the capital stock, to produce an additional unit of output.

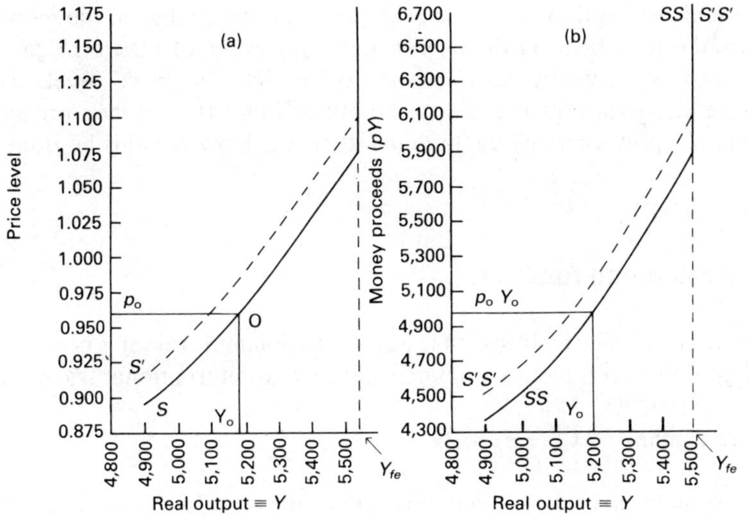

Figure 15.2 The aggregate supply function

because, as output (Y) rises, so does the labour input required to produce an additional unit of output. Hence with a given money wage the price level (p) and the value of money proceeds (pY) which will just induce businessmen to produce any given level of output rises as the level of output rises.

What is the meaning of the point of discontinuity? At some level of output, which we have called Y_{fe}, labour will be fully employed. In the short run, therefore, Y cannot exceed Y_{fe} whatever the expected level of prices (p) or money proceeds (pY). Hence at this point of discontinuity the curves become vertical.

In what circumstances will the aggregate supply curve shift and in what way? The parameters of the curve are listed as (i)–(iv) on page 248 and the behaviour hypothesis it reflects is listed at (e). Of these parameters (a) to (c) are constant in a short-run analysis. Hence only the money wage rate is available as a source of shifts unless we permit, as we shall *not* do, the business behaviour hypothesis to change. What, then, is the effect on the curve of, say, an increase in the money wage rate (W_h) to some new higher value W_h'?

We know from an earlier analysis that, given the production function, the state of technique and the capital stock, any level of real output will entail a particular marginal labour cost (input requirement) for additional output. Hence the price level which will just induce businessmen to produce the given level of output will, from the relation $p = W(\partial N/\partial Y)$, rise if W increases. It follows that any level of output will be associated with a higher value of money proceeds (pY) if the money wage rate is W_h' rather than W_h. Hence the SS curve of Figure 15.2b shifts *upwards* in the manner shown by the dashed line $S'S'$. This line will, of course, coincide with the original curve for all values of money proceeds greater than a certain figure (6,100 on our figure) at the point of discontinuity given by Y_{fe}. For a cut in money wages from W_h' to W_h the argument, at this formal level, is simply reversed. The $S'S'$ curve becomes the SS curve.

The reader, relaxing one of the assumptions of the short-run analysis, should now work out the consequences for the SS curve of a greater value for K ($\equiv$ the real stock of capital).

The reader should also work out for this example – and the change in the money wage rate already discussed – the effect on the aggregate supply curve of Figure 15.2a.

Of course the *SS* curve by itself cannot determine the price level. To show the simultaneous determination of prices (p), output (Y) and thus money proceeds (pY) we must superimpose upon it an aggregate demand curve. How can this be done?

The aggregate demand function

We know, from our earlier analysis, that aggregate demand, relating now to our simplest model, and ignoring government economic activity and international trade, is given by:

$$\text{aggregate demand} \equiv C_p + I_p \equiv D$$

Now I_p (real planned investment) depends upon the rate of interest. For a given money supply, following the analysis of Chapter 11, the rate of interest depends upon the two liquidity functions (L_1 and L_2) and the level of *money income*. The higher is money income, the higher in general is the rate of interest.

Suppose, for example, we choose the level of real output Y_0 in Figure 15.2. Then the equilibrium price level (to satisfy businessmen) will be p_0 and the equilibrium value of money proceeds is $p_0 Y_0$, which is the money income received. This assumes, of course, that production plans are always realised. With a given money supply this immediately determines a rate of interest (r_0), which, via the investment function, gives us the value of real planned investment (I_{p0}). From the consumption function, since we know output (Y_0), we know real planned consumption (C_{p0}). We thus know:

$$C_{p0} + I_{p0} \equiv \text{aggregate demand in real terms} \equiv D$$

at the price level p_0. This enables us to plot, by repeated experiment in this way, a curve relating $C_p + I_p \equiv$ real planned expenditure to the price level (p). Such a curve is depicted in Figure 15.3a. Equally, simply by multiplying real planned expenditure by the price level to which it refers, we can obtain $p(C_p + I_p) \equiv$ money value of real planned expenditure at any level of output (Y). This curve is plotted on Figure 15.3b.

Both these curves (which are obviously simply related) are forms of the aggregate demand function. This function, like the aggregate supply function, is more usually expressed in terms of employment (N) than output (Y). The transformation, if it is required, can, however, very easily be made through the production function which, in its short-run version, gives a unique relation between Y and N, as Figure 15.1 reminds us.

What do we take as given in drawing these curves? Obviously they reflect the influence of:

(a) a given consumption function
(b) a given marginal efficiency of investment schedule
(c) a given money supply
(d) given L_1 and L_2 (liquidity preference) functions
(e) a given production function
(f) a given state of technique and capital stock
(g) a given money wage rate

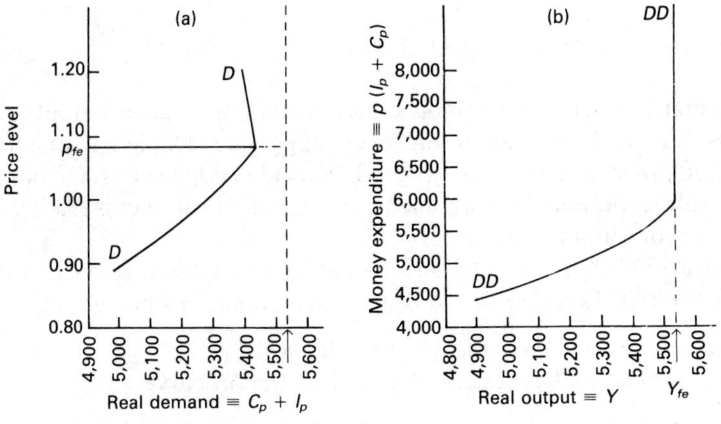

Figure 15.3 Aggregate demand functions

This is a lengthy list and the fact that it is so reflects the complicated chain of reasoning which we used to construct the curves. Examination of this list also reveals that the items (e)–(g) on which the aggregate demand curve depends are also determinants of the aggregate supply curve. It therefore follows that, in some cases, changes which shift the former curve will also shift the latter. These two curves thus have a degree of interdependence – a point which must be kept very carefully in mind. This interdependence arises from the definition of the functions which the reader needs to keep constantly in mind. To put matters concisely:

1. The aggregate supply function tells us how much output businessmen will plan to supply at any given price level.
2. The aggregate demand function tells us how much businessman will *sell* if they produce their planned output at a given price level.

Finally, we should add that, although the construction of these aggregate demand functions is complicated, we have in fact constructed them on an implicit simplifying assumption which must now be brought into the open. This implicit assumption is that the distribution of income, which, as the reader will recall, is a parameter of our consumption function, is constant. In certain cases, as we shall see later, this is a very strong assumption. Nevertheless in the *formal parts of our analysis* we shall retain it.

Because the aggregate demand functions are complicated concepts, we need to interpret them with considerable care. To see how to interpret them consider Figure 15.4b. In this we have superimposed the aggregate demand function which relates $p(C_p + I_p)$ to Y on the aggregate supply function of Figure 15.2b.

Suppose now that businessmen expect money proceeds to be OA. From the aggregate supply function they will produce output of Y_A. Money income will therefore be $p_A Y_A = OA$. Given this level of money income, the value of the money supply and the two liquidity preference functions (L_1 and L_2), this will in the money market determine a rate of interest r_A which, via the given MEI schedule, tells us the rate of planned investment (Ip_A). Real planned consumption (C_{pA}) depends, by hypothesis, only on real income (Y_A). Hence this too is known. Thus we have determined $D_A \equiv C_{pA} + I_{pA}$. Multiplying this by the price level (P_A) gives us the value of money expenditure. As we have drawn the curves we have:

$$P_A D_A > P_A Y_A$$
$$\text{money expenditure} > \text{expected proceeds}$$

In such a situation competition will induce businessmen to expand output until the curves intersect at Y_e. At Y_e (the equilibrium level) aggregate demand is equal to aggregate supply. Expected proceeds and actual proceeds coincide and businessmen have no incentive to expand or contract output. This argument, as the reader can see, is readily reversed for a hypothetical level of output in *excess* of Y_e.

Now in Figure 15.4b both thc *DD* and *SS* curves are upward-sloping to the right. The validity of the analysis therefore depends upon *two* conditions being met:

(a) the *DD* curve must lie *above* the *SS* curve for all $Y < Y_e$
(b) the *DD* curve must be *less* steeply sloped than the *SS* curve

The first condition is met by our model. Assume a very low (but not zero) planned real output. Then, if the consumption function is linear and autonomous consumption positive, planned real consumption will exceed output. Since the price level is low the interest rate (*ceteris paribus*) will also be low and planned real investment $p(C_p + I_p)$ will exceed the value of expected proceeds (pY). But what of the second condition?

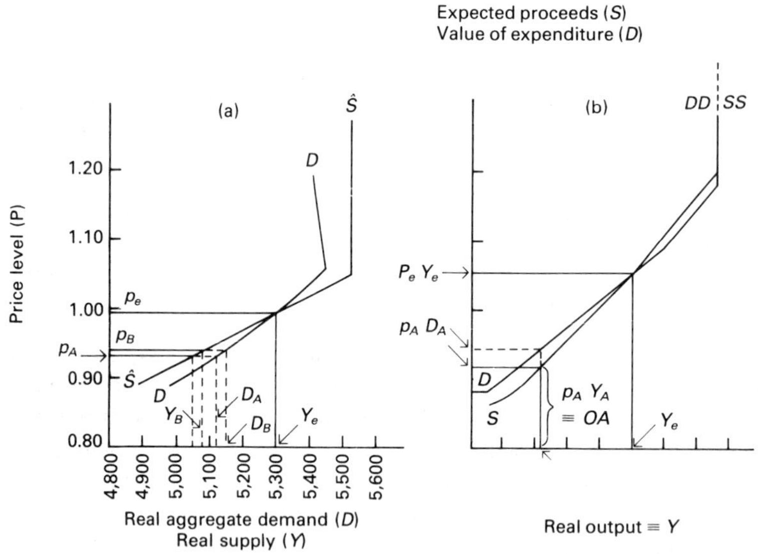

Figure 15.4 Aggregate demand and supply

By construction $pD \equiv p(C_p + I_p)$. Assume, to simplify matters, that I_p does not react to the rate of interest. Then, as output rises, pD rises for two reasons: (i) because the price level (p) rises; (ii) because as Y rises so does C_p. Similarly aggregate supply S ($\equiv pY$) increases as Y increases (i) because p (the price level) rises, and (ii) because Y rises. Obviously since C_p rises by *less* than Y, then pD rises by *less* than S as Y increases. This is simply another way of saying that the slope of *DD* is flatter than the slope of *SS*.

Hence both our conditions are satisfied: pD does lie *above* S for low values of Y *and* the slope of DD is *flatter* than that of SS even if investment does *not* fall as the rate of interest rises. If we now allow for this latter effect our conclusion is simply strengthened. Now look at the curves on Figure 15.4a. The aggregate supply curve $\hat{S}$ needs no further explanation. What of the aggregate demand curve? Again assume businessmen to expect a low price level (say p_A) and thus produce output Y_A. As we have shown above, real planned expenditure (D_A) will exceed Y_A. Thus at a low price level (p_A) the D curve must be to the right of the aggregate supply curve $\hat{S}$.

Now suppose businessmen expect a price level higher than p_A (say p_B). Accordingly they produce output Y_B. If the rate of interest was at its minimum at p_A and remains at its minimum level at p_B (i.e. we are on the flat part of the L_2 function) $C_p + I_p$ will rise by an amount determined by the increase in Y and the marginal propensity to consume. Hence at the *higher* price level (p_B) the value of $C_p + I_p$ will be *greater*. The D curve slopes *upwards to the right*. Hence to cut the $\hat{S}$ curve it must slope upwards, as p rises, at a *faster rate* than the $\hat{S}$ curve. This can be shown to be the case by an argument analogous to that used above in relation to the curves of Figure 15.4b.

Where the D and S curves cut we determine the equilibrium values of the price level (p_e) and real output (Y_e). This point, obviously enough, gives the value p_eY_e which we found in Figure 15.4b. In short, Figure 15.4a gives no *more* information than Figure 15.4b. Its advantage is simply that it gives, explicitly rather than implicitly, the equilibrium value of the price level.

It should be noted that, at some point, the D curve of the two diagrams *reverses* its direction of slope. Why is this? The explanation is not hard to seek. At p_{fe} the $\hat{S}$ curve becomes vertical for reasons we have already explained and output (Y) is at its full-employment ceiling. Hence real planned consumption is also at its ceiling for the given consumption function. Now as p rises above p_{fe} the rate of interest rises and I_p falls. Hence $C_p + I_p$ *falls* and the D curve bends backwards to the left.

The introduction of aggregate demand and supply curves of the kind dealt with here clearly involves some unavoidably intricate argument. The reader is therefore exhorted to go very carefully over this analysis and that of the section following. Then, after completing the chapter, he or she should construct the numerical model given in the questions and exercises. In this way it is relatively simple to understand the central lessons of aggregate demand and supply analysis which are that:

1. *The equilibrium level of prices is simultaneously determined with the equilibrium levels of output, employment and the rate of interest.*
2. *The aggregate demand and supply functions depend on many of the same determinants.*
3. *An increase in aggregate supply increases aggregate demand but typically by less than the increase in supply.*

A numerical example of the construction of aggregate demand and supply schedules

The purpose of this section is to give a precise illustration of the construction of the model of the previous section.

To do this, it is convenient to begin with the aggregate supply schedule. We thus require a simple approximation to an aggregate production function. Let us write this as:

$$Y = F + eN - fN^2 \tag{15.4}$$

where $Y \equiv$ real output and $N \equiv$ labour input and we are assuming that the stock of capital (K) is invariant, as is the state of technique.

Now if both goods and factor markets are purely competitive and employers seek to maximise profits, labour will be demanded until the real marginal product of labour ($\partial Y/\partial N$) is equal to the real wage (W_h/p) – that is, until:

$$\frac{\partial Y}{\partial N} = \frac{W_h}{p} \tag{15.5}$$

where $W_h \equiv$ the historically given money wage rate.

If we now differentiate the production function 15.4 we obtain:

$$\frac{\partial Y}{\partial N} = e - 2fN \tag{15.6}$$

which provided $f > 0$, falls as N increases we must expect. Combining 15.5 and 15.6 yields:

$$p = \frac{W_h}{e - 2fN} \tag{15.7}$$

and thus yields a functional relation between p ($\equiv$ the price level) and N ($\equiv$ employment) which, since, from 15.4, any given value of N implies a unique level of Y, could also be written as a functional relation between p and Y: that is, as an aggregate supply schedule.

Table 15.1 Illustrative calculation of aggregate supply schedules

(1) Price level p	(2) Labour input N	(3) Aggregate real supply Y	(4) *Money proceeds (to 4 significant figs)* pY
0.89	50	4,873	4,332
0.91	60	4,964	4,513
0.93	70	5,051	4,699
0.95	80	5,136	4,898
0.98	90	5,219	5,091
1.0	100	5,300	5,300
1.03	110	5,379	5,517
1.05	120	5,456	5,744
1.08	130	5,531	5,994
1.11	130	5,531	6,110

Note: Figures have been rounded and $N = 130$ defines full employment.

Sources: col. (2) derived from labour demand function:

$$N^D = 500 - 50\frac{W_h}{p}$$

col. (3) derived from production function.
col. (4) = col. (1) × col. (3).

This is illustrated in Table 15.1, taking the following assumed numerical values for the coefficients of 15.4 and for the historically given money wage rate (W_h):

$$F = 4{,}400 \qquad f = 0.01$$
$$e = 10 \qquad W_h = 8.0$$

Notice that from this table we can easily construct aggregate supply schedules relating p to Y or pY to Y. The former type of function is illustrated in Figure 15.5, the latter we can readily construct for yourself. Notice also that at each point on the aggregate supply schedule businessmen are assumed to be maximising profit.

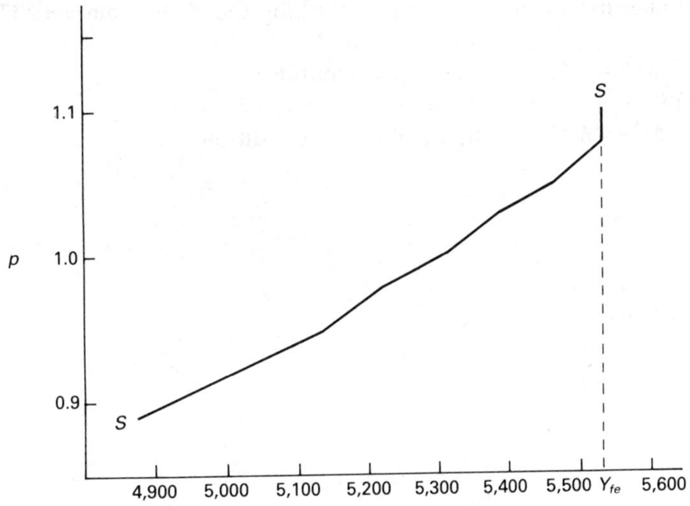

Figure 15.5 Aggregate supply curve

We now turn to construct the aggregate demand schedule. To do this we first define:

$$\text{real aggregate demand} \equiv D \equiv C_p + I_p \tag{15.8}$$

Retaining our simple consumption hypothesis, we may write:

$$C_p = A + cY \tag{15.9}$$

which gives us the familiar linear propensity to consume schedule. If we use a similar linear approximation to the investment hypothesis – such as, for example:

$$I_p = H - br \tag{15.10}$$

we can construct a schedule relating I_p to r. Since H is a positive constant, I_p will have some maximum value associated with the minimum interest rate which the community will accept: that is, the value of r_{min}. To fix our ideas, let us assume that, numerically, we have:

$A = 100 \quad H = 1{,}000 \quad r_{\min} = 2.0$ per cent
$c = 0.8 \quad b = 10$

Given this information we can construct Figures 15.6 and 15.7, which depict the consumption and investment hypotheses.

From 15.9 and 15.10 by making use of the identity 15.8 we can obtain:

$$D \equiv C_p + I_p = (A + H) + cY - br \tag{15.11}$$

which reminds us that real aggregate demand depends upon *both* real income (Y) and the interest rate (r). Thus to find D for any given Y we must also know r.

To find r we make use of the equations describing the money market. These are:

$$M^S = M_0 = \text{the supply hypothesis} \tag{15.12}$$
$$M^D = KpY + Z - dr = \text{the demand hypothesis} \tag{15.13}$$
$$M^S = M^D = \text{the equilibrium condition} \tag{15.14}$$

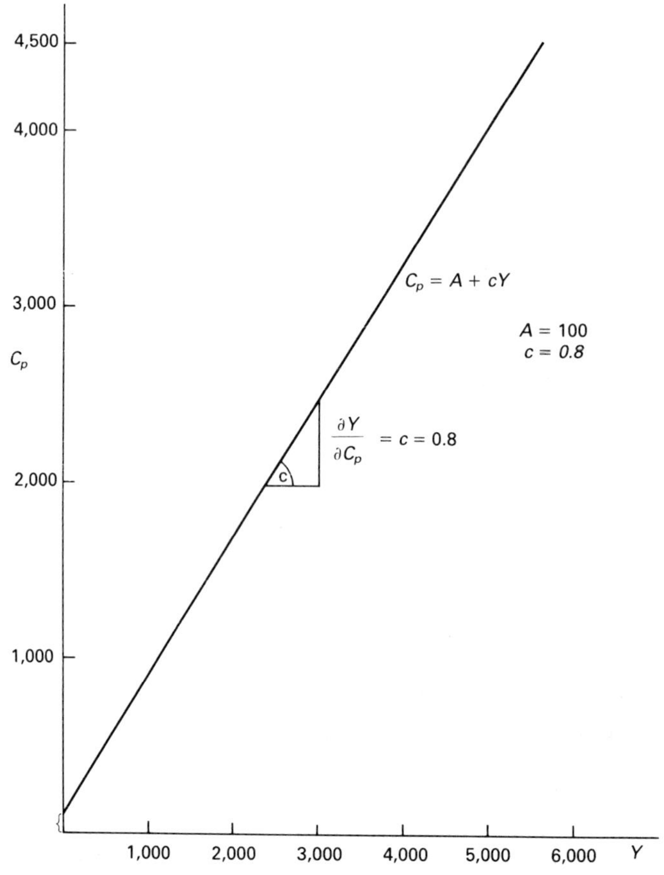

Figure 15.6 Consumption hypothesis

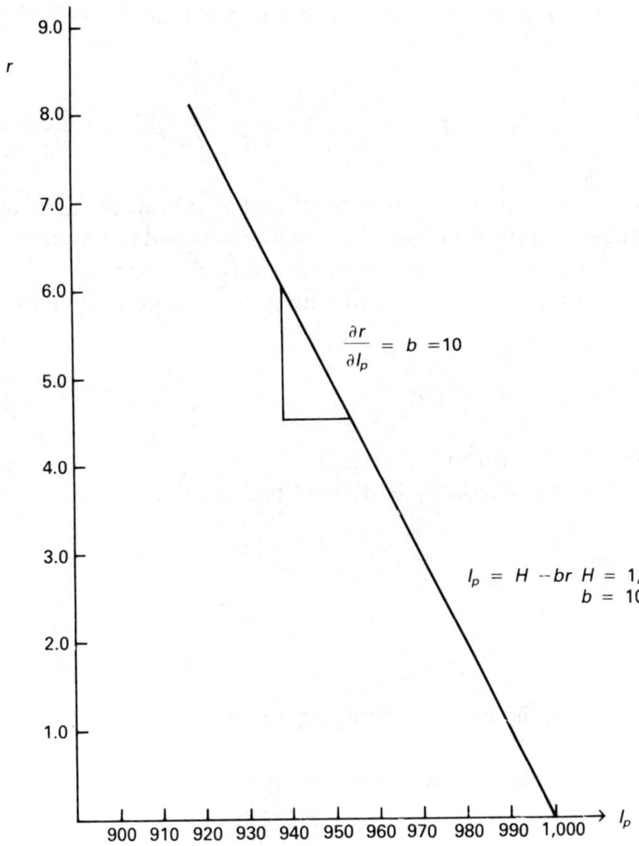

Figure 15.7 Investment hypothesis

As the reader can readily check, substitution of 15.12 and 15.13 into 15.14 yields the following solution for r:

$$r = (KpY + Z - M_0)\,\frac{1}{d} \tag{15.15}$$

Inserting this into 15.11 yields the following rather formidable-looking expression for D:

$$\begin{aligned} D &= (A + H) + cY - \frac{b}{d}(KpY + Z - M_0) \\ &= \left[A + H - \frac{b}{d}(Z - M_0)\right] + cY - \frac{b}{d}KpY \end{aligned} \tag{15.16}$$

Again assuming numerical values for the demand and supply of money functions, we can now calculate D for any value of Y and pY. Unfortunately Y and pY remain to be determined.

From the aggregate supply function, however, we already know that a given value of p implies a given value of Y and thus pY. Thus if Y in 15.16 is replaced by the aggregate supply function relating Y to p – written purely for convenience as $Y = s(p)$ – then 15.16 becomes:

$$D = \left[A + H - \frac{b}{d}(Z - M_0)\right] + cs(p) - \frac{b}{d} Kps(p) \qquad (15.17)$$

which clearly gives D as a function of p while yet emphasising that aggregate demand depends upon aggregate supply (via both the consumption and investment functions) and on the characteristics of the demand and supply functions for money.

Taking the following numerical values for the money market equations:

$$M_0 = 2{,}500 \qquad K = 0.25$$
$$Z = 1{,}375 \qquad d = 50$$

we can calculate D, as is shown in Table 15.2.

If the aggregate demand schedules as defined are schedules relating:

p and D

or

pD and D

are now superimposed on the corresponding aggregate supply schedules from Table 15.1, we obtain Figure 15.8.

It is easy to see from the diagram that the aggregate supply and demand schedules intersect at the values:

$p = 1.0$; $Y = 5{,}300$; $D = 5{,}300$; $pY = 5{,}300$: $pD = 5{,}300$

Table 15.2 Illustrative calculation of real aggregate demand
(figures rounded)

(1) Price level p	(2) Aggregate real supply Y	(3) Value of aggregate supply pY	(4) Rate of Interest r	(5) Real planned consumption C_p	(6) Real planned investment I_p	(7) Real aggregate demand D	(8) Value of aggregate demand pD
1.11	5,531	6,110	8.1	4,525	919	5,444	6,043
1.08	5,531	5,994	7.5	4,525	925	5,450	5,886
1.05	5,456	5,744	6.0	4,465	940	5,405	5,675
1.03	5,379	5,517	5.1	4,403	949	5,352	5,513
1.0	5,300	5,300	4.0	4,340	960	5,300	5,300
0.98	5,219	5,091	3.0	4,275	970	5,245	5,140
0.95	5,136	4,898	2.0	4,209	980	5,189	4,930
0.93	5,051	4,699	2.0	4,141	980	5,121	4,763
0.91	4,964	4,513	2.0	4,071	980	5,051	4,596
0.89	4,873	4,332	2.0	4,000	980	4,980	4,432

Sources: col. (2) derived as in Table 15.1; col. (3) derived as in Table 15.1; col. (4) derived from equation (15.15) subject to r_{min} 2.0 per cent; col. (5) derived from equation (15.9); col. (6) derived from equation (15.9); col. (7) derived from identity (15.8); col. (8) = col. (1) × col. (7).

Moreover a glance back at Table 15.2 reminds us that this equilibrium entails:

$r = 4.0$ per cent; $C_p = 4{,}340$; $I_p = 960$

Now consider a price level other than $p = 1.0$ – say $p^* = 0.91$. From Figure 15.8a, or alternatively from Table 15.1, we find:

aggregate supply $\equiv Y^* = 4{,}964$

Similarly from Figure 15.8, or alternatively from Table 15.2, we find:

aggregate demand $\equiv D^* = 5{,}051$

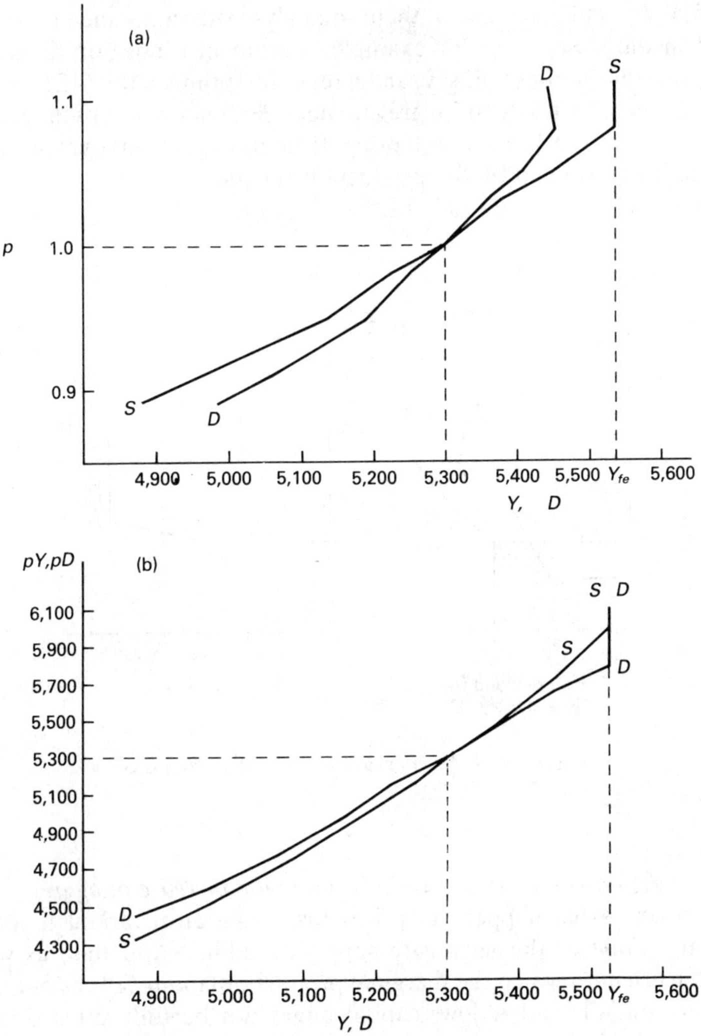

Figure 15.8 Aggregate demand and supply schedules

hence the *excess* demand at the *disequilibrium* price p^* is $D^* - Y^* = 87$ or, in value terms, $p^*(D^* - Y^*) = 4{,}596 - 4{,}513 = 83$. Clearly, where $p^* < p$ we shall always have $D^* > Y^*$ and conversely where $p^* > p$. In short, Figure 15.8 correctly indicates *not only*:

(a) the nature of the equilibrium solution, *but also*
(b) the *extent* of the disequilibria which will exist at prices other than the equilibrium price

Moreover, and this is the fundamental lesson of Keynesian economics, it makes clear, as our method of deriving the aggregate demand schedule emphasises, not only the interdependence of aggregate demand and aggregate supply, but also the precise nature of the interdependence.

The determination of prices

Now that we have explained the relationship between our curves in the two segments of Figures 15.2–15.4 we shall make use of them to analyse the simultaneous determination of prices and real income. Suppose, for example, we are in a position depicted by Figure 15.9b. Assume now that because of, say, an increase in optimism the MEI schedule shifts to the right. What happens? Clearly the aggregate demand functions in both sections of Figure 15.9 shift. Output rises from Y_0 to Y_1 and prices from p_0 to p_1. Employment, of course, also rises by an amount determined by the production function.

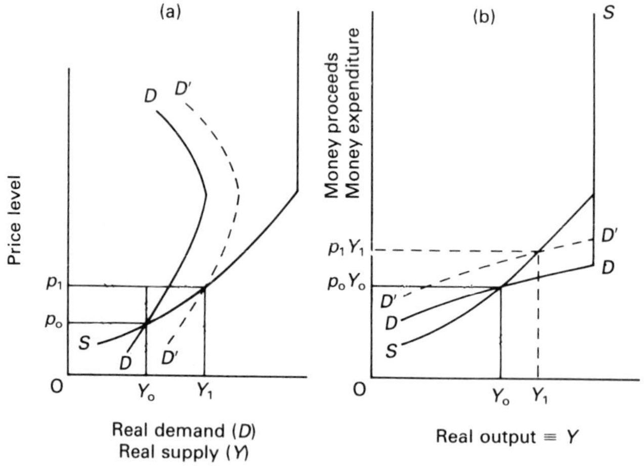

Figure 15.9 An increase in the MEI schedule

There is, however, *no simple relationship between the increase in aggregate demand and the increase in prices*. What happens to prices (assuming an invariant money wage rate) depends upon the *slope* of the aggregate supply schedule. And this, as we have seen, depends upon the *extent* to which the marginal product of labour falls as output expands. If employment were initially rather low, capital might not be fully utilised. Machines, for example, might all be in use but be running at reduced speeds. In such a situation the marginal productivity of labour might fall very little and thus prices rise by very little, as output and employment expand. If this is so the increase in aggregate demand will go, in the main, to increasing output and employment. Conversely, if the initial equilibrium were close to full employment, the fall in the marginal product of labour might be marked. In such a situation the increase in prices might be relatively large, and the increase in output and employment relatively small.

Inflation and money wage changes

A special problem arises if aggregate demand increases from a position of equilibrium *at* full employment. This is illustrated in Figure 15.10b, where the D curve, initially at DD, moves to $D'D'$. Here output, in the short run, *cannot* increase. Yet at the initial (i.e. old equilibrium) price level the quantity of output demanded now exceeds that supplied. There is, in short, a situation of *excess demand*. Such a situation is a disequilibrium one characterised by inflationary pressure. We are, at present, assuming a perfectly competitive system in the goods market. Hence we shall expect the price level to rise. Since this, with a given money wage rate (W_h) implies a fall in real wages, an excess demand for labour will emerge.

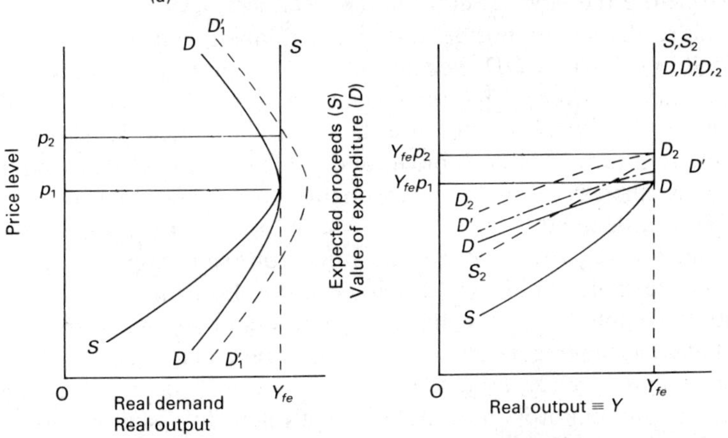

Figure 15.10 A shift in the aggregate demand function at full employment

So far, by regarding W_h as given, we have not specified how the labour market responds to excess demand for labour at full employment. The simplest assumption is that money wage rates are bid up by excess demand and thus tend to rise *pari passu* with prices so that the real wage is invariant as long as:

$$N^D \equiv \text{demand for labour} \geqslant N_f \equiv \text{full employment}$$

Given this assumption, the distribution of income between wage-earners and profit-recipients is also invariant. Hence prices will rise until the interest-rate mechanism has reduced aggregate demand to the level of full-employment aggregate supply. Descriptively we may say that prices and wages rise proportionately, thus *shifting both* aggregate demand and supply schedules. The rise in prices increases the demand for money, and this, given the nominal money supply, raises the rate of interest, bringing about an *induced* fall in planned investment. Since C_p is constant at the level determined by Y_{FE}, aggregate real demand ($D \equiv C_p + I_p$) falls. At the new equilibrium price level (p_2) the interest rate will have increased sufficiently to equate D with Y_{FE} and hence p_2D (≡ money expenditures) with p_2Y_{FE} (≡ the value of aggregate supply). Hence the new equilibrium will be characterised by:

a higher price level (p_2)
a higher money wage rate (W_{h2})

with real output and real wage ($\equiv W_{h2}/p_2$) unaltered.

It is now important to notice what is implied by our earlier statement that both schedules *shift*. Since the original aggregate demand and supply curves were constructed on the basis of W_h, *both now have as a parameter the new money wage rate* W_{h2}. Thus the final equilibrium is characterised by new DD and SS curves labelled D_2D_2 and S_2S_2 in Figure 15.10b. The curve $D'D'$ is thus no longer relevant; nor is the initial aggregate supply curve. The reader should construct for himself the appropriate new curve for Figure 15.10a in which the curve $D_1'D_1'$ corresponds to $D'D'$ in Figure 15.10b and thus indicates the aggregate demand schedule *after* the initial shift but *before* money wages and prices have risen and hence before the new equilibrium has been attained.

In addition the reader should not be misled into thinking that the analysis is reversible: that is, if D_2D_2 shifted back to DD (because of a decline in business optimism) we should revert to the original price level (p_1), the original money wage rate (W_h) and the original aggregate supply curve (SS).This is because though at the present level of abstraction it is not unreasonable to assume that both prices and money wages are flexible *upwards* at full employment, it is almost certainly unreasonable to assume that wages are flexible *downwards*. Hence if demand falls so that $N^D < N_f \equiv$ full employment, the new money wage rate W_{h2} must be regarded – at least as a first approximation – as invariant: in short the money wage rate exhibits downward rigidity in the short run.

Finally it should be noted that this analysis assumes not only that there is a determinate price level (p_2) at which aggregate demand is once again equal to aggregate supply (which depends on the analysis already discussed) but *also that the system will remain at this price level*. This second assumption is implicit; it is equivalent to assuming that the system is *dynamically stable*. The precise meaning of this will become clearer in later chapters. The reader, however, may for the moment simply assume that although the DD curve cuts the SS curve from above it is still easy to invest the system with dynamic properties which ensure that, once disturbed from equilibrium, the system will *not* return to it, i.e. that it will not remain at p_2. This implies, in the context of the present example, that an inflationary price rise once started never stops. Our method of analysis, though verbally it may appear dynamic, is comparative statics. Logically, however, we cannot compare equilibrium positions, as we have been doing, unless the system under study is *dynamically stable*, for if it is not, no equilibrium will be established. A basic assumption of our method is thus dynamic stability, which implies, in this particular case, that prices will (at p_2) cease to rise: in short that the inflationary price rise is finite.

Starting again from equilibrium we may ask: What happens if the money wage rate is increased to a new constant level? The money wage rate is a parameter of *both* the aggregate demand and aggregate supply curves. Hence *both* curves must shift.

Consider first the *SS* curve. Given the profit-maximising behaviour of businessmen and the unchanged production function, the *SS* curve must shift upwards, for any level of output will now be associated with a higher price level and thus a higher level of expected proceeds. Since the price level is higher, the money income generated by any level of output is now correspondingly higher. The nominal money supply is constant, by assumption. Hence given the two liquidity functions (L_1 and L_2) the rate of interest associated with any level of output will be higher. Hence, at any level of Y, aggregate demand in real terms ($D \equiv C_p + I_p$) will be *smaller*. On the other hand the price level has *risen*. Has the value of money expenditure pD associated with any given Y risen or fallen? The answer to this question is not immediately obvious, for, though the price level has risen, real planned investment (and thus real aggregate demand) has fallen.

Fortunately it is not difficult to establish that money expenditure must have risen. To see this assume the contrary. Then $pD \equiv p(C_p + I_p)$ has fallen at any level of Y, though p has risen. Since C_p depends only on Y (through the consumption hypothesis) the fall in $C_p + I_p$ must be due to a fall in I_p. But for I_p to fall *either* the MEI schedule must have shifted (while we have assumed it to be constant) *or* the rate of interest must have risen. The rate of interest, however, will only rise if, with given L_1 and L_2 functions, money expenditure rises and thus increases the demand for active balances. Hence we have a contradiction: for $p(C_p + I_p)$ to *fall* requires $p(C_p + I_p)$ to *rise*. Hence $p(C_p + I_p)$ *cannot fall*, for the very mechanism which brings about a fall in one of its components (I_p) – and thus raises the problem of its direction of change – depends upon the change being positive. Hence the aggregate demand curve *DD* shifts upwards.

If $p(C_p + I_p)$ cannot *fall*, can it remain unchanged for any level of output (Y)? The argument which excludes a fall excludes this possibility also.

Since *both* the aggregate demand and aggregate supply curves are shifting upwards, what is the nature of the final equilibrium? In general the new equilibrium will be characterised by:

(a) a higher price level
(b) a higher level of money income
(c) a higher level of the rate of interest
(d) a lower rate of real planned investment
(e) a lower level of real output
(f) a lower level of employment

In short the new *DD* and *SS* curves will intersect to the *left* of the initial equilibrium value of Y and at a *higher* value of money income.

Are there any circumstances in which predictions (e) and (f) would be inappropriate? There are two possibilities. If the initial equilibrium in the money market were at the minimum interest rate (r_{min}) and remained at that level *after* the change in the money wage rate, then I_p would not fall and $C_p + I_p$ would be unchanged at any level of Y. The same result would follow if the rate of interest changed in the manner discussed earlier but the marginal efficiency of investment schedule was completely interest inelastic. In both these cases (which could occur together) the aggregate demand and supply functions would shift upwards by an equal amount. Hence, though predictions (a) and (b) remain generally appropriate, (c)–(f) in some special circumstances might be inappropriate.

Does it follow from this that a cut in money wages – even if it could be arranged – would *necessarily* increase output and employment? The answer is: no. Admittedly a lower level of the money wage rate implies a shift to a lower *SS* curve and a shift to a lower *DD* curve.

But we must be careful not to be misled by our formal analysis. What is the mechanism involved? If the money wage rate is reduced, then, at *any* level of real output, the price level consistent with profit maximisation will fall proportionately. Any level of real output will thus entail a lower level of money income than before. This will lower the demand for transactions balances. So much is certain. But the rate of interest will fall only if it is not already at its minimum. Hence the rate of interest may *not* fall. If it does not there will be no increase in real planned investment and thus in output. Admittedly this is essentially one of the special cases already discussed under money wage increases. In general a cut in the money wage rate, if that could be arranged without an outbreak of industrial strife or a wave of bankruptcies, would, given the assumptions of our model, tend to increase output and employment.[1] There is, however, nothing in the model which guarantees that even the most severe money wage cut would enable the system to reach full employment. To see this let us revert temporarily to our earlier *IS/LM* analysis.

Suppose initially we are in equilibrium at Y_0 – a level of output substantially below Y_{fe} (see Figure 15.11). The rate of interest is r_0. If we now cut the money wage rate, the effect is to reduce the equilibrium interest rate at each level of output and raise the maximum level of output which can be financed with a given money supply. As a result the *LM* curve shifts to a new position LM_1. Output is now Y_1 and the rate of interest r_1. Employment has increased but it is still considerably below full employment.

As we have constructed the figure, r_1 is equal to $r_{\min}$. *Hence any further cut in the money wage rate cannot reduce it.* Hence output cannot rise above Y_1. This difficulty occurs whenever the rate of interest which *would* equate planned saving out of full-employment income with planned investment (called r_{fe} on Figure 15.11) is *less* than $r_{\min}$. A special case of this occurs when r_{fe} is negative.

This is a point of considerable importance. In depressions business people tend to be pessimistic. The *IS* curve, therefore, because the MEI schedule is low, is located far to the

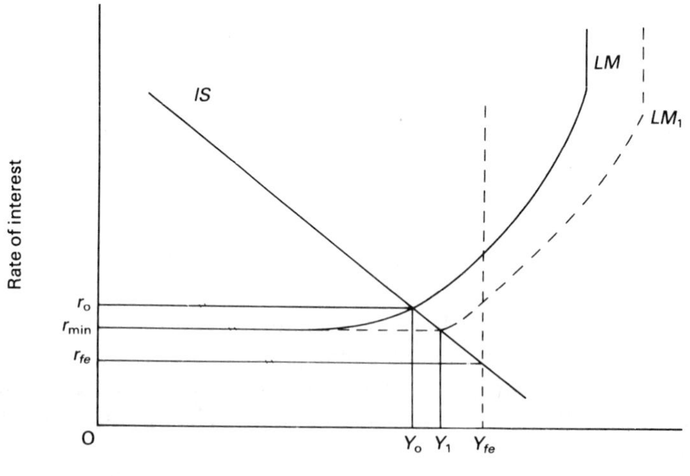

Figure 15.11 Money wage cuts and employment

[1]Our formal model is slightly biased in favour of money wage cuts since it assumes income distribution constant. If a wage cut shifts distribution in such a way as to bring about a fall in the consumption function (which is quite possible) this would offset the interest effect.

left. The rate of interest is in consequence likely to be at, or near to, its minimum.[1] It follows that cuts in the money wage rate will, in these circumstances, bring little or no fall in the rate of interest and thus little or no increase in employment. This point is significant because it has in the past often been argued that, to eliminate unemployment, it is essential to reduce money wage rates. At its crudest this argument is based upon a fallacy of composition. A *single* business, if it can reduce its wage rate, can reduce prices and sell more output, thus hiring more workers. This is true because if a *single* business reduces the wage rate it pays, the reduction in workers' money incomes will not affect significantly the demand for *its* product. If all businesses do it, however, workers' incomes, and hence their demand for all products, must fall. Hence once again, what is true for the one is not true for all taken together – as our more formal analysis demonstrates. In contrast to this argument our model tells us that:

(a) a cut in the money wage rate *may* increase employment but will not necessarily do so
(b) however far this money wage cut is taken, it *may* not prove possible, by this method, to reach 'full employment'

In this analysis we have implicitly proceeded on the basis of a consumption function which omits the real value of households' assets as a determinant of C_p. This was done for simplicity. Suppose, however, we replace our implicit function:

$$C_p = H + cY$$

by

$$C_p = H' + cY + dA \quad (d > 0)$$

where A is defined – as in Chapter 9 – as the real value of households' assets. Our analysis will now be correct only if A is unaffected by changes in the price level (p); and this will be correct only if the nominal value of the assets entering A varies precisely with the price level.

In practice, households hold many assets (e.g. currency, bank deposits, building society deposits) which have values fixed in nominal terms. They also hold bonds whose market value, given the nominal money supply, is either invariant or increasing as p falls (since the lower p, the lower, *ceteris paribus*, is the rate of interest). Incorporating this into our discussion means that we must expect the consumption function (as implicitly defined) to *shift* as p changes, for a fall in p must, to some extent, make households better off and a rise in p make them worse off. This is the basis for what is sometimes called in the literature 'the Pigou effect'.

Suppose we write the nominal value of such assets as L. Then our more complete consumption hypothesis becomes:

$$C_p = H' + cY + d\frac{L}{p} \quad (d > 0)$$

and L/p is the 'Pigou-effect' term.

Now if such a term exists and $d > 0$ then, logically, a cut in money wages (which reduces p) will raise L/p and hence C_p. Since there is, in logic, no limit to the extent of the cut in money wages and hence the fall in p, there is no limit to the rightward shift in the consumption schedule which can be brought about by money wage cuts. Hence there must

[1] In post-1945 recessions this statement is doubtful, particularly since we are also interpreting the interest rate to mean the *nominal* interest rate. It was approximately correct after 1932.

be some cut in the money wage rate which will restore full employment by shifting the *IS* curve of Figure 15.11 sufficiently far to the right. Formally, then, our earlier argument and, in particular, our conclusion (b) on page 265 is destroyed.

In practice, however, as a matter of policy, it may not be destroyed in the sense that it may be correct to argue that money wage cuts are an *inefficient* method of restoring full employment since:

(a) they are, to put it mildly, difficult to carry out
(b) their efficacy depends upon the value of the parameter d, which may well be small, and the other possible consequences of a rise in L/p.

Consider for a moment the meaning of L as those financial assets, held by households, whose values are fixed in nominal terms. Any such asset is the liability of some institution (e.g. a bank, building society, or the state). A rise in the real values of households' assets is thus a rise in the real value of some bodies' liabilities. If these bodies respond to a rise in their real liabilities by reducing their real expenditure, the rise in C_p will be partly offset. Indeed if debtors and creditors react symmetrically to variations in L/p the effect on real aggregate demand must be zero.

It is thus arguable that, for policy purposes, though not in logic, the case against money wage cuts remains. It must, however, be emphasised that this conclusion in so far as it rests upon the implicit assumption that $D \equiv C_p + I_p$ is relatively insensitive to changes in L/p, implies empirical judgements about the magnitude of the parameter d and the extent to which its influence is offset by the reactions of debtors.

Preliminary summary

The analysis of the preceding sections may be set out formally as follows. First by assuming:

(a) that businessmen seek to maximise profits
(b) that they are operating in a purely competitive system

we showed that, given the money wage rate (W_h), businessmen would adjust output (and hence employment) until:

$$p \frac{\partial Y}{\partial N} = W_h$$

which, since $\partial Y/\partial N$ is, via the short-run production function, uniquely related to Y, enables us to write, given W_h:

$$Y = S_1(p)$$

or

$$pY = S_2(p)$$

as alternative forms of the aggregate supply function.

We next defined aggregate demand as:

$$D \equiv Cp + I_p$$

and hypothesised the behaviour relations:

$$C_p = f_c(Y)$$
$$I_p = f_i(r)$$

Assuming the nominal money supply to be given ($\equiv M^S$) we then adopted the money demand hypothesis:

$$M^D = L(pY, r)$$

Equating M^D and M^S, i.e. requiring equilibrium in the money market, we now obtain an expression for r as a function of pY, M^S:

$$r = L'(pY, M^S)$$

Thus the aggregate demand function, on substitution, can be written:

$$D = f_c(Y) + f_i L'(pY, M^S)$$

As we have already seen, Y (or pY) can be obtained as a function of p from the aggregate supply hypothesis. Hence:

$$D = f_c S_1(p) + f_i L'[S_2(p), M^S]$$

which is the form of the aggregate demand function employed in Figures 15.4a, 15.8a and 15.8b. Notice that:

1. This function *explicitly* depends on the aggregate supply hypothesis; it thus not only emphasises the interdependence of aggregate demand and supply but specifies the *precise nature of the interdependence*.
2. D is now expressed, given M^S, as a function of p alone – albeit a complicated one since it depends upon p in two ways.
3. Since Y (provided employment is less than full) rises with p, then because of the consumption function hypothesis, D also will rise with p: that is, the D curve will be upward-sloping, as we have drawn it.

This last point is worth some emphasis since in some expositions schedules called 'aggregate demand' are depicted sloping downwards with respect to the price level. Reasons for thinking that these curves are misleadingly named when called 'aggregate demand' curves are given in the appendix to this chapter, which explains their derivation. At this point we merely note that they are *not* aggregate demand functions as we have defined them.

When, as in the earlier figures, the relevant aggregate demand and aggregate supply schedules are superimposed, we then see, in a slight paraphrase of Keynes's own words, that 'the volume of output is given by the intersection between the aggregate demand function and the aggregate supply function'. Simultaneously determined are the equilibrium values of the price level, the interest rate, the real wage rate, consumption, investment and the demand for money. Moreover at any price level *other* than the equilibrium price level, the discrepancy between the relevant points on the two schedules gives a measure of excess demand (or excess supply) in the goods market either in real terms $(D - Y)$ or in value terms $(pD–pY)$.

As we have seen, our theory implies a precise relationship between aggregate demand and aggregate supply such that given p ($\equiv$ price level) there will be a given value of Y ($\equiv$ real aggregate supply) and a given value of D ($\equiv C_p + I_p \equiv$ aggregate demand). The specification of the nature of this interdependencce is the crucial lesson of the whole analysis since Keynes's aims were twofold. That is, he sought to show:

(a) the nature of the interdependence between D and Y
(b) that this interdependence was *not* of a form commonly described by Say's law

Say's law, which is usually paraphrased as stating that 'Supply creates its own demand', is ambiguous and can be interpreted in two very different ways.

The first of these, which we shall call *Say's identity*, interprets it as saying that aggregate demand is equal to aggregate supply for all positive values of p. In this case the aggregate demand and supply schedules would coincide and p ($\equiv$ the price level) would be indeterminate.

The second proposition, which we shall call *Say's law*, interprets it as saying that the economic system is so constructed, in institutional and behaviouristic terms, that the aggregate demand and supply schedules always intersect at a value of p ($\equiv$ price level) which implies $Y = Y_{fe}$: that is, that if output departs from the full-employment level, forces are automatically set to work which, if allowed to operate freely, will restore full employment. What kind of system this implies is discussed more fully in Chapter 18, where we present a brief sketch of Keynes and his predecessors. At the moment we are only concerned to make clear that the Keynesian theory which we have presented is a denial of both Say's identity and Say's law.

We must now re-emphasise that both the aggregate demand and supply functions which we have constructed depend upon the money wage rate, which we have taken as given. Unless we can give an account of how this gets determined our theory must remain rather empty since its predictions depend upon the value of a variable for which we have, so far, given no explanation.

In Keynesian analysis, from which our model is derived, it is assumed that *the money wage rate is an exogenous variable (determined outside the model) by a process of industrial bargaining between employees (organised in trade unions) and employers (sometimes but not always organised in associations)*. What is envisaged in this assumption, shorn of its institutional complexities, is that unions bargain for a rate of *money wages*. This does *not* mean that unions do not take prices into account at all: that is, possess a *money illusion*. It means that they bargain for money wages simply because the economic and institutional system is such that they cannot easily bargain for a real wage.

Once a level of money wages has been determined by bargaining, W in our model takes a particular value which we have called W_h. At this negotiated level of the money wage rate the whole of the work-force then offers itself for employment and the supply curve of labour is a horizontal straight line up to 'full employment' and a vertical straight line *at* 'full employment'. This supply curve is depicted in Figure 15.12.

The demand for *labour* curve can then be superimposed upon the supply curve. The derivation of this curve we leave as an interesting and difficult exercise for the reader. The excess of full-employment labour supply (N_f) over the quantity of labour actually employed (N_0) is then *involuntary unemployment*: that is, it is an index of the number of persons

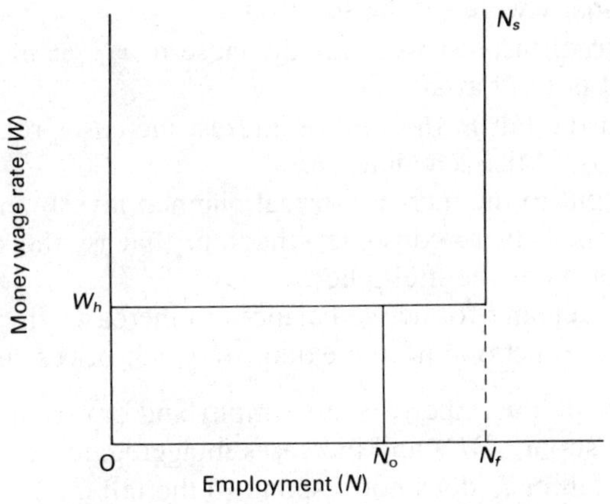

Figure 15.12 The labour supply function

prepared to work at the existing money (and real) wage who cannot obtain employment.

There are, of course, other forms of unemployment. For example, some unemployment is *seasonal* – such as that in the catering and holiday industries. In addition some unemployment is *structural*: that is, due to long-run changes in the commodity composition of demand involving, say, the transfer of workers from declining industries (such as mining) to expanding industries (such as chemicals). Observed unemployment will therefore tend to exceed the N_f–N_0 of our figure because of the presence of structural and seasonal elements.

The quantity of money and the price level

Now that we have a theory of the price level let us see how it works – that is, what predictions it generates – by asking one of the oldest questions in economics: namely, what are the consequences of an increase in the money supply?

We look first at aggregate demand, and then at aggregate supply. The way the nominal money supply is determined is not explained until Chapter 24, which also shows how the central bank by buying (selling) bonds on the open market can increase (decrease) the money supply. *We now simply assume that, by buying bonds, the central bank increases the nominal money supply*. In terms of our *IS*/*LM* curve analysis, the *LM* curve moves to the right. There is, in general, an expectation that (i) the equilibrium rate of interest will decline, and (ii) the level of output will increase. In terms of our *DD*/*SS* analysis, the *DD* curve tends to shift upwards, for any level of prices will now, for a given level of real income, imply a lower rate of interest and thus greater real aggregate demand.[1] Hence the new aggregate demand curve will in general lie to the right of our original curve.

How big will the increase in demand be? The answer must depend upon:

1. The extent to which the rate of interest falls as a result of the increase in M^S, which depends upon
   (a) the slope of the L_2 function

[1]This, as the reader will be aware, assumes (i) that the demand for idle balances is not infinitely interest elastic, and (ii) that the investment schedule is not completely interest inelastic.

(b) *where* we originally were on the function
Obviously if the rate of interest were intially close to r_{min} it might fall very little. If it were *at* r_{min} it could not fall at all,

2. The extent to which the fall in the rate of interest increases real planned investment:[1] that is, the slope of the MEI schedule,
3. The response of output to the increase in real planned investment which depends upon the slope of the propensity to consume schedule: that is, the marginal propensity to consume which determines the multiplier,
4. The response of the demand for active balances to increases in output (= real income) determined by the L_1 function and the extent to which prices rise as output increases.

Obviously, in view of all this, there is no simple and invariant relationship between increases in the money supply (M^S) and increases in aggregate demand. There may be no response (if r does not fall or I_p does not respond to the fall in r): or there may be a large response (if r falls considerably and I_p responds largely to reductions in r). To make a useful prediction we must know the *slopes* of the functions over the relevant ranges, which are of course questions of fact.

Suppose we *do* know the relevant functions. Then we can work out the response of aggregate demand and thus the shift in the *DD* schedule. We already know that what happens when aggregate demand increases (the *DD* curve shifts) is in general (i) an increase in output and employment, and (ii) an increase in the price level.

The precise results now depend upon the nature of the *SS* function, the slope of which depends on the production function and where we were originally on it. Clearly we may have either:

(a) a large increase in output (and hence) employment with a small price increase, *or*
(b) a small increase in output (and hence) employment with a large price increase[2]

Thus, although there is a relation between the money supply (M^S) and the level of prices (p), there is no simple relationship between increases in the former and increases in the latter. In particular, unless the increase in the money supply takes place at 'full employment', prices will *not* rise in the same proportion as the money supply and they will not necessarily do so even at full employment. This is an important conclusion because one popular theory of the price level, the *quantity theory of money*, in its simplest form at least, asserts this proportionality proposition.

This neo-Keynesian analysis of the consequence of an increase in the nominal money stock (M^S) needs to be qualified in two ways. The first of these relates to *the way in which the increase in the money stock occurs*, the second to *the scale of the increase*.

Our analysis specifically relates to an increase brought about by *open-market operations*: that is, by the central bank purchasing bonds from private portfolios and thus raising bond prices (lowering the interest rate). Hence, by assumption, the initial impact is through individuals' capital accounts and the impact on aggregate demand is taken to be indirect, i.e. via the fall in the interest rate.

Conceivably, however, the increase in the money stock might have entered the system as someone's income. For example, an increase in government expenditure entailing a deficit might be financed by money creation up to some given change in the nominal money stock. In this case we have *both* fiscal *and* monetary expansion and there is a direct impact on

[1]Notice that if the consumption function contains a 'Pigou' term which incorporates the value of bond holdings, then a fall in the interest rate, by increasing bond values, will raise consumption.

[2]Or, if r initially equal r_{min}, no change in either output or prices. The same result will also follow it planned investment is completely interest inelastic.

aggregate demand. Hence the expansionary effect will be greater than in the case we have discussed.

Finally, there is the case, of no practical relevance but sometimes postulated by 'monetarists', in which the addition to the nominal money stock takes the form of money (typically notes?) dropped in some random manner by helicopter. In this case the finders receive a 'windfall' (i.e. unexpected) gain roughly analogous to winning a football pool when one believed that one's coupon had not been posted. In this case, too, there is likely to be some direct impact on aggregate demand (i.e. an impact *not* induced by the fall in the interest rate). This, however, seems sure to be purely temporary. Indeed, since in the new equilibrium of the system, output, the price level and the interest rate must be such as to generate a demand for money (M^D) equal to the (increased) supply of money (M^S), the outcome will be identical with that for the open-market purchase case even though the immediate impact differs and the dynamic path followed by the economy in moving to its new equilibrium may also differ.

In general, then, the way in which the new money enters the system *may* need to be considered in analysing the results of an increase.

This caveat, however, is likely to be significant only where the scale of the increase in M^S *is marginal*. What scale of change is 'marginal' in this sense? No clear-cut answer to this question can be given, but the underlying point is clear enough: for example, if the increase in M^S *doubled* the money stock (so that M^S became $2M^S$), the fact of *doubling* would probably be much more important for the result than the method (say open-market operations or helicopter) by which the doubling was achieved.

This is only one way, and perhaps the less important one, of interpreting 'marginal'. *The second is to recall that our analysis depends upon an invariant demand for money function, an invariant investment function and an invariant consumption function (on the aggregate demand side) and an investment aggregate supply function. All these functions depend upon transactors' expectations*. It seems reasonable to argue that 'large' changes in M^S will change these expectations and thus change the functions on which the analysis is constructed. By a 'marginal' change we mean one which is sufficiently small *not* to induce any significant changes in expectations and thus in the behavioural relations of the system.

This proviso is extremely important, for it emphasises that in using our theory we proceed by changing some exogenous variable (in this case the nominal money supply) and then, *on the assumption of given and invariant behaviour functions*, predict the consequences for the endogenous variables – notably output, the price level, employment and the interest rate. This formal method of proceeding is correct; and, up to a point, it is useful. We must, however, always be prepared to ask whether, in practice, our invariance assumptions hold or whether the exogenous change may induce a shift in one or more of the behaviour relations of the model. Formal analysis, in short, needs to be supplemented by an intuitive understanding of the social and economic systems and this may lead us to believe that the formal analysis, in certain circumstances, is incomplete and thus potentially misleading.

Final summary

In this chapter we have extended our model slightly in order to show that the price level, hitherto regarded as exogenously given, is more properly regarded as an endogenous variable, determined, along with other endogenous variables, in a general-equilibrium model.

In order to explain the determination of the price level, we constructed aggregate demand and supply schedules. The intersection of these then depicted the determination of the equilibrium value of p ($\equiv$ the price level) and Y ($\equiv$ real output). The assumptions underlying these curves have already been discussed in some detail. The essential point to note is that the schedules are interdependent in the sense that the aggregate demand schedule depends on the aggregate supply schedule but that the latter does *not* depend upon the former. Indeed this method of presenting an essentially Keynesian macro-static model is undertaken principally to make clear:

(a) the precise nature of the interdependence entailed in Keynesian theory
(b) that this interdependence does not take a form compatible with either Say's identity, or Say's law, as we have defined them

These are crucial points since they are the very core of Keynes's analysis and the central message of Keynesian economics.

We then used the aggregate demand/supply analysis, albeit on a number of restrictive assumptions, to work out the consequences of:

(a) an increase in business optimism
(b) a cut in the money wage rate
(c) an increase in the nominal money supply

Our analysis of (b) – but not necessarily our policy conclusion – we qualified by extending our simple consumption hypothesis so as to include a 'Pigou-effect' term. Our analysis of (b) we shall, in Chapter 18, compare with an alternative analysis arising out of what is called 'the quantity theory of money'.

Questions and exercises

1. The following relations describe the complete Keynesian model used in this chapter to provide a numerical example:

GOODS MARKET

$S_p = -A + (1 - c)Y$	saving function	(15.I)
$I_p = H - br$	investment function	(15.II)
$S_p = I_p$	equilibrium condition	(15.III)

MONEY MARKET

$M^S = M_0$	money supply	(15.IV)
$M^D = K(pY) + Z - dr$[1]	demand for money	(15.V)
$M^D = M^S$	equilibrium condition	(15.VI)

[1]Assume that $r_{min} = 2.0$ per cent.

LABOUR MARKET

$N^D = X - g\left(\frac{W}{p}\right)$	demand for labour	(15.VII)
$N^S = f_n(W)$[1]	supply of labour	(15.VIII)
$W = W_h$	money wage rate	(15.IX)
$Y = F + eN - fN^2$	production function	(15.X)
$\frac{\partial Y}{\partial N} = e - 2fN$	marginal product of labour	(15.XI)
$U = N_f - N$	definition of involuntary unemployment	(15.XII)

[1]Interpret to mean the supply of labour infinitely elastic at the ruling money wage rate up to full employment and infinitely inelastic at full employment.

You are given the numerical values of the constants and coefficients of the functions (set out below):

A	= 100	X	= 500
c	= 0.8	g	= 50
H	= 1,000	W_h	= 8
b	= 10	F	= 4,400
K	= 0.25	e	= 10
Z	= 1,375	f	= 0.01
d	= 50	r_{min}	= 2.0 per cent
M_0	= 2,500	N_f	= 130

(a) Construct and graph aggregate supply schedules relating Y to pY and N to pY
(b) Construct and graph aggregate demand curves relating Y to pY and N to pY for the following values of N: N = 50, 60, 70, 80, 90, 100, 110, 120, 130.

Use these schedules to verify the equilibrium values of:

$Y \equiv$ real income
$pY \equiv$ money income
$N \equiv$ employment

given in the text.

2. Verify also the equilibrium values of:

$C_p \equiv$ real planned consumption
$I_p =$ real planned investment
$r \equiv$ the rate of interest
$\frac{W}{p} \equiv$ real wage rate
$U \equiv$ involuntary unemployment
$p \equiv$ the price level

What is the maximum money income (pY) which can be financed with the given money supply?

3. Suppose the money wage rate (W_h) is cut to reduce involuntary unemployment (U):
   (a) Will full employment ($N_f = N$) be restored?
   (b) If not, what will be the value of U?
   (c) What rate of interest (r) is necessary to reach full employment?

4. What is the relationship between equations (15.VII), (15.X) and (15.XI)? Explain in economic terms and show how (15.VII) can be derived from (15.X).

5. Use the model of question 1 to find N (employment) for all integral values of W (money wage rate) from 6 to 10. Graph and interpret the resulting curve. Is this a demand curve for labour in terms of the *money wage rate*? What is its approximate elasticity at $W_h = 8$? Can it be superimposed on the supply curve of Figure 15.12.

6. Use the model to analyse the consequences of an increase in the money supply from 2,500 to 2,700. What reduction in the given money wage rate W_h would achieve the same result? Use your answer to discuss the relative advantages of increases in the money supply and cuts in the money wage rate as methods of reducing involuntary unemployment. Would fiscal policy be a more effective weapon than either?

7. Define the share of wages in the total product as:

$$\frac{N \times W}{Y \times p} \equiv \frac{\text{wage bill}}{\text{money income}}$$

Find the share of wages when (i) $W_h = 8$; (ii) $W_h = 6$.

8. In terms of our model, has involuntary unemployment any single cause? Comment on the view that it can exist only if the money wage rate is 'too high' or the consumption function is 'too low'.

9. 'Unemployment equilibrium can occur if, and only if, money wage rates are inflexible.' Discuss. On what assumptions would this statement be correct?

10. 'In so far as the central bank controls the money supply it is the *nominal* money supply which it controls. It is the public which determines the *real* money supply.' Elucidate and appraise.

11. In Figure 15.4b the aggregate supply and aggregate demand curves appear to coincide at values of expected proceeds in excess of $Y_{fe}p_{fe}$. If this were so, expected proceeds would be indeterminate over the relevant range. From the numerical model:
    (a) Evaluate pY_{fe} and $p(C_p + I_p)$ at full-employment output for prices in excess of p_{fe}.
    (b) Show that with output at full employment (Y_{fe}) and $p \geqslant p_{fe}$, aggregate supply pY exceeds aggregate demand $[p(C_p + I_p)]$.
    (c) On the basis of these results reinterpret the relevant portions of Figure 15.4b.

12. Suppose the money wage rate were higher, the lower the level of unemployment. Redraw Figure 15.2 on this assumption. Analyse its implications.

13. Modify the saving hypothesis of question 1 to read

$$S_p = -A + (1 - c)Y + b\left(\frac{M^S}{p}\right) \quad (b = -0.1)$$

How would you interpret the modification? What kind of behaviour hypothesis is implied? Does the introduction of the new term change the conclusions of our analysis with regard to the effect of money wage cuts on involuntary unemployment? Why?

14. A businessman of your acquaintance tells you: 'If I could cut my wage rate I could lower prices and sell more. If I sold more I could employ more people. All businessmen are in my position. It is obvious that a cut in money wages reduces unemployment.' Write him a reasoned explanation of his error.

15. What does it mean to say that an individual suffers from 'money illusion'? Give a precise definition.

16. Which, if any, of the following consumption hypotheses implies a 'money illusion'? Explain carefully.

$$C_p = A + cY + b(M^S/p)$$
$$C_p = A + c(pY) + b(M^S/p)$$
$$p(C_p) = pA + c(pY) + bM^S$$
$$p(C_p) = B + c(pY) + bM^S$$

17. A cut in money wages distributes real income away from wage-earners and profit-recipients and to those persons whose incomes are fixed in money terms. Why? How would this modify your analysis of money wage cuts?

18. 'A 10 per cent cut in money wages means a 10 per cent cut in prices...In real terms therefore everything is as it was. There is no effect on output or employment.' Discuss critically.

19. What predictions would you suggest for a cut in money wages in an economy engaging in international trade? Why?

20. Discuss the assertion that the rise in unemployment is the result of excessive wage claims.

21. Replace equation 15.V of question 1 by:
$$M^D = K(pD) + Z - dr$$
and rework question 1. Interpret the new hypothesis and show that the equilibrium results are unaffected. Comment on the disequilibrium positions.

Suggested reading

*P. Davidson and E. Smolensky, *Aggregate Supply and Demand Analysis* (Harper & Row, 1965) chs 9–13.

J. M. Keynes, *The General Theory of Employment, Interest and Money* (Macmillan, 1936) ch. 18.

*More advanced reference.

APPENDIX: ON ALTERNATIVE AGGREGATE DEMAND CURVES

I.

The aggregate demand schedule employed in the main text gives D ($\equiv$ real aggregate demand) as a function of p ($\equiv$ the price level). It is obtained as follows:

$$D \equiv C_p + I_p \tag{1}$$

$$C_p \equiv c(Y) \qquad \left(0 < \frac{\partial C}{\partial Y} \leqslant 1\right) \tag{2}$$

$$I_p = i(r) \qquad \left(\frac{\partial I}{\partial r} < 0\right) \tag{3}$$

$$M^D = L(r, pY) \qquad \left(\frac{\partial M^D}{\partial r} < 0; \quad \frac{\partial M^D}{\partial (pY)} > 0\right) \tag{4}$$

$$M^S = \bar{M} \tag{5}$$

$$M^D = M^S \tag{6}$$

Using 4 – 6 to solve for r we obtain:

$$r = L'(pY, \bar{M}) \tag{7}$$

Hence:

$$\begin{aligned} D &\equiv C_p + I_p \\ &\equiv c(Y) + iL'(pY, \bar{M}) \end{aligned} \tag{8}$$

Now apart from D, equation 8 contains two endogenous variables, namely p and Y. We cannot, therefore, relate D to p, as the aggregate demand schedule conceptually requires, unless *either*:

(a) Y is known, *or*
(b) Y is eliminated

Clearly route (a) is inappropriate since we should then have a curve relating D to p for a given value of Y, when our aim is to treat Y as an endogenous variable to be determined, along with p, by the intersection of the aggregate demand and supply schedules. We therefore choose alternative (b) and eliminate Y by inserting the aggregate supply hypothesis which relates Y to p. This entails the further assumptions that:

$$Y = f(K, N); \quad \frac{\partial Y}{\partial K} \text{ and } \frac{\partial Y}{\partial N} > 0 \quad \frac{\partial^2 Y}{\partial K^2} < 0 \quad \frac{\partial^2 Y}{\partial N^2} < 0 \tag{9}$$

$$p\frac{\partial Y}{\partial N} = W_h \tag{10}$$

$$K = \bar{K} \tag{11}$$

Equation 10 reflects two assumptions. The first is institutional, in that it implies that the goods market is purely competitive; the second is behaviouristic, in that it hypothesises that businessmen seek to maximise profits.

Equation 11 states that, in the short run, the capital stock is invariant. Equation 9 is the production function. Inserting 11 into 9 enables us to write:

$$Y = f(\bar{K}, N)$$

and since, for any given K, $\partial Y/\partial N$ is a function of N(or Y) we may now rewrite 10 as:

$$pf(Y) = W_h$$

or

$$Y = f(p, W_h) \tag{12}$$

This in turn, taking the value of W_h as given, yields:

$$Y = S_1(p) \tag{13}$$

or

$$pY = S_2(p) \tag{13*}$$

which are our forms of the aggregate supply function. Inserting 13 into 8 now gives the aggregate demand functions:

$$D = cS_1(p) + iL'[pS_1(p), \bar{M}] \tag{14}$$

or

$$pD = pcS_1(p) + piL'[pS_1(p), \bar{M}] \tag{14*}$$

which gives D (or pD) as a function of p given W_h and $\bar{M}$ (≡ the nominal money supply).

The two schedules 13 and 14 are drawn in Figure 15.13. Notice that, at any price level which does not equate D and Y, say P_0, the horizontal distance btween D_0 and Y_0 provides a measure of excess demand (or supply) in the goods market: that is, involuntary stock accumulation or decumulation.

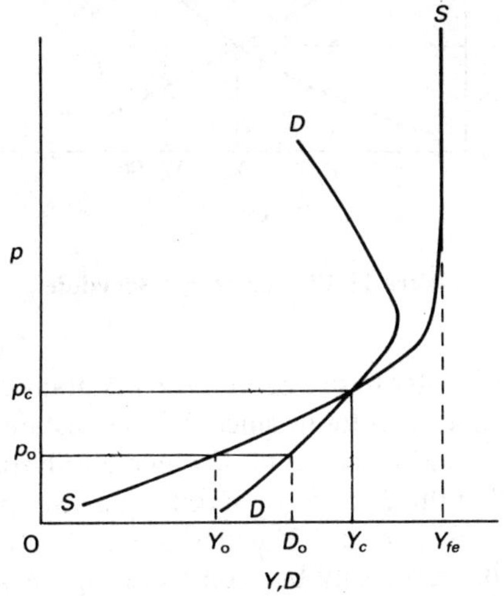

Figure 15.13 Aggregate demand and supply schedules

The aggregate demand schedule constructed in this way has the following pedagogic advantages:

(a) it corresponds, save for the use of Y rather than N on the horizontal axis and the unstarred rather than starred versions, with Keynes's own formulation
(b) it makes explicit the dependence of aggregate demand on aggregate supply
(c) it correctly identifies situations of disequilibrium in the goods market

II.

The alternative schedule found in the literature and identified as an 'aggregate demand curve' follows the same procedure as far as 8. That is, it obtains:

$$D = c(y) + iL'(pY, \bar{M}) \tag{8}$$

However, confronted with the necessity of eliminating Y it does so, not by making use of the aggregate supply function as we have done, but by inserting the condition $D = Y$: that is, that the goods market is *always* in equilibrium. Thus it obtains:

$$Y = c(Y) + iL'(cY, \bar{M})$$

and eliminates not Y but D. The resultant curve (see Figure 15.14) relates Y to p on the assumption that *both* the money *and* goods markets are in equilibrium.[1]

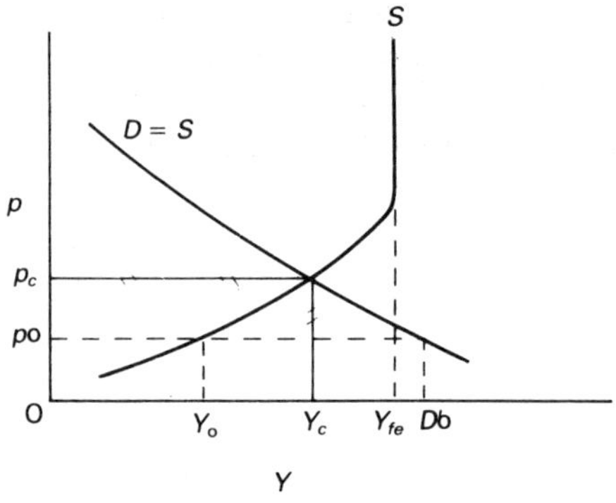

Figure 15.14 The $D = S$ schedule

The reader will have no difficulty in seeing that the resultant curve *must* slope downwards from left to right, for the higher is p then, since M^S is constant ($= \bar{M}$), the higher is p the higher is r and the lower is I_p and the level of Y which equilibrates the goods market. This curve, which we have labelled the $D = S$ (demand equals supply) curve, is, of course, the locus of all the pairs of values of p and Y which are compatible with equilibrium in the familiar *IS/LM* diagram. This can easily be seen from Figure 15.15.

In this figure, recalling that p is a parameter of the *LM* curve, we have drawn *LM* schedules for $p = p_0, p_1, p_2, p_3$, where $p_0 < p_1 < p_2 < p_3$. Since the greater the value of p the greater for any Y is the demand for money, the higher will be the associated interest rate in the money market. Given the *IS* curve, this has the usual consequences for the equilibrium value of Y. Clearly the locus of pairs of r and Y can be used to trace out a curve relating Y to p, which is the $D = S$ curve already described.

Now return to Figure 15.14. It is trivial that the equilibrium position $p = p_eY = Y_e$ depicted in Figure 15.14 must be identical with the equilibrium position depicted in Figure 15.13 since, in equilibrium $D = S$ in both cases and the models are otherwise identical. Consider, however, a non-equilibrium price level, say p_0. The $D = S$ curve tells us that, in this situation:

(a) the quantity of output demanded is D'_0
(b) that excess demand is apparently therefore D'_0–Y_0, *even though*
(c) excess demand is assumed to be identically zero at all points on $D = S$

[1]In terms of behaviour this implies assuming that output is independent of p: that is, the producers simply supply whatever is demanded at any price level. The retention of the aggregate supply schedule in the diagram, however, shows that this behaviour is not being assumed.

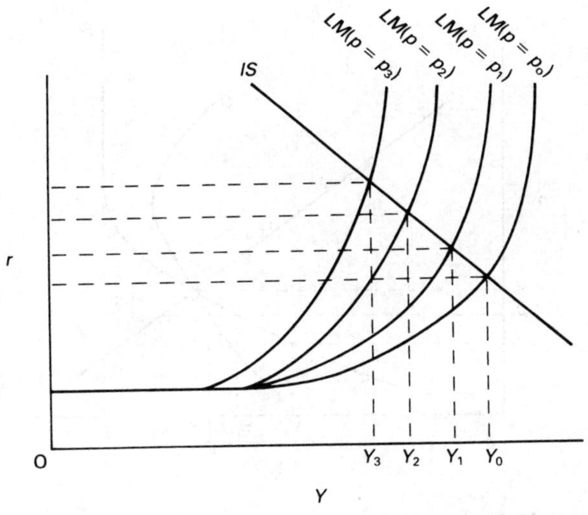

Figure 15.15 Constructing the $D = S$ schedule

Obviously D_0'–Y_0 in Figure 15.14 is *not* a correct measure of the excess demand in the goods market which will exist if $p = p_0$. For if $p = p_0$ and supply plans are carried out, this will generate a level of money income $p_0 Y_0$ which is *not* the level of money income implied by the $D = S$ curve at p_0. This is, of course, $p_0 D_0'$, which implies:

(a) a level of r other than that which will actually rule
(b) a level of Y which is not equal to Y_0

Hence the $D = S$ curve incorrectly describes all positions of disequilibrium in the goods market and is correct only in the case of equilibrium.

The $D = S$ curve when defined as an 'aggregate demand' curve suffers also from the disadvantages:

(a) that it encourages the notion that aggregate demand and supply are independent, *and thus*
(b) assigns an incorrect sign to the derivative dD/dp (≡ the change in demand resulting from a change in the (expected) price)

Since the purpose of Keynes's analysis was to clarify the form of the interdependence between D and S, (a) is a serious defect from the pedagogic point of view. Moreover, since in partial-equilibrium analysis demand curves are treated as independent of supply curves and the quantity demanded as independent of the quantity supplied, a student may be too easily led into treating general-equilibrium analysis in the same way as partial-equilibrium analysis.

Disadvantage (b) may also be serious. For suppose businessmen expect a higher price than p_0 – say p_1 – they will expand output to Y_1 on Figure 15.16. However, according to the $D = S$ curve, demand *falls* from D_0' to D_1'. Since consumption is dependent on Y, which has risen, readers may find this puzzling. They may even be misled into thinking that demand falls because the rise in r consequent upon the higher level of money income, now $p_1 Y_1$, reduces investment sufficiently to offset the increase in consumption. Nothing of the kind is being asserted. Indeed all that the $D = S$ curve tells us is that if p and r are higher I_p will be

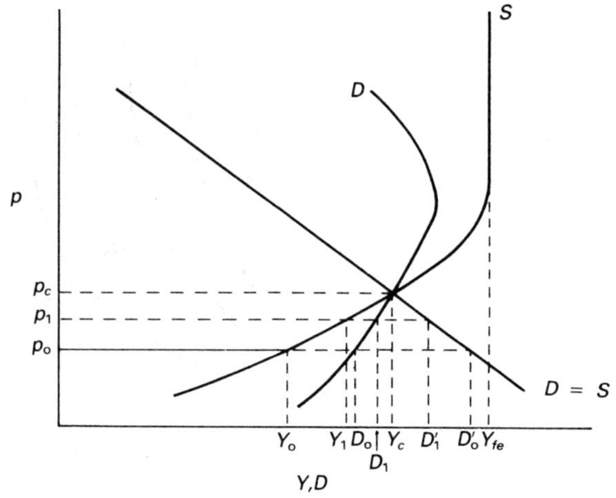

Figure 15.16 Aggregate demand and supply and $D = S$ schedule

lower and hence, via the multiplier, the *equilibrium* value of income, defined by $D = Y$, must also be lower.

This, of course, is not to say that the $D = S$ curve may not, for some purposes, be a useful teaching device. It is, on the contrary, simply to suggest that, even though definitions are matters of choice, it is not helpful to define, as the aggregate demand curve, a schedule which assumes that aggregate demand is equal to aggregate supply and which obscures the relationship between the quantity of output produced and the quantity demanded.

Chapter 15*

Aggregate Supply: A Further Look

Introduction

In the last chapter, we constructed the aggregate supply schedule on the assumptions that:

(a) businesses aimed to maximise profits
(b) the market system was one of 'pure competition'
(c) a short-run production function existed, while both the stock of real capital ($\bar{K}$) and the money wage rate (W) were given: the former as the result of history, the latter as the result of a bargaining process yet to be discussed in any detail

On this basis we constructed a schedule relating aggregate planned output (Y) to the level of money proceeds (pY) expected by businesses. This is the schedule depicted in Figure 15.2b (p. 249), which shows that if businesses expected proceeds to be p_0Y_0 their planned output would be Y_0. The diagram is repeated here.

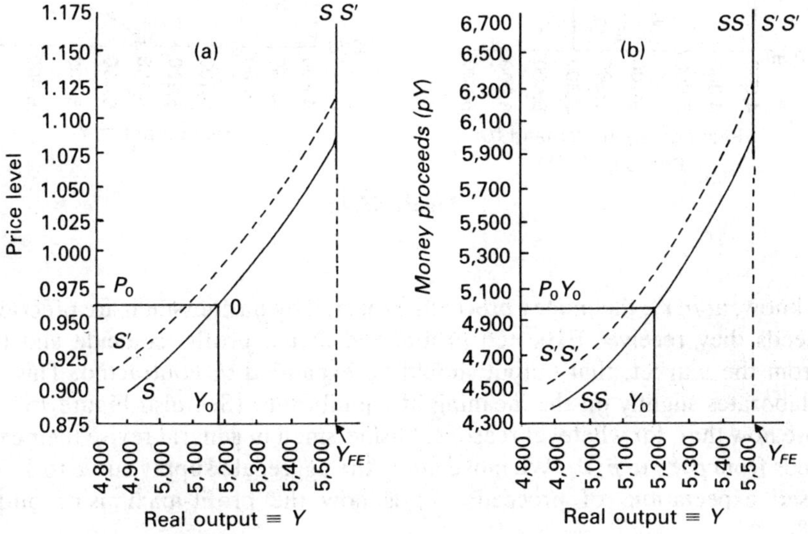

Figure 15.2b

This analysis, however, has thus far not considered the nature of the business expectations which determine the level of output businesses will plan to produce. The purpose of this chapter is to remedy this omission and, in particular, consider three questions:

1. How far the observed behaviour of output is to be explained by changes in aggregate supply rather than aggregate demand?
2. How do businessmen form their expectations?
3. Since the future is necessarily uncertain, in what ways do increases (decreases) in the uncertainty attaching to businessmen's expectations affect the analysis.

We shall, of course, consider these questions in the context of our neo-Keynesian theory, which, as the reader will recall, stresses the interdependence of aggregate demand and supply and specifies the form this interdependence takes.

Aggregate demand and supply recalled

In Figure 15.4b (p. 252) we demonstrated how *equilibrium* output was determined by Y_3 by the intersection of aggregate demand and supply schedules at p_eY_e. For convenience, this diagram is reproduced here.

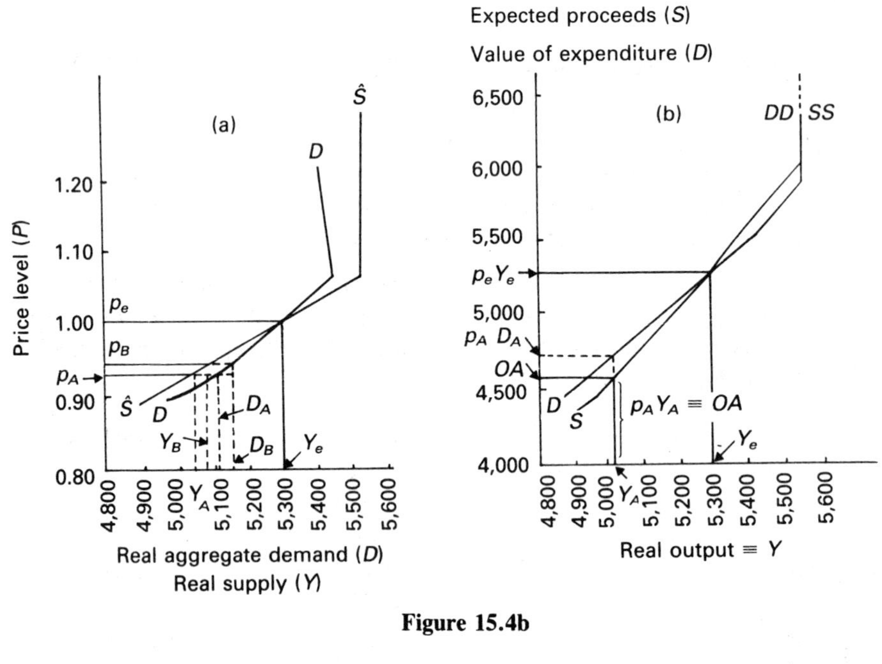

Figure 15.4b

As we know, at p_eY_e, the money proceeds expected by businessmen are precisely equal to the proceeds they receive. Expected profits and actual profits coincide and there is no signal, from the market, that output should be expanded or contracted. This, of course, simply elaborates slightly on the meaning of equilibrium. (See also Figure 15*.1.)

Suppose now that, for whatever reasons, businessmen in general revise their expectations of proceeds from p_eY_e to p_xY_x. We move *along* the aggregate supply curve to Y_x since, with the revised expectations of proceeds, Y_x is now the profit-maximising output. What happens?

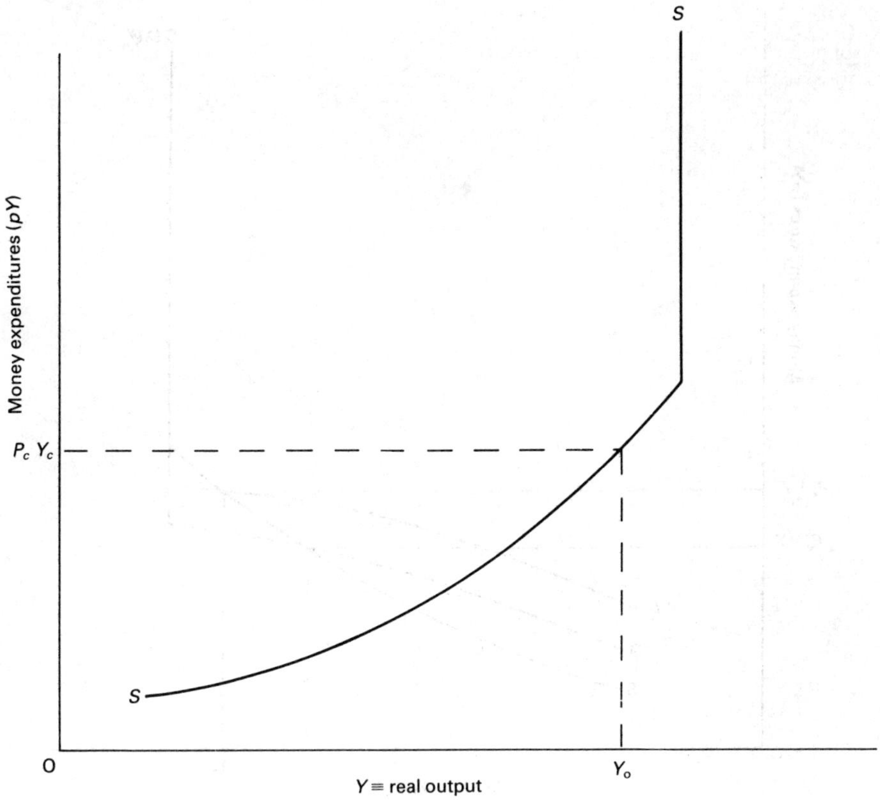

Figure 15*.1 Aggregate supply and expected proceeds

According to Figure 15*.2, with output Y_x, aggregate demand will be *less* than aggregate supply and the market process will generate signals, in the form of unplanned increases in stocks and shortfalls in realised profits, which must, after some time, cause businessmen to revise downwards their expectations regarding money proceeds and hence their planned level of output.

This analysis, however, is based upon the assumption that the money supply and the consumption, investment and money demand functions are all invariant.

The plausibility of these assumptions can obviously be questioned since, if businessmen suddenly become more optimistic about expected proceeds (the quantity of output they can sell at profit-maximising prices), it seems not unreasonable that they should also become more optimistic regarding investment prospects. This would shift the investment function in a way favourable to aggregate demand. The same increased optimism *could* affect both the consumption function *and* the money demand function. Thus aggregate demand may respond to an increase in aggregate supply not only via induced movements determined by given and invariant behaviour relations – which are what is shown in the *DD* curve of the figure – but also via a *shift* in the *DD* curve to, say, *D'D' due to changes in the underlying behaviour relations resulting from a generalised change in private-sector expectations*.

The position of *D'D'* is sure to be to the left of *DD*. But beyond that it is arbitrary since we have no quantified theory which can tell us by how much, say, the investment function

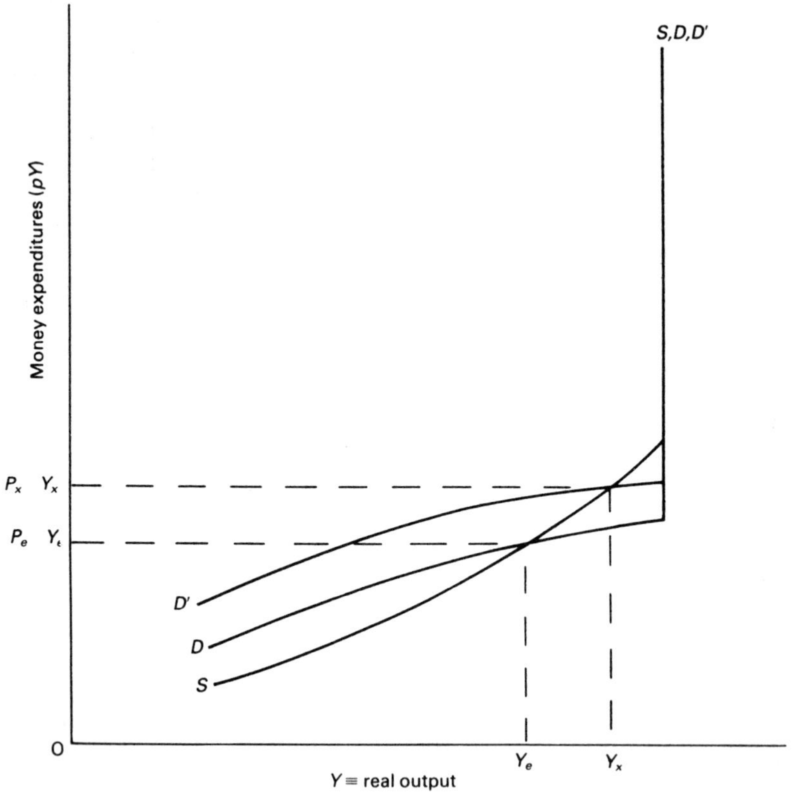

Figure 15*.2 Equilibrium aggregate output and expected proceeds

shifts in response to an expectation-induced movement *along the aggregate supply schedule.* Conceivably *D'D' may be such as to produce equilibrium at* Y_x. But this is only one possibility.

Suppose, however, that over some range of outputs – say Y_1 to Y_2 in Figure 15*.3 – the interdependence of transactors' expectations is such that the *DD* and *SS* curves approximately coincide, in the sense that a movement along *SS* is accompanied by a shift in *DD* which validates the selected output. In this case:

(a) output is indeterminate as long as $Y_1 \leqslant Y \leqslant Y_2$, *which entails that*
(b) the level of output can be determined (in the range Y_1 to Y_2) only from the supply side, *so that*
(c) businessmen's expectations of proceeds are crucial in determining Y

Of course, there may be no such range of indeterminancy as $Y_1 - Y_2$ or, what is much the same thing, the range may be extremely small. But if there *is* such a range and it *is* at all large the importance of business expectations is obvious since pessimistic expectations suggest a value of Y in the neighbourhood of Y_1 (a recession level), while optimistic expectations suggest a value near Y_2 – an approximate 'full-employment' level.

Just how far the observed movements in output in the UK are movements within a range such as $Y_1 - Y_2$ rather than the response of output to market signals generated by changes in aggregate demand is unknown. It seems possible, however, that such expectations shifts are

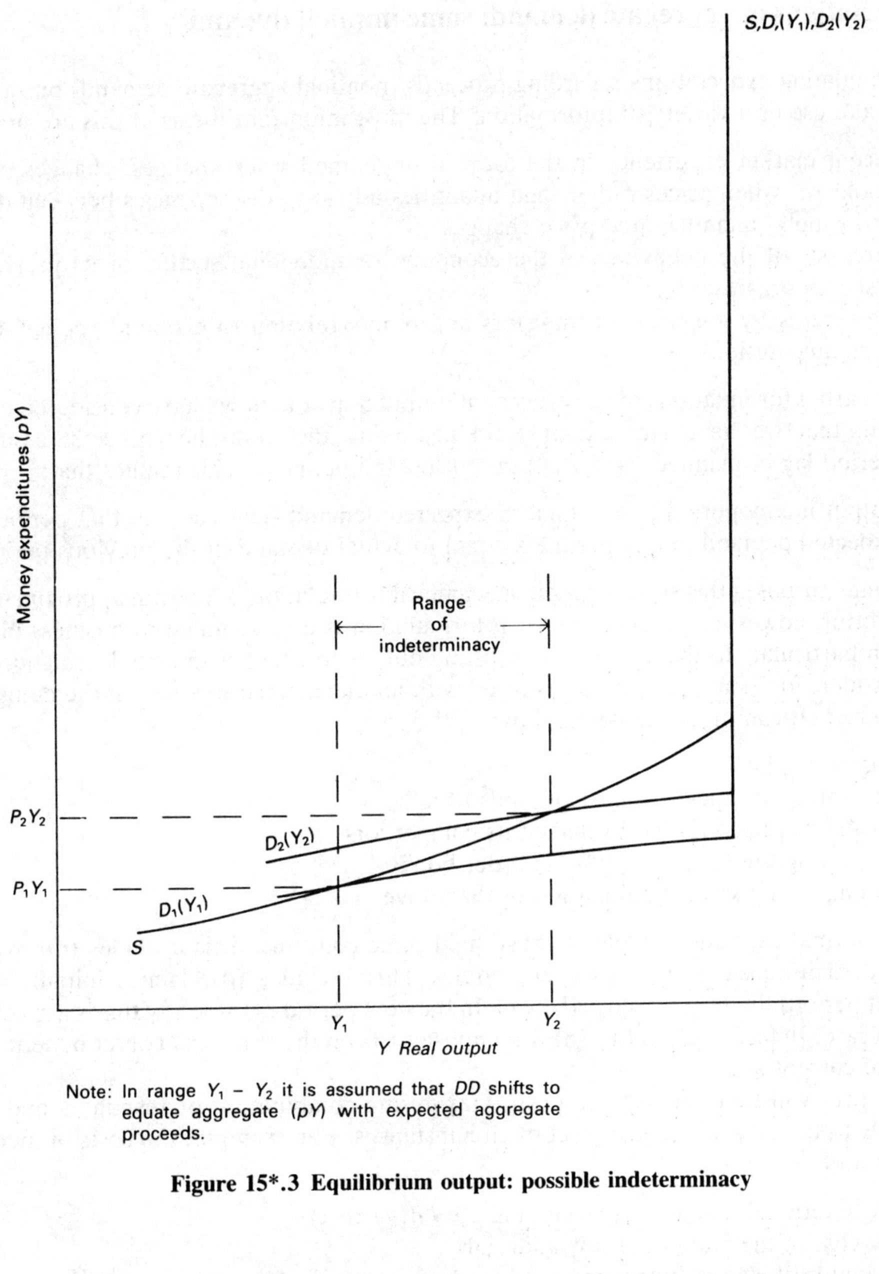

Note: In range $Y_1 - Y_2$ it is assumed that *DD* shifts to equate aggregate (*pY*) with expected aggregate proceeds.

Figure 15*.3 Equilibrium output: possible indeterminacy

of some importance. For example, surveys of business expectations conducted by the CBI in 1982 suggest that industry as a whole is generally pessimistic in its expectations about aggregate demand. If this pessimism were, for some reason, replaced by more optimistic expectations, and output increased, would there then, as *DD* insists, be excess supply, accumulation of unplanned stocks and a forced return to the initial position, or might there, as *D'D'* suggests, be an increase in aggregate demand sufficient to absorb the increase in output?

Clearly expectations, and how they are formed, are matters of considerable significance.

Expectations of aggregate demand: some implicit dynamics

In formulating expectations regarding proceeds (nominal aggregate demand) businessmen can make use of a variety of information. The most important forms of this are probably:

(a) recent market experience in the form of unplanned stock changes, changes in order books or, when prices rather than quantities adjust to discrepancies between demand and supply, unanticipated price changes
(b) forecasts of the behaviour of the economy (or individual sectors of it) prepared by research organisations
(c) statements by government ministers and others relating to economic policy and the economic outlook

In our earlier formulations of the process of output adjustment we have considered only the first, in that we have (for example, in discussing the multiplier process) assumed a one-period lag in planned (= actual) output behind demand. This implies that:

(a) output in any period is set equal to expected demand (proceeds) in that period
(b) expected demand in any period is equal to actual demand in the previous period

For some purposes this sort of simple mechanical formulation is a useful approximation. It is doubtful, however, whether any such formulation is a good guide to business planning and, in particular, to the process of adjusting output to changes in actual demand.

Consider, for example, a business faced with an unexpected increase in the demand for its product. It can meet the demand by:

(a) raising output
(b) permitting its stock of finished goods to fall
(c) raising its price relative to that of its competitors
(d) permitting the lengthening of its order books
(e) by employing some combination of the above

In our formal dynamic models we have held price constant. This excludes (c). We have ignored such considerations as order books. This excludes (d). Hence initially (in the current period) the firm employs (b) and, in the next period (a). Clearly this is a special and simple case. In fact, each of (a)–(d) will impose costs on the firm, *and* confer benefits in the form of current and future profits.

The firm will then choose the profit-maximising combination of responses and this is unlikely to be the same in every set of circumstances. For example, the costs of increasing output are:

(a) the additional labour cost (including the *hiring* cost)
(b) the cost of the additional raw materials
(c) the interest cost in borrowing funds to finance the first two options

There are also the possible *firing* costs (redundancy payments) which may be incurred if the increase in demand proves to be temporary.

Taken together, the costs of increasing output are considerable and are unlikely to be accepted when there is any considerable measure of *uncertainty* about the persistence of any observed increase in demand. By the same type of argument, firms may be reluctant to dispose of employees if demand is observed to fall since if they do so they incur *firing* costs and, should the fall in demand reverse itself, the cost of *hiring* replacements for the workers they have only just recently dismissed.

In short, output may not always adjust rapidly or mechanically to a change in expected demand because of the uncertainty attaching to business expectations. And expected demand may not adjust rapidly or mechanically to actual demand. Moreover, *both* processes are likely to differ according to:

(a) the nature of recent economic experience
(b) the policies adopted and actually carried out by the government

To fix our ideas suppose that, for something like a decade, the economy has been operating at, or close to, 'full-capacity' utilisation or 'full employment'. If demand now falls (for whatever reason), we may expect:

(a) output to respond rather slowly since firms' typical experience is of 'full-capacity' utilisation and they will expect the authorities to act to restore this state of affairs so that the shortfall is temporary
(b) employment to respond more slowly still since firms will expect that labour temporarily surplus will soon be needed again – so it makes sense to avoid 'firing' and 'hiring' costs
(c) firms, in the very short run, to be prepared to accumulate (temporarily?) unwanted stocks

Of course, if the fall in demand *is* semi-permanent, firms' expectations will eventually change, output will adjust, indeed, will initially, over-adjust since stocks are excessive, and there will be a belated 'shake-out' of labour.

These dynamic processes will be conditioned in one way or another by the pronouncements and actions of government ministers and the central bank which may either speed up or retard the formation of 'correct' demand expectations and may either increase or decrease the uncertainty inevitably attaching to firms' demand expectations.

At the moment of writing the UK is in deep recession, and experience, since 1973–4, has been of relatively low and declining levels of capacity utilisation. Suppose now the authorities were to increase government expenditure and reduce taxation: in short embark on a programme of fiscal expansion. How would firms be likely to respond?

Opinions differ on this issue and it is probably correct to argue that the outcome would depend in some measure on who carried out the policy and how the policy was presented. But assuming these problems away, it is hard to believe that firms would:

(a) revise their expectations of demand at all quickly
(b) adjust output at all rapidly to any revised expectation of demand

Indeed, in the real world we might expect the early response to be a tendency to increase prices and allow order books to grow larger. Because of the influence on expectations of close to a decade of recession (depression) we cannot expect reflationary policies to work in the simple and mechanical way suggested by our expository model or as they did from 1950 to 1970 in an economy unused to any but small and temporary deviations from 'full-capacity' working.

Thus the expectations of businessmen, the confidence with which they hold them and the way they revise them, via the aggregate supply function, are of importance in determining the speed with which, and the path by which, output approaches its equilibrium level. We must therefore be careful that, in the interest of pedagogic simplicity, we do not give the impression that the dynamics of adjustment constitutes a simple mechanical process independent of the current position of the economy, recent economic experience and the pronouncements and actions of the authorities.

Money wages and inflation: more implicit dynamics

In constructing the aggregate supply schedule we took the money wage rate ($\equiv W$) as given and assumed it to be determined by some (not very well defined) process of bargaining. On this assumption, any expansion in output was accompanied by a rise in the price level due to the operation of the principle of diminishing marginal labour productivity. The money wage rate itself remained unaltered.

In practice, of course, the wage rate is unlikely to remain unaltered. This means that the dynamic multiplier process by which the economy moves from one equilibrium to another will typically involve changes in the money wage rate, which is, as we know, a determinant (parameter) of the aggregate supply schedule. Hence a movement *along* the aggregate supply schedule due, say, to an expansionary fiscal policy is likely to be accompanied by upward *shifts* in the schedule resulting from increases in the money wage rate which derives from the 'bargaining' process.

This means that the outcome of an expansionary policy by the authorities consists in:

(a) a movement *along* the aggregate supply curve, which can be termed 'reflation'
(b) a succession of upward *shifts* in the aggregate supply curve, which *since they increase the equilibrium price at each level of output* can be termed 'inflation'

Notice that these do *not* strictly divide the expansion in nominal GNP resulting from the dynamic workings of the multiplier into output and price-level changes since reflation will typically entail some price increase. As a crude approximation, however, we may think in these terms.

What this means is that in considering the consequences of any expansion of nominal demand, we need to ask:

1. How far is this met by an expansion of *output*?
2. How far is this met by a rise in *prices*?

We may also ask the strictly dynamic question:

3. How are output and price increases distributed during the operation of the dynamic multiplier? That is, does the expansion initially involve output changes in the main with price changes emerging later in the process, or the reverse of this, or some other more complex pattern?

Clearly these issues relate to the dynamics of our theory and, in particular, to the dynamics of the price level. This, of course, is usually called the theory of inflation and is considered, in some detail, in Chapter 21 with the ultimate purpose of answering these and other questions. The purpose of this brief discussion is not to anticipate the analysis offered there but:

(a) to remind readers of the relationship between the theory of aggregate supply and the theory of inflation
(b) to emphasise that *any* macroeconomic theory requires an aggregate supply hypothesis
(c) to show, once again, why a movement *along* a schedule may, in practice, lead to *shifts* in it
(d) to recall the simplistic nature of the dynamic 'multiplier' illustrations given earlier in the book.

Summary

The purpose of this chapter has been to examine the aggregate supply schedule of Chapter 15 in a rather less formal way and by doing so to show:

(a) the role of changes in business expectations
(b) the role of the uncertainty (confidence) with which the expectations are held

As a result we found the behaviour underlying the aggregate supply schedule to be important, particularly in explaining the time path followed by the economy in moving from one equilibrium to another: that is, the dynamics of the multiplier process.

Also, we noted that the theory of aggregate supply (as we have presented it) rests upon a theory of money wage determination so that, in dynamic form, it involves the theory of inflation.

Finally our brief review emphasised that the dynamic path of output and price adjustments in the multiplier process was unlikely to be invariant to the initial level of output and recent economic experience.

Questions and exercises

1. 'Business expectations are now so lacking in confidence that any expansionary policy will simply increase imports and domestic prices rather than output and employment.' Elucidate and appraise.

2. What light, if any, do the CBI surveys throw on business expectations?

3. 'The speed with which output responds to an increase in demand depends crucially upon businessmen's view of its permanence.' Elucidate. How do you think it would respond next year?

4. 'Any increase in output brings a corresponding increase in income. If businessmen expanded output, they would find that the demand was there.' Discuss critically.

5. Can you define an *operational* index of business uncertainty?

6. 'Successful profit maximisation requires a businessman to take complicated decisions on the basis of very unclear *market signals*.' Explain with particular reference to the decision to expand output.

7. 'If an increase in optimism shifts the *investment demand schedule*, it is highly likely that it will also shift the *demand for money schedule* and the *consumption function*.' Discuss and, in the light of your discussion, criticise the analysis in the text.

8. 'Business cycles have nothing to do with demand. They reflect the propensity of businessmen to suffer from alternate waves of optimism and pessimism.' Discuss critically.

9. 'The proposition that *supply creates its own demand* is a useful approximation to the real world.' Discuss critically.

10. 'The economy is never static. Recessions either become depressions or recoveries.' Elucidate. Which would you predict for the UK, and why?

Suggested reading

M. N. Baily, 'Stabilization Policy and Private Economic Behaviour', *Brookings Papers on Economic Activity*, 1 (1978).

E. F. Denison, *Accounting for Slower Growth: the United States in the 1970s* (Brookings Institution, 1980).

*S. J. Nickell, 'The Influence of Uncertainty on Investment: Is it Important?', *Economic Journal* (March 1977).

D. C. Rowan, 'Macroeconomic Policy and Industrial Performance', paper delivered at the International Symposium on Industrial Policies for the 1980s (Madrid, May 1980.)

*Advanced reference.

Part III

Monetarist Macroeconomics

Chapter 16
The Quantity Theory of Money

In Chapter 15 we completed our account of the static 'neo-Keynesian' model by examining the relationship such a model predicts between an assumed exogenous change in the nominal money stock and the endogenous response of the price level.

In this chapter we contrast these predictions (summarised on pp. 266–72) with those of the *quantity theory of money*. Accordingly we begin by setting out the essentials of this theory.

The quantity equation and the quantity theory

The quantity theory begins with the identity:

$$\begin{array}{c}\text{value of total}\\ \text{purchases of final output}\end{array} \equiv \begin{array}{c}\text{value of total}\\ \text{sales of final output}\end{array} \tag{16.1}$$

which states that, in any period, the values of sales and purchases are equal – as *ex post* they must be since they are (as we know) alternative ways of describing the same transactions.

In a money economy, purchases must involve a transfer of money from purchasers to sellers. If the nominal money supply ($\equiv M^S$) over the relevant period is, on average, equal to a particular value we can then define:

$$\begin{aligned} V_y &\equiv \text{income velocity of money} \\ &\equiv \frac{\text{value of purchases of final output}}{M^S} \end{aligned} \tag{16.2}$$

so that:

$$\text{value of total purchases of final output} \equiv M^S\, V_y \tag{16.3}$$

where

$$V_y \equiv \text{income velocity}$$

which equals the number of times, on average, a unit of M^S changes hands in making purchases of final output.

The value of total sales of final output can now be divided into the quantity of real final output sold ($\equiv Y$) and the average price ($\equiv p$) of a unit of output. We thus have:

$$\text{value of total sales of final output} \equiv pY \tag{16.4}$$

Combining 16.3 and 16.4 gives us the identity usually described as the quantity equation, which is, of course:

$$M^S V_y \equiv pY \tag{16.5}$$

Notice that, since 16.5 is an *identity*, thus far no *theory* has been developed. What 16.5 does is provide a conceptual framework in terms of which a theory *can be developed*. In particular, if the left-hand side of 16.5 is identified with aggregate nominal expenditure, it suggests that, rather than dividing this into nominal consumption and nominal investment and then developing theories to explain their planned values, as we did in Chapters 9–10 we should approach matters by developing a theory to explain the magnitude of the nominal money stock (M^S) and income velocity (V_y).

In short, to complete the analogy with our earlier approach we can write:

$$\text{aggregate demand} \equiv \text{aggregate supply}$$

which, as before, is our condition for equilibrium in the goods market, and then, using 16.5, write this as:

$$M_p^S V_{yp} = pY \tag{16.6}$$

where

$$M_p^S \equiv \text{planned value of } M^S$$
$$V_{yp} \equiv \text{planned value of } V_y$$

Since an elementary neo-Keynesian theory would write its analogue of 16.6 in the form:

$$p(C_p + I_p) = pY \tag{16.6K}$$

where

$$C_p \equiv \text{planned real consumption}$$
$$I_p \equiv \text{planned real investment}$$

the formal relationship between the two approaches is clear. So, too, is the way in which the quantity theory approach emphasises the significance of the nominal money stock and the rate at which households and firms plan to turn over the nominal money stock in their collective possession – that is, their decisions regarding velocity.

The quantity theory approach and aggregate demand

It is easy to see that one way of using 16.6 is to employ the left-hand side of the equation to develop a theory of aggregate demand in nominal terms. To do this we require a theory of the determination of the money supply and a theory of the determination of velocity.

A particularly simple version of the quantity theory assumes that:

(a) the nominal money supply is an exogenous variable, the proximate determinant of which is the central bank
(b) planned velocity is a behavioural *constant* equal to $\bar{V}_y$.

The quantity theory in this form asserts that:

(a) there is a constant relationship between the value of aggregate demand and the nominal money stock, *which*
(b) holds not only on average but also at the margin, so that a given proportional increase in M^S yields an identical proportional increase in nominal aggregate demand.

Notice that this formulation assumes that *causation runs from* M^S (the exogenous variable) *to* aggregate demand and from aggregate demand to aggregate supply (pY).

Now pY is the value of aggregate supply and, in equilibrium, this must be equal to $M^S V_y$. The quantity theory, however, does not entail a specific aggregate supply hypothesis which can tell us how much of a given proportionate change in pY is to be explained in terms of a proportionate change in Y and how much is to be explained by the proportionate change in p. We can, however, distinguish two limiting cases.

The first of these occurs when it is assumed that output (Y) is constant at some level consistent with, say, an approximation to 'full employment'. We shall examine later the circumstances in which such an assumption might be plausible. We then have:

$$\begin{aligned} M^S V_y &= pY \\ V_y &= \bar{V}_y \quad \text{(a constant)} \\ Y &= Y_{fe} \quad \text{(a constant)} \end{aligned}$$

so that:

$$M^S \frac{\bar{V}_y}{Y_{fe}} = p \tag{16.7}$$

or

$$M^S \bar{Q} = p \quad \left(\text{where } \bar{Q} = \text{constant} \equiv \frac{\bar{V}_y}{Y_{fe}}\right)$$

This yields the conclusions typically associated with the quantity theory: namely, that (i) prices are proportionate to the nominal money stock, and (ii) the rate of change of prices is equal to the rate of change of the money stock. In a more sophisticated form these propositions are the basis of what is now called 'monetarism'.

The alternative limiting case is the one we introduced, for purely pedagogic purposes, in Chapter 8: namely, that the price level (p) is a constant. We now have:

$$\begin{aligned} M^S V_y &= pY \\ V_y &= \bar{V}_y = \text{(a constant)} \\ p &= \bar{p} = \text{(a constant)} \end{aligned}$$

so that:

$$M^S \left(\frac{\bar{V}_y}{\bar{p}}\right) = Y \qquad (16.8)$$

or:

$$M^S(\bar{Q}') = Y \quad \left(\text{where } \bar{Q}' \equiv \frac{\bar{V}_y}{\bar{p}}\right).$$

In this case the quantity theory is extended from a theory of aggregate demand to a theory of the determination of output.

Logically (as opposed to empirically) there is no reason to prefer 16.7 to 16.8 or vice versa. Empirically, however, 16.8 may be a better approximation to the response of aggregate supply in the *short run* and 16.7 in the *long run*. It is, in any case, well worth noting that, in popular discussion, the quantity theory is typically associated with the proposition that it is prices (*not* output) that are proportional to the nominal money stock (M^S).

In this conventional and naive form the quantity theory consists in:

(a) the assertion that aggregate demand in nominal terms is proportional to the nominal money stock
(b) the assertion that the aggregate supply relationship takes a particular form in which output is constant at its 'full-employment' level.

The quantity theory and the demand for money

The basic quantity equation 16.5 is capable of a further interpretation *in that it can be regarded as specifying a demand function for money*. We write:

$$M^S V_y = pY \qquad (16.5)$$

In equilibrium we require the demand for money to equal the supply. Hence:

$$M^D = M^S$$

where M^D is the nominal demand for money.

Substituting this relationship in 16.5 yields:

$$M^D V_y = pY$$

or

$$M^D = \frac{1}{V_y}(pY)$$

which, if $V_y = \bar{V}_y$, as we are assuming, predicts that:

$$M^D = L(pY) \quad (16.9)$$

where L is a positive constant $\equiv 1/V_y$. This implies that M^D has elasticities of unity (i.e. is homogeneous of degree one) with respect to L, Y and p.

The hypothesis that V_y (or its reciprocal L) is a behavioural constant is fairly readily tested since estimates of V_y can be obtained by dividing the nominal GDP in any period by the average value of 'the' nominal money stock over the same period. The estimates so obtained are not unambiguous since 'the' nominal money stock is capable of a range of definitions[1] running from legal tender money (currency) through currency plus various categories of bank deposit to still broader definitions which embrace such assets as deposits with building societies, the National Savings Bank and National Giro. However, on the basis of conventional definitions, estimates of V_y ($\equiv 1/L$) can be constructed both for the interwar years and for the thirty-odd years since the end of the Second World War.

Speaking very broadly the proposition that V_y changed only very slowly and in a fairly predictable manner was a useful approximation until roughly the onset of the 1930s depression. Since then, however, V_y ($\equiv 1/L$) has exhibited very considerable variation, with some systematic tendency to move pro-cyclically: that is, to expand in periods in which output is rising relatively fast (in relation to its 'typical' rate of growth or 'trend'), and to fall when output is rising less fast or is itself falling.

In short, therefore, the data suggest that the hypothesis that V_y is a constant – which is basic to the naive version of the quantity theory – is not well grounded. Money demand functions of the form of 16.9, like the proposition that nominal aggregate demand is proportional to the nominal money stock, cannot be accepted. It is therefore hardly surprising that in its naive form the quantity theory became discredited.

The finding that V_y was *not* a stable *number* does not, of course, exclude the possibility that it is a *stable function of a relatively small number of variables*. It is therefore not surprising that the quantity theory has been reformulated along these lines by a group of distinguished economists, among whom Milton Friedman is the best known. The reformulation consists (formally speaking) in replacing L (the reciprocal of V_y) by a function so that the money demand hypothesis $M^D = L(pY)$ becomes:

$$M^D = f(????)\,(pY)$$

with:

$$L = f(????) \quad (16.10)$$

Precisely which variables should enter this function is still in dispute. The typical approach to the problem has been to emphasise the role of money as an asset and argue that L must, as a result, be a function of the rates of return on alternative assets including goods. Thus a somewhat simplified version of Friedman's reformulation would be:

[1]See Chapter 22.

$$L \quad = f\left(r, \hat{g}_r, r_e, \hat{g}_e, \frac{\hat{d}p}{p}\right) \tag{16.11}$$

where, as before:

$r \equiv$ nominal rate of return on bonds, *and*
$r_e \equiv$ nominal rate of return on equities
$\hat{g}_r \equiv$ expected percentage nominal capital gain on bonds
$\hat{g}_e \equiv$ expected percentage nominal capital gain on equities
$\frac{\hat{d}p}{p} \equiv$ expected nominal rate of return on goods (i.e. expected rate of change in prices)

with all the marginal response coefficients negative.

If this hypothesis is inserted into the quantity theory equation with $M^S = M^D$ we have:

$$M^S = f\left(r, \hat{g}_r, r_e, \hat{g}_e, \frac{\hat{d}p}{p}\right) pY \tag{16.12}$$

Clearly 16.12 can no longer be used to predict nominal aggregate demand from M^S since, to do so, we need to know r, g_r, r_e, $\hat{g}_e$ and $\hat{d}p/p$, all of which are variables. *A fortiori*, since it cannot be used to predict aggregate demand, then, even if the form of the aggregate supply relation is assumed to be known, it cannot be used to predict the consequences of a change in the nominal money stock (M^S) on prices or output. What the quantity theory now provides is a theory of the demand for money and no more; and, as we shall see, it is arguable how far this theory differs from the 'neo-Keynesian' theory outlined in Chapter 11.

To provide more than this, 16.12 must become a single equation in a fully developed theory, and, in so far as any such theory yields predictions at variance with those we have derived from our neo-Keynesian model, these will result not only from 16.12 but from the other hypotheses of the theory as well. In the next chapter we shall show how 16.12 – or a simplified version of it – becomes part of a 'monetarist' model and in what circumstances the predictions of the naive quantity theory hold in such a model.

The demand for money: quantity theory and Keynesian approaches

The reformulated quantity theory interpreted as a money demand function is given by:

$$M^D = f\left(r, \hat{g}_r, r_e, \hat{g}_e, \frac{\hat{d}p}{p}\right) pY \tag{16.13}$$

In what ways does this differ from the Keynesian formulation of Chapter 11?

As we have seen, both approaches emphasise the role of money as an asset rather than simply as a means of making payments. The 'neo-Keynesian' approach, however, concentrates on financial assets as substitutes for money and uses 'bonds' as a portmanteau term for financial assets bought and sold on organised financial markets. The hypothesis of 16.13 extends this notion a little by specifically including 'equities' and thus the expected return on them ($\equiv r_e + \hat{g}_e$). But this extension is fully consistent with the earlier approach. What is distinctive is the formal inclusion of the expected return on goods ($\hat{dp}/p$) – *and thus the emphasis which is placed on goods as a substitute for money*. Here again there is no formal theoretical contradiction with the Keynesian approach. There is nothing in the neo-Keynesian theory which would exclude a role for $\hat{dp}/p$. It is, however, the case that Keynesian economists have not, in general, emphasised it. Their emphasis has been placed more upon $\hat{g}_r$ (and, *a fortiori*, $\hat{g}e$).

At the same time, Keynesian analysis, as we have seen, typically implies that $\hat{g}_r$ is, itself, related to r via the assumption that wealth owners have some idea, however imprecise, of a 'safe' or 'normal' level of interest rates. If a similar analysis is extended to equities then, on Keynesian arguments, $\hat{g}_r$ and $\hat{g}_e$ need not appear in 16.13 since, given the 'safe' or 'normal' level of r and r_e, $\hat{g}_r$ and $\hat{g}_e$ would be known if r, r_e are given. Moreover, as we saw earlier, this implies that the interest elasticity of the demand for money ($\equiv \partial M^D/\partial r \times r/M^D$) grows (in absolute value) as r falls and, in the limiting case, tends to infinity at some low level of r. In short, the Keynesian analysis contains a crude theory of interest-rate expectations and, from this, derives specific predictions about the interest elasticity of money demand of which the so-called 'liquidity trap' is a special case.

By contrast 16.13 does not imply any such theory. Although it recognises the importance of $\hat{g}_r$ and $\hat{g}_e$, it offers no explanation of their determination. Nor does it imply any particular form of the interest elasticity. In practice, money demand functions derived from the quantity theory approach usually treat this elasticity as a constant (that is, as independent of r) and expect it to be of small absolute value numerically: *that is, they place reduced emphasis on financial assets as substitutes for money*.

Although 16.13 includes both $\hat{g}_r$ and $\hat{g}_e$, which are essentially short-run phenomena, its frame of reference is typically long run rather than short. In order to interpret it in this way, but at the same time make it consistent with the observed tendency for velocity to rise in cyclical upswings and fall in downswings, it is not uncommon for the theory to be rewritten as:

$$M^D = f\left(r, r_e, \frac{\hat{dp}}{p}\right) \tilde{p}\tilde{Y} \tag{16.14}$$

where:

$\tilde{Y} \equiv$ *permanent* income
$\tilde{p} \equiv$ *permanent* prices

and *permanent* variables can be identified, very approximately, with the *long-run* trend values of the variables concerned. If we now assume tht $M^D = M^S$ we have:

$$M^S = f\left(r, r_e, \frac{\hat{dp}}{p}\right) \tilde{p}\tilde{Y}$$

so that $V_y \equiv pY/M^S$ is given by:

$$V_y = \frac{pY}{\tilde{p}\tilde{Y}} \times \frac{1}{f(r, r_e, \frac{\hat{dp}}{p})} \tag{16.15}$$

Clearly when pY coincides with its 'trend' ($\equiv \tilde{p}\tilde{Y}$) then $pY/\tilde{p}\tilde{Y} = 1$ and $V_y = 1/f(r, r_e, \hat{d}p/p)$ is its *long-run* value.

However, in the upswing of a cycle in output in which $pY > \tilde{p}\tilde{Y}$, V_y will *exceed* this 'trend' value, and conversely when, in a recession, $pY < \tilde{p}\tilde{Y}$. Thus redefining p and Y in this way makes it possible to give 16.13 a *long-run* interpretation while maintaining its consistency with 'stylised' observations of short-run behaviour.

Thus some versions of the reformulated quantity theory use, or imply, definitions of p and Y which differ from those typical of Keynesian analysis. In other cases pY is replaced by nominal wealth where the assets are valued at replacement costs rather than current market prices.

Finally, and perhaps most importantly, economists of quantity theory persuasion regard money demand functions as highly stable and thus potentially very reliable elements of any theory of macroeconomic behaviour.

It is natural for the reader to ask which of the two theories, or more strictly the functional representations of them, better explains the observed facts and can thus claim to be more powerful. This is not a question which has been entirely settled mainly because the functional forms typically employed in empirical studies of money demand do not specify, with any precision, the different hypotheses.

An alternative and perhaps more useful question is: What do we know empirically about the money demand function? In Table 16.1 we have summarised the results of some recent studies of money demand functions in the UK.

As the reader will note, the functional forms employed in these studies are extremely simple, while many variables which theory suggests to be relevant (notably $\hat{g}_r$, $\hat{g}e$ and, in some instances $\hat{d}p/p$), have been omitted. If, however, we think in terms of a function of the form:

$$\begin{aligned} M^D &= kr^{\partial 1}\, p^{\partial 2}\, Y^{\partial 3}\, (\hat{d}p/p)^{\partial 4} \\ \log M^D &= \log k + \partial_1 \log r + \partial_2 \log p + \partial_3 \log Y + \partial_4 \log \hat{d}p/p \qquad (16.16) \end{aligned}$$

so that the empirical work yields estimates of the elasticities ∂_1, ∂_2, ∂_3 and ∂_4, it seems that there are some reasons for thinking that, in the UK:

$$\begin{aligned} \partial_1 &\simeq -0.4 \\ \partial_2 &\simeq 0.8 \\ \partial_3 &\simeq 1.0 \end{aligned}$$

while ∂_4 is uncertain both as to sign and magnitude – no doubt, at least in part, because the 'expected rate of inflation' ($\equiv \hat{d}p/p$) cannot be observed and has been proxied by different investigators in different ways.

Table 16.1 UK money demand functions: selected results

Investigators	Data period	Monetary aggregate	Income variaible	Income elasticity	Interest rate elasticity	Price elasticity
1. Goodhardt and Crockett (1970)[1]	1955III–1969III	M_1	GDP	1.25	−1.05*	**
			GDP	1.09	−0.80ᵠ	**
2. Hacche (1974)[2]	1963IV–1972IV	M_1	TFE	0.70	−0.06*	1.0^{π}
					−0.21ᵠ	1.0^{π}
3. Hamburger (1977)[3]	1963I–1976IV	M_1	GDP	0.67	−1.07†	**
4. Coghlan (1978)[4]	1964I–1976IV	M_1	TFE	1.01	−0.30*	0.71
5. Rowan and Miller (1979)[5]	1963II–1977II	M_1	TFE	0.56	−0.08†	0.67

GDP ≡ gross domestic product
TFE ≡ total final expenditue
* ≡ interest rate defined as 3 months local authority bill rate
† ≡ interest rate defined as 3 months Eurodollar rate
ᵠ ≡ interest rate defined as rate on Consols
** ≡ no estimate
π ≡ constrained to be unity

Note: The results given are the values of the elasticities when adjustment to any change is complete.

[1] *Bank of England Quarterly Bulletin* (June 1970)
[2] *Bank of England Quarterly Bulletin* (September 1974)
[3] 'The Demand for Money in an Open Economy: Germany and the United Kingdom', *Journal of Monetary Economics*, vol. 3 (1977)
[4] *Bank of England Quarterly Bulletin* (March 1978)
[5] 'The Demand for Money in the United Kingdom 1963–1977' *Southampton University Discussion Paper*, no. 7902 (1979).

Conclusions

1. The quantity theory is usually identified in popular discussion with its naive form in which:

   (a) income velocity (V_y) is treated as a behavioural constant
   (b) the level of real output (Y) is taken as determined by, say, the full-employment condition
2. In this case the price level (p) is proportional to the nominal money stock (M^S) both on average and at the margin. Moreover, by explicit assumption, real output (and hence employment) is unaffected by the nominal money stock – a condition usually described by the statement that '*money is neutral*', i.e. *the nominal money stock, from which causation is assumed to run, determines only the absolute level of prices and money wages, and exerts no influence on 'real' variables*.
3. In this form the quantity theory consists essentially in a simple theory of nominal aggregate demand *plus* the assumption of invariant output.
4. If output is allowed to grow over time at, say, x per cent per annum then, if the nominal money stock is assumed to grow at, say, m per cent, the naive quantity theory predicts that the price level will rise at the percentage $m-x$.
5. The naive form of the quantity theory is not tenable; hence the proposition that V_y is a constant *number* has been replaced by the proposition that V_y is a stable *function* of a small number of variables.
6. This revision entails that the quantity theory ceases to provide (of itself) *either* a theory of prices *or* a theory of aggregate demand. Instead it provides a theory, similar in some respects to the Keynesian theory of Chapter 11, of the demand for money.
7. The quantity theory approach is now significant mainly because:

   (a) it stresses the role of the nominal money stock in explaining aggregate demand and hence the role of the rate of change in the nominal money stock in explaining the rate of growth in prices
   (b) because it has led a group of economists to develop a macroeconomic theory called 'monetarism', *which not only bases itself on (a) but also*
   (c) retains the hypothesis that, over the horizon of time relevant for the theory, money is neutral in the sense already described, i.e. does not affect the equilibrium values of real variables

In the next chapter we shall consider 'monetarist' theory in some detail.

Questions and exercises

1. 'The elementary quantity theory sweeps the whole of the theories of consumption, investment and liquidity preference into the single ragbag of income velocity. It thus explains virtually nothing and obscures virtually everything.' Elucidate and discuss.

2. From *Economic Trends* construct data for quarterly changes in

   (a) the money supply
   (b) GNP at current prices

   for the period 1960–80.

How far are the observed changes in GNP explained by the money supply and how far are they explained by changes in observed income velocity? Comment on your results.

3. From *Economic Trends* for the years 1950–80 use annual data for GNP and M^S to calculate annual observations for V_y ($\equiv$ income velocity). Plot the resultant observations against a similar series for the rate of interest on long-term government securities. Is V_y a function of r? If so, is the observed relation compatible with (i) the liquidity preference theory of Chapter 11, (ii) the revised quantity theory? How stable is V_y? Compare your results with those of Artis and Lewis, *Monetary Control in the United Kingdom* (1981, p. 28).

4. Assume the money demand function of the naive quantity theory, that is:

$$M^D = kpY \quad \text{(where } k = \text{constant)}$$

On this basis construct the usual *IS/LM* diagram. How does the *LM* curve differ from the usual construct? State your assumptions carefully and generate predictions for

(a) an increase in business optimism

(b) an increase in government expenditure

How do the predictions differ from those of our 'Keynesian' model? Why?

5. 'The quantity theory predicts that an increase in the money supply brings about a proportional increase in prices and leaves the rate of interest unaltered.' Explain. On what assumptions is the statement correct?

6. 'Reputable quantity theorists never regarded income velocity as a constant. On the contrary they regarded it as a function of a number of variables.' Elucidate. Develop a 'velocity function' and explain your choice of independent variables. How far, if at all, does your 'new quantity theory' differ from the Keynesian?

7. 'The quantity theory assumed that aggregate demand depended only on the money supply and was thus independent of the money wage rate. Keynes denied this.' Explain. Use aggregate demand and supply analysis to show how aggregate demand depends on the money wage rate.

8. Typically the quantity theory regards causation as running *from* changes in the nominal money supply *to* changes in GNP. How far do you think this is reasonable? What reasons are there for arguing the reverse direction of causation – that is, the nominal money supply responds to changes in GNP? What evidence would you cite in favour of either view?

9. 'The quantity theory of money emphasises the substitution of money for goods. The Keynesian approach, by contrast, emphasises the substitution of money for bonds or, more generally, interest-earning financial assets.' Discuss.

10. Re-examine the data you have constructed to answer question 3. Does your graph suggest a stable demand function for money or not?

11. 'Keynesian theory predicts that the (absolute value of the) interest elasticity of the demand for money *increases* as *r declines*. The quantity theory does not entail this prediction.' Explain and appraise.

12. 'For an exogenous change in the nominal money supply to have a predictable effect on GNP we require *more* than a stable demand function for money.' Discuss.

13. The following macrostatic model incorporates a money supply function:

$$
\begin{array}{rcllr}
Y & = & C_p + I_p & & (1) \\
C_p & = & c_0 + c_1 Y + c_2 r & (0 < c_1 < 1;\ c_2 \leqslant 0) & (2) \\
I_p & = & i_o + i_1 Y + i_2 r & (i_1 > 0;\ i_2 < 0) & (3) \\
M^S & = & M_0 + \alpha_1 pY + \alpha_2 (r - r^*) & (\alpha_1 \alpha_2 \geqslant 0) & (4) \\
M^D & = & m_0 + m_1 pY + m_2 r & (m_1 > 0;\ m_2 < 0) & (5) \\
M^D & = & M^S & & (6) \\
p & = & \bar{p} & & (7) \\
r^* & = & \bar{r}^* & & (8)
\end{array}
$$

Solve the model for Y, treating $p = \bar{p} =$ constant, and from your solution obtain expressions for the 'multipliers':

$\dfrac{dY}{dM_0} \equiv$ an autonomous increase in the nominal money supply

$\dfrac{dY}{dm_0} \equiv$ an autonomous increase in liquidity preference

Analyse your results and discuss, in particular, the influence of the parameters m_1, m_2, α_1, α_2. In your discussion identify the result for:

(a) the liquidity-trap assumption
(b) the naive quantity theory assumption

What difference does the introduction of a money supply function make?

14. In the light of your results in question 13 re-examine your answer to question 12.

15. Discuss the assumptions regarding central bank and commercial bank behaviour which might lie behind the money supply function of equation 4 of question 13. Can you think of any? Are they sensible?

16. From the model of question 13 obtain an expression for:

$\dfrac{dM^S}{d_{i0}} \equiv$ change in money supply resulting from an increase in autonomous investment

Interpret your result in the light of your discussion in question 8.

17. 'A *ceteris paribus* increase in government spending has virtually no effect on real or money incomes. It simply raises the interest rate' (MONETARIST). 'A *ceteris paribus* increase in Government spending raises income by the full multiplier' (KEYNESIAN). What is meant by *ceteris paribus* in these statements? Can you reconcile them? What, if any, are the issues of substance?

18. Write an essay setting out the main areas of disagreement between Professors Friedman and Kaldor. Are the disagreements due to issues of fact, matters of interpretation or disputes over analysis?

19. Using quarterly data for the UK for 1960–1983 plot the rate of change of 'money' (per cent) and the rate of change of prices (per cent). Comment on your data.

Suggested reading

*M. J. Artis and A. R. Nobay, 'Two Aspects of the Monetary Debate', *NIESR Review* (August 1969).

A. B. Cramp, 'Does Money Matter?', *Lloyds Bank Review* (Penguin, 1973).

D. Fand, 'Some Issues in Monetary Economics', *Banca Nazionale del Lavoro Quarterly Review* (September 1969).

*M. Friedman, in *Studies in the Quantity Theory of Money* (Chicago University Press, 1956).

*M. Friedman, 'Comment', *Lloyds Bank Review* (October 1970).

*M. Friedman, 'The Role of Monetary Policy', *American Economic Review* (May 1968).

H. G. Johnson (ed.), *Readings in British Monetary Economics* (Oxford University Press, 1972) pp. 3–109.

*N. Kaldor, 'The New Monetarism', *Lloyds Bank Review* (July 1970).

*N. Kaldor, 'Rejoinder', *Lloyds Bank Review* (October 1970).

J. M. Keynes, *The General Theory of Employment, Interest and Money* (Macmillan, 1936) ch. 21.

D. W. Laidler, *The Demand for Money* (International Textbooks, 1969) chs 1–5.

D. Savage, 'The Channels of Monetary Influence: A Survey of the Empirical Evidence', *NIESR Review*, no. 83 (February 1978).

D. Savage, 'Some Issues of Monetary Policy', *NIESR Review*, no. 91 (February 1980).

*More advanced reference.

Chapter 17
Monetarist Macroeconomics

Introduction

The job of this chapter is to give an account of 'monetarist macroeconomics': that is, the macroeconomic theory typically held by those economists who are identified (or identify themselves) as 'monetarists'. This is not an easy thing to do for at least two reasons.

The first is that the term 'monetarist' (like the term 'Keynesian') not only has no very precise meaning but has become part of the small change of political dispute. Indeed the two terms have become elements in a continuing but not notably constructive polemic so that both now carry political overtones which are liable to distort or obscure their meaning. Polemics have no place in a textbook. We must, as a result, try to offer a definition of 'monetarism' which is clear and, by virture of its clarity, free from polemical taints. Once this has been done (if indeed it can be done) we can cease to use the words 'monetarism' and 'monetarist' in anything but a precise way and concentrate on those propositions which, in our view, serve to define it.

Unfortunately, setting out these propositions is far from straightforward since economists who are usually identified as 'monetarist' and who are happy enough to accept the identification do not have identical views. In what follows we have therefore sought to identify 'monetarism' with a *minimum* number of propositions which we believe 'monetarists' would typically accept. These propositions we define as 'monetarist macroeconomic theory' even though some 'monetarists' accept additional propositions which are equally at variance with our earlier analysis and equally important in their implications for policy.

As we have seen, a macroeconomic theory must contain both a theory of aggregate demand and a theory of aggregate supply. Accordingly we begin with the 'monetarist' analysis of the former.

Monetarism and aggregate demand

The three main economic propositions underlying the 'monetarist' theory of aggregate demand are:

1. The nominal money stock (M^S) – however narrowly or broadly defined – is a variable subject to control by the monetary authorities. This is the central bank, itself subject to control by the government.
2. The demand for money (*in real terms*) is a stable function of a small number of variables and is homogeneous of degree zero in prices (i.e. is unaffected by the price level).
3. Causation runs primarily *from* the nominal money stock (M^S) – as this is set by the central bank – *to* money expenditures.

The first of these propositions we have already met in Chapter 16, at least by implication, since there we treated the nominal money supply as an exogenous variable. We are now marginally expanding the meaning of this assumption by asserting that the *nominal* money stock (*not the real money stock*) can be set by the central bank. Precisely why this is theoretically plausible will emerge when, later, we turn to discuss the theory of the supply of money. For the present, the reader is asked to take its plausibility on trust.

The second has again been anticipated by some of our discussion in Chapter 16, since it implies that the demand for money, in real terms, can be written – using the notation of Chapter 16 – as:

$$\frac{M^D}{p} = f\left(r, \frac{\hat{dp}}{p}\right)Y \tag{17.1}$$

which states that the *real* quantity of money demanded (M^D/p) depends only upon real income (Y), the rate of interest on 'bonds' (now once again a convenient shorthand for financial assets other than money), which we denote by r, and the expected rate of price change ($\hat{dp}/p$) which is, of course, the expected rate of return on goods.

If we wished to give this function a particular form, it would be sensible to use:

$$\frac{M^D}{p} = kr^{\delta_1}Y^{\delta_2}\left(\frac{\hat{dp}}{p}\right)^{\delta 1} \tag{17.2}$$

which, in nominal terms, is:

$$M^D = kr^{\delta_1}Y^{\delta_2}\left(\frac{\hat{dp}}{p}\right)^{\delta_3}p \tag{17.3}$$

Clearly 17.3 is a special case of the function postulated in Chapter 16 in that the elasticity of M^D with respect to p is set to unity. Thus the condition that the demand for *real* balances (M^D/p) is homogeneous of degree zero with respect to prices is equivalent to saying that the demand for *nominal* balances is homogeneous of degree one.

Aggregate demand in nominal terms is now explained in 'monetarist' theory by arguing that it will be determined by:

(a) the nominal money stock (M^S), which is set by the central bank
(b) the actions of transactors which equate M^D to M^S by adjusting the value of nominal aggregate demand

The reader should note that this is virtually identical with an earlier account of the naive quantity theory in which income velocity (V_y) was taken to be a behavioural constant, whereas 17.2 implies that this assumption has been replaced by the notion of a *stable velocity function.* However, in Chapter 16 we argued that once this was done relations like 17.2 could *not* be used to predict nominal aggregate demand from the nominal money supply since, in order to do this, it was necessary to know the values of r, $\hat{d}p/p$ and, if $\delta_2 \neq 1$, Y. How has this logical difficulty been overcome?

Monetarists, to provide a theory of nominal aggregate demand, tend to assume that *either* δ_1 and δ_3 are very small (in absolute value), *or* variations in r and/or $\hat{d}p/p$ are small. Since the second of these would be hard to reconcile with observation, the implicit assumption must typically be that δ_1 and δ_3 are small. Notice that, as δ_1 and δ_3 tend to zero, income velocity (V_y) tends to a constant – our familiar condition for the naive quantity theory under which M^D is *not* interest elastic. Thus, although 'monetarist' *theory* embraces what we called the 'reformulated quantity theory' – and thus a non-zero interest elasticity – 'monetarist' *practice*, in the sense of policy proposals, typically regards invariant (or very slowly changing) income velocity as a good first approximation to the behaviour of the macro-system.

The 'monetarist' theory of nominal aggregate demand is, on this interpretation, extremely simple since it explains the level of demand by the nominal money stock (M^S) and the 'near enough constant' income velocity of money. This implies, since δ_1 and δ_3 are assumed to be small, that variations in nominal aggregate demand are overwhelmingly to be explained by variations in the nominal money stock, which are, in their turn, to be explained by central banking actions. Since the central bank is almost invariably a creature of government, the potentially ideological content of the 'monetarist' analysis becomes apparent: for it can be paraphrased by the argument that it is preponderantly governments, by permitting (or arranging for) fluctuations in the nominal money stock (a variable which they indirectly control), that are responsible for fluctuations in nominal aggregate demand and hence for the aggregate supply responses which they call forth. It follows that if some of these responses are unwelcome – for example, take the form of falls in output (and increases in unemployment) or increases in the price level – the responsibility for these lies preponderantly with the government. Why do we say 'preponderantly' rather than 'exclusively'? This is because, as we shall see more clearly later in this book, central banking (and hence governmental) control over the nominal money stock is far from precise, while the behaviour of observed income velocity indicates that the approximation that is 'near enough constant' is very rough indeed.

The implication of this 'monetarist' analysis for policy is discussed in Chapter 28. We now consider its relation with our earlier neo-Keynesian approach.

Monetarism, aggregation and 'crowding out'

It must be obvious from what has been said that the 'monetarist' theory of aggregate demand is itself highly aggregative in the sense that it runs in terms of total nominal expenditure (M^SV_y) and not in terms of the sub-aggregates such as consumption, investment and government expenditure which we found it necessary to distinguish when formulating a 'Keynesian' model.

To see this let us revert to the earlier analysis, assume an economy which does *not* enter into international trade, and accordingly write the nominal value of aggregate demand (pD) thus:

$$p[C_p + I_p + G_p] \equiv pD \qquad (17.4)$$

where

C_p = real planned consumption
I_p = real planned investment
G_p = real planned government expenditure on goods and services
p = price level

By contrast, the 'monetarist' theory writes:

$$M_p^S V_{yp} \equiv pD \tag{17.5}$$

where

M_p^S = planned value of the nominal money stock
V_{yp} = planned value of income velocity

which asserts, at least by implication, that nothing is to be gained (in terms of explaining pD) by developing theories of consumption and investment decisions. This implies, of course, that the 'monetarist' approach via M^S and V_{yp} is at least as useful in explaining pD as the 'Keynesian' approach. We do not need theories of consumption and investment, according to this view, to explain aggregate demand but only if we wish to explain its distribution.

Whether theories of the 'monetarist' form (that is, equation 17.5) are more successful in explaining the observed behaviour of nominal expenditures (pD) than the more complex 'Keynesian'-type theories is a question of fact which has led to very considerable controversy among economists and remains an arguable issue. It is, however, obviously the case that, *if the 'monetarist' view holds and V_y is 'very roughly' a constant, then an increase in real planned investment (I_p) or in real planned consumption (C_p) with no changes in M^S will have a multiplier, in nominal terms, of 'very roughly' zero.* Precisely the same proposition holds for an increase in real government expenditures.

Why do we obtain 'zero multipliers' and what do they mean? Clearly if M^S and V_y are given, then pD is determined quite independently of the values of C_p, I_p and G. If G is exogenous, as we have hitherto typically assumed, then any increase in the nominal value of C_p(or I_p) must be precisely offset by a consequential reduction in nominal I_p (or C_p). Alternatively any increase in nominal government expenditure (pG) must be precisely offset by an equivalent decline in nominal $C_p + I_p$. In short, the monetarist model entails that:

an increase in nominal {consumption / investment / government expenditure} 'crowds out' an equivalent amount of {investment / consumption}

with the converse (i.e. 'crowding in') in the case of a decrease.

Notice that this proposition, if correct, entails that the authorities cannot manipulate nominal aggregate demand (pD) by fiscal means and is therefore of direct relevance to policy.

Thus far we have spoken of 'crowding out' only in nominal terms. The alternative is to think of 'crowding out' in real terms. Strictly speaking, the latter is the more fundamental concept. It is, however, fairly obvious that 'nominal crowding out' implies 'real crowding out' if the increase in pC_p, pI_p or pG is *not* assumed to *lower* the price level ($\equiv p$) or a decrease to raise it. This seems a relatively weak assumption.

Obviously, however, the converse does not hold, in the sense that the absence of complete 'nominal crowding out' does not entail the absence of 'real crowding out'. For this to occur it is sufficient for the price level (p) to rise in the same proportion as nominal aggregate demand, entailing no change in real aggregate demand ($\equiv D$).

How does 'crowding out' occur? What mechanism or mechanisms lie behind the 'crowding-out' proposition? Two possibilities are readily demonstrated by means of the *IS/LM* approach. They are, as readers can identify by recalling our earlier analysis:

(a) a demand function for money which is of zero interest elasticity, *or*
(b) an *IS* curve of infinite interest elasticity – that is, a horizontal *IS* curve.

The first of these two cases, put in formal terms, occurs because the money demand function is of the form:

$$M^D = kpY$$

so that $V_{yp} \equiv 1/k$ is *not* a function of the interest rate.

Equating M^D and M^S (taken to be exogenous) gives:

$$M^S = kpY \qquad (17.6)$$

so that pY is proportional to M^S and the *LM* curve is a vertical straight line drawn at the level of money income (pY) which satisfies equation 17.6.

This situation is depicted in Figure 17.1, and it is easy to see that any change which shifts the *IS* curve leaves the equilibrium value of pY unaltered. In short, on this assumption, 'nominal crowding out is complete'.

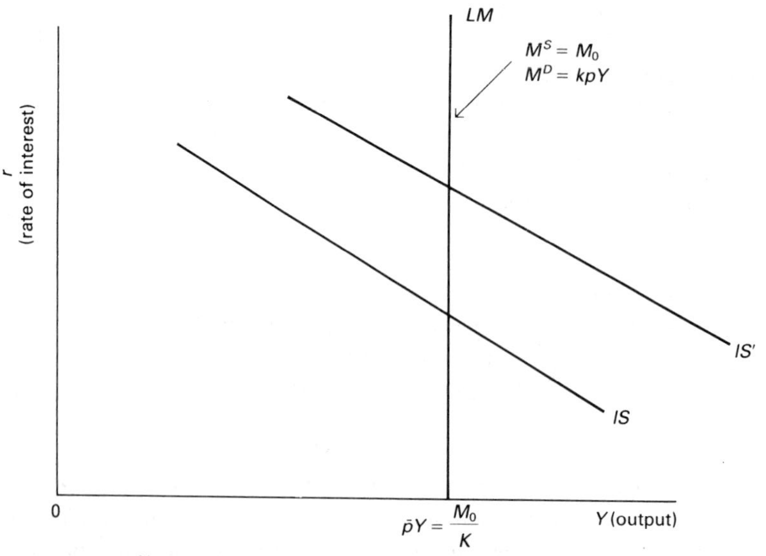

Note: p ($\equiv$ price level) is assumed to be invariant at $\bar{p}$

Fig. 17.1 The interest-inelastic demand for money

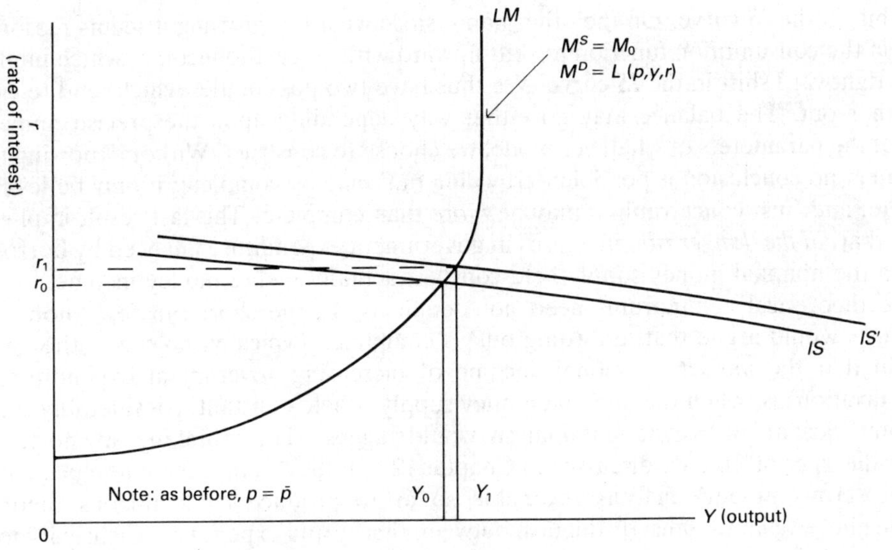

Fig. 17.2 The highly interest-elastic *IS* schedule

Suppose, for example, the government increases G by ΔG so that the *IS* curve shifts to *IS'*. The interest rate will rise to reduce the nominal value of real planned investment and consumption by an amount equal to ΔG. A similar argument holds if the *IS* schedule shifts because of an autonomous increase in consumption and/or investment. *Unless* M^S *is increased the multiplier of the system is zero.*

The second possibility is depicted in Figure 17.2. This shows a 'very nearly' horizontal *IS* curve. The slope of the *IS* curve depends, of course, on the properties of the consumption and investment functions. The more responsive both are to a change in the interest rate and the greater is the marginal propensity to consume, the greater is the slope. A horizontal curve in fact may imply $\partial C_p/\partial Y \equiv$ marginal propensity to consume $= 1$. The curve depicted permits $\partial C_p/\partial Y < 1$ and the response of investment and consumption to a change in r to be less than infinite.

In Figure 17.2 we have permitted the money demand function (and thus the *LM* curve) to display interest elasticity. It is nevertheless apparent that, because the *IS* is so flat, a comparatively large rightward shift in the curve to *IS'* yields a negligible change in either income or the rate of interest. In the limiting case of a horizontal *IS* curve, the multiplier is, of course, zero and 'nominal crowding out' is complete.

The *IS*/*LM* analysis is essentially short run in the sense that wealth is treated as invariant. If a longer-run approach is adopted, *and* the demand for money regarded as a positive function of wealth, it is possible to argue that even if:

(a) the *LM* schedule is interest elastic, *and*
(b) the *IS* schedule is of an interest elasticity greater than zero but less than infinity

increases in government expenditure will still *in the 'long run'* be 'crowded out'.

Suppose, for example, the government increases its expenditure and finances the increase by borrowing. As the deficit continues, the private sector is acquiring government bonds, which are an element in private wealth. The growth in wealth increases the demand for money. Hence the *LM* curve shifts to the left and it is possible that this shift will offset the initial shift in the *IS* curve. On the other hand, since wealth is growing it seems reasonable to expect the consumption function to shift upward with respect to income, which implies a further rightward shift in the *IS* curve. We thus have two possibilities which tend to cancel each other out. The balance may go either way depending upon the precise numerical values of the parameters of whatever model we choose to construct. Without knowing these parameters no conclusion is possible: 'crowding out' *may* be complete; it *may* be less than complete; and, just conceivably it may be *more* than complete. This last result implies, of course, that, *in the 'longer run'* increases in government expenditure financed by borrowing but with the nominal money supply held constant actually *reduce* money income.

These theoretical conundrums need not detain us. In the short run few 'monetarist' economists would argue that 'crowding out' is complete. Typically, however, they would maintain that the impact on money income of increasing government expenditure (or cutting taxation) is, when the nominal money supply is held constant, considerably smaller than some variants of 'Keynesian' analysis would suggest. Their thinking, in short, tends *towards* the 'special' case we discussed in Chapter 12; but they cannot claim it to be general.

Is the 'crowding-out' analysis reversible so as to produce an analogous theory of 'crowding in'? Again we must distinguish between theory and experience. Clearly if income velocity is a behavioural *constant*, a cut in government expenditure, by shifting *IS* to the left, simply reduces the interest rate. Alternatively, if the *IS* curve is very flat, even if money demand is interest elastic, neither income nor the rate of interest will be much changed. Thus 'crowding-in' is complete (in the first case), approximately complete (in the second) and both cases are simple inversions of those already discussed. Thus in theory (at least as we have reviewed it) 'crowding-out' implies 'crowding-in'.

What of experience? Using data to test the 'crowding-out' thesis is a difficult matter since the first essential is to construct a model of the economy (that is, a set of equations) and estimate, by appropriate statistical techniques, the values of the coefficients (which represent households' or firms' behaviour) in the model. This done, the model can then be used for 'experiments' to tell us whether, *in the model*, 'crowding-out' occurs and how long, in terms of calendar years and quarters, it takes to be, say, 80 per cent complete. Unfortunately there are a great many macroeconomic models of this kind and they yield rather different conclusions. We cannot, therefore, be too confident of the upshot. However, the main models of the UK economy do not offer any strong support for the hypotheses over the sort of period (say two years) which might be relevant for policy. This is demonstrated more fully in Chapter 27.

Monetarist analysis and aggregate supply

As we have already seen, the monetarist analysis of nominal aggregate demand assigns a leading role to the nominal money stock and, while not asserting that income velocity is, in theory, a constant, not uncommonly argues empirically that constancy of velocity is an acceptable 'first approximation'. Assuming this to be so, an x per cent change in the nominal money stock causes an approximately x per cent change in nominal aggregate demand and hence in the equilibrium nominal value of aggregate supply (pY). But how do 'monetarists' see this being distributed over output (Y) and the price level (p)? In short, what is the monetarist theory of aggregate supply and in what way, if any, does it differ from the theory we set out in Chapters 15 and 15* and treated as an element in the 'Keynesian' model?

The theory of aggregate supply which we put forward in Chapter 16 consisted essentially of three elements:

(a) the assumption that businessmen seek to maximise profits
(b) the short-run production function hypothesis under which both (i) the capital stock and (ii) the state of technique are given so that output (Y) is a given function of the labour input (N), as is the marginal physical product of labour ($\partial Y/\partial N$)
(c) the assumption that the money wage (W) is given – which implies that *involuntary unemployment can be positive in equilibrium* – that is, that the labour market does *not* operate so that everyone who wishes to work at the ruling real wage is able to do so.

Monetarist theory accepts the first two. However, the monetarist view of the working of the labour market differs sharply, in that it assumes that the labour market *does* operate so *that everyone who wishes to work at the ruling real wage is able to do so.* In short, if the labour market is in equilibrium, *involuntary unemployment* is zero. This means, in terms of our earlier definition, that the labour market operates in such a way as to ensure 'full employment'. All this comes about because (i) the money wage rate is *not* taken to be rigid but assumed to be, like any other price, determined by demand and supply, and (ii) it is also assumed that a fall in the money wage rate (W) does *not* entail a corresponding proportionate fall in prices (p) and thus an invariant real wage – a result which follows from the assumption that nominal aggregate demand is determined by the nominal money stock and income velocity and is thus independent of the money wage rate.

We can use our earlier diagrammatic apparatus to demonstrate this independence of aggregate demand and supply in monetarist theory (see Figure 17.3). Assuming (for simplicity) that V_y is constant and the nominal money supply (M^S) is set by the central bank, then nominal aggregate demand (pD) = $M^S V_y$. *Hence real aggregate demand is inversely proportional to the price level.* In the diagram the $D_M D_M$ curve shows real aggregate

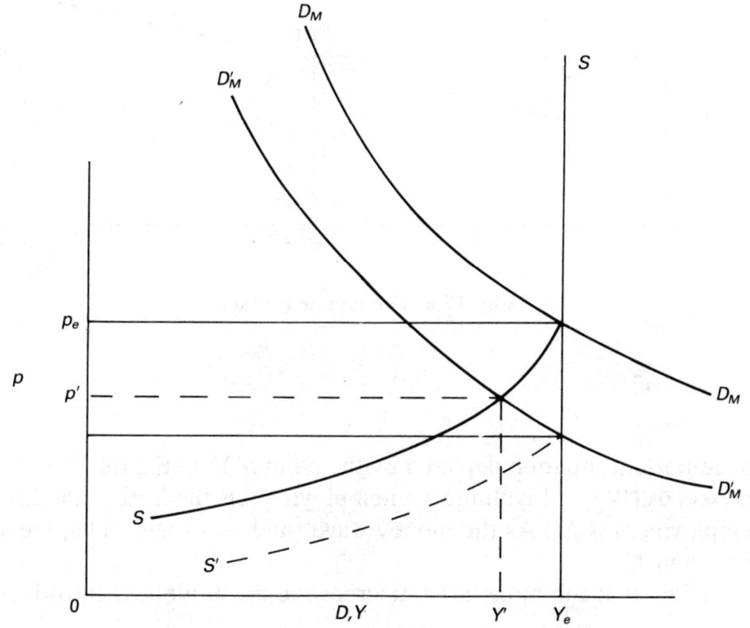

Fig. 17.3 Aggregate demand and supply: a 'monetarist' view

demand as a function of price. Note that, unlike our earlier Keynesian formulation, this curve slopes downwards. It is *independent* of aggregate supply and (given V_y) is determined entirely by M^S.

The $D_M D_M$ curve is now superimposed on the aggregate supply curve of our earlier theory and determines the equilibrium price level (p_e) and output (Y_e). This level of output we know will correspond to 'full employment' in the sense of the absence of 'involuntary unemployment'.

Suppose now that the nominal money stock is reduced so that we have a new aggregate demand curve $D'_M D'_M$. This cuts the aggregate supply curve at a point defined by ($p'Y'$). But clearly this does not correspond to 'full employment', which requires Y_e (as before) and p'_e. How does the system adjust to achieve this result?

We know that, at Y', people are involuntarily unemployed. Hence the nominal wage falls. But the nominal wage is a parameter of the aggregate supply function (SS). Hence this schedule must shift to the right until it reaches the position $S'S'$ at which the equality of demand and supply in the goods market yields Y_e and p'_e as required.

Behind this process, the adjustment of the labour market occurs as in the usual demand–supply analysis. This is illustrated in Figure 17.4, where the *real* wage (W/p) is plotted on the vertical axis and the quantity of labour on the horizontal. N^D and N^S are the demand and supply curves for labour. In equilibrium employment is E_e and the real wage $(W/p)_e$.

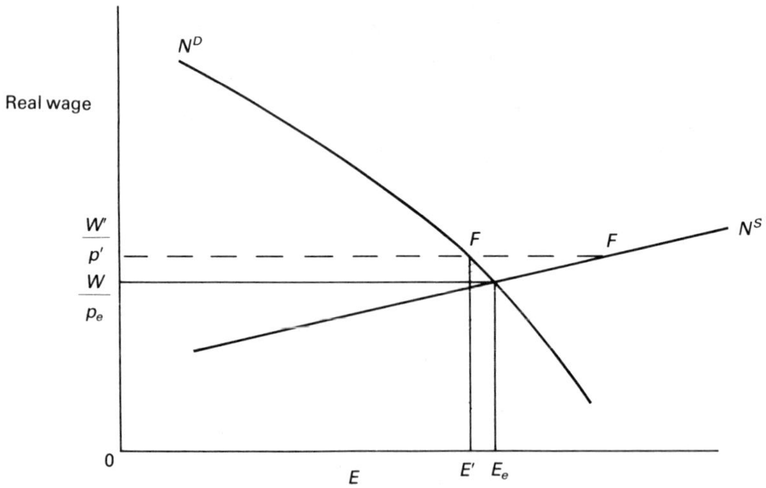

Fig. 17.4 The labour market

At the disequilibrium situation depicted by the point $p'Y'$ in Figure 17.3, the real wage is W'/p' which exceeds $(W/p)_e$. Involuntary unemployment is the horizontal distance denoted by FF and employment is E'. As the money wage (and real wage) falls, the system moves towards $(W/p)_e$ and E_e.

We may conclude that the monetarist macroeconomic model, by introducing:

(a) complete money wage and price flexibility
(b) making nominal aggregate demand independent of aggregate supply

ensures that:

(c) the equilibrium value of real output is independent of nominal aggregate demand (and hence the nominal money stock) and is in effect determined in the labour market
(d) in equilibrium, involuntary unemployment must be zero

so that:

(e) any unemployment existing in equilibrium must be due *either* to seasonal factors or to persons changing jobs who are 'voluntarily' unemployed while they search for work they regard as acceptable.

Notice also that, if the labour market does *not* operate as monetarists envisage and the money wage rate is inflexible rather than flexible, the monetarist theory of aggregate demand is compatible with an equilibrium (such as $p'Y'$) in which involuntary unemployment (due to inadequate nominal aggregate demand) is positive.

Monetarism: some intuitive dynamics

Formal dynamic theory is restricted to Part IV of this book. This is why, in presenting the 'Keynesian' model, we did not attempt to discuss either inflation or economic growth, even though both are problems of major (some would say obsessive) contemporary concern. Pedagogic rules are, however, made only to be relaxed. Accordingly, and primarily because it can be argued that it is to their differing views about the dynamics of the macroeconomic system that the dispute between 'Keynesians' and 'monetarists' can mainly be ascribed, we here give a brief, informal and restrictive account of 'monetarist' dynamics.

Consider now an exogenous reduction in the nominal money supply (M^S). As we have seen, the monetarist position is that, in the new equilibrium, real income (Y) will be invariant at a level determined by the production function and the requirement for labour-market equilibrium. Hence the price level (p) will have risen by the same proportion as the nominal money stock. Money is 'neutral' or, as is sometimes said, 'money is a veil'. If we assume this to be correct, we can now ask the important questions:

1. By what path does the system move to its new equilibrium?
2. How long, in terms of calendar time, does the system take to reach its new equilibrium or move, say, 90 per cent of the way to it?

Why are these questions so important? Consider the second of them and suppose that it took 100 years for prices to adjust from their initial equilibrium level to the new and lower level appropriate to the reduced value of the nominal money stock. Since the value of output (pY) must conform to total expenditure (businessmen can hardly agree to the accumulation of unwanted inventories for a period of this length), then, since the price level (by assumption) adjusts slowly, output (Y) must be below its 'full-employment' level for each of the 100 years. After the 100 years have elapsed, assuming M^S remains unchanged at its new reduced level, the system will be back to 'full employment'. The monetarist theoretical result holds. But it is a result which, *ceteris paribus*, looks much less interesting the longer (in terms of calendar time) it takes to materialise. Would anyone be much interested in a prediction of the form: an 8 per cent cut in the nominal money supply today will, *ceteris paribus*, after 100 years, have reduced the price level by 8 per cent, thus reducing the rate of inflation in each year by an average of 0.08 per cent per annum?

So far we have only argued about the length of time required for the system to adjust fully (or approximately) to its new equilibrium. What of its adjustment path? Suppose, for example, an 8 per cent cut in the nominal money supply leads with no appreciable delay to an 8 per cent cut in aggregate demand. We know that the sum of the percentage changes in price and output must be 8 per cent for each year of adjustment. But we do *not* know how this will be distributed over them. Yet it is obviously a matter of crucial significance.

Consider, for example, a dynamic path which is characterised by very slowly adjusting prices and money wages. For each of the first ten years, prices do not adjust at all. Thereafter they adjust by 0.09 per cent per annum, so that, after a further ninety years, they have fallen by approximately 8 per cent. This is a pretty unappetising path since, for a decade, output must bear the whole of the adjustment by falling 8 per cent; it then recovers very slowly (by 0.09 per cent per annum) over each of the next ninety years. It would be much more appetising if prices responded rapidly to the reduction in the money stock. Suppose, for example, the reduction of 8 per cent in the money stock led to an initial fall in prices of, say, 7 per cent followed by a further reduction of 0.0101 per cent per year. In this case the initial fall in output is only 1 per cent and, though further recovery is even slower, this matters very little since so little recovery is required.

It is possible, therefore, that 'monetarist' theory in the *qualitative* form *may* be relevant, if at all, only to some very long 'long run'. Of course, our choice of 100 years is entirely arbitrary and may be attacked as a way of ridiculing a theory and thus implicitly urging its rejection. This was not the intention. The '100 years' illustration was selected as a means of emphasising the importance of thinking about the time span over which, in practice, monetarist 'neutrality' may be regarded as an acceptable approximation. A century may be absurdly long. But what of a decade: or a quinquennium? Alternatively we may ask: How much of any (theoretically) necessary response in prices will be completed after 1, 2, 3, 4, ..., 10 years, and by what path?

Although not all monetarists accept his position, Milton Friedman's original argument was that the lag connecting a change in the nominal money supply to the price change was not only 'long' but also 'very variable'. The meaning of 'long' in terms of calendar time is nowadays rarely stated with any claim to precision and will certainly differ between countries. Contemporary comment in Britain suggests a lag of two to three years. This is a substantial advance on earlier estimates which were of the order of one to two years and may reflect the growing dismay which the economic experience of 1979–82 has produced rather than the results of any systematic research.

Most monetarists also take the view that, in the adjustment to any reduction in the nominal money stock, *the burden in the early stages falls upon output and employment*. Prices and money wages are fully 'flexible' only in the 'long run'. 'Eventually', after a process of adjustment which is agreed to be 'very variable', price adjustment is expected to be complete and real output is restored to its initial equilibrium position.

Obviously enough, the importance attached to monetarist 'neutrality' propositions depends upon the meaning we attach to 'eventually'. If our best estimate were that it would take 1,000 years for the adjustment to neutrality to be, say, 90 per cent complete, we would regard the analysis of small interest. The picture would be very different if 'neutrality' held over, say, one calendar year. Evidence about the meaning of 'eventually' is, in the nature of things, obtainable only from macroeconometric models, and the results yielded by these differ not only *between* models but also *over time*. For what they are worth, however, a number of models seem to suggest that it takes three years or so for a reduction in the nominal money stock to have any appreciable impact on the price level, and this suggests that if 'neutrality' holds at all it may well take a decade or more for the economy to approach 'acceptably close' to it. This is perhaps why some critics of 'monetarism' argue that many of its propositions should have added to them the phrase 'after ten to twenty years' if they are not to be seriously misleading as well as highly controversial.

Neo-Keynesian economists would probably accept that, over some period of time, the 'neutrality' proposition may be a useful approximation. Keynes himself did so. Many of them would deny, however, that the period of time over which the proposition is a useful first approximation is of any relevance for our understanding of the economy over the sort of horizon which typically concerns us – let alone the period which is relevant for the conduct of policy in a democratic system.

Monetarism and economic stability

Not very surprisingly, in view of their 'neutrality' prediction and its underpinnings, monetarists tend to believe that the economic system is 'stable'. This does not mean that output would not fluctuate 'cyclically' in relation to productive capacity – we saw in Chapter 6 that in the UK economy it has done. But it does imply that the fluctuations would be mild and be politically and socially 'acceptable' in the important sense of not generating political and social changes which modify the system to a significant degree. The monetarist view, therefore, is that the private sector of the economy would, if left to itself, generate only 'acceptably small and acceptably shortlived' fluctuations in output and employment.

The implications of this position are immediately obvious. Keynesian economics is 'interventionist', in the sense that those who accept it tend to believe that:

(a) the performance of the economy can be 'improved' by government action

which is sometimes extended to the proposition that:

(b) in the absence of such intervention the economy's performance would be intolerable and lead to a breakdown of the social and political system

In short, it is not only argued that a modern 'mixed' economy *can* be managed effectively and *thus* should be, *but that its survival probably depends upon such management being undertaken.*

With greater or lesser confidence, monetarists tend to deny both propositions. Indeed, they often go further, arguing that attempts at anti-cyclical demand management, however well intentioned, are either ineffective or actively harmful and in many instances have increased the severity of cyclical fluctuations.

We discuss the implications of this position for economic policy later in the book. It is clear, however, that apart from the function of controlling the nominal money stock, monetarists see little, if any, role for government intervention in the workings of the macroeconomic system. Market processes and utility maximisation can be relied upon to give us a result which, if unattractive to many, is nevertheless the best that is attainable.

Monetarism: a comparative summary

Though, as we have warned the reader, any short account of 'monetarism' (such as we have given) is sure to be incomplete and thus runs the risk of being misleading, we have set out in Table 17.1 a comparison of what appear to be the most important elements of 'Keynesian'

Table 17.1 Comparison of 'Keynesian' and 'monetarist' views

Variable, function or prediction	'Keynesian' position	'Monetarist' position
M^S (= nominal money supply)	Primarily endogenous	Primarily exogenous Controllable within workably narrow limits
M^D (= money demand function)	Relatively interest elastic Interest elasticity an inverse function of r. Not very stable in the short run	Relatively interest inelastic Usually regarded as a constant Stable
Investment function	Relatively interest inelastic Unstable	Relatively interest elastic Stable
Consumption function	Relatively interest inelastic Stable	Relatively interest elastic (via wealth) cash-balance effect Relatively stable
Money wages	Relatively inflexible	Flexible
Prices	Mark-up on wage costs	Flexible
Output (short run)	Variation in Y primarily explained by shifts in investment function	Variation in Y primarily due to variation in M^S
Output (long run)	—	Unaffected by fiscal policy or money stock
Fiscal policy	Effective in influencing Y	Ineffective in influencing Y
Long run	Too long in calendar time for propositions of 'neutrality' of money to be important	May be quite short, i.e. less than 5 years
Labour market	Involuntary unemployment consistent with equilibrium	Involuntary unemployment zero in equilibrium

and 'monetarist' positions. The reader should find this helpful, particularly if the references suggested at the end of the chapter are also looked at.

Summary

The revival of the quantity theory of money has led to the emergence of a body of thought on macroeconomics which is typically referred to as 'monetarism'.

In the *short run* the theory:

(a) emphasises the role of changes in the nominal money supply (M^S) in explaining the behaviour of nominal and real income

(b) argues that, because of 'crowding out', fiscal policy is relatively ineffective as a means of influencing either nominal or real income.

In the *longer run* the theory argues that:

(c) both wages and prices are flexible
(d) equilibrium in the labour market will be reached only when involuntary unemployment is zero, *so that*
(e) *longer-run* equilibrium entails that, via the production function, the level of employment determines real output, *so that*
(f) since employment depends only on the real wage (W/p) the quantity of money (in nominal terms) determines only the absolute level of prices (p) (that is, money is 'neutral').

Finally, 'monetarists' believe that the *longer run* may be quite short in terms of calendar time and that, left to itself, the private sector of the economy is 'stable', in the sense we have discussed.

Questions and exercises

1. 'Monetarism entails a change in macroeconomic policy only because of its long-run results. And the long run is too long to be of any practical interest.' Elucidate and appraise.

2. 'Any reduction in the money stock – or, more realistically, its rate of growth – will have a much more rapid impact on prices under a regime of a "floating" exchange rate.' Elucidate and appraise.

3. 'Because the lags in the impact of monetary policy are so long and so unreliable and because changes in the money stock have such powerful effects, anti-cyclical manipulation of the money stock should never be attempted. The money stock should grow steadily at an appropriate rate.' Elucidate. How would you calculate the 'appropriate' rate for the UK? State your assumptions carefully.

4. 'Inflation is always and everywhere a monetary phenomenon.' Explain the relation between this statement and 'monetarist' theory. Has the statement any testable meaning?

5. How close a relation existed between the rate of change of prices in the UK and the rate of change of the nominal money stock (i) from 1950 to 1972, and (ii) from 1972 to 1982? Does the relation support the 'monetarist' case?

6. At the moment of writing (1982) registered unemployment in the UK exceeds 3 million and 'true' unemployment is alleged to exceed 4 million. What proportion of this would you consider to be 'involuntary'? Give your reasons.

7. 'If we all had complete confidence in "monetarist" theory, the rate of inflation would adjust very quickly indeed to any change in the rate of growth in the nominal money stock.' Do you agree? Give your reasons for agreeing or disagreeing.

8. According to 'monetarists' trade unions cannot cause inflation but only unemployment. Elucidate and appraise in the light of your answer to question 4.

9. 'If money is neutral, so is the rate of change of money. This entails that real output and its rate of growth are independent of the rate of inflation. If this is so, why do we worry about it?' Elucidate and appraise.

10. 'Since it became such a popular doctrine, "monetarism" has typically succeeded in reducing output – or its rate of growth – raising unemployment and bringing the Western economies to the brink of a major depression.' Do you agree? Give your reasons for or against. If you agree, where has 'monetarist' theory been most misleading?

11. 'Monetarists are all agreed that if the "money stock" is "properly" controlled, wonderful results will follow. Unfortunately, they find very considerable problems in defining both the "money stock" and what is meant by "proper".' Elucidate and evaluate with special reference to UK experience.

12. 'The crucial assertion of "monetarists" is that the money demand function is stable. Since it is not, there is little more to be said.' Evaluate this contention with special reference to empirical studies of the money demand function.

13. Outline the *transmission mechanism* linking an increase in the nominal money supply to an increase in nominal aggregate demand in (i) neo-Keynesian theory, and (ii) 'monetarist' theory. Do they differ in any important ways?

14. 'By and large "Keynesians" believe in *discretionary* monetary policy employed, say, for anti-cyclical purposes; monetarists oppose discretion and support some simple "rule" for steady monetary growth which should be announced by the authorities.' Elucidate and appraise.

15. 'To tell us whether monetary policy is "easy" or "tight" we must look at the money stock. This is the correct indicator of policy.' Do you agree? Give your reasons for or against and explain why a 'monetarist' might agree, while a 'Keynesian' might prefer to use interest rates.

16. Use the *IS/LM* analysis to show that the contention in question 15 implies that fluctuations in income occur mainly because of fluctuations in the position of the *IS* curve. Does the alternative hold if the fluctuations originate in fluctuations in the *LM* schedule?

17. Analyse, from a 'monetarist' standpoint, the consequences of an increase in the nominal money stock in an 'open' economy. Assume a 'pegged' rate of exchange.

18. Repeat the analysis of question 17 on the assumption of a 'floating' rate. Under which regime is monetary policy more powerful? Why?

19. Was monetary policy 'tight' or 'easy' in the UK between 1979 and 1981? Explain your choice of 'indicator' of monetary policy and apply it to the relevant data.

20. 'In an *open* economy it is the *exchange rate* which is the best *indicator* of *monetary policy*.' Elucidate and appraise giving clear definitions of the words in *italics*.

Suggested reading

Bank of England and HM Treasury, Replies to Questionnaire on Monetary Policy, in Treasury and Civil Service Commission, *Memoranda on Monetary Policy* (HMSO 1979–80).

J. A. Bispham, 'The New Cambridge and "Monetarist" Criticisms of "Conventional" Economic Policy Making', *NIESR Review*, no. 74 (February 1975).

A. P. Budd. 'The Debate on Fine Tuning: The Basic Issue', *NIESR Review*, no. 74 (February 1975).

J. Burton, 'The Varieties of Monetarism and their Policy Implications', *Three Banks Review* (June 1982).

T. Congdon, 'Why has Monetarism Failed so Far?', *The Banker* (March–April, 1982).

K. Cuthbertson, *Macroeconomic Policy: The New Cambridge, Keynesian and Monetarist Controversies* (Macmillan, 1979) esp. pp. 1–12 and ch. 5.

G. E. J. Dennis, *Monetary Economics* (Longman, 1981) chs 5, 6.

D. Higham and J. Tomlinson, 'Why do Governments Worry About Inflation?', *Westminster Bank Review* (May 1982).

Lord Kaldor and N. Trewithick, 'A Keynesian Perspective on Money', *Lloyds Bank Review* (January 1981).

*D. E. W. Laidler, in *Demand Management* ed. M. Posner (Heinemann, 1978).

*D. E. W. Laidler, 'Monetarism: An Interpretation and an Assessment', *Economic Journal* (March 1981).

*T. Mayer, *The Structure of Monetarism* (Norton, 1978).

M. Panić, 'Monetarism in an Open Economy', *Lloyds Bank Review* (July 1982).

R. Tarling and F. Wilkinson, 'Inflation and the Money Supply', *Cambridge Economic Policy Review*, no. 3 (1977).

* More advanced references.

Chapter 18

Keynes, the Classics and the 'New Classicism'

In the last chapter we attempted to give an outline of 'monetarist' macroeconomics and to contrast this with the 'Keynesian' model we developed in earlier chapters. In developing any model – whether 'Keynesian', 'monetarist', or what you will – there is always a risk of losing sight of its overall structure in the necessarily rather detailed examination of its component parts. This chapter is designed to guard against this risk by:

(a) recalling the principal characteristics of our Keynesian model
(b) contrasting this with the model which is typically used to exemplify pre-Keynesian (or 'classical') macroeconomics
(c) offering a brief account of what is nowadays called 'New Classicism' – a doctrine which, basing itself on a theory of how expectations are formed, denies the relevance of 'Keynesian' economics and has powerful implications for the conduct of economic policy.

The structure of the model

In considering the structure of any theory the first step is to ask two questions:

1. Which variables does the model explain or determine? (These we call the *endogenous* variables,)
2. Which variables does the model take as given – that is, determined outside the system? (These we call the *exogenous* variables.)

Let us now look at the first of these questions, remembering that any model of this type is constructed not only of a set of *hypotheses* about behaviour but also of a set of assumptions about the institutional environment.

As we already know from our manipulation of the model, it contains *nine endogenous* variables. These are:

$Y \equiv$ real output
$C_p \equiv$ real planned consumption
$I_p \equiv$ real planned investment
$r \equiv$ rate of interest
$p \equiv$ price of a unit of output
$N^D \equiv$ quantity of employment demanded (employed)
$U \equiv$ the quantity of involuntary unemployment
$M_p^D \equiv$ quantity of money demanded
$\frac{W}{p} \equiv$ real wage rate

To determine the equilibrium values of these variables we need to know (i) the values of the *exogenous* variables; (ii) the functional relationships which constitute the behaviouristic hypotheses of the theory; and (iii) any relationships between the variables which exist by definition.

In the short-run model, the variables which we take to be given – that is, determined outside the system and hence by definition *exogenous* – are:

$M^S \equiv$ the nominal quantity of money – determined by central banking policy
$W_h \equiv$ the value of the money wage rate – determined by an institutionalised process of bargaining between employers and employees
$K \equiv$ the real capital stock
$T \equiv$ the state of technique
$A \equiv$ the real value of households' assets
$\alpha \equiv$ the distribution of income

Notice here that, in purely formal terms, the variables we take to be *exogenous* are at choice. It would, for example, be a simple matter to regard the money supply (M^S) as *endogenous*. To do this we would need to formulate a behaviour hypothesis for the central bank which, given the institutional structure of the banking system, would permit us to write the money supply as a function of some endogenous variables on which the central bank bases its policy. A simple, but not necessarily plausible hypothesis, might regard the central bank as providing a greater nominal quantity of money, the higher is the market rate of interest. This would give us a behaviour function of the form: $M^S = f(r)$, with $\partial M^S/\partial r > 0$, to replace our more familiar formulation $M^S = M_0$. Equally we could develop a hypothesis about the labour market which would make W_h an endogenous variable. This, at this stage of our analysis, we do not choose to do.

Though we shall proceed retaining our classification of M^S and W_h as *exogenous*, it should be clear to the reader that since we need not do so, part of the skill in building models is concerned precisely with deciding *which* variables are to be taken as exogenous. A sensible decision depends partly on knowledge of the institutional and social environment in which our model is to operate and partly upon the type of problem on which we wish our model to throw light. To put matters concisely, what is involved is 'judgement'; there are therefore no rules – simple or complex – which can be set out to ensure that any model constructed will be relevant.

Once we have taken our decision on this matter, in addition to the values of the *exogenous variables*, we require certain behaviour assumptions. These are:

(a) a consumption hypothesis which explains consumption behaviour
(b) an investment hypothesis which explains investment behaviour

(c) a liquidity preference hypothesis which explains behaviour with respect to the demand for money
(d) a profit-maximisation hypothesis which explains the demand for labour in terms of the real wage rate and also underlies some versions of (b)
(e) a labour-supply hypothesis which explains the supply of labour
(f) the 'technical' relation, specified by the production function, which relates the inputs of labour (N) to quantities of real output (Y)

Our model, despite its heroic level of simplification, thus contains *fifteen* variables, of which nine are endogenous and six exogenous. An elementary knowledge of mathematics tells us that, to determine the value of any variable, a single equation is required; for two variables we need two independent equations; for fifteen variables fifteen independent equations. Hence, if we wish, and it is often convenient to do so, we can write down our model in terms of fifteen equations. These equations, which the reader will readily recognise from previous chapters, are set out in Table 18.1.

Although this mathematical method of expressing a model is undoubtedly convenient and useful, it may also help to set out the model in terms of a diagram. This is done in Figure 18.1. (Notice that although the figure does not explicitly show the interdependence of the three markets, certain variables are shown as affecting more than one market. This reflects the interdependence which is a feature of the model.)

Taken together, the table and the figure make it clear what the structure of our system is. They also make it plain that by (i) taking as given the values of *six* exogenous variables, (ii)

Table 18.1 The Keynesian model

	Equation	Meaning	Chapter references
1.	$Y = C_p + I_p$	Equilibrium in goods market	8
2.	$C_p = f_1(Y, A, \alpha, r)$	Consumption hypothesis	9
3.	$I_p = f_2(K, r)$	Investment hypothesis	10
4.	$M_p^D = L_1(Y_p) + L_2(r)$	Demand for money hypothesis	11
5.	$M^S = M_0$	Supply of money assumption	11
6.	$M_p^D = M^S$	Equilibrium in money market	11
7.	$N^D = f_3(W/p)$	Demand for labour depends upon the real wage	15
8.	$N^S = f_4(W)$	Supply of labour depends upon money wage	15
9.	$Y = f_5(T, K, N)$	Production function hypothesis	7 and 15
10.	$W = W_h$	Money wage rate determined by 'historical' bargaining process	15
11.	$T = T_0$	State of technique given	10 and 15
12.	$K = K_0$	Stock of capital given	10 and 15
13.	$A = A_0$	Real value of household assets given	9
14.	$\alpha = \alpha_0$	Income distribution given	9
15.	$U \equiv N^S - N^D$	Definition of involuntary unemployment	15

Note: the subscripts after the function signs inserted in equations 2, 3, 7, 8 and 9 are used merely to remind the reader that the functions are not the same in each equation.

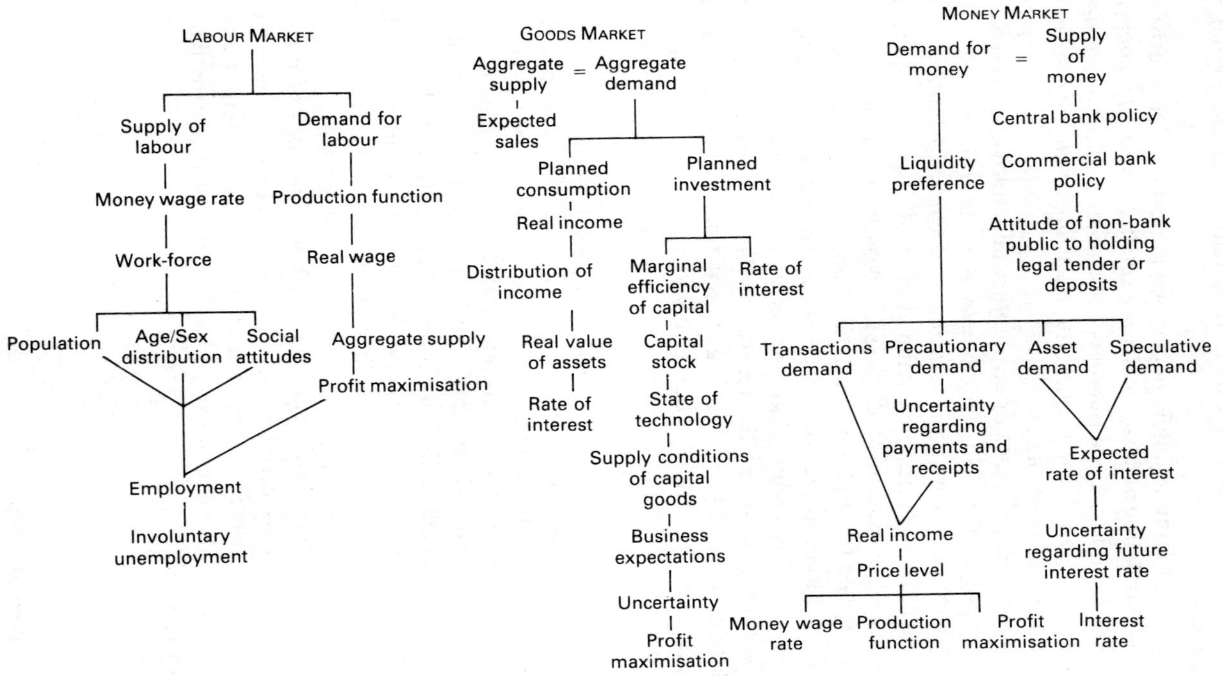

Figure 18.1 The model in outline

assuming *six* functional relations which reflect behaviour, (iii) adding the *two* equilibrium conditions for the goods and money markets, and (iv) *one* definitional identity, we can determine the equilibrium values of each of the fifteen variables and hence of the nine *endogenous* variables. Suppose we operate the model in this way and the resulting equilibrium levels of output and employment are Y_0 and N_0. Suppose further that $N_0 < N_f$ so that involuntary unemployment (U) exists. It is natural to ask: What 'causes' this involuntary unemployment?

If we look at our system we immediately notice two important characteristics. First, the *equilibrium values of all the endogenous variables are simultaneously determined.* Hence, *in a system of this type, crude notions of causation are obviously inappropriate simply because the value of any endogenous variable depends upon the value of all the exogenous variables and all the assumed functional relations.*

For example, to 'explain' the existence of involuntary unemployment (U) we can point to (i) too small a money supply; (ii) too high a money wage rate; (iii) too low a propensity to consume schedule; (iv) too low a marginal efficiency of capital schedule; (v) too high a liquidity preference schedule; or (vi) some combination of all these. The conclusion is that, if it makes sense to speak of 'causation' at all in a system of this kind, no single 'cause' can in general be isolated to explain the equilibrium value of any single endogenous variable. The reader is thus well advised to drop the concept of causation and think instead merely of the properties of the system. This means that instead of asking what 'causes' involuntary unemployment, we ask what would be the result, for the equilibrium value of U, if (say) some exogenous variable changed or some functional relationship shifted. This, as the reader will recall, is precisely the form of question we have in fact been asking.

The second point to notice is that this is the only form of question it is meaningful to put to the model.

It is obviously not meaningful to ask, for example, what would happen if the rate of interest (r) changed, for r is an endogenous variable determined within the system. It therefore cannot change its equilibrium value unless some change occurs in the exogenous variables and/or the functional relations. This does not mean, and must not be interpreted to mean, that it is not meaningful to ask how a businessman (or a group of businessmen) would behave, in given and specified circumstances, when confronted by different interest rates. We asked precisely this form of question in building up our investment function. But in this case we were considering only investment behaviour. We thus treated planned investment (I_p) as a dependent variable and the rate of interest, r, as an independent variable. In the system as a whole, however, the equilibrium values of *both* I_p and r are dependent variables. Endogenous variables are, in short, dependent variables *within the system as a whole.* This point, which is sometimes hard to grasp, is important. The reader will find Figure 18.1 helpful in this context and will also find it instructive to work the exercise at the end of this chapter.

Pre-Keynesian macroeconomics

In contrast with our 'Keynesian'-type model, pre-Keynesian macroeconomic theory predicted that the equilibrium level of output would always be such as to provide 'full employment' in the sense that everyone willing to work at the real wage rate ruling in the economy was able to do so. Thus the principal prediction of pre-Keynesian macroeconomics was that, in equilibrium, involuntary unemployment (U) would be zero. How was this result reached? In what main way, or ways, did pre-Keynesian macroeconomics differ from Keynesian?

According to pre-Keynesian theory in its simplest form, the economy consisted of three markets: those for labour, goods and money. To show the nature of pre-Keynesian theory we consider each in turn.

In the labour market the quantity of labour *demanded* by businessmen is taken to be a *decreasing* function of the real wage. This proposition, which we have already discussed in Chapter 17, assumes that businessmen maximise profits and that there is a given short-run production function exhibiting diminishing marginal physical productivity of labour. Hence:

$$N^D = f^D\left(\frac{W}{p}\right) \tag{18.1}$$

On the supply side of the market individuals are assumed to offer their labour until the real wage exactly offsets the marginal disutility of working. If, as seems plausible, the marginal disutility of work rises as the amount of work done increases, then the quantity of labour offered by a given work-force will be an *increasing* function of the real wage. Hence:

$$N^S = f^S\left(\frac{W}{p}\right) \tag{18.2}$$

For equilibrium in the labour market we require:

$$N^S = N^D \tag{18.3}$$

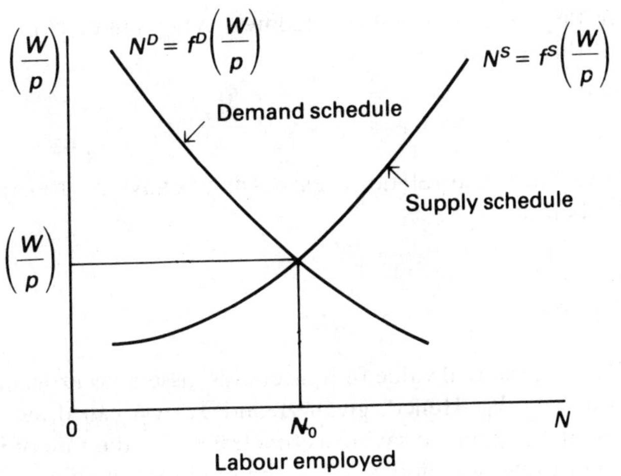

Figure 18.2 The equilibrium in the labour market

Hence when the labour market is in equilibrium we have a determinate (and equal) quantity of labour supplied and demanded and a determinate real wage. This is illustrated in Figure 18.2 where:

N_0 is the equilibrium quantity of employment

$\left(\frac{W}{p}\right)_0$ is the equilibrium quantity of real wage

Note that since, at N_0, *all those who wish to work at the real wage* $(W/p)_0$ *are doing so, there is no involuntary unemployment.* N_0 thus corresponds to *full employment*. Given our production function and taking, as we must in short-run analysis, K and T as given, it is easy to see that the equilibrium level of real output (Y_0) is determined once N_0 is known. This is demonstrated in Figure 18.3.

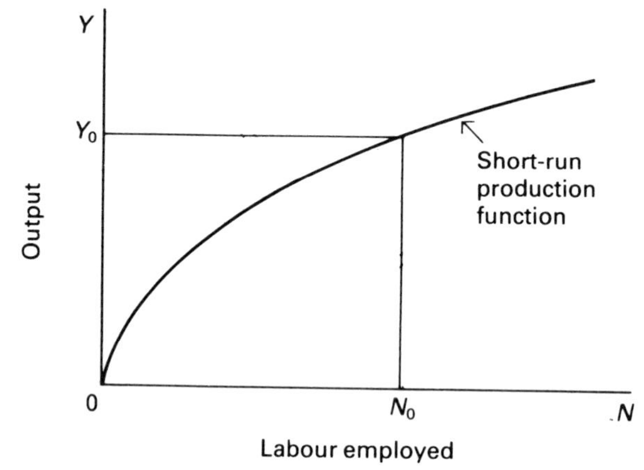

Figure 18.3 The determination of output

We now know the value of output (≡ income). Will planned expenditure equal this value in real terms? If this is so then:

$$I_p = S_p \tag{18.4}$$

We now need two functional relations, expressing behaviour, to explain I_p and S_p. Let us write, as we did before:

$$I_p = f(r) \tag{18.5}$$
$$S_p = f(Y, r, A) \tag{18.6}$$

As before we treat A, the real value of households' assets, as *exogenous*. From Figure 18.3 we already know $Y = Y_0$. Hence, given A and Y_0, we can draw, on Figure 18.4, both planned investment and planned saving as functions of r (the rate of interest). We thus find r_0, the equilibrium value of r, and S_{p0}, I_{p0}, the equilibrium values of S_p and I_p.

In the money market, as before, we take the nominal money supply to be exogenous:

$$M^S = M_0, \tag{18.7}$$

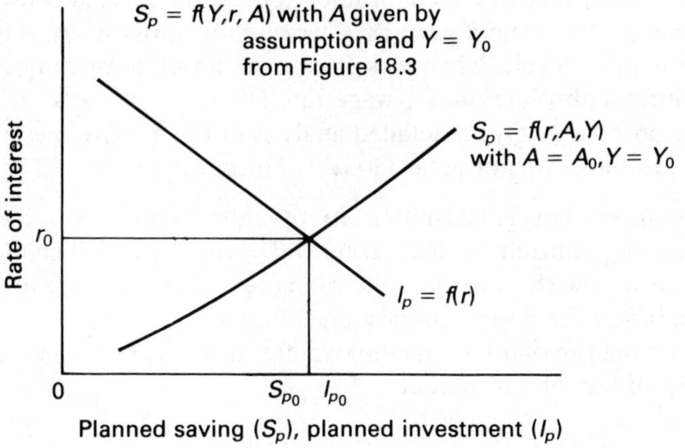

Figure 18.4 Equilibrium in the goods market

To explain the demand for money we make use of the elementary quantity theory and write:

$$M_p^D = L\,pY \tag{18.8}$$

where L is the proportion, assumed to be constant, of their money incomes (pY) that people wish to hold command over in the form of money. Notice that 18.8 entails a *behaviour* assumption – namely, that people *do* hold L constant.

Finally, we impose the equilibrium condition:

$$M^S = M_p^D \tag{18.9}$$

These three equations enable us to determine M^S, M^D and equilibrium money income $(pY)_0$ which, since we already know Y_0, immediately gives the equilibrium price level p_0. This is shown in Figure 18.5.

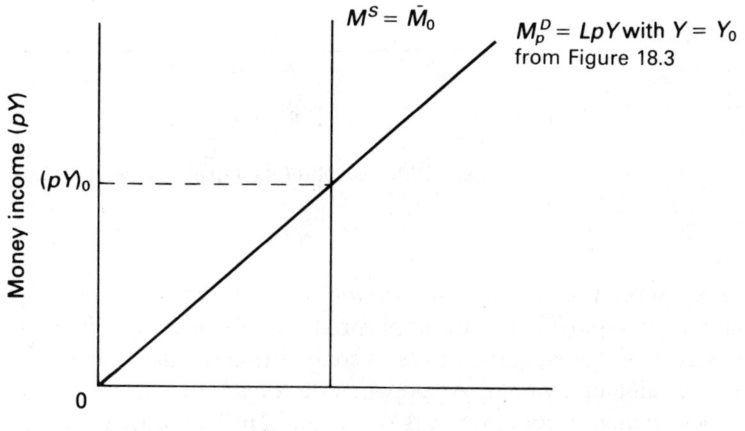

Figure 18.5 The determination of money income

Clearly once we know p_0 (the equilibrium price level) – we also know W_0 (the equilibrium money wage rate) – for, from Figure 18.2, we already know W_0/p_0 (the ratio of the money wage rate to the price level), whence, knowing the absolute price level (p_0), we can easily find the equilibrium absolute money wage rate (W_0).

It is not our purpose to give a detailed analysis of this pre-Keynesian system. Certain of its properties are, however, of great interest. For example:

1. If the labour market is permitted to operate freely – on the usual competitive assumptions – equilibrium in this market will *always* be at full employment, in the sense that all those who wish to work at the ruling real wage are able to do so. In short there can in equilibrium be no involuntary unemployment.
2. This suggests that involuntary unemployment, if it occurs, reflects some intervention in the working of the labour market.

This possibility is illustrated in Figure 18.6, which again depicts the labour market. If the real wage, say because of government or union intervention, is fixed at $\bar{W}/p$ then the quantity of labour demanded is N_1^D and that offered is N_1^S. Involuntary unemployment is then $N_1^S - N_1^D \equiv U$.

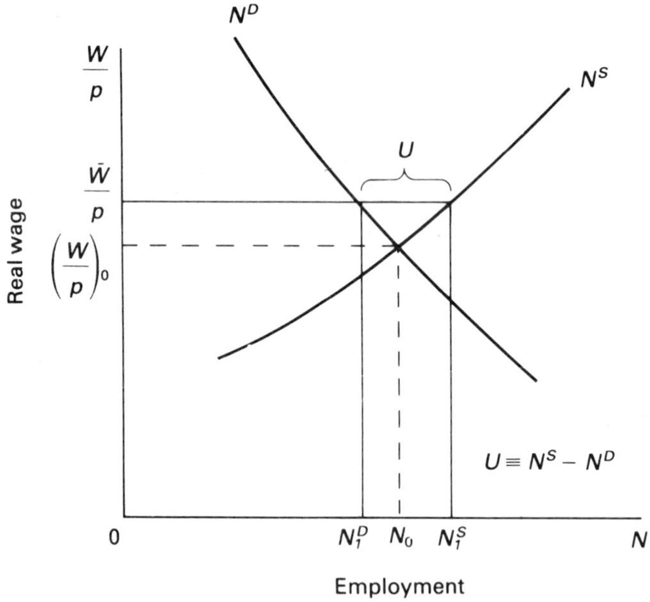

Figure 18.6 Involuntary unemployment

It is easy to see that a policy *implication* of pre-Keynesian theory was that, to eliminate involuntary unemployment, the appropriate action was to *eliminate intervention* in the labour market, so allowing the forces of competition to push real wages down to $(W/p)_0$ and thus restore full employment. Again when the wage rate was not flexible the implication of pre-Keynesian macroeconomics was that a cut in money wages – by reducing the real wage rate – would restore full employment, which, as we have seen, is not necessarily so in our (Keynesian) model. In addition it is worth noting that, in pre-Keynesian macroeconomics, the quantity theory of money holds. Suppose, for example, the money supply is doubled. Then from equation 18.8 or Figure 18.4, equilibrium money income $(pY)_0$ also doubles. Since equilibrium real income (Y_0) is determined by the level of employment, which depends only on the real wage, then if both p_0 and W_0 also double, the system will once again be in equilibrium with prices and money wages twice their previous level but with employment, output, the real wage and the rate of interest unaffected. It follows that the *equilibrium* values of these variables, and of S_p and I_p, do not depend upon the money supply, which influences only the equilibrium value of p and W – *absolute* prices and money wages. For this reason it is sometimes said that in pre-Keynesian macroeconomics 'money was a veil'. The pre-Keynesian system also carried the implication that rising prices (inflation) were to be explained by an increasing money supply.

Though our formal analysis shows the quantity theory of money to hold when the nominal money supply is doubled, at least one mystery remains. Plainly, in the new equilibrium we must have:

$$M_p^D = p_0 Y_0$$

but this simple deduction leaves unexplained the *mechanism* which raises prices from p_0 to $2p_0$. To put the same point rather differently: since, in a competitive system, prices rise only if aggregate demand exceeds aggregate supply just *how* does the doubling of the money supply cause aggregate demand (at p_0) to exceed aggregate supply (at p_0)? Equations 18.5 and 18.6 appear to provide no explanation. Nor, since 18.8 hypothesises that the demand for money is *not* a function of the interest rate, can the interest-rate mechanism be the explanation. This is the mystery.

A simple and appropriate solution to the mystery is provided by rewriting Figure 18.6. This involves recalling that $A(\equiv$ the real value of households' assets) must, in a model containing only three types of assets, be capable of disaggregation as follows:

$$A \equiv \frac{M^S}{p} + \frac{B_0}{p} + K$$

where

$$\frac{M^S}{p} \equiv \text{real value of households' money balances}$$

$$\frac{B_0}{p} \equiv \text{real value of households' bonds}$$

$$K \equiv \text{households' holdings of real assets}$$

Then, with B_0/p and K held constant, a doubling of M^S from M_0 to $2M_0$ must raise A by doubling M^S/p. This shifts the savings (consumption) schedule. We expect the marginal response coefficient relating planned consumption (C_p) to real assets (A) to be positive. Hence $\partial S_p/\partial A$ will be negative. Hence because of the 'cash-balance' effect subsumed in equation 18.6 there *is* a mechanism which will cause excess demand at the initial price level p_0 – though the existence of such a mechanism is not obvious at first glance.

In short, the 'classical pre-Keynesian' model's central hypothesis was that an increase in real money (real cash) balances caused households to substitute money for goods. By contrast the Keynesian model implies that an increase in real cash balances M/p leads households to substitute money for bonds.

The remaining properties of pre-Keynesian macroeconomics can readily be established by manipulating the model set out in the questions and exercises at the end of this chapter.

What is the structure of pre-Keynesian macroeconomics? The *exogenous* variables are:

$M^S \equiv$ the nominal quantity of money
$K \equiv$ real capital stock
$T \equiv$ state of technique
$A \equiv$ real value of households' assets

The *endogenous variables* are:

$Y \equiv$ real output
$C_p \equiv$ real planned consumption
$I_p \equiv$ real planned investment
$r \equiv$ rate of interest
$p \equiv$ price of a unit of output
$N^D \equiv$ quantity of labour demanded
$N^S \equiv$ quantity of labour supplied
$W/p \equiv$ real wage rate
$M_p^D \equiv$ nominal quantity of money demanded
$U \equiv$ the quantity of involuntary unemployment

There are thus *fourteen* variables, *ten* endogenous and *four* exogenous. To determine them we have the nine equations (18.1 – 18.9) *plus*:

$$K = \bar{K} \qquad (18.10)$$
$$T = \bar{T} \qquad (18.11)$$
$$A = \bar{A} \qquad (18.12)$$

and also the production function and the definitional identity $N^S - N^D \equiv U$. This gives us the fourteen equations we need.

Keynesian and pre-Keynesian macroeconomics: the 'Keynesian revolution'

All models are logically similar in that given (i) the values of a set of *exogenous variables,* (ii) a number of *behaviour assumptions* – including, where relevant, such technical relations as a production function – and (iii) any necessary definitions, *each* model determines the equilibrium values of its *endogenous variables.* In this sense our 'Keynesian' and 'classical' models are alike. However, they differ sharply in their *predictions* and, as a result, in their *policy implications*. From, very roughly, the end of the Second World War to the mid-1970s, economic policy in most Western countries, and more particularly in Britain, was dominated by 'Keynesian' thinking, as was the teaching of macroeconomics. Because both differed so sharply from what had gone before it became common to describe these two developments as 'the Keynesian revolution'. As we have seen, there are formal similarities between what we have identified as 'monetarism' and the 'classical' model. It is therefore hardly surprising that the growing influence of 'monetarist' ideas and the resurgence of the 'classical' faith in the capacity of market processes to ensure that the 'invisible hand' would maintain 'full employment' should often be called a 'monetarist' or 'new classical' counter-revolution. What is the justification for this colourful language?

The essential contribution of 'Keynesian' economics is to provide an explanation of the interdependence between aggregate demand and aggregate supply which does *not* entail that, in equilibrium, there will be no involuntary unemployment. On the contrary, 'Keynesian' analysis asserts that equilibrium may occur at any level of employment within the upper limit imposed by the size of the work-force. There is, it is argued, no mechanism – that is, no 'invisible hand' – which makes the system tend *automatically* towards a full-employment equilibrium.

This prediction was obviously easy to reconcile with the very severe unemployment – much of it 'involuntary' – which characterised the interwar years. Moreover its implication that, to attain 'full-employment', conscious intervention in the working of the economic system was necessary, was acceptable to many individuals deeply concerned at the social and economic costs of persistent mass unemployment. So, too, was the *type of intervention*, typically expansionary fiscal and monetary policies, which the theory implicitly advocated.

In direct contrast, 'classical' macroeconomics, which predicted that persistent *involuntary unemployment* on any scale was impossible, appeared to have little to offer. In general it was *anti-interventionist* and thus tended to criticise the interventionist proposals of others. For example, fiscal expansion, advocated by some, was attacked with a version of the 'crowding-out' hypothesis known as 'the Treasury view'.

It was of course no easy matter to reconcile the principle prediction of the 'classical' theory with the chronic persistence of massive involuntary unemployment. In view of the structure of the theory, the 'classical' diagnosis tended to emphasise the impediments to the smooth working of markets in general and the labour market in particular. This was logical enough since, according to the theory, a 'competitive' labour market *must* eliminate involuntary unemployment so that, if involuntary unemployment were observed, it *must* be because of the absence of a sufficiently 'competitive' labour market. Thus 'classical' macroeconomics emphasised the need for money wage flexibility and implied that the labour market *should be made competitive* to ensure it. Provided this was done, then a reduction in the money wage, by reducing the real wage, would restore 'full employment'.

This was of course not a policy prescription favoured by 'Keynesians', whose sceptical view of the efficiency of money wage reductions in raising employment has been discussed earlier.

The acceptance of 'Keynesian' macroeconomics was a relatively slow process. It had not gone very far by the outbreak of the Second World War, which – as wars invariably do – substantially modified conventional objections to fiscal expansion and, by 1941, had produced the first 'labour shortage' in Britain since the end of the First World War. However, after the Second World War 'Keynesian' economics and the 'maintenance of full employment' as an objective of policy became part of the 'conventional wisdom' accepted by both Conservative and Labour administrations, honoured by both in the observance rather than the breach for more than a quarter of a century.

It is not possible to say with any certainty to what degree our relative success in maintaining 'full employment' from 1945 to, say, 1973 is attributable to the 'Keynesian revolution'. My personal view is that a good part of it is. If this is correct then not only has the 'Keynesian revolution' made a significant impact on our lives – which is undeniable – but that impact has also been largely beneficial. In particular, those who remember the interwar years can hardly be blamed for believing that few men, by their work, can have conferred greater benefits on the Western World than Lord Keynes.

Be this as it may, it is hardly surprising that the regular attainment of historically low percentages of unemployment (between the late 1940s and the early 1970s) encouraged some economists to argue that this resulted not *from* policy but from the basic stability of the macroeconomic sytem operating *despite* policy. Moreover, with unemployment reduced to acceptable levels, it was perhaps natural for economists to attach greater importance to other problems, notably inflation and the recurrence of balance-of-payments 'crises'.

Although the argument that the authorities' commitment to the 'full-employment' objective *and* 'Keynesian' policies had little to do with our relative success in maintaining high employment is almost certainly mistaken, the gradual increase in the importance attached to controlling inflation is readily comprehensible. After all, prices have been rising in the UK – very nearly continuously – since 1935. Moreover, it is obvious that, if the authorities will *always* adjust nominal aggregate demand to maintain output and employment then the price level (in a static analysis) or its rate of change (≡ inflation) (in a dynamic analysis) are unconstrained: for by fiscal or monetary means the authorities will *validate* whatever price level or inflation rate occurs.

Typically, economists of 'monetarist' persuasion regard inflation as a more important problem than unemployment. This concern with the problem of the day enhanced the appeal of the theory to commentators and politicians in much the same way as the appeal of 'Keynesianism' was enhanced forty-odd years ago by its concern with reducing unemployment. 'Monetarism', moreover, argued that inflation was essentially a monetary phenomenon originating, primarily, in the behaviour of the nominal money stock, which, it further asserted, was a variable susceptible to control by the authorities. The theory, in practical terms, thus not only identified the current problem, inflation, as the urgent one but also offered a relatively simple theoretical explanation of its origin and an (apparently) fairly simple and relatively costless policy for its control and eventual elimination. The growth of its influence is, as a result, not a matter of any great surprise.

When we say that 'monetarists' tend to 'regard inflation as a more important problem than unemployment', we mean that they are more willing to accept reductions in output (and related increases in unemployment) as a consequence of anti-inflationary operations on aggregate demand than are non-monetarists. This is not because they are less interested in economic welfare but because, as we have seen, their theory suggests that any deviations from the 'full-employment' equilibrium of the real economy will be in theory temporary and in practice very shortlived. They also believe that the amount of additional unemployment which might have to be accepted in order to reduce the inflation rate by, say, 2–3 per cent is small. Their critics dispute both propositions. They believe that the increase in unemployment which would have to be accepted in order to reduce inflation by 2–3 per cent is, in practice, likely to turn out to be large and certainly not 'very shortlived'.

It is not hard to see how these two opposed views relate to what we have called the 'neo-Keynesian' and 'classical' positions.

The 'new classical' approach

The 'new classical' group is, intellectually, distinct from 'monetarism', as we have identified that macroeconomic approach. Its central element is a theory of 'rational expectations'.

Combining this theory with the proposition tht markets typically 'clear' and, in particular, that the labour market does so leads to the following conclusions:

1. Money is not only 'neutral' in the long run but also in the short run, which, in terms of calendar time, will be very short indeed.
2. *Anticipated* policy changes aimed at increasing output will have no effect on anything but prices.
3. Governments can only influence output and employment by continually 'surprising' economic transactors.

How does the theory lead to these results? We can do no more than offer a very brief sketch.

'Rational expectations' can be interpreted as a method of forming expectations which typically leads to 'correct' results. This does not mean that the future values of all variables are exactly equal to what transactors as a whole expect. It simply means that the inevitable prediction errors are unsystematic: that is, there is no persistent tendency to over- or under-predict. Obviously, if there were such a tendency, transactors would be led to modify their expectations-generating theory. The point about unsystematic or random errors is that they convey no information about how this should be done.

If the economy about which expectations are being formed is describable by a 'model' – as it must be if behaviour is regular – then it is easy to see that 'rational expectations' will be formed on the basis of this model. Non-systematic or random errors arise because the model is not exact. All systematic elements – *including the policy decisions of government* – are predicted on the basis of the model: that is, 'rational' expectations are formed about them.

Now suppose that the 'model' on which the 'rational' expectations are formed is 'classical', in the sense that the macroeconomy is expected to operate at 'full employment'. Then, using a circumflex to denote expected values, we have, to explain expected output ($\hat{Y}$) and prices ($\hat{P}$):

$$\hat{Y} = Y_{fe} = \text{planned level of output}$$

$$\hat{P} = \frac{\hat{M}^S \hat{V}_y}{\hat{Y}}$$

and, applying, for expositional purposes, the naive quantity theory assumption of constant income velocity:

$$\hat{V}_y = \bar{V}$$

Now $\hat{M}^S$ is the predicted level of the nominal money stock derived from the transactors' 'model' of how the monetary authority will behave. It is obvious that if $M^S \neq \hat{M}^S$, p will *not* be equal to $\hat{p}$ and transactors (as a group) will be 'surprised'. How will they react?

A variety of stories can be told about this. A common one is that if firms find, say, $p > \hat{p}$ (since $M^S > \hat{M}^S$) *each firm* will interpret this 'signal' as a rise in the price of *its own output in relation to all other outputs. In short it will mistake a rise in the absolute price level for a rise in its own relative price and will therefore be under some incentive to expand output.* This gives an aggregate supply relation of the form:[1]

[1] This relation is sometimes called the 'surprise' aggregate supply function.

$$
\begin{aligned}
Y - Y_{fe} &= f(p - \hat{p}) \\
&= f^*(M^S - \hat{M}^S)
\end{aligned}
$$

which simply states that output will rise above its 'full-employment' trend level whenever $M^S > \hat{M}^S$: that is, the monetary authorities cause a positive 'surprise'. *Notice that it is the unanticipated element in M^S which influences output; the anticipated part influences the level of prices only.*

How can output expand above the 'full-employment' level, which (as we know) is given by the equality of labour demand and supply at the ruling real wage? As firms bid for more labour, the money wage rises. *More labour will be forthcoming if workers do not appreciate that prices (p) are now above their expected value ($\hat{p}$). Assume this is so. Then Y will 'temporarily' be above Y_{fe} and employment 'temporarily' above 'full employment'.*

Why do we say 'temporarily'? Clearly $Y–Y_{fe}$ is positive only because *both* firms *and* workers are fooled (or misled) by the signals coming from the goods and labour markets. But this cannot be expected to persist. *It is not possible to fool all of the transactors all of the time.* Firms will learn that $p > \hat{p}$ did *not* imply a favourable movement in their relative prices; and workers that the rise in money wages did *not* entail a rise in real wages. Hence Y will return to Y_{fe}; and employment to its initial level.

Thus monetary (and fiscal) policies can only influence real activity in so far as they are (i) unanticipated, and (ii) as a result mislead transactors into taking action which is misguided. Thus, if people adjust their expectations quickly and find out rapidly when they have taken action which is mistaken, it is easy to see that output should fluctuate in a narrow range around Y_{fe} and that the price level should adjust rapidly to an anticipated change in the nominal money stock.

There is of course much more to 'new classicism' than the arguments sketched in the preceding paragraphs. However, it is not hard to see how 'rational expectations' can be used to provide a foundation for monetarist analysis (though one which not all monetarists accept) and why it implies that, even over relatively short periods of calendar time (say one to two years), changes in the nominal money stock will have significant effects on prices only.

Summary

In this chapter we have offered a brief review of the relation between 'Keynesian' and 'pre-Keynesian' macroeconomics. In two important senses this review has been unfair to the latter since:

(a) we have not discussed the very great debt Keynes himself owed to his predecessors, on whose work he necessarily built, *while*
(b) pre-Keynesian theory has been presented in a decidedly skeletal way – a process which does it considerably less than justice.

The importance of the comparison lies in its demonstration that:

(a) the theories generate very different predictions, *and so*
(b) imply different attitudes to policy

Our discussion emphasises the relationship between 'monetarism' (as we have interpreted it) and pre-Keynesian macroeconomics. It also gives a very brief outline of what is called 'new classicism' – a body of theory which supports the main 'monetarist' and 'pre-Keynesian' positions while advancing reasons for thinking that *systematic* policy interventions by the authorities will have little impact on real variables within the system. Notice that while 'new classicals' accept 'monetarism', by no means all 'monetarists' accept 'rational expectations' analysis, which is the essence of 'new classicism'.

As we have seen, the behaviour of the labour market lies at the centre of the controversy. The 'new classical' view is that this 'clears' virtually continuously so that 'involuntary unemployment' is negligible. This contention, in its emphasis on 'rational' (i.e. profit- and utility-maximising) behaviour, is met by the arguments of the 'new Keynesians'. They also rely upon the assumption of maximising behaviour to *explain why the labour market will not 'clear'* in the sense described earlier and hence why money wages are 'sticky'.

Which of the two theories ('Keynesian' and 'monetarist/pre-Keynesian') is the more relevant is a question upon which the reader must reach his or her own conclusion. In doing so, however, it is essential to recognise that:

1. Whichever model is judged to be the more relevant now *may* well *not* be the more relevant in ten years' time since *both* human behaviour *and* the institutional framework within which it must operate are subject to change.
2. Whichever model the reader selects as the more relevant must be continuously tested against observation. The reader's allegiance to any model *must* be conditional on performance and *not* absolute. Unless this holds the theory will become a dogma.

In short, what is essential is to ask continuously: Which theory has the greater ability to explain why the economy operates as it does and not in some other way?

Questions and exercises

1. 'In pre-Keynesian economics the rate of interest was the variable which equated planned saving with planned investment. In Keynesian economics the variable which does this is income.' Explain.

2. In the pre-Keynesian model of pages 326–32 what would be the consequences of a government deficit? Does pre-Keynesian theory tend to support the notion of a balanced budget? If so, why?

3. 'In *both* Keynesian and pre-Keynesian macroeconomics a cut in money wages will raise employment if, and only if, it reduces the real wage.' Explain. Why does a cut in money wages always reduce the real wage in pre-Keynesian economics?

4. 'Variables are properly classified as exogenous or endogenous only in relation to an economic *model* containing a number of equations. The classification "dependent" and "independent" by contrast refers to a single equation.' Do you agree? Illustrate your answer by reference to Keynesian and pre-Keynesian theories.

5. Use the pre-Keynesian model below to find the equilibrium values of:

$$Y \quad \frac{W}{p} \quad W \quad p \quad S_p \quad I_p$$

From it develop predictions of the consequences of:

(a) an increase in autonomous consumption of 100 per period
(b) an increase in the desired ratio of money to money income to 0.5
(c) a shift in the investment function amounting to 100 per period

Compare your predictions with those you would derive from a Keynesian model.

PRE-KEYNESIAN MODEL

$S_p = -A + (1-c)Y$ $I_p = H - br$ $S_p = I_p$	goods market	$A = 100,\ (1-c) = 0.2$ $H = 1{,}000,\ b = 10$
$M^S = M_0$ $M^D = kYp$ $M^D = M^S$	money market	$M_0 = 2{,}650$ $K = 0.25$
$N^D = X - \ell\left(\frac{W}{p}\right)$ $N^S = Q + n\left(\frac{W}{p}\right)$ $N^S = N^D$	labour market	$X = 500,\ \ell = 50$ $Q = 20,\ n = 10$
$Y = F + eN - fN^2$	production function	$F = 4{,}400,\ e = 10$ $f = 0.01$

6. 'In pre-Keynesian economics the function of the rate of interest was to determine how a given output should be distributed between consumption and capital accumulation'. Explain.

7. In what sense, if any, is it true to say that pre-Keynesian macroeconomics *assumed* full employment or a 'natural' level of unemployment?

8. 'Saving is spending just as much as consumption is. Moreover since saving entails capital accumulation – which in the *long run* makes us all better off – we should encourage saving at the expense of consumption.' What sort of theory is implied by these statements?

9. '*Monetarism* is nothing new. It is simply pre-Keynesian macroeconomics in clothes sufficiently unfamiliar and ill-fitting to look new.' Discuss critically.

10. 'Say's law stated that supply created its own demand. It was fundamental to pre-Keynesian theory.' Where – if anywhere – do you find such an assumption in the model pages 326–32 of the chapter? Examine the view that Say's law is not a single assumption but a statement about the workings of a price system.

11. If A (the real value of households' assets) is interpreted as $A \equiv M/p + B_0/p + K$, is it still correct to say that, in a Keynesian model, flexible wages will restore full employment if and only if $r_{fe} > r_{min}$? If not, why not?

12. Rewrite the pre-Keynesian model of pages 326–32 by replacing equation 18.8 with:

$$M_p^D = L_1(pY, r)$$

where L_1 is now a liquidity function such that $\partial M^D/\partial r < 0$. Show that the quantity theory of money still holds and reinterpret the mechanism whereby a doubling of the money supply produces excess demand in the goods market.

13. 'In a Keynesian system with no cash-balance effect, an increase in the money supply leads households to substitute money for bonds. In the "pre-Keynesian system" the substitution was in favour of goods.' Explain. Construct a more general model containing both forms of substitution. In such a model will money wage cuts eliminate involuntary unemployment?

14. In question 11, B_0/p denotes the real value of bond holdings and B_0 the nominal values. Hence B_0 depends upon B, the *quantity* of irredeemable bonds in the system and r, the rate of interest such that:

$$B_0 = \frac{\bar{B}}{r}$$

where $\bar{B}$ is the quantity of irredeemable bonds each paying a coupon income of £1 per year in perpetuity. Explain the identity above. What assumption is entailed in the statement on page 331 that B_0/p is constant: What difficulties would arise if it were not made?

15. 'Rational expectations theorists cannot explain cyclical fluctuations unless some *ad hoc* element is added to their theory, for, if their theory holds, deviations of output from its "full-employment" trend should be random.' Elucidate and appraise.

16. 'Admittedly the typical businessman is not too bright but is he really so silly as to mistake absolute price changes for relative price changes when information on prices is so readily available?' Consider this comment and its relevance for the aggregate supply hypothesis of the 'new classicals'.

17. Write down your expected value of real GDP for next year? On what information is the expectation based? What 'model' did you use in forming your expectations? Did it contain elements *not* present in 'neo-Keynesian', 'monetarist' or 'new classical' theories? What were they?

18. 'If the nominal money supply grows faster than expected, so will prices. And, because of this "surprise", output will expand faster than its trend value.' Elucidate. How does this analysis apply to UK experience between 1979 and 1983?

19. 'The expected rate of increase in the money supply is, of course, the target rate of increase announced by the authorities.' Is it? If it is, what does this imply for your answer to question 18?

20. 'Rational expectations theory assumes that we *know* how the economy works. We have *done* all the learning we need to do. We have not *a* model but *the* model. To put it mildly, this assumption lacks descriptive realism.' Elucidate and appraise with particular reference to the impact of macroeconomic policy changes.

Suggested reading

J. Burton, 'The Varieties of Monetarism and their Policy Implications', *Three Banks Review* (July 1982).

F. H. Hahn, 'Reflections on the Invisible Hand', *Lloyds Bank Review* (April 1982).

R. F. Harrod, *The Life of John Maynard Keynes* (Macmillan, 1951) particularly ch. II.

D. G. Mayes, 'The Controversy over Rational Expectations', *NIESR Review,* no. 96 (May 1981).

R. L. Meek, *Economics and Ideology and Other Essays* (Chapman & Hall, 1967) pp. 179–95.

*M. Parkin and R. Bade, *Modern Macroeconomics* (Philip Allan, 1982) chs 26–31.

* More advanced reference.

Part IV

Some Dynamic Problems

Chapter 19
Economic Growth

In developing the analysis of earlier parts of this book we made use of the assumption that the *capacity* of the economic system to produce output was given.

We justified this convenient simplification by explicitly confining our analysis to a 'short run' – defined as a period over which capacity was invariant – and arguing that this assumption, over a time span of, say, one or two years, though it obviously introduced an error, did not introduce an error so great as to vitiate the analysis. The empirical justification for this position was, of course, that although capacity does grow continuously it grows only very slowly.

The theory of Part II of this book is thus, in essentials, a theory of aggregate demand. It explains how much of the (given) productive capacity will be utilised. In the short-run theory, output can be increased – up to the limit imposed by 'full capacity' – only by increasing the extent to which the given capacity is utilised (that is, by increasing employment). An alternative way of describing the theory is thus to call it a theory of unemployment, or a theory of capacity utilisation.

In the long run, by contrast, capacity itself must be treated as a variable simply because, though it grows only slowly, slow growth over a long period is significant. It is, indeed, not much of an oversimplification to say that:

(a) in the short run output grows only when the extent to which capacity is utilised *increases*
(b) in the *long run* it grows because capacity itself increases

The relevance of this view was made clear in our outline in Chapter 6. This is that to explain the behaviour of output we need (i) a theory to explain the rate at which *capacity grows*; and (ii) a theory to explain why the *proportion of capacity utilised fluctuates. In this chapter we concentrate on the first of these problems – the problem of economic growth.*

Now both growth and fluctuations are essentially *dynamic problems* – that is, they involve the time *rates of change* of such variables as income, employment, investment, consumption, and so on. The purely *static* analysis of the book so far does not permit the introduction of rates of change. It runs only in terms of equilibrium levels. Hence our earlier analysis, though essential and valuable, necessarily requires extension to deal with these new problems. The nature of these extensions will become clear as we proceed in this and the following chapter.

The definition of economic growth

In developing our theory of 'economic growth' we need to be as precise as possible. The term 'growth' is usually used in relation to real output. There are, however, a variety of 'growth concepts' even in relation to output. Are we, for example, interested in gross or net output? Is it simply real output which interests us or is it output per head of the population? Alternatively, should we look at output per head of the work-force or, recognising that hours worked on average per year per worker have a long-run tendency to decline, should we look at output per man-hour-year? Do we mean by growth the absolute or proportional (percentage) increase in the variable which interests us?

There is no single correct answer to these questions for the excellent reason that the concept which is relevant depends, as always, upon the question we are asking. For example, if our concern is with *economic welfare,* net output per head is probably the appropriate variable, while if we are interested in productivity we may prefer gross output per man-hour-year.

In the present context our concern is with the broad aspects of 'economic growth'. We shall therefore discuss the determinants of the proportional (percentage) rate of growth in the capacity of the economy to produce real net output. To see the relationship between this concept and the others mentioned here the reader should refer back to Chapter 6. In terms of this, our aim is to explain the *slope* of the capacity growth line.

The growth of productive capacity

As far back as Chapter 7 we introduced, and in some degree explored the meaning of, the concept of a production function. The notion behind this function, it will be recalled, was that, assuming businessmen to employ labour and capital optimally – that is, to obtain maximum output from any given inputs – there was a stable relationship between real net output (Y), the real capital stock (K), the quantity of labour employed (N) and the state of technique or productive know-how (T). In formal terms this hypothesis was expressed in functional notation by writing:

$$Y = f(K, N, T) \tag{19.1}$$

In Chapter 15 we made use of this hypothesis – though since our analysis was *short run* we took both the capital stock (K) and the state of technique (T) to be given and constant. Now, working in the *long-run* context we treat all three as variables. Hence thinking now of 'full-capacity' output and writing this as Y_c we can state that:

$$Y_c = f_1(K, N_f, T) \tag{19.1a}$$

where $N_f \equiv$ quantity of labour input corresponds to 'full employment'.

It is intuitively obvious that *if* (19.1) is a meaningful way of expressing a relation between capital, labour and net output – and we shall assume that it is – then the proportionate rate of growth in full-capacity output must depend in some way upon the proportionate rates of growth in capital, the work-force and the state of technique. Formally, using lower-case letters for proportionate rates of growth in the variables, we may say that:

$$y_c = f_2(k, n_f, t) \tag{19.2}$$

This conclusion, which we stated much earlier in Chapter 7, is, as we noted above, intuitively obvious. Nevertheless, since we have, admittedly very crudely, estimated that between 1950 and 1973 capacity grew at about 3 per cent per annum it immediately suggests a question: just how much did k (the rate of capital accumulation), n_f (the rate of growth of the work-force) and t (the rate of improvement in technique) contribute to our estimated 3 per cent growth in capacity? This question clearly has important implications for policy – particularly if we want, as at the moment of writing it seems that we do, to accelerate economic growth. It is also important because it is an issue on which economists are by no means unanimous. In explaining the rate of capacity growth some economists emphasise the role of capital accumulation; others emphasise technical improvement. Plainly both these factors – and the rate of growth of the work-force – play *some* part in explaining growth. The issues are their relative importance and the degree to which they are independent of one another.

A production function hypothesis

The question of the relative importance of technical change, capital accumulation and growth in the work-force in determining the rate of growth in capacity is an empirical one. We must therefore look at our observations of what *has* happened and, from them, try to discover the contributions to past growth of each factor. To do this effectively we must approach the data with a theory formulated precisely enough to permit us to measure the parameters of the production function itself. There is, as the reader will doubtless notice, a precise analogy here with our theory of consumption. In developing this theory we began first with a very general notion of a consumption function. Next we postulated a *particular form* of consumption function which permitted us to estimate the value of the 'marginal response coefficients' relating real planned consumption to such variables as real income, the real value of households' assets and the rate of interest. How can we proceed from the general notions of the previous section to a particular production function hypothesis?

In order to develop the notion of the consumption function we placed *restrictions* upon it which seemed to us, for various reasons, to be plausible. Thus we argued that $\partial C/\partial Y$ (≡ marginal propensity to consume) would be positive but less than unity. What restrictions can we place on the form of the production function of 19.1?

Economic theory tells us that, if businessmen maximise profits, they will employ labour until the marginal physical product of labour is equal to the real wage. It follows that – at least over the observed range – the marginal product of labour (≡ $\partial Y/\partial N$) must always be positive.

We also expect, and indeed assumed throughout Chapter 15, that the marginal product of labour will fall if, with the capital stock and technique constant, additional labour is employed.

Symmetrically we are entitled to argue that, if businessmen try to maximise profits, they will employ capital up to the point at which *its* marginal product (≡ $\partial Y/\partial K$) is equal to *its* cost to the businessman. Since the latter is positive, so too will be the former. Moreover we may expect the marginal product of capital to fall if, with a given work-force and state of technique, additional capital is employed.

These considerations give us *four* conditions which we can immediately require any new – and less general – production hypothesis to satisfy.

In Chapter 7 we introduced – and indeed in some degree discussed – a *particular* production function of the form:

$$Y = TK^{\alpha}N^{1-\alpha} \quad \text{(where } 0 < \alpha < 1\text{)} \tag{19.3}$$

This function, as we showed in Chapter 7, satisfied each of the four requirements we have set out above. Are there any other conditions we can impose?

As a matter of empirical observation the share of the national income accruing to wage-earners seems to be relatively constant over long periods of time. This means that, since with only two factors of production what does *not* go to labour *must* go to capital, we can plausibly require the additional condition that (i) our function must be such that the shares of labour and capital are constant; and if so, then (ii) each factor is paid its marginal product.

In Chapter 15 we saw that a businessman who aimed at maximising profit would employ labour until the marginal product of labour (in real terms) was equal to the real wage. If each worker is paid this real wage, then the total receipts of labour (wage bill) are given by:

$$\begin{aligned} \text{wage bill} &\equiv \text{no. of employed workers} \times \text{real wage} \\ &= \text{no. of employed workers} \times \text{marginal product of labour} \\ &= N \times \frac{\partial Y}{\partial N} \end{aligned}$$

Analogously the *share* of wages is given by:

$$\frac{\text{wage bill}}{\text{real income}} = \frac{N \times \partial Y/\partial N}{Y}$$

Now *if* the function entails, on this reasoning, a *constant share of wages* (and profits) in the national income, it will, on assumptions which, at this level of generality, are quite plausible, satisfy *five* restraints which empirical observation and economic theory suggest that we should impose. It would therefore seem a reasonable function in terms of which to seek to explain growth – at least as a first approximation. In practice it is easy to show that, on our assumptions about factor rewards, the function at 19.3 *does* entail constant shares of wages and profits. Indeed, as an arithmetic example easily illustrates, the following conditions always hold:

$$\frac{\text{wages bill}}{\text{income}} = 1-\alpha$$

$$\frac{\text{profit bill}}{Y} = \alpha \tag{19.4}$$

For a numerical illustration put $\alpha = 0.5$, $T = 10$, $K = 100$ and $N = 10{,}000$. Then:

$$\begin{aligned} Y = TK^{\alpha}N^{1-\alpha} &= 10 \times (100)^{\frac{1}{2}} \times (10{,}000)^{\frac{1}{2}} \\ &= 10 \times 10 \times 100 \\ &= 10{,}000 \end{aligned}$$

The marginal product of labour is given by the expression:[1]

$$\frac{\partial Y}{\partial N} = (1-\alpha)TK^{\alpha}N^{-\alpha} = 0.5 \times 10 \times 100^{\frac{1}{2}} \times 10{,}000^{-\frac{1}{2}}$$
$$= 5\left(\frac{10}{100}\right)$$
$$= 0.5$$

whence:

$$\text{wage bill} \equiv N \times \frac{\partial Y}{\partial N}$$
$$\equiv 10{,}000 \times 0.5$$
$$= 5{,}000$$

The *share* of wages is given by:

$$\frac{\text{wage bill}}{Y} \equiv \frac{N \times (\partial Y/\partial N)}{Y} = \frac{5{,}000}{10{,}000} = 0.5 = 1-\alpha$$

which is the proposition set out at 19.4.

It follows that the function $Y = TK^{\alpha}N^{1-\alpha}$ satisfies the *five* important conditions which we can reasonably require of it. To what 'growth hypothesis' (analogous to 19.2) does this function lead? By making use of fairly elementary mathematics this is easily found to be:[2]

$$y_c = t + \alpha k + (1 - \alpha)n_f \tag{19.5}$$

To check 19.5 as before put $\alpha = 0.5$, $T = 10$, $K = 100$, $N = 10{,}000$. Then $Y_0 = 10{,}000$, as we showed in the paragraph above.

Now put $T = 10.001$, $K = 121$, $N = 12{,}100$. We have:

$$Y_1 = 10.001 \times (121)^{\frac{1}{2}} \times (12{,}100)^{\frac{1}{2}}$$
$$= 10.001 \times 11 \times 110$$
$$= 12{,}101.210$$

According to 19.5 we have:

$$y_c = t + \alpha k + (1 - \alpha)n_f$$
$$= \frac{0.001}{10.0} + \alpha\left(\frac{21}{100}\right) + (1 - \alpha)\,\frac{2{,}100}{10{,}000}$$
$$= 0.01 \text{ per cent} + 0.5 \text{ (21 per cent)} + 0.5 \text{ (21 per cent)}$$
$$= 21.01 \text{ per cent}$$

[1] This formula is obtained by differentiating the production function partially with respect to N.

[2] This formula holds precisely only for indefinitely small values of the independent variables. It is obtained by logarithmic differentiation of the production function.

Now the percentage increase in Y is given by:

$$\frac{Y_1 - Y_0}{Y_0} = \frac{12{,}101.210 - 10{,}000}{10{,}000} = \frac{2{,}101.210}{10{,}000} = 21.0121 \text{ per cent}$$

which taken correct to two decimal places, is the result obtained from 19.5.[1]

It follows that the function 19.3 (first introduced in Chapter 7) is not only plausible (since it meets the *five* requirements we put upon it) but also leads to a simple 'growth hypothesis'. This simple growth hypothesis tells us that:

$\frac{\partial y}{\partial k} \equiv$	marginal response coefficient relating the rate of growth in output to the rate of capital accumulation	=	share of profits in the national income
$\frac{\partial y}{\partial n} \equiv$	marginal response coefficient relating the rate of growth in output to the rate of increase in the work-force	=	share of wages in the national income

This means, since these shares are easily measured, that it is not difficult to estimate the marginal response coefficients – a result which puts us well on the way to calculating the relative importance of k, n and t in explaining the rate of growth in actual output and thus, adding the full-employment assumption, the rate of growth of *full-capacity* output.

The growth in output and capacity output

The previous section of this chapter, though rather difficult, is an essential preliminary to an attempt to assess the relative importance of t, k and n in explaining growth. If we accept the rather heavy load of assumptions entailed, we can now write our growth hypothesis:

$$y = t + \text{share of profits} \times k + \text{share of wages} \times n \qquad (19.5)$$

The two shares can readily be obtained from national income estimates. We therefore have:

- $y \equiv$ the rate of growth of actual output – is conceptually measurable, and indeed data exist in most countries for estimating purposes.
- $k \equiv$ the rate of growth of the real capital stock, and is also conceptually measurable and in some countries – notably the USA – data exist for estimating purposes.
- $n \equiv$ the rate of growth of labour input – is similarly capable of estimation.

Hence in 19.5 of the *six* terms five are susceptible to measurement (in principle) and estimation (in practice). It follows that t – the rate of change of technique – can be estimated as a residual: that is, as the difference between the *observed* rate of increase in output and the contributions explained by the *observed* rate of increase in capital (multiplied by its

[1]Which, we recall, does not hold precisely for other than indefinitely small changes.

marginal response coefficient) and the *observed* rate of increase in labour (multiplied by its marginal response coefficient).

There are now several studies of the growth in output which are based on production functions of the form of 19.3 and growth hypotheses of the form 19.5. Many of them are rather technical. In what follows we set out some of their results, adjusted so as to fit our model. Because of the need for adjustment the results are illustrative only.

According to US data the share of wages (the marginal response coefficient of the growth in employment) is about 0.77. The corresponding marginal response coefficient for the growth of capital is therefore 0.23. Between 1929 and 1957, real national product in the USA grew at the compound rate of 2.93 per cent per annum. During the same period employment grew at an estimated 1.31 per cent. However, the average hours worked per employee fell. Hence the input of labour (corrected for the change in hours) grew at only 1.08 per cent. Over the same period capital accumulated at the rate of 1.88 per cent. Hence rewriting 19.5 we have:

$$
\begin{aligned}
t &= y - \text{share of profits} \times k - \text{share of wages} \times n \\
&= 2.93-(0.23 \times 1.88)-(0.77 \times 1.08) \\
&= 2.93-0.4324-0.8316 \\
&= 1.666
\end{aligned}
$$

Thus on this calculation it seems that something like 57 per cent (i.e. 1.67/2.93 × 100/1) of the growth in the US national product between 1929 and 1957 is to be explained by the process of technical improvement. Capital accumulation accounts for only a little more than 14 per cent, while the growth of labour input accounts for about 28 per cent.

The calculation set out above, though it has the appearance of precision, is in reality extremely crude. If these figures are meaningful at all – and the reader should by now be aware that the method involves a heavy load of assumptions by which it stands or falls – they do no more than indicate orders of magnitude. Nevertheless *if* these orders of magnitude are even approximately correct, they are interesting, for they suggest that the role of capital accumulation in promoting growth may be less significant than is commonly supposed. Suppose we assume that they are both meaningful and accurate as far as orders of magnitude are concerned. Then, plainly, provided we can calculate the rate of growth of the full-employment labour input, we can readily calculate the rate at which full capacity grew in the period. It follows that in explaining the rate at which actual output grew we have developed – in operational terms – a method of explaining the rate of growth in 'full-capacity' output.

It is of course arguable that the method we have used is erroneous, and in consequence the conclusions drawn are also erroneous. At this stage the reader is simply asked to take note of two points:

(a) the estimated contribution of technical progress to observed growth reflects the assumptions involved and, in particular, the assumption that the rate of technical progress is independent of the rate of capital accumulation and work-force expansion
(b) the method we have employed has been subjected to very considerable criticism on this and other grounds in the professional literature

Unfortunately many of the criticisms of the method are technically difficult and thus beyond the scope of this book. The reader, therefore, is asked to consider our results *not* as generally accepted estimates of what are agreed to be the relevant coefficients, but rather as an illustration of *one way among many* in which the production function concept can be made operational and the results which follow from adopting it. It is certainly *not* claimed that the method used is the best way of approaching the problem. Nor are we arguing that economists as a whole are agreed that it is the best way or that the best way of approaching the problem is the subject of a professional consensus.

Accelerating growth: capital accumulation

In recent years there has been growing dissatisfaction with the rate of growth of output in the UK. As a result considerable thought has been given – and is still being given – to how the rate of growth might best be increased. What light does our earlier analysis throw upon this problem?

According to our data for the US economy, we have our expression for the rate of growth of output in which the relevant orders of magnitude appear to be broadly as follows:

$$y_c = t + \alpha k + (1-\alpha)n_f$$
$$= 1.7 + 0.25k + 0.75n_f$$

Can we make use of this approximation to interpret UK experience?

If the concept of a production function is applicable and *if* the form of the production function is appropriate – both of which are open to considerable doubt – there remains the problem of whether parameter values derived from US data are useful approximations in the UK case. Simply as an illustration we shall assume that they are. It follows that a 1 per cent increase in k (from, say, 2 to 3 per cent) would add only one-quarter of 1 per cent to the growth rate y_c.

Now k, by definition, is the proportional rate of capital accumulation per year. This is annual net investment (I) divided by the capital stock (K). In a closed economy, *ex post*, $I \equiv S$, where $S \equiv$ net savings. In general saving plans are carried out. Hence:

$$I = sY$$

where $s \equiv$ the proportion of income the community plans to save. It follows that:

$$k \equiv \frac{I}{K} = s\frac{Y}{K}$$

In short, the rate of capital accumulation depends upon two factors:

(a) the average (which for convenience is now put equal to the marginal) propensity to save $= s$

(b) the output/capital ratio (Y/K)

We may now take the output/capital ratio – in terms of annual output – to be about ⅓. Hence if the average net propensity to save is around 0.09, the percentage rate of capital accumulation will be 3 and, to raise it to 4, the proportion of income saved must be raised to 0.12. And this, since the marginal response coefficient ($\partial y_c/\partial k$) is assumed to be a quarter, will add only one-quarter of 1 per cent to the rate of growth in output. Alternatively we may

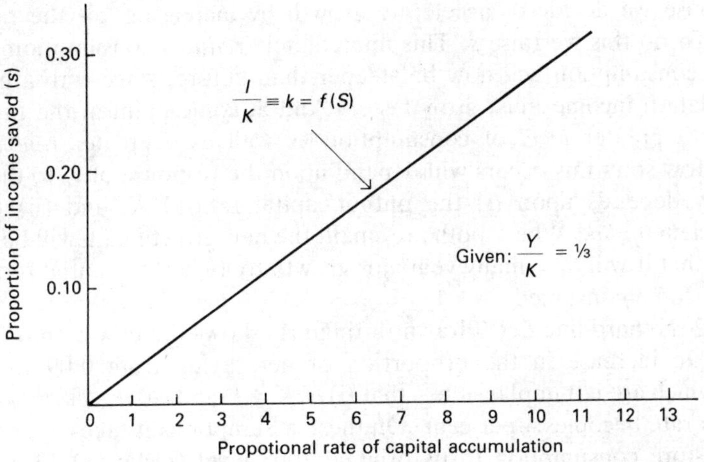

Figure 19.1 The rate of capital accumulation and the saving ratio

say that, on these figures, to raise the growth rate in output by 1 per cent – from, say, 3 per cent to 4 per cent – by raising the rate of capital accumulation would, *ceteris paribus*, require an increase in s from 0.09 to about 0.21 – a very large increase indeed. This is an important and suggestive result, as a simple diagram makes plain (see Figure 19.2).

Suppose the economy is growing with continuous 'full employment' at 3 per cent per annum (in terms of real net output) with a given s. Then consumption will be growing at the same rate of 3 per cent since it is, *ex hypothesis,* a constant proportion $(1-s)$ of output. On Figure 19.2 we plot time on the horizontal axis and the logarithm of real consumption on the vertical. The dashed line CC thus gives the path of consumption when income is growing at 3 per cent per annum. Obviously in 1965 consumption is OA.

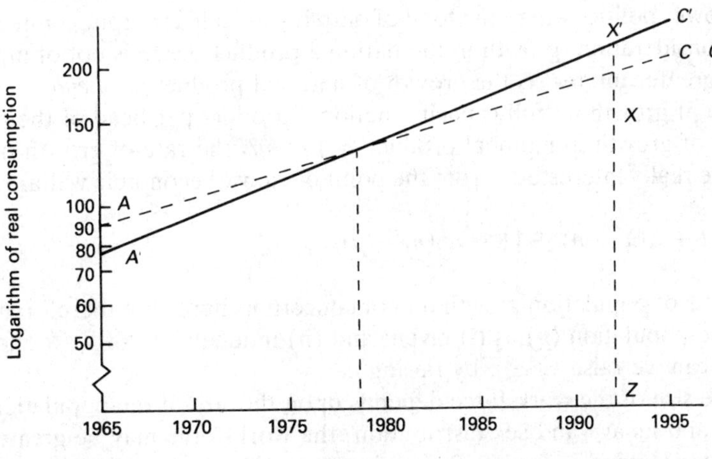

Figure 19.2 Capital accumulation and the rate of growth of consumption

In 1965 suppose we decide to accelerate growth by increasing k – the rate of capital accumulation. To do this we raise s. This immediately *reduces* consumption to OA'. The growth path of consumption will now be steeper than before, since with a higher rate of capital accumulation income must grow faster. And at some point in the future we shall begin to enjoy a greater *level* of consumption as well as a greater *rate of growth* in consumption. How soon this occurs will depend upon the response of y_c to the change in s and this clearly depends upon (i) the output/capital ratio Y/K, and (ii) the marginal response coefficient $\partial y_c/\partial k$. Where both are small, the new growth path will be little steeper than the old so that it will take many years for growth to 'offset' the initial reduction in the proportion of income consumed.

In Figure 19.2 the hard line $C'C'$ drawn through A' shows the new path of consumption resulting from an increase in the proportion of net saving from 0.09 to 0.21 on the assumptions – which are not implausible – that (i) $Y/K = \frac{1}{3}$, and (ii) $\partial y_c/\partial k = 1/4$, so that the 3 per cent growth rate becomes 4 per cent. On these assumptions it takes approximately: (i) 3½ years to restore consumption to its original 1965 level (OA); (ii) 13½ years before consumption on the *new* growth line becomes equal to what it would have been on the *old* at the point where CC and $C'C'$ cut; while (iii) not until 1992 does total consumption for the years 1965–92 become equal under the two systems.

From this analysis two conclusions follow. First, any attempt to accelerate growth in Britain primarily by raising the rate of capital accumulation seems likely to bring rather poor returns. Second, such a policy has considerable costs in terms of consumption forgone.

Accelerating growth: labour input

From 19.5 it is obvious that one way of increasing y_c (the rate of growth of full-capacity output) is to increase n_f (the rate of growth of the 'fully employed' work-force). In general, of course, we are not much interested in the growth of net national product as such. Suppose, for example, net national product in real terms *quadrupled* while the population *quintupled*. National product *per capita* – an index of *potential* economic welfare – would have *fallen* despite the immense growth in output. Apart, therefore, from the area of international power politics where the total of output – as well as output per head – seems to be a relevant consideration, growth in the national product *per se* is not of major interest. What is of far greater interest is the growth of national product *per head*.

Now the rate of growth in 'full-capacity' national product per head of the population is simply the rate of growth in national product (y_c) *minus* the rate of growth of population (p). Thus we are really interested – from the point of view of economic welfare – in raising:

$$y_c - p = t + \alpha(k - p) + (1 - \alpha)(n_f - p) \tag{19.6}$$

The determinants of population growth do not concern us here. We therefore take the rate of growth of the population (p) as (i) given; and (ii) independent of y_c, k and n_f.

We now ask can we raise $y_c - p$ by raising n_f?

Obviously the size of the work-force depends upon the size of the population. But given the population and its age and sex distribution, the work-force may be greater or smaller depending on the extent to which the various age/sex groups *participate* in economic activity. This in turn depends upon a whole host of factors – many of which are social rather than economic. It is clear, however, that if we could raise the rate of *participation* – that is, the proportion of the population in the work-force – then while the participation rate is rising n_f can rise independently of p. Equally obviously this process must have a limit if only because not more than 100 per cent of the population can, as a matter of logic, enter the work-force. In practice, of course, nothing like the whole population *is* or *can be* in the work-force. Moreover, though participation rates do change quite markedly for particular age/sex groups, the overall percentage changes rather little. This is because while participation rates for some groups, notably females, have tended to rise, the participation rates for males over 64 and for boys and girls below 20 have tended to fall. In general we no longer work until we die and we require, and increasingly receive, a good deal more, and longer, education before we go to work.

It seems, therefore, that though, as a matter of theory, we could hope to raise $y_c - p$ by raising n_f (by policies designed to increase participation rates) this is likely to be very difficult in practice, if not impossible. Indeed the increasing demands for education allied to the trend towards earlier retirement may well, on balance, reduce the overall participation rate. This conclusion is strengthened by the reflection that, in thinking of n_f simply as 'persons', we are neglecting the obvious point that n_f is really a measure of labour input which is 'persons' multiplied by the *average hours worked per period per person.* Secularly average hours worked are tending to fall. Hence for any given p the rate of growth of labour input seems if anything likely to decline. This is doubly unfortunate, for as we have already shown $\partial y_c/\partial n_f$ (the marginal response coefficient relating the growth of output to the growth of labour input) is probably quite large – of the order of 0.75. Hence not only are we denied an opportunity of raising $y_c - p$ by raising n_f but we must, in practice, look forward to a fall in n_f in relation to p which will tend to reduce the rate of growth in output per head. It follows, therefore, that the principal hope of raising $y_c - p$ must rest in bringing about an increase in t (the rate of improvement in productive technique).

Accelerating growth: innovation

Improving productive technique – 'know-how' – consists in bringing about a change in productive methods such that for any given input of labour and capital services a larger output can be obtained. This process is continuous for the economy as a whole, and as our earlier discussion suggests is probably the most important source of growth in real net output per head.

At this stage a qualification is essential. Above (p. 349) we estimated t (the rate of improvement in 'know-how') as a residual. Our estimate therefore attracts any errors in our estimates of the remaining five elements in equation 19.5. Two conclusions follow. First, we should not be too dogmatic in asserting that our estimate of t is of the right order of magnitude. Second, t – as we have estimated it – is a 'catch-all'. *It is in fact that part of the observed growth in output which cannot be explained, on our theory, by the growth in capital and labour inputs.* It may therefore contain a great deal more than is usually implied in the phrase 'technical change'. Despite these qualifications, until a more refined analysis shows our conclusion to be in error, we can, with proper caution, retain it.

The process of improving 'know-how' – which gives us a positive value for t – consists of a number of related activities. These can be classified into three processes:

(a) the *development* of knowledge which, if used in production would permit a greater output from a given input of labour and capital
(b) the *application* of this new knowledge to the actual process of production
(c) the *reduction of the spread* in actual production methods between those employed by the most efficient and least efficient firms

It follows that, to increase t, we need to increase the rates at which these three processes are taking place.

How we may hope to raise t needs an extensive examination beyond the scope of this book. At this stage it is sufficient for the reader to note that, contrary to what is often believed, *invention* (process (a) above) is only a part – and possibly not the most important part – of improving 'know-how'. From this it follows that increasing the rate of invention may not be the most useful way of increasing t – that is, of raising the rate of improvement in technique.

Summary

We began this chapter by recalling that in Chapter 6 we 'estimated' – very roughly – that the capacity of the UK economy probably grew at about 3 per cent per annum or a shade more up to 1973. We argued that since 1973 the rate has been significantly lower.

We then tried to develop a meaningful theory to explain the observed rate of growth. The centrepiece of this theory is the concept (introduced in Chapter 7) of an aggregate production function relating the rate of output per period to the inputs of capital and labour services per period and the state of productive technique. We then developed this theory in the form of a *particular* production function. We chose this function because it satisfied (cf. Chapter 7) a number of conditions which economic theory and empirical observation suggested to be important. Using this theory, and the assumption that both labour and capital were paid (as wages or profits) their marginal products, we then attempted to estimate the relative contributions of:

k ≡ the annual rate of capital accumulation
n ≡ the annual rate of growth in labour input
t ≡ the annual rate of improvement in technique

to the observed rate of growth in real net output. From the estimates yielded by this exercise we then set out some observations on past growth and discussed, in a brief and general way, some of the problems of seeking to raise the rate of expansion in 'full-capacity' output in the UK.

Questions and exercises

1. The following figures show that in the period 1973–7 many countries, including the UK, experienced sharp falls in their rates of growth in output per employee.

	Real GDP per employee (per cent annual growth)		*Output per man-hour in manufacturing (per cent annual growth)*	
	1960–73	*1973–7*	*1960–73*	*1973–8*
USA	2.1	0.3	3.2	1.7
Canada	2.4	0.5	4.6	2.5
Japan	8.8	2.7	10.0	3.5
Italy	5.8	−0.2	7.2	2.6
UK	2.6	0.4	3.9	0.2

Use the analysis of this chapter to suggest possible explanations.

2. 'The production function $Y = TK^{\alpha}N^{1-\alpha}$ assumes that the rate of technical progress is independent of the rate of capital accumulation. This is absurd.' Discuss these statements.

3. In a group of firms which employed business consultants the average increase in net productivity achieved, as a result of their advice, was of the order of 50 per cent. Does this surprise you? What light, if any, does it throw upon the production function used in the text?

4. One reason for using the production function $Y = TK^{\alpha}N^{1-\alpha}$ is that, if each factor is paid its marginal product, the shares of the factors are invariant at α and $1-\alpha$. Is this marginal productivity assumption reasonable?

5. How 'stable' *is* the share of labour? Use the Blue Book to calculate the share of labour for each year from 1950 to 1980. Plot your results on a graph. Is there a trend? Is the share 'stable'? What is the estimated value of $1 - \alpha$?

6. Look at the data in question 1, and add a measure of unemployment in each country. Does this help you to suggest reasons for the sharp decline in growth rates?

7. The following hypothetical data are observed for the economy of Erewhon. What is the production function? What results would we get if we assumed it was of the form $Y = TK^{\alpha}N^{1-\alpha}$?

Year	*Y*	*Capital stock (K)*	*Employed persons (N)*	*Wage bill*	*Profits*
t	350	500	100	175	175
t+1	356	520	96	178	178
t+2	355	530	90	177.5	177.5
t+3	357	534	90	178.5	178.5
t+4	365	540	95	182.5	182.5
t+5	375	550	100	187.5	187.5
t+6	390	560	110	195	195

8. In question 7, which assumption in our earlier analysis must be abandoned? Why? What is your estimate of the average propensity to save? How do you obtain it?

9. 'The present preoccupation with economic growth is simply a fashion. If people were aware of the economic and social costs of growing faster the fashion would be very shortlived indeed.' Discuss in the light of (i) our earlier analysis; (ii) the costs of pollution; (iii) your own social preferences.

10. 'The so-called "technical progress coefficient" we derive from assuming a production function and applying it to observed data is really nothing more than a measure of our ignorance.' Elucidate and appraise.

11. 'The Soviet Union is a major industrial power today only because its planners imposed immense privations on its people during the interwar years.' Explain.

12. How would you attempt to measure 'labour productivity'? What relation is there between this concept and 'output per man employed'? In what circumstances, if any, is the latter a proper indicator of the former?

13. How would you expect output per man-hour to behave

    (a) in a *recession* which is generally expected to be temporary?
    (b) in a *recession* which it is feared will persist for some years?
    (c) in a cyclical expansion from a cyclical trough?

    Give your reasons and compare your predictions with UK experience.

14. 'The rate of growth of *capacity* output, since it depends on net investment, must depend upon the rate of growth of *actual* output. It therefore depends upon demand as well as supply considerations.' Elucidate and appraise.

15. Critically examine the assumptions underlying our method of estimating the rate of growth of capacity output.

16. 'If businessmen expected the UK economy to grow faster, they would act in such a way as to ensure that it did.' Elucidate. Do you agree?

17. 'Whatever one does with the figures, the UK comes close to the bottom of the international growth league.' Is this so? If it is, how would you seek to explain it (i) in terms of the analysis of this chapter; (ii) in other terms? Are your explanations testable?

18. 'In most UK industries the least efficient firm is only about one-quarter as efficient as the most efficient.' If this is correct, what does it suggest about the process and rate of innovation and what policy measures might bring about an increase in it?

19. 'If unemployment in the UK were to rise to 10 million, inefficient managers and workers would be unemployed and inefficient firms would be bankrupt. Output per person employed would therefore be much higher than it is now observed to be. But this would not necessarily indicate any increase in productivity.' Elucidate and appraise.

Suggested reading

*E. F. Denison, *The Sources of Economic Growth in the United States and the Alternatives Before Us* (Brookings Institute, 1962).

E. F. Denison, *Why Growth Rates Differ: Postwar Experience in Nine Western Countries* (Brookings Institute, 1967).

E.F. Denison, 'Effects of Selected Changes in the Institutional and Human Environment upon Output per Unit of Input,' *US Survey of Current Business* (January 1978).

E. F. Denison, 'Explanations for Declining Productivity Growth', *US Survey of Current Business* (August 1979).

E. F. Denison, *Accounting for Slower Growth: the United States in the 1970s* (Brookings Institute, 1980).

* More advanced reference.

J. C. R. Dow, *The Management of the British Economy* (Cambridge University Press, 1964) particularly chs 14–16.

W. A. H. Godley and J. R. Shepherd, 'Long-Term Growth and Short-Term Policy', *NIESR Review* (August 1964).

A. Maddison, *Economic Growth in the West* (Allen & Unwin, 1964).

A. Maddison, 'How Fast can Britain Grow?', *Lloyds Bank Review*, no. 79 (January 1966).

NIESR, 'Policies for Faster Growth', *NIESR Review* (February 1962).

NIESR, Special Issue on Britain's Comparative Productivity, *NIESR Review* (August 1982).

D. C. Paige, 'Economic Growth: the Last Hundred Years', *NIESR Review*, no. 16 (1961).

Chapter 20
Fluctuations in Economic Activity

In Chapter 19 we developed an account of the process whereby, over the long run, the capacity of the economy to produce output grows. In this chapter we consider why, as a matter of observation, the growth path followed by the economy involves *fluctuations* in the extent to which, in any given year, the *available capacity* is utilised. The problem of economic *fluctuations* is often discussed under the heading of the theory of economic *cycles*. What then is a cycle?

In Chapter 6 we defined a *cycle as a repeated wavelike movement in the value of any economic variable over time*. Most economic series when plotted against time exhibit such movements. The cycles, however, are not regular, i.e. their *periodicity* – the length of time over which they repeat themselves – is not constant. Nor do the individual series move in step. Nevertheless the wavelike movements exhibit a sufficient degree of regularity to make it reasonable to speak of 'cycles'.

In this chapter we shall be concerned only with cycles in *macroeconomic variables*. Microeconomic variables such as the output of new houses, pigs, machine-tools and many others also display cyclical fluctuations and these variables sometimes display a pattern of fluctuations dissimilar to that of the macroeconomic concepts.

In Figure 20.1 are plotted quarterly estimates of real gross domestic product in the UK. Through the resultant curve is drawn a dotted line *gg* representing the long-term rate of growth in gross domestic product. This we call the 'trend', which passes through the data for 1955–6. Clearly output exhibits considerable fluctuations around its 'trend' *gg*. In short, there is a cycle in gross domestic product. This in some periods, for example the year 1959, rises *faster* than the trend, while in others, for example 1956–8, it either rises more *slowly* or even, as in 1951–2 and 1979–81, actually *falls*. Obviously whenever output grows *faster* than the trend rate of increase in capacity, the proportion of capacity employed *rises*. It follows, therefore, as indeed was noted in Chapters 6 and 19, that fluctuations in the output of the UK economy *around its rising trend* can be viewed as fluctuations in the proportion of productive capacity employed. Since the theory which we developed in Chapters 8–12 argued that aggregate output would adjust, up to the limit of 'full capacity', to aggregate demand, it is clear that, to explain why cycles of this kind occur, we need to explain why aggregate demand fluctuates over time. In short, we have to try to explain the determinants

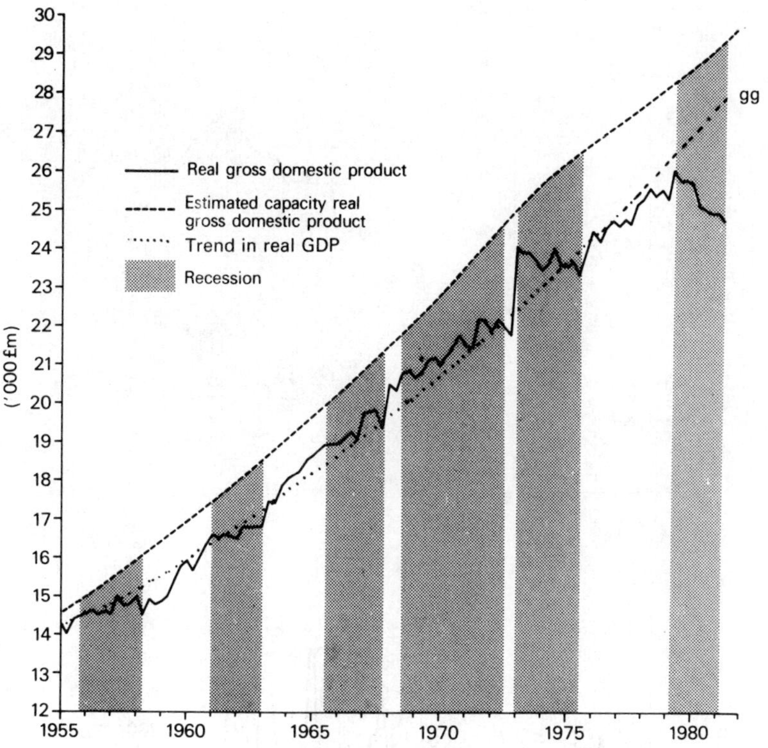

Source: *Economic Trends,* Annual Supplements.

Figure 20.1 Real GDP, trend and estimated 'capacity'

of the *time rates of change* of such variables as consumption, investment, exports, imports and government expenditure. Our earlier analysis was *static* and *timeless* and sought to explain only the equilibrium levels of these variables. Hence in this chapter we need to develop our theory in a *dynamic* way – that is, in a way which *essentially and explicitly involves time.*

In Figure 20.2 we have again plotted the behaviour of consumption, gross investment in fixed capital, investment in inventories, exports and imports.[1] The reader should recall that though these series too exhibit fluctuations, the timing and form of these do not correspond at all precisely to the fluctuations in gross domestic product. In some cases the fluctuations are more marked. In others they are less. Fluctuation, however, is general.

The terminology of fluctuations

In order to discuss cycles in economic activity we need a terminology in which to do so. This terminology is a matter of choice. But if we do not adopt one we run the risk of confused description from which can come only a confused and confusing analysis.

[1] The figure is substantially an expansion of Figure 6.7.

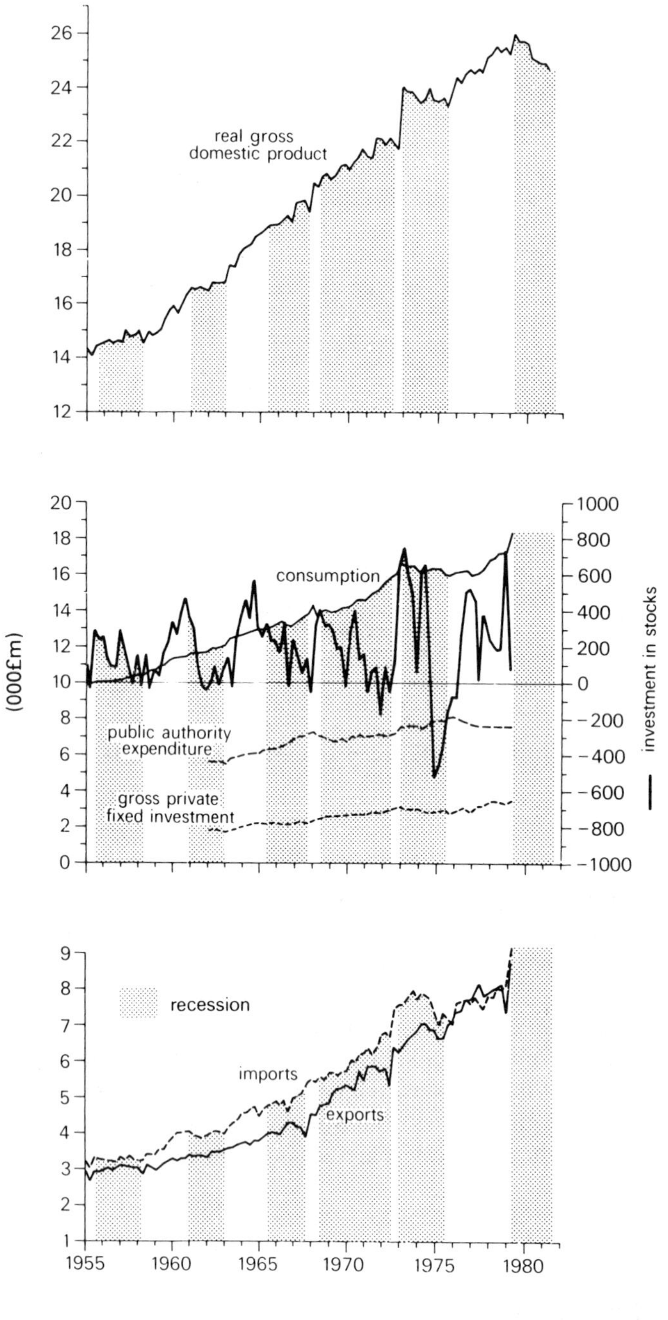

Source: *Economic Trends*, Annual Supplements.

Figure 20.2 Expenditures on GDP

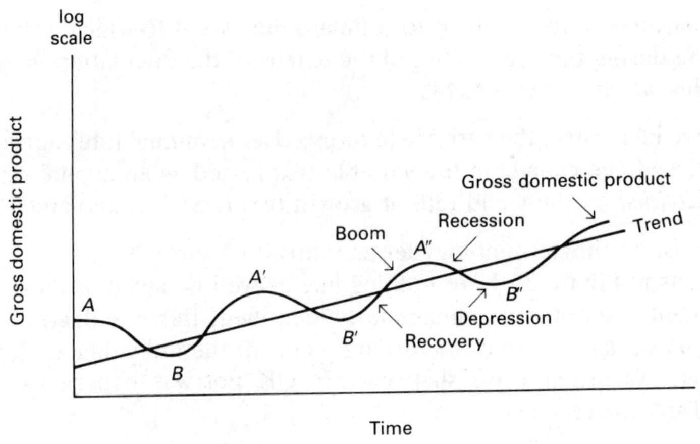

Figure 20.3 'Ideal' cycle in gross domestic product around a rising trend

In Figure 20.3 is set out an 'ideal' cycle in gross domestic product around a rising trend. This cycle we divide into two main *phases:*

(a) the *upswing* – in which output rises *faster* than the trend and, as a result, the proportion of capacity employed is *rising*
(b) the *downswing* – in which output rises *more slowly* than the trend and, as a result, the proportion of capacity employed is *falling*

The reader should notice that output may not fall absolutely in the *downswing*; it may not even cease to rise. What falls is the *proporton of capacity employed.* At some point the upswing ceases and becomes a downswing. This we call:

(c) the *upper turning-point* – represented by points A, A' and A'' on the graph

Equally, at some point the downswing ceases and becomes an upswing. This we call:

(d) the *lower turning-point* – represented by points B, B' and B'' on the graph

A single cycle runs from upper turning-point to upper turning-point (or lower to lower). The time taken for this cycle we call:

(e) the *length* or *periodicity of the cycle* – this is represented by the distances AA', $A'A''$, BB', $B'B''$ on the graph

Notice that, as we have constructed our Figure 20.3 the periodicity of the cycle is constant. In practice, as Figures 20.1 and 20.2 make clear, the periodicity of economic fluctuations is *not* regular.

There are a number of other terms commonly used to describe economic fluctuations which are not always given precise meanings. Such terms are: *recovery, boom, recession, depression.* In terms of Figure 20.3 we define these as follows:

(f) *recovery* – that part of the upswing below the trend
(g) *boom* – that part of the upswing above the trend
(h) *recession* – that part of the downswing above the trend
(i) *depression* – that part of the downswing below the trend

Finally, we need a concept to enable us to compare the extent to which different economic variables fluctuate during the cycle. We call the extent of the fluctuation in any time series its *amplitude*. This we shall measure by:

(j) the percentage increase in the variable (expressed as an annual rate) during the upswing *minus* the percentage change in the variable (expressed as an annual rate) during the downswing *divided* by the trend rate of growth (expressed as an annual rate)

To illustrate the use of this terminology let us return to Figure 20.1.

The observations in Figure 20.1 are nothing like as well behaved as those of our 'ideal' cycle. Turning-points cannot be unambiguously identified. In some degree, therefore, we must take arbitrary decisions about the turning-points of the individual cycles in real gross domestic product. Accordingly we shall classify UK postwar experience as we did in Chapter 6 (see Table 20.1).[1]

Table 20.1 Approximate cycle datings*

Peak	Trough
1951III	1952III
1955IV	1958II
1961I	1963I
1965III	1967IV
1968III	1972III
1973I	1975III
1979II	1981II

*Based on real GDP deviations from logarithmic trend.
Source: *Economic Trends*, Annual Supplements.

On the basis of this classification it seems that the UK economy by 1972 had (i) completed five cycles, while (ii) the periodicity of the completed cycles varied between 15 and 23 quarters, i.e. roughly 4–6 years.

It is worth noticing that while the upper turning-points of cycles 1 and 2 lay near the 'full capacity' growth line, that of cycle 3 did not. Moroever, in terms of the proportion of the unused (or excess) capacity they represent, the lower turning-points in cycle 2 and possibly cycle 3 are lower than the corresponding turning-point of cycle 1.[2] Booms are not proceeding as far as they did and depressions are going rather further. Finally it seems, as the reader can confirm, that the *amplitude* of the UK cycles, as we have defined it, has been tending to increase.

The postwar cycles in UK economic activity are of course a great deal less severe than those experienced in the interwar years. The cycle, however, has obviously not disappeared. It therefore requires explanation. What does a theory of cyclical fluctuations need to provide?

First, any such theory must explain why, at some point, a cumulative upward movement begins. Second, it must explain why, at some point, the cumulative upward movement ceases and in some cases (e.g. 1951, 1955 and 1979) reverses itself.

[1] The reader is invited to identify the turning-points of cycles since 1971 and to compare these datings and his or her own estimates with those set out in *Economic Trends* and in *NIESR Review*, no. 98 (November 1981) table 1.

[2] This is, as the reader should check, even more marked with the lower turning-points of cycles 5 and 6.

Elements of cycle theory

According to our static theory of aggregate demand, the principal elements in demand independent of the level of income (output) are (i) investment; (ii) exports; (iii) government expenditure. It is these elements which, given stable propensities to consume and import, the money supply, the two liquidity functions, the money wage rate and the production function, determine the equilibrium level of output. This suggests that it is likely to be *fluctuations* in these elements – or some of them – to which we must look to explain fluctuations in output.

According to our analysis, the rate of real planned investment depends upon the rate of interest and the schedule of the marginal efficiency of investment. As a matter of observation (cf. Chapter 10) the *amplitude* of investment fluctuations is very severe. Since interest rates change comparatively little in the cycle, while the response of planned investment to changes in the rate of interest is probably rather small (and slow) severe fluctuations in investment can only be explained, in terms of our theory, by cyclical shifts in the schedule of the marginal efficiency of investment – to the right in upswings, to the left in downswings. Why should such shifts occur?

In developing our theory of investment we emphasised the subjective nature of the schedule of the marginal efficiency of investment. In particular we pointed out that the position of the schedule depended upon (i) businessmen's *expectations* (which could be optimistic or pessimistic); and (ii) businessmen's *uncertainty* regarding their expectations. One possible explanation of fluctuations in planned investment over the cycle thus runs in terms of expectations and uncertainty. Suppose, for example, the economy starts upwards from its lower turning-point as a result, let us say, of an expansionary government budget. Since, by assumption, there is plenty of spare capacity, output and employment expand. The multiplier operates and a cumulative recovery begins. This tends to raise profits, to make businessmen more optimistic and to reduce their uncertainty regarding prospects over, say, the next two or three years. In these circumstances it seems entirely plausible that the MEI schedule should shift to the right. If it does, investment increases, thus adding the effect of the investment multiplier to the budget multiplier. And this may further increase investment by producing greater optimism and reducing uncertainty.

In upswings, output expands faster than capacity. In the early stages, when excess capacity is present, the additional output can be produced from the capacity already in existence. As expansion proceeds, and excess capacity is reduced, businessmen need to increase their capacity by undertaking investment. This takes two forms. First, there is investment in fixed capital such as factory buildings, plant and equipment. Second, there is investment in inventories which must be increased, as output rises, if the process of production is to proceed smoothly.

Thus to our *expectational* (or psychological) explanation of fluctuations in investment we can add a second or *capacity* element which is primarily technical in character. These two elements provide a plausible explanation of why, once a recovery has started, it will be fed and sustained by an expansion of investment in fixed capital and in stocks. The result is a cumulative process of expansion – the upswing – which proceeds from recovery to boom.

The pattern of investment behaviour explains the cumulative process of expansion. It does not, however, explain why expansion ceases and possibly gives way to contraction. Why should expectations reverse themselves? Why should businessmen suddenly plan to reduce the rate at which they add to capacity? A theory which seeks to answer these questions is set out in later sections. In the meantime, however, we need simply note that if investment behaves as we suggest, the cumulative upswing and the cumulative downswing are not hard to understand. The awkward problems are the turning-points.

What part do exports play in explaining the cycle? Our exports are part of other countries' imports and, as we saw in Chapter 14, these depend on the incomes of other countries. Hence if the incomes of *other countries fluctuate*, so will their demand for our exports. This will bring our export multiplier into operation (see Chapter 14). It follows that the existence of international trade is a means of transmitting the cyclical fluctuations of the rest of the world to Britain and, via our demand for imports (the exports of the rest of the world), our cyclical fluctuations to the rest of the world.

During the latter half of the nineteenth century, and during the first four decades of the twentieth, there is evidence to suggest that cyclical movements in exports were probably the major element in generating cycles in British economic activity. In the postwar period this evidence is much less marked. Domestic investment is now the dominant element in the cyclical process, though, since investment usually starts to rise *after* the upswing has begun, it is clear that the cyclical fluctuation of investment cannot easily explain the lower turning-point.

This brief sketch of the generation of cyclical fluctuations leaves us with three problems to explain:

1. Why does an upswing halt?
2. Why does it reverse itself?
3. Why do recoveries begin?

The dynamic theory of investment: the accelerator hypothesis

In this section we develop with more precision, and in more formal terms, the *capacity* element in the dynamic theory of investment sketched in the previous section.

Consider a businessman who produces, and has produced for many years, 10,000 pairs of shoes. To produce these shoes he requires 10 machines. One machine wears out each year and each year is replaced by an identical machine. See Table 20.2.

Table 20.2

Year	Total output (pairs of shoes)	Total no. of machines required	Annual capital depreciation (in terms of machines)	Gross investment (in terms of machines)	Net investment (in terms of machines)
1	10,000	10	1	1	0
4	10,000	10	1	1	0
7	11,000	11	1	2	1
8	11,000	11	1	1	0

Suppose now that in year 7 the demand for shoes rises to 11,000 pairs. In the very short run the businessman may satisfy this demand by using his existing 10 machines more intensively – say by working double shifts. By assumption, however, to maximise profits at an output of 10,000 pairs he requires 10 machines. Hence to maximise profits with an output of 11,000 pairs he requires 11 machines.

If he adds the new machine he undertakes *net investment* of one machine. As a result we have (i) a doubling of *gross* investment; and (ii) an increase in *net* investment from zero to one machine. Suppose now demand remains at 11,000. The businessman has adjusted his stock of machines completely to this output. He has no need for further machines. Hence net investment falls to zero: gross investment falls to the one machine required for replacement. It follows from this simple example that the level of *net* investment depends upon the *change in output*. When output is rising net investment is positive. When output is constant net investment is zero.

Let us now generalise this argument to the economy as a whole. We begin with the assumption that the desired (because most profitable) stock of fixed capital bears a fixed relation to output. Formally:

$$K^* = \alpha Y \tag{20.1}$$

where

- K^* is the desired stock of fixed capital
- Y is annual output
- α is the (average) ratio of K^* to Y and the marginal ratio of $\Delta K^*/\Delta Y$

Now let Y_t and Y_{t-1} stand for output in years t and $t-1$ and K^*_t and K^*_{t-1} stand for desired capital at the end of years t and $t-1$. We have:

$$K^*_{t-1} = \alpha Y_{t-1} \tag{20.2}$$

$$K^*_t \quad = \alpha Y_t \tag{20.2a}$$

whence:

$$K^*_t - K^*_{t-1} = \alpha(Y_t - Y_{t-1}) \tag{20.2b}$$

We assume (as we did in our numerical example) that the capital stock actually in existence at the end of year $t-1$ (which we call K_{t-1}) was optimally adjusted to the output of that period. It follows that:

$$K_{t-1} = K^*_{t-1} \tag{20.2c}$$

and:

$$K^*_t - K_{t-1} = \alpha(Y_t - Y_{t-1}) \tag{20.2d}$$

This tells us that the desired capital stock for year t will exceed the capital stock in existence at the end of the previous year by an amount which depends upon (i) the capital/output ratio α; and (ii) the change in output between the two years.

Now to bring the actual capital stock to the desired level – raise K_{t-1} to K^*_t – businessmen will undertake net investment. How much will they undertake in the year? This depends upon the *speed* at which they adjust the capital stock. Hence we can write, more generally:

$$I_t = \lambda\alpha(Y_t - Y_{t-1}) \tag{20.2e}$$

where:

I_t ≡ net investment in year t
λ ≡ a coefficient measuring the *speed of response* (with $0 < \lambda \leqslant 1$)
$\lambda\alpha$ ≡ the accelerator coefficient, which we shall call V

In our numerical example $K_{t-1} = 10$ and $K^*_t = 11$ for $Y_t = 11{,}000$;

$$Y_{t-1} = 10{,}000 \text{ and } \alpha \frac{K}{Y} = \frac{1}{1000}$$

so that:

$$I_t = \lambda \frac{1}{1000} (11{,}000 - 10{,}000) \tag{20.2en}$$

Since we argued that net investment would be *one* machine, we made, in our numerical example, the special assumption that λ was unity. That is, that the shoe manufacturer's speed of response was such that he adjusted his capital stock *completely* during a single year. This may – or may not – be the case. It is commonly assumed,[1] with the result that the accelerator theory is often written:

$$I_t = \alpha(Y_t - Y_{t-1})$$

which gives it a rather narrow technical interpretation and obscures the element of time response completely. We shall write it:

$$I_t = V(Y_t - Y_{t-1}) \tag{20.2f}$$

where:

$$V \equiv \lambda\alpha$$

so that V, our accelerator coefficient, depends upon two elements:

α ≡ the optimum (most profitable) capital/annual output ratio
λ ≡ the speed with which businessmen seek to adjust actual capital to the optimum

The implications of this version of the *capacity* theory of investment are important. First, *net* investment determined by the accelerator will be positive if, and only if, output is *rising*. Second, *net* investment will *fall* if *the rate at which output is rising* declines. Third, *net* investment (due to the accelerator) will be *zero* if output is *constant*. Fourth, *net* investment will be negative if output is *falling*.

So far we have interpreted this *accelerator* theory only in relation to investment in fixed capital. It can, however, readily be adapted to the task of explaining investment in inventories. To do this we introduce the assumption that businessmen seek to maintain stocks in a fixed ratio to output. Thus we have:

$$S^*_t = \alpha'(Y) \tag{20.2g}$$

[1] For ease of exposition we shall adopt this assumption in our formal examples.

where:

$S^*_t \equiv$ the desired (optimal) level of stocks
$\alpha' \equiv$ the desired (optimal) ratio of stocks to output
$Y \equiv$ output

The formal structure of the argument is then identical with that already put forward. It yields:

$$I_{st} = V'(Y_t - Y_{t-1}) \tag{20.2h}$$

where:

$I_{st} \equiv$ net investment in inventories
$V' \equiv$ the (inventory) accelerator coefficient

In the UK the ratio of stocks to gross domestic product (at annual rates) is about 0.4. Since businessmen probably plan to adjust stocks fairly quickly, the speed of response coefficient is probably close to unity. Hence V' may, with some degree of plausibility, be thought of as being about 0.4.

Adding the two components of accelerator net investment we obtain:

$$I_t + I_{st} = (V + V')(Y_t - Y_{t-1}) \tag{22.2i}$$

for the sum of accelerator investment. This, simply because it is investment *induced* by the change in output, is often called *induced investment.* Naturally enough *some* net investment is only very loosely related to changes in output. This is the case with very long-range investment. It is also likely to be the case with investment aimed at the production of new products. Net investment which is not induced in this way we call *autonomous.* This we shall write as H.

Our complete investment hypothesis may now be written as:

$$\begin{aligned}(\text{gross investment})_t &\equiv (\text{net investment})_t + (\text{replacement})_t \\ &\equiv H_t + I_t + I_{st} + R_t \\ &\equiv H_t + (V + V')(Y_t - Y_{t-1}) + R_t\end{aligned} \tag{20.2j}$$

where R_t depends upon the proportion of the capital stock requiring replacement in any year. Since R_t probably changes only slowly, it follows that it is the induced component plus any changes in autonomous investment due to changes in business expectations which, on our hypothesis, explains the cyclical fluctuations in gross investment.

The impact of the *accelerator* may best be seen by combining it with the simple multiplier. To do this we take autonomous investment and replacement as constant and specify the following model:[1]

$$\begin{aligned}
R_t &= \bar{R} \text{ for all periods} & \bar{R} &= 20 \\
H_t &= \bar{H} \text{ for periods } t,\ t-1, \text{ and } t-2 & \bar{H} &= 30 \\
H_t &= \hat{H} \text{ for periods } t+1 \text{ and thereafter} & \hat{H} &= 40 \\
I_t &= V(Y_{t-1} - Y_{t-2}) + H_t + R_t & V &= 0.8 \\
C_t &= A + cY_{t-1} & A &= 100.\ c = 0.5
\end{aligned}$$

[1] Notice that this model contains a *consumption lag* and no output lag.

Two points are worth noticing about this model. First, we have made *induced investment* (I_t) depend upon the *past* change in output rather than the current change. This is probably more realistic. Second, we have assumed that households base their current expenditure on consumption on the *last* period's income.

We can now write down the equation for gross output as:

$$Y_t = A + cY_{t-1} + V(Y_{t-1} - Y_{t-2}) + R_t + H_t \tag{20.2k}$$

In equilibrium, by definition, output is constant. Hence $Y_t = Y_{t-1} = Y_{t-2}$. Call the *initial* equilibrium level $\bar{Y}_1$. We obtain, on substituting this into 20.2k:

$$\bar{Y}_1 = A + c\bar{Y}_1 + V(\bar{Y}_1 - \bar{Y}_1) + \bar{R} + \bar{H} \tag{20.2ka}$$

$$\bar{Y}_1 = (A + \bar{R} + \bar{H})\frac{1}{1-c}$$

$$= (100 + 20 + 30)\frac{1}{1 - 0.5}$$

$$= 300$$

In the new equilibrium ($\bar{Y}_2$) we have:

$$\bar{Y}_2 = A + c\bar{Y}_2 + V(\bar{Y}_2 - \bar{Y}_2) + \bar{R} + \hat{H} \tag{20.2kb}$$

$$= (A + \bar{R} + \hat{H})\frac{1}{1-c}$$

$$= (100 + 20 + 40)\frac{1}{1-0.5}$$

$$= 320$$

Two points emerge from this elementary substitution. They are:

(a) the *equilibrium* levels of output are unaffected by the accelerator
(b) the *change* in equilibrium levels is given by the simple static multiplier with which we became fully familiar in Chapter 9

To illustrate the *dynamic* behaviour of the system – how it moves over time – the simplest procedure is to construct a table (see Table 20.3). Examination of this table brings out a number of points:

1. On our assumptions the system moves to its new equilibrium by a series of fluctuations.
2. The movement begins with an upswing which lasts until period $t + 4$. But, as the rate at which output rises during this upswing falls away, as it does by period $t + 3$, the rate of induced investment begins to fall, as it does in period $t + 4$.
3. This fall in induced investment itself slows the rise in output, and by period $t + 5$ causes output actually to fall.
4. By period ? the fall has been checked and output has once again started upwards.[1]

The reader should also notice that although net investment depends upon output via the accelerator relation, its induced component nevertheless begins to fall *before* output. This is, of course, because it depends not on the *level* of output but its *rate of change*.

[1] You should calculate the period for yourself.

Table 20.3 Dynamic multiplier and accelerator

Period	Income Y	Planned consumption C_p	Replacement R	Gross investment: Autonomous H	Gross investment: Accelerator induced $I = V(Y_{t-1} - Y_{t-2})$	Planned saving S_p	Actual saving S_A
t	300	250	20	30	Nil	50	50
$t+1$	310	250	20	40	Nil	50	60
$t+2$	323	255	20	40	8	55	68
$t+3$	309.9	261.5	20	40	10 4	61.5	70.4
$t+4$	333.07	265.95	20	40	7.12	65.95	67.12
$t+5$	327.47	266.585	20	40	0.936	66.435	60.936
$t+6$			20	40			
$t+7$			20	40			
$t+8$			20	40			
$t+9$							
$t+10$							
⋮							
$t+n$	320	260	20	40	Nil	60	60

Date: $\frac{\partial C_p}{\partial Y} \equiv C = 0.5;\ V = 0.8.$

Assumptions: (i) constant prices; (ii) constant interest rates.

Note: The reader is invited to work out period $t+6$, $t+7$, $t+8$ from the equation:
$Y_{t+6} = A + cY_{t+5} + \bar{R} + \hat{H} + V(Y_{t+5} - Y_{t+4})$

This table demonstrates that a model which contains *both* the multiplier and the accelerator may generate quite realistic cycles. Thus the accelerator–multiplier model *can* explain why, if output starts on an upswing, it will reach an upper turning-point and why, if it starts on a downswing, it will eventually turn up – that is, reach a lower turning-point.

The results in Table 20.3 depend, however, upon the particular values we have selected for the marginal propensity to consume ($c = 0.5$) and the accelerator coefficient ($V = 0.8$). Both these values are probably on the low side. Suppose we take a more realistic value for V. What would happen?

V is, as we have shown, the (marginal) capital/output ratio. If this is equal to the average ratio, a plausible guess would put its numerical value between 3.0 and 4.0, say 3.5. Retaining all our other assumptions unchanged, how does the model behave now? We can easily construct a table to show (Table 20.4).

A glance at this table shows that the system now behaves very differently. The system starts upwards, as before, in period $t+1$. But it never turns down. In short it rises without limit, or, as the same point is usually put, it *explodes. Notice also that the two models differ only in their dynamic behaviour for the static equilibria described by both are identical.*

In fact, with our basic equation (20.2) there are a number of possible dynamic paths of output. Which is relevant depends on the values of c (the marginal propensity to consume) and V (the accelerator coefficient). The possibilities can be classified as follows:

1. Damped fluctuations ultimately converging to new equilibrium (Table 20.3).
2. Explosion with fluctuations *never* converging to new equilibrium (Table 20.4).
3. Constant fluctuations around new equilibrium *never* converging to new equilibrium (Figure 20.4).
4. No fluctuations: smooth convergence ultimately reaching new equilibrium (Figure 20.4).
5. Explosive fluctuations *never* reaching new equilibrium (Figure 20.4).

Table 20.4 Dynamic multiplier and accelerator

				Gross investment				
Period	Income Y	Planned consumption C_p	Replacement R	Autonomous H	Accelerator induced $V(Y_{t-1} - Y_{t-2})$	I_p	Planned saving S_p	Actual saving S_A
t	300	250	20	30	Nil	50	50	50
$t + 1$	310	250	20	40	Nil	60	50	60
$t + 2$	345	255	20	40	30	90	55	90
$t + 3$	437.5	272.5	20	40	105	165	72.5	165
$t + 4$	652.25	318.75	20	40	277.5	333.5	118.75	333.5
$t + 5$								
$t + 6$								
$t + 7$								
$t + 8$								

Data: $\frac{\partial C_p}{\partial Y} \equiv c = 0.5;\ V = 3.0;$

Note: The reader is invited to work out periods $t + 5$, $t + 6$, $t + 7$ from the equation:
$Y_{t+5} = A + cY_{t+4} + \bar{R} + \hat{H} + V(Y_{t+4} - Y_{t+3})$

This is decidely awkward, for we can hardly suppose that the values of c and V are likely to be precisely those required to produce path 3 – the only path generating cycles of constant amplitude such as, in broad terms, we tend to observe. This makes the accelerator–multiplier model a much less satisfying explanation of the cyclical fluctuations in output, though it has its place in any full explanation. For we obviously cannot exclude values of V of the order of 3.0. And such values, when inserted into our model, make it *dynamically unstable.* It does not fluctuate (as we would like it to). Nor does it ever reach its new static equilibrium of 320. Since an *explosive* system seems, empirically, absurd, while it equally seems that empirically plausible values of V imply an explosive system, it is clear that we need to find some way of (i) putting a *ceiling* to the upswings of a *potentially* explosive system and explaining why it should ever turn down, and/or (ii) putting a *floor* to the system's downswings and explaining why it should ever turn upwards. This we shall attempt in the next section.

Before we discuss the problem of *ceilings* and *floors* we need to make one or two points about the accelerator itself.

Both in our tables and in our exposition we have given a formal and mechanical interpretation of the accelerator. Pedagogically this is permissible. The accelerator hypothesis, however, seeks to describe human behaviour. Purely mechanical interpretations should therefore be avoided. In particular the following points, glossed over in our discussion, should be kept in mind:

1. The accelerator theory is a *capacity* theory of investment. The accelerator coefficient may therefore take a lower value in recovery (where there is *ex hypothesis* considerable excess capacity in the economy) than in booms (when excess capacity is far less and still diminishing). Our model in treating V as constant may therefore seriously oversimplify matters.

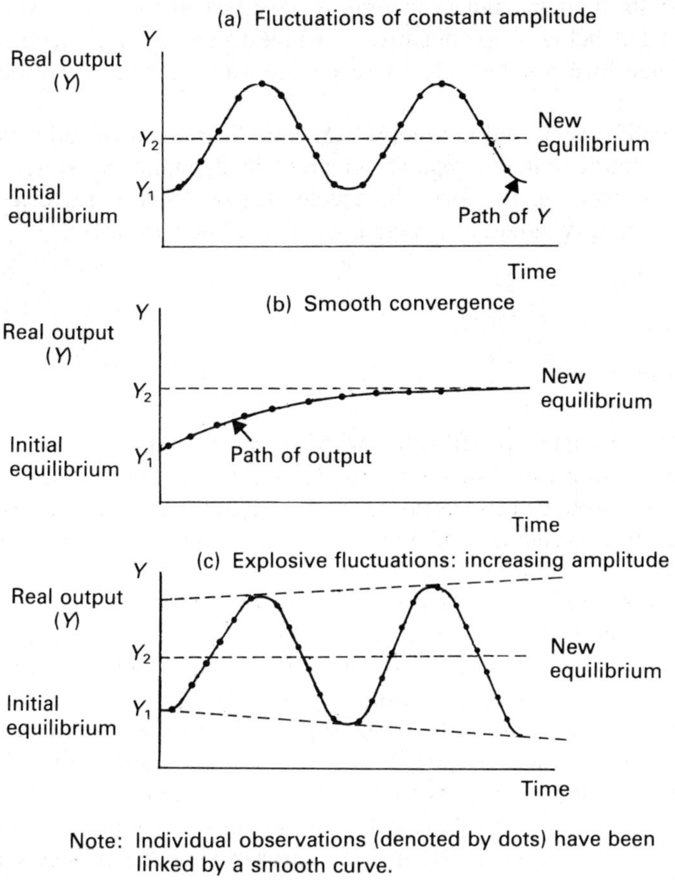

Figure 20.4 Classification of dynamic paths of output: multiplier–accelerator model

2. The accelerator theory also contains room for the influence of *expectations* and *uncertainty*. In the early stages of recovery, although businessmen may *observe* a given change in output they may not *expect* the new level of output to persist or, if they do expect it to do so, they may not be very *confident* of their expectation. Hence they may not revise their optimal capital stock (K^*) fully in accordance with the new level of output or, alternatively, may proceed cautiously in adjusting actual K to K^*.[1] Either attitude would reduce the value of V in the early stages of an upswing, a possibility of which we take no account in our table.

[1] Our tables asume λ ($\equiv$ speed of response parameter) to be a constant equal to unity. In fact λ may vary over the cycle.

3. It is obvious that gross investment in fixed capital can never be negative. This means that induced net investment, which according to the accelerator theory will be negative in the downswing if output falls, cannot exceed, in absolute value, the value of replacement investment (R_t). To put this formally we have $I_t = V(Y_{t-1} - Y_{t-2})$ in the upswing and $I_t = V(Y_{t-1} - Y_{t-2})$, provided $R_t + I_t \geqslant 0$, in the downswing.

This obvious constraint implies that, over the cycle as a whole, the accelerator may behave *asymmetrically*. In short, if the fall in income is very fast in the downswing, since gross investment cannot fall below zero, negative net investment cannot exeed R_t in absolute value, and may therefore not be able to reach the value indicated by our accelerator equation.

Despite these qualifications and the theoretical complications involved in realistic values for V, there is no doubt that the *capacity* element in dynamic investment theory is an important one. In a more flexible form the accelerator principle must form a part of any dynamic investment theory aimed at explaining cyclical fluctuations.

Ceilings and floors

In the last section we came up with the awkward problem that realistic values of the accelerator coefficient imply *explosive* systems. How can we constrain such systems?

In an upswing real output can rise as fast as it likes up to the position of 'full capacity'. At this point it has reached its *ceiling*. The maximum rate of increase then becomes the rate of increase in capacity – in the UK rather more than 3 per cent per annum.[1] This rate of increase must be less than the rate enjoyed during the upswing, for if it were not 'full capacity' would never be reached. Hence, the annual percentage increments in real output *along* the *ceiling must* be less than those in the upswing. Hence accelerator-induced investment must fall and a downswing begin.

The existence of a full-capacity ceiling thus serves two purposes in our theory. First, it explains why a theoretically explosive system cannot proceed upwards without limit. Second it explains why, if the economy attempts to 'crawl along the ceiling', it will eventually turn downwards: that is, it explains why there will be an upper turning-point. In practice, in the UK, booms are sometimes checked by official action before the ceiling is reached. This happened in 1960. A check of this kind slows the rate of growth and this, via the accelerator, reduces induced net investment and a downturn begins.

Why does the downswing not proceed for ever? What checks this? In the first place, although gross investment *can* fall to zero it is unlikely to do so, for this implies that *all* firms in the economy have zero gross investment. This is improbable. If some do not have zero gross investment, then since none can have *negative* gross investment, gross investment as a whole will be positive. Moreover, even if gross investment *does* fall to zero, there will still be a floor to income since, on our usual consumption function hypothesis, there will be some level of income so low that, for the community as a whole, all income will be consumed (i.e. $C_p = Y$). In the second place, some net investment is, in our terminology, *autonomous*: that is, it is unaffected by the recent behaviour of output. A part at least of this will continue even in depressions. Hence gross investment will not, in general, fall to

[1] Based on the experience of 1950–73.

zero in a depression but to some positive value which we may call I_{min}. It follows that, with a given consumption function, the minimum level of output is:

$$Y_{\min} = \left[I_{\min} \times \frac{1}{1-c}\right] + \left[\frac{A}{1-c}\right]$$

where $A \equiv$ autonomous consumption, and c, as usual, denotes the marginal propensity to consume.

Once Y reaches $Y_{\min}$ it ceases to fall. Hence the induced net investment due to the accelerator, which was *negative* when income was falling, *rises* to zero. As a result output rises above $Y_{\min}$ and, probably after some time lag, accelerator-induced investment becomes positive.

Thus even when the value of the accelerator coefficient implies, mathematically, an explosive system, there are good reasons for thinking that the existence of (i) a full-capacity ceiling, and (ii) a minimum level of output, will not only constrain fluctuations in a manner more in accordance with experience but also explain both the upper and lower turning-points. The plausibility of this line of reasoning is strengthened by the observation that, for example in 1960, the British authorities have intervened to check booms before they reach the ceiling and to restart growth or check recessions (1959, 1963 and 1972).

Growth and fluctuations

In this chapter, by means of a rather brief excursion into dynamics, we have sought to set out the elements of a theory which explains cyclical fluctuations in aggregate demand and thus in output and the proportion of productive capacity employed. In the previous chapter we discussed some aspects of the rate at which, in the long run, 'full-capacity' output grew over time. This separation of the related problems of growth and fluctuations is legitimate up to a point. It carries, however, a risk that the reader may unconsciously assume that the two problems are independent. To see the importance of this consider the proposition:

> *if* we could eliminate the cyclical fluctuations in output, *then* we could grow just as fast as we have done in the past

This implies that the long-term 'trend' rate of growth in capacity is entirely independent of the cyclical process. This may or may not be the case. At present economists cannot give a very confident answer one way or the other. It is *possible* that, by reducing or eliminating fluctuations, we *might* grow faster. Equally it is *possible* that we might, as a result, grow more slowly. The cycle *may* be the cost of growth; or it may not. Our discussion throws no light on this issue. Nor does it imply one answer rather than another. Two things are, however, sure. The first is that in *estimating* the long-term rate of growth in capacity we are using observations obtained from the fluctuating path followed by the UK economy. Our estimate is therefore not independent of the cycle. The second point is that the question is one of considerable practical importance, for, during the last few years, the elimination of the cycle, and the maintenance of steady, sustainable growth, at high levels of employment and capacity utilisation have been sharply downgraded as policy objectives.

The balance of payments in the cycle

So far in discussing the cycle we have virtually ignored external considerations. What is likely to happen to the balance of payments during a cycle?

Suppose aggregate demand goes through a cycle due in the main to fluctuations in gross investment. Exports, we may assume, expand throughout the cycle at a rate governed primarily by the rate of growth in output in the rest of the world. For simplicity assume this to be constant at, say, 4 per cent per annum. In the upswing of domestic output, imports will rise for two reasons. First, the rate of imports, per annum, depends upon incomes via the marginal propensity to import. This we saw in Chapter 14. Hence as the level of income rises so does the level of imports. In the second place, as output expands there will be induced investment in inventories. In the UK inventories have a significant import content – possibly of the order of 0.3 or 0.4. Hence there will be an accelerator-induced rise in imports. It follows that the import function which we developed earlier ignores some important *dynamic* elements in import demand. Instead of writing – and thinking of – our import function in the form:

$$(\text{imports})_t = F + zY_{t-1}$$

which is a dynamic version of our earlier function, we *should* write and think of a function of the form:

$$(\text{imports})_t = F + zY_{t-1} + z'V'(Y_{t-1} - Y_{t-2})$$

where:

$z \equiv$ marginal propensity to import
$z' \equiv$ marginal share of imports in inventory investment
$V' \equiv$ inventory investment accelerator coefficient

Given an import function of this form it is clear that imports are likely to rise very fast in an upswing. The rise is likely to be considerably faster than that in either gross domestic product or exports. Hence upswings in UK output are likely to be accompanied by a sharp deterioration of the balance of payments on current account.

In Figure 20.5 we have set out data for two postwar periods which lend some support to this theory.

This analysis, brief as it is, is still suggestive. It explains why UK upswings tended to cause balance-of-payments difficulties which sometimes compelled the authorities to intervene to check the boom. It also shows that one way of *temporarily* easing the external position is to halt expansion. For if the growth in output is stopped inventories cease to rise and perhaps even fall. Either way the import bill is sharply reduced and the balance of payments strengthened. This policy, which has been called, somewhat tartly, 'strength through stagnation', was essentially that of Mr Selwyn Lloyd in 1961–2 and Mr Callaghan in 1966–7. It was, of course, a temporary expedient and no more. For once a further upswing began, as it did in early 1963, the mechanism began again to operate, the import bill rose sharply and external difficulties reappeared, as they did for example in 1964 and 1965, and in 1972.

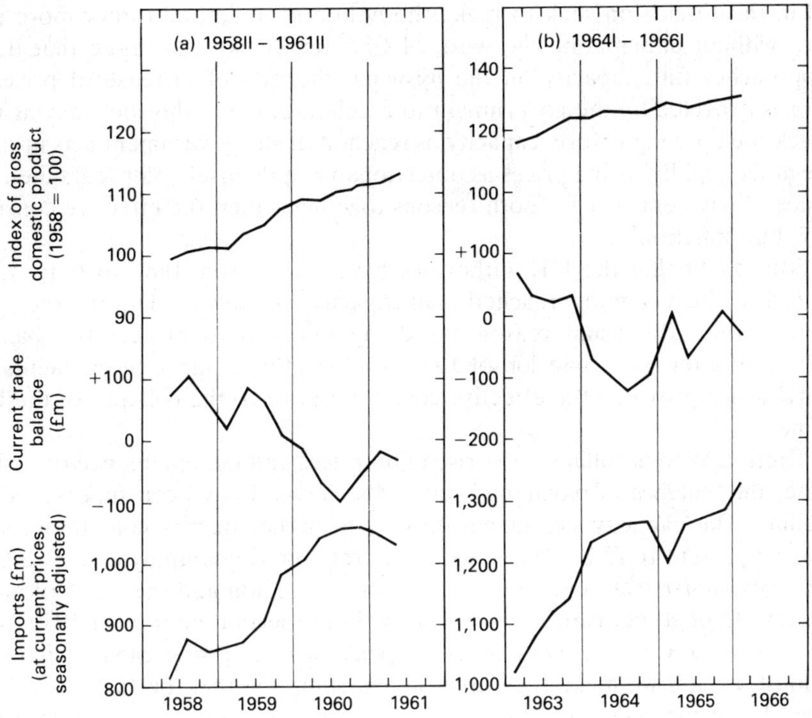

Source: index gross domestic product – *National Institute Economic Review* (November 1967); current trade balance (£m) – *Economic Trends* (September 1967) imports (£m) – *Economic Trends* (September 1967).

Figure 20.5 Imports and the current balance in two UK expansions

More about the ceiling and its impact on policy

In our rather formal discussion of the cycle we have sketched a theory which (i) regards the dynamic structure of the economic system as *explosive*, but (ii) *constrains* the system within a 'ceiling' and a 'floor'. Hitherto we have interpreted the upper constraint as being the 'capacity' of the economy to produce output. However, once we admit the possibility of official intervention, 'capacity' becomes only one of a number of possible upper constraints. We must now ask, with the UK economy particularly in mind, is 'capacity' the relevant upper constraint?

The first alternative upper constraint may, rather loosely, be referred to as the 'balance-of-payments' constraint. If, as we argued in the previous section, the UK's current-account balance, and indeed overall balance, on external account deteriorates sharply in upswings, the government may, in order to protect the country's overseas reserves and preserve the rate of exchange, intervene to check the upswing of the cycle *before* full capacity is reached. In such a case it is *not* the 'capacity' constraint which is effective but the 'balance-of-payments' constraint.

The second possible upper constraint may be thought of, again rather loosely, as the 'inflation' constraint. We shall discuss the problem of rising prices more fully in the next chapter and in this discussion seek to make the notion of 'inflation' rather more precise. Nevertheless, without anticipating the work of Chapter 21, we can argue that if, as the economy approaches full 'capacity' in the upswing, the rate of increase of prices *either* accelerates *or* is expected by the government to accelerate, the authorities may again take action to check the upswing before 'capacity' is reached. If the government acts in this way, because it regards 'rapidly' rising prices as objectionable in themselves or fears their impact on the balance of payments (or for both reasons together), then the effective constraint is *not* 'capacity' but 'inflation'.

There is little doubt that the UK authorities have acted, from time to time, to check expansions *before* the economy reached 'full-capacity' operation. During the 'pegged' exchange-rate period, the usual reason for doing this was to protect the balance of payments. Indeed, after the expansion of 1958–9, it was the 'balance of payments' rather than 'capacity' which provided the effective constraint prior to the collapse of the Bretton Woods regime.

Since the Bretton Woods collapse, the rise in oil prices and the emergence of a 'floating' exchange rate, the 'balance-of-payments' ceiling has increasingly been superseded by the 'inflation' ceiling. The 'capacity' ceiling has thus not been the effective constraint for nearly two decades. At present (end-1982), for example, registered unemployment (which, on a comparative basis, *understates* unemployment) is over 3 million and the index of industrial production some 15 or so per cent *below* its 'peak' in the second quarter of 1979. Since its level then was only about 3½ per cent *above* its 'peak' in 1973, excess capacity in industrial production must, even if we make the implausible assumption that the 1973 'peak' defined 'full capacity', be of the order of 20 per cent or more. Nevertheless, the authorities are continuing to follow a restrictive policy, defending this decision primarily in terms of controlling inflation and being applauded by many – perhaps most – commentators for doing so. There could be no better demonstration of the dominance of the 'inflation ceiling'.

Typically, until the early or mid-1970s, UK governments attempted to control the economy by what were rather generally accepted macroeconomic policies so as to:

(a) reduce the amplitude of 'cyclical' fluctuations
(b) contain expansions before they seriously infringed the 'balance-of-payments' constraint

This was essentially a short-run anti-cyclical stabilisation policy aimed at moving the economy, over time, as smoothly as possible along the line *bb* in Figure 20.6.

The long-run objective of the authorities was to ensure that:

(c) *bb* and *pp* grew at the same rate as *ff* (i.e. had the same slope on Figure 20.6)
(d) *pp* and *bb* were, in any period, as least as great as *ff* so that the economy could grow along the 'capacity' growth path

Stabilisation involves managing aggregate demand countercyclically. This means *reducing* demand in the later stages of the upswing (as the economy approaches *bb*) and *stimulating* demand in downswings. Clearly this raises difficult problems of *timing*. If restraint is imposed too late, the downswing may be made steeper. Conversely, if demand is stimulated too late, the expansion may become unmanageably fast.

The road to instability is paved with good intentions. We know, in quantitative dynamic terms, far less about the economy than we would like and probably far less than we think we know. As a result, using the full benefit of hindsight, even during the relatively very successful years from 1948 to 1973, it is not hard to find periods in which the authorities made errors in both the timing and magnitude of their 'anti-cyclical' policies. Thus the

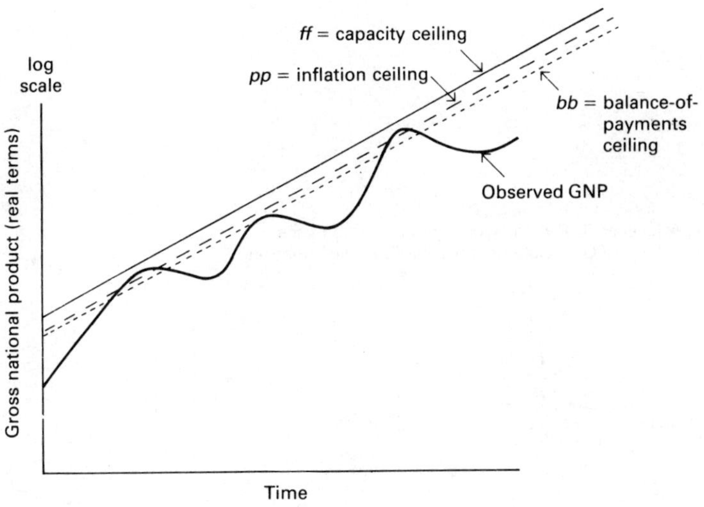

Figure 20.6 The growth cycle: schematic presentation

observed cycle in UK output, for this period, may appear as it does partly because of errors in macroeconomic policy.

Since the mid-1970s, stabilisation has been of considerably smaller importance in the authorities' plans. The policy horizon has become *medium term* rather than *short run* as a consequence. And the dominant constraint has typically been the authorities' beliefs regarding the *pp* curve – which, it appears, has since 1973–4 fallen fairly sharply in relation to both the *bb* and *ff* curves, even though, since 1976, the former has probably declined fairly sharply in relation to the latter simply because of the emergence of an overvalued pound sterling.

We might illustrate the contemporary position in terms of our *ff, bb* and *pp* lines as in Figure 20.7. Here *bb* has fallen in relation to *ff* because of the rapid deterioration in the UK's 'competitiveness' since 1976. Similarly *pp* has shifted downwards, for reasons which are not yet fully understood, because a given rate of growth in prices seems now to be compatible with a much lower level of 'capacity utilisation' than was formerly the case. The dominant constraint is now provided by *pp* and, in the *medium term* , the economy is expected to grow along some path like *pp* (that is, with a low level of 'capacity utilisation': perhaps 2.7–3.4 million unemployed) and well below *bb* – which implies a current-account surplus. Ultimately, it is hoped (and believed) that by keeping within a fairly stringent inflation ceiling, *pp* will shift upwards towards *bb*. The problem would then be to raise *bb* – and a *pp* of 'acceptable' slope – closer to *ff*.

The wisdom (or otherwise) of this shift in the approach to policy clearly depends very much on how inflation is to be explained. Accordingly, we discuss the problem of inflation in the next chapter. It is, however, worth noting that if our theory of the cycle has any merit it may be difficult to keep the economy growing along a path such as *pp* rather than declining into a fairly deep depression. This risk becomes the greater, the more that other countries follow similar policies for similar reasons.

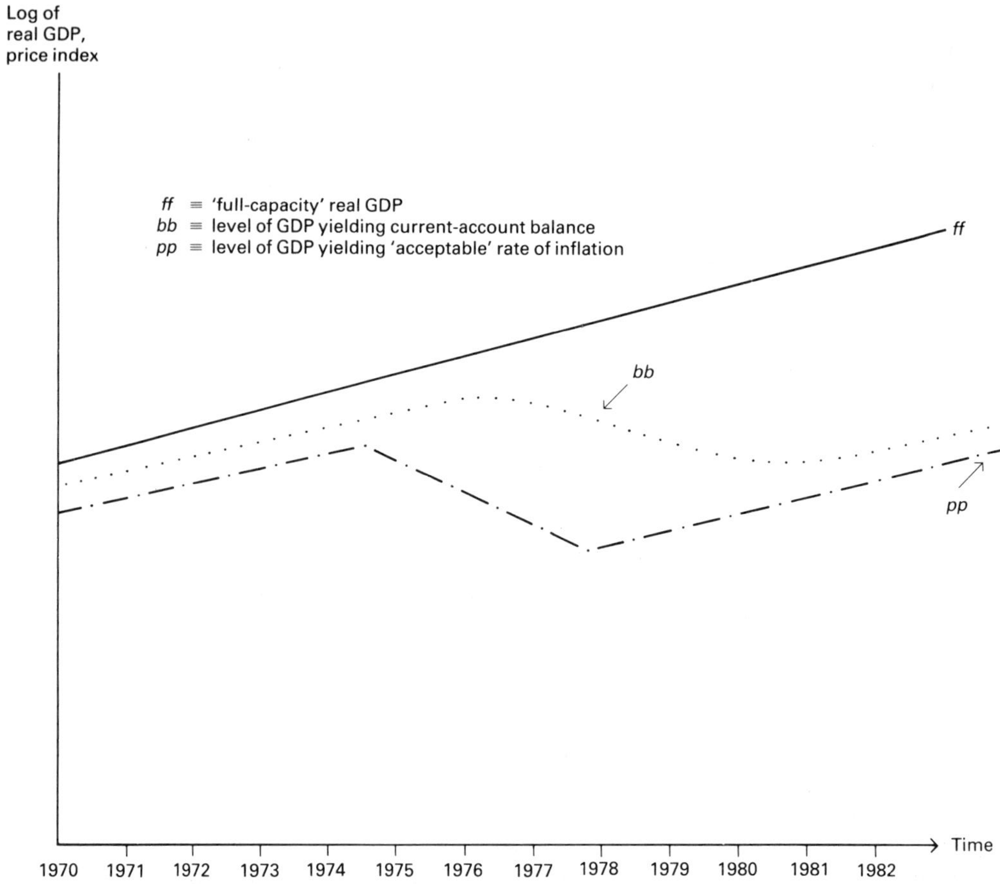

Note: schematic illustration not to scale

Figure 20.7 UK macroeconomic policy and the changing constraints

Summary

The aim of this chapter has been to explain why 'mixed-capitalist' economies in general, and the UK in particular, experience fluctuations in the level of economic activity which may, rather loosely, be termed 'cyclical'. To do this we sketched a dynamic theory of investment based, in large measure, upon the accelerator hypothesis. Since the accelerator hypothesis suggested an unstable economic system we found reasons for thinking that the fluctuations of the system were constrained by (i) the ceiling of 'full-capacity' growth, and (ii) the floor provided by a minimum level of output. In discussing the accelerator hypothesis we provided an illustration of the distinction between dynamic and static economic models, for although both our accelerator models (of Tables 20.3 and 20.4) yielded identical static equilibrium results, the first model (with $V = 0.8$) was *stable* while the second (with $V = 3.0$) was *unstable*. From this it is possible to deduce that a wide range of dynamic models, with differing *dynamic* behaviour, nevertheless yield the *same equilibrium results*. From this it may be inferred that the *comparative static* method of analysis employed in earlier chapters is valid if, and only if, the model being discussed is *dynamically stable*. Then, because it is a matter of great importance to the UK, we examined the likely behaviour of the balance of payments on current account during the cycle and developed a dynamic import function. This led us to postulate a 'balance-of-payments' constraint. The main analysis was conducted in real terms and assumed constant prices and interest rates.

Questions and exercises

1. Interpret the following two models. Give a verbal explanation of each equation.

Model I	Model II
$Y_t = C_t + I_t$	$Y_t = C_t + I_t$
$C_t = A + cY_{t-1}$	$C_t = A + cY_t$
$I_t = H_t + R_t + v(Y_t - Y_{t-1})$	$I_t = H_t + R_t + v(Y_{t-1} - Y_{t-2})$

   Using the values of c, v, H_t, R_t given in the text construct tables showing the behaviour of both systems from periods t to $t + 8$. What are the static equilibria of the two systems? Do they differ? Are both systems stable?

2. 'The accelerator coefficient is simply the marginal capital/output ratio.' Do you agree? If not, why not?

3. 'Since the accelerator depends on the ratio K/Y, while K is a *stock* independent of the length of the period for which Y (which is a *flow*) is defined, the accelerator coefficient with respect to monthly income is *four times* as large as the accelerator with respect to annual income. It is therefore meaningless to talk of stability in terms of the accelerator coefficient.' Examine this view.

4. How would you attempt to test the accelerator hypothesis? Write down a function for investment in fixed capital incorporating the accelerator hypothesis and any other hypotheses which seems to you to be worth investigating.

5. Plot on a graph the quarterly figures for real investment in inventories in the UK from 1957 to 1980. What difficulties are there in interpreting this series? Is it consistent with the hypothesis that businessmen seek to maintain a constant ratio of stock to output? What leads you to take your view? (Use data from *Economic Trends*.)

6. 'Booms in investment in fixed capital reflect waves of innovation. Hence if there were no investment booms there would be no technical progress.' Do you agree?

7. In the market for peanuts we have (i) a relation between the quantity demanded and price of the form $Q_t^D = A + bP_t$ where $b < 0$; and (ii) a relation between the quantity supplied and price of the form $Q_t^S = Z + gP_{t-1}$, where $g > 0$, $P(t) \equiv$ price in period t.

   Find the equilibrium price in terms of A, Z, g and b. Since the equilibrium price must be positive what must be the sign of $A - Z$, and what does this mean in economic terms?

   Assign numerical values to A, b, Z and g and plot the resulting demand and supply curves on a graph. Assume that, in some period $t = 0$ price departs from equilibrium. Trace out the subsequent movements of price and quantity. Is your system stable? What is the economic interpretation of the lag between supply and price?

8. 'In the UK, investment turns up after output and turns down after output has flattened out.' Is this so? If it is, what kind of investment theory does it suggest? What starts UK expansions and what stops them?

9. 'Observed investment in stocks consists of both planned and unplanned elements. Since we can never identify these two components we can never hope to test any theory of planned investment in inventories.' Do you agree? Can you suggest any way of estimating unplanned inventory accumulaton?

10. 'The desired ratio of stocks to output must, if businessmen are rational, depend significantly upon the cost of borrowing.' Explain. If this is so, what implications has it for our inventory accelerator?

11. Assume that $K_t{}^*$ (the desired level of inventories at the end of period t) responds both to output (Y_t) and the rate of interest (r_t) so that:

$$K_t{}^* = f(Y_t, r_t)$$

Assume further that planned investment in inventories in period t (I_{pt}) depends upon the difference between the inventories desired at the end of the period t ($K_t{}^*$) and actual inventories at the end of period $t - 1$ (K_{t-1}) so that:

$$I_{pt} = \lambda(K_t{}^* - K_{t-1})$$

Unplanned inventory accumulation (I_{ut}) is simply the difference between output in period t (Y_t) and demand in period t (D_t) so that:

$$I_{ut} = Y_t - D_t$$

Since businessmen adjust output to expected demand D^* we have

$$I_{pt} + I_{ut} \equiv \text{observed investment in inventories}$$

$$\equiv \lambda(K_t{}^* - K_{t-1}) + D_t{}^* - D_t$$

(a) Which of these variables are observable?
(b) What is the meaning of λ?
(c) Can you offer an explanation of $D_t{}^*$ in terms of observable variables? (*Hint*: refer to the beer production model of Chapter 2.)

In the light of your answers reconsider questions 9 and 10.

12. What is meant by 'autonomous' investment? What kinds of investment do you think are likely to fall into this category? If you can think of none, does this mean that you think that all investment is 'induced'?

13. 'The electorate must realise that – as a nation – we can no longer spare the productive resources necessary to provide an efficient Health Service' (Election Address, 1982). Critically evaluate this contention with special reference to (i) the cyclical position of the economy, and (ii) the concept of 'scarcity' it implies.

14. Examine Figure 20.6 carefully. On what assumptions are the slopes of the *pp* and *bb* lines the same as those of the *ff* line? Do you consider these assumptions realistic?

15. 'In terms of industrial output excluding the North Sea we must, by now, be operating at at least x per cent *below* full capacity. In terms of manufacturing production the position is probably marginally worse; and in terms of GDP marginally better.' Calculate the percentage of excess capacity in each area in the UK in the first half of 1982. Explain and defend your methods.

16. 'UK governments in their attempts to manage demand invariably intervene too late and usually intervene too sharply.' Examine the record of the last four UK Chancellors and seek to establish or refute this contention.

17. Compare the *dynamic* investment theory of pages 364–72 with the theory advanced in Chapter 10. Can you reconcile the two approaches? What difficulties do you meet in making a reconciliation? Is the accelerator coefficient a function of the interest rate? If so, why?

18. It is stated in the text that V ($\equiv$ the accelerator coefficient) is equal to the marginal capital/output ratio. On what assumptions is this correct? In the text what unstated assumption is being made about the value of λ ($\equiv$ speed of response)? What is the relation between V and $\partial Y/\partial K$?

19. 'The case for the devaluation of sterling is stronger the greater the gap between the *ff* line and the *bb* line of Figure 20.6.' Elucidate.

20. Reconstruct Figure 20.1 for the period 1960–80. Date the 'peaks' and 'troughs' of the cycles and construct a curve of 'full-capacity' growth. Compare your datings with those given in *NIESR Review*, no. 98 (November 1981). Explain and defend your method of constructing the 'full-capacity' growth curve and compare your estimates of 'excess capacity' with those given in the *NIESR Review.*

21. Use the theory of the production function to relate the coefficient α of equation 20.1 to the marginal product of capital ($\partial Y/\partial K$).

22. To the model of 20.2k (p. 368) add the hypothesis of an output lag such that:

$$Y_t = D_{t-1}$$
$$D_{t-1} \equiv C_{t-1} + I_{t-1} + H_{t-1} + R_{t-1}$$

Construct a revised version of Table 20.3. Does it modify the general conclusions derived from Table 20.3? If so, how and why?

Suggested reading

F. R. Brechling and J. N. Wolfe, 'The End of Stop–Go', *Lloyds Bank Review* 1965).

J. C. R. Dow, *The Management of the British Economy, 1945–60* (Cambridge University Press, 1964) chs 14–15.

*G. Haberler, *Prosperity and Depression* (United Nations, 1946) introduction, chs 1, 8.

P. N. Junankar, *Investment: Theories and Evidence* (Macmillan, 1972) chs 3, 6.

J. M. Keynes, *The General Theory of Employment, Interest and Money* (Macmillan, 1936) ch. 22.

R. C. O. Matthews, *The Trade Cycle* (Cambridge University Press, 1959) particularly chs 1–3.

NIESR, 'The British Economy in the Medium Term', *NIESR Review,* no. 98 (November 1981).

* More advanced reference.

Chapter 21
Rising Prices and Inflation

Thus far our discussion of the problem of prices in our macroeconomic model has had two principal characteristics. It has been:

(a) *highly aggregative*, in that we have discussed only a single domestic price referred to as 'the' price of output
(b) *static*, in the sense that we have been concerned with the determination of the equilibrium *level* of prices

Throughout the rest of this book we shall continue to retain the assumption of a single domestic price: that is, we shall continue to proceed as in (a) a procedure which implicitly takes output to be single homogeneous commodity.

However, in attempting to analyse the problem of inflation, we *must abandon static analysis since, by definition, inflation – which is the rate of change of prices – is a concept which essentially involves time and thus requires a dynamic theory rather than a static theory of the price level.*

To fix our ideas, we now define:

$$\frac{p(t)-p(t-1)}{p(t-1)} \times 100 \equiv \frac{\Delta p(t)}{p(t-1)} \times 100 \equiv \dot{p}(t) \equiv \text{percentage rate of inflation}$$

where $p \equiv$ the price level, and (t), $(t-1)$ are the periods of calender time to which the observations are applicable. The general form of this relationship is:

$$\frac{X(t) - X(t-1)}{X(t-1)} \times 100 \equiv \frac{\Delta X(t)}{X(t-1)} \times 100 \equiv \dot{x}(t) \equiv \text{percentage rate of change in } X \quad (21.1)$$

and this is a form we shall apply in later sections of this chapter.

Armed with this notation we now proceed to develop the theory of inflation.

Inflation and market behaviour

Inflation, by definition, is the process of price increase. The obvious point of departure, therefore, in any attempt to explain the experience reviewed earlier, is to ask in what circumstances prices will rise. Clearly this depends upon the way prices get determined. And this, in its turn, depends upon the nature of the markets involved.

There is of course an immense diversity in market forms, from the organised commodity markets in, say, tea, coffee, tin and rubber – which approximate to continuous competitive trading in a homogeneous commodity – to, say, the housing market – which has very different characteristics. Doing, regrettably, rather serious violence to reality, we ignore this diversity and regard markets as falling into only two types, both of which can be thought of as limiting cases. These are:

(a) markets in which prices are said to be *flexible*, meaning that prices change if and only if excess demand (supply) exists
(b) markets in which prices are *not flexible* in this sense but change if and only if *either* costs change, *or* businessmen, in setting prices, change the 'mark-up' they apply to costs

In the first case we say that prices are *flexible*; in the second we say that they are *cost-determined*. In practice many prices are partly *flexible* and partly *cost-determined* so that the logical distinction between the two processes is, commonly, empirically blurred. For expositional purposes we shall ignore this and continue to treat them as limiting cases.

The *flexible* price case is illustrated in Figure 21.1, which depicts the demand and supply curves for peanuts. Here *DD* is the demand curve; *SS* is the supply curve and p_0 the equilibrium price.

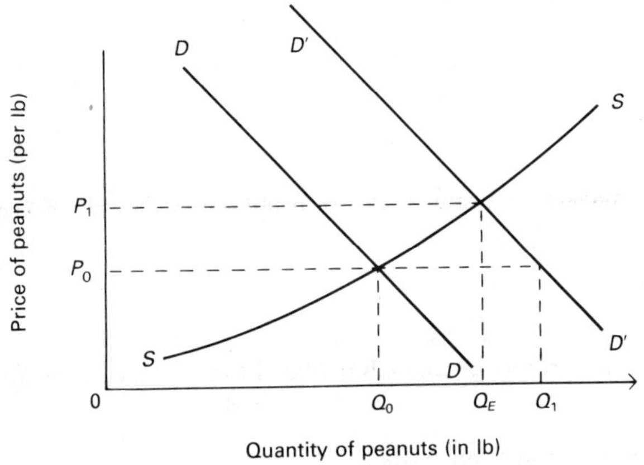

Figure 21.1 The market for peanuts

Suppose now that the demand curve shifts to $D'D'$. At p_0 the quantity demanded is Q_1 and the quantity supplied is Q_0. Hence there is *excess demand* (in quantity terms) of Q_0Q_1 and, in value terms, of $p_0\,(Q_0Q_1)$. It is now assumed that prices are bid up in the market and that firms expand output so that the new equilibrium is reached at p_1Q_E.

How fast will prices rise? This depends upon the *dynamic characteristics* of the theory which we have not yet specified. One simple hypothesis is that the rate of price increase (in proportionate terms) depends upon the proportion of excess demand to total supply.

Formally this can be written:

$$\frac{p(t) - p(t-1)}{p(t-1)} = f\left(\frac{D - S}{S}\right) \quad \left(\text{with } \Delta p(t) \gtrless 0 \text{ if } D - S \gtrless 0\right) \tag{21.2}$$

where $D \equiv$ quantity *demanded*, and S that *supplied* at the initial market price in period $t-1$.

This hypothesis is shown in Figure 21.2 on the simplifying assumptions that the function in 21.2 is both linear and symmetric in the sense that price responds to *excess supply* in the same way (with sign reversed) as it responds to *excess demand*. These assumptions are not necessarily realistic.

Thus Figures 21.1 and 21.2 illustrate a market in which:

(a) prices rise (fall) if and only if excess demand (supply) is present
(b) the proportionate (or percentage) rate of changes of prices is a linear function of excess demand (supply) in the market

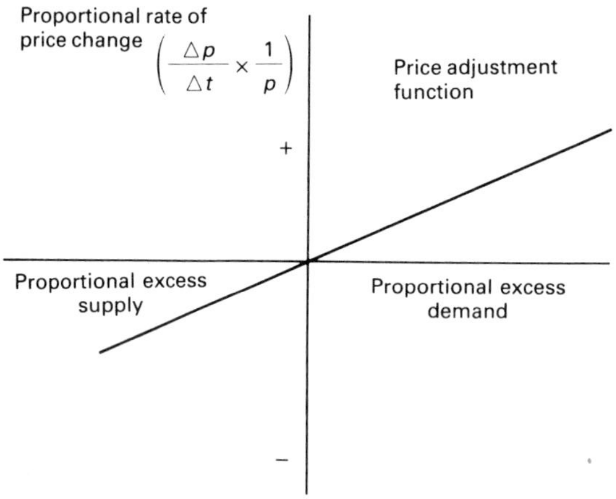

Figure 21.2 The market for peanuts: excess demand and the rate of price change

Analogously, strict interpretation of what we have called *cost-determined* pricing requires:

(a) prices to be set by a 'mark-up' on costs
(b) the 'mark-up' itself to be independent of the excess demand/supply in the market over a relatively wide range of market situations

Formally we have:

$$p = c(1 + q) \tag{21.3}$$

where $c \equiv$ costs per unit of output, and $q \equiv$ proportionate 'mark-up' set by businessmen, so that it becomes obvious that prices can change if and only if either costs ($\equiv c$) or the mark-up ($\equiv q$) changes.

What are 'costs'? In the simplest case we may regard costs as consisting in:

(a) labour costs
(b) the costs of inputs obtained from abroad

so that:

(c) costs are the (appropriately weighted) sum of labour costs and import costs

By labour costs we mean, of course, labour costs per unit of output so that if $W \equiv$ nominal wage cost per worker and $X \equiv$ output per worker then:

$$\text{the proportionate rate of change in wage costs} \equiv \frac{\Delta W(t)}{W(t-1)} - \frac{\Delta X(t)}{X(t-1)}$$

$$\text{the percentage rate of change in wage costs} \equiv \left(\frac{\Delta W(t)}{W(t-1)} - \frac{\Delta X(t)}{X(t-1)}\right) \times 100 \equiv \dot{w} - \dot{x} \qquad (21.4)$$

Thus if prices are cost-determined, the proportionate rate of change of prices is given by:

$$\frac{\Delta p(t)}{p(t-1)} = \frac{\Delta W(t)}{W(t-1)} - \frac{\Delta X(t)}{X(t-1)} + \frac{\Delta q(t)}{1+q(t-1)} \qquad (21.5)$$

for an economy which does *not* engage in international trade – and by the following extension where it does:

$$\frac{\Delta p(t)}{p(t-1)} = \pi\left(\frac{\Delta W(t)}{W(t-1)} - \frac{\Delta X(t)}{X(t-1)}\right) + (1-\pi)\frac{\Delta p_m}{p_m(t-1)} + \frac{\Delta q(t)}{1+q(t-1)} \qquad (21.6)$$

where $p_m \equiv$ price of imports in domestic currency, $\pi \equiv$ weight of wage costs in total costs, and $0 < \pi < 1$. Clearly 21.5 simply assumes $\pi = 1$.

Which of our two very simple models of price determination is the more plausible? We now think of our economy as containing *two* highly aggregative markets: one for goods, and one labour. Typically, in developed and highly industrialised economies of the Western type, it is plausible to regard prices as cost-determined rather than flexible. We thus have *two* possible market structures:

	Method of price formation	
	Goods market	*Labour market*
Type 1	Cost-determined	Flexible
Type 2	Cost-determined	Cost-determined

Corresponding to those two types are two types of inflationary process. Of these, type 1 is the more realistic and it is type 1 which we shall seek to analyse. Before doing so, however, we must recall that our approach is an oversimplification since, as we remarked earlier, its classificatory scheme reflects *only two limiting forms of price determination, whereas most important markets display elements of both*.

In addition, in a trading economy (such as the UK) in which imports constitute an important input into the productive process, we need to say whether import prices are to be regarded as 'cost-determined' or 'flexible'. This is an awkward question since imports consist partly of industrial products (which typically have 'cost-determined' prices) and partly of primary products sold on organised markets (where prices are 'flexible'). The latter case is less important than it may at first appear since prices on these markets respond to *world excess demand/supply* which, as a first approximation, can be regarded as independent of the behaviour of the UK economy and thus not responsive to domestic excess demand/supply. On these arguments, import prices can be regarded as the equivalent of 'cost-determined' for any single economy (other perhaps than the USA), even though some are certainly 'flexible' from the point of view of the world economy.

Import prices, however, are determined by the exchange rate as well as the prices set by overseas producers. Hence, if the exchange rate is 'flexible' (as we have defined this concept), so too are import prices. In a full analysis this must be taken into account.

Initially, however, we ignore this complication: that is, we develop our theory of inflation in the context of a 'closed' economy in which $\pi = 1$.

An inflationary process: type 1

Since we are assuming a 'closed' economy, we know that π ($\equiv$ the weight attaching to wage costs) in 21.6 is equal to unity. In a model of type 1, prices will rise only if costs rise. And this requires *either* a rise in wage costs ($\equiv W/X$) *or* a rise in the 'mark-up' ($\equiv q$) *or* some combination of the two. In practice, the UK experience shows little or no evidence of 'mark-up' inflation. The realistic case is therefore a rise in wage costs per unit of output or, more simply, a percentage increase in money wages ($\dot{w}$) *greater* than the percentage increase in productivity ($\equiv \dot{x}$). How are we to explain this phenomenon?

For the moment, let us take the rate of growth in output per man (productivity) as given so that, in our familiar formal terms:

$$\dot{x} = \bar{\dot{x}} \tag{21.7}$$

meaning that (provisionally) $\dot{x}$ is taken to be *exogenous*. For simplicity assume $\bar{\dot{x}}$ = zero.

Now all we have to do is to explain the rate of change in money wages ($\dot{w}$) in order to explain the rate of change in wage costs.

According to our earlier assumptions, the labour market operates in accordance with our *flexible* model. Hence *money* wage earnings should rise if *excess demand* for labour is present. In formal terms we are assuming that:

$$\frac{W(t) - W(t-1)}{W(t-1)} \equiv \frac{\Delta W(t)}{W(t-1)} = f\left(\frac{N^D - N^S}{N^S}\right)_t \tag{21.8}$$

or, in percentage terms:

$$\frac{\Delta W(t)}{W(t-1)} \times \frac{100}{1} \equiv \dot{w} = f\left(\left[\frac{N^D - N^S}{N^S}\right]\frac{100}{1}\right)_t \tag{21.8a}$$

where $N^D \equiv$ quantity of labour demanded, and $N^S \equiv$ quantity of labour supplied.

Suppose now that, for whatever reason, excess demand for labour appears (i.e. $N^D - N^S > 0$). What happens?

Clearly W (≡ wage earnings per unit of labour) rise. Hence W/X (≡ wage cost of a unit of output) rises. Prices are, by assumption, cost-determined. Hence the increase in wage costs per unit of output is passed on and, since we are assuming no import costs, prices rise in the same proportion as wage costs: that is, the real wage per unit of output is unchanged.

Let us suppose that this process occurs and that, in real terms, the demand for output is, like the real wage, unaffected. Then it seems that wages – and hence prices – will continue to rise at the same rate *ad infinitum* as long as we have $N^D - N^S > 0$ and invariant, which, since we know that N^D (≡ the demand for labour by employers) is determined by the planned level of output, will be the case as long as real aggregate demand is unaltered.

Thus this model suggests that:

1. The price *level* is potentially *explosive* in the sense that if $N^D > N^S$ it will rise without limit.
2. Any rate of change of wages/prices may exist (positive or negative) according to whether excess demand is positive or negative.

We now need to ask two questions.

1. How *relevant* is a simple model of this kind?
2. What does it *implicitly assume about behaviour*?

To fix our ideas let us interpret the first of these questions to mean how realistic is it:

(a) to regard the demand for output – and hence the derived demand for labour (≡ N^D) – to be independent of the absolute level of prices and wages
(b) to treat wage/price behaviour as symmetric with respect to excess demand supply

Consider (a) first. Our static model states that the higher the price level, the higher will be the nominal demand for money (for transactions and precautionary purposes). Hence, unless the nominal money supply rises *pari passu* with the price level, the rate of interest will tend to rise, which:

(a) will *reduce* the market value of bond holdings and thus consumption
(b) via the cost of borrowing, will tend to *reduce investment*

If the nominal money supply does *not* rise with the price level, then the *real value* of money holdings must fall. Similarly, the *real value* of assets the nominal value of which is fixed in terms of the unit of account (e.g. National Savings or building society deposits) will also fall, and in the case of long-term bonds this real decline will be compounded by the fall in market value due to the increase in the interest rate. Thus the 'real-balance' effect (the fall in the real value of money holdings) is extended into a general 'wealth effect' which must be expected to reduce real planned consumption and, possibly, real planned investment.

In addition, provided income-tax allowances are not adjusted in such a way to offset its impact, 'fiscal drag' – which results because the proportion of income taken in tax is typically an increasing function of *nominal* incomes – will tend to lower real personal disposable income in relation to real personal income and thus reduce consumption.

Thus even in our simple economy, which (by assumption) does not engage in international trade, it is reasonable to argue that real aggregate demand, and hence N^D, will fall if the price level rises and hence that the rise in the price level will reduce – and ultimately eliminate – the excess demand for labour. *This means that what we have called type 1 inflation does have a stop. The existence of international trade strengthens this conclusion. In practice, however, the stop may be a long time in coming*. This is partly because, for reasons we shall review later, there is some observed tendency for the nominal money supply to adjust, at least in part, to any price increase; and partly because it may require a rather large change in prices to reduce aggregate demand (and hence $(N^D - N^S)/N^S$ to a significant extent: that is, interest cost effects and wealth effects – even supplemented by 'fiscal drag' – may be *quantitatively* rather small.

Hence, although a type 1 model will, in principle, have a *stable* price level, any inflationary process which does occur may prove to be persistent.

Now consider (b): that is, whether the response of money wage earnings to excess demand/supply is symmetrical, as we have thus far assumed.

Generally speaking, economists tend to argue that symmetry is an implausible assumption and that, in practice, money wage earnings tend to be 'sticky' downwards. This implies that our construction of Figure 21.2 is slightly misleading and should be replaced by *either* a function consisting in two linear sub-sections of unequal slope *or* by a non-linear formulation, as is done in Figure 21.3. This modification increases the descriptive realism of the theory; it does not, however, modify it in any essential way.

Once we have abandoned symmetry and extended our analysis to encompass the impact of price changes on real aggregate demand, we can regard the inflationary process of type 1 as having considerable relevance to the experience of the UK and at least some other developed Western economies. Taking this to be so, we need to press our examination of it rather further by looking harder at the behaviour implied by our wage-adjustment hypothesis (equation 21.8).

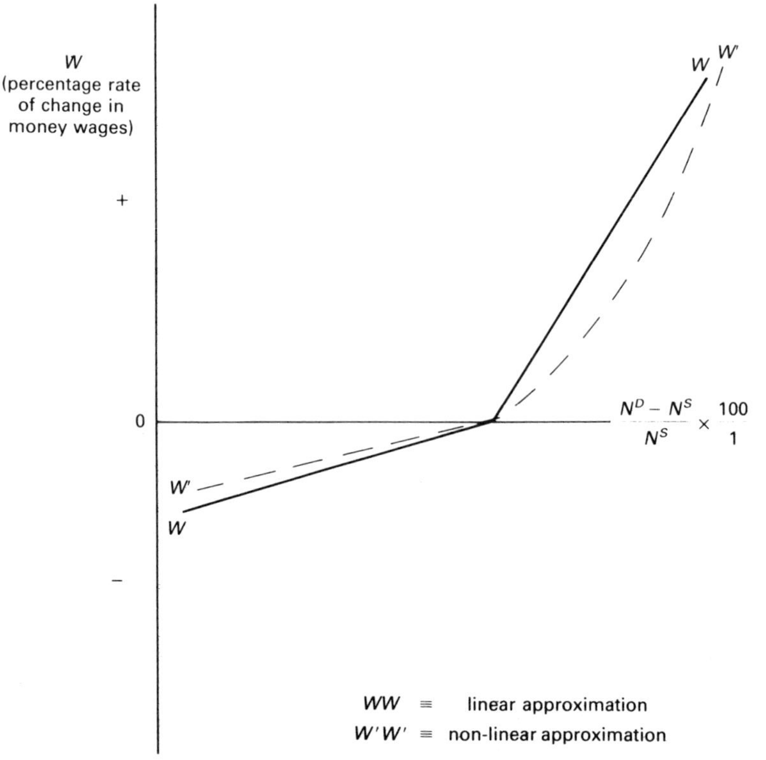

Figure 21.3 Asymmetric wage-adjustment schedules

Economic behaviour and the wage rate

Our interpretation of flexible wages has been encapsulated in:

$$\frac{\Delta W(t)}{W(t-1)} = f\left(\frac{N^D - N^S}{N^S}\right)_t \tag{21.8}$$

where are are now assuming that the functional form is probably non-linear, as in Figure 21.3. Unfortunately N^D and N^S are not directly observable. We must therefore first ask whether this fundamental part of our theory can be made meaningful by finding directly observable data which provide plausible proxies for $(N^D - N^S)/N^S$. Once this has been done the theory is testable since statistical series of wage and salary earnings are available.

One possibility would be to use the *difference* between reported job vacancies ($\equiv V$) and registered unemployed ($\equiv U$) as an index of $N^D - N^S$ and use the size of the work-force as an empirical representation of N^S. This means writing:

$$\frac{N^D - N^S}{N^S} \approx f\left(\frac{V - U}{N}\right)$$

where $N \equiv$ the work-force as usually defined.

Alternatively we can, since, empirically, $V–U$ is inversely related to U, use the level of recorded unemployment as a proxy for $N^D - N^S$ and write:

$$\frac{N^D - N^S}{N^S} \approx f\left(\frac{U}{N}\right)$$

or, reverting to the percentage formulation:

$$\left(\frac{N^D - N^S}{N^S}\right) \times 100 \approx f\left(\frac{U}{N} \times 100\right)$$

where $U/N \times 100$ is readily recognised as the percentage of the work-force unemployed and is defined as u.

Our theory is now operational since data for $\dot{w}$ and for u exist so that the hypothesis:

$$\dot{w}(t) = f[u(t)]$$

is testable by observation.

This relationship is typically thought to take the form set out in Figure 21.4. *This curve is essentially a labour-market or wage-adjustment curve*. Its slope and position reflect the behaviour of employers and employees (typically organised in unions) in negotiating wage settlements. Thus, if the curve shifts upwards or downwards, it is, *on the basis of our theory*, not possible to say whether the observed shift is to be explained by employers 'pulling' up wages harder or by employees 'pushing' up wages harder. Some additional evidence is required to justify a diagnosis of this kind. Thus, in attempting to influence (typically to lower) the position of this curve, some commentators have argued in favour of a tax on employers who grant 'inflationary' wage increases, others for policies designed to limit union claims, and still others for both.

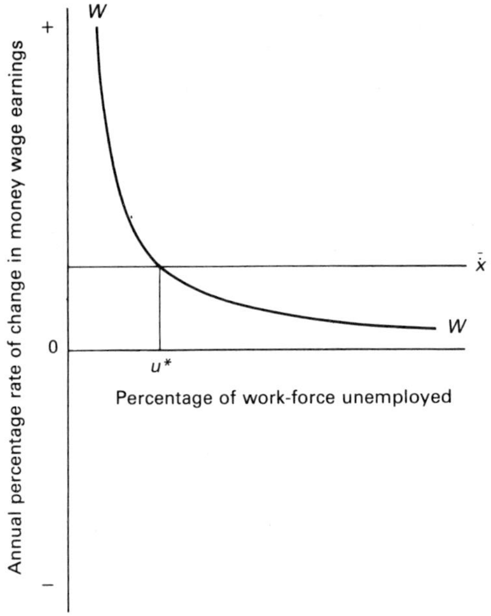

Figure 21.4 Wage-adjustment curve (hypothetical)

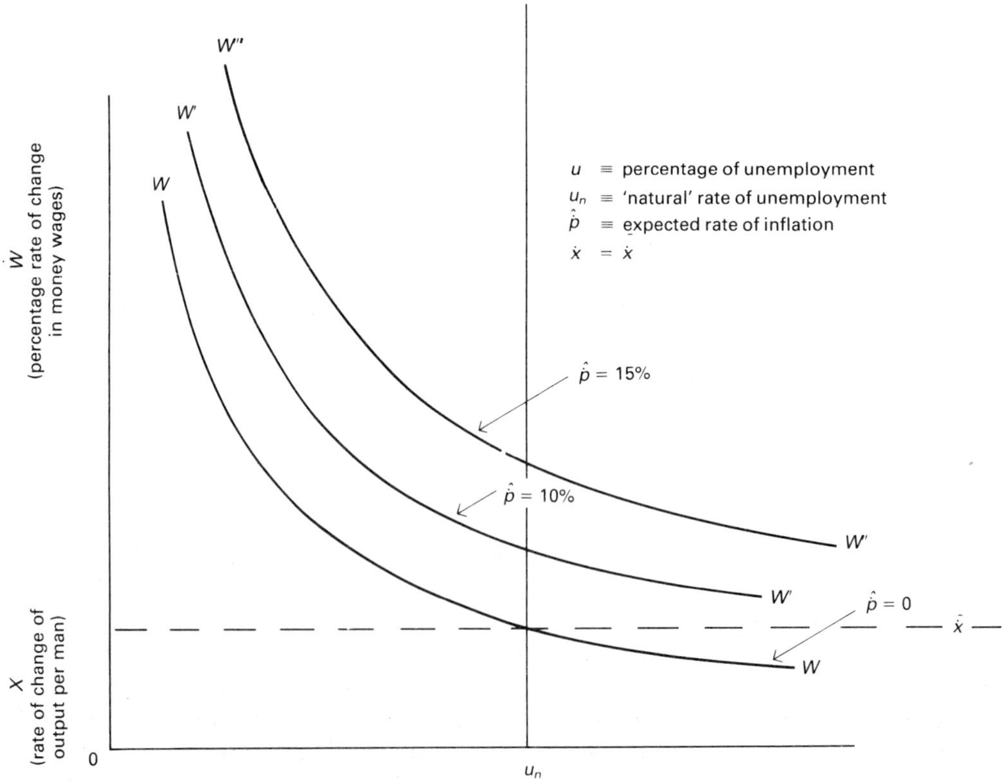

Figure 21.5 The wage-adjustment schedule and expectations of inflation

As we have constructed it, the *WW* schedule appears to make possible a 'trade-off' between the percentage of unemployment and the percentage rate of growth in wage earnings. By accepting more of the former we can have less of the latter – provided, of course, the schedule itself is stable.

Superimposed on the *WW* schedule in Figure 21.5 is a horizontal line which represents the (assumed exogenous) rate of change in productivity. Where the two schedules intersect $\dot{w} = \bar{\dot{x}}$,, so that the rate of change in wage costs per unit of output is zero. As drawn, this occurs at u^*. If $u < u^*$, $\dot{w} - \bar{\dot{x}} > 0$ (i.e. wage costs per unit of output are rising). If $u > u^*$, they are falling.

Suppose this relation to hold. Then since prices are an invariant mark-up on wage costs, $\dot{p} = \dot{w} - \bar{\dot{x}}$ and a schedule like *WW* can be constructed with $\dot{p}$ rather than $\dot{w}$ on the vertical axis. This, of course, depicts a 'trade-off' between $\dot{p}$ (≡ inflation) and the percentage of unemployment derived from the 'trade-off' depicted by the *WW* schedule.

As set out here, this rather crude theory asserts that $\dot{w}$ depends *only* on u. No other variables enter the function. Is this plausible? A moment's reflection says that it is not: for it implies that the past history of wages and prices has no influence on $\dot{w}$, in the sense that a given level of unemployment will be associated with the same rate of increase in wages where, for some time, $\dot{p} = 0$, as it would if $\dot{p}$ has been running at, say, 100 per cent. Observation says that this is absurd; and so does economic theory since it implies that neither employers nor employees have any interest in the *real wage* but suffer from a *total money illusion*.

Assume *WW* in Figure 21.5 to be the schedule relevant when, for (say) a decade or more, actual inflation has been zero. How would we construct $W'W'$ defined as the schedule which would be relevant if, for a decade or more, $\dot{p}$ had been (say) 10 per cent? In these circumstances it is reasonable to expect wage-earners to adjust their claims so as to attempt to take account of the rate of inflation *they expect to rule during the duration of the contract*. They may *not* expect 10 per cent since their forecast of inflation may *not* result simply from past experience of $\dot{p}$. It would be surprising, however, if their expected rate of inflation were not in the neighbourhood of 10 per cent. Broadly similar arguments will hold for employers since any employer will be more ready to agree to a given wage claim if he expects, say, 10 per cent inflation.

On these arguments, our simple wage hypothesis will become:

$$\dot{w} = f(u, \hat{\dot{p}}) \tag{21.9}$$

where $\hat{\dot{p}} \equiv$ the rate of inflation expected by transactors in the labour market.

It follows that inflationary expectations (i.e. $\hat{\dot{p}}$) are a parameter of any *WW* schedule the position of which depends upon (i) the level of $\hat{\dot{p}}$, and (ii) the elasticity of wage earnings (W) with respect of prices (P), which is, of course, the marginal response coefficient $\partial\hat{\dot{w}}/\partial\hat{\dot{p}}$, which we take to be positive.

Accordingly, in Figure 21.5 $W'W'$ is drawn above *WW* since the former assumes $\hat{\dot{p}} = 10$ per cent and the latter $\hat{\dot{p}} = 0$. Similarly, if $\hat{\dot{p}} = 15$ per cent the relevant wage-adjustment curve would lie above $W'W'$ at, say, $W''W''$.

Thus $\dot{w}$ depends crucially upon expectations of inflation ($\hat{\dot{p}}$). Hence inflation itself, since as we have seen, it depends upon $\dot{w}$, also depends crucially on $\hat{\dot{p}}$.

Moreover, any 'trade-off' between unemployment and the rate of inflation defined by a wage-adjustment curve is *conditional upon the invariance of the values of* $\hat{\dot{p}}$ and $\partial\dot{w}/\partial\hat{\dot{p}}$ used in its construction. If *either* of these changes, then the *WW* schedule must shift and, therefore, the initial apparent 'trade-off' become irrelevant. This implies that any 'trade-off' may be a very short-run phenomenon indeed, as we shall now demonstrate.

Expectations and the 'augmented' wage-adjustment curve

The addition of the term in $\hat{p}$ to the wage-adjustment (*WW*) schedule is commonly said to 'augment' it with an expectations variable. The influence of this variable on $\dot{w}$, however, depends on the value of $\partial\dot{w}/\partial\hat{p}$. To fix our ideas let us assume, for expositional convenience, that the rate of wage adjustment is inversely related to u and linear in $\hat{p}$, so that:

$$\dot{w} = \frac{a_0}{u} + a_1\,\hat{p} \quad \left(\frac{\partial\dot{w}}{\partial u} < 0;\ \frac{\partial\dot{w}}{\partial\hat{p}} = a_1 > 0\right) \tag{21.10}$$

Can we, on theoretical grounds, say anything about the *magnitude* of a_1?

Whatever may be true in the *short run*, sooner or later, we must expect a_1 to approach unity since workers, via their unions, seem sure to press for compensation for the $\hat{p}$ they anticipate, while employers, whose concern is with the real wage, provided they have the same value of $\hat{p}$ (i.e. employers' and workers' expectations coincide), seem likely to offer it. Hence a plausible 'long-run' hypothesis is:

$$\dot{w} = \frac{a_0}{u} + \hat{p}$$

or:

$$\dot{w} - \hat{p} = \frac{a_0}{u}$$

where $\dot{w} - \hat{p} \equiv$ percentage change in the expected real wage, $\hat{p}_w \equiv$ rate of inflation expected by workers, and $\hat{p}_e \equiv$ rate of inflation expected by employers coincide at $\hat{p}$.

In the short run a_1 may well differ from unity since $\hat{p}_w$ and $\hat{p}_e$ may *not* coincide and the outcome (and character) of recent wage bargaining may make workers (and employers) more or less 'forceful'. In the short run, therefore, the market may exhibit $a_1 < 1$.

Now consider the implications of $a_1 = 1$: that is, the 'longer-run' situation. Since:

$$\dot{w} - \hat{p} = \frac{a_0}{u}$$

it is clear that the expected rate of change of real wages is now determined by the level of unemployment (in percentage terms) or, since employment and output are related through the short-run production function, by the percentage shortfall of output ($\equiv Y$) *below* capacity output (Y_c) i.e. $(Y_c - Y)/Y_c$ per cent, sometimes called the (percentage) 'output gap'.

For the real wage settlement ($\dot{w} - \hat{p}$) emerging from the market to be validated, it is necessary for $\hat{p} = \dot{p}$. Given our theory this requires, for any value of $\hat{p}$ whatsoever, a given level of unemployment. We define this level as:

$$u_n \equiv \text{natural rate of unemployment}$$

which is sometime called, for reasons that we shall explain in a moment, the non-accelerating inflation rate (percentage of) unemployment (NAIRU). The ideas underlying this can be seen as follows. From our price-adjustment hypothesis:

$$\dot{p} = \dot{w} - \hat{x}$$

(since q = the 'mark-up' percentage is invariant), and from the 'augmented wage equation' with $a_1 = 1$:

$$\dot{w} = \frac{a_0}{u} + \hat{p}$$

so that:

$$\dot{p} = \frac{a_0}{u} + \hat{p} - \bar{\dot{x}}$$

To find u_n we set $\dot{p} = \hat{p}$ so that:

$$\dot{p} - \hat{p} = 0 = \frac{a_0}{u_n} - \bar{\dot{x}}$$

and thus:

$$u_n = \frac{a_0}{\bar{\dot{x}}}$$

that is, u_n is *smaller* the *greater* is $\bar{\dot{x}}$.

Now u_n is independent of $\dot{p}$; hence a vertical line drawn through u_n represents the 'longer run' trade-off between $\dot{p}$ and u, which obviously means that, in the 'longer run' no trade-off exists. If, in the 'longer run', the labour market is also assumed to operate so that, at u_n, everyone who wishes to work at the ruling real wage is able to do so, u_n can also be said to correspond to 'full employment' in the sense that involuntary unemployment is zero. Moreover, as our argument above shows, u_n is the only possible position of 'long-run' equilibrium in the important sense that at u_n: (i) the inflation rate is constant since $\dot{p} = \hat{p}$ at u_n, and (ii) $\dot{p}$ *can* be zero *provided it is expected to be zero* (i.e. $\hat{p} = 0$). This is because, whenever $u \neq u_n$, then $\dot{p} \neq \hat{p}$, and as a result expectations of inflation sooner or later will be revised. To see this postulate a simple rule for revising expectations such as:

$$\Delta\hat{p} = f(\dot{p} - \hat{p}) \left(\text{with } \frac{\partial(\Delta\hat{p})}{\partial(\dot{p}-\hat{p})} > 0\right)$$

Thus expectations are revised (by a fairly crude error-learning process) so that if inflation is higher (lower) than expected, expectations are revised upwards (downwards). Of course, expectations are *not necessarily revised by the whole of the error*. Moreover the revision process may be very slow. To see what this means, let us make the special assumption that the revision process is given by:

$$\hat{p}(t) - \hat{p}(t-1) = \lambda\,[\dot{p}(t-1) - \hat{p}(t-1)] \quad (\text{with } 0 < \lambda \leqslant 1) \tag{21.12}$$

with $\lambda = 1$, as a special assumption for expositional purposes so that $\hat{p}(t) = \dot{p}(t-1)$.

Suppose now $u < u_n$ and $\hat{p} = 0$. Since $u < u_n$, $\dot{w} - \hat{p} > \bar{\dot{x}}$. Hence $\dot{p} > \hat{p}$. Hence $\hat{p}$ is revised upwards. However, as long as u remains *less than* u_n, then $\dot{w} - \hat{p} > \bar{\dot{x}}$, so $\dot{p} > \hat{p}$. Hence $\hat{p}$ continually increases and so does $\dot{p}$. Thus $u < u_n$ entails *accelerating* inflation; and, by an identical argument, $u > u_n$ entails *decelerating* inflation. Hence u_n is alternatively described as NAIRU. An illustration of accelerating inflation is given in Table 21.1, where we have assumed:

u_n = 6.0 per cent
u = 4.0 per cent
$\bar{\dot{x}}$ = 3.0 per cent
$\hat{\dot{p}}(t) = \dot{p}(t-1)$, i.e. $\lambda = 1$

This discussion shows the crucial importance of inflationary expectations in the theory of inflation and how the introduction of $\hat{\dot{p}}$ into the wage-adjustment hypothesis weakens the case for the existence of a 'longer-run' trade-off between inflation and unemployment. The analysis also suggests that *reducing* the rate of inflation in circumstances in which expectations (i.e. the value of $\hat{\dot{p}}$) respond only very slowly to experience, ministerial exhortation and/or other signals may be a very costly process indeed.

Table 21.1 Expectations and the wage-adjustment curve*

			u_n = 6.0 per cent				
Period	Rate of change of productivity %	Percentage unemployment %	Rate of change of money wages %	Rate of change of wage costs %	Rate of change of prices %	Expected change in real wage %	Actual change in real wage %
0	3.0	4.0	6.0	3.0	3.0	6.0	3.0
1	3.0	4.0	9.0	6.0	6.0	6.0	3.0
2	3.0	4.0	12.0	9.0	9.0	6.0	3.0
3	3.0	4.0	15.0	12.0	12.0	6.0	3.0
4	3.0	4.0	18.0	15.0	15.0	6.0	3.0
5	3.0	4.0	21.0	18.0	18.0	6.0	3.0

*Hypothetical data.

To see the latter point suppose that the economy is operating at u_n but that, for whatever reasons, $\dot{p}$ is unacceptably high. To reduce $\dot{p}$ (i.e. to decelerate) the authorities adopt policies which raise u well above u_n, as illustrated in Figure 21.6.

In this diagram *WW* is the wage-adjustment schedule applicable to an expected rate of inflation equal to the (unacceptable) rate actually ruling. A glance back at Table 21.1 shows that, if $u > u_n$, inflation falls not only because, on *WW*, $\dot{w} - \hat{\dot{p}} < \bar{\dot{x}}$ (entailing that $\dot{p}$ falls) but also because, as $\dot{p}$ falls, so does $\hat{\dot{p}}$ – which moves us to a lower 'short-run' curve such as, say, W′W′. If expectations are very sticky ($\hat{\dot{p}}$ adjusts very slowly to reductions in $\dot{p}$, entailing positive forecasting errors) the declaration process is seriously retarded. This implies that $u > u_n$ would have to be maintained for a long time – entailing very considerable excess positive forecasting errors) the deceleration process is seriously retarded. This implies that u $\dot{p}$. Plainly, if expectations ajusted *more* rapidly, any given retardation could be attained at much lower cost in terms of involuntary unemployment and lost output. Finally, if expectations could be influenced appropriately so that $\hat{\dot{p}}$ became equal to the (lower) rate of inflation desired by the authorities ($\equiv \dot{p}^*$) immediately, *unemployment need never be raised above* u_n. These considerations are distressing since (as Chapter 6 shows) prices have been rising virtually continuously since 1935 – so that the expectation of positive and significant rates of inflation is likely to be well entrenched and thus slow to respond to short-term experience. Only people close to or beyond the age of retirement have experienced anything other than a rising price level in the UK and probably few can recall much of the experience.

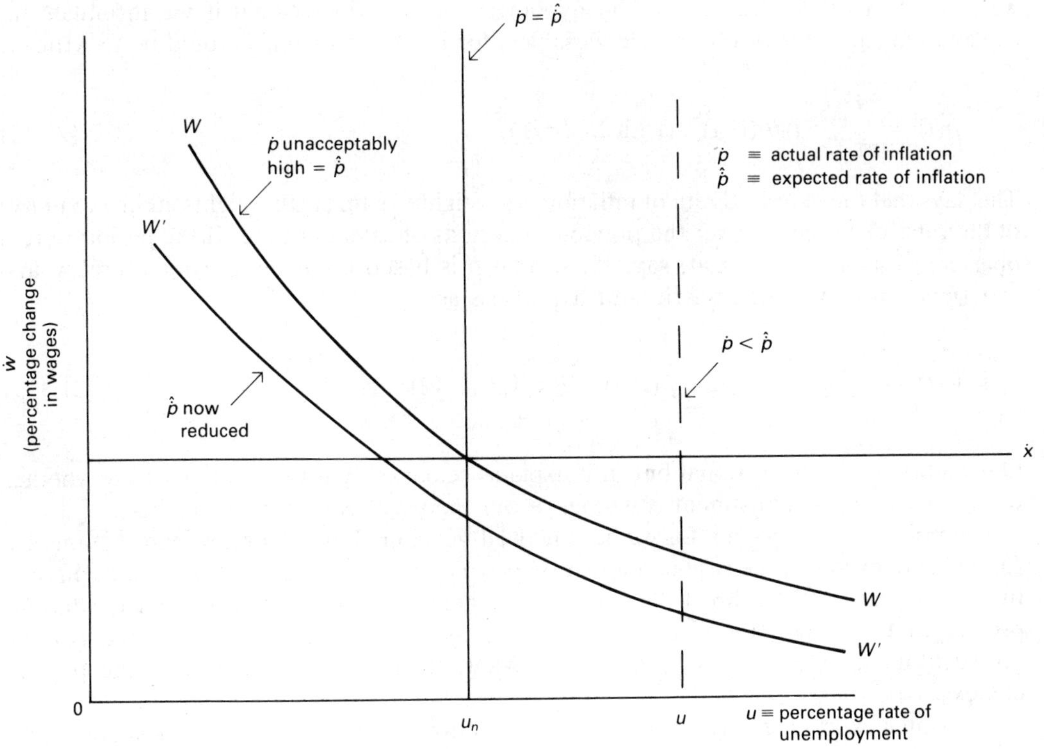

Figure 21.6 Reducing inflation: the importance of expectations

Finally, the reader should note that once expectations of inflation enter the analysis it is not hard to explain why we should observe relatively high values of u (which are probably considerably in excess of u_n) together with 'unacceptably' high rates of inflation: that is, the phenomenon typically described as 'stagflation'.

The formation of expectations

We have now argued that, in explaining inflation ($\equiv \dot{p}$), expectations of inflation ($\equiv \hat{\dot{p}}$) are crucial. Unfortunately we cannot, in general, observe expectations – only their consequences. It is thus difficult to test theories in which expectational variables play an important role since attempts to do this are invariably *conditional* upon some theory of how expectations are formed and thus test *two* hypotheses jointly. For example, to test our wage-adjustment hypothesis:

$$\dot{w} = \frac{a_0}{u} + a_1 \hat{\dot{p}}$$

we have data on $\dot{w}$ and u. But the hypothesis is only operational if we formulate an explanation (in terms of observable variables) for $\hat{\dot{p}}$. One possibility would be to write:

$$\hat{\dot{p}}(t) = \sum_{i=1}^{i=n} h_i\dot{p}\ (t-i) \quad (\text{with } \Sigma h_i = 1) \tag{21.13}$$

This says that the expected rate of inflation is a weighted sum (with weights adding to unity) of the rates experienced over the previous n periods of calendar time. If the period were a quarter, we might guess n at, say, 12, so that $\hat{\dot{p}}$ is based upon the previous three years' experience of $\dot{p}$. We then rewrite our hypothesis as:

$$\dot{w}(t) = \frac{a_0}{u(t)} + a_1\ \Sigma h_i\ \dot{p}(t-i) \quad (i = 1,2,\ldots,12) \tag{21.13a}$$

Our theory is now operational but, if it explains remarkably little, we cannot say whether our theory of wage adjustment is wrong, or our theory of expectations, or both.

This point is worth noting: for we have no well-developed theory of how expectations are formed and, except in the case of a few surveys which seek to measure expectations directly by questionnaires, little direct data relating to them. This means that many expectations proxies in economics are rather *ad hoc*: that is, look 'reasonably' plausible (to the investigators) in the context of the time. What, then, looks 'plausible' in the present context?

In forming expectations regarding the future, most of us look back at the past and, more particularly perhaps, the recent past. The formulation at 21.13 therefore makes some sense in general terms. It might make even more if the lag terms (or weights) were distributed so that more recent values of past inflation [$\equiv \dot{p}(t-i)$], were more heavily weighted.

There are, however, obvious difficulties in basing $\hat{\dot{p}}$ only on past values of $\dot{p}$. Suppose we expected unemployment to rise, surely this would modify our views? Or, suppose a change in budget policy is announced, would not this modify an expectation of $\dot{p}$? On this line of argument the hypothesis of 21.13 needs to be supplemented by our forecast (derived, of course, from our economic theory) of the impact on future $\dot{p}$ of recent 'news'. Admittedly, it is hard to say what items, among the welter of information and misinformation produced daily by the media, constitute 'news' in this sense, and not all of us have a very clear idea of the relevant economic theory. Nevertheless it seems plausible to argue that transactors typically expect the immediate future values of $\dot{p}$ to be much like those of the (more or less) recent past *unless* the recent 'news' implies very strongly that this will *not* be the case. Even when the 'news' does suggest, say, a fall in $\dot{p}$, the influence of recent experience may be strong and, as a result, $\hat{\dot{p}}$ may be slow to adjust, with consequences we have already discussed for the persistence of past levels of inflation.

This is of course a pragmatic and rather cautious view. As against this we can argue that, despite the diversity of opinion, the economy behaves *as if* transactors had a well-developed theory of inflation which leads them to make forecasts of $\dot{p}$ such that *errors* in forecasts have no systematic component, i.e. there is no recurrent tendency to over- or under-predict and thus cause transactors to revise their theory. Such systematic over- or under-prediction will, of necessity, arise if $\dot{p}$ is changing *and* forecasts are based *entirely* on past experience as, say, in 21.13. For $\hat{\dot{p}}$ is simply a weighted average of past values of $\dot{p}$ and will *over-predict* if $\dot{p}$ is falling and *under-predict* if $\dot{p}$ is rising. Where there are no systematic errors, and forecasts are based upon a well-developed theory, we can say that expectations are approximately 'rational' in the sense of what is called 'rational expectations' theory.

In this latter case expectations of $\dot{p}$ may be revised very rapidly. Suppose, simply as an example, that transactors behaved as if they believed, with great confidence, that:

$$\dot{p}(t) = f[\dot{M}^S(t-1)] \tag{21.14}$$

where $\dot{M}^S$ = the percentage rate of change of the nominal money stock. Then any change in $\dot{M}^S$ will lead to a rapid revision of the expected rate of inflation since:

$$\hat{\dot{p}}(t) = f[\dot{M}^S(t-1)] \tag{21.15}$$

This would, in theory, make it possible for a rapid reduction in the rate of inflation (via the reduction in $\hat{\dot{p}}$) – even if the percentage rate of unemployment remained invariant – provided that only $\dot{M}^S$ was reduced, since the economy would move immediately to a *lower* wage-adjustment curve and hence to a *lower* rate of change in wage costs and prices.

The extent to which transactors do possess 'rational expectations', based on this or some more complex theory, is an empirical matter on which the evidence is far from clear cut. A cautious judgement which nevertheless seems consistent with recent UK experience is that transactors do not and hence that estimates of $\hat{\dot{p}}$ are adjusted rather slowly and mainly on the basis of recent changes in $\dot{p}$. And this, as we have seen, entails that inflation rates – particularly perhaps where downward adjustments are in question – exhibit very considerable inertia.

Theory and UK experience

Our model of type 1 inflation consists essentially in a price equation and a wage equation. A simple version of this can be written:

$$\dot{p}(t) = a_0 + a_1\,\dot{w}(t-i) + a_2\,\dot{p}_m\,(t-j) + a_3\,\dot{x}\,(t-k) \tag{21.16}$$

$$\dot{w}(t) = b_0 + b_1\,\hat{\dot{p}}(t) + b_2\left(\frac{N^D - N^S}{N^S}\right)(t-l) \tag{21.17}$$

where $\dot{p}_m \equiv$ the percentage rate of change in import prices; and we write $t-i$, $t-j$ etc., to indicate that lags are likely to be present and are of unknown length.

To complete the model we need an expectational hypothesis and this, in many investigations, took the form of 21.13, say:

$$\hat{\dot{p}}(t) = \sum_{m=1}^{m=n} h_m\,\dot{p}(t-m)$$

Until the late 1960s models of this kind usually worked quite well and produced, when estimated by econometricians, results in broad conformity with our theory, in that the marginal response coefficients a_1, a_2, a_3, b_1, b_2 were of the correct sign and of plausible magnitude. Moreover they typically suggested a value of b_1 in the neighbourhood of 0.5–0.6 and thus implied a 'short-run' trade-off between the percentage of unemployment and the percentage rate of inflation. It thus became common to advocate managing the economy so that $(N^D-N^S)/N^S$ (often proxied by u) yielded an 'acceptable' value for $\dot{p}$ on the assumption that both functions were stable.

After the late 1960s, relations of this kind performed increasingly poorly and typically under-predicted the values of both $\dot{w}$ and $\dot{p}$. Moreover the evidence suggested that the relationship between $\dot{w}$ and the excess demand for labour was becoming increasingly unreliable, while the coefficient b_1 (the elasticity of wages in nominal terms to expected prices) was moving towards unity. In some investigations $\dot{w}$ even appeared to react *perversely* to unemployment. Thus experience from the beginning of the 1960s to the beginning of the 1980s appears to support the proposition that wage-earners obtain, on average, complete compensation for expected price changes (i.e. the coefficient on $\hat{\dot{p}}$ is very close to unity) but little else.

The findings that $\dot{w}$ is *not* – as it once was – reliably related to unemployment or alternative measures of excess demand in the labour market throws considerable doubt on the proposition that there exists a relatively stable 'natural rate of unemployment' (NAIRU). It thus throws considerable doubt on the argument that, by raising u above u_n, a deceleration in inflation can be obtained. No doubt, over some periods, a fall in $\dot{w}$ *will* coincide with a rise in u – as it did in 1980–2. But it is not hard to find periods in which a rise in u has been accompanied by a rise in $\dot{w}$ or no response whatsoever.

The upshot of recent research is, as a result, scarcely comforting. Raising unemployment has, it appears, an unreliable and very temporary effect – if any at all – in reducing $\dot{w}$, while the finding that $\dot{w}$ responds one for one to $\hat{\dot{p}}$ indicates that, even if a stable relation between $\dot{w}$ and u were to reappear, any resultant 'trade-off' would be very shortlived indeed. The 'longer-run' wage-adjustment curve is, it seems, undoubtedly vertical. Its *position*, however, is quite unstable – so unstable that the proposition that $\dot{w} - \hat{\dot{p}} = \mathrm{f}(u)$ cannot be accepted, so that the 'natural rate of unemployment' (which we called u_n) is revealed as a 'will-o'-the-wisp'.

One consequence of these research findings is that contemporary macroeconometric models often contain equations for the explanation of $\dot{w}$ which are dominated by whatever proxy is used for $\hat{\dot{p}}$. Thus a Treasury model contains an equation of the following form:

$$\dot{w} = \sum_{i=0}^{i=11} \alpha_i \, YH(t-i) + \sum_{j=1}^{j=11} B_j \dot{p}(t-j) + \text{time trend}$$

with $\Sigma\, \alpha_i = 0$ and $\Sigma\, B_j = 1$, where $YH \equiv$ a variable which measures the pressure of demand. This implies that the long-run influence of YH (over eleven quarters) is zero.

Typically these equations forecast poorly and, as a result, when contemporary macroeconomic models are used to make short-term forecasts – like, for example, the Treasury offer twice-yearly – it is not unusual for the wage equation to be dropped and $\dot{w}$ given a fore-cast value based upon 'informed judgement' rather than the model itself.

A more important consequence is that an appropriate anti-inflationary policy is hard to specify since $\dot{w}$, and hence $\dot{p}$, depend crucially on expectations (i.e. $\hat{\dot{p}}$), which are not easily influenced by policy actions if they are derived, primarily, from past experience of $\dot{p}$. However, we postpone our consideration of policy until the final part of this book.

Summary and conclusions

Inflation ($= \dot{p}$) is typically analysed in a framework which assumes that:

(a) prices are cost-determined
(b) wages are flexible

Fairly simple models of this type had good explanatory power until the late 1960s. Moreover these models generally suggested that:

(c) the price elasticity of wages was of the order of 0.5 – 0.6
(d) that $\dot{w}$ was reliably responsive to the percentage rate of unemployment

As a result, inflationary processes were dampened and there appeared to be a reliable and sensitive short-term 'trade-off' between $\dot{w}$ (and hence $\dot{p}$) and u so that to reduce the former it was only necessary to increase u by a relatively small amount.

As an example of such a wage-adjustment relation we give the following result due to Dicks-Mireaux and based on data from 1946 to 1959:

$$\dot{w}(t) = 3.90 + \hat{p}(t) + 2.78 \left(\frac{N^D - N^S}{N^S}\right) (t - 1/4)$$

with:

$$\hat{p}(t) = 0.30\,\dot{p}(t) + 0.16\,\dot{p}(t-1)$$

where the period of observation is a year and $t - 1/4$ denotes the twelve months ending three months (one quarter) before the current year.

The reader can easily see that this result has marginal response coefficients which conform in sign and magnitude to our earlier hypotheses.

The reliability of the 'short-run' trade-off implied by this result over the 'longer period' was always a matter of doubt, for it was hard to see how workers could, indefinitely, tolerate a price elasticity of wages less than unity since this implied that inflation entailed an apparent acceptance of a continuing fall in the expected real wage. Theorists therefore argued that:

(e) the 'longer-run' elasticity of wages with respect to prices must be unity, *so that*
(f) any 'trade-off' between $\dot{w}$ and u was relevant only to the 'short period' in which the elasticity was less than one

This was the assertion that the 'longer-run' wage-adjustment curve was a vertical line drawn through a particular level of unemployment known as the 'natural rate' (NAIRU). This theory led to the propositions that:

(g) $u < u_n$ entailed accelerating inflation
(h) $u > u_n$ entailed decelerating inflation
(i) $u = u_n$ was compatible with any level of inflation expected by transactors

In elementary versions of this theory u_n is a function of the rate of change of productivity and the marginal response coefficient $\partial(\dot{w}-\dot{p})/\partial u$ – as we have seen – and is typically regarded as a quantity which changes only very slowly.

Recent empirical work which takes into account the experience of the last twenty years typically finds that:

(j) the price elasticity of wages *is* close to unity, *but that*
(k) there is no reliable relationship between $\dot{w} - \dot{p}$ and u, *so that*
(l) the so-called 'natural rate of unemployment' is highly unstable

The conclusions are dispiriting since they suggest that:

(m) the principal determinant of inflation ($\dot{p}$) is expectations of inflation ($\hat{\dot{p}}$), *so hence*
(n) no reliable mechanism for decelerating inflation exists, *since*

(o) we do not know *either* how expectations are formed *or* how they can be (appropriately) influenced, *while*
(p) raising u to a level above the (highly variable) u_n is plainly unreliable

In short macroeconomics lacks an empirically supported theory of inflation which not only complicates policy but leaves the field open to ideologues and dogmatists who are invariably in very ample supply.

If we look at long-run time series, there is an association between the rate or change of prices ($\dot{p}$) and the rate of change of the nominal money stock ($\dot{M}^S$). Such an association does not, however, establish causation. We cannot say whether $\dot{M}^S$ *caused* $\dot{p}$, or $\dot{p}$ *caused* $\dot{M}^S$, or some combination of both, without further enquiry. Historically, for example, the level of output per worker has been related to the growth of population. This, however, does not imply that raising the rate of population growth will raise the rate of growth of output per head; nor does it imply the reverse.

Questions and exercises

1. 'The *natural* rate of unemployment is supposed to change slowly since it is determined by *real* forces and institutional arrangements.' What do you think these 'real forces' and 'institutional arrangements' are?

2. 'We *could* have a tolerable rate of inflation if we operated the economy close to the *natural rate* of unemployment which cannot be more than x per cent.' Discuss critically. How would you attempt to estimate x?

3. Even if, over the typical cycle, the *average* values of $\dot{w}$ and $\dot{x}$ were equal we should still have rising prices because wage behaviour is asymmetric.' Elucidate and appraise.

4. 'High rates of inflation are harmful because they reduce economic growth.' Do you agree? Give your reasons for accepting this proposition. Is there any empirical evidence to support it?

5. 'At any point on the vertical line drawn through u_n on Figure 21.6 actual inflation is equal to expected inflation and the economy is operating at the *natural* rate of unemployment. No special significance, or so it seems, attaches to $\hat{\dot{p}} = \dot{p}$ at $\dot{p}$ = zero. So why all the fuss about reducing inflation rather than stabilising it?' Elucidate. How would you answer this criticism?

6. 'Incomes policies, to be effective, *must* change inflationary expectations.' Elucidate and appraise.

7. 'The only effective incomes policy is four million unemployed for four years. After that we might reduce it to three million.' Analyse the model and assumptions behind this statement.

8. 'An elasticity of wages with respect to prices less than unity is patently absurd. Those who believe in this will believe in anything.' Elucidate and appraise.

9. 'Incomes policies *never* work. The politicians ensure this, for the Opposition always appeals to the electorate by promising their removal.' Review UK experience in the light of this comment. To what conclusions does it lead you?

10. 'The only thing worse than a high rate of inflation is the sort of policies which are typically imposed to reduce it. Quite apart from their *short-run* effects, which are unpleasant enough, these policies ensure the UK's continuing industrial decline.' Critically appraise these contentions.

11. 'Reducing inflation means more than simply reducing the observed rate of inflation. Any persistent deflation will do that. For a genuine success we must radically reduce inflationary expectations and/or modify the wage/price process.' Elucidate and appraise.

12. '*Full-employment* policies *plus* union wage bargaining *inevitably* generate permanent inflation. To eliminate inflation at least *one* must go. The real question is which?' Do you agree? If so, which is your preferred alternative? What does it entail?

13. 'The analysis of the *augmented* wage-adjustment curve suggest that *any* equilibrium rate of inflation ($\hat{\dot{p}} = \dot{p}$) entails the same level of unemployment and thus the same level of *real* activity.' Elucidate, and discuss the relationship between this result and 'classical' macroeconomics.

14. In the second quarter of 1979 the Thatcher–Howe administration embarked on a policy of reducing the rate of inflation. Use data for the second quarters of 1980, 1981, etc., to estimate the elasticity of the rate of inflation with respect to:
    (a) registered unemployment
    (b) employment

    Comment on your estimates. What do they suggest, if anything, about the 'costs' of the post-1979 policy?

15. 'No country which engages in international trade on any significant scale can, for long, maintain a rate of inflation significantly above (or below) the general international experience.' Elucidate and appraise in the light of the empirical evidence. Does the exchange-rate regime matter?

16. 'Very little observed unemployment is *involuntary*. Most of it is either structural or seasonal or arises from perfectly rational attempts by individuals to find themselves better jobs – a process which is clearly *voluntary*.' Give clear definitions of the *italicised* terms. Do you accept this statement? How would you test it?

17. 'The most effective steps we could take to reduce unemployment would be (i) to reduce, by at least 25 per cent, the *real* value of social security benefits, and (ii) to reduce the scope of the *black economy*.' What analysis – if any – do you think lies behind this statement? Is there any evidence to support it?

18. Many contracts between employers and employees involve fixed scales of wages which can be renegotiated rather rarely. Can you explain why *both* employers *and* employees are willing to enter into such arrangements? What do they gain?

19. 'Wage contracts which are for a year or more and which overlap in time entail precisely the sort of aggregate wage *stickiness* which ensures that *monetarist*-type anti-inflation policies will be slow to work and impose significant *transitory* and *permanent* costs on the community.' Elucidate and appraise.

20. '*Keynesians* and *monetarists* have at least this in common: neither has an acceptable theory of inflation.' Do you agree? Give your reasons for agreement or disagreement.

21. 'A 10 per cent devaluation or depreciation in sterling *ceteris paribus* sooner or later produces a 10 per cent increase in domestic prices.' Discuss critically with special reference to the meanings of 'sooner', 'later' and *ceteris paribus*.

22. 'In the long run, the rate of wage increases will be entirely independent of the level of unemployment. The rate of inflation will be determined by expectations and the long-run wage-adjustment curve horizontal.' Elucidate and appraise.

Suggested reading

J. A. Bispham, 'The Nature of the Inflation Process', *NIESR Review*, no. 100 (May 1982).

J. Burton, *Wage Inflation* (Macmillan, 1971).

J. D. Byers, in *Perspectives on Inflation: Models and Policies*, ed. David Heathfield (Longman, 1979).

A. J. H. Dean, 'Incomes Policies and Differentials,' *NIESR Review*, no. 83 (February 1978).

*L. A. Dicks-Mireaux, 'The Interrelationship between Cost and Price Changes, 1946–1959', *Oxford Economic Papers*, vol. 13 (October 1961).

L. A. Dicks–Mireaux and J. R. Shepherd, 'The Wage Structure and Some Implications for Incomes Policy', *NIESR Review*, no. 22 (1962).

*J. C. R. Dow, 'An Analysis of the Generation of Price Inflation' *Oxford Economic Papers* (October 1956).

J. C. R. Dow, *The Management of the British Economy, 1945–60* (Cambridge University Press, 1964).

J. C. R. Dow and L. A. Dicks-Mireaux, 'Price Stability and the Policy of Deflation', *NIESR Review*, no. 3 (1959).

*J. C. R. Dow and L. A. Dicks-Mireaux, 'The Determinants of Wage Inflation: UK, 1946–56', *Journal of the Royal Statistical Society*, Series A, vol. 122 (1959).

S. G. B. Henry and P. A. Ormerod, 'Incomes Policies and Wage Inflation: Empirical Evidence for the UK 1961–77', *NIESR Review*, no. 83 (February 1978).

S. G. B. Henry, M. C. Sawyer and P. Smith, 'Models of Inflation in the United Kingdom', *NIESR Review*, no. 77 (August 1976).

D. Higham and J. Tomlinson, 'Why do Governments Worry about Inflation?', *Westminster Bank Review* (May 1982).

*D. E. W. Laidler and M. Parkin, 'Inflation – A Survey', *Economic Journal* (December 1975).

R. G. Lipsey, *An Introduction to Positive Economics* (Weidenfeld & Nicolson, 1971) appendix to ch. 33.

A. Marin, 'The Phillips Curve (Born 1958–Died?)', *Three Banks Review* (December 1972).

NIESR, 'Some Aspects of the Present Inflation', *NIESR Review* (February 1971) pp. 38–49.

OECD, *The Problem of Rising Prices* (Paris, 1970).

W. B. Reddaway, 'Rising Prices for Ever?', *Lloyds Bank Review* (July 1966).

*R. M. Solow, *Price Expectations and the Behaviour of the Price Level* (Manchester University Press, 1969).

*More advanced references.

Part V
The Determination of the Money Supply

Chapter 22
Money, Debt and Liquidity

In our outline of the liquidity preference theory of interest we have already put forward a definition of the money supply. This definition, however, was stated dogmatically and the principles underlying it were never discussed. At the same time we made reference to the concept of liquidity. Our task in this chapter is to examine the concepts of money and liquidity in more detail and thus explain and justify the brief references made in the course of our earlier analysis.

The functions of money

Modern economic organisation is based upon a highly complex division of productive function. This in turn depends upon the process of exchange. *The supreme importance of money is that it facilitates exchange.* It thus makes possible the extreme division of productive function upon which our material well-being rests. Money, accordingly, must be regarded as a most useful and revolutionary invention.

Every purchase involves the creation, expression and settlement of a debt. Consider, for example, the purchase of a tennis racquet. Once the racquet has been chosen by the purchaser and received by him, a debt is created which is owed by the purchaser to the seller of the racquet. The value of this debt must be expressed in terms of some unit comprehensible to both parties. The unit in which debts (prices) are expressed is known as the *unit of account*. In Britain the unit of account is the pound sterling; in India the rupee; in the USA the dollar; in the Soviet Union the rouble.

Historically the pound, as its name implies, was related to a certain weight of metal. Modern units of account are, however, essentially abstract concepts. There is no 'pound', 'dollar' or 'rouble'. The abstract unit of account is also found in primitive monetary systems, for even where the unit of account was a 'slave', a 'goat', or a 'bottle of gin', it remained an abstract concept of a 'standard' or 'normal' slave, goat or bottle of gin to which any given slave, goat or bottle of gin might, or might not, correspond.

Once the debt has been expressed in terms of the unit of account, the next problem is that of settlement. If the money of the society is purely a money-of-account, settlement proceeds by barter. In this case money's single function is to provide a unit in which prices may be expressed. Modern moneys, however, do more than this. They furnish a *means of settling indebtedness*. For settlement of debt something must pass from the debtor to the creditor which, either by law or custom, the latter is compelled or prepared to accept in settlement. The *things* which pass must, of course, have values expressed in terms of the unit of account or directly related to it. Those *things* which are acceptable by law in settlement of debt are known as *legal tender money*; those *things* which are generally acceptable as a matter of custom we call *customary money*.

The third function of money is to act as an *asset* or *store of value*. Once society develops a *thing* (or *things*) which acts both as a means of settling indebtedness and unit of account (two attributes which together constitute a *medium of exchange*) then those *things* can be held by individuals as assets or stores of value. *To hold money thus becomes one way of holding wealth.* As earlier analysis has made clear, this function of money in acting as an asset is the fundamental one for monetary theory, whether 'Keynesian' or 'monetarist'.

It is convenient to summarise our brief discussion of money's functions by a simple diagram (see Figure 22.1).

On the basis of this analysis, how best can money be defined? Essentially money is as money does. Hence we may define *money* as *anything legally or customarily acceptable in settlement of debt*.

Our next step must be to consider what are the 'things' which, in developed economies, perform the functions of money.

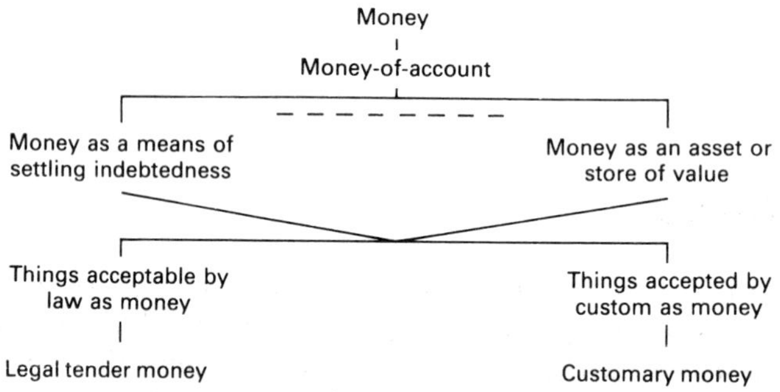

Figure 22.1

The characteristics of modern money

In the early stages of monetary development the things which served as money were commonly familiar and widely used commodities. As one example of a *commodity-money* we may take slaves, which as recently as the first decade of the present century still performed monetary functions in parts of West Africa.

An efficient money needs to possess, in as high a measure as possible, the attributes of (i) portability, (ii) divisibility, (iii) durability, (iv) homogeneity, and (v) stability in value. Slave money was deficient in most of these. Admittedly, slaves, in view of their ability to walk, were portable. On the other hand they were not divisible; moreover, being subject to the hazards of accident, disease, escape and suicide they were not always very durable. Again, slaves were scarcely homogeneous, a state of affairs which gave unlimited opportunities for disputing whether a particular slave was, or was not, a 'standard' slave in terms of the unit of account. Finally, slave moneys were additionally defective in that a successful slave-raiding war, or outbreak of disease, could cause sharp fluctuations in their supply and thus their value. Many of the early commodity-moneys shared these defects in greater or lesser degree. Hence slave-moneys, goat-moneys, cattle-moneys and their like were gradually replaced by the precious metals which possessed the desirable qualities to a greater extent.

The precious metals, even after the introduction of coinage, remained essentially *commodity-moneys*. The unit of account was defined in terms of a weight of metal. The relative values of coins were determined by their metal content. Money as we know it today came later. It was a development of paper money and *representative* paper moneys were a stage in its evolution.

Modern moneys are what is called *token* or *fiat* moneys. The distinguishing feature of fiat moneys is that, in sharp contrast to commodity-moneys or representative moneys their monetary values greatly exceed their intrinsic values and they are not, in law, convertible into anything other than themselves. An admirable example of such money is provided by the pound note. The cost of printing such a note is considerably less than a penny. Its value, as a commodity, is virtually zero. Indeed, apart from its possible use as a rather unattractive wallpaper, it is difficult to see any non-monetary employment for a note at all. Legally, the pound note is convertible only into other notes or coins, though, as a matter of fact, the Bank of England will in certain circumstances exchange such notes for other currencies at a rate of exchange which the British authorities choose and may alter.[1] The value of the pound note, in its monetary function, thus depends upon its scarcity and this is preserved by legal and institutional arrangements, examined later. On the other hand, notes are legal tender throughout the UK. And, together with *token* coin, despite their intrinsic worthlessness, they provide a currency which possesses in high measure those attributes of portability, divisibility, durability and homogeneity which our earlier discussion has shown to be desirable. Thus, as money has developed, the *things* which serve as money have become specialised to their monetary functions and are now virtually valueless apart from them.

What are the things which serve as money in the UK? First, there are the notes issued by the Bank of England and declared to be legal tender by the state. Second, there are token coins issued by the state and declared to be limited legal tender. These, under law, must be accepted in full and final settlement of debts. It is, however, a matter of common experience that debts may also be settled by means of cheques. A cheque is an order to a banker, signed by the drawer, ordering the banker to transfer a stated sum, standing to the credit of the drawer in the bank's books, into the possession of the payee. *A cheque is not in itself money*. What performs the monetary function when a payment is made by cheque is the *bank deposit* which the cheque is merely an order to transfer. Bank deposits are not, of course, legal tender. Anyone can refuse to accept a cheque offered to him and demand payment in legal tender notes and coin. Nevertheless, in many developed societies cheques are very widely accepted and bank deposits form the principal means of payment. Bank deposits are, in fact, the outstanding example of *customary money*. Plainly, only those deposits subject to transfer by cheque can be regarded as money.

The line of reasoning so far followed in this section can be set out very briefly in the form of a skeleton diagram (see Figure 22.2). The reasoning underlying the diagram leads us, of course, back to the definition of the money supply given earlier. For the things which are

[1]The reader will know that this relates to the period of a 'pegged' exchange rate.

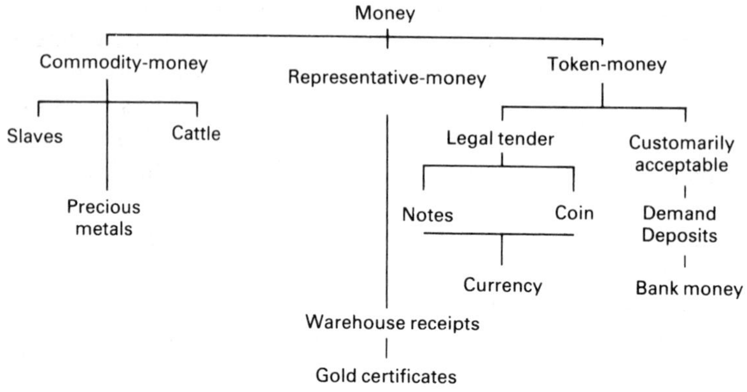

Figure 22.2

money in Britain are *coin, notes* and *demand deposits* with the banking system. More than this, however, it suggests a further question: granted that coin, notes, and demand deposits are money, what precisely are they? What, in other words, is the essential nature of the *things* which serve as money?

Notice that we are here including only demand (i.e. current-account) deposits in our definition of money. Since these typically earn no interest this procedure is identical with that we adopted in our discussion of liquidity preference.

It is, however, common knowledge that innumerable definitions of 'money' exist which include other assets. Some of these we discuss later. It is nevertheless the case that the adoption of a more inclusive definition of money – for example, in the UK *either* M_3 *or* sterling M_3 – does not in any essential way modify our earlier short-term theory of the determination of nominal interest rates. It simply makes it more complicated since each new asset has an 'interest rate' to be explained.

Money as debt

It is convenient to begin an examination of modern money with *notes*, which are of course the principal form of legal tender. What then is a British pound note?

British notes are issued by the Bank of England, whose *liabilities* they are. They are in fact paper tokens of indebtedness which represent claims against the Bank. These claims (or titles to wealth) mean that the Bank *owes* the *bearer* of the note the sum stated on its face. Notes are therefore no more than IOUs made payable to the bearer on demand which, as a matter of convenience, are issued in certain fixed values and printed upon paper. They differ, of course, from the IOUs of private persons, which are claims against the issuer, in that the Bank is under no obligation to convert *its* IOUs into anything other than different types of its own obligations; a private individual's IOU must, if payable on demand, be converted into legal tender money.

The fact that bank notes are merely tokens of the Bank's indebtedness to the bearer is immediately apparent from contemplation of the notes themselves, for Bank of England pound notes still carry the inscription: 'I promise to pay the bearer on demand the sum of one pound' and this promise is signed: 'For the Gov^{R} and Comp^{A} of the Bank of England' by the Chief Cashier of the Bank. Bank of England notes are not legally convertible into anything other than the notes or deposits of the Bank of England. The promise is, in consequence, completely meaningless. It is in practice no more than an anachronistic survival of the days when Bank of England notes were legally convertible into gold: that is, when the pound note was *representative* rather than *fiat* money. Nevertheless, although the promise is specious, it has the merit of making plain the essential nature of a note which is, as we have already said, the token of a debt owed by the Bank to the bearer of the note, payable on demand, and not legally convertible into anything other than a similar note or notes of identical origin, though possibly of different denomination.

If a note is an inconvertible token of indebtedness payable to the bearer on demand, what is a *coin*? Token coins may best be regarded as notes which are, purely as a matter of convenience, printed upon metal. Some countries do, in fact, make little use of coin and provide small change by issuing notes of very low denomination. In general, however, coins are preferred since small denomination notes, as a consequence of repeated use, become torn and dirty and ultimately present an appearance which is at once unlovely and unhygienic. If coins are tokens of indebtedness printed on metal, whose obligations are they? In Britain, token coins are manufactured by the Mint. They are issued to the banks and the public through the Bank of England. In principle, therefore, they are the obligations of the state. In law, somewhat paradoxically, there is no obligation upon the state to convert coin into notes. In practice, however, the full convertibility of coin into notes is maintained by various administrative devices. The difference between the cost of producing coin, including the cost of the metal, and its monetary value is known as 'seignorage' and is treated as part of the income of the state.

We have thus reached the position that *legal tender money* in Britain (currency) consists of acknowledgements of indebtedness issued either by the state or the Bank of England. What then is *customary* money?

Demand deposits are acknowledgements of indebtedness in precisely the same way as are notes and coins. If John Smith has a demand (current-account) deposit standing in his credit in the ledgers of Lloyds Bank, this means that Lloyds Bank is in debt to John Smith for this sum which the Bank has *borrowed* from him. A bank deposit of this type differs from a note in a number of significant ways. First, it is the debt, not of the state or a state-owned insititution, but of a private banking company. Second, it is not inconvertible since Lloyds Bank is obliged, if John Smith demands it, to convert the deposit into legal tender. Third, a deposit, which is merely a book entry in the bank's ledger, has no 'bearer'. Its transfer from one person to another is made by the bank only on the instructions of the holder. Fourth, a deposit is less vulnerable to loss, theft, or damage than legal tender money, though it is exposed to the hazards (negligible in developed economies) of banking failure. From these attributes we can see that a bank deposit (current account), though not legal tender, is a very *convenient* form of money which can easily be transferred in settlement of indebtedness. This accounts for its widespread popularity. In essentials it is, of course, like legal tender money, no more than an acknowledgement of indebtedness and a promise to pay legal tender to the (deposit) holder on demand.

In Tables 22.1 and 22.2 we offer some data which show:

(a) the relative importance of demand deposits in our definition (generally called M_1) of the money supply
(b) the relative importance of M_1 and sterling M_3 which is the 'broad' definition usually employed in the UK

Table 22.1 Composition of UK 'money supply': selected dates, 1963–80 (in £ million)

Date	Notes and coin in circulation with public		UK private-sector sterling sight deposits		Money stock Unadjusted	Money stock Seasonally adjusted
	£m	% of total	£m	% of total	£m	£m
1963I	2,248	33.7	4,424	66.3	6,672	6,790
1965I	2,401	32.6	4,957	67.4	7,358	7,450
1967I	2,751	35.4	5,022	64.6	7,773	7,890
1969I	2,914	34.9	5,425	65.1	8,399	8,510
1971I	3,324	34.3	6,367	65.7	9,691	9,820
1973I	4,170	33.8	8,163	66.2	12,333	12,300
1975I	5,448	37.0	9,287	63.0	14,735	14,780
1977I	6,801	34.8	12,765	65.2	19,566	19,700
1979I	9,140	33.2	18,355	66.8	27,495	27,440
1980I	9,692	33.2	19,481	66.8	29,173	29,300

Note: for details of construction consult *Bank of England Quarterly Bulletin*, table 11.1, various issues; and *Bank of England Statistical Abstract*, no. 2 (1975) table 12.1.

Table 22.2 UK monetary data: selected dates, 1963–81 (seasonally adjusted data in £ million)

Date	M_1	Sterling M_3	M_1/Sterling M_3 %
1963I	6,740	10,550	63.9
1965I	7,280	11,380	64.0
1967I	7,490	12,050	62.1
1969I	8,490	15,740	53.9
1971I	9,820	18,020	54.5
1973I	11,350	21,280	53.3
1975I	14,880	35,560	41.8
1977I	19,540	40,720	48.0
1979I	27,580	52,360	52.7
1980I	29,370	59,250	49.6
1981I	31,850	69,900	45.6

Note: horizontal lines indicate change in banks included in data.
Source: *Economic Trends*, Annual Supplements.

Debts and liquidity

All token money, it seems, is debt but not all debt is money. What is the relationship between the debts which are money and the debts which are not?

Money, as we know, serves as an asset or store of value. So, too, do a variety of other acknowledgements of debt such as National Savings Bank deposits, bonds, debentures and shares. It is obvious, therefore, that as assets these claims are all, in differing degrees, substitutes for money. Money, however, alone possesses the property of being generally acceptable in settlement of debt. Hence the holder of money may, at any time, convert his holding into any other type of asset he wants. In doing so, he *shifts* his money holding to someone else in exchange for, let us say, a bond. In a market economy money is therefore the most readily *shiftable* of assets and one which, in view of its general acceptability, enjoys, from the point of view of any individual, a perfect market. Moreover, if the price level in general is stable (or relatively so) money can be converted into other assets without loss: that is, money enjoys *capital certainty*. These two attributes, *shiftability* and *capital certainty*, are the determinants of *liquidity*. Because money possesses them in greater measure than other claims on real goods it is the *most liquid of all assets* and an object of *liquidity preference* on the part of the public. These ideas are familiar to us since we have already sketched them briefly in our outline of the liquidity preference theory of interest.

Now it is easy to see that *all assets*, from second-hand running shoes to British government bonds, possess *some* measure of shiftability and price certainty. The liquidity of any asset is therefore a matter of degree. The greater the measure of shiftability and price certainty possessed by an asset, the greater its substitutability for money, or, to put the same point rather differently, the greater its 'moneyness'. All assets are liquid, but some are more liquid than others. In general, claims of various kinds are relatively liquid assets when compared with goods.

If shiftability is a necessary condition for liquidity, what confers it upon an asset? This question can best be answered by taking a look at a particular asset as an example, let us say a government bond.

The holder of a bond who wishes to sell it experiences few difficulties. There are well-organised markets for dealing in claims including bonds. These are the stock exchanges. Disposal of a bond therefore entails little more than a telephone call to a broker. Since bond prices are quoted daily, dealings in bonds frequent, while bond markets contain many participants, any individual wishing to sell his bond holding will know the price he will obtain within very narrow limits, for, unless he is a Rockefeller or a Getty, sale of his holdings is unlikely to influence market prices. Bonds are clearly very readily shiftable because they enjoy an active, highly organised and near-perfect market. We may conclude that *marketability* confers *shiftability*.

Marketability is, as we have seen, a sufficient condition for shiftability. This, however, does not make it a necessary condition. Some assets, because of *special institutional arrangements*, are also highly shiftable even though they are non-marketable. A good example of such an asset is provided by National Saving Bank deposits. These are wholly without a market. Nevertheless, their conditions of issue are such that any holder of them can demand their conversion into legal tender by the state. They can, in other words, be shifted since, provided the depositor gives the necessary notice, the Post Office will convert them into legal tender. Fixed (or time) deposits with the commercial banks are further examples of the same type of shiftability even though they are not marketable. Assets of this kind are shiftable because they are encashable.

As regards the first attribute of liquidity, namely shiftability, we reach the general conclusion that it can be conferred either by the existence of a market or by special institutional arrangements. What of the second attribute, *capital certainty*? The prices of marketable assets are subject to fluctuation, though those of encashable assets are not. National Savings Bank deposits and fixed deposits with the commercial banks are examples of encashable assets whose money values are invariant. Marketable assets, however, do fluctuate in price, though some, such as bonds, fluctuate relatively less than most. Shares and debentures which, provided they are *quoted* on the stock exchange, enjoy a good measure of marketability, experience wider price fluctuations than bonds, while commod-

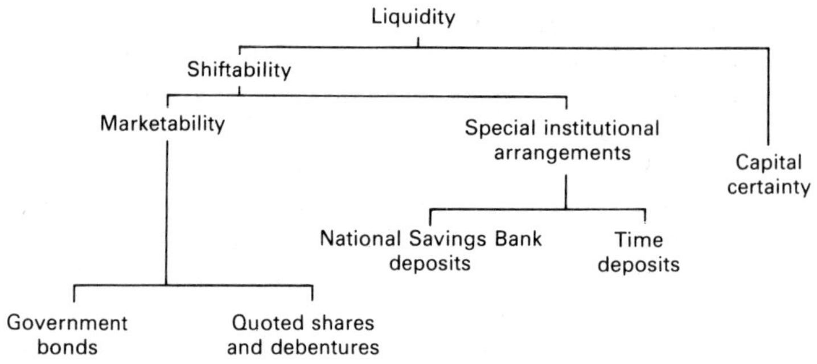

Figure 22.3

ities, the markets for which are usually imperfect, are particularly subject to price changes.

From this discussion, despite its brevity, we are sufficiently familiar with the meaning of liquidity to attempt a rough liquidity ranking of assets, a ranking in order of their moneyness. We set it out, in diagrammatical form, in Figure 22.3.

Now, keeping in the forefront of our minds the reasoning underlying this layout, we may attempt a purely ordinal ranking. This is set out in Table 22.3. This table is confined to claims (or acknowledgements of debt) since real assets are, in general, less liquid than claims.

Table 22.3 retains our earlier convention that only demand deposits are to be defined as 'money'. As we noted earlier, there are a number of more inclusive definitions in general use, while in theory, by including one (or more) additional types of asset in our widest existing definition, we can always develop a new one. Thus if we have definitions called M_1,

Table 22.3 The liquidity ranking of claims

Type of asset	Liability of	Classification	General grouping
Coin	State	Money	Liquid Assets
Notes	Central bank		
Demand deposits	Commercial banks		
National Savings Bank deposits	National Savings Bank	Near-moneys	
Time deposits	Commercial banks		
Bonds	State	Marketable government securities	
Local government bonds	Local government		
Debentures (quoted)	Corporate enterprises	Marketable securities	
Preference shares (quoted)	″ ″		
Ordinary shares (quoted)	″ ″		
Debentures (unquoted)	″ ″	Non-marketable securities	
Preference shares (unquoted)	″ ″		
Ordinary shares (unquoted)	″ ′		

M_2, M_3 we can always define an M_4, etc., *ad infinitum*. Thus it is logically conceivable that we should have an M_{27} or even an M_{396}. No definition can be *wrong*; it can only be more or less useful. Clearly, 'moneyness' is a matter of degree. We cannot assert that our definition (which corresponds to M_1) is *correct* and all others *erroneous*. But if we adopt, say, M_2 or sterling M_3 as our preferred definition, we must ensure that our *theory* is adjusted in any way which may be necessary.

At present the Bank of England provides numerical estimates of *four* money stock concepts. It also provides *two* estimates of the stock of private-sector liquidity (known as PSL 1 and 2) which could easily be called M_4 and M_5. Unless 'monetarism' and the 'monetarist' approach to macroeconomic policy become discredited in official eyes, these definitions are likely to be increased in number, or redefined, or both, since the search for some nominal money stock concept which, if controlled, will perform as 'monetarist' theory suggests seems sure to continue. The present set of definitions is thus likely to prove temporary. Nevertheless the reader should be familiar with it since to do so is an essential preliminary to following much of the current controversy. In Table 22.4 we set out some recent data on the present definitions.

Table 22.4 Money and liquidity: UK selected dates (1973–81) (seasonally adjusted, £ million)

Date	M_1 £m	PSL 2 %	Sterling M_3 £m	PSL 2 %	Private-sector liquidity totals: PSL 1 £m	% of PSL 2	PSL 2 £m
1973I	12,450	25.5	26,590	54.4	27,844	57.0	48,868
1975I	14,880	23.7	35,560	56.5	38,193	60.7	62,889
1977I	19,540	26.0	40,720	54.1	43,284	57.5	75,230
1979I	27,580	28.0	52,360	53.1	56,264	57.0	98,584
1980I	29,370	26.7	59,250	53.8	63,725	57.8	110,109
1981I	31,850	25.5	69,900	55.9	72,744	58.2	124,979

Note: for definitions of PSL 1 and PSL 2 see the article in *Bank of England Quarterly Bulletin* (September 1979); for details of items included in PSL 1 and PSL 2 consult *Financial Statistics*, various issues.
Source: *Economic Trends*, Annual Supplements.

The reader will also perceive that Table 22.3 treats shares of all kinds as debts. In law, shares are evidence of residual ownership and not debt, and holdings of ordinary shares are deemed to confer both ownership and control. This distinction between evidence of ownership (shares) and evidence of debt (debentures) cannot be taken very far without experiencing difficulties due to the existence of such hybrid varieties as participating preference shares, redeemable preference shares, and the like. Shares are traded like evidences of debt. Their holders compare them as assets directly with evidences of debt and probably think of them as such. Moroever, with the increasing divorce between effective control of enterprises and their legal ownership, there is some reason to suppose that the management of enterprises thinks of shareholders as creditors rather than owners. For all these reasons, as well as convenience, we have treated shares of all types as debts.

Finally, the reader will notice that although Table 22.3 lists thirteen categories of claim, it is far from comprehensive. Two points are worth noting in this respect. First, the reader may derive much benefit from considering, in the light of our discussion, where claims which we have not listed would be placed in the table. Second, the table suggests that, in developed economies, there exists a highly complex network of claims arising from the fact that the liabilities of one group are the assets of another. This second point emphasises the level of abstraction at which we discussed interest theory in Chapter 11.

Summary

In this chapter we have been concerned to justify the definition of the money supply we put forward in Chapter 11. To provide such a justification we had first to examine the function of money in a modern developed economy and then indicate which *things* performed these functions. The answer we found was consistent with our earlier definition.

Next we asked what *were* the things which constituted the money supply? Our examination showed that modern money consists of debt issued either by the central bank (in Britain the Bank of England) or the commercial banks (in Britain such banks as Lloyds, National Westminster, and so on). In short, modern money, which is an asset to its holder, is the liability of some banking institution on which it is a claim.

After this we considered the characteristics of money as an asset and found that, *given reasonable price stability*, money was the most 'liquid' of all assets. This justified our earlier argument that, in a model assuming constant prices, money was *perfectly liquid* and, as an asset, provided a way of holding wealth, which, at zero or negligible storage costs, possessed also a convenience yield. This sustained our earlier argument that to induce them to sacrifice this convenience (overcome this liquidity preference) and hold wealth in the form of claims which were *not* money, wealth-owners would require to receive a reward in the form of a rate of interest.

Additionally we showed that although, in our highly simplified model, there is by assumption only *one* type of interest-bearing claim (bonds), in reality there is a whole range of claims. This complication we shall continue to ignore, basing our theory, as in Chapter 11, on the assumption that only three forms of asset exist: namely, money, bonds and goods. It is, however, this wide range of claims which leads to a considerable variety of money stock definitions.

Questions and exercises

1. Rank the following assets in order as to 'shiftability' and 'capital certainty'. Give your reasons. Then insert them into their appropriate place in Table 22.3.
   (a) building society deposits
   (b) shares in BL
   (c) an IOU from the most honest person you know
   (d) a traveller's cheque issued to you by Barclay's Bank
   (e) a 1980 model *Triumph Acclaim*
   (f) a portrait of one of your ancestors by an unknown artist (believed 'in the family' to be Gainsborough)
   (g) a Norman Castle on Romney Marsh

2. It is sometimes hard to change notes into coin. In what circumstances, if any, would a pound note exchange for less than 100p in coin? Why do these circumstances rarely, if ever, arise?

3. Can a millionaire ever be short of money? If so, how?

4. 'The introduction of a decimal currency – as expected – raised all prices and made us all worse off.' Discuss.

5. Suppose prices are expected to rise by 12 per cent during the year. On this assumption reconsider the ranking of assets given in Table 22.3. Is money's ranking affected? If so, why?

6. Is a credit card money? Does the issue of Barclaycards increase the money supply?

7. 'Price certainty' is said to exist when an asset can be sold on a large organised market with frequent quotations. Is 'price certainty' related to 'capital certainty'? Give your reasons.

8. Can you describe an asset which has complete 'capital certainty' but virtually no 'liquidity'?

9. 'To hold long-term bonds confers *income certainty*: to hold short-term bonds or Treasury bills confers *capital certainty*.' Elucidate. Use your explanation to estimate the way in which (i) the childless widow of a retired senior civil servant, and (ii) a bank, would distribute a portfolio of £100,000 over (a) money; (b) Treasury bills; (c) long-term bonds. Would it matter if this widow was not childless?

10. 'A banker is a man who is in the fortunate position of having his IOUs acceptable as money.' Explain.

11. 'Non-demand deposits can always be converted into demand deposits if the holder wishes at small cost and with negligible delay. There is therefore no point in distinguishing M_1 from concepts such as sterling M_3.' Elucidate and appraise.

12. 'The quantity of M_1 at any time is determined by the non-bank public subject to the obvious constraint that $M_1 \leq M_3$. There is therefore no way the authorities can control M_1 other than by controlling the demand for it.' Do you agree? If so, what variables would have to be controlled by the authorities to control the demand for M_1?

13. 'The capacity of financial institutions to innovate must not be underestimated. How long will it be before building society deposits become subject to transfer by cheque? And what will we then mean by the *money supply*?' Discuss. What other assets in your view are likely to change their 'character' in this way and so to require inclusion in 'money' or 'liquid assets'?

14. 'Money – *narrowly defined* – will *never* be deliberately held as an asset since there are other assets with known values in terms of the unit of account which yield interest.' Elucidate. Does this point invalidate the theory of Chapter 11? If not, why not?

15. Explain and evaluate the contention that liquidity preference theory determines not the level of 'the rate of interest' but the difference between the rate of interest on time deposits with banks and that on bonds.

16. Plot the 3-months Treasury bill rate and the 2½% Consol rate on a graph. Use quarterly data for the period 1960–80. Define the long rate *minus* the short rate as the 'rate gap'. Describe its behaviour.

17. In the light of question 16, how would you attempt to develop a theory explaining the rate gap?

18. Plot the rate of return on equities against the 2½% Consol rate. Define the former *minus* the latter as the 'yield gap'. Can you extend the theory you put forward to answer question 16 to explain the 'yield gap'?

19. Evaluate critically the money stock and private-sector liquidity definitions employed by the Bank of England. Which seems to you the 'useful' policy target? Why?

20. 'The only unambiguous definition of *money* is legal tender currency. This is the definition which economists should employ.' Elucidate and appraise.

Suggested reading

Bank of England, 'Components of Private Sector Liquidity', *Bank of England Quarterly Bulletin* (September 1979).
Bank of England, 'Transactions Balances – A New Monetary Aggregate', *Bank of England Quarterly Bulletin* (June 1982).
G. E. Dennis, *Monetary Economics* (Longman, 1981) ch. 1.
HM Treasury, *Economic Progress Report*, no. 123 (July 1980).
W. T. Newlyn, *The Theory of Money* (Oxford University Press, 1971) ch. 1.
R. S. Sayers, *Modern Banking* 7th edn (Oxford University Press, 1967) chs 1, 2, 7, 8.

Chapter 23
Commercial Banks and the Money Supply

In the previous chapter we saw that modern money consists of two components: (i) demand deposits with the commercial banks; (ii) notes. Of these the first, and most important component, consists of liabilities of the *commercial banks*, the second of liabilities of the *central bank*. Since we have defined the money supply as:

> the nominal value of demand deposits and notes held by the non-bank public

it follows that, to explain its determination, we must examine the behaviour of the commercial banks and the central bank, for, just as an individual controls the nominal value of the IOUs he or she issues, so do banks and, in doing so, the latter control the money supply.

Commercial banks: definition and functions

A bank may be defined as an institution which:

(a) accepts deposits which are subject to transfer by cheque
(b) makes loans and advances

Since deposits are tokens of indebtedness *by* banks, while advances are tokens of indebtedness *to* banks, it is clear that, like other financial institutions which borrow from the public in order to acquire a portfolio of financial assets, banks are dealers in debts. Commercial banks are, broadly speaking, those which perform the two functions above by dealing mainly with households and enterprises. *The special significance of commercial banks which distinguishes them from other financial institutions such as life assurance offices lies in the fact that the principal type of liability which they issue to the public, demand deposits, is customary money and in developed societies is the most important kind of money.* By increasing or reducing their borrowing from the public, i.e. by expanding or contracting their deposit liabilities, commercial banks can plainly exert an important influence on the money supply; or, to put the matter another way, they can act as either manufacturers (or destroyers) of money.

Commercial banks, like other privately owned enterprises, are concerned to earn profits for their shareholders. In explaining their behaviour, therefore, the first question we need to ask is how do their profits arise?

Commercial banks have three main sources of revenue. These are:

(a) the interest *received* on their asset portfolio
(b) charges made for the operation of current accounts
(c) the commissions earned by them on the provision of particular services

Against the sum of these must be set two main items of expenditure:

(d) the interest *paid* by banks to induce persons to hold their deposits
(e) their operating expenses, i.e. salaries of managers and clerks, stationery, rent, and so on

If we look at the revenue items it is easy to see that the income received from interest on the asset portfolio must be of major importance.

We are already familiar with the fact that different types of claim carry different rates of return. This is true of bank assets. Notes and coin, for example, provide no money return to their holder. Treasury bills usually offer a relatively low return. Securities (government bonds) are typically more remunerative, returning perhaps 8–15 per cent, while advances, the most remunerative of all bank assets, might provide 15–20 per cent. Plainly, given the magnitude of its asset portfolio, any commercial bank will enjoy a higher average rate of return the greater is the proportion of the higher-yielding assets in its portfolio. Hence, bearing in mind that they aim to maximise profits, commercial banks might be expected to aim at holding a large part of their portfolios as advances and securities.

Commercial banks, however, must, when selecting their asset distributions, take full account of their obligations to depositors. Holders of a bank's deposits are its creditors to the extent of their balances in its books. It is the obligation of the bank to pay its creditors, i.e. encash its deposits if asked to do so by giving legal tender money (notes) on demand (to holders of demand deposits) or at the end of a stated period (to holders of time deposits). Any bank's ability to do this depends upon the liquidity of its asset portfolio. The greater the liquidity of the asset portfolio, the greater the bank's ability to encash its deposits if called upon to do so: that is, the greater its ability to meet the fundamental obligation of deposit banking.

In modern developed economies the rates of return on financial assets tend to be inversely related to their liquidity. Hence, while the need to earn profits pulls commercial banks towards high-yielding (illiquid) asset portfolios, the need to keep liquid pulls them in the reverse direction. The distribution of assets actually chosen by banks thus represents a compromise between the *conflicting claims of profitability and liquidity*. This argument is illustrated in Table 23.1, which, on the basis of assumed rates of return on the various categories of asset, presents a clear contrast between liquid and illiquid asset portfolios.

It is easy to see that distribution *A* offers the bank concerned a higher average return (9.65 per cent) than distribution *B* (approximately 3½ per cent). On the other hand *A* is markedly less liquid a portfolio than *B*.

Notes, coin and demand deposits at the central bank may be regarded as constituting the *cash holding* of the bank. Deposits at the central bank are included since, like notes, they are central bank liabilities and the central bank will convert them into legal tender on demand. The ratio of cash to total liabilities (the cash ratio) is one rather crude index of the

Table 23.1 Alternative asset distributions of bank *X†**

Liabilities	(1)	Assets			Return in per cent per annum (2)	*Asset distributions* *A* (3)	*B* (4)
1. Shareholders' funds	100	Liquid Assets	Cash	Coin	0	50	500
Capital reserves				Notes	0	25	400
				Deposits at central bank	0	85	100
			Treasury bills		8	200	400
2. Deposits							
Demand	1,000	Risk assets	Earning assets	Government securities	10	520	120
Time	500			Advances	12	720	80
TOTAL LIABILITIES	1,600	TOTAL ASSETS				1,600	1,600

*Certain assets such as bank premises have been neglected.
†The rates of return assumed in col. (2) have been chosen arbitrarily. However, they are not unreasonable historically:

	Distribution *A*	*B*
Average rate of return on asset portfolio	9.65%	3.35%
Ratio of cash to total liabilities	10%	62½%
Ratio of liquid assets to total	22½	87½%

liquidity of an asset portfolio. With distribution *A* this ratio is 10 per cent, with *B* 62½ per cent. A second rough measure of liquidity is the ratio of cash plus Treasury bills[1] to total liabilities. This is sometimes called the 'liquid assets' ratio. The table shows this ratio to be 22½ per cent in *A* and 87½ per cent in *B*. Both ratios, of course, are greater in the lower-yielding portfolio *B*. It is also clear that there are, in principle, an infinite number of differing asset portfolios possible. The selection of bank portfolios is thus, though it always requires a compromise between profitability and liquidity, a highly complicated matter. Can we be more precise regarding the likely ratios?

Each business day the customers of any bank are drawing out and paying in legal tender money. Since receipts and payments do not match precisely, the bank will need, as till money, certain minimum working balances. Moreover, beyond these minimum working balances, banks will require a secondary precautionary reserve to cover unexpected demands on deposits. Since cash provides no income the bank will economise in cash to the limit of its ability and, where possible, hold its *secondary reserves* in the form of readily shiftable interest-bearing assets of high capital certainty such as Treasury bills. In making its decisions regarding the cash and liquid asset ratios a bank will rely heavily upon past experience. Past experience will give a good guide to the minimum of till money required. And past experience will provide a fair guide to the probable fluctuation in deposits. Thus, on the basis of its accumulated experience over the years, any bank is likely to develop fairly fixed notions regarding its desired cash and liquid asset ratios. In some cases, particularly in the UK, the conventional cash and liquid asset ratios, over the years, became

[1]Or other assets of equivalent 'liquidity'.

– at least in the case of the cash ratios – very close to unwritten laws. In most countries with highly developed financial systems there is a considerable degree of stability in these ratios.

Once the bank has assured itself of sufficient cash and liquid assets, the remainder of its portfolio can be allocated beween government securities and advances. These are sometimes called 'illiquid' or 'risk' assets.

This brief discussion of the principles underlying banks' choice of asset leads to the following conclusions:

1. Banks' asset portfolios represent a compromise between the claims of profitability and liquidity.
2. In developed financial systems banks commonly establish conventions regarding:
   (a) the desired ratio of cash to total (or deposit) liabilities
   (b) the desired ratio of liquid assets to total (or deposit) liabilities
3. These conventions are based on the accumulated experience of the past and usually change only rather slowly.

Deposit creation in which the commercial banks are active

We have already spoken of the commercial banks' ability to vary the money supply by the creation or destruction of deposits. How and why are deposits created and destroyed?

In examining these questions it is convenient to begin with the assumption that the commercial banking system consists of a single bank. Suppose this is so: How can that bank's deposits increase? We may distinguish two general cases: that in which the bank is the active or initiating agent; and that in which it is passive. Let us consider the former category first.

Commercial bankers in general are in the happy position that their IOUs are accepted as money by the community. To purchase an asset from a member of the public and thus increase its earnings, our bank has merely to draw a cheque upon itself. Since the recipient of the cheque must bank with it, the consequence of such a purchase is to increase its deposit liabilities by the amount of the cheque paid to whoever is selling the asset to the bank, and increase the bank's assets by the value of the asset purchased, plainly an equal amount. Such a transaction can be illustrated very simply.

We assume our single bank to begin operations with its liabilities and assets in the following position:

BANK *X*: POSITION 1
(*£m*)

Liabilities		*Assets*	
Deposits	1,000	Cash	100
		Securities	400
		Advances	500
	1,000		1,000

Bank *X* now decides to purchase £10 million of government securities. It does so by sending an order to its broker, who purchases these securities in the market from John Smith and Peter Robinson each of whom receives a cheque for £5 million drawn by Bank *X* on itself. Both these individuals have accounts with Bank *X* into which they will pay the cheques.

Their deposits, Bank *X*'s liabilities, will accordingly rise by £10 million. At the same time Bank *X*'s security portfolio will expand by £10 million. Thus we reach position 2:

BANK *X*: POSITION 2
(*£m*)

Liabilities		*Assets*		
Deposit (pos. 1)	1,000	Cash		100
plus J. Smith	5	Securities (pos. 1)	400	
plus P. Robinson	5	*plus* purchases from		
		J. Smith	5	
	1,010	P. Robinson	5	410
		Advances		500
Total liabilities	1,010	Total assets		1,010

This simple transaction has had the following obvious consequences:

1. Bank *X*'s deposit liabilities *and hence the money supply* have increased by £10 million,
2. The public is now holding an additional £10 million of money,
3. Bank *X* is now holding an additional £10 million of *earning assets*.

Moreover, it has had the additional consequence, which is not too obvious, of *reducing Bank X's cash ratio from 10 per cent in position 1 to 9.9 per cent in position 2.*

Now it can be objected to this example that Messrs Smith and Robinson would probably not be willing to hold the whole of their additional money balances in the form of bank deposits but would keep a portion of them in notes and coin. Let us suppose that this is the case and Smith and Robinson decide to hold one-fifth of their increased money balances in the form of legal tender. With this assumption we reach position 2a:

BANK *X*: POSITION 2A
(*£m*)

Liabilities		*Assets*		
Deposits (pos. 1)	1,000	Cash (pos. 1)	100	
		less withdrawals by		
plus J. Smith	4	J. Smith	1	
plus P. Robinson	4	P. Robinson	1	98
Total deposits		Securities (as pos. 2)		410
(pos. 2a)	1,008			
		Advances		500
	1,008			1,008

Corresponding with position 2a, the additional money holdings of Robinson and Smith would be:

	J. Smith	*P. Robinson*	*Total*
Bank deposits	4	4	8
Notes or coin	1	1	2
	5	5	10

In this case (2a) we have the additional consequences that:

(a) Bank *X*'s *cash holding* has been reduced
(b) Its cash ratio has fallen rather more sharply to approximately 9.7 per cent

Hence, on the basis of this simple example, we are justified in reaching the following tentative conclusions:

1. A bank may increase its deposits and hence the money supply by purchasing any asset from the public.
2. Such an increase in its deposits will involve a fall in its cash to deposits ratio.
3. The fall in this ratio will be greater, the greater the proportion of the increase in the money supply which the public wishes to hold in the form of legal tender notes and coin.

Let us now see what will happen if Bank *X* grants additional advances for, say, £10 million. Let us suppose such advances are granted first of all as a loan to the *XYZ* Manufacturing Co. Ltd. Since the advance is made as a *loan* the balance of the *XYZ* Co. rises by £10 million. Hence deposit liabilities increase by £10 million, while there is an equal increase in advances. We move, therefore, from position 1 to position 3:

BANK *X*: POSITION 3
(*£m*)

Liabilities			*Assets*		
Deposits (pos. 1)	1,000		Cash		100
plus new deposits			Securities		400
of *XYZ* Co.	10	1,010	Advances (pos. 1)	500	
			plus new advance		
			of *XYZ* Co.	10	510
Total liabilities		1,010	Total Assets		1,010

If the advance is granted as an overdraft the matter is a little more complicated since the *granting* of the overdraft does not itself alter the bank's balance-sheet. Indeed, all that is likely to occur is the receipt by the *XYZ* Co. of a letter from Bank *X* authorising it to overdraw its existing balance up to £10 million if it wishes to do so. Only as the *XYZ* Co. makes use of this facility by drawing cheques in favour of, say, Robinson and Smith is there any change in deposits and the amount of advances. For example, let us suppose the *XYZ* Co. pays £8 million to Smith and £2 million to Robinson. Then we have a new position 3a:

BANK *X*: POSITION 3A
(*£m*)

Liabilities			*Assets*		
Deposits (pos. 1)	1,000		Cash		100
plus J. Smith	8		Securities		400
plus P. Robinson	2	1,010	Advances (pos. 1)	500	
			plus overdraft		
			XYZ Co.	10	510
		1,010			1,010

It is clear from comparison of positions 2, 3 and 3a that granting an advance, whether in the form of a loan or an overdraft, has the same effect on the balance-sheet position of Bank *X* as the purchase of an equivalent amount of securities, though, in the case of an overdraft, the balance-sheet is not altered until the overdraft facilities are actually used. Our tentative conclusions are thus perfectly general. If Bank *X* sets out to increase its earning assets the consequences are first an increase in its deposit liabilities, and hence in the money supply, and second a fall in its cash ratio.

What are the limits upon bank expansion of this type? We have already noticed that banks tend to maintain a conventional (or legally imposed) cash ratio. As long as this is the case, the planned cash ratio, *given the extent* of the bank's existing cash holding, is sufficient to define a maximum of deposit liabilities and to place a limit upon *active* deposit creation by banks. To see this, we need only to look back to position 1. At that stage Bank *X*'s cash ratio was 10 per cent. If 10 per cent had been the Bank's planned ratio, the expansions in our examples would never have taken place since each involved a *fall in the actual cash ratio*. The effect of adopting a rigid cash ratio convention is thus to remove final control of the volume of its deposits from Bank *X*. Whatever its cash holding Bank *X* will now buy (or sell) securities and grant (or recall) advances until its cash holdings represent 10 per cent of its deposits. This means that the money supply is determined by (i) the cash ratio, which determines the volume of bank deposits which can be based upon a given cash holding; and (ii) whatever influences determine the magnitude of the bank's cash holdings.

Deposit creation in which the commercial banks are passive

Now that we have seen how a bank may create deposits actively, let us examine how deposits may alter when the bank is passive.

There are certain assets which a commercial bank will always purchase if offered to it by an individual (or enterprise) and thus create a deposit in his or her (its) favour. These assets are (i) legal tender notes and coin; (ii) the obligations of other banks; (iii) foreign exchange. To illustrate these possibilites let us start again from position 1 and assume that the public now decides that it would rather hold £10 million of its existing money holdings as bank deposits than as notes. Accordingly it pays £10 million to the credit of its account with Bank *X*. Thus we reach position 4.

BANK *X*: POSITION 4
(*£m*)

Liabilities			*Assets*		
Deposits (pos. 1)	1,000		Cash (pos. 1)	100	
			plus new cash	10	
New deposits	10	1,010			
			Securities		400
			Advances		500
		1,010			1,010

The consequences of this decision on the part of the public are:

(a) to increase their deposits with Bank *X* by £10 million
(b) to increase Bank *X*'s cash holdings by £10 million
(c) to leave the public's money holdings (the money supply) unaltered – the public are now holding an additional £10 million of deposits (bank money) but £10 million less of legal tender money (notes)
(d) to increase Bank *X's* cash ratio from 10 per cent to 10.9 per cent

Bank *X* if it wishes can now set about restoring its cash ratio to 10 per cent by undertaking an *active* expansion of deposits through, for example, the purchase of £90 million worth of additional securities. With the bank's cash ratio restored to equilibrium we reach position 5:

BANK *X*: POSITION 5
(£m)

Liabilities			*Assets*		
Deposits (pos. 1)	1,000		Cash (pos. 1)	100	
plus passively created	10		*plus* new cash	10	110
plus actively created	90	1,100	Securities (pos. 1)	400	
			plus new purchases	90	490
			Advances		500
		1,100			1,100

In position 5 we can see that Bank *X*, by purchasing an additional £90 million of securities, has expanded its deposits sufficiently to restore its desired cash ratio of 10 per cent. This final position is reached, it is worth noticing, by an expansion in which the bank was first passive and then active.

The second type of asset which the bank will always purchase is a claim upon another bank. We have assumed Bank *X* to be the only commercial bank in the system. The only other bank on which claims may be issued is therefore the central bank. Let us assume that John Smith has a cheque drawn on the central bank for £10 million. This he pays into his account at Bank *X*. We reach position 6:

BANK *X*: POSITION 6
(£m)

Liabilities			*Assets*	
Deposits (pos. 1)	1,000		Cash	100
plus J. Smith	10	1,010	Claim on central bank	10
			Securities	400
			Advances	500
		1,010		1,010

At the conclusion of the day's business Bank *X* will present its claim upon the central bank and the central bank will credit Bank *X*'s account with itself. Accordingly we reach position 7:

BANK *X*: POSITION 7
(£m)

Liabilities		*Assets*		
Deposits (pos. 6)	1,010	Cash (pos. 6)	100	
		plus new deposit		
		at central bank	10	110
		Securities		400
		Advances		500
	1,010			1,010

Again we see that Bank *X*'s cash holding has increased £10 million. This is because Bank *X* holds part of its cash in the form of deposits at the central bank. Such deposits from its point of view are cash. Hence its cash holdings have increased and its cash ratio risen once more, as in position 4, to 10.9 per cent. Once again it can undertake an active expansion to position 5.

If John Smith had received his deposit at Bank *X* not because of a £10 million cheque on the central bank but because he had sold £10 million worth of foreign exchange we should have had a similar process. This is shown below at position 6a and 7a:

BANK *X*: POSITION 6A
(£m)

Liabilities			*Assets*	
Deposits (pos. 1)	1,000		Cash	100
J. Smith	10	1,010	Foreign exchange	10
			Securities	400
			Advances	500
		1,010		1,010

At the close of business Bank *X* will sell the foreign exchange to the central bank. This is usually done since commercial banks hold only small working balances of foreign exchange and sell any surplus to the central bank. Thus we reach position 7a which is identical with position 7:

BANK *X*: POSITION 7A
(£m)

Liabilities		*Assets*		
Deposits (pos. 6a)	1,010	Cash (pos. 6)	100	
		plus new deposits		
		at central bank	10	110
		Securities		400
		Advances		500
	1,010			1,010

This last case is very important because when any country's balance of payments is in surplus, i.e. its inhabitants are receiving more foreign exchange than they are paying out, there will be net sales of foreign exchange to the commercial bank(s). It is therefore essential to notice that not only does the country concerned gain foreign exchange in such circumstances but there is: (i) an equal rise in both the deposits and cash holdings of the commercial banks; and (ii) a rise in the cash ratio.

We may thus conclude that a passive expansion of commercial bank deposits, commercial bank cash holdings, and a rise in the cash ratio of commercial banks may be brought about by:

(a) an increase in the public's preference for holding their money as bank deposits rather than notes and coin (position 4)[1]
(b) deposit by the public at the commercial banks of cheques drawn upon the central bank (positions 6 and 7)
(c) net sales by the public to the commercial banks of foreign exchange resulting from a surplus on the balance of payments (positions 6a and 7a)

Any one of these will make possible an active (secondary) expansion by the commercial banks (position 5).

In practice the public's preferences regarding the form in which they wish to hold their stocks of money are fairly stable in the short run. Hence the principal short-run determinants of the cash holdings of the commercial banks and, in consequence, of the money supply are: first, the behaviour of the central bank; second, the state of the balance of payments.

Several commercial banks

Our analysis so far has been based upon the simplifying assumption of a commercial banking system consisting of a single bank – Bank *X*. Do our conclusions hold if more than one bank is introduced? This is an important question, for, as a matter of fact, there are no countries where the commercial banking system consists of only one bank. In order to answer it we therefore present a single example involving not only Bank *X* but also Banks *Y* and *Z*. Our single assumption is that each bank maintains a 10 per cent ratio.

We begin our example by assuming (position 1) that Banks *Y* and *Z* each have a cash ratio of 10 per cent. Bank *X*, however, has recently experienced a £10 million increase in both deposits and cash giving it a ratio of 10.9 per cent. What happens when Bank *X* expands its advances portfolio by, say, £30 million in order to restore its cash ratio? (See Table 23.2.)

As these advances are spent it is plain that not all the deposits created will be with Bank *X*. Since the banks are of roughly equal size it is reasonable to assume that one-third of the advances are paid to customers of *Y* and *Z*. Each of these banks will therefore experience a £10 million increment in deposits against which they will hold £10 million worth of cheques drawn on *X*. At the end of the day's business these cheques will be presented to *X* for payment. *X* will settle in cash and will thus find its cash reserves reduced by £20 million. *This cash, is, however, not lost to the commercial banks as a whole*. It merely passes from *X*

[1]This is *not* a change in liquidity preference, which relates to the public's plans to hold money rather than bonds.

Table 23.2

Position 1

Bank X			Bank Y			Bank Z		
Dep. 1,010	Cash	110	Dep. 1,000	Cash	100	Dep. 1,000	Cash	100
	Securities	400		Securities	600		Securities	200
	Advances	500		Advances	300		Advances	700
1,010		1,010	1,000		1,000	1,000		1,000
Cash ratio 10.9%			Cash ratio 10%			Cash ratio 10%		

Position 2
(After Bank *X* has expanded advances by £30 million)

Bank X			Bank Y			Bank Z		
Dep. 1,020	Cash	90	Dep. 1,010	Cash	110	Dep. 1,010	Cash	110
	Securities	400		Securities	600		Securities	200
	Advances	530		Advances	300		Advances	700
1,020		1,020	1,010		1,010	1,010		1,010
Cash ratio 8.8%			Cash ratio 10.9%			Cash ratio 10.9%		

Position 3
(After Banks *Y* and *Z* have expanded their security portfolios by £15 million)

Bank X			Bank Y			Bank Z		
Dep. 1,030	Cash	100	Dep. 1,020	Cash	105	Dep. 1,020	Cash	105
	Securities	400		Securities	615		Securities	215
	Advances	530		Advances	300		Advances	700
1.030		1,030	1,020		1,020	1,020		1,020
Cash ratio 9.7%			Cash ratio 10.3%			Cash ratio 10.3%		

Position 4
(After all adjustments have been completed)

Bank X			Bank Y			Bank Z		
Dep. 1,040	Cash	104	Dep. 1,030	Cash	103	Dep. 1,030	Cash	103
	Securities	400		Securities	627		Securities	227
	Advances	536		Advances	300		Advances	700
1,040		1,040	1,030		1,030	1,030		1,030
Cash ratio 10%			Cash ratio 10%			Cash ratio 10%		

Increase in bank deposits (position 4 – position 1)
Bank *X* (1,040–1,010) – £30 million
Bank *Y* (1,030–1,000) – £30 million
Bank *Z* (1,030–1,000) – £30 million
Total commercial banking system – £90 million.

to *Y* and *Z*, who now find both their cash holdings and cash ratios increased. This brings us to position 2.

In position 2 both *Y* and *Z* are under some incentive to expand their earning assets. Let us assume that each decides to expand its earning assets by purchasing £15 million-worth of securities. Each will now lose cash to the other two. *Y*'s losses to *Z* will be exactly offset by *Z*'s losses to *Y*. Each, however, will lose one-third of £15 million to *X*. In other words *X* will gain deposits and cash to the value of £10 million. In this way we reach position 3. Finally, by further adjustments we reach position 4 in which each bank has restored its cash ratio to 10 per cent and the *commercial banking system* as a whole is fully adjusted to the £10 million increment in its cash base which was the cause of the expansion.

It is easy to see that the expansion of deposits (and hence the money supply) has been precisely £90 million. This, of course, is identical with the result obtained in an earlier example which was based upon a single bank. This suggests that our 'three-bank' analysis allows us to draw the following conclusions:

1. A system of deposit banks, *provided all expand together*, may increase deposits in response to an increment in their cash holdings to the full limit imposed by their cash ratio.
2. Hence, if in our earlier examples, Bank *X* is considered to stand for the commercial banking system, the conclusions reached in these examples may perfectly properly be applied to a 'commercial banking system' comprising several banks.

Our three-bank analysis, however, also tells us rather more, for it is an obvious inference from the losses in cash experienced by Bank *X* (position 2) that in a multi-bank system a single bank cannot, *unless the other banks also participate*, go very far in expanding deposits. With this lesson in mind the reader may safely apply all the conclusions, reached in our earlier analysis merely on the basis of Bank *X*, to a commercial banking system as a whole.

Questions and exercises

1. 'The principal function of commercial banks is to bring borrower and lender together'. Discuss.

2. Use the *Bank of England Quarterly Bulletin* to prepare a table giving the rates of interest on (i) Treasury bills; (ii) trade bills; (iii) short-term bonds; (iv) medium-term bonds; (v) long-term bonds; (vi) company debentures; (vii) industrial ordinary shares.
   Are the lower rates to be obtained on the more 'liquid' assets? Can you explain why ordinary shares yield less than bonds? To explain this, which assumption of our model have you to abandon?

3. 'A banker's business is founded on confidence.' Explain.

4. Why do some countries have a comparatively small proportion of bank deposits in their money supply?

5. 'An individual bank has little ability to expand the money supply unless all the other banks expand in step.' Elucidate.

6. Use the *Bank of England Quarterly Bulletin* to compare the liabilities and assets of the London clearing banks with the hypothetical structure of Table 23.1. Would our arguments need substantial revision before they could be applied to the clearing banks? If so, what revisions would you propose?

7. Write short notes on: (i) Treasury bills; (ii) government bonds; (iii) advances. What are the principal characteristics of each asset from the point of view of the banker? Base your notes on chapter 6 of the Radcliffe Report (see below).

8. 'A banker can lend no more than he can borrow.' 'A banker can create money and lend it where he will.' Comment. Are these two statements reconcilable?

9. In what circumstances would money lose its liquidity premium? Why?

10. Use the *Bank of England Quarterly Bulletin* to examine the proposition that commercial banks tend to maintain stable asset/deposit ratios.

Suggested reading

Bank of England, 'Monetary Control – Provisions', *Bank of England Quarterly Bulletin* (September 1981).
G. E. J. Dennis, *Monetary Economics* (Longman, 1981) ch. 7.
HM Treasury, *Monetary Control*, Cmnd 7858 (HMSO).
HM Treasury, *Economic Progress Report*, no. 137 (September 1981).
W. T. Newlyn, *The Theory of Money* (Oxford University Press, 1971) chs 1–3.
Radcliffe Report (HMSO, 1959) chs 1–3.

Chapter 24
Central Banking and the Money Supply

In the previous chapter we found that there were three determinants of the money supply:

(a) the *asset preferences* (cash/deposit ratio) of the commercial banks
(b) the *preferences of the non-bank public* regarding the *form* in which they wish to hold their *money* (i.e. as deposits or notes)
(c) the *cash reserves* of the commercial banks

Of these (a) and (b) can as a first approximation be regarded as invariant in the short run. Hence the money supply is determined by the *cash reserves* of the commercial banks.

The importance of the central bank in developed monetary systems arises from the fact that it can control the cash reserves of the commercial banks. It follows that, in the short run, it is the policy of the central bank with regard to these reserves which determines the money supply.

We must now see how the power of the central bank to control the cash reserves of the commercial banks arises.

The central bank and its functions

The central bank is an institiution, often but not always owned by the state, which has the overriding duty of conducting the monetary policy of the government. It is, in terms of our model, the duty of the central bank to control the money supply (and thus the rate of interest) in a manner which has an effect on aggregate demand which the government deems to be appropriate. *The general and overriding function of the central bank is thus discretionary monetary control.* Its particular functions, from which its capacity to perform its main function derive, are the following:

1. It is the sole source of *legal tender money* (notes) which are central bank liabilities.
2. It acts as *bankers' bank* in that commercial banks keep accounts with the central bank just as individuals and enterprises keep accounts with commercial banks.
3. It is the *government's banker* and keeps the main government accounts and provides the government with economic and financial advice.

4. It *holds the gold and foreign exchange reserves* of the country.[1]
5. It acts, if the need arises, as *lender of last resort*.
6. With a 'pegged' exchange rate, it operates so as to maintain the 'pegged' rate chosen by the government, while under a 'floating' rate system, it may intervene in the market for a variety of reasons.
7. It manages the *government debt* (usually known as the National Debt).

Just as the borrowing and lending activities of the commercial banks were reflected in their balance-sheets, so too are the functions of a central bank. To see this consider the (highly simplified) central banking balance-sheet set out in Table 24.1

Table 24.1 Balance-sheet of central bank of Erehwon

Liabilities			Assets	
Notes			Gold and foreign exchange	100
with public	50		Securities	100
with banks	50	100		
Deposits				
of bankers	50			
of government	50	100		
Total liabilities		200	Total assets	200

Note: This balance-sheet neglects the following items which appear on central bank balance-sheets:
Liabilities: capital and reserves; other liabilities.
Assets: premises and equipment; other assets

On the liabilities side we have first *notes*, a part of which is in the tills of the commercial banks, a part of which is held by the *non-bank public* and thus, by definition, forms part of the money supply (function 1).

The second liability consists of *deposits* – partly owned by the *commercial banks* and partly by the *government* (functions 2 and 3).

As *assets* it holds first *gold and foreign exchange* (function 4) and, second, *government securities*, which reflect past lending to the state (functions 1 and 3).

Retaining this balance-sheet let us now assume that (i) commercial banks have demand deposits equal to their total deposits; (ii) have a planned cash/deposits ratio of 10 per cent. Then, since the commercial banks' *cash* (≡ note holdings *plus* deposits at the central bank) are 100, total commercial bank deposits are 1,000 and demand deposits 1,000. Since the non-bank public holds 50 units of notes, the money supply (≡ demand deposits *plus* notes held by the non-bank public) is 1,050 units.

We have, in short, the position shown in Table 24.2.

We shall use this table, in the whole of what follows, to explain the consequences of central banking operations. From the table it is plain that if the central bank can vary the cash holding of the commercial banks it can vary the money supply. Let us see how this can be done.

[1]This is not true of the UK where reserves are held by the Exchange Equalisation Account.

Table 24.2 Position 1

Central Bank				Commercial banks					Non-bank public	
Liabilities		Assets		Liabilities		Assets				
Notes		Gold and foreign		Demand		Cash			Holdings	
with public	50	exchange	100	deposits	1,000	notes	50		of notes	50
with banks	50					deposit at		100	of deposits	1,000
Deposits		Securities	100			central bank	50		Total money supply	1,050
of bankers	50					Securities	500			
of government	50					Advances	400			
	200		200		1,000			1,000	Securities	5,000

Behaviour assumptions:

1. Banks preferred cash ratio $\equiv \dfrac{\text{Cash}}{\text{Deposits}} = 10\% = q$

2. Non-bank public's preferred ratio of legal tender to customary money $\equiv \dfrac{\text{Notes}}{\text{Deposits}} = 5\% = \alpha_1$.

Other assumption:

$$\text{total gross debt outstanding} \equiv \text{central bank holding} + \text{commercial bank holdings} + \text{non-bank public holdings}$$
$$\equiv 100 + 500 + 5{,}000$$
$$\equiv 5{,}600$$

The control of commercial bank cash: open-market operations

Suppose the central bank purchases, in the open market, 10 units of bonds from members of the public. To pay for these it draws cheques on itself. These are paid into the commercial banks who present them to the central bank for payment. The central bank in response then credits the commercial banks with 10 units in its books. As a result, starting from position 1 (Table 24.2) we reach position 2 (Table 24.3). What has happened is this:

(a) in the central bank's balance-sheet assets (securities) have increased by 10 units – so have liabilities (bankers' deposits)
(b) in the commercial banks' balance-sheet assets (cash) have increased by 9.5 units – so have liabilities (demand deposits)
(c) in the non-bank public's balance-sheets assets are unchanged *but* money holdings are *up* by 10 units, bond holdings *down* by a similar amount

We thus see that, as a result of an *open-market purchase* of 10 units, there has been a *primary increase* in the money supply of 10 units.

Adjustment, however, cannot stop at the position depicted by Table 24.3 for the *actual* cash/deposits ratio now exceeds the *planned* cash/deposits ratio of 10 per cent. Moreover the non-bank public is now holding too high a ratio of notes/deposits.

If the banks try to restore the cash/deposit ratio to its planned value they will expand their assets (by buying securities and/or making advances) and thus their deposits until the cash/ratio is restored to its planned value. This is known as the *secondary* increase in the money supply.

After the secondary expansion, the final position (3) is reached. This is shown in Table 24.4.

It follows that our open-market operation (purchase) has produced an increase in the money supply which is a multiple of itself. We have:

$$\text{total increase in money supply} \equiv \Delta M^S = 70$$

of which:

$$\text{primary increase} \equiv X_1 = 10 \text{ units}$$
$$\text{secondary increase} \equiv X_2 = 60 \text{ units}$$

There is, in short, a credit multiplier at work which we can define as:

$$\text{credit multiplier} \equiv \lambda \equiv \frac{\Delta M^S}{X_1} \equiv \frac{\text{total increase in money supply}}{\text{open-market purchase}}$$

We can easily set up a *model* of this credit multiplier as follows. By definition we have:

$$M^S \equiv D + C_h \qquad (24.1)$$

where $D \equiv$ commercial bank deposits, $C_h \equiv$ non-bank public's holding of notes.

Assume the public's preferred ratio of

$$\frac{C_h}{D} = \alpha_1 \qquad (24.2)$$

Table 24.3 Position 2

Central bank					Commercial bank					Non-bank public	
Liabilities			Assets		Liabilities		Assets				
Notes			Gold and foreign		Deposits	1,009.5	Cash			Holdings	
with public		50.5	exchange	100			notes	49.5		of notes	50.5
with banks		49.5					deposit at		———	of deposits	1,009.5
Deposits			Securities	110			central bank	60	109.5		
of bankers		60					Securities		500	Money	
of government		50					Advances		400	supply	1,060
		210		210		1,009.5			1,009.5	Securities	4,990

Table 24.4 Position 3

Central bank					Commercial bank					Non-bank public	
Liabilities			Assets		Liabilities		Assets				
Notes			Gold and foreign		Deposits	1,066.67	Cash			Holdings	
with public	53.3		exchange	100			notes	53.17		of notes	53.33
with banks	53.17	106.5					deposits at			of deposits	1,066.67
Deposits			Securities	110			central bank				
of bankers	53.5							53.5	106.67	Money supply	1,120.0
of government	50	103.5					Securities		550	Securities	4,940.0
							Advances		410		
		210		210		1,066.67			1,066.67		

Then:

$$M^S = D(1 + \alpha_1) \tag{24.3}$$

Now:

$$D = \frac{C_b}{q} \tag{24.4}$$

where $C_b \equiv$ commercial bank cash holdings, $q \equiv$ commercial bank planned cash ratio, so that:

$$M^S = (1 + \alpha_1)\frac{C_b}{q} \tag{24.5}$$

But:

$$C_b \equiv N + B_d - C_h \tag{24.6}$$

where $N \equiv$ notes issued by central bank, $B_d \equiv$ bankers' deposits at the central bank, $C_h \equiv$ notes held by non-bank public, so that, if we substitute in 24.6 from 24.2 we get:

$$C_b = N + B_d - \alpha_1 \frac{C_b}{q}$$

$$C_b = (N + B_d)\frac{q}{q + \alpha_1} \tag{24.7}$$

Hence we have, on substituting again into 24.5:

$$M^S = (N + B_d)\left(\frac{q}{q + \alpha_1}\right)\left(\frac{1 + \alpha_1}{q}\right)$$

$$= (N + B_d)\left(\frac{1 + \alpha_1}{q + \alpha_1}\right) \tag{24.8}$$

An open-market purchase of X_1 increases $N + B_d$ by X_1. Hence the credit multiplier is given by:

$$\frac{\Delta M^S}{X_1} \equiv \lambda = \left(\frac{1 + \alpha_1}{q + \alpha_1}\right) \tag{24.9}$$

In our example:

$$\alpha_1 = 1/20 = 0.05$$
$$q = 1/10 = 0.10$$

therefore:

$$\lambda = \frac{1.05}{0.15} = 7 \tag{24.9n}$$

Hence, as Table 24.4 shows: the total increase in the money supply is **70** units, of which, rounding up the figures, the increase in deposits is **66.67** units, and the increase in notes held by the non-bank public is **3.33** units, while the increase in the banks' cash is **6.67** units.

This model, it should be noticed, contains *two* behaviour assumptions (equations 24.2 and 24.4), the former relating to the non-bank public, the latter to the commercial banks. Assuming these to hold we can generalise our conclusion by saying that:

1. *Any* purchase (sale) of an asset by the central bank from (to) a member of the non-bank public brings about:
   (a) a primary increase (decrease) in the money supply equal to the value of the purchase (sale)
   (b) a secondary increase (decrease) in the money supply which is a multiple of the primary increase (decrease)
2. The magnitude of the total change in the money supply depends upon
   (a) the value of the open-market operation
   (b) the commercial banks' preferred cash ratio
   (c) the (marginal) ratio in which the non-bank public prefers to hold deposits and notes

As presented here, the argument is formally symmetrical: an open-market purchase of X_1 increases the money supply by λX_1; an open-market sale of X_1 reduces the money supply by λX_1. In practice this may not be so. In general a central bank can always *compel* a contraction: it cannot, however, *compel* an expansion. In some circumstances the commercial banks may prefer – perhaps because of uncertainty – to hold a cash/deposit ratio *above* the 10 per cent they usually prefer. Hence it is possible that the secondary expansion resulting from a given open-market *purchase* may be less than the contraction resulting from a corresponding open-market sale. This qualification is worth noting.

What assets does the central bank buy and sell? Primarily, as our example suggests, it buys and sells government securities. Purchases (sales) of this kind, conducted on the market by the central bank's broker, are called open-market purchases (sales). They are the most important single device which the central bank can use to control the money supply.

In addition the central bank buys (sells) foreign exchange at whatever rate of exchange it wishes to maintain. Net purchases (sales) of foreign exchange from the non-bank public have an influence on the money supply of the type we have already discussed. However where there is a fixed rate of exchange which the central bank (on government instructions) seeks to maintain, the bank has no option but to act as residual buyer or seller. If, for example, at the ruling rate of exchange the demand for foreign exchange in terms of the domestic currency exceeds the supply, *either* the rate of exchange will move *against* the domestic currency to equate supply and demand, *or* the central bank must sell whatever foreign exchange is necessary to satisfy demand. In conducting such residual net purchases (or sales) the central bank is *passive*. It provides to (sells) or takes off (purchases from) the market whatever is necessary to maintain the price (rate of exchange). By contrast in open-market operations the central bank is *active* in the sense that, unless it is compelled to maintain an invariant rate of interest (fixed price for bonds) it chooses *when* open-market operations are necessary and the scale on the direction in which they should be conducted.

To illustrate: suppose that, to maintain the rate of exchange at its existing level, the central bank has to purchase 10 units (in terms of domestic currency) of foreign exchange. Starting, as before, from position 1 (Table 24.2) we reach position 2a (Table 24.5).

Comparison of this table with Table 24.3 (position 2 of the earlier example) shows only one variation: namely, that in this case it is the central bank's holdings of *gold and foreign*

Table 24.5 Position 2a

Central bank					Commercial bank						Non-bank public	
Liabilities			Assets		Liabilities		Assets					
Notes			Gold and foreign		Deposits	1,009.5	Cash				Holdings	
with public		50.5	exchange	110			notes		49.5		of notes	50.5
with banks		49.5					deposit at				of deposits	1,009.5
Deposits			Securities	100			central bank		60	109.5		
of bankers		60					Securities			500	Money supply	1,060
of government		50					Advances			400	Securities	5,000
		210		210		1,009.5				1,009.5		

Table 24.6 Restriction of money supply by means of variation in required reserve ratio

Central bank					Commercial bank						Non-bank public	
Liabilities			Assets		Liabilities		Assets					
Notes			Gold and foreign		Deposits	750.1	Cash				Holdings	
with public	37.4		exchange	100			notes		56.3		of notes	37.4
with banks	56.3	93.7					deposits		56.3	112.6	of deposits	750.1
Deposits			Securities	100			Securities			280.4		
of banks	56.3						Advances			357.1	Money supply	787.5
of government	50	106.3									Securities	5,219.6
		200		200		750.1				750.1		

$$\text{Commercial bank's cash ratio} = \frac{112.6}{750.1} \times 100 \simeq 15\%$$

exchange which have risen by 10 units, *not* its holdings of government securities. Apart from this, positions 2 and 2a are identical. Hence since position 2, via a *secondary* expansion, led to position 3 so will position 2a. This illustrates the proposition that *any* purchase (sale) of assets by the central bank from the non-bank public has the same consequences for the money supply.

Table 24.5 shows that the central bank is holding, on behalf of the community, increased foreign reserves. An increase in reserves occurs whenever a country receives more foreign exchange (as export proceeds) than it pays out (in import costs). Hence, since this is simply a situation in which exports − imports > zero, the balance of payments is in surplus. We may add to our two previous propositions:

3. A balance-of-payments surplus (deficit) causes the central bank to purchase (sell) foreign exchange equal to the value of the surplus (deficit) in domestic currency.
4. This brings about:
   (a) a primary increase (decrease) in the money supply equal to the surplus (deficit)
   (b) a secondary increase (decrease) in the money supply determined in the usual way.
5. As long as the balance of payments is in surplus (deficit) there will be a tendency for the money supply to undergo an expansion (contraction) which is a multiple of the surplus (deficit).

Finally it is worth noting that, if there is a *surplus* on the balance of payments of 10 units per period, the central bank can offset the impact of its consequential *passive* purchases of foreign exchange on the money supply by undertaking *active* open-market *sales* of 10 units per period. This keeps its total assets, and hence the money supply, constant. Such a policy is sometimes called *neutralisation*.[1] Its distinguishing characteristic is that the central bank's domestic assets (in our model, securities) change in the opposite direction to its external assets (gold and foreign exchange). In short, disequilibrium on the balance of payments does not prevent the central bank from determining the money supply, though it may make it harder for it to do so in the short run. But no central bank can indefinitely accumulate or decumulate reserves. In the longer term the central bank's powers of neutralisation are limited.

Controlling bank cash: other devices

In some countries (Australia was a notable example) the central bank, in its task of controlling the money supply, was faced by (i) very large surpluses (deficits) on external account due primarily to sharp fluctuations in the price of exports; and (ii) a market in securities which was too small to permit the massive open-market operations necessary to achieve a reasonable measure of neutralisation. In these circumstances central banks are usually given special legal powers which enable them to control the commercial banks. Two types are particularly well known. They are:

(a) powers to *vary* the ratio which commercial banks are *required* to maintain between cash and deposits – known as the power to employ 'variable reserve ratios'

[1]The Exchange Equalisation Account automatically provides for neutralisation in this sense.

(b) powers to *freeze* a part of commercial bank deposits at the central bank, thus removing them, by *definition*, from the commercial banks' *cash* – the frozen deposits are then defined as 'special deposits' or 'special account deposits', or some such classification.

Essentially what happens in these cases is that the central bank, finding itself unable to control the money supply by dealings with the non-bank public, obtains legal powers to exert direct control over the cash holdings of the commercial banks.

In our model, equation 24.8 gave an expression for the equilibrium money supply in terms of:

$N + B_d \equiv$ notes issued by the central bank *plus* bankers' deposits at the central bank

$q \equiv$ the preferred cash/deposits ratio of the commercial banks

$\alpha_1 \equiv$ the ratio of the public holding of notes to deposits

Variation in the reserve ratio illustrated formally in terms of the model consists of an *enforced* variation in q. In such a case there is no *primary* change in the money supply. The total change is the *secondary* expansion or contraction forced upon the banks. Clearly if q is *raised* a *contraction* must result. If q is reduced an expansion may (if the banks wish) take place. This asymmetry simply reflects our earlier argument concerning open-market operations. We can use equation 24.8 to illustrate. This is:

$$M^S = (N + B_d)\left(\frac{1 + \alpha_1}{q + \alpha_1}\right)$$

or, using position 1:

$$M^S = (150) \times 7 = 1{,}050$$

where:

$$q = 0.10$$
$$\alpha_1 = 0.05$$
$$N = 100$$
$$B_d = 50$$

Suppose q is now said to become 0.15. In numerical terms the money supply becomes, as a result of a *secondary* contraction:

$$M_1^S = 150\left(\frac{1.05}{0.20}\right) = 787.5 \quad \text{or} \quad \lambda = 5.25$$

Clearly the variable reserve ratio device is potentially at least one of great power, though in practice reserve ratios are unlikely to be varied as drastically as this example would suggest.

The alternative device, which we shall call that of *special deposits*, simply freezes a part of commercial deposits (B_d). Suppose 10 units are so frozen. B_d now becomes 40 and our model yields for the new equilibrium money supply:

$$M_2^S = (100 + 40) \times 7 = 980$$

Table 24.7 Effect of a call to special accounts of 10 units

Position 2B									
Central bank				Commercial banks					
Liabilities		Assets		Liabilities		Assets		Holdings of non-bank public	
Notes		Gold and foreign		Deposits	1,000	Cash		Notes	50
with public	50	exchange	100			notes	50	Deposits	1,000
with banks	50	Securities	100			deposit at		Money supply	1,050
Deposits						central bank	40	Securities	5,000
bankers						Special deposits	10		
(i) free	40					Securities	500		
(ii) special	10					Advances	400		
government	50								
	200		200		1,000		1,000		

$$\text{Cash ratio} = \frac{90}{1{,}000} < 10\%$$

Table 24.8 Final position

Liabilities		Assets		Liabilities		Assets		Holdings of non-bank public	
Notes		Gold and foreign		Deposits	933.3	Cash		Notes	46.7
with public	46.7	exchange	100			Notes	53.3	Deposits	933.3
with banks	53.3	Securities	100			Deposit at		Money supply	980
Deposits						central bank	40	Securities	5,050
bankers						Special deposits	10		
(i) free	40					Securities	450		
(ii) special	10					Advances	380		
government	50								
	200		200		933.3		933.3		

Cash ratio = 10%

In short the *variable reserve ratio* device changes the *multiplier* leaving the quantity of bank cash initially unaltered. The *special deposit* device changes *bank cash* (by freezing what before was a part of it) leaving the *multiplier unaltered*. Neither device has any *primary* effect on the money supply and both make it unnecessary for the central bank to conduct open-market operations.

These procedures, for a given change in the money supply from position 1 (Table 24.2) are illustrated in Tables 24.6 and 24.7.

Lender of last resort

The central bank's function as lender of last resort is, in the UK, primarily of historical interest, for strictly speaking this function refers to the obligation on the central bank to lend, virtually without limit, if the stability of the financial system is ever called into question. A hypothetical example may serve to illustrate what is implied.

Suppose we begin, as usual, in position 1 as set out in Table 24.2. In this situation we assume that the non-bank public becomes doubtful of the capacity of the commercial banking system to encash deposits on demand: that is, to meet its obligations. There is, in short, a crisis of confidence.

Now the public will hold bank deposits (customary money) only so long as it is confident of the banks' capacity to encash deposits on demand. If the public thinks that the banks may *not* be able to encash deposits, it will rush to cash them. In terms of our model, there will be a catastrophic shift in α_1, i.e. the ratio in which the public wishes to hold notes and deposits.

Now the banks have deposit liabilities of 1,000 units and hold cash only 100 units. Hence when the public has encashed 100 units of deposits we reach position 2c shown in Table 24.9. In this position, the banks' cash is zero. Deposits, however, are still 900 units. If the public insists on trying to encash further deposits then, *unless the banking system can find additional cash*, the banks must suspend payment. In this event the banking system, and with it the monetary system, will collapse. Deposits will no longer serve as customary money save possibly at a discount in terms of notes. Such a financial collapse would, beyond all doubt, have immense economic and social consequences. In a situation of this kind it is the duty of the central bank to act as lender of last resort and, by doing so, to ensure the liquidity and hence stability of the banking and monetary systems.

To illustrate what acting as *lender of last resort* means, assume that, after encashing 100 units of deposits, the public insists on cashing a further 300 units. To meet this demand, which the banks cannot meet, the central bank lends to the banks, say, 400 units. The banks take these loans in the form of notes and pass 300 units to the public. Thus we reach position 3c (Table 24.10). Here we see that the central bank's liabilities (notes) have risen by 400 units above the figure at position 2b. Against this they have a corresponding asset ('advances to commercial banks') of 400 units.

The commercial banks' liabilities have risen by 100 units, the net result of a 400 unit increase in liabilities *to* the central bank and a 300 unit decrease in their liabilities to the non-bank public.

The money supply is unaltered in total. However, the public now holds only 600 units of deposits (as against its original 1,000), and, as a results, has 450 units of notes (as against its original 50).

Table 24.9 Operation as lender of last resort: position 2c – the crisis

Central bank					Commercial banks					Holdings of public	
Liabilities			Assets		Liabilities		Assets				
Notes			Gold and foreign		Deposits	900	Cash			Notes	150
with public	150		reserves	100			notes		Nil	Deposits	900
with banks	Nil	150					deposit at				
							central bank		Nil		
Deposits			Securities	100			Securities		500	Money supply	1,050
of bankers	Nil						Advances		400	Securities	5,000
of government	50	50									
		200		200		900			900		

Table 24.10 The lender of last resort: position 3c

Central bank					Commercial bank					Holdings of public	
Liabilities			Assets		Liabilities		Assets				
Notes			Gold and foreign		Deposits	600	Cash			Notes	450
with public	450		reserves	100	Loan from		notes	100		Deposits	600
with banks	100	550			central bank	400	deposits at				
							central bank	Nil	100		
Deposits			Securities	100			Securities		500	Money supply	1,050
of bankers	Nil		Advances to				Advances		400	Securities	5,000
of government	50	50	commercial banks	400							
		600		600		1,000			1,000		

As long as the 'crisis of confidence' persists, the central bank must continue to act as lender of last resort. Once the non-bank public is sure that it *can*, if it wishes, always convert deposits into notes on demand, it will no longer wish to do so. Notes will be deposited at the commercial banks. As a result they will pay off their loans from the central bank and the system will revert to position 1 – the position which existed *before* the crisis of confidence occurred.

This example illustrates, in simple terms, the 'classic' case of a central bank acting as lender of last resort in a financial panic. Such situations are nowadays rare – at least in developed economies. Essentially the example illustrates a situation in which the central bank is compelled, in order to preserve the financial and monetary system, to act as *residual lender*. This it commonly still does, though not usually in a situation in which confidence has collapsed. *It now acts as residual lender in situations in which it has, deliberately, compelled the commercial banks to borrow from it.* This sounds perverse. How can it occur?

Suppose we are in position 1 and the central bank wishes to contract the money supply. We assume that it cannot undertake open-market sales so it 'freezes' in special deposits, say, 10 units of what was bank cash.

In this situation the banks have a cash ratio *below* their preferred ratio. The result must be a secondary contraction. But this cannot be carried out instantly, for, if the central bank cannot sell 10 units of securities on the open market neither can the commercial banks, while to reduce advances necessarily takes time. Hence to maintain their cash ratio the commercial banks borrow from the central bank. It *must*, to meet its obligations as lender of last resort, act as a *residual lender*. Hence it lends. But although it will never refuse to lend, *it can charge whatever rate it likes on its loans*. In the postulated circumstances it will charge a rate sufficiently high to compel the banks to get out of debt to it (carry out their secondary contraction) as quickly as they can. Such a rate is sometimes called a *penal* or *penalty* rate. Its object is twofold: (i) to compel contraction; and (ii) to raise interest rates.

The general conclusion is that whenever a central bank acts as residual lender it can, if it wishes, raise interest rates and compel contraction by charging the banks a penalty rate for their advances. For in such circumstances the banks, compelled to borrow at a rate higher than that at which they *can* currently lend, will (i) raise their own lending (and borrowing) rates, and (ii) embark on a secondary contraction. In our formal discussion of the rate of interest we saw that it was a price equating the demand to hold money with the supply of money. A contraction in the money supply *ceteris paribus* raises the rate of interest. This analysis is quite consistent with the above example. Indeed the example can best be viewed by the reader as an illustration, in institutional terms, of the formal analysis of Chapter 11.

The rate at which the central bank will lend is known by various names in various countries. In Britain, for example, it was called 'Bank Rate'[1] and, for historical reasons, was charged not on loans made *directly* to the banks but on advances made *indirectly* through the *discount houses*. In Australia the rate is known as the 'central bank rate'. Unlike Bank Rate, it is not published. Often it is called 'the central bank discount rate' because the *method of lending* takes the form of the purchase *by* the central bank *from* the commercial banks of a particular government debt known as a *Treasury bill*. Since the initial purchase of the Treasury bill from the Treasury by the commercial bank is called 'discounting' its sale to the central bank is called 'rediscounting'. In short, each financial system has its own individual institutional arrangements and its own nomenclature. These details, though fascinating and important, do not concern us in this context. What matters is

[1]Now replaced by 'Minimum Lending Rate'.

the essential nature of the operation and this is, at our present level of abstraction, very much the same in all systems.

We may conclude by saying that:

1. *Historically* the role of the central bank as *lender of last resort* arose because of the need to protect the financial and monetary system from 'crises of confidence'.
2. *Contemporaneously* central banks rarely have to act as lender of last resort in this sense, though they often act, frequently as a matter of deliberate choice, as *residual lender*.
3. The central bank must *always* be prepared to act in this way.
4. Whenever it does it *can charge whatever rate it thinks fit*.
5. This power gives it a measure of direct control over interest rates which is quite compatible with the theory set out in Chapter 11.

Government fiscal operations and debt management

Suppose, in any period, we have a situation in which:

T	$-$	$(G + R)$	$=$	10
tax receipts	$-$	(government expenditure)	$=$	10

Then the government is running a *surplus* at the rate of 10 units per period. It follows that the public is paying into the government account (at the central bank) a net sum of 10 units. Starting, as usual, from position 1 we reach position 2d (Table 24.11).

As a result of the surplus:

(a) government deposits are up by 10 units, bankers' deposits are down by 10
(b) the money supply is down by 10 units
(c) commercial bankers' cash ratio is *below* their preferred ratio

Clearly a secondary contraction will tend to follow from position 2d. What does the government do with its surplus? It has two choices: first, it can continue to hold higher balances idle; or, second, it can use these balances to repay some of its debt by buying up some of its outstanding obligations in the market.

Obviously by acting on the second choice the government can lower its annual interest bill (reduce R). It will therefore repay debt (by purchase) and the central bank will advise it as to which debt to repay. Strictly this is not one question but two. For the government has two types of choice:

1. Shall it repay debt held by the central bank or debt held outside the central bank?
2. What type of debt (short-term or long-term) shall it repay?

Our model contains only one kind of government debt – long-term bonds. We cannot therefore deal with question 2, though in practice government debt in many differing maturities is outstanding and the choice of which to repay may influence the relative interest rates on the debts of different maturities. We can, however, ask question 1 in terms of our model.

Suppose the 10 units are used to repay the debt held by the central bank. We reach position 3d (Table 24.12).

Table 24.11 The impact of a surplus of 10 units: position 2d

Central bank					Commercial bank					Non-bank public	
Liabilities			Assets		Liabilities		Assets				
Notes			Gold and foreign		Deposits	990	Cash			Holdings	
with public	50		exchange	100			notes	50		of notes	50
with banks	50						deposit at			of deposits	990
							central bank	40	90		
Deposits			Securities	100			Securities		500	Money supply	1,040
of bankers	40						Advances		400	Securities	5,000
of government	60										
	200			200		990			990		

Table 24.12 Repayment of debt held by the central bank: position 3d

Central bank					Commercial banks					Non-bank public	
Liabilities			Assets		Liabilities		Assets				
Notes			Gold and foreign		Deposits	990	Cash			Holdings	
with public	50		exchange	100			notes	50		of notes	50
with banks	50	100					deposit at			of deposits	990
							central bank	40	90		
Deposits			Securities	90			Securities		500	Money supply	1,040
of bankers	40						Advances		400	Securities	5,000
of government	50	90									
		190		190		990			990		

Table 24.13 Repayment of debt held by non-bank public: position 4d

Central bank					Commercial banks					Non-bank public	
Liabilities			Assets		Liabilities		Assets				
Notes			Gold and foreign		Deposits	1,000	Cash			Holdings	
with public	50		exchange	100			notes	50		of notes	50
with banks	50	100					deposit at			of deposits	1,000
							central bank	50	100		
Deposits			Securities	100			Securities		500	Money supply	1,050
of banks	50						Advances		400	Securities	4,990
at government	50	100									
		200		200		1,000			1,000		

From this position a secondary contraction must follow.

Alternatively, suppose the 10 units are used to repay debt held by the non-bank public. We reach position 4d, which, from the monetary point of view, must lead to a restoration of position 1 (Table 24.13).

Generalising this result we may say that:

(a) a government surplus in any period brings about a primary decrease in the money supply equal to the surplus
(b) if the surplus is used to repay debt held by the central bank the primary decrease will be followed by a secondary decrease
(c) if the surplus is used to repay debt held by the general public (or the commercial banks) there will be no change in the money supply, which will return to its original value

It is a simple matter for the reader to work out the corresponding propositions with regard to a *deficit*. Here the result turns on whether the *deficit* is financed by *borrowing* from the central bank or the public.

This analysis shows that, in advising the government on debt operations, even of the limited kind permitted by our model, the central bank can exert an important influence on the money supply and the rate of interest.

The money supply and the monetary base

If we look back at equation 24.8 we find that:

$$M^S = (N + B_d) \left(\frac{1 + \alpha_1}{q + \alpha_1} \right)$$

where the expression $(1 + \alpha_1)/(q + \alpha_1)$ is a form of 'multiplier' and is a function of the two ratios α_1 and q. What of the *multiplicand*?

We did not give $N + B_d$ a special name. It is, however, one definition, perhaps the most common, of what is called the *monetary base*. Thus equation 24.8 gives the nominal money supply (M^S) as the product of the monetary base ($\equiv MB$) and a multiplier which in equation 24.8 we called λ. Hence:

$$M^S = MB \times \lambda$$

is both forms of the so-called 'base-multiplier' theory and of 24.8.

We have also argued, partly for simplicity in exposition, that the central bank, by open-market operations and perhaps other devices, can determine MB. As a piece of simple theory, this is acceptable. It is, however, not uncommon for particular central banks to argue that their control over MB is in fact so imperfect that seeking to control the nominal money supply by setting the value of MB so that, given the authorities' best estimate of λ, some target level of the money stock ($\equiv M^{S*}$) will be attained, is impractical. Indeed, the Bank of England has argued in very much this way during the controversy over monetary control in the UK which led to the introduction of a new method of control in August 1981.

Limitations of space prevent any detailed discussion of UK financial institutions or monetary control methods. The reader should therefore supplement the discussion in this and the following chapters by a careful reading of the references marked with an asterisk. Although the details differ very considerably you should find the simple model of the text very relevant to the UK controversy.

Summary

In this chapter we have attempted to show what a central bank is, how a central bank can control the nominal money supply, and some of the devices it employs to do so.

Our method has been to erect a *model* of the central bank and its associated commercial banking system. No monetary system is precisely like this model. Nevertheless, the model displays many of the essential features of developed monetary systems sufficiently well to be useful in gaining a *general* understanding of the principal central banking techniques and operations. Typically, however, each national monetary system possesses individual characteristics and complexities. A full understanding of any system therefore requires a detailed knowledge of the institutions which comprise it. The reader is thus urged to study the references given at the end of this chapter for a fuller account of the UK system.

We may now ask whether we were justified, for example in Chapters 11 and 12, in treating the nominal money supply as a variable determined independently of all other variables in the model and thus *exogenous*. Undoubtedly this is a convenient pedagogic device – akin to assuming that the consumption function is such that real planned consumption depends on real income alone. Unfortunately convenient expository assumptions can be misleading. Now that we know that the principal proximate determinant of the money supply is central banking policy we must ask how misleading it is to write:

$$M^S = \bar{M} \equiv \text{some exogenously determined quantity}$$

The short answer to this question is that it may well be very misleading indeed, and is certain to be misleading in some degree. The principal reason why this is so is that the central bank, in managing the nominal money supply, typically does so with certain objectives in mind. One of these, which in practice seems to be of considerable importance, is preserving the orderly operation of money and capital markets ($\equiv$ market for long-term funds). Hence central banks commonly seek to prevent large fluctuations in r. Thus if r is above what they think it ought to be, or is rising faster than they think is desirable, they tend to carry out open-market purchases. Since r responds to changes in money income, this means that the nominal money supply, via central bank actions, is to some extent functionally related to other variables within the system. Thus it might be more realistic to write, instead of our usual hypothesis, a nominal money supply function of the form, say:

$$M^S = M_0 + \alpha_1 pY + \alpha_2(r - r^*) \quad (\alpha_1, \alpha_2 > 0)$$

where:

r^* = the central bank's target long-term interest rate
M_0 = autonomous element in M^S

Typically, in the chapters which follow, we shall *not* do this. We shall retain, in the interest of simplicity, the assumption that the nominal money supply is exogenous. The reader is therefore warned, at this stage, that this is done for expository purposes only and that, in practice, the money supply has a substantial endogenous element.

Questions and exercises

1. Use the model of this and earlier chapters to explain the consequence for the money supply and interest rate of a government deficit of 10 units financed by borrowing from the non-bank public. What happens to the public's holdings of government securities?

2. Suppose the central bank wishes to reduce the money supply by 140 units. Use the model of pp. 433–6 to calculate (i) the size of the necessary open-market sales, and (ii) the size of the increase in the cash ratio necessary to obtain the same result.
   In what circumstances would bond sales by the *banking system* as a whole be greater under method (ii) than method (i)?

3. Study chapter 3 of the Radcliffe Report. How applicable is our model to the conditions it describes?

4. How would you define the 'monetary base' in the UK? Give your reasons.

5. When the Exchange Equalisation Account buys foreign exchange it borrows the sterling in the market by issuing Treasury bills. Conversely when it sells foreign exchange it uses the proceeds to buy Treasury bills. Add the Exchange Equalisation Account to the model of this chapter and analyse the consequences of a balance-of-payments surplus of 10 units. Assume a 'pegged' exchange rate.

6. 'It is, broadly speaking, true to say that private individuals cannot put into a modern banking system anything which is not there already.' Do you agree? If not, why not? If so, why?

7. 'An increase in saving raises bank deposits.' 'The notion that an increase in saving will raise bank deposits rests upon a crude and elementary confusion of *stock* and *flow* concepts.' Discuss.

8. 'In recent years the banks have lost deposits to both building societies and hire-purchase companies.' Are such deposit losses possible? If so, how? If not, why not?

9. In what circumstances would you advise the Bank of England to conduct open-market sales? Why?

10. Analyse the consequences for income, employment, the rate of interest and the balance of payments of open-market purchases by the central bank (i) as a 'Keynesian' and (ii) as a 'monetarist'. If your predictions differ, say why this is so.

11. 'If banks sell securities to finance an increase in advances, then the nominal money supply is unaffected. However, idle balances are activated or, what is the same thing, velocity is increased.' Elucidate and appraise.

12. 'The basic cause of inflation is simply this: the creation of money gives profits to banks, while the cost of creating it is negligible. Small wonder that they create it as hard as they can go.' Elucidate and appraise.

13. 'The more precisely the central bank attempts to control the money stock, the greater the short-term fluctuations in interest rates are likely to be.' Do you agree? Use the *Bulletin of the Board of Governors of the Federal Reserve System* to obtain data on US experience between 1979 and 1982 and comment on this in the course of your analysis.

14. How successful has the Bank of England been in controlling the rate of growth of sterling M_3 in accordance with government targets? Use monthly data for 1978–82 as the basis for your answer.

15. The balance-sheet identity of our notional central bank is (from Table 24.1) given by:

    notes + deposits ≡ gold and foreign exchange + government securities

    Rearrange this, using your own notation, to give the sources of the monetary base. Then examine these in order to discuss how far the central bank can control the monetary base in the 'short run'.

16. Compare your discussion in answering question 15 with the views in the government's *Monetary Control* and in my own, 'Implementing Monetarism: Some Reflections on the UK Experience' (both in the suggested reading).

17. What was the supplementary deposit scheme? How did it work? In what way – if any – did it encourage 'cosmetic' changes in sterling M_3?

18. 'As soon as one seeks to control a monetary aggregate, the banks and the non-bank public conspire – in perfectly legitimate ways – to change its character and thus its economic significance.' Elucidate and appraise with particular reference to UK experience.

19. 'If sterling M_3 grows faster than the target set by the Chancellor, nothing is more certain than that interest rates will rise.' Do you agree? Give your reasons. Can the quotation be reconciled with the theory of Chapter 11?

20. 'In the UK, the authorities adjust the monetary base to the money supply. They attempt to control the latter by setting an interest rate which, at the forecast level of nominal GNP, will induce the public to demand the *target* money stock.' Elucidate and appraise.

Suggested reading

*M. J. Artis and M. K. Lewis, *Monetary Control in the United Kingdom* (Philip Allan, 1981) chs 1, 4, 6, 7.

Bank of England, 'An Account of Monetary Policy', *Bank of England Quarterly Bulletin* (March 1978).

Bank of England, 'External and Foreign Currency Flows and the Money Supply', *Bank of England Quarterly Bulletin* (December 1978).

Bank of England, 'Monetary Base Control', *Bank of England Quarterly Bulletin* (June 1979).

*Bank of England, 'Methods of Monetary Control', *Bank of England Quarterly Bulletin* (December 1980).

Bank of England, 'Monetary Control: the Next Step', *Bank of England Quarterly Bulletin* (March 1981).

Bank of England, 'The Monetary Base: A Statistical Note', *Bank of England Quarterly Bulletin* (March 1981).

*More advanced reference.

Bank of England, 'The Operation of Monetary Policy', *Bank of England Quarterly Bulletin* (June 1981).

Bank of England and HM Treasury, *Money in Britain: 1959–1969* (Oxford Univesity Press, 1970).

Bank of England and HM Treasury, Reply to Questionnaire on Monetary Policy, Treasury and Civil Service Committee, *Memoranda on Monetary Policy* (1979–80).

Bank of England and HM Treasury, *Monetary Control*, Cmnd 7858 (HMSO, March 1980).

G. E. J. Dennis, *Monetary Economics* (Longman, 1981) chs 7, 10.

W. T. Newlyn, *The Theory of Money* (Oxford University Press, 1971) ch. 3.

Radcliffe Report (HMSO, 1959) ch. 4.

Radcliffe Committee: Memoranda of Evidence vol. 1 (HMSO, 1960) pp. 35–42.

D. C. Rowan, 'The Evolution of British Monetary Policy 1951–1972', *Manchester School* (February 1973).

*D. C. Rowan, 'Implementing Monetarism: Some Reflections on the UK Experience', *Banca Nazionale del Lavoro Review* (June 1981).

*More advanced reference.

Chapter 25

More About the Money Supply: The Formation Table Approach

Introduction

The analysis of the previous chapter leads to the conclusion that it is useful to decompose the money supply into two elements:

(a) the monetary base ($\equiv N + B_d$), which is to be treated as a multiplicand
(b) a 'multiplier' (which we denote by λ)

so that:

$$M^S \equiv MB \times \lambda \tag{25.1}$$
$$\Delta M^S \equiv \lambda \times \Delta MB + MB \times \Delta\lambda \tag{25.2}$$

where $MB \equiv$ monetary base $\equiv N + B_d$.

Now 25.1 and 25.2 are identities. They contain no assumptions about economic behaviour. A *theory*, however, can be developed using the framework of 25.1 and 25.2 and we developed such a theory in Chapter 24 by showing that, in our simple system:

$$\lambda \equiv \frac{1 + \alpha_1}{q + \alpha_1}$$

and assuming that q and α_1 were behavioural constants so that λ is also constant, as well as assuming that MB was determined by the central bank.

This entails replacing the identity 25.1 by the equation 25.1a and the identity 25.2 by the equation 25.2a:

$$M^S = MB \times \lambda \tag{25.1a}$$
$$\Delta M^S = \lambda \times \Delta MB \tag{25.2a}$$

This 'monetary base:multiplier' approach to money supply theory concentrates upon distinguishing the behaviour of three sectors of the economy – namely, the central bank, the commercial banks and the non-bank public. Moreover it is an approach which is 'liability orientated' since it asks what determines the magnitude of commercial banks' liabilities (≡ *deposits* in our simplified scheme) and what determines the non-bank public's holdings of central bank liabilities (≡ *notes* in our illustration).

Now it is obvious, since liabilities ≡ assets, that we could have approached the money supply problem from the asset side. In other words we could have asked, using:

$$\Delta M^S \equiv \Delta D + \Delta C_h \tag{25.3}$$

what asset changes correspond to ΔD *and* ΔC_h?

This is, in fact, an important element in what is called the 'Formation Table Approach', which consists essentially in:

(a) decomposing ΔD and ΔC_h into the corresponding asset changes, *and then*
(b) employing the public sector's financing identity to rearrange the asset changes in a particular way.

Notice that this procedure does not involve any new theory of the behaviour explaining how the money supply is determined. It simply provides an alternative framework in terms of which to describe ΔM^S *or, reverting to levels rather than changes,* M^S. There are no particular behaviour assumptions which are associated with the formation table and thus there is no identifiable 'formation table theory'. Nevertheless, the formation table emphasises factors which are somewhat obscured in the 'monetary base:multiplier' framework and, perhaps for this reason, has led to controversies regarding the determination of the money supply and its control.

The formation table approach

The formation table typically relates to ΔM^S rather than M^S. Hence we begin our exposition by setting out an expression for ΔM^S in the notation of Chapter 24 and using the data in Tables 24.2–24.4 to provide a numerical illustration. Thus:

$$\Delta M^S \equiv \Delta D + \Delta C_h \tag{25.3}$$
$$70 \equiv 66.67 + 3.33 \tag{25.3n}$$

We now employ the commercial banks' balance-sheet to explain ΔD in terms of asset changes. This gives:

$$\Delta D \equiv \Delta C_b + \Delta GS_b + \Delta A_b \tag{25.4}$$
$$66.67 \equiv 6.67 + 50 + 10 \tag{25.4n}$$

Similarly we employ the central bank's balance-sheet to provide the counterpart to ΔC_h. Thus:

$$\Delta C_h \equiv \Delta GFE_{cb} + \Delta GS_{cb} - \Delta Dep_{g.cb} - \Delta C_b \tag{25.5}$$
$$3.33 \equiv 0 + 10 - 0 - 6.67 \tag{25.5n}$$

where:

ΔGFE_{cb}	$\equiv$	change in central bank's holdings of gold and foreign exchange
ΔGS_{cb}	$\equiv$	change in central bank's holdings of government securities
$\Delta Dep_{g.cb}$	$\equiv$	change in government's holdings of central bank deposits

Substituting 25.4 and 25.5 into 25.3 gives:

$$\Delta M^S \equiv \Delta GS_b + \Delta GS_{cb} - \Delta Dep_{g.cb} + \Delta A + \Delta GFE \qquad (25.6)$$
$$70 \equiv 50 + 10 - 0 + 10 + 0 \qquad (25.6n)$$

At this stage 25.6 can be rewritten in a more familiar form. To do this we identify:

(a) ΔA with bank lending to the *private sector*
(b) $\Delta GS_b + \Delta GS_{cb} - \Delta Dep_{g.cb}$ with net bank lending to the *public sector*

Hence an alternative way of looking at 25.6 is to write:

$$\Delta M^S \equiv \begin{matrix}\text{bank lending}\\ \text{to}\\ \text{public sector}\end{matrix} + \begin{matrix}\text{bank lending}\\ \text{to}\\ \text{private sector}\end{matrix} + \begin{matrix}\text{change}\\ \text{in}\\ \text{overseas reserves}\end{matrix} \qquad (25.7)$$
$$70 \equiv 60 + 10 + 0 \qquad (25.7n)$$

and, defining:

$$\begin{matrix}\text{domestic credit}\\ \text{expansion}\end{matrix} \equiv DCE \equiv \begin{matrix}\text{bank lending}\\ \text{to}\\ \text{public sector}\end{matrix} + \begin{matrix}\text{bank lending}\\ \text{to}\\ \text{private sector}\end{matrix} \qquad (25.8)$$

to obtain:

$$\Delta M^S \equiv DCE + \begin{matrix}\text{change in}\\ \text{overseas reserves}\end{matrix} \qquad (25.9)$$
$$70 \equiv 70 + 0 \qquad (25.9n)$$

which is a much simplified form of the tables published monthly in *Financial Statistics* and *Economic Trends* and quarterly in the *Bank of England Quarterly Bulletin* which analyse the expansion in sterling M_3.

Now it is obvious that 25.9 can be further extended by using the public sector's financing identity. This can be written:

$$G + R + \Delta D_{g.cb} \equiv T + B \qquad (25.10)$$

where G, T, R have their usual meanings and B denotes borrowing.

Defining:

$$\text{PSBR} \equiv G - T + R \equiv B - \Delta D_{g.cb} \qquad (25.11)$$

we recall that:

$$B \equiv \Delta GS_b + \Delta GS_{cb} + \Delta GS_h \equiv \text{total sales of government debt} \tag{25.12}$$

so that:

$$\left.\begin{aligned} PSBR &\equiv \Delta GS_b + \Delta GS_{cb} + \Delta GS_h - \Delta D_{g.cb} \\ \text{and:} \\ PSBR - \Delta GS_h &\equiv \Delta GS_b + \Delta GS_{cb} - \Delta D_{g.cb} \end{aligned}\right\} \tag{25.13}$$

where $\Delta GS_b \equiv$ sales of government debt to the non-bank public.
Thus:

$$\Delta M^S \equiv (PSBR - \Delta GS_h) + \Delta A + \Delta GFE \tag{25.14}$$

which is essentially the form given in UK official statistics.
In terms of our example in Chapter 24 we have $\Delta GS_b + \Delta GS_{cb} + \Delta GS_h = 0$ and $\Delta Dep_{g.cb} = 0$. Hence $G + R - T$ is also zero. Thus PSBR is zero; $\Delta GS_h = -60$. Whence:

$$\begin{aligned} \Delta M^S &\equiv PSBR - \Delta GS_h + \Delta A + \Delta GFE \\ &\equiv (0 + 60) + 10 + 0 \\ &\equiv 70 \end{aligned} \tag{25.15}$$

This is the form in which the formation table is usually published, though, since our model is highly simplified, the official UK tables are rather more complex.

The formation table and the PSBR

As we have sought to emphasise, the formation table is a framework within which observed changes in the money stock can be analysed in terms of:

(a) bank lending to the public sector
(b) bank lending to the private sector
(c) the balance of external transactions, i.e. the change in overseas reserves in our simple model

It does not, unlike the 'monetary base:multiplier' approach, typically make particular assumptions about portfolio behaviour (in our elementary model the assumptions that q and α_1 are constants of behaviour). On the other hand, it places emphasis upon domestic credit expansion and, in particular on bank lending to the public sector. Moreover, as we have seen, it expresses the latter as $PSBR - \Delta GS_h$. Thus it is possible – though incorrect – to interpret the formation table as implying that an increase in the PSBR brings about an increase in the rate of change in the money stock. The formation table, of course, implies nothing of the sort, for:

$$\Delta\Delta M^S \equiv \Delta PSBR - \Delta\Delta GS_h + \Delta\Delta A + \Delta\Delta GFE \tag{25.16}$$

where $\Delta\Delta \equiv$ the change in the change in any variable to which it is applied.

Clearly, unless there is a theory which specifies the relationship between $\Delta PSBR$ and the other items on the right-hand side of 25.16 it is not possible to predict the relationship between $\Delta\Delta M^S$ and $\Delta PSBR$. The formation table approach offers no such theory (though a theory which leads to the prediction of a positive relation would not be difficult to formulate). In practice, in the UK the short-term relationship between the PSBR and ΔM^S has been unreliable. This is shown by Figure 25.1, which uses data for the PSBR and ΔM^S, where the latter is defined, in accordance with UK practice, as Δ sterling M_3.

Of course, over the relative *long run*; assuming the PSBR to be typically positive, we might quite reasonably expect a relationship between the sum of the PSBRs and the money supply. This is because government debt is an element in private-sector wealth. As long as PSBR > 0, the total of debt outstanding is increasing. Hence wealth is increasing and, if M^S is invariant, so too is the ratio of government debt to money in non-bank private-sector portfolios. To persuade portfolio owners to accept such a shift in the debt/money ratio, we would expect the rate of interest on debt to have to increase. Alternatively, if the rate of interest is to remain unaltered, the debt money ratio must be preserved by allowing the money supply to grow in the same proportion as the holdings of government debt by the non-bank private sector. Thus, in the long run, the greater the total of government debt outstanding, the greater will typically be M^S and/or the interest rate on such debt. This amounts to saying that non-bank portfolio owners have stable asset demand functions in the *long run* which depend on only a small number of variables – in this brief account only on wealth and the interest rate. In the short run, however, asset demand functions are relatively unstable, shifting with every response of expectations to the 'state of the news', and changes in wealth are small. Hence, although it is reasonable to expect a long-run positive relation between government indebtedness and M^S, a stable *short-run* relation between ΔM^S and the PSBR is *not* to be expected and, as we have seen, in practice is not observed.

The formation table and monetary control

The 'monetary base:multiplier' analysis leads to the conclusion that the nominal money supply is determined by:

(a) central bank policy (which determines the monetary base)
(b) the asset preferences of: (i) the commercial banks (summarised by q), and (ii) the non-bank public (summarised by α_1)

which determines the 'multiplier' which has to be applied to the monetary base.

In our version of the analysis, which is deliberately simplified for pedagogic purposes, q and α_1 are treated as constants. In principle, however, there is no difficulty in thinking of q and α_1 as stable functions of a number of variables. In short, the 'monetary base: multiplier' theory can be made more realistic if we wish and is in no way restricted to the simplicities of our formulation. Its characteristic is that it seeks to explain the money supply in terms of the behaviour of identified sub-sectors of the economy and, treating the central bank as 'exogenous' in this context, specifies the relevant behaviour of the remaining two sectors in terms of readily observable variables and readily comprehended decisions. Its implication is therefore that causation runs *from* the monetary base *to* the money supply. To control the

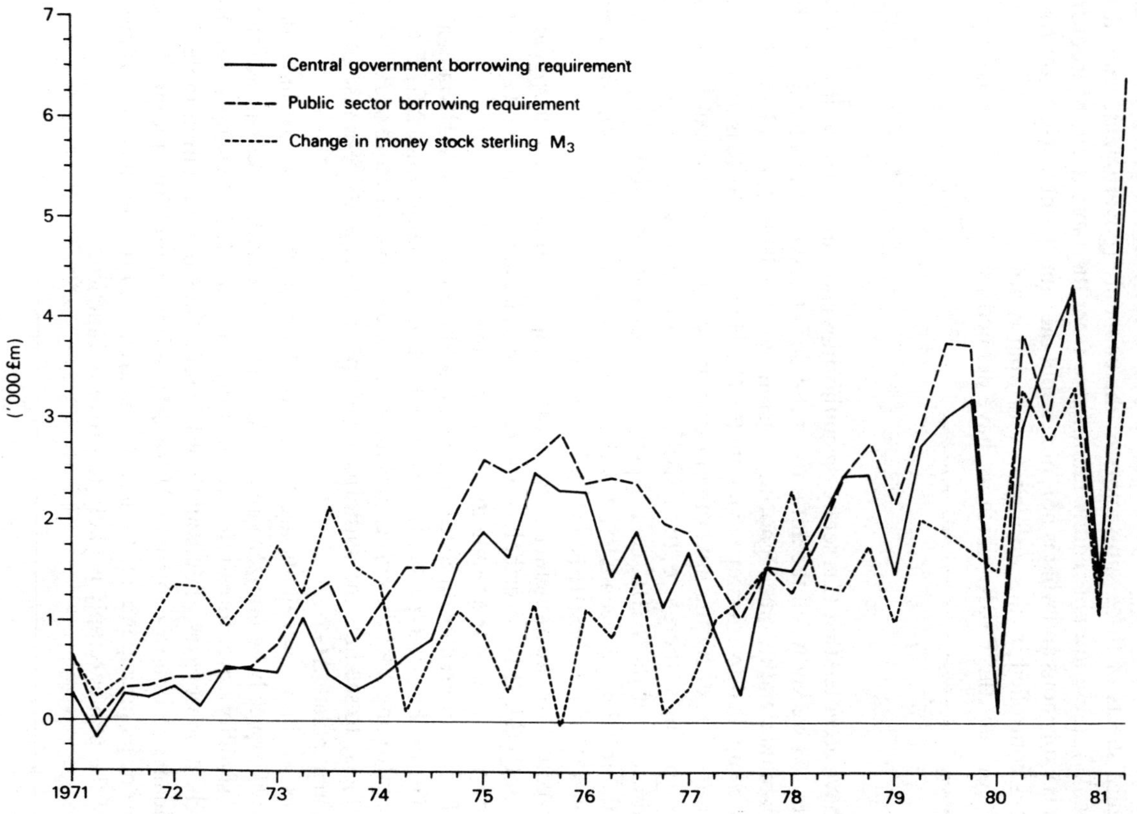

Source: *Economic Trends*, Annual Supplement, 1982, table 148.

Figure 25.1 The public sector borrowing requirement and changes in the money stock

latter quantity, the central bank must set the former. Conversely, if the central bank wants to set not the money supply but the rate of interest, M^S must be allowed to adjust to whatever money demand is at that rate and the monetary base must be adjusted to the money stock.

By contrast, since it implies no particular theory, the formation table implies relatively little about control of the money stock. Although its most common form (25.15) derives from the balance-sheets of three sub-sectors to the economy (government, central bank, commercial banks), these are not readily identifiable from the table itself. Moroever, it is not clear what is exogenous and what is not, nor, to put the same point in a less controversial manner, what is controlled by the authorities and what is not.

To see this, consider the PSBR, which we have defined as:

$$PSBR \equiv G + R - T$$

Typically we have accepted that G is set by the authorities and can thus be written as $\bar{G}$. But T cannot be set. As we know, all the authorities can do is to determine a legal relationship between tax liabilities and income. Ignoring evasion, we thus have $T = f(Y)$ and a similar argument can be applied to transfer payments ($\equiv R$). Hence the PSBR is an endogenous variable which can be set by the government only in so far as income can be accurately forecast. Not surprisingly, therefore, the PSBR is not controllable within rather wide limits, and official forecasts of the PSBR can display large percentage errors. Thus even if we could specify the relation between $\Delta PSBR$ and $\Delta\Delta M^S$, and, as we have seen, we cannot do this, control of ΔM^S via the PSBR is a doubtful proposition.

Admittedly, control of the monetary base is not so simple, in practice, as it appears in our example in Chapter 24. It is nevertheless a simpler matter than attempting to manipulate the PSBR – to what is, on our arguments, an uncertain end.

Problems of equal or greater difficulty arise with seeking to control ΔM^S via controlling ΔA, ΔGS_h and/or ΔGFE. In a 'perfectly clean float' of the exchange rate, ΔGFE is always zero. Thus in controlling ΔM^S the authorities must operate via one or more of $PSBR$, ΔA or ΔGS_h. It is not easy to see how the authorities can obtain any speedy response of ΔA; nor how they can manipulate ΔGS_h.

Moreover, as we know, no floats are 'perfectly clean' in the sense we have defined. Hence ΔGFE will typically be non-zero and occur because the authorities (in the interest of exchange-rate stability) are forced to offset shifts in the demand/supply for foreign exchange which, in most cases, they could not foresee. Thus the formation table does not give much guidance as to how control of M^S or ΔM^S – if the authorities require it – can be achieved. Indeed, its principal contribution in this area is to remind us how formidable a task control of the money supply is likely to prove in practice.

Summary and conclusions

The formation table provides a framework within which to analyse observed changes in the money supply. It does not offer a theory of the determination of the money supply in the sense that it is not associated with any particular set of behaviour assumptions.

The formation table is obtained by: approaching ΔM^S from the assets side of the relevant balance-sheets, making use of the balance-sheets for the central bank's, the commercial banks' and the public sector's financing identity, to yield:

$$\begin{aligned}
\Delta M^S \quad &\equiv \quad \begin{array}{c}\text{bank lending}\\ \text{to}\\ \text{public sector}\end{array} + \begin{array}{c}\text{bank lending}\\ \text{to}\\ \text{private sector}\end{array} + \begin{array}{c}\text{change in external}\\ \text{reserves}\end{array} \\
&\equiv \quad \begin{array}{c}\text{public}\\ \text{sector}\\ \text{borrowing}\\ \text{requirement}\end{array} - \begin{array}{c}\text{purchases of}\\ \text{bonds by}\\ \text{non-bank}\\ \text{public}\end{array} + \begin{array}{c}\text{change in}\\ \text{bank loans or}\\ \text{advances to}\\ \text{private sector}\end{array} + \begin{array}{c}\text{change in}\\ \text{external}\\ \text{reserves}\end{array} \\
&\equiv \quad \text{domestic credit expansion} + \text{change in external reserves}
\end{aligned} \tag{25.14}$$

Plainly this way of presenting the data emphasises the role of the PSBR in 'explaining' ΔM^S and has led to the assertion that an increase in the PSBR will typically entail a greater increase in the money stock.

The formation table, which does not provide or imply any theory of the relationship between the elements on the right-hand side of 25.14 cannot, in logic, be used to derive any such prediction.

In practice the *short-run* relationship (in the UK) between PSBR and ΔM^S is unreliable with respect to both sign and magnitude. Theory would suggest, however, a positive relationship in the long run since:

(a) government debt holdings constitute wealth to the non-bank private sector
(b) it is reasonable to regard the long-run money demand to be a function of wealth as well as income, prices and the rate of interest.

Unlike the 'base-multiplier' approach sketched in Chapter 24, the formation table does not suggest a method of controlling the money stock, only what is implied if it is controlled.

Questions and exercises

1. 'A given PSBR implies a given change in sterling M_3. Hence the budget is the most important weapon in the fight to achieve our money stock targets.' Elucidate and appraise in the light of both theory and UK experience.

2. How important have external influences on the money supply been in the UK? Use the identity:

   $$\Delta M^S - DCE \equiv \text{external flows}$$

   to estimate the external influences. How would you explain their impact in 1979 and 1980?

3. 'A perfectly clean float isolates the domestic money supply from the impact of reserve flows. But it does not eliminate the impact of other net external flows.' Elucidate.

4. According to *Monetary Control* the main ways in which the authorities can control the money supply are via 'interest-rate' and 'fiscal' policy. Elucidate. Can you reconcile the underlying 'theory' with the 'base-multiplier' approach?

5. Why is the PSBR so difficult to forecast? Given this difficulty, how can the money supply be controlled in the UK?

6. What are the main difficulties with 'monetary base' control?

7. 'It would be possible to bring about an immense reduction in the nominal money supply by issuing a form of government debt, encashable on demand at no penalty, which offered a yield greater than bank deposits.' Do you agree? Explain your reasons. Would the change in the money supply be 'cosmetic' or 'economically meaningful'?

8. 'The empirical relationship between the PSBR and changes in the nominal money stock is not close and, if anything, is negative.' Review the data. Do you agree? If so, comment on the discussion in *Monetary Control*.

9. 'Central bankers always worry about *orderly markets*. As a result they never raise interest rates quickly enough to control the money stock.' Elucidate and appraise.

10. 'The proper target for the UK monetary authorities is not M_1, M_3 or sterling M_3. It is M_2.' What is M_2? Would it, in your opinion, be superior to controlling M_1, M_3 or sterling M_3? Give your reasons.

11. 'A policy which seeks to control M_1 is simply a policy which seeks to control nominal GNP, of which M_1 is an indicator.' Is this so? What does it imply about (i) the demand function of M_1 balances, and (ii) the income velocity of M_1 balances? Is there evidence to support these implications?

12. Using data from the Annual Supplements of *Economic Trends*, plot the quarterly observations of income velocity for M_1, M_3 and sterling M_3. Which is the 'most stable'? Justify your interpretation of 'most stable' and say whether the exercise throws any light on the choice of a monetary target.

13. Using Bank of England data, plot changes in the 'monetary base' against changes in M_1, M_3 and sterling M_3. Is there any evidence of a stable multiplier? Would you expect a stable multiplier?

14. Some items in the sources of the 'monetary base' are particularly difficult to forecast. Which do you think they are? How does the inability to forecast complicate 'monetary-base control'?

15. In October 1979 the US Federal Reserve began to try to control 'the' money supply by setting the quantity of bank reserves. What have the results been since then? What light do they throw on the consequences of introducing 'monetary-base control'?

Suggested reading

*M. J. Artis and M. K. Lewis, *Monetary Control in the United Kingdom* (Philip Allan, 1981) ch. 4.

Bank of England, 'DCE and the Money Supply', *Bank of England Quarterly Bulletin* (March 1977).

*More advanced reference.

Bank of England, 'External and Foreign Currency Flows and the Money Supply', *Bank of England Quarterly Bulletin* (December 1977).
Bank of England, 'Monetary Base Control', *Bank of England Quarterly Bulletin* (June 1979).
Bank of England, 'Methods of Monetary Control', *Bank of England Quarterly Bulletin* (December 1980).
Bank of England, 'Monetary Control: the Next Steps', *Bank of England Quarterly Bulletin* (March 1981).
Bank of England, 'The Operation of Monetary Policy', *Bank of England Quarterly Bulletin* (June 1981;.
Bank of England and HM Treasury, *Monetary Control,* Cmnd 7858 (HMSO, 1980).
*S. G. B. Henry *et al.*, 'Money and the PSBR', *NIESR Review*, no. 94 (November 1980).
HM Treasury, 'The Impact of Recession on the PSBR', *Economic Progress Report*, no. 130 (February 1981).
HM Treasury, 'Public Sector Borrowing Requirements', *Economic Progress Report*, no. 126 (October 1980).
HM Treasury, 'New Monetary Control Arrangments', *Economic Progress Report*, no. 137 (September 1981).
HM Treasury, 'Monetary Policy and the Economy', *Economic Progress Report*, no. 123 (July 1980).
Lord Kaldor, Memorandum on Monetary Policy, (response to a questionnaire), Treasury and Civil Service Committee, *Memoranda on Monetary Policy* (HMSO, 1979–80).
M. Friedman, in ibid.
D. W. Laidler, in ibid.
Bank of England, in ibid.
Board of Governors, US Federal Reserve System, in ibid.
Midland Bank, Annual Monetary Surveys, in *Midland Bank Review* (Summer issues).
D. Savage, 'Some Issues of Monetary Policy', *NIESR Review* no. 91 (February 1980).

*More advanced reference.

Part VI
Macroeconomic Policy

Chapter 26
Economic Analysis and Economic Policy

In the earlier chapters of this book we have tried to do two things.

The first is to show *how* economists seek to develop – and *test* – theories which explain how the economic system operates.

The second is to set out the essential elements of the two main approaches to macroeconomic theory which command extensive support among professional economists. These we have called 'neo-Keynesian' (Chapters 8–15) and 'monetarist' (Chapters 16–18). This method has been adopted since, though a synthesis of the two will probably emerge, there is as yet no professional consensus as to the form of this synthesis. It is thus not possible to present a single macroeconomic model which commands general acceptance.

As the reader will recall, what we have called 'positive economics' is concerned with propositions of the form:

if X occurs in some specified context *S, then Z* occurs

In this chapter we discuss *economic policy*. Clearly policy recommendations are propositions about what the authorities *ought* to do. In terms of our earlier distinction, they are therefore *normative*. Hence any policy recommendation contains three elements:

(a) a *value judgement* which defines what is desirable
(b) a *theory or model* of how the economic system works
(c) a recommended *policy action* which is consistent with *both* (a) and (b)

It is therefore reasonable to expect that policy proposals should set out clearly:

(a) the objective to be attained
(b) the economic model
(c) the reasons for thinking that the recommended course of action is consistent with both

Unfortunately, if we exclude a few well-established research organisations such as, *inter alia*, the National Institute of Economic and Social Research (NIESR), the London Business School (LBS) and Cambridge Econometrics (CE), this is not generally the case. Even in those newspapers which claim, probably correctly, to be read and taken seriously by 'top people', clear expositions of policy proposals are commonly lacking. Elsewhere, and more particularly perhaps in political or quasi-political discussions, the whole process of analysis supporting the favoured policy is either severely truncated or, deliberately or inadvertently, suppressed. We are, as a result, often confronted with statements which implicitly claim strong support from positive economics even though such support, if it exists at all, may be tentative in the extreme. Other statements not only do this but also imply an unstated value judgement. As an example of the former there is the statement that 'inflation reduces economic growth', which is frequently alleged to be a well-established economic rule of general applicability. This statement *may* be correct. But it is not a prediction of either 'monetarist' or 'neo-Keynesian' macroeconomic theory. Nor do the available empirical investigations offer much support for it. It is therefore not 'well established' and the claim that it is is spurious. As an example of the latter, we can take the assertion that 'economics make it clear that quantitative import restrictions are unsound' – which is obviously absurd since positive economics can do no more than predict the most probable consequences of imposing quantitative import restrictions in a defined way. Whether these predicted consequences are 'unsound' or not cannot be decided by an appeal to observation alone. It necessarily involves some set of value judgements defining 'soundness' and 'unsoundness'.

Both forms of statement are potentially extremely misleading. Nevertheless statements of both types are common even in what is usually regarded as 'informed comment'.

The reader is therefore warned that policy recommendations, whether implicit (as in our first example) or explicit (as in our second), should be met with critical but constructive scepticism. This is best achieved by keeping firmly in mind the following questions:

1. *What model* underlies the recommendation?
2. *What reasons*, theoretical and empirical, are there for accepting this model?
3. *What value judgements* are implied?

and applying them to each policy proposal which is encountered.

Suppose now that we are confronted by a particular policy recommendation explicitly aimed at a stated objective: for example, suppose that the Chancellor of the Exchequer is urged to take some action (call it A) in a given situation (call it S) in order to achieve an objective B. This immediately raises the issue in positive economics of whether, in context S, A will lead to B. Suppose we decide that, given our degree of understanding of the macroeconomic system, B is a probable outcome of doing A in context S. This does not end the matter, for (as we know) changing some exogenous (policy-determined) variable A will change not only whatever endogenous variable defines B but also *all other endogenous variables* within the system. For example, if A were government expenditure on goods and services and B real output, we would expect any change in B to be accompanied by change in the price level, the interest rate, the rate of inflation, the rate of exchange, tax receipts, transfer payments, and so on. If we are to evaluate policy A we therefore need to ask:

4. What other results, apart from B, will flow from taking action A?
5. Are those other results desirable or undesirable in terms of the value judgement on the basis of which A was recommended?

In most cases it will be found that although policy A will produce result B, which (by assumption) is a desirable outcome, it will also produce other results (say $B_1, B_2, B_3, \ldots, B_j$) which, in terms of the same value judgement, are *not* desirable. This immediately raises two issues:

6. Is the occurrence of B sufficient to compensate for the undesirable outcomes $B_1, B_2, \ldots, B_j$?

7. Does there exist some alternative policy to A (let us say A') which, while producing B, also produces less of the undesirable outcome $B_1, \ldots, B_j$?

Clearly question 6 relates to the *value judgement* underlying the policy recommendation, for only if we know this can we calculate whether the gain in 'welfare' from attaining B is greater than the loss in 'welfare' arising from $B_1, \ldots, B_j$.

Question 7 is, however, again a matter of *positive economics*. It asks: Is there a more *efficient policy* than A for producing the desired result B? And this is an issue which can, in some cases, be determined independently of the precise form of the value-judgement scale.

Suppose, for example, that both A and A' produce B *and* also the undesirable changes $B_1, B_2, B_3, \ldots, B_j$, denoted by $B_{1A}, \ldots, B_{jA}$ and $B_{1A}', \ldots, B_{jA}'$. If each of the $B_{1A}, \ldots, B_{jA} \geqslant B_{1A}', \ldots, B_{jA}'$, clearly A' is the *more efficient policy* even when our knowledge of the value judgement extends no further than the proposition that B is desirable and $B_1 - B_j$ undesirable. In general, however, we cannot expect each of $B_{1A}, \ldots, B_{jA}$ to be equal to or greater than $B_{1A}', \ldots, B_{jA}'$. When they are not, then to rank the two policies we shall then need:

(a) a precise *quantitative description* of *all* the results of both policies – which requires a *quantitative* and *dynamic macroeconomic model*
(b) a detailed definition, in terms of $B, B_1, \ldots, B_j$, of the value judgements – for these are necessary if we are to evaluate the total outcome

Given (a) and (b) it is obviously possible to tell the Chancellor, first, whether *either A* or A' is, on balance, beneficial, and second, which is the more beneficial (that is, which is the more efficient given (b)).

In general, of course, economists are *not* given (b). In relation to macroeconomic policy they concern themselves with *positive economics*: that is, with formulating and estimating the coefficients of a dynamic macroeconomic model capable of specifying, in the necessary detail, the *complete* dynamic consequences of given policy actions. Armed with this information, it is possible for the authorities to make relevant choices *consistent with their value judgements* which, in a democratic society, we may reasonably expect to reflect the value scales of the electorate. Conversely, of course, if we do have a fairly clear idea of (b) we can, in the light of the information provided by our model, examine whether the authorities' policies are consistent with (a) and (b).

This argument is, unfortunately, something of a simplification since there is more than one macroeconomic model capable of predicting the dynamic consequences of policy actions taken in given circumstances; and the predictions of the different models do not always agree. *In short, there is no single model which commands universal approval.* And this is hardly surprising considering the complexity of the economic system and the relatively trivial amount of resources typically devoted to improving our understanding of it. *In practice, therefore, in the present state of economic knowledge, we simply do not know enough about the workings of the macroeconomic system to make, with any great degree of confidence, precise numerical predictions about the consequences of policy changes.*

This does not mean that the existing models are of no value and need not be studied. On the contrary, the predictions of these models perform two important tasks. The first of these is to set limits on our uncertainty about the results of a given policy action. For example, if one model of the economy yields a multiplier (after eight quarters) for government expenditure on goods and services of 2.1 and a second model yields multiplier (again after eight quarters) of 0.72, it may be reasonable to regard these estimates as giving upper and lower limits. These limits (which are purely hypothetical) are uncomfortably broad. Nevertheless they permit the models to perform a second task: namely, to impose useful restraints on dogma. In our example they would exclude dogmatic assertions that the eight-quarter multiplier is 4 or zero. And restraints on dogmatism are particularly important where the subject is one (like economics) on which everyone has views but which few have seriously studied and fewer still have attained any understanding.

In the next chapter we shall review the predictions of some of the major macroeconomic models of the UK as a preliminary, in our final chapter, to offering a review of what we identify as 'neo-Keynesian' and 'monetarist' approaches to macroeconomic policy.

The objectives of macroeconomic policy

In the UK the objectives of economic policy since the Second World War have been:

(a) the maintenance of 'full employment', sometimes paraphrased as a 'high level of employment'
(b) the maintenance of a rate of growth in real output which is 'acceptable'
(c) the maintenance of a 'tolerable' rate of increase in the general price level

In the context of a 'pegged' exchange rate such as obtained until 1973, the pursuit of these objectives was subject to a balance-of-payments constraint which entailed that, over the typical output 'cycle' of, say, 4½–5½ years, the overall balance of payments must be in balance in the sense that there must be no long-run tendency to external deficit or, since our surplus is necessarily the deficit of some other country or group of countries, no long-run tendency to accumulate a significant surplus. In the context of a 'flexible' or 'floating' rate this constraint is, formally speaking, absent. However, since, as we know, the behaviour of the exchange rate has implications for output and the price level, the external situation remains a matter of importance.

Not one of the concepts listed above is easy to define in numerical terms in a way which is free from controversy. And the time is past when UK governments committed themselves to numerical targets. In earlier editions of this book we assumed that:

(a) 'full employment' was defined as 1.6 per cent of the work-force unemployed
(b) an 'acceptable' growth rate was defined as the (then) government target of 4 per cent
(c) a 'tolerable' rate of inflation was defined as a rate of annual price increase less than 2 per cent.

These would now seem absurdly ambitious. Let us therefore, simply to fix our ideas, adopt the essentially arbitrary interpretations of:

(a) 'full employment' as 1 million (say 4 per cent of the work-force) registered unemployed
(b) 'acceptable' growth in real output as 2–2½ per cent
(c) 'tolerable' inflation as less than 9 per cent.

Notice that these objectives are essentially 'short run'. For example, in the longer run the rate of growth in output depends primarily on the rate of growth of the economy's capacity to produce. This depends, as we have seen, on factors which change only relatively slowly, and which, if they respond to policy at all, do so in ways which are not well understood. Growth rates, even prior to the present recession, have, as Table 26.1 shows, fallen sharply throughout the Western world since 1972–3, and thus far economists have been unable to provide a convincing analysis of this decline.

Given that we are thinking in 'short-run' terms, can we be rather more precise about what we mean by 'short run'?

Table 26.1 Rates of economic growth: selected countries

	Growth rate of output per civilian employee		Changes in growth rate (percentage points)
	1950–73	1973–7	
USA	2.1	0.3	−1.8
Canada	2.6	0.5	−2.1
Japan	7.8	2.7	−5.1
France	4.6	2.9	−1.7
West Germany	5.0	3.3	−1.7
Italy	5.3	−0.2	−5.5
UK	2.5	0.4	−2.1
Australia	4.6*	1.6	−3.0

*Based on industrial production.

Sources: E. F. Denison, 'Explanations for Declining Productivity Growth', *Survey of Current Business* (August 1979): Reserve Bank of Australia, *Statistical Bulletin*, various issues.

Essentially what is at issue here is the *horizon* over which governments plan their policies. Typically, in a democratic society, this horizon is likely to be relatively short since the interval between general elections (or similar opportunities for peaceful transfers of power) is of the order of 4½ years at a maximum. By the 'short run' we are therefore thinking of a horizon no longer than this. Again to fix our ideas, let us take an arbitrary definition of the typical policy horizon of two years or eight quarters.

Our approach therefore envisages policy as seeking to achieve its objectives by taking actions planned with a horizon of the order of two years.

The reader should also note that although all governments accept policy objectives of *the form we outlined above* (thought not necessarily our numerical interpretations of them), *the relative importance they attach to them may well differ*. This is a matter of major importance since it is commonly the case that the objectives are inconsistent so that, say, a policy to reduce unemployment towards the target level of 4 per cent may involve the probability of inflation rising from, say, 9 per cent to a measurably higher figure. In this case governments have to decide how much additional inflation they are prepared to accept in order to reduce unemployment or, what is the same thing, how much additional unemployment they will accept in order to reduce inflation. What is at issue here is the rate at which the government will 'trade-off' one objective against another; and this, plainly enough, is a matter of their value judgements.

The reader should note carefully that our approach rests upon the implicit assumption that the government – acting through the 'authorities' (whom we define as the central bank *plus* the Treasury) – has a major responsibility for the working of the economy. This assumption is so familiar and so generally accepted that in many cases we are unaware that we are making it. *It needs to be stressed, however, that it is an assumption and one which is not necessarily acceptable*.

Finally the reader should note that this assumption is commonly extended into a second and more dubious assertion to the effect that:

(a) *given* the forms of action open to them (that is, the instruments under their control), *and*

(b) *given* the extent of our understanding of the way the economic system works, *then*
(c) *it is possible for the authorities to improve the performance of the economic system by conducting macroeconomic policy*

Both assumptions are readily justified by our 'neo-Keynesian' analysis (in Chapters 8–15) and, within narrower limits, by the 'monetarist' approach (in Chapters 16–18). It may well be, however, that both are erroneous and that we are deluding ourselves in thinking otherwise. It may be that our level of economic understanding is so poor that our attempts to manage the economy – whether on 'neo-Keynesian' or 'monetarist' lines – do more harm than good.

In what follows we shall proceed on the assumption that we do have sufficient understanding of the economic system to make it possible to formulate and conduct an effective and efficient macroeconomic policy.

The instruments of macroeconomic policy

The usual classification of the means of influencing the economy at the disposal of the authorities distinguishes:

(a) monetary policy
(b) fiscal policy
(c) exchange-rate policy (where the rate is 'pegged')
(d) other forms of intervention

Monetary policy

This is defined as discretionary action taken by the authorities (typically by the Bank of England) aimed at influencing (i) the nominal money supply, and/or (ii) nominal interest rates, and/or (iii) the ease with which, at any given set of interest rates, money can be borrowed – which is usually termed 'availability'. In our theoretical sections we have applied demand/supply analysis to the money market, which (as we have seen) implies that the authorities can in principle set *either* the nominal money stock *or* 'the' interest rate but *not* both. At a rather formal level of analysis this is correct. However, it assumes that 'the' interest rate is determined in a market by demand/supply. In practice, however, many interest rates are determined administratively and, in the short run, are only loosely related to market forces. Hence, to a limited extent, the authorities can influence *both* the quantity of money *and* its cost. This explains why we refer to both in our definition. Finally, we introduce 'availability' because, in the financial system as it is, individual fund markets exhibit imperfections. This means that, since interest rates do not adjust to 'clear' the market (that is, all borrowers who will pay the ruling rate can borrow what they wish), funds have to be rationed. This is a familiar situation to would-be borrowers, from both commercial banks and building societies.

Fiscal policy

This is defined as the discretionary manipulation by the authorities of (i) government expenditure on goods and services, (ii) the function relating the tax yield to GDP, and (iii) the function relating transfer payments to GDP. Because tax yield and transfers are related to GDP the observed fiscal deficit or surplus is not a good indicator of the expansionary or contractionary impact of fiscal policy. Suppose, for example, that we write:

$$G = \bar{G} \quad \text{(a familiar assumption needing no explanation)}$$

and:

$$\begin{aligned} T &= t_0 + t_1 Y \quad (0 < t_1 < 1) \\ R &= R_0 + R_1 Y \quad (-1 < R_1 < 0) \end{aligned}$$

so that the fiscal deficit is given by:

$$\begin{aligned} D &\equiv \bar{G} + R_0 + R_1 Y - t_0 - t_1 Y \equiv -S \quad \text{(where } S \equiv \text{surplus)} \\ &\equiv \bar{G} + (R_0 - t_0) + Y(R_1 - t_1) \end{aligned}$$

Clearly the observed deficit depends upon Y, and if Y changes because some exogenous variable (say income in the rest of the world) changes, the deficit will also change. *The observed change will, however, have nothing to do with changes in policy which is defined as discretionary action taken to change $\bar{G}$, t_0, t_1, R_0, R_1 – the elements under the control of the authorities.*

To avoid this difficulty we typically employ – as an indicator of overall fiscal policy – what is called the 'full-employment' or 'high-employment' surplus. This is defined as:

$$S_{fe} \equiv (t_0 - R_0 - \bar{G}) + Y_{fe}\,(t_1 - R_1) \equiv -\, D_{fe}$$

This restricts the influence of Y to the relatively small – and in principle calculable – change in 'full-employment' income. Thus a change in S_{fe} must be primarily due to discretionary changes in t_0, R_0, $\bar{G}$, t_1, R_1: that is, to fiscal policy changes as we have defined them. Moreover, as the reader can readily verify by referring back to Chapter 13, an *increase* in S_{fe} is a factor which *reduces* aggregage demand (unless 'crowding in' is complete) and a *reduction* in S_{fe} a factor tending to increase it.

Hence ΔS_{fe} is an indicator of the expansionary/contractionary impact of fiscal policy, and although in practice not always easy to estimate, conceptually it is a superior indicator to the change in the observed surplus, which is of course ΔS, where $S \equiv -D$.

Exchange-rate policy

This consists in variation in the 'pegged' rate of exchange – a jump in the 'occasionally jumping peg'.

Other forms of intervention

This is a residual or catch-all concept. It covers, in principle, all the forms of intervention *not* included under the other headings. It follows that the range of possible forms of intervention is virtually limitless. In practice, however, the forms most usually discussed are:

(a) 'incomes policy' – itself hard to define
(b) 'import quotas', which are quantitative restrictions on imports of defined classes of goods (possibly on *all* forms of imports) which require imports to be licensed
(c) tariffs – taxes imposed upon imports distinguished by commodity type and/or country of origin

In the present context this last one is relatively unimportant.

This gives us a sufficiently clear idea of the meaning of commonly used terms to consider the next issue, which is to specify the problems facing the authorities in seeking to use these instruments to manage the economy.

The policy problem

Now that we know the objectives of policy and the principal instruments at the authorities' disposal, let us consider what is involved in formulating and implementing macroeconomic policy. To clarify the problem let us assume that the economy is characterised by:

(a) an invariant long-term rate of growth in real output
(b) a marked 'cycle' of more or less regular periodicity

Let us also assume that the authorities have a single objective – namely, to maintain unemployment at 4 per cent of the work-force. This involves:

(a) dampening and (for perfect success) eliminating the 'cycle'
(b) raising the trend growth curve to coincide with the curve drawn at 4 per cent unemployment (see Figure 26.1).

Consider the problem of dampening the cycle. In periods in which output is below trend, we need to increase aggregate demand, and vice versa in periods in which output is above trend. The required path of anti-cyclical stabilisation might thus look something like Figure 26.2, though this rather simplifies the problem by assuming that output adjusts immediately to demand.

This diagram makes an obvious but extremely important point. *The first of these is that, to be successful, interventions must be correctly timed.* For, if they are not, there is a risk that the authorities' actions will be out of phase with the system so that they increase demand when output is *above* trend and reduce it when output is *below* trend. This *would increase the amplitude of the cycle* and, far from stabilising the economy, destabilise it. In short, as we have already pointed out, the *dynamics of stabilisation policy are crucial.*

The reader should note that, in practice, policies aimed at stabilisation have often proved destabilising. Governments have frequently intervened by 'too much too late', and found

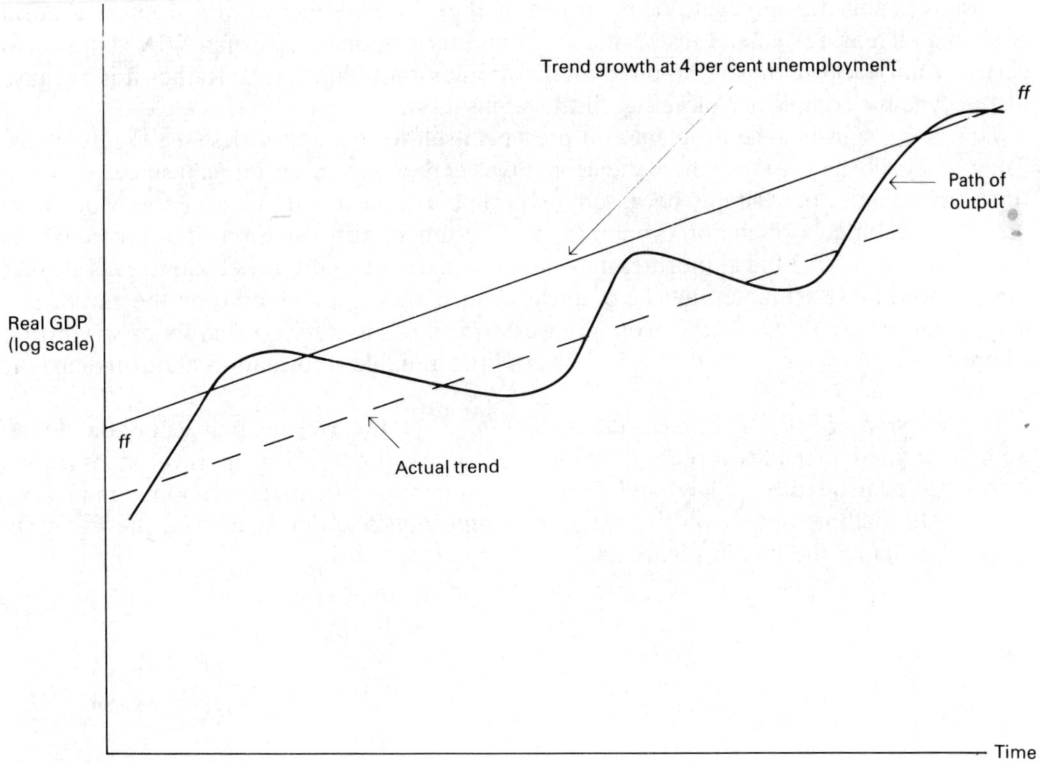

Figure 26.1 The growth cycle and policy

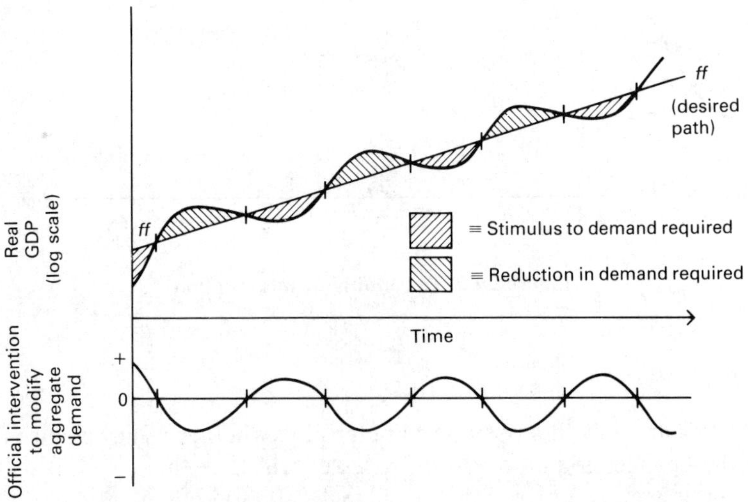

Figure 26.2 Economic stabilisation and 'full' employment: the path of official intervention

themselves reducing aggregate demand just as the economy turns down from its cyclical peak and increasing demand just as the economy starts upon its upswing. Why is this? It is certainly not because those who direct policy are ignorant blunderers. Rather it is because of the dynamic complexity of anti-cyclical stabilisation.

To see this consider the problem as it presents itself to the authorities (see Figure 26.3). Their *first problem* is to say where the economy is *at present*. This is difficult since statistical time lags calendar time simply because it *takes* time to collect and process data. Moreover, the initial estimates of major economic series often require revision. To illustrate. At time Z on Figure 26.3 the authorities may have estimates of where the economy was at, say, time Z_0. But these estimates may be of uncertain accuracy. At Z, therefore, the authorities may be fairly sure of where the economy was *prior* to Z_0 and have some series suggesting where it was at Z_0. They will have relatively little reliable information about its current position.

The *second problem* is to forecast the path of the economy over the policy horizon, which we have defined to be of two years. This involves forecasting the exogenous variables (other than those controlled by policy) and then, using a quantitative macroeconomic model, to forecast the path of output on the *basis of existing policies*. Let us assume the forecasts made at Z define the line in Figure 26.3.

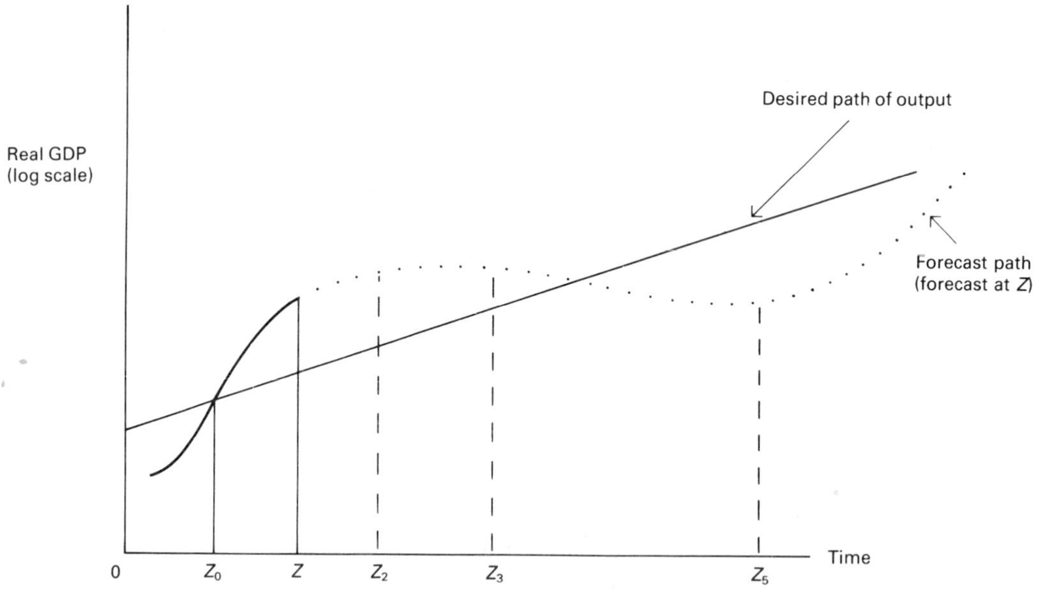

Figure 26.3 The timing of intervention

The authorities are now in a position to determine whether policy changes are desirable and to plan the changes required. Both processes will take time. And it will take further time to obtain ministerial approval for any changes and to implement them. It may be, say, as late as Z_2 before the recommended changes in policy actually occur.

Economists typically refer to the period $Z_0 - Z_2$ as the 'inside lag' since it is the lag *inside* the policy-making and implementing authority. It can be thought of as being the sum of a *recognition lag* (the period required to recognise the need for a policy change, i.e. $Z_0 - Z$) and as *planning lag* ($Z - Z_2$).

Whatever action the authorities take at Z_2, output will typically not respond immediately. Output tends to lag demand. And it will take some time for aggregate demand itself to respond to whatever combination of monetary and fiscal policies was used to reduce demand at Z_2. Finally, by assumption, our ultimate target is not output but unemployment, which, like employment, tends to lag output. Action at Z_2 may not become effective, therefore, until Z_3. Moreover, depending on the form of the dynamic response, the action taken at Z_2 may still be operating to reduce aggregate demand at, say, Z_5, where the need is to increase it. The lag between the policy change (at Z_2) and the response of the economy as measured by, say, output or unemployment is called the *outside lag*. It is not a single discrete lag of the form, say, 'output this month equals demand last month' but rather a time form, as is illustrated in Figure 26.4.

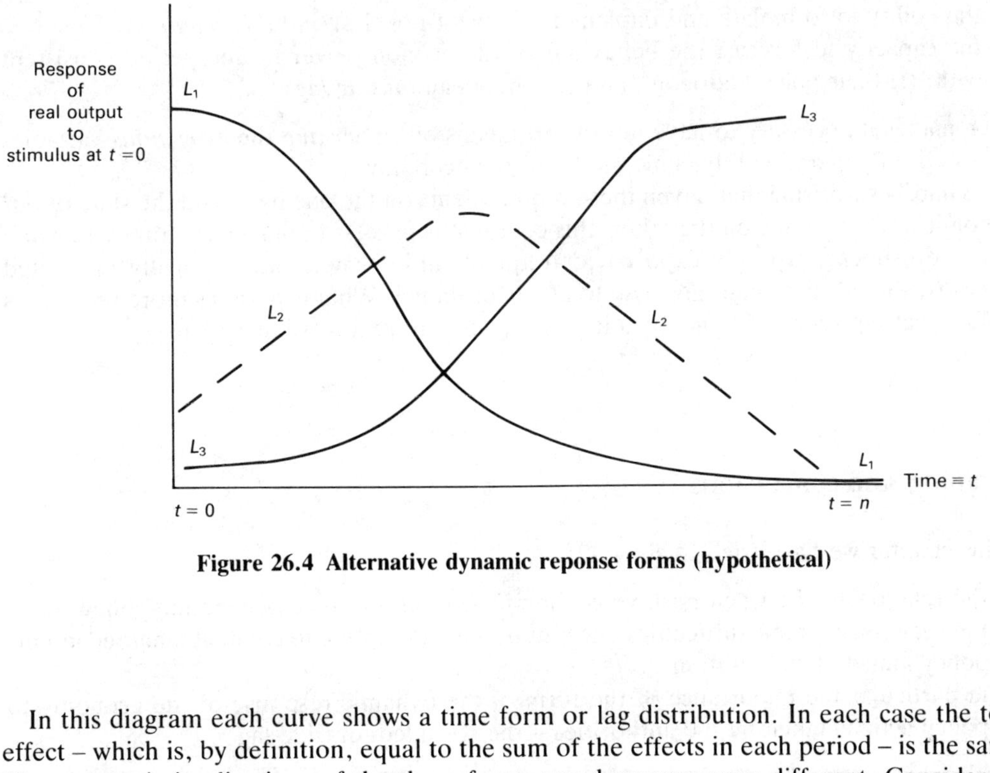

Figure 26.4 Alternative dynamic reponse forms (hypothetical)

In this diagram each curve shows a time form or lag distribution. In each case the total effect – which is, by definition, equal to the sum of the effects in each period – is the same. The economic implications of the three forms are, however, very different. Consider the form denoted by L_1L_1. Here most of the effect occurs in the first few periods. The reverse is true for L_3L_3, while L_2L_2 is an intermediate case. A simple way to identify lag forms is by use of the *mean lag*, which we define as:

mean lag ≡ period of time by which *half* the total effect has occurred

Clearly L_1L_1 has a mean lag dramatically shorter than L_3L_3.

The *total* lag in policy can now be thought of as:

inside lag + outside lag ≡ total lag

Notice that if the *outside lag* is of the form of L_3L_3, anti-cyclical policy will be extremely hard to conduct since the effect of intervention will take a long time to appear. Thus intervention at Z_2 may be having its greatest impact between Z_4 and Z_5. Thus the *form* of the *outside lag* – or the mean outside lag – is an important influence on the difficulty of conducting an anti-cyclical policy. For if L_3L_3 *is* the relevant form, the authorities must obviously intervene very strongly at Z_2 in order to have a significant early impact, and then reverse their policy as the impact of the intervention at Z_2 provides a stimulus in excess of what is required.

It is therefore essential, for policy to be successful, that the authorities should be confident that they have good information as to the form of the *outside lag* and that this form should be invariant to policy.

Thus for successful conduct of macroeconomic policy the authorities need:

(a) the ability to diagnose the current position of the economy and be confident in their diagnosis
(b) the ability to formulate and implement relevant policies, *and this requires*
(c) the capacity to forecast the behaviour of the economy over a time period consistent with: (i) their policy 'horizon', and (ii) the mean *outside lag*

which makes it necessary to have not only a means of forecasting the *exogenous* variables but also a fully quantified dynamic model of the economy.

It is hardly surprising that, given these requirements on the one hand and the state of our economic understanding on the other, this continuous process of diagnosis, forecasting and policy adjustment, typically exposed to frequent, ill-informed and politically motivated criticisms, should sometimes give rise to errors of timing. What is perhaps more relevant is the fact that between 1950 and 1970 it was, in general, relatively successful.

Summary and conclusions

In this chapter we have tried to show:

(a) the relationship between positive economic analysis and macroeconomic policy
(b) the very considerable difficulties encountered in attempting to conduct macroeconomic policy aimed at stabilisation
(c) in particular the importance of the form of the dynamic response of the economy to policy actions taken by the authorities – the so-called 'outside lag'

Clearly what is crucial to the issue of how far – if at all – the authorities should be expected to intervene is the extent of our knowledge of the dynamic responses of the system to changes in monetary and fiscal policy or other policy actions.

In the main, this knowledge is derived from macroeconomic models developed through a continuing process of economic research. In the next chapter we shall examine the responses to policy changes which are implied by three important models of the UK economy. Because economic research is a continuing process directed towards increasing our understanding, the models are continuously developed and refined. The reader is therefore warned that although our discussion is based upon the models in their most recent form (1982), it is far from representing any final word. Modifications must and will occur and these may well modify the models' behaviour in ways relevant for policy.

Questions and exercises

1. 'Since government expenditure cannot be turned on or off like a tap, anti-cyclical fiscal policy is mainly a matter of varying tax rates.' Discuss with special reference to UK experience from 1950 to 1973.

2. 'Monetary policy is easy to adjust but works slowly and not very reliably. By contrast fiscal policy changes are relatively rapid and reliable in their impact but extremely hard to make.' Would you expect this statement to be correct? Give your reasons.

3. 'Monetary policy works through changing interest rates, and very few transactors worry about them when considering expenditure decisions.' Discuss critically. What does the empirical evidence suggest?

4. 'We never know enough to take appropriate policy actions at the proper time. We always wait – and ultimately overreact.' Explain why this pattern of behaviour is likely. If it were typical, how would policy affect the 'cycle'?

5. Explain the cyclical path of the PSBR assuming unchanged fiscal policy. How would you define a 'cyclically adjusted' PSBR? Compare your account with that of HM Treasury.

6. 'If the tax and transfer functions are shifted in a manner that changes their marginal responses with respect to income, the so-called *full-employment* budget surplus may signal expansion when the change is, in fact, contractionary.' Construct a diagram to demonstrate this result. Do you think it is an important criticism of the 'full' or 'high' employment budget surplus as an indicator of fiscal stance?

7. 'After June 1979 monetary policy was extremely tight. This was an important element in generating the recession of 1979–82.' How would *you* assess the 'ease' or 'tightness' of monetary policy in an open economy like the UK? Does your indicator of monetary policy support the quotation? If not, which indicator would?

8. 'A restrictive monetary policy operates via the exchange rate. Its principal impact is through *competitiveness* and the current-account balance and it probably does lasting damage to our export potential.' Elucidate and appraise in the light of UK experience.

9. 'The UK economy will have an extraordinary and sustained recovery from 1984 onwards.' 'It will be extraordinary if the UK economy shows any marked recovery during the decade.' Which view do you support, and why? What elements in your analysis are crucial in determining your position?

10. 'Our recovery from the 1979–82 recession will *not* be led by a reflationary fiscal policy but by increase in....' With which major expenditure component(s) would you complete this sentence? Give your reasons, and explain why any increases you predict are not 'crowded out'.

Suggested reading

C. Allsopp and V. Joshi, 'Alternative Strategies for the UK', *NIESR Review*, no. 91 (February 1981).

Bank of England, 'Why is Britain in Recession?', *Bank of England Quarterly Bulletin* (March 1978).

J. A. Bispham, 'The New Cambridge and "Monetarist" Criticisms of "Conventional" Economic Policy Making', *NIESR Review*, no. 74 (November 1975).

F. T. Blackaby, 'British Economic Policy 1960–1974: A General Appraisal', *NIESR Review*, no. 77 (May 1977).

A. P. Budd, 'The Debate on Fine Tuning: The Basic Issues', *NIESR Review*, no 74 (November 1975).

J. C. R. Dow, 'Fiscal Policy and Monetary Policy as Instruments of Control', *Westminster Bank Review* (May–November 1960).

J. C. R. Dow, *The Management of the British Economy 1945–60* (Cambridge University Press, 1964) chs 1, 4, 5, 14.

W. Eltis, 'The Failure of the Keynesian Conventional Wisdom', *Lloyds Bank Review* (October 1976).

W. Eltis, 'The Keynesian Conventional Wisdom', *Lloyds Bank Review* (July 1977).

HM Treasury, 'Monetary Policy and the Economy', *Economic Progress Report*, no. 123 (July 1980).

HM Treasury, 'The Impact of Recession on the PSBR', *Economic Progress Report*, no. 130 (February 1981).

Lord Kahn, 'Mr Eltis and the Keynesians', *Lloyds Bank Review* (April 1977).

NIESR, 'The British Economy in the Medium Term', *NIESR Review*, no. 98 (November 1981).

Radcliffe Report (HMSO, 1959) ch. 6.

D. Savage, 'The Channels of Monetary Influence: A Survey of the Empirical Evidence', *NIESR Review*, no. 83 (February 1978).

D. Savage, 'Some Issues of Monetary Policy', *NIESR Review*, no. 91 (February 1980).

D. Savage, 'Fiscal Policy: Description and Measurement', *NIESR Review*, no. 99 (February 1982).

G. D. N. Worswick, 'The End of Demand Management', *Lloyds Bank Review* (March 1978).

Chapter 27
Macroeconomic Models in the UK

Introduction

The purpose of this chapter is to use three of the major macroeconomic models of the UK economy to obtain estimates of its dynamic response to defined policy actions.

The three models selected for this examination are those of the Treasury (HMT), the National Institute of Economic and Social Research (NIESR), and the London Business School (LBS). There are, of course, many other models in existence – for example, the models of Cambridge Econometrics (CE), the University of Liverpool (L) and the Cambridge Economic Policy Group (CEPG). However, no model seems to outperform the others on a systematic basis. We therefore concentrate our attention on those which are best known and most accessible. This selection does not imply superiority. Nor does it, in the case of HMT, imply that it is *this* model which dominates policy formation by the government of the day.

What is a model?

During the course of this book we have constructed a number of models, each of which consists of a number of equations. Some of these are definitional identities. Others contain hypotheses about behaviour. Typically, however, our models are qualitative in the sense that they do not contain estimates of the numerical magnitudes of the coefficients relating to economic behaviour (the marginal response coefficients) such as, for example, the marginal propensity to consume. Moreover, each relationship is treated as exact (that is, for example, the marginal propensity to consume is treated as an exact number (say 0.8), not as a number estimated to be 0.8 ± (say) 0.1), while the equation contains no error term which captures those influences on the dependent variable which are *not* explained by the hypothesis. Thus our consumption function in Chapter 9 takes the form (say):

$$C_p = a_0 + a_1(Y-T+R) + a_2r + a_3W$$

with $0 < a_1 \leqslant 1$, $a_2 < 0$ and $a_3 > 0$ while an estimated form might be written:

$$C_p = 1{,}072 + 0.8(Y-T+R) - 0.02r + 0.007W + u$$

where each numerical estimate is the *most probable* value of the coefficient, but is subject to a margin of error, and u is the error term resulting from the failure of the variables $(Y - T + R)$, r and W, the constant and the marginal response coefficients, to explain the observed values of C_p. In practice, of course, estimated equations of this type are also dynamic, which means that all variables are dated and lag forms of greater or lesser complexity are involved. As an example we offer the equation in an early version (1974) of the HMT model which explained real planned consumers' expenditure. This is:

$$C_p(t) = \alpha_0 + \sum_{i=0}^{i=9} \alpha_{1i} (N\tilde{W}\tilde{F}\tilde{P}\ (t-i)) + \sum_{j=0}^{j=2} \alpha_{2j} (N\tilde{W}\tilde{P}GG\ (t-j) + \sum_{k=0}^{k=10} \alpha_{3k} (N\tilde{O}\tilde{P}Y\ (t-k)) + R\tilde{P}\tilde{I}M\ (t) + J(t) + \text{error term}$$

where:

$N\tilde{W}\tilde{F}\tilde{P}$	≡	net wages and forces pay	(all at 1970 prices)
$N\tilde{W}\tilde{P}GG$	≡	net grants to persons	(all at 1970 prices)
$N\tilde{O}\tilde{P}Y$	≡	other personal income	(all at 1970 prices)
$R\tilde{P}\tilde{I}M$	≡	imputed rent	(all at 1970 prices)
J	≡	effect of HP regulations	(all at 1970 prices)
net	≡	net of taxes	

Here each of the α_{1i}, α_{2j}, α_{3k} represent the combined influences of a *static* (or long-run) marginal response coefficient *and* the form of its distribution over time. Thus, according to HMT, we have:

(a) $\Sigma\, \alpha_{1i} = 0.932$, with each α_{1i} becoming smaller as i increases
(b) $\Sigma\, \alpha_{3k} = 0.735$, with α_{3k} initially increasing with k, reaching a peak at $k = 3$ and then declining as k approaches 10.

These two patterns of coefficients are displayed in Table 27.1.

Table 27.1 Lag distributions: an illustration

Quarter	α_{1i}	α_{3k}
0	0.30	0.08
1	0.23	0.10
2	0.10	0.12
3	0.09	0.12
4	0.07	0.11
5	0.05	0.09
6	0.04	0.06
7	0.027	0.02
8	0.015	0.015
9	0.01	0.01
10		0.01
Total	0.932	0.735

Source: *Treasury Macroeconomic Model Technical Manual* (1974) p. 11.3.

Contemporary macroeconomic models contain a great many equations. For example, HMT now contains 640 endogenous variables and thus 640 equations including definitional identities. Despite their magnitude, however, these models *are no different in principle from the models developed earlier in this book* in that *given*:

(a) the values of the exogenous variables, i.e. variables *not* explained by the model
(b) any *past* values of the endogenous variables (i.e. variables which *are* explained by the model such as GDP, prices, employment)

they determine the current values of the *endogenous variables*.

The reader need not therefore be dismayed either by their magnitude or by the rather forbidding appearance of some equations. Of course, there are very complex econometric problems involved in estimating the many coefficients designed to capture the regularities of economic behaviour. But econometrics is a study in itself which does not concern us here. Neglecting this, these models differ from, say, the model discussed in Chapter 12 only because:

(a) they determine many more endogenous variables – and thus require correspondingly more equations
(b) they are dynamic and thus involve lags in relationships
(c) the coefficients are estimated numerically from past data by econometric techniques
(d) each behaviour equation contains an error term

Conceptually, therefore, they do not contain any economic (as opposed to econometric) principles with which the reader is not familiar.

What can models do?

Macroeconomic models can be used in three main ways. These are:

(a) to *track* the behaviour of the economy over time
(b) to *formulate forecasts* of its future behaviour
(c) to *provide estimates* of the economy's response to defined policy actions

Consider the first function.

If, for any period, we are given the current and past values of the *exogenous* variables and the past values of the *endogenous* variables, the model will determine for us the current value of every endogenous variable. The same process can be carried out for the next period, the period after that, and so on. In this way, given the necessary values of the exogenous variables, the model will generate a path over time for each endogenous variable. Thus a quarterly macroeconomic model will generate quarterly values of its endogenous variables.

Suppose now that, in operating the model, we do not use it to make forecasts but to 'explain' the past. We do this by inserting into the model the *actual historically observed values of the exogenous variables*. The model then generates values for the *endogenous* variables (as we have explained) and these can be compared with their actual observed values. That is, we compare the *track* or *path* of any endogenous variable which interests us as this is calculated by the model with the actual observed path or track of this variable. In this way we get a picture of the model's ability to *track* the actual behaviour of the economy.

Figure 27.1 illustrates this process by comparing a major model's tracks for real GDP, the rate of price change and unemployment from 1978I to 1981II with the actual observed values of these variables.[1] The differences are, of course, the *errors* generated by the model. The reader can see from these tracks how well the model is able to explain our recent experience with these variables.

Why should we do this?

Clearly if a model's tracking performance is 'poor', we shall have little confidence in its usefulness for forecasting and little interest in estimates of its responses to policy actions. What is meant by 'poor'? No unambiguous interpretation can be given and it is therefore not easy to suggest any single criterion.

It seems, however, reasonable to expect the model to do better than simple and mechanical methods of generating forecasts.

For example, suppose we forecast some important variable (say real GDP) by arguing that real GDP in the *next* quarter would be equal to what it is in *this* quarter *plus* half the difference between its value in this quarter and the quarter before this. Then, writing $Y(t)$ for this quarter's real GDP, we have:

$$Y(t+1) = Y(t) + 0.5\,(Y(t) - Y(t-1))$$

as the relation or 'model' we use for forecasting.

This kind of relationship is sometimes called a 'naive model'. The expression is somewhat misleading since no economic theory is employed in its construction, and economic theory typically *is* employed in developing large macroeconomic models. Clearly there is a virtually unlimited range of 'naive models' which *could* be used in forecasting. If we are to have any confidence in our macroeconomic model it must *outperform* any 'naive model' with which we compare it in the sense that:

(a) its tracking errors must, on average, be 'smaller' than those of any 'naive model' we use for comparison

Since 'errors' can be valued in a variety of ways, this requirement is, again, not entirely unambiguous. We shall, however, simply assume that an appropriate means of evaluating errors can be agreed. 'Small' means small on this agreed scale.

As we have seen, real GDP and other important economic series follow a path over time which contains 'cycles'. Each 'cycle' has an upper and lower turning-point. If our interest in models derives from a wish to engage in anti-cyclical stabilisation, then we require our macroeconomic model to perform 'better' than alternative 'naive models' in tracking the 'cycle'. This entails that:

(b) it tracks the main 'cyclical' turning-points better than any 'naive model' we consider using, *and*
(c) signals fewer – or at least no more – false 'turning-points' in the major economic series

Taken together conditions (b) and (c) ensure that the model effectively tracks the main 'cyclical' fluctuations in the important economic series *without* adding additional 'cycles' which have no counterpart in the real world.

Provided a model passes 'tests' of this sort in respect of the *main* macroeconomic variables, its powers of systematic description – for this is what *tracking* is – are acceptable. It is now worth examining its *forecasting* ability.

[1]These tracks were obtained from the latest (Autumn 1981) published version of the Treasury's macroeconomic model. However, in no way whatsoever do the values derived from the model carry the approval of HM Treasury, which has no responsibility whatever for them. All exogenous variables, of course, take their observed values.

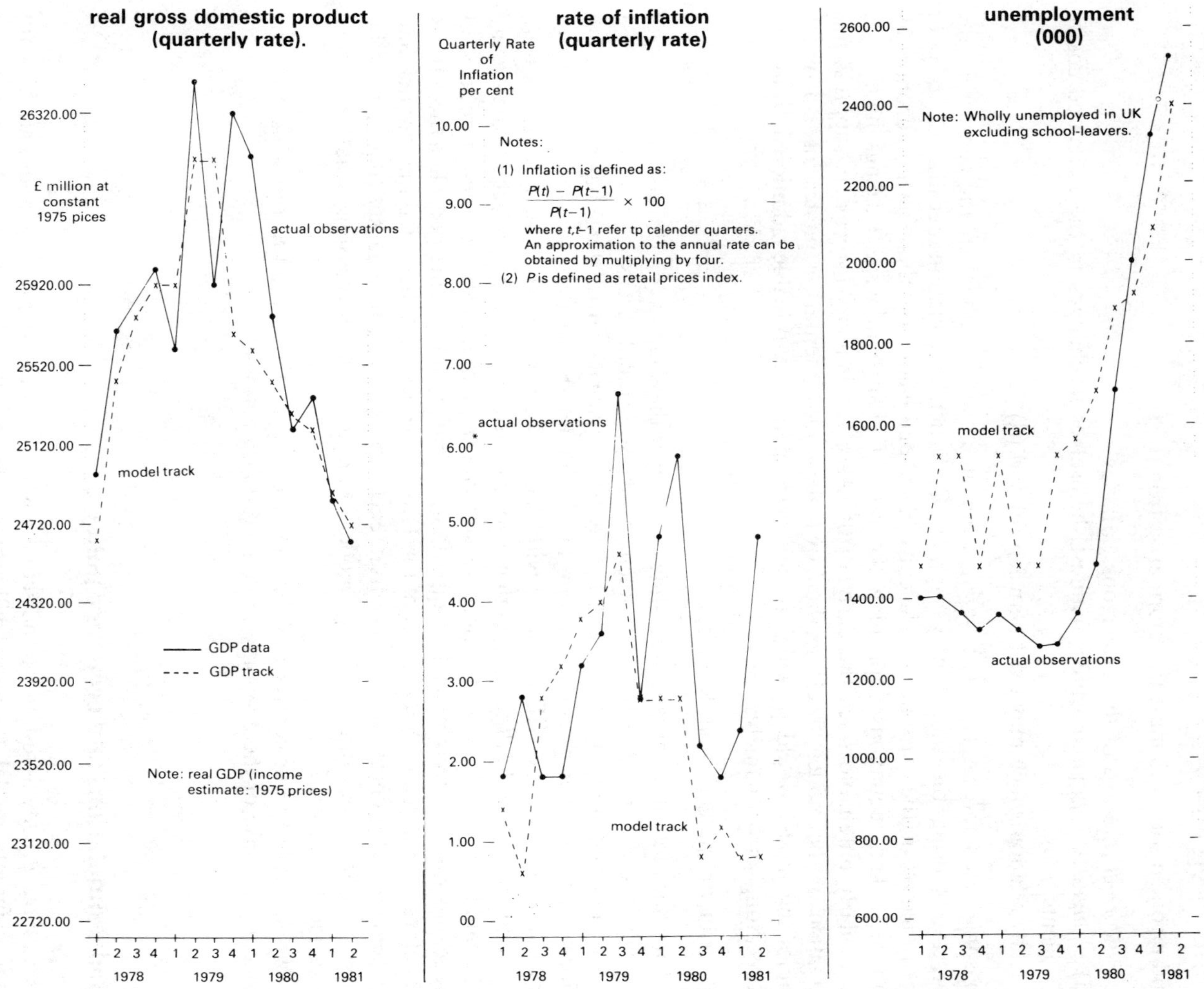

Figure 27.1 GDP, the rate of inflation and unemployment 1978–81

Clearly the model will generate predictions of the future values of the main variables provided it is first given forecasts of the *exogenous* variables which enter into the model. Its forecasts of endogenous variables are thus *conditional* upon:

(a) the forecast values of the *exogenous* variables, including, of course, those variables set by the authorities (e.g. the parameters of taxation functions)
(b) the model itself

and errors in forecasts must therefore arise from:

(c) *incorrect forecasts* of the exogenous variables
(d) *changes in behaviour* which manifest themselves in changes in the estimated coefficients, *plus*
(e) any relation which may exist between (c) and (d).

In some cases forecasts do not derive from an invariant model in the sense that the forecasters using the model may suppress a particular equation because of its poor performance in the past and replace its calculated value by their own 'judgemental' forecasts. Thus equations explaining the rate of change in wage earnings have been particularly unreliable since the early 1970s. As a result many forecasters suppress this equation of the model, inserting their own 'best judgemental' estimates instead of the values the model would provide. In this case there is a possible additional source of 'forecasting' error, namely:

(f) errors in 'judgemental' forecasts

The allocation of observed forecasting errors over the sources (c)–(f) raises a number of difficult theoretical and technical problems which we cannot discuss.

An important study by Professor M. J. Artis (see suggested reading) has attempted to allocate forecasting *differences* between models under the headings we have mentioned. Thus, in comparing the NIESR model with that of the LBS, most of the differences were accounted for by *model differences* – that is to say, differences in the underlying theory and in estimation – and by differences in *judgement*. Differences between forecasts of exogenous variables were much less important. A similar pattern emerged when the NIESR model was compared with a version of the HMT. It should also be noted that 'model' and 'judgement' differences tended to offset each other – which suggests that it may be important, in forecasting with any model, *who does* the forecasting: that is, whose 'judgements' are used.

We now turn to our central problem: How can a model be used to throw light on the dynamic response of the economy to defined policy actions?

Model simulations and economic policy

As we have already noted, when the actual observed values of the exogenous variables are inserted into the model, the model will provide a historical time path for all the endogenous variables in it. These 'tracks' can be compared with the actual observed values of these variables (the actual 'track') in order to see how far the model is able to 'explain' past experience.

Suppose we conduct the following experiment. For a period of time – say 1969II–1979IV – we insert into the model the actual observed values of the exogenous variables. This gives us a 'track' for each endogenous variable over the time period 1969II–1979IV. Now, over precisely the same period of time, we run the model again but, in doing so, change the value of some policy-determined exogenous variable (say public-sector expenditure on goods and services) by a fixed amount – say £1 billion in 1969II prices. This means that if the original 42 values of public expenditure on goods and services in real terms were $X_1, X_2, X_3, \ldots, X_{42}$ the new values will be:

$$X_1 + £1\text{b},\ X_2 + £1\text{b},\ \ldots,\ X_{42} + £1\text{b}$$

We shall, in short, be imposing a defined policy change on the model *without altering the values of any of the other exogenous variables*: that is, we are carrying out a *ceteris paribus* experiment identical in form with the analytical experiments we have conducted throughout this book, but because our model is now so much more complex, it is considerably more complicated and thus not susceptible to an analytical as opposed to numerical solution.

With the new values of public expenditure, the model will generate a new *track* for each endogenous variable for the period 1969II–1979IV. *If we compare this new track with the original track, the difference between the values of any endogenous variable we choose to examine indicates the impact, on that variable, of our specified change in policy taking place at a particular period of time.* We can thus obtain a profile – over 1969II–1979IV – of the dynamic response of any endogenous variable which interests us to any policy change we care to make.[1] For example, instead of increasing public-sector expenditure, we could have reduced tax rates or increased the nominal money supply. Alternatively we could have imposed combinations of policy changes. Whatever we do, the model will generate a corresponding time path for the endogenous variables and this can always be compared with the *track* (usually called the 'control path') which the model generates when the exogenous variables, including those set by the authorities as policy instruments, take their actual observed values. *The difference between the 'control path' and the second track is, for any endogenous variable, its dynamic response.* Notice that, by this technique, we can ask such questions as, for example: By how much will real GDP have risen after, say, 5, 8 or 23 quarters (or, in our example, any other number up to 42) as a result of a £1 billion increase (at constant 1969II prices) in the rate of public-sector expenditure?

This kind of experiment is called a 'simulation' since the model is being used to simulate the response of the economy to a given change in policy occurring at a particular time (1969II in our example).

Notice that simulations of this type do *not tell us what the dynamic response of the economy would be to the policy change. They tell us what the response of the model is.* If the model performs well (in tracking), we may feel confident that there is a useful degree of correspondence between the two. Unfortunately, even if the model has tracked well in the past, it may still mislead us about the impact of a given policy change imposed *now* or at some time in the future. *In short, although the results of simulations of this kind are suggestive, they are certainly not definitive.* This point is obvious enough since identical policies simulated on different models frequently yield significantly different dynamic responses. It is nevertheless worth stressing since what is obvious is all too often overlooked.

[1] In the case of real GDP these responses are dynamic multipliers.

This obvious but important point can be clarified by recalling the main assumptions underlying simulations of this kind. They are:

1. The observed regularities of economic behaviour, reflected in (i) the functional forms, and (ii) the coefficients of the model, are 'reliable'. *This means that they do not change over time in a way not allowed for in the model's structure.*
2. They are also 'reliable' in the sense that they are 'policy-invariant'. *This means that they should not change in response to the policy itself.*

Clearly, if (1) does not hold, simulations over 1969II–1979IV may be seriously misleading if we try to formulate policy in, say, 1984 on the basis of what they tell us. For, if behaviour changes, the model's equations will be less useful than before and, unless, by chance, the consequential errors offset each other in their impact on the 'key' endogenous variables which interest us, the model must mislead.

Point (2) is, superficially at least, a special case of (1). It does, however, raise an important point about models themselves. To see this, let us ask: *What is it that the equations of the model actually do*?

Essentially any equation, let us say a household consumption function, measures the observed results of households' *responses* to defined variables such as income, taxes, transfers, interest rates, and so on. The observations which the model uses are the *results* of households' decisions. The model does not 'explain' why these decisions were what they were. And it is clear that an immense array of variables which might, theoretically, influence these decisions do not appear in the model. *The most important of these are the values of variables expected in the future*. For example, the readiness of households to increase real consumption in response to an increase in real income is likely to depend to a significant extent on how far the increase is regarded as a temporary or permanent change. Thus, in general, the observed behaviour of any group of transactors identified in the model reflects their expectations. *Moreover we must expect these expectations to be formed on the basis of all the information available to them, which must include information about government economic policy*. Hence, if policy is changed (as simulations assume), expectations *may* change in a way which will modify the decision pattern on which the model's equations are based.

In logic, it is tempting to say that some such process *must occur* – and hence to argue that simulations of policy changes are *necessarily* misleading. However, we need not press the argument this far. It is sufficient for us to note that policy simulations are likely to be less useful when the policy change is *either* on a very large scale *or* of an unfamiliar variety, since significant revisions in expectations seem more probable in both these cases.

We may sum up by saying that, although macroeconomic models can be used to simulate the results of policy changes, the simulations are suggestive, not definitive, and are probably most reliable when:

(a) the assumed policy changes are relatively 'small'
(b) they are of a familiar form

We also suggest that, for most existing models, the simulations are more reliable over, say, periods up to three years than periods of, say, ten years or so.

Finally we should note the technical point that, because of their mathematical forms the response of any model to a given policy change may depend, in some measure, on *when* the change is assumed to occur simply because, on different dates, the ruling economic conditions may differ in ways which influence the response.

Model simulations: some examples

The purpose of this section is to set out (in tabular form) and discuss some simulation results from the HMT and NIESR macroeconomic models. Sadly, comparable results for the LBS model are not available. In examining the 'results' two points must be stressed at the outset.

1. As we have seen, the results are obtained by treating *each marginal response coefficient as being known precisely in numerical terms. In practice these coefficients are not known precisely*: they lie within limits given by the underlying statistical theory. *This means that the simulation results are 'expected' or 'mean' values and must be interpreted as having a range of errors which may be quite large. Small differences between models in their simulation results for any variables are, as a result, probably of no significance.*
2. The results must be treated as *illustrative* of the response of particular models and not *definitive* for a number of reasons. The first of these is simply that models are typically in a process of continuous evolution. As a consequence, any model has a number of versions none of which it is possible to identify as 'the' model. It follows that when we refer to the HMT, NIESR and LBS models we are using an expression which is not well defined and thus potentially misleading. The second reason is that any given version of the same model can be used, for any purpose, in a number of ways. This holds for simulations, even though, since the exogenous variables take their historically observed values in any simulation, no ambiguity arises under this head. It holds because any investigator may, for perfectly proper reasons, think it wise to 'adjust' particular equations of the model in certain ways before proceeding. Since any two users of, say, the HMT model may choose to impose different 'adjustments', it is clearly unwise to talk about 'the HMT model' without keeping this reservation in mind, particularly since it is not always easy to discover just what 'adjustments' have been made.

In what follows we report the results of two simulations of policy changes. Here we can face an additional problem in trying to make comparisons *across* models. This is because not all models use the same conceptual framework, in the sense that some models disaggregate futher than others. For example, in the HMT model it is possible to simulate the consequences of a change in VAT since this tax appears separately in the model. In contrast the NIESR model does not distinguish between VAT and other indirect taxes. It can, as a result, only simulate the results of some approximation to a change in VAT in the form of a change in indirect taxes. Given the other limitations of simulations, this 'imperfect comparability' problem may not matter a great deal. It provides, however, one more reason why the reader should be cautious in imputing too much precision to comparative simulation results.

Now that we are aware of their limitations, what do the available results actually suggest?

The first set of results we present compares the consequences, according to versions of the HMT and NIESR models, of a 5 per cent increase in the basic rate of tax. *This policy change can be regarded as a form of restrictive fiscal policy*. It follows that a 'neo-Keynesian' analysis would suggest a fall in output. A 'monetarist' approach would add that any fall in output would be very shortlived and probably rather small: that is, 'crowding in' would be fairly speedy.

Now consider Table 27.2.

According to this table the HMT simulation suggests that the restrictive fiscal policy reduces real GDP by £300m (at 1975 prices) by the fourth quarter; by some £540m by the eighth quarter and by £722m (about 0.8 per cent of GDP) by quarter 16. There is no sign of

Table 27.2 Simulation 1: fiscal policy change (the effects of a 5 per cent increase in the basic rate of tax: floating exchange rate)
(All data are deviations or percentage deviations from the control values).

	£mns. Absolute deviation in 1975 prices						Percentage deviation			
	Exports		Private fixed investment		GDP		average earnings		consumer prices	
Quarter	HMT	NIESR	HMT	NIESR	HMT	NIESR	HMT	NIESR	HMT	NIESR
1	−9	—	−14	−12	−97	−46	—	—	—	—
4	−81	−11	−77	−40	−314	−197	0.7	0.2	−0.7	−0.1
6	−151	−21	−72	−60	−450	−226	0.6	−0.5	−1.3	−0.3
8	−226	−23	−62	−80	−539	−237	−0.6	−1.0	−1.9	−0.5
12	−343	−16	−76	−79	−689	−245	−3.3	−2.6	−3.5	−1.2
16	−422	−14	−74	−51	−722	−165	−6.0	−4.6	−6.1	−2.4

*ratio of U.K export prices to competitors' export prices. Negative change denotes improvement
†ratio of U.K. unit labour cost to unit labour costs in competitor countries. Negative change denotes improvement.
Note: Current account balance deteriorates in HMT by quarter 16 after initially improving. In NIESR Current Account improves steadily throughout.

'crowding in', though there is some sign of the rate of increase in the deviation in output itself falling after twelve quarters. Not very surprisingly employment falls by about 460,000 and unemployment rises by nearly 290,000. See Table 27.2 (opposite).

As we expect, since policy is restrictive, nominal wage earnings do not rise as fast as they otherwise would have done. Nor do prices. By the end of year 4 (i.e. quarter 16) both are 6 per cent below their control values. Thus the rate of price/wage inflation is lower (on average) by about 1.4 per cent per annum.

The external impact of the policy is interesting. Our usual analysis would lead us to expect an induced fall in imports as GDP falls and thus some improvement on current account. On the other hand, domestic nominal interest rates should also fall, promoting a capital outflow. Which influence, according to HMT, will dominate? Apparently the former since the effective exchange rate *appreciates* markedly. Indeed it more than offsets the impact of reduced earnings on 'competitiveness', the index of which *falls* by some 12 per cent by quarter 6 – a level at which it roughly remains.

According to NIESR, the results are very different. As expected, real GDP does fall, but by only about one-third of the HMT estimate. Moreover, by quarter 16, the NIESR model, though widely regarded as being very 'Keynesian', is showing some signs of 'crowding in'. Again the changes in employment and unemployment are far less than HMT suggests, while the average decline in the rate of inflation over the four years is less than half that suggested by HMT. Clearly the NIESR response, though qualitatively similar, is heavily damped in relation to HMT. There are also marked differences in the external response, for, according to NIESR, both 'competitiveness' and the current-account balance *improve*, while the appreciation of the effective exchange rate is negligible. In short, according to the NIESR model, fiscal policy, at least as defined by this simulation, is much less powerful than HMT suggests and has differently signed external effects.

It would be helpful if a comparable simulation were available in published form for a recent version of the LBS model, for this is presumably the research basis for the somewhat 'monetarist' stance typically adopted by the LBS and its staff. No such simulation had been published by end of 1982. However, a simulation of *an increase* in government expenditure financed by the issue of bonds does exist. This makes it clear that, whatever may or may not

Table 27.2 *continued*

Deviation in 000				Effective exchange rate		'Competitiveness' index	
Employment		Unemployment		percentage deviation		percentage deviation	
HMT	NIESR	HMT	NIESR	HMT	NIESR	HMT†	NIESR*
−11.7	−4	6.9	2	3.6	0.2	3.6	−0.2
−107.2	−36	66.5	27	8.2	1.2	9.1	−0.8
−192.5	−65	120.5	53	11.1	1.2	12.0	−0.5
−274.5	−89	172.5	76	10.4	1.1	10.0	−0.3
−397.3	−121	248.1	106	15.6	1.8	11.3	−0.5
−464.9	−122	288.3	111	18.2	2.0	11.4	−0.3

Sources: table adapted from: R. Bladon-Hovell, C. Green and D. Savage, 'The Transmission Mechanism of Monetary Policy in Two Large-Scale Models of the U.K. Economy', University of Manchester Discussion Paper No. 22 (May 1981), reprinted in *Oxford Bulletin of Economics and Statistics* (February 1982).

occur in some very 'long run', the LBS model gives no sign of 'crowding out' during the first four years after the policy change. Admittedly, none of the dynamic GDP 'multipliers' is large – the maximum value of around 1.3 occurring after ten quarters. But, after quarter 4, the smallest value exceeds unity and there is no sign of the 'monetarist' prediction of the multiplier converging to zero. Paradoxically, the LBS model also predicts that, over a three-year period, *the increase in government expenditure reduces prices* and, even after four years, the increase in the consumer price index is less than ¼ of 1 per cent: in short it is negligible. Finally, although the LBS model predicts an increase in the interest rate, with the nominal money supply constant, this amounts to less than 1 percentage point even by the end of four years. The only possible conclusion seems to be that, over the sort of horizon over which simulation results can, perhaps, be taken fairly seriously, the LBS model behaves in a very 'non-monetarist' way indeed, in that an expansionary fiscal policy change *does* affect real variables, while it tends to *reduce* rather than increase the price level.

In Table 27.3 we present the results of the second 'policy change': a 5 per cent increase in nominal interest rates. As we have noted, this change too is restrictive. On a 'Keynesian' view, we would expect output to fall partly through 'cost of capital' and 'wealth' effects influencing private investment and consumption, and partly because a rise in domestic rates, by attracting capital inflows, raises the exchange rate, tends to weaken 'competitiveness' and thus reduces exports. Since, with a given demand function for money, an increase in nominal interest rate entails a fall in the money supply, the 'monetarist' prediction is that, in the 'long run', only the price level is changed. Real variables are unaffected. Hence on a 'monetarist' view the effect of the restrictive policy on output should again be shortlived. There should, however, be a substantial impact on inflation.

According to Table 27.3, the HMT model is, relative to the NIESR model, extremely responsive to monetary policy changes. For example, real GDP falls with HMT by some £1.6b (1.75 per cent) after three years. Most of this fall occurs in the first two years. Moreover a very significant proportion of it is to be explained by the decline in exports – presumably resulting from the severe appreciation (some 48 per cent) in the effective exchange rate and the similar (44 per cent) deterioration in UK 'competitiveness' which

Table 27.3 Simulation 2: monetary policy change (the effect of a 5 per cent increase in interest rates: floating exchange rate)
(All data are absolute or percentage deviations from control values)

	Absolute Deviations in 1975 prices £mns						Percentage deviations			
	Exports		Private fixed investment		G.D.P.		Average earnings		Consumer prices	
Quarter	HMT	NIESR	HMT	NIESR	HMT	NIESR	HMT	NIESR	HMT	NIESR
1	−65	−5	−13	−4	−111	−42	−0.1	—	−0.3	—
4	−364	−56	−104	−129	−494	−422	−1.0	−0.4	−4.1	−0.6
6	−624	−68	−306	−189	−934	−263	−3.4	−1.2	−6.8	−1.0
8	−874	−45	−415	−215	−1360	−342	−7.0	−2.2	−9.1	−1.3
12	−1124	−8	−585	−218	−1617	−304	−14.1	−3.4	−13.0	−2.3
16	−826	−16	−317	−201	−765	−203	−19.8	−6.3	−15.6	−3.9

†Negative change denotes improvement.
*Negative change denotes improvement.

Source: as for Table 27.2.

have taken place by quarter 6. Employment falls by more than 950,000 and unemployment rises by 610,000. Overall, then, the impact of the (admittedly Draconic) assumed 'tightening' of monetary policy on real variables is very marked in HMT.

So, too, are the responses of nominal variables. For example, if HMT is to be believed, by quarter 12 average nominal earnings are 14 per cent *lower* and, by quarter 16, *20 per cent lower* than they would have been in the absence of the policy change. Prices are some 16 per cent lower by quarter 16. Thus the policy reduces the rate of inflation per year by about 4 per cent on average and generates an average reduction in real wages of roughly 1 per cent per annum over the four years.

The NIESR model is much less responsive: for example, the fall in output is at its maximum only about one-quarter of that suggested by HMT and is reached much earlier – in fact by quarter 4. Thereafter the restrictive impact appears to decline. Employment falls by only about a sixth of the HMT estimate and unemployment rises by a little over a quarter. In short, according to NIESR, the impact on these major real variables is considerably muted when compared with HMT's forecasts.

In the HMT model much of the reduction in aggregate demand is explained by the fall in exports. With the NIESR model exports fall very considerably less. *Indeed, the maximum fall shown by NIESR is only about 6 per cent of the maximum fall suggested by HMT.* In NIESR the current-account balance *improves*; in HMT it *deteriorates*. And according to NIESR the effective exchange rate appreciates by very little and 'competitiveness' deteriorates only very marginally.

The international aspects of the process whereby monetary policy 'tightening' is transmitted to the economy as a whole plainly differ very greatly in the two models. This is, it seems, an area in which economists are in serious disagreement.

Finally, as we would expect, the average reduction in inflation is, at about 1 per cent, considerably smaller in the NIESR model and the average annual fall in real wages only about ½ per cent.

Unfortunately, no comparable simulation exists in published form for the LBS model. We are therefore unable to say how any recent version of this model reacts dynamically to any given easing or tightening in monetary policy.

Table 27.3 *continued*

Absolute Deviations in 000 of persons				percentage deviations				in £millions	
Employment		Unemployment		Effective exchange rate		'Competitiveness' index		Current account balance	
HMT	NIESR	HMT	NIESR	HMT	NIESR	HMT†	NIESR*	HMT	NIESR
−14.3	−4	8.5	2	29.1	1.7	29.1	1.5	280	42
−144.0	−68	89.5	47	39.2	4.8	38.2	2.9	7	272
−326.7	−106	205.6	90	47.9	2.0	43.6	—	−286	26
−580.5	−141	368.4	120	43.1	1.7	34.2	−0.1	−960	113
−961.6	−165	610.5	144	44.7	3.0	25.5	0.9	−1207	271
−871.3	−161	547.8	144	12.1	3.2	−9.9	0.4	−1409	289

Simulation experiments are being conducted, more and more frequently, with all the principal macroeconomic models. By the time this book appears, therefore, it is highly probable that new results will enable a far more comprehensive review of the dynamic responses of the three 'main' models to given policy changes. The somewhat scanty results we record here do, however, enable us to reach some tentative conclusions.

The first of these is that none of the models – and certainly not that of the supposedly 'monetarist' LBS – supports the 'monetarist' contention that fiscal policy changes have no impact on the 'real' sector of the economy. This suggests that, if 'crowding out' (or 'crowding in') occurs at all, it does so only after a period of time in excess of four years. Thus, even over what we have called a 'medium-term' *policy horizon*, there is little reason for expecting 'crowding out' if these three models are assumed to be, broadly speaking, useful representations of the behaviour of the economy.

The second is that, although the HMT and NIESR models give very different quantitative results, they are, for many variables, *qualitatively* similar. It may therefore be sensible to think of the HMT model as setting the *upper* limit for a given policy response and the NIESR model the *lower*. Thus the 5 per cent increase in the basic rate of tax could be thought to reduce real output by between £700–250m (at 1975 prices) by the end of three years and a 5 per cent increase in interest rates by between £1.6b and around £300m. These ranges are, of course, uncomfortably wide. Both, however, exclude zero (a result which often seems to be implied by the defenders of the policies followed between 1979 and 1982) and the sort of 'multipliers' commonly suggested by very naive models of an alleged 'Keynesian' type. Moreover, the uncomfortable fact that the range is wide should remind us very forcefully that the dogmatism on macroeconomics which is our daily diet is totally out of place.

The third conclusion is that the models appear to differ particularly sharply in their handling of the international sector. This is important since, as we have seen, the UK is an extremely 'open' economy on both current and capital accounts. For example, in HMT, the main impact of monetary policy appears to occur via the effective exchange rate, the 'competitiveness' position and the response of exports. In the NIESR model these channels are relatively unimportant. This discrepancy immediately points up a crucial area for research. It also suggests that, if HMT *is* a good approximation to the economy's response, the implication is that a restrictive monetary policy is likely to involve considerable longer-run costs and may to this extent be inefficient as a restrictive device. According to

NIESR, the risks of using monetary policy are much smaller. In view of the contemporary emphasis on 'monetarism' the significance of this issue is clear.

In short, comparative simulations are useful in that:

1. They probably define a *range* within which the response of the economy lies.
2. The calculated *range* – because it is large – itself should be a safeguard against dogmatism.
3. The *results* are probably sufficiently reliable to permit some extreme assertions (e.g. the 'crowding-out' of fiscal policy changes) to be refuted.
4. Any major differences in the responses of different models offer useful indications of where additional research is urgently needed.

Summary

This chapter gives a very brief account of the main contributions of macroeconomic models to:

(a) explaining the past
(b) forecasting
(c) predicting the consequences of particular macroeconomic policy actions

In doing this we have paid particular attention to the last and attempted to show how the consequences of policy actions can be simulated, as well as implicit assumptions underpinning any simulation experiments.

Although simulations of policy actions obviously have their limitations, we illustrated them by reference to two simulations conducted with versions of the HMT and NIESR models. We also commented on a few results from a recent (as yet unpublished) experiment with the LBS model.

Our conclusion was that these experiments had a value in that they were able to:

(a) *refute* extreme theoretical predictions
(b) *suggest* a range of dynamic responses within which the response of the UK economy probably lies
(c) *identify* areas in which economic understanding seemed particularly weak
(d) *emphasise* the folly and potential economic costs of adopting dogmatic positions about the consequences of fiscal and monetary actions.

Questions and exercises

1. 'Macroeconomic models cannot tell us anything about policy since any change in policy will change the model'. Discuss.

2. 'If policy is *systematically* anti-cyclical – and transactors are *rational* – policy will be ineffective.' Is this so? What is meant by 'rational' in this context?

3. How would you evaluate the 'errors' generated by a model? Which of the sets of results set out in Table 27.4 do you prefer, and why?

Table 27.4

Time	Actual value	Predictions of Model 1	Model 2	Model 3
t	100	102	99	102
$t+1$	106	107	105	107
$t+2$	112	109	111	109
$t+3$	113	117	113	122
$t+4$	113	109	112	124
$t+5$	107	109	104	106
$t+6$	102	106	102	103
$t+7$	103	111	101	103
$t+8$	100	98	99	95
$t+9$	87	81	84	85

4. 'There are plenty of large macroeconomic models around. But their results are usually *massaged out* of all recognition before any forecasts are published.' Elucidate. What corresponds to 'massaging' in our discussion?

5. From the successive issues of the LBS *Economic Outlook* obtain forecasts for real GDP, industrial production and unemployment for the quarters of 1982. Is there any systematic tendency to revise forecasts?

6. 'We don't need models to forecast recession or recovery. Some economic series systematically lead the cycles. And these are reliable indicators of cyclical movement.' Study the cyclical indicators as given in *Economic Trends.* Do they, in your opinion, confirm or deny this statement?

7. 'The stock market is dominated by skilled professional investors concerned to forecast profits. Thus the market always correctly forecasts the cycle.' Elucidate. Examine the behaviour of equity prices in the UK and comment on your findings.

8. 'Most so-called *cyclical* indicators signal as many false cycle turning-points as real ones.' Do they?

9. 'Simulations are fun. But they probably tell us nothing about the economy as opposed to the economists who built the model being simulated.' Elucidate and appraise.

10. What do the NIESR and HMT models suggest about the impact of monetary policy?

11. 'Ministers believe devoutly in crowding out. Models don't.' Discuss. Which view do you accept, and why?

12. If monetary policy *really* works as the HMT model suggests, what consequences would you expect to follow the fall in interest rates in July–August 1982? Give your reasons?

13. 'In the HMT model it is international capital flows which respond to monetary policy and it is the consequences of these that bring about changes in demand.' Elucidate.

14. 'It is obvious, from the Treasury's own model, that any severe tightening of monetary policy must do great damage to our export industries.' Discuss in the light of Table 27.3. By what percentage do real exports decline? Assume that the policy change occurs at the beginning of 1976.

15. According to the HMT model (Table 27.3) the restrictive monetary policy causes a 45 per cent appreciation in the effective exchange rate by quarter 12 which declines to 12 per cent by quarter 16. Can you suggest a theoretical explanation for this movement?

16. Using the 1976I values of all the variables, use Table 27.3 to calculate the interest elasticities of: (i) real GDP, (ii) private fixed investment, (iii) consumer prices, as suggested by HMT for quarters 4, 8, 12, 16. Is (ii) the interest elasticity of a (dynamic) investment demand schedule? If not, why not?

17. With a *fixed exchange rate*, the HMT model gives the results shown in Table 27.5 for a 5 per cent increase in interest rates.

Table 27.5

Quarter	Exports	Private fixed investment	Real GDP	Consumer prices (%)	Average earnings (%)	Employment	Unemployment
1	—	−2	−17	—		−2.0	1.2
4	−4	−35	−11	—	0.1	−7.2	4.5
8	−8	−131	−60	0.1	0.1	−26.9	16.7
12	−13	−106	−25	0.1	—	−26.3	16.1
16	−9	5	68	−0.1	−0.2	7.8	−4.7

Compare these results with those in Table 27.3. Can you offer a theoretical explanation of the main differences? What do you infer about a 'floating' versus a 'pegged' exchange rate? Use these results to deduce the approximate change in consumption in quarters 8, 12 and 16.

18. With a *fixed exchange* rate, the NIESR model is more responsive than HMT to a 5 per cent increase in interest rates. See, for example, Table 27.6. Compare these results with those of Table 27.3 What does the NIESR model suggest about the merits of a 'floating' or 'pegged' exchange rate?

Table 27.6

Quarter	Private fixed investment	Real GDP	Average earnings (%)	Consumer prices (%)	Employment	Unemployment
1	−6	3	—		—	—
4	−133	−137	−0.2	—	−42	27
8	−233	−338	−0.9	−0.1	−114	96
12	−230	−316	−2.5	−0.8	−152	182
16	−208	−237	−4.7	−1.9	−156	139

19. 'With a fixed exchange rate, *tightening* monetary policy has little impact on real or nominal variables. But with a *floating* rate it is extemely powerful.' Elucidate theoretically and discuss critically in the light of the simulation results.

20. 'The NIESR and HMT models yield very similar results for a 5 per cent increase in the basic rate of tax when the exchange rate is *pegged*. In both GDP *falls* by some £230 million (at 1975 prices), and unemployment *rises* by about 95,000. However, in the former, prices *fall* by some 1½ per cent while HMT suggests a ½ per cent *rise*.' Do these results surprise you? What general conclusions do they – together with Tables 27.2 and 27.3 – suggest about the two models?

21. 'The alternatives to basing policy decisions on model simulations are to base them on ministerial *hunches* or the currently fashionable economic mythology. Of the three, I prefer models.' Which do you prefer? Why?

22. How would you use the HMT or NIESR model to identify the origins of the 1979–82 recession and the part played by government policy changes in bringing it about?

Suggested reading

*M. J. Artis, 'Why do Forecasts Differ?', paper presented to Bank of England Panel of Academic Consultants, no. 17 (February 1982).

Bank of England, 'Why Do Forecasts Differ?', *Bank of England Quarterly Bulletin* (March 1982).

F. T. Blackaby, 'Forecasting and Economic Policy', *NIESR Review*, no. 100 (May 1982).

R. Bladen-Hovell, C. Green and D. Savage, 'The Monetary Transmission Mechanism in HMT and NIESR Models', University of Manchester Discussion Paper (1981), reprinted in *Oxford Bulletin of Economics and Statistics* (February 1982).

S. Brooks, 'Systematic Econometric Comparisons; Exports of Manufactured Goods', *NIESR Review*, no. 97 (August 1981).

A. Dean, 'Errors in National Institute Forecasts of Personal Incomes, Inflation and Employment', *NIESR Review*, no. 78 (November 1976).

J. S. E. Laury *et al.*, 'Properties of Macroeconomic Models of the UK Economy: A Comparative Study', *NIESR Review*, no. 83 (February 1978).

D. G. Mayes, 'Forecasting and Economic Policy', *NIESR Review*, no. 100 (May 1982).

*C. Mowl, 'Simulations in the Treasury Model', *Treasury Working Paper*, no. 15 (October 1980).

NIESR, 'The Medium Term: Prospects and Problems', *NIESR Review*, no. 94 (November 1980) pp. 9–15.

M. J. C. Surrey and P. A. Ormerod, 'Formal and Informal Aspects of Forecasting with an Econometric Model', *NIESR Review*, no. 81 (August 1977).

F. Teal and D. R. Osborn, 'An Assessment and Comparison of two NIESR Econometric Model Forecasts', *NIESR Review*, no. 88 (May 1979).

*More advanced references.

Chapter 28
Macroeconomic Policy: Two Approaches

Introduction

The aim of this chapter is to give an account of 'neo-Keynesian' and 'monetarist' approaches to the conduct of macroeconomic policy with special reference to the UK. This is done, not with the intention of demonstrating that one approach is superior to the other, but in order to show, as clearly as possible, in what ways the two approaches differ and what issues in positive economics stand behind these differences.

Inevitably the analysis in this chapter draws upon that of earlier chapters. Some repetition is therefore unavoidable. This has, however, been kept to a minimum by giving cross-references to the arguments of earlier chapters in footnotes rather than by repeating the arguments themselves. The reader is strongly advised to make full use of these cross-references and to supplement them by reading material listed at the end of relevant chapters.

The policy framework

Our policy framework regards the authorities as having a small number of macroeconomic variables as *target variables*. At any given time the authorities will have target *values* for these target variables. The broad aim of any interventionist macroeconomic policy is then to maintain these target variables as close as possible to their target values by the use of:

(a) monetary policy
(b) fiscal policy
(c) any other forms of intervention which are technically possible and which, from time to time, seem desirable (e.g. the introduction of some form of 'incomes policy' *or* the imposition of quantitative restrictions upon imports)

Thus the authorities set (a) and (b) in accordance with their overall objectives, the rate at which they will 'trade off' one objective against another where both cannot simultaneously be attained, *and their understanding of the dynamic response of the economy to policy actions: that is, their explicit or implicit macroeconomic model.*

In terms of this framework, how can we explain the observed fact that reputable economists frequently put forward quite different policy recommendations even when they are agreed about the existing position of the economy?

In the first place, the economists may have different objectives, *either* in the sense that they do not have the same target variables, or, where they have the same target variables, they nevertheless have differing 'trade-offs' between them.

In the second place, as we have seen, policy proposals are conditional upon forecasts of *exogenous variables*. Where economists' forecasts differ then, *ceteris paribus*, so will their policy recommendations. For example, if one economist forecasts zero growth in world trade over the next four years, while another forecasts growth at a steady 8 per cent, their proposals are likely to differ sharply.

In the third place, the policy proposals may derive from *different models of how the economy responds to policy changes*.

Finally, the policies proposed may be based upon very different assumptions regarding the appropriate policy 'horizon'. Some economists, for example, typically conduct their analysis in terms of a relatively 'short' horizon – let us say of 1½–2 years. Others are accustomed to thinking in a 'medium-term' framework which might yield a policy 'horizon' of 4½–5½ years. Our review of simulations with two prestigious models gives good reason to suppose that, where this is the case, policies will differ markedly.

Consider the first possibility. This clearly relates to value judgements and not to positive economics, for if I am prepared to accept a 50 per cent increase in unemployment in return for a 1 per cent fall in inflation, while you will accept only a 10 per cent increase in unemployment, this, ultimately, is likely to be a matter of our social and political preferences. We cannot hope to resolve our differences by appeals to observation.

By contrast, the second and third possibilities do relate to positive economics in the sense that, in principle, any differences are capable of resolution by appeals to observation.

In principle, for example, it should be possible to identify which of two (or more) methods of forecasting the exogenous variables of the models gives the better results and thus seems likely to provide the more reliable guide.

Again, *in principle*, it should be possible to determine, by appeals to observation, which of the available macroeconomic models is, given the value of the exogenous variables, the most reliable means of forecasting the values of the *target variables*.

Is it similarly possible, even in principle, to estimate the most 'useful' definition of the 'policy horizon'? This is a complicated issue, as a simple illustration makes clear.

Obviously, if two economists offer opposed recommendations regarding the most 'useful' policy period, they may do so because:

(a) they differ in: (i) their choice of target variables, and/or (ii) the rate at which they will 'trade off' one target variable against another
(b) they possess different models of the economy

As we have seen, economic research can do nothing to resolve (a), which relates to value judgements, while we have already pointed out that (b) is, *in principle*, a matter for positive economic research. Suppose now that two economists accept the same model *and* hold identical value judgements in the form of (a). Can they still – with logic – recommend different 'policy horizons'?

A 'short' policy horizon implies more or less continuous adjustment of macroeconomic policy and thus, *assuming that policy is successful*, a relatively smooth path for real GDP over time yielding some positive 'trend' rate of growth; 'cyclical' fluctuations in such a system would be very small. By contrast a 'medium-term' policy horizon implies the virtual absence of anti-cyclical stabilisation; 'cyclical' fluctuations would (by assumption) tend to be larger. Again, over the longer term, real GDP would exhibit some positive 'trend' rate of growth.

There is no reason why the two 'trend' rates of growth should be identical. Possibly the 'trend' would be greater if the 'cyclical' fluctuations around it were smaller. Alternatively the 'cycle' might be the unavoidable cost of growth. Clearly it would be possible for our two economists to hold opposed views in this issue – an issue which is not typically determined by existing macroeconomic models, which tend to take 'trends' as exogenously given.

Suppose, however, they do not: that is, they are entirely agreed as to the relationship between 'cyclical' fluctuations and growth. It is nevertheless possible for them to recommend differing policy horizons since one may *prefer* a smooth (but relatively flat) growth path of real GDP and the other *prefer* larger fluctuations accompanied by faster long-run growth.

The selection of the most 'useful' policy horizon thus involves *both* values *and* the model of the economy. Our earlier analysis is thus formally applicable. However, the notion of 'value judgements' has now to be extended to embrace 'cyclical' fluctuations and the rate at which we are prepared to 'trade off' present against future real GDP. In the same way the notion of the 'model' has got to be extended from, say, the interpretations of the previous chapter, to embrace a quantitative theory of growth which can explain the relationship between 'cyclical' fluctuations and the 'trend' rate of growth in real GDP.

It thus follows that the definition of the most 'useful' policy horizon is not a matter which can be settled by positive economic analysis alone, *even in principle*. Unless the underlying value scales can be shown to be very similar, they may influence matters even where there is no significant disagreement about the relevant economic 'model'. On the other hand, since in practice there is probably rather more disagreement about the relevant 'model', it is probably this element – in principle susceptible to positive economic analysis – which accounts for most of the disagreement about 'policy horizons'.

Unfortunately, it does not follow that what is possible in principle is also possible in practice. For example, economic data are often not available in the form required. It is often of dubious quality. With some series major revisions are not uncommon. Hence the research techniques which can be employed are restricted and the models commonly rather crude. As a result highly reputable investigators of complete integrity and great technical ability may not be able to discriminate between two contrasting hypotheses' ability to explain the observed facts and hence, *a fortiori*, between alternative macroeconomic models. Doubtless, as economic research proceeds, our ability to discriminate will improve. In the meantime, however, it is important for the reader to understand that, because of the limitations of our economic understanding, highly reputable economists may, in a given state of economy, put forward very different policy recommendations even though they possess similar (or identical) value judgements.

This set of circumstances has two important consequences. These are:

1. Dogmatic assertions about policy (which imply dogmatic certainty regarding the workings of the economy) are entirely out of place. We do not know enough to justify dogmatism; we merely know enough to regard any dogma encountered as deriving either from ignorance or the wish to mislead.

2. Because reputable economists can – and do – make different policy recommendations, it is essential, when these appear, to identify how far these arise from disagreements about positive economics and, as precisely as possible, the forms such disagreements take.

In the next section of this chapter we begin on the task of applying the second point to disagreements between 'Keynesians' and 'monetarists'.

The 'Keynesian' approach[1]

As we have seen, the 'Keynesian' approach rests upon the hypotheses that:

(a) there is no 'automatic' mechanism which ensures that the economy will, on average over a typical 'cycle' in real GDP, operate at an 'acceptable' level of capacity utilisation
(b) government intervention is necessary to ensure such a result
(c) successful intervention is a practical possibility

Typically 'Keynesians' have identified 'intervention' mainly with the control of aggregate demand (via monetary and fiscal policy) supplemented, on occasions, by changes in the (pegged) exchange rate and by an 'incomes policy' of some not very well defined form. Thus, from (say) 1950 to 1973, a period in which policy was dominated by 'Keynesian' thinking and the exchange regime was that of an occasionally jumping peg:

(a) *fiscal policy* was the principal means of controlling aggregate demand in the UK
(b) *monetary policy* – defined in terms of nominal interest rates rather than some concept of the nominal money stock – was used primarily to influence the balance of payments on capital account
(c) adjustments to the 'pegged' exchange rate were made occasionally (1949, 1967), and typically reluctantly and tardily, in an attempt to adjust discrepancies in international 'competitiveness' arising from cumulative movements in UK costs relative to the costs of the UK's main overseas competitors.

In the main – and certainly prior to, say, 1971 – the principal constraint facing the UK authorities appeared to be the state of the balance of payments. Thus 'cyclical' expansions were often checked by the emergence of current-account – and overall – deficits, forcing the authorities to 'tighten' monetary policy to protect the capital account and use fiscal policy (aided by monetary policy) to reduce demand and thus the current-account deficit. This was the pattern of experience which came to be known as 'stop–go'.

'Stop–go' emerged in a period in which macroeconomic performance was, by recent (let alone 1982–3) standards, extremely successful. Not only was employment typically at a very high level (unemployment averaged about 1.8 per cent between 1951 and 1971) but economic growth in terms of real GDP (and output per man) was historically high. Perhaps as a result many eonomists of 'Keynesian' persuasion believed that the economy could be 'fine-tuned', in the sense that it was possible to adjust policy precisely enough *and* frequently enough to restrict fluctuations around the trend growth in 'full-employment' output to very minor magnitudes.

[1]This section draws mainly upon Chapters 9–15, 21.

Thus the 'Keynesian' approach assumed that:

(a) aggregate demand could be 'fine-tuned', *with*
(b) a short policy horizon – perhaps 4–6 quarters

and considered its most effective instrument for doing this to be fiscal policy. Budgets therefore tended to be supplemented by 'mini-budgets' and by the use of techniques permitting rapid variation in indirect taxes without the need for a new budget.

In addition, it was also believed that:

(c) the expectations-augmented 'Phillips curve' was relatively stable, *and*
(d) offered a reliable 'trade-off' between unemployment and the rate of wage/price change, *which suggested that*
(e) expected inflation adjusted rather slowly to observed inflation, *and*
(f) the elasticity of money wages with respect to expected prices was significantly less than unity

Finally, as we have seen, monetary policy was defined in terms of nominal interest rates and *not* the nominal money stock, primarily because 'Keynesians' tended to regard the money demand function as unstable over their typically short-term 'policy horizon'.

By any recent standard the UK economy performed relatively satisfactorily between 1950 and 1972. How far this was *because* of policy or *in spite* of policy is arguable. *But that its performance was remarkably good when compared with either* the interwar years *or the years from (say) 1973–79 let alone 1979–82 can hardly be disputed.*

The assumptions (a) – (f) which we have imputed to the 'Keynesian' approach became significantly less acceptable after 1972. Quite apart from the major shocks to the system provided by the increases in oil prices and, to a lesser degree by entry into the EEC, it became clear that the 'Keynesian' version of the expectations-augmented Phillips curve was becoming increasingly unreliable for two distinct reasons.

In the first place, the *positive elasticity* of money wages to expected prices appeared to be increasing towards – if not to – the value of unity (the value typically assumed by 'monetarists'). In the second place, the *negative* relationship between the rate of money wage change and the level of unemployment – hitherto relatively reliable qualitatively *and* quantitatively – was breaking down. This entailed that the control of wage/price changes by manipulating the level of unemployment between narrow limits itself became increasingly unreliable. The rate of increase in money wages (and thus in prices) appeared to vary independently of the level of unemployment and to become impossible to forecast or explain on the basis of Phillips-type theory. 'Keynesian' explanations of inflation thus became increasingly unsatisfactory, while at the same time the actual rates of inflation rose to levels comparable with or above those experienced during the extremely shortlived 'Korean war boom'.

It had of course always been apparent that the manipulation of aggregate demand with the dominant aim of maintaining 'full employment' entailed validating whatever price/wage changes occurred. To be continuously acceptable, therefore, such a policy required *either* a tolerably low rate of change in wages/prices *or* a willingness to live with whatever rate of inflation occurred. The latter was certainly not generally acceptable. Hence 'Keynesian' analysis and policy prescriptions implied *either* continuous money wage restraint on the part of organised labour and employers *or* some form of direct policy control which could *ensure* effective wage restraint.

Keynes wrote against a background of persistent depression, widespread involuntary unemployment and stable (or even falling) prices. Although the existence of a potential 'inflation' problem was recognised in early postwar discussions, it received little sustained attention presumably because, despite the maintenance of continuous 'full employment', inflation rates (apart from the brief Korean war boom) were relatively low between 1950 and 1972. The inflationary problem – or so it seemed – was not urgent. Moreover, the 'Phillips-curve' analysis suggested that, if we wished, inflation could be controlled. *The analysis certainly did not consider the possibility that we might experience very high levels of unemployment together with very high rates of inflation: that is, what is now called 'stagflation'*. It is thus not really surprising that 'incomes policies' – which eventually had to be introduced on several occasions – were typically rather desperate *ad hoc* expedients which carried little or no suggestion of lasting into the 'medium term' or 'longer run'. Small wonder then that they were perceived to be temporary and that their 'successes' were also temporary and commonly followed by the collapse or withdrawal of the policy and by sharp increases in the rate of growth in money wages.

Because of the breakdown of the Phillips-curve analysis, it can be argued that contemporary 'Keynesian' macroeconomics is in an unsatisfactory state since, although assumptions (c) – (f) are no longer tenable – beyond the general recommendation of an 'incomes policy' 'Keynesians' have little to say about the control of inflation. Moreover, since 'incomes policy' is quite commonly left undefined, what they have got to say has a rather small operational content and sometimes comes close to defining 'incomes policy' tautologically. This is hardly surprising since the principal achievement of British politicians and the British media during the last decade has been to politicise the process of wage determination. As a result a rational economic analysis of 'incomes policy' would find it hard to obtain a hearing, and, empirically, the rate of change of money wages – though typically related (with a unitary marginal response coefficient) to the expected rate of change of prices – varies markedly from year to year in a manner which thus far defies systematic analysis.

In short, although many (probably most) 'Keynesian' economists regard an 'incomes policy' as a necessary element in any policy aimed at eliminating or controlling inflation, there is no consensus as to what this means in operational terms.

Although the 'expectations-augmented Phillips curve' has had to be abandoned in the form defined above, 'Keynesians' retain the hypothesis that the labour market does not 'clear' and hence that *involuntary* unemployment can (and does) exist. At the moment this is written, registered unemployment exceeds 3 million, while special schemes are believed to reduce the number registered by some 450,000. A further 400–500,000 do not appear to have registered. Hence in the usual sense, unemployment may be around 3.7–3.9 million. 'Keynesians' would argue that much of this unemployment is *involuntary*.

Because 'Keynesians' view the labour market as very slow to adjust, they believe that the 'short'- and 'medium'-term trade-off between inflation and unemployment is now not only unreliable but also typically unfavourable. As a result they forecast that attempts to reduce inflation by reducing the rate of expansion in nominal aggregate demand will result in severe reductions in output (and increases in unemployment), persistently reduced levels of economic activity in relation to capacity, and relatively small (and probably temporary) reductions in the rate of inflation.

We may thus summarise the present 'Keynesian' approach to policy by saying that it involves only two departures from the relative optimism and confidence of the consensus of the 1960s. Both are major, however. They are:

(a) a somewhat reduced confidence in the ability of the authorities to 'fine-tune' the economy and a correspondingly greater willingness to contemplate rather longer 'policy horizons'

(b) the emphasis on the need for a permanent 'incomes policy' rather than occasional *ad hoc* interventions.

The 'monetarist' approach[1]

If we look back to Chapters 16–18 we see that we identified the 'monetarist' position in regard to policy as being based upon the hypothesis that the private sector is inherently stable in the sense that:

(a) 'cyclical' fluctuations around the trend of GDP would be mild even in the absence of anti-cyclical interventions by government
(b) the trend would itself represent an average level of capacity utilisation corresponding, if not to 'full employment' (as hitherto interpreted), then to the 'natural rate' of unemployment

Plainly, on these bases the *need* for macroeconomic intervention (as defined by 'Keynesians') is much less. In addition many 'monetarists' argue that the difficulties of carrying out a successful anti-cyclical policy in a dynamic economy are so great that, whatever the intention of the authorities, intervention is just as likely to intensify 'cycles' as it is to dampen them. On *both* grounds, therefore, 'monetarists' are against intervention and, in particular, against attempts at 'fine-tuning'.

Accepting (a) and (b) is equivalent to accepting that real variables are determined through the usual market mechanisms in a way which leads to a roughly constant level of capacity utilisation at the 'natural rate' of unemployment. Not surprisingly, therefore, 'monetarists':

(c) deny that fiscal or monetary policy can alter the equilibrium values of 'real' variables
(d) identify policy with 'monetary policy'
(e) regard the proper 'target' of macroeconomic policy as the price level (or its rate of change)

In the 'short run' it is, of course, true that 'monetarists' predict that if 'monetary policy' is used in an attempt to reduce inflation the early impact will be on output and employment. Prices will respond only after a lag commonly believed to be in the order of 1½–4 years. Not very surprisingly, therefore, 'monetarists' typically:

(f) think in terms of a policy horizon of, say, 2–4 years – essentially a 'medium-term' scale compared with that implicit in the 'Keynesian' notion of the 'fine tuning'

Given this basic approach, the monetarists' crucial propositions are that:

(g) over a period of time consistent with this policy horizon, the nominal money stock (or its rate of growth) is controllable by the authorities[2]
(h) because the money demand function is hypothesised to be highly stable, 'monetary policy' is better defined in terms of the nominal money stock than in terms of the nominal interest rate

[1]Based on Chapters 16–18, 21.
[2]See Chapters 24 and 25 and the references there cited.

Where, as in the UK, the economy is 'open', 'monetarists' typically support the acceptance of a floating (that is, market-determined) rate of exchange and regard this rate as tending to the value which equates the prices of internationally traded products whatever their country of origin. This doctrine is more familiarly known as the *theory of purchasing power parity*, and 'monetarists' hypothesise that although floating exchange rates are manifestly subject to violent short-term movements for a whole range of reasons, over the *medium term* (2–4 years, say), purchasing power parity tends to dominate.

Clearly, propositions (a)–(c) – which we have identified as basic – rest upon a particular view of how the labour market works. This is to the effect that rigidities in the labour market are shortlived and that, over a period of, say, two years, the market clears in the sense that there is no involuntary unemployment *and* unemployment is at the so-called 'natural' rate. This implies that the real wage is equal both to the marginal product of labour and the marginal disutility of working.

'Monetarism' is a theory developed from the *quantity theory of money*. At its simplest its aim is to explain the behaviour of prices using the money stock as the exogenous (causal) variable and the price level as the endogenous (dependent) variable. To relate inflation to the rate of change of nominal money clearly requires some theory to explain the rate of growth of real output and the rate of growth in income velocity, for, by definition:

$$\dot{M}^S + \dot{V}_y \equiv \dot{p} + \dot{Y}$$

where:

$\dot{M}^S \equiv$ rate of growth of the nominal money stock
$\dot{V}_y \equiv$ rate of growth of income velocity
$\dot{p} \equiv$ rate of growth of price
$\dot{Y} \equiv$ rate of growth of real output

Over the years in which 'monetarism' was being formulated, in most developed Western countries, $\dot{Y}$ was relatively steady, i.e. 'cycles' were mild. Also capacity utilisation was typically high. It is arguable that 'monetarists' tended to accept these observed regularities as the inevitable consequence of market forces, whereas 'Keynesians' believed them to result, in significant measure, from successful 'Keynesian' stablisation policies. 'Monetarists' thus regarded policy as being concerned with $\dot{p}$ (≡ inflation) and the control of inflation as entailing the control of $\dot{M}$ and $\dot{V}_y$ and predominantly the former. Thus, just as 'Keynesian' theory derived from the need to explain (and then eliminate) persistent depression – and attained acceptance, at least in part, because it promised to do both – 'monetarism' drew its strength, at least in part, from the need to explain (and then reduce) the rates of inflation experienced in the Western world after 1972. 'Keynesianism' tended to minimise the importance of inflation or potential inflation; 'monetarism' tended to minimise the output and employment costs of anti-inflationary policy.

'Monetarist' theory of inflation is essentially that of the 'natural-rate' hypothesis. This implies that:

(i) the 'natural rate' is either a constant or changes slowly and in a manner which is predictable

for if this does not hold, the 'natural-rate' hypothesis has no obvious empirical interpretation and thus offers no guide to policy.

Table 28.1 Tabular summary of 'Keynesian' and 'Monetarist' positions

Variable, function or issue	'Keynesian' view	'Monetarist' view
1. M^S (≡ nominal money supply)	Very significant endogenous element Hard to control in short run	Controllable by central bank within acceptably narrow limits
2. M^D (≡ nominal money demand)	Unstable in short run Significant interest elasticity	Stable Interest elasticity small
3. $\dot{w}$ (≡ rate of change of money wages)	Probably unit response with respect to $\hat{p}$ Otherwise highly unstable due to an increasingly politicised bargaining process	Stable expectations-adjusted 'Phillips curve' with constant (or very slowly changing) 'natural' rate of unemployment ($\partial\dot{w}/\partial\hat{p} = 1$)
4. $\hat{p}$ (≡ expected rate of inflation)	Primarily dependent on past experience of $\dot{p}$ Slow to adjust to changes in $\dot{p}$	Dependent on *both* past values of $\dot{p}$ and $\dot{M}^S$ Adjusts relatively rapidly to changes in both
5. q (≡ rate of exchange)	Eclectic explanation of determination Emphasises short-run fluctuations in private capital flows arising from changes in expectations Regards purchasing power parity as relevant mainly in the very long run	Exchange rate moves to equalise prices of internationally traded goods (purchasing power parity) This influence dominant in medium term Since price levels are determined in each country by M^S, essentially a 'monetary theory' of the exchange rate
6. Labour market	Does *not* clear in relevant policy period Involuntary unemployment possible and may be severe	Clears (to a close approximation) over policy period Involuntary unemployment typically negligible and temporary

continued opposite

Paradoxically, if the 'natural-rate' theory *does* hold, then the economy will typically be operating at the 'natural rate' of unemployment and the rate of growth in output (≡ $\dot{Y}$) will be determined by 'real' forces, i.e. productivity, thrift, technological change. *Both* the level of unemployment *and* the rate of growth of output are, on this analysis, independent of the level of inflation provided it is anticipated ($\dot{p} = \hat{p}$). Hence 'monetarism' is a macroeconomic theory aimed at explaining (and eliminating) inflation, even though it is an implication of 'monetarism' that the performance of the 'real' economy is unaffected by the level of $\dot{p}$ *as long as it is fully anticipated*.

This apparent theoretical contradiction need not detain us. It is, however, important to note that in so far as 'monetarists' believe that fairly substantial reductions in the rate of inflation *can* be achieved over, say, 2–4 years by reducing the rate of change of the nominal money stock, this implies that

(j) the expected rate of inflation ($\hat{p}$) responds relatively rapidly to (i) any decline in actual inflation ($\dot{p}$), and/or (ii) the decline in the rate of change of the nominal money stock ($\dot{M}^S$), and/or (iii) the expected rate of change of the nominal money stock ($\hat{\dot{M}}^S$)

Table 28.1 *continued*

Variable, function or issue	'Keynesian' view	'Monetarist' view
7. Determination of real and nominal endogenous variables	All simultaneously determined within the model	Real and nominal variables separable Former determined by 'real' forces; nominal variables by M^S: that is, money determines money values
	MACROECONOMIC POLICY	
8. Policy horizon	Short: 1–2 years	Medium term: 4–5 years
9. Control of nominal aggregate demand	Control by fiscal and/or monetary policy Emphasis on fiscal policy	Fiscal policy nullified by 'crowding out(in)' Control by monetary policy
10. Operating target of monetary policy	Nominal interest rate	Nominal money stock (M^S)
11. Control of inflation	Essentially by modification of wage-bargaining process by 'incomes policy'	Essentially by controlling rate of growth in M^S (i.e. $\dot{M}^S$) by stabilising $\dot{M}^S$ at a level equal to 'trend' rate of growth in real GDP 'Incomes policy' unworkable and unnecessary if $\dot{M}^S$ is correctly controlled
12. Costs of reducing inflation	Severe costs in terms of fall in real output, increase in unemployment and in social friction Costs likely to be persistent and to contain a permanent element	Costs relatively small if policy of 'gradualism' is followed Costs transitory

for, if this does not hold, any significant reduction in the rate of inflation would require unemployment substantially above the 'natural' rate to persist for a considerable time.

Empiricism and the two approaches

In Table 28.1 we offer a summary of the main elements in what we have called the 'Keynesian' and 'monetarist' positions.

From this table it is apparent that the disagreements crucial for contemporary policy relate to items 3 and 4, both of which are, in principle, matters susceptible to empirical research. Economic research is of course a continuous process and, by the time this book appears in print, new research findings may have modified the present position. At the moment of writing, however, the majority view appears to be that no stable 'augmented Phillips curve' exists in the UK, and in particular the 'natural' rate of unemployment appears to change as much, if not more, than actual unemployment. This implies that continuing to accept the 'monetarist' view on this matter is an act of faith rather than reason.

Because what transactors *expect* cannot be directly observed, the empirical investigation of item 4 is a controversial and difficult matter. The evidence currently available suggests, however, a 'slow' rather than 'rapid' rate of adaptation in $\hat{p}$.

Thus taken together 3 and 4 seem to imply that the 'monetarist' theory of inflation is not well grounded. But if 'monetarist' explanations are increasingly untenable, 'Keynesian' explanations scarcely seem to exist, for to assert that $\dot{w}$ is to be explained primarily by $\hat{p}$ *and* a quasi-political bargaining process is not very helpful. Nor is it very helpful to propose an 'incomes policy' as a means of constraining the bargaining process if no specifications of what such a policy means and how it is to be implemented are offered.

We have taken issues 3 and 4 simply as examples of theoretical differences which are, in principle, resolvable by appeal to observation and which have been, and are continuing to be, investigated by the methods of positive economics. Similar problems arise with items 1, 2, 5, 8, 9, 10 and 12.

We cannot, however, examine now *either*:

(a) *how* economic research might hope to resolve these issues, *or*
(b) *what* conclusions the available research studies seem to support

Both are of course matters of extreme importance. Readers, however, must investigate them for themselves. It is hoped that Table 28.1 – together with the references at the end of this chapter – will help you to do so, though, because research is a continuing process, our references may well need supplementation by the time this book appears.

Finally, it is hoped that the discussion in this chapter will remind the reader of the complex issues which lie behind differences over economic policy and which are commonly obscured in 'popular' writing. Given these complexities, it is far from surprising that economists often disagree. What matters is that we understand *why* they disagree and *whether* – and if so, *in what way* – any disagreement can be resolved by appeals to observation.

It has been the overriding purpose of this book to promote this understanding.

Questions and exercises

1. 'If men are *rational* and so reduce their real wage demand when unemployed, *involuntary unemployment* must be both negligible and shortlived.' Discuss with special reference to the meanings of *rational* and *involuntary*.

2. Can you suggest ways in which what we have called the 'Keynesian' and 'monetarist' views of the determination of the 'expected rate of inflation' (i.e. $\hat{p}$) could be tested by observation?

3. 'If we cannot reflate the economy because of the risk of recurring inflation, this can only mean that the recession of 1979–82 – and the policies which were largely responsible for it – have made no permanent impact on the inflationary mechanism and have therefore failed.' Elucidate and appraise.

4. 'If additional public-sector investment is inflationary, as government ministers endlessly allege, so is additional private-sector investment or consumption.' Critically evaluate this statement.

5. What is meant by an 'incomes policy'? What are the main problems in (i) devising such a policy, and (ii) implementing it?

6. 'It is stretching the British talent for understatement to the limit to describe macroeconomic policy since mid-1979 as a *costly failure.*' Write a reasoned assessment of policy over this period. Does your assessment support the quotation or not? Give your reasons.

7. The pound sterling was (mid-1982) agreed to be 'seriously overvalued'. How would you seek to estimate the extent of 'overvaluation'? What, in your view, would be an 'equilibrium' rate of exchange for the UK?

8. 'Foreign exchange markets suffer, in the short run, from speculation which is destabilising rather than stabilising. Hence depreciations (or appreciations) go too far: that is, they overshoot the equilibrium rate.' Do you agree? Give your reasons. What evidence is there from the recent experience of the pound, the yen and the US dollar to support this statement?

9. 'Keynes was right to argue that we are always the slaves of some defunct economist. The issue now is which economist it is: Milton, Maynard, or both?' Elucidate and appraise.

10. Write a critique of the most recent budget from the point of view of: (i) a 'Keynesian', and (ii) a 'monetarist'. In what ways would their assessments differ, and why?

11. All Western countries are now trying to deflate their economies with the object of reducing inflation. What are the risks of these policies? And what are their implications for world trade?

12. 'Involuntary unemployment is, like compulsory physical training, an excellent discipline for other people.' Examine critically with particular reference to the short- and long-run 'costs' of unemployment.

13. 'There would be a very sharp reduction in unemployment if the rate of benefit was reduced by 25 per cent.' Can you devise a model to support this conclusion? What does it imply about the 'natural' level of unemployment?

14. 'Businessmen and government ministers are always talking about the *real wage*. But they never say whether they mean what the firm pays to the worker, what he ends up with after taxes, national insurance and so on, or what the worker actually costs the firm.' What is the relation between these concepts? Which is relevant for what purpose? Do they move together?

15. 'The debate about whether governments should or should not intervene in the working of the economy is an academic exercise of no importance whatever. Public opinion will – sooner or later – force them to intervene or deliberately sacrifice office. And what politican will do the latter?' Discuss critically. What are the implicit assumptions about the working of the economy and the political system?

16. What is 'structural' unemployment? How important do you think it is in explaining the present unemployment level? Give your reasons.

17. 'The discovery of North Sea oil *necessarily* entails the accelerated decline of British manufacturing industry.' Can you formulate a theory which sustains this conclusion?

18. 'The stock market *always* predicts the upswings in the UK's cycle. Unfortunately it predicts a good many others as well.' Is this so? If it is, what do the mid-1982 levels of equity prices in the world's stock markets suggest for the world economy in subsequent years?

19. 'There is some doubt whether *Keynesianism* was a "success" between 1950 and 1973. Our recent experience, by contrast, permits no such doubts about *monetarism.*' Discuss with particular reference to the meaning of 'success' and recent UK experience.

20. Use the discussion of aggregate supply in Chapters 15 and 15* to predict the response of output, employment and prices to an expansion of public-sector investment.

21. Outline the 'monetarist' theory of the impact on the rate of interest of an increase in the rate of growth of the nominal money stock. Distinguish between the 'short'- and 'long'-run impacts and between the 'real' and 'nominal' rate.

22. Discuss the contention that the overvaluation of sterling is due not to the Thatcher-Howe monetary policy but to the existence of North Sea oil. What do the various macroeconomic models suggest?

23. What economic experience would, in your view, compel the abandonment of 'monetarist' theory?

24. What economic experience would, in your view, compel the abandonment of 'Keynesian' theory?

25. Review UK economic experience since 1950 in the light of your answers to the two previous questions.

Suggested reading

T. Barker, 'Long-Term Recovery: A Return to Full Employment', *Lloyds Bank Review* (January 1982).

F. T. Blackaby, 'British Economic Policy 1960–74: A General Appraisal', *NIESR Review*, no. 80 (May 1977).

F. T. Blackaby, 'The Reform of the Wage Bargaining System', *NIESR Review*, no. 85 (August, 1978).

S. Brooks, *The Economic Implication of North Sea Oil*, NIESR Discussion Paper no. 38.

F. H. Hahn, Memorandum on Monetary Policy, in Treasury and Civil Service Committee, *Memoranda on Monetary Policy* (HMSO, 1979–80).

C. Hawkins and G. McKenzie (eds), *The British Economy: What Will Our Children Think* (Macmillan, 1982).

S. G. B. Henry and P. A. Ormerod, 'Incomes Policy and Wage Inflation: Empirical evidence for the UK 1961–77', *NIESR Review*, no. 85 (August 1978).

HM Treasury, 'Revenue from the North Sea', *Economic Progress Report*, no. 131 (March 1981).

HM Treasury, 'Revenue from the North Sea', *Economic Progress Report*, no. 143 (March 1982).

R. L. Major, 'Britain's Trade and Exchange Rate Policy', *NIESR Review*, no. 90 (November 1979).

G. Maynard, 'Microeconomic Deficiencies in UK Macroeconomic Policy', *Westminster Bank Review* (July 1982).

Midland Bank, 'Macroeconomic Policy in the UK – Is There an Alternative?', *Midland Bank Review* (Winter 1981).

Midland Bank, 'Economic Outlook', *Midland Bank Review* (Summer 1982).

S. A. B. Page, 'The Value and Distribution of the Benefits of North Sea Oil and Gas, 1970–1985', *NIESR Review*, no. 82 (November 1977).

C. F. Pratten, 'Mrs Thatcher's Economic Experiment', *Lloyds Bank Review* (January 1982).

Index